HEAR THE ROAR!
THE UNOFFICIAL AND
UNAUTHORISED GUIDE TO
THUNDERCATS

HEAR THE ROAR!
THE UNOFFICIAL AND
UNAUTHORISED GUIDE TO
THUNDERCATS

DAVID CRICHTON

First published in the UK in 2011 by
Telos Publishing Ltd
139 Whitastable Road, Canterbury, Kent, CT2 8EQ
www.telos.co.uk

This Edition 2020

Telos Publishing Ltd values feedback. Please e-mail us with any
comments you may have about this book to: feedback@telos.co.uk

ISBN: 978-1-84583-164-6

British Library Cataloguing in Publication Data.
A catalogue record for this book is available from the British
Library.

CONTENTS

Introduction   7

Part One - The Making of *ThunderCats*   9
     1: Eye of the Beholder: Producing *ThunderCats*   11
     2: The Formula: The Writers' Story   49
     3: The Garden of Delights: The Art of *ThunderCats*   124
     4: Swan Song: The Music of *ThunderCats*   148
     5: Out of Sight: The Voices Behind the Characters   171

Part Two - Episode Guide   207
     6: Book of Omens: The Complete Story Guide   209
     Season One: 1985   210
     Season Two: 1986-1989   290

Part Three - Character Profiles   349
     7: Good and Ugly: An A-Z of the *ThunderCats* Universe   351

Part Four – Merchandise   389
     8: All that Glitters: The Toy Story   391
     Toy Guide   410

Part Five – *SilverHawks*   415
     9: *SilverHawks*: Partly Metal, Partly Real   417

Part Six - The *ThunderCats* Legacy   439
     10: Return to Thundara: The Ongoing Saga   441

Appendix A - *ThunderCats 2011*   464

Appendix B - *ThunderCats Roar*   473

Photo Gallery   481

INTRODUCTION

On 23 January 1985, a new syndicated television serial entered the vocabulary of playgrounds across America. The pilot episode of *ThunderCats* introduced a group of feline nobles who had fled their planet due to its imminent destruction – finding a new home in a distant galaxy, they set out to survive, using only teamwork and the mystical power of the Sword of Omens. Within the year, the series had become an international phenomenon, dominating the action/adventure genre and overwhelming the toy shelves with a monumental marketing effort. While viewers followed the on-screen adventures of Lion-O and his fellow ThunderCats in their endless battle with the demon-priest Mumm-Ra, a talented group of creative individuals were working tirelessly behind the scenes; pushing the boundaries of the medium. Their work resulted in a masterpiece of children's entertainment and, over a four year period, *ThunderCats* captivated a generation of children across the world, beginning a legacy that continues to thrive decades after the show's original broadcasts. To the children of the 1980s, one phrase will always epitomise the adventures of youth: *Thunder, Thunder, Thunder, ThunderCats Ho!*

Hear the Roar! is the first ever comprehensive guide to the *ThunderCats* phenomenon. With the benefit of exclusive in-depth interviews with the key creative talents involved, it gives a detailed account of the creation and production of this outstanding piece of American televisual history; presents a full episode guide to the show; explores why it continues to be celebrated over a quarter of a century after its initial broadcast, while many of its contemporaries have faded from public memory; and looks ahead to a new era as Cartoon Network prepares to air a 21st Century revival.

In short, this is the book for which all *ThunderCats* fans have been waiting!

For Becci, Sophie, Millie, Margot, Ian, Marie, and Julie

In loving memory of Eric and Dorothy Scattergood,
and Irene and William Crichton

With thanks to all of my contributors for their time and generosity.

Special thanks to Lee Dannacher and Peter Lawrence, without whom
this book would not have been possible.
Also to Stephen James Walker and David Howe from Telos for their patience and
professionalism.

I'm also grateful to the following individuals for their assistance
in the research of this guide:

Nathan Baker
Caroline Chang
Rick Goldschmidt
Angie Hill
Mark Sheard
Neil Sheldon
Andrew Marczenko

This book is dedicated to the many talented individuals who
created *ThunderCats* and *SilverHawks*. It stands in memory of:

Adolph Caesar
Lee Dannacher
Mike Germakian
Earl Hammond
Bob Haney
Earle Hyman
Bob McFadden
Mike Moore
Romeo Muller
William Overgard
Stephen Perry
Howard Post
Sigmund 'Siggy' Singer
Ted Wolf

PART ONE
THE MAKING OF *THUNDERCATS*

1. EYE OF THE BEHOLDER
Producing ThunderCats

Over 20 years before *ThunderCats* first aired, the formation of a small company named Videocraft International marked the first step on the road toward its inception.

In 1948, graphic designer Arthur Rankin Jr had begun a career at the ABC television network (which was in its infancy, beginning broadcasts that same year). Within a few short years, Rankin had been promoted to the role of art director at the network, before leaving in 1952 to pursue his own business interests. While searching for new accounts for his company, Rankin forged links with a New York advertising agency, Gardner Advertising, and it was here that he met a fellow employee, Jules Bass. Bass was increasingly dissatisfied with his career at the agency (his first job since leaving college) and a creative collaboration with Rankin began that would last for four decades.

Both Rankin and Bass were eager to specialise in animated television productions for children and, with the formation of their company, Videocraft International, in 1961, the search began for a portfolio of work to produce for domestic markets. The first project undertaken by the new company was an animated series based on the Pinocchio tales. 130 five-minute episodes of *The New Adventures of Pinocchio* were produced by Videocraft utilising the stop-motion animation format (achieved by the minute manipulation of animatic figurines). With the success of the *Pinocchio* series, Videocraft continued to increase and diversify their output. It was in 1964 that the company entered the lucrative holiday specials market and their legacy was assured with the production of the one-hour special *Rudolph the Red Nosed Reindeer*. With the success of the genre and Videocraft's 'Animagic' format (the name given to the Japanese-produced stop motion technique pioneered by the company), Arthur Rankin Jr and Jules Bass continued to produce new holiday specials each year and enchanted a generation of children with their visual storytelling.

In 1968, the Videocraft International brand was replaced with the eponymous Rankin/Bass moniker, which would become synonymous with their catalogue of work.

Continuing to produce new animation for children until the late-1980s, Arthur Rankin Jr and Jules Bass were the ideal working partners, each playing to their own individual strengths and seldom seen together at their offices in New York. During their long collaboration, Rankin's art background lent itself to the direction, art production and animation of Rankin/Bass projects (including creating links with Japanese animation studios). Bass, meanwhile, would typically involve himself in the writing, editing and music production for their catalogue of work. In addition, both men ran an extremely tight ship, involving themselves in all aspects of production across their careers.

'We did all of that,' explains Arthur Rankin. 'The animation was done in our Tokyo studios; I was in charge of those studios. Bass and I worked as a perfect team. We were partners for over 40 years, and that was a long run in our business. We'd interchange and both perform each other's duties. To see both of us at a meeting would always be shock, because one of us obviously wasn't necessary! We were a family, Rankin/Bass was a complete family, nobody ever left us, we stayed together forever and ever. Romeo Muller wrote a lot under our direction, Lee Dannacher directed all of the voice tracks on *ThunderCats*, and she was with us forever. Peter Bakalian was also a close associate, and also the Japanese crew. We never went anywhere else, we made animation together and films together. We stayed together and everyone liked everyone else.'

Asked about the vast success of the company, Rankin says that he is incredibly proud of his achievements, adding that there is no formula for success: 'You do the best you can. Sometimes, they are better than the things you've done before. Our holiday specials, all of them, have been on the air [in the US] for 30 to 50 years. *Rudolph* is having its forty-seventh annual transmission. Every year, it's the longest-running, highest-rated film in the history of the medium. People ask if I knew it would be a success, and I say, "Yeah of course, I always plan on those things", but I had no idea – it was booked for two runs and here we are, 47 years later, and it's still going! I don't know why some things catch on and some don't. We had humanity in all of our stuff – in all of our stories the bad guy usually becomes a good guy; especially in the holiday specials, the antagonist becomes part of the team and life goes on with a smile.'

Asked about his breakthrough production, Rankin recalls: 'My next door neighbour in Greenwich was a man named Johnny Marks. He had written a song called "Rudolph the Red Nosed Reindeer". That was a very popular song and I said, "Why don't we try to form a musical adaptation of the song with a story?" Johnny was reluctant at first, because he lived off his ASCAP earnings – when your song is played anywhere in the world, a penny drops, and he liked that income and thought some of it might be jeopardised – but I convinced him it would all help, and of course, all these years later, it has.'

Throughout the '60s, '70s and '80s, Rankin/Bass continued to develop cherished properties, dominating the market and securing their place in the hearts of millions of children. 'After the success of our Christmas shows, the network would call and say, "Give me one, we want one of those," recalls Rankin. 'I'd say, "One of what?" They'd say, "You know, one of those things you do." So we'd go and find things, like a McGinley book – *A Year Without Santa Claus*; that won a Pulitzer prize – or our other material like *The Hobbit* by Tolkien; we won everything for that, including a Peabody. So we worked on different storylines. My main capacity is as an artist and an art director and I was always looking for new designs for pictures, asking, "How can we do this picture?" *The Wind in the Willows* was completely different from *ThunderCats*, obviously; *The Hobbit* was based on drawings by Arthur Rackham. I was always looking for a different way to present a story visually.'

The following biography issued by Rankin/Bass was included in the many pages of literature sent to interested parties to promote the *ThunderCats* series:

> Rankin/Bass Productions was formed in 1961 to produce commercial and television films. The company's first and most well-known production was RUDOLPH THE RED-NOSED REINDEER, a one-hour television special, created in dimensional 'Animagic'. It premiered on the NBC network in December 1964. It is still on the air (CBS) and holds the record as the longest-running single film ever made for

television.

The success of RUDOLPH spawned a series of animated Specials, including THE LITTLE DRUMMER BOY, 'TWAS THE NIGHT BEFORE CHRISTMAS, FROSTY THE SNOWMAN and THE HOBBIT, just to name a few. There have been 33 to date.

The team continues to write, produce and direct special programmes. Their current effort is for CBS-TV and will premiere December 1985. It is a musical hour, in 'Animagic', based on L Frank Baum's THE LIFE AND ADVENTURES OF SANTA CLAUS.

Rankin/Bass is also well known for animated motion pictures, such as the critically acclaimed THE LAST UNICORN.

In the area of live-action films, they have produced a dozen theatrical and television motion pictures, including THE LAST DINOSAUR, THE BERMUDA DEPTHS and THE SINS OF DORIAN GRAY.

In series for television, they created the two big hits of the 'bubble gum rock era' – THE JACKSON 5IVE and THE OSMOND BROTHERS – among others.

Their current activity includes the 65 episode THUNDERCATS series for air September 1985 and SILVERHAWKS – 65 episodes for the fall of 1986.

Arthur Rankin Jr came to the company via the ABC-TV Network where he was credited with over 1,000 programmes as head art director.

Jules Bass began his career with Gardner Advertising, in New York, as a commercial television producer.

Together the team has won innumerable awards, including the prestigious Peabody Award for THE HOBBIT.

Today Rankin/Bass has over 600 employees engaged in New York, California and Japan working on over 150 films. Future plans include a new animated series for children, set for broadcast in 1987, several feature film projects in both animation and live action and continued activity in the Specials area.

Creating *ThunderCats*

The evolution of the *ThunderCats* series was a truly collaborative process. The involvement of Rankin/Bass in developing the property began early in 1984 with a routine meeting between Jules Bass, Lee Dannacher (Bass's producer) and Stanley Weston, president of Leisure Concepts Inc (LCI), a licensing agent that marketed Rankin/Bass products. The purpose of the meeting was for Weston to pitch for the development of a children's television series; but, as Dannacher explains, *ThunderCats* was not initially on the agenda:

'Jules and Arthur had developed a relationship with [a distribution company called] Telepictures. We were in an extraordinary amount of development; we were producing *Wind in the Willows* and we had development with all three networks, including HBO. It was crazy. Telepictures had come in and we were developing shows with them like *Machine Men* ... Arthur and Jules had no prior involvement in the

13

merchandising world, so Telepictures brought in Stan Weston and Leisure Concepts Inc to the table for all of these other shows. One day, Stan walks in and I'm in Jules' office and he has this whole satchel of cute little fuzzy things, because R/B was known for its holiday specials, the Romeo Muller thing. He's lining up these fuzzy things and I'm bored already. I look across the table at this portfolio, and he has huge posters of characters that are half cats, half people. While he's giving this pitch to Jules, I'm unloading his portfolio at the other side of the room saying, "Jesus, this is good". So Jules starts looking at them. They were very dark, very detailed, very comic book; the dark, DC comic style of very detailed work. It just looked so cool, and Jules made fun of me because I'm a cat lover and he hated cats. He said, "You just like those because you love cats". This is not crediting myself with the idea; I was just bored with the fuzzy things.'

Established in 1978, Telepictures Corporation was formed by Michael Garin. Initially a small outfit, the company soon became involved in distributing Rankin/Bass's back catalogue as well as working hand-in-hand with them in developing new series. 'At that time,' notes Dannacher, 'Telepictures was elbowing Arthur and Jules and saying, "These other ideas are wonderful: Nicole Hollander's *Sylvia*, [a] King Tut [idea] etc". These were the shows we were in development with, but they really wanted an action/adventure, Monday through Friday idea. Stan Weston [says] it was all [down to me that *ThunderCats* came about], because I was bored and pulled [those pictures] out of the portfolio. It instantly hit Arthur and Jules, "This is it", nobody else was [doing anything like it]. There was *Masters of the Universe*, but [nothing else] .That's why I adored Arthur and Jules – for seeing a good idea, and then knowing how to develop it.'

Arthur Rankin expands on the growing collaboration between Rankin/Bass and Telepictures. 'They syndicated the shows and they did very well,' he admits. 'Telepictures and our company [complemented each other], because what we didn't have, they had. They had the best sales force in the television industry and they could take a series like the old *Lucy-Desi* series and sell it on a market-by-market basis, and they were interested in doing some of it themselves. Mattel called us into a meeting and wanted us to take one of their shows and syndicate it for them, and as we were walking back to our cars, I said, "We don't have to do that, we can do [our own show] – we have everything that they're trying to buy from us. We have animation, we have the best, that's why they've called us in, so why don't we do our own?" And that's how *ThunderCats* came about.'

Prior to Stan Weston's impromptu presentation of the *ThunderCats* series to Rankin/Bass, the idea had first emerged from one of Weston's regular contributors, serial inventor Tobin 'Ted' Wolf. Wolf had conceived a series that revolved around humanoid cat people, tentatively entitled *ThunderCats*. He had taken his idea, along with preliminary sketches of the characters, to Weston, who immediately saw potential in the concept.

Wolf's daughter, Janice, tells her father's story: 'He got a degree in mechanical engineering thanks to the GI bill after World War II, where he was wounded in the Battle of the Bulge and was awarded the Purple Heart medal. He was originally the engineer for Westinghouse, then got into inventing toys for different companies before opening his own toy invention company. That was back in the days when remote-control and battery-operated toys were brand new – he had hundreds and hundreds of patents from many different companies. He also invented the battery-operated portable record player we teenagers used to take to the beach. My father was a self-made man; he was raised in foster homes and orphanages from a young age. He was living on the streets of New York as a teenager, and enlisted in the army when the war broke out.

'My father had a mind that never stopped working. I don't remember specifically when his thinking switched from toys to television, but somewhere in the early '80s he came up with the idea of a cast of superheroes with the features of cats and humans combined. My dad partnered with a man named Stan Weston, who was the power, I believe, behind [the] GI Joe [toys]. My dad took the idea to Mr Weston, who had the marketing connections. He was the marketing half of the partnership and my dad was the creative half. Stan Weston took it to Jules Bass.

'ThunderCats came at the end of my father's career. He retired, travelled, cruised and enjoyed life. My father was totally shocked at how successful ThunderCats was. None of us had any idea. What was really nice was that the success never changed him. He'd run the idea past me, and my first reaction had been, "Hmmmm", but I'd told him I thought it was great. I had no clue either that ThunderCats would catch on the way it did. In 2001, I was walking down a dirt road in a little beach town outside of Maceio, Brazil, and these little children ran up to me and started shouting, "ThunderCats! ThunderCats! ThunderCats!" When ThunderCats had taken off, my dad had had a gold necklace made for me with the ThunderCats logo on it. I had no idea it was so recognisable, even in rural Brazil! My father owned the copyright for ThunderCats, and I inherited it when he died in 1999.'

Stan Weston recalls that Ted Wolf was a long-time artist friend: 'He showed me some boards of one idea – ThunderCats. I told him I loved the title and the basic look, storyline, etc and that I thought I could sell it for TV. One day, I stopped by the NY office of Jules Bass – just to chat, By chance, one of his assistants asked, "What's in your bag?" I showed them the presentation on ThunderCats. After a series of events and many weeks later, they decided to [commit] the production budget. We handled the merchandising as well as receiving a separate fee per episode for the idea itself, and the show went on to become a *big* hit.'

With Rankin/Bass and Telepictures' commitment to produce and develop the series, the task of turning Ted Wolf's sketches and loose ideas into a workable format fell to Jules Bass and Lee Dannacher. For his part, Arthur Rankin would oversee the visual presentation of the series, travelling to Tokyo to assemble an animation team capable of producing 65 episodes of the ThunderCats series. 'I never wrote for the show, but I designed it,' says Rankin. 'Designing a show and doing character drawings etc is as a result of what the writer puts on paper, and if we didn't like that, we'd change it, but if we liked it, we'd design characters, backgrounds, movements and equipment that they'd have. Overseeing that was mainly my job, and I worked in the Tokyo studios. I spent a lot of time in Japan and lived there for a while.'

To capitalise on the numerous markets that were interested in the growing action/adventure genre for children (both domestically in the US and abroad), Telepictures would fund the production of the series and syndicate it to countless networks across the world, including over 100 stations in the US alone. Sales and marketing forces were mobilised to secure new buyers, and the ThunderCats franchise began to take shape. To enable the up-front cash injection the series would require, Telepictures used the 'barter' method to secure advance funds from advertisers. Originating in the US, this popular model offered stations the opportunity to broadcast episodes of the series in return for secured airtime that could be sold to advertisers in advance. In the 1985 issue of the *Television/Radio Age* journal, the Vice President of Marketing at Telepictures, Dick Robertson, made the following summary of the situation: 'We have put up $15 million to make 65 episodes of *ThunderCats*. Frankly, the stations have laid out zero cash.' Robertson (who would later become President of Warner Brothers Domestic Television Distribution) was hugely influential in framing the business model that *ThunderCats* adopted, and he successfully placed the series with some of the top broadcasters across the world. To further entice broadcasters, Telepictures decided upon the innovative use of profit-sharing for stations that were willing to commit financially to a series like *ThunderCats*, prior to its success having been determined. Interviewed in a 1984 issue of *Pagano* (p VI-1), Telepictures' President, Michael Garin, described his philosophy: 'Broadcasters who share the risk by signing up early to air the series before there is even a script should also be able to share in the programme's profits if it is a success.'

With contracts secured, Rankin/Bass began enlisting the services of talented creative personnel to move the *ThunderCats* series into active production. Jules Bass would be heavily involved in both story development and shaping the series' execution, but day-to-day running of the Rankin/Bass production schedule would fall to Lee Dannacher in the role of supervising producer.

'I had shown up in New York in 1972, aged 21, with little direction and the rent to pay,' she admits. 'I had studied at university and had received a degree in Sociology, so [I thought that] whatever I was going to do, it was going to be a serious career. But the rent had to be paid, so my sister got me my first job in commercial production. I had been a dancer for a while; I was in a ballet company. But [I had] no film experience and no animation experience at all.

'So my background was commercial production, but then I wanted to get serious, so I became a production manager for documentaries. Around 1978, Jules and Arthur were developing a part-live action and part-animation show with Woody Allen for ABC, and a mutual friend introduced me. I was pretty much at production coordinator level at the time, and they hooked me up. Jules and Arthur hired me to help on a show that was never sold, but after having stayed with them for a little over six months, I really got on well with both guys and they kept me on.

'You have to understand that Arthur and Jules ran a two-man show. It was not at all what we think of as a production company. Basically it was just the two guys, and they would expand the staff when they sold a show and it was in production, but almost all the time everything was off-site. The writers would come in for meetings, but we never had a production studio in the way it's known in Hollywood. When I joined them, it was just the three of us, and it stayed that way with a secretary and occasional production assistants right through until we produced *ThunderCats*. We produced an extraordinary amount. They'd already amassed a huge library by 1978 when I joined, then subsequent to that, from 1978 to 1984, there were continual holiday productions in the Animagic format. There were a lot of flat-cel animations that were two hours in format, but they were made for television. They included *Flight of the Dragon*, *Wind in the Willows* and the Tolkien properties, *Return of the King* and *The Hobbit*. Then throw in their live-action productions, one shot in Bermuda, one in Canada, and a whole slew of things in production. But it was really just me, Arthur Rankin and Jules Bass, with people coming in on-site. It was a small office at 1 East 53rd Street, and it was this darling little building tucked in from 5th Avenue. The building was, at that time, the Museum of Broadcasting building, and it was this small, classic townhouse structure –

the museum has since expanded greatly and is somewhere else in New York now, but we had these lovely offices up there. We never had to have a storyboard department or an art department; that was all subcontracted out originally.

'Jules and Arthur knew [from the start] that I knew nothing about animation, but I believe it was Jules who, the first time they were heavy into production, looked at me and said, "Come on over to the studios, you might learn something". So, I went into a sound recording studio with him, and that was it. I fell in love; sound production was what I was going to do for the rest of my life. It was so different from anything I'd ever experienced, producing the acting, the orchestra recording. It was this wonderful film-making that was happening only at the soundtrack level. Almost 100 percent of all other animation producer/directors at the time (at the level of Arthur and Jules) were animators to start with. We were the only studio in New York, except for the Independent Animation World. The other ones out in LA, including Disney, did things differently. Arthur and Jules were never animators … Arthur was an art director, so there lay his talents, his instincts. Jules was a producer, but he would also hand-model for the commercials, because they both started out in the commercial world, producing for television. They weren't animators from the get-go and never were, but they developed, over time, into these consummate producer/directors. So they devised a very unique method for animation – it was to develop the concept. They'd either buy a concept or look at something like *Rudolph* or *Frosty* and get extremely good instincts in bringing in the writer who'd be able to write for that particular thing, like Len Starr or Bill Overgard – all those old guard [writers]. Then they'd go out and canvass the best art designer – a lot of their work was handled by Paul Coker, who was a genius in his field and handled all the Christmas specials … Arthur developed an extraordinary love for Asia and the Middle East – we thought it was because of the geishas over there, but he just laughs and says it was everything else, the culture etc. Arthur developed strong ties with the animation companies over there.'

With producers in place, Rankin/Bass turned their attention to sourcing a lead writer and designer to craft the world of *ThunderCats* in words and imagery. To help construct a series bible (a document used to convey to fellow writers the set-up, characters and locations used within a series) and work on the pilot scripts, Jules Bass enlisted the help of head writer Leonard Starr. A well-respected comic book artist and writer, Starr was able to imbue the series with the required mythology, and pilot scripts were commissioned immediately. 'Leonard was a friend,' explains Arthur Rankin. 'He did some of that, but not all of it. He was a participant in the early days. Jules Bass was also very important in *ThunderCats'* development, and they worked together to form the premise of the show.'

The following document is the outline of *ThunderCats* prepared for Jules Bass by Leonard Starr. This represents the very first incarnation of the series in written form, and, while aspects differ substantially from the finished programme (notably names and descriptions), the cornerstone of the series' plot would be developed with relatively few changes:

THUNDERCATS

A wagon train of spaceships is making its way through the universe, seeking colonisation on a new planet, their own planet, Thundera (accent on second syllable) being doomed. Aboard the lead ship, the commander, Jagu-R, an elderly warrior type with jaguar spots etc., is checking astral charts on a tele-screen. Standing beside him is young prince Lion-L. He is about ten years old and human-like except for his leonine mane of hair. Also in the control room are the other nobles of Thundera – Cheet-A, Panth-R, Tige-R, Wiley-KT – the THUNDERCATS. Jagu-R tells them that they will be responsible for the young prince's safety as he, Jagu-R, is too old to survive a trip to a new galaxy since even in the suspension capsules the aging process continues, though much slowed down. They vow loyalty to young Lion-L, smiling indulgently as the youth brashly declares himself capable of taking care of himself.

The THUNDERCATS all have specific characteristics; Cheet-A has superspeed, so that in action she is virtually a blur. Panth-R is the nightfighter, possessing exceptional acrobatic ability and martial skills. Tige-R is the master of camouflage, capable of merging with any background. Wiley-KT is mischievous and a troublemaker, unable to resist pranks, often fouling up the activities of the others, who then have to pull his fat out of the fire. (Unlike the drawing of Wildcat, he should be smaller, a feline Dead End kid.) Suddenly the wagon train is attacked. Jagu-R recognises the enemy ships. They are mutants from the planet Plun-Darr – Monkey-men, Jackalmen, Reptilians, etc. Normally at war with each other as well as the Thunderians, they have joined forces for this attack. Why? Jagu-R knows. They are after the 'Eye of Xanth', the source of the THUNDERCATS' power. Although it has held the mutants at bay for many centuries, the mutants wish to capture it for themselves before it leaves their galaxy. Once that is achieved, each of the mutants scheme to get it for themselves. Jagu-R holds the 'Eye of Xanth' aloft. It is embedded in the hilt of a mighty sword. It can be looked into (or through) to see the past, the future, and the presence of danger in the present. (The 'Eye' is lidded and normally closed, but opens when bidden or danger threatens.)

Jagu-R shouts orders to the rest of the wagon train of spaceships to form a circle, which they do, but to no avail. The mutants' ships are too many and too powerful for the THUNDERCAT ships; essentially freighters carrying pilgrims and their possessions to a new land. The lead ship is also hit. Seeing that the damage is irreparable, Jagu-R orders the THUNDERCATS into their suspension capsules, where they will remain until Jagu-R can find a planet on which to land the damaged ship, a journey that can take centuries. (Prince Lion-L's capsule is the same size as the adult THUNDERCATS, as he will be fully grown by the time the ship lands. The sword with the 'Eye of Xanth' is placed at his side.) Next to Lion-L's capsule is one for his nursemaid or Nanny. It is somewhat like a sheepdog, but with space creature characteristics (horns, scaly feet, etc). Its name is Snarf and it persists in thinking of Lion-L as a child even when he has become a fully grown superhero, worrying about his going out in bad weather, making him finish his food, clumsily trying to pull him out of harm's way, thereby occasionally messing him up. He can also be fierce when pressed, overcoming his natural gentleness when Lion-L is in danger.

Quickly checking the astral charts, Jagu-R sees that their only hope is a tiny blue planet, the third in orbit around an insignificant sun. It will have to do. The length of the journey is shown by Jagu-R growing older at the controls, his feeble, shaking finger putting the ship on automatic as he zeroes in on Earth, finally turning to dust within his costume.

The ship crashes, in the African jungle, scattering the suspension capsules containing the THUNDERCATS. Lion-L's capsule bursts open and the sword goes flying out of sight. Snarf comes to first, tries to waken Lion-L by nudging him, licking his face. Lion-L groggily revives. Snarf gleefully nips back to his own capsule bringing back toys – space equivalents of teddy bears, rattles, etc. Lion-L, seeing that he is now fully grown, waves them off with disdain. He sees the other capsules scattered about, recognises the other THUNDERCATS through the transparent face plates. He is about to pry them open when the mutants appear, teleported down from their spaceships. They want the 'Eye of Xanth'. Lion-L is mystified, doesn't know what they're talking about. The mutants know that it must be around somewhere, and they now also see their chance to destroy the other THUNDERCATS while they're still asleep in their suspension capsules. As the mutants set about doing this, hacking at the capsules with swords, battle-axes, Lion-L, in a fury, leaps forward to stop them. But there are too many of them and he is unarmed. They fling him aside, laughing.

Snarf has been rooting around in the underbrush and now finds the sword. He rushes back to Lion-L, nudges him with it. Without looking to see what it is, Lion-L pushes him away angrily. This is no time for his stupid toys. But the 'Eye' on the hilt opens, begins to glow. The spirit of Jagu-R hovers over it and his spectral voice booms out. 'Pay heed, for this is the "Eye of Xanth", the source of the THUNDERCATS' power!' Lion-L stares at the spirit awestruck ... he seems to remember ... he touches the sword tentatively ... and it virtually comes alive in his hand, the 'Eye' glowing fiercely. With a lion-like roar, he rushes the mutants. While battling, he touches each of the THUNDERCATS' capsules as the opportunity allows with the tip of his sword, and as the capsules fly open, the THUNDERCATS spring forth, each fighting the mutants in his or her special way.

The mutants now haven't a chance and, cowering, they teleport themselves back to their ships. The THUNDERCATS congratulate their young prince, who has done well his first time out. Now they must set about building their castle, 'The Cat's' Lair', in preparation for whatever dangers await them on the new planet.

Once this brief, two page summary was approved for development, Leonard Starr structured an expanded 11 page document, which included additional profiles of the programme's heroes and villains as well as a description of the various terrains on 'Third Earth'. A memo from Leonard Starr to Jules Bass reveals their collaboration in pitching the many themes of the series:

MEMO TO: Jules Bass
FROM: Leonard Starr
DATE: March 12, 1984
RE: Bible

Jules – One of the things that made Spiderman a success was to give him some of the problems his readers have – trouble with his girl when he could get one, pimples, his aunt keeping after him to tidy up his room, get some decent clothes, etc.

With Lion-L, it could be that by waking up an adult without having gone through the process of growing up there's a great deal that he doesn't know. Some things he discovers for himself, other things must be explained by the older, wiser THUNDERCATS. It's an opportunity for humour, and also a way of slipping in the 'message' so that we don't seem to be aping *He-Man*'s way of attaching the lesson by way of epilogue. There's also precedent in folklore for this kind of muscle-bound innocent – Siegfried and Parsifal leap to mind – so there may be some kind of basic appeal for this kind of character, especially for a young audience.

In general, I see this epic as being somewhat of a cross between Tolkien and *Star Wars*. Hope it works for you.

Best, Len

For the visual progression of the series, the company approached Stan Weston about the possibility of using his long-term collaborator Mike Germakian to design the principal worlds and characters required, along with marketing materials including logo and poster designs. 'Mike was LCI's Creative Director for over 20 years,' acknowledges Weston, 'as well as my best friend until the sad day he left us. At LCI we depended on logical 3-D presentations to help us sell any given idea/product. Usually I would discuss my thinking with Mike, then he would get back to me with his rendition of the same idea. Usually he was right on. We had an uncanny connection when it came to visualisations of ideas/concepts. If memory serves me, I loaned Mike to Rankin/Bass on temporary duty in the early creative time of *ThunderCats*. I am sure he contributed a lot.'

Mike Germakian was indeed loaned to Rankin/Bass, where he took an office and worked through the huge amount of material required to get the series ready for animation. Although his contract no longer exists, the terms and payments received are detailed in an identical contract prepared for his work on the subsequent Rankin/Bass series *SilverHawks*:

We hereby agree to hire your services and you agree to render such services for us as an employee for hire to develop and render characters, set and concepts ... We agree to pay you and you agree to accept for the above services the sum of $7,500 (Seventy-Five Hundred Dollars.) ... You represent that you have entered into a separate agreement with LEISURE CONCEPTS INC, under which you will receive a % of its net income from the exploitation of Leisure Concept's rights in the series.

The referenced agreement with LCI included half of the 3% revenue that the company received, the other half going to Stan Weston. This made Germakian one of the few employees engaged by Rankin/Bass to receive a share in the success of the series, which was not standard in employee contracts, favouring flat fees for services rendered.

With pre-production gaining momentum, the *ThunderCats* concept envisaged by Ted Wolf became a new and more structured entity overseen by the team at Rankin/Bass. After the opening scripts had been written, further scriptwriting and editing would begin to be overseen by British writer Peter Lawrence.

'I think Ted Wolf came to Jules and Arthur, however he got there, with four or five characters that were mutated human cats, and that was it,' surmises Lawrence. 'Maybe he called them *ThunderCats*, I'm sure he did, and one was based on a lion, but I very much doubt that he even had Cheetara.'

Dannacher agrees that the character line-up changed as the series developed: 'I had to fight very hard to get Cheetara in the series as the only woman, because this was the early '80s and I was the only woman at the table. Whether it was at Rankin/Bass with the writers, certainly with Telepictures and certainly over in Japan. The glass ceiling was so low at that time for women. So I remember sitting with all the writers at the first big writing meeting and we didn't have a woman in the 'good guy column' and just very minor bad guy girls, so I had to fight very hard at that time to get Cheetara's role up there. Then, they weren't going to give her a weapon. I remember having a fun fight with Bill Overgard about that, and finally he came in at the next meeting and she had this stick. Obviously, her skill was her speed, but she had this stick to work with, and Bill said, "Lee, does that satisfy you?"'

A Full-Scale Production

Sixty-five episodes of *ThunderCats* had been commissioned by Telepictures – a common number for syndicated children's programming as, with episodes 'stripped' across the five weekdays each week, this would comprise a 13-week run. The show was due to transmit from September 1985, preceded by a pilot in January of that year (though production was continuous through 1984/85). The pilot would be structured so that stations could run it either as two standard half-hour episodes ('Exodus' and 'The Unholy Alliance') or as one hour-long feature presentation. It would be written by Leonard Starr and would serve to introduce viewers to the world of the *ThunderCats*. The pilot would then be repeated in the autumn, before an unbroken run of new episodes would begin.

'All stations ran the episodes to the same 13 week schedule,' explains Lee Dannacher. 'Weekly, we continued to deliver final episode masters to Telepictures (who would, in turn, distribute them to the individual stations) right up to the final week ... but we didn't miss an airdate! Although there were some under-the-wire, "just caught Fed-Ex at midnight" kind of scenes. I believe the independent stations, as well as the companies that controlled multiple stations (like Metromedia), had the option of running the *ThunderCats* one hour special as a stand-alone, sometime prior to the series start date in September. The airdates for the one-hour special could have fluctuated between stations, but when the series premiered on 9 September 1985, all stations ran five original episodes for each of the next 13 weeks. It was glorious! By mid-season, we were hearing taxi-cab drivers talking about "this new cat show that's on...!" I forget when the [ratings] numbers came out (because syndication is so different than network broadcast seasons – as they were in the '80s, anyway), but I think it was shortly after the last episodes aired in mid-December 1985 – when all the trades had huge ads announcing the ratings and *ThunderCats* was number one!'

While Jules Bass was busy in New York assembling a cast of professional voice artists, Arthur Rankin had secured the involvement of Japanese animator Masaki Iizuka. Under Iizuka's direction, his newly-founded Pacific Animation Corporation (based in Tokyo) would handle the complete run of episodes, outsourcing various stages of production to other animation companies in Hong Kong, Taiwan and Korea.

'When we had amassed these materials,' notes Dannacher, 'Arthur would take [the project] over and employ the perfect animation studio that would eventually produce the animation. Japanese animation didn't have the American sensibilities; things like timing and how they would work through a script. Japanese animation is renowned, but if you look at the films, the pacing is very slow. They'd spend forever looking at a sunset, whereas American television at the time needed a different pace and sensibility with comedy. The Japanese animators didn't understand our comedy and we didn't get theirs. So Arthur and Jules, which was genius, decided to produce it almost like a radio play to time. We'd first record the actors, then we'd edit down the best takes. If you take a 30 minute show, we'd start with 40 minutes, but we'd need commercial breaks, so we'd format that, insert the breaks for action and lock it in as a 22 minute show, and it would then be sent to the animators, who would have to conform that show to the Rankin/Bass timing. Basically, the shows were perfectly timed and sent over. Even the comedy was very well explained. We'd send the material with a locked-in soundtrack to the animation studios and, at that stage, we're just sitting in a darkened studio, we'd spot the sound effects, doors opening and closing, magical effects etc, so the animators would know, "That's when they need the fairy to do a turn" and they'd see what was in our heads and why we left ten or 15 seconds. Plus the animators had to work hard to work that way. Usually, they'd get dialogue without any editing and it would be up to them how long they'd take on different scenes. We sent the locked soundtrack and spotted all the music (which also had distinct timings), so when the animators sent their answer prints back to the States, we'd have a fully formatted show that just needed tweaking and final editing. We might send a show over that was two minutes too long, but that's all we needed to cut. We'd do that and then send it to the network. When I'd explain that to animators, they'd say, "I'd never work on a show like that; someone's trying to tell me how long to animate a scene before I know what to do with it?"'

Dannacher attributes a huge proportion of the eventual success of *ThunderCats* to the efforts and talents of Pacific Animation Corporation and Masaki Iizuka: 'Up until 1985, [Rankin/Bass] hadn't been doing any action adventures *per se*. There was action in *Flight of Dragons* and *Return of the King*, but as for that new explosion of Monday to Friday shows (*Masters of the Universe* etc), we'd not done that genre. So from that point on, Masaki would say, "Well Lee, I know how to do this better than you," because they'd been doing that genre for a long time. He took over the production of sound effects and the production of storyboards, which had always, before that, been done by our artists in the States. So, all of a sudden, our whole relationship with Masaki-san and PAC changed remarkably; a lot of responsibility went to his side of the ocean. It was great, because he did it so well.

'I'd known Masaki for a long time, at least four or five years before *ThunderCats*, and we'd been through the live action shows together. The four of us knew each other very well ... When we got to the *ThunderCats* stage, we were heavily into development and production on many shows that were ongoing, so the four of us were insanely busy working with a lot of people outside of our offices ... Telepictures were saying, "We've bought your library, we're going to distribute the heck out of that," and they were in co-development on a lot of productions, and we were also in development with a lot of networks like HBO. Telepictures were going to get funding from outside of the normal studios because they wanted to do their own programming for their own syndication unit, so we were developing shows like *Machine Men* (we were going to ride the popularity of robots at the time). Arthur and Jules had already built up a working relationship and bond with Telepictures for almost a year through 1983, and they got to know us and we got to know them. Then they started muscling in – "Come on you guys, this is hot, the 65 half hours, Monday through Friday, we really want to do something there". They had already started having toy meetings on the other shows we were developing, and they were saying, "Look at what this can be". Arthur and Jules were blinking. All through the '60s they'd been in productions where it was just the two of them and a guy that was sort of my role. But they knew what series production meant; you gave your life away to it. It was one episode after another after another.

'I remember a meeting where we had the story ideas [for *ThunderCats*] already, and Masaki came over to New York. [Arthur and Jules] sat us down in a meeting and they said, "This is fabulous, we know your work, we can do this, but we (Arthur and Jules) are not going to be in the daily grind of it. We'll all develop it together, establish the whole thing, the worlds, everything. The four of us will do all of that together. [But] it's your ball game for the rest of it. Can you guys handle it?" [Masaki and I] looked at each other, and we're starting to say yes, but they said, "No ... think about it!" So, we went off for a long walk in Central Park, where I'm saying, "I think I can do it, can you do it?" And Masaki said, "I think I can do it". But we stopped off at a bar, and four tequilas later, we were absolutely sure we could do it; it was great!

'Arthur and Jules had been in series production before, with their Saturday morning series (like *The Jackson 5ive* and *Kid Power*). They knew first-hand the relentless schedule of series production. So I believe what they wanted from us was a firm commitment we would be there for the long haul. Of course, none of us anticipated [that we would actually] sell and start production on *SilverHawks* before we were even finished with [the 65 episodes of] *ThunderCats* ... or [that we'd follow] up with the four shows of *The Comic Strip* while still finishing up *SilverHawks* and producing the second [65-episode] *ThunderCats* order! So none of us, in any way, knew then what the "long haul" was truly going to be! Our decision … was really [answering the question], did we truly want to commit? Loyalty was everything at Rankin/Bass, and Masaki and I had been mentored by Arthur and Jules for long enough that once we were committed (and they knew this about us) nothing would get in our way. Arthur's golden rule for us to live by was: On Quality; On Time; On Budget … That golden rule resonated with me for the "long haul" of all our series work, and if I can say so, I don't believe Masaki and I ever let him down in that commitment over the next five years.

'Jules and Arthur were the consummate producer/directors. I discovered later that in Hollywood, the animation studios had 50 people doing the work that just Jules and Arthur were doing. So they were very well rounded. They were really showmen. I hate to use that word, because it will sound like I am assigning them to the past, but they came up with the ideas; they had extraordinary instincts for great ideas that were presented to them. Their instincts for finding the other talent, whether the actors, writers, storyboards or artists, were so good. From '78 to '84 when we started *ThunderCats*, they taught me all of those different responsibilities. A supervising producer out in LA might be one of two or three [working on a given production]. One would have the responsibility for budgets, scheduling and coordination and liaison with networks, merchandising and publishing. Another would supervise the making of the soundtrack and the artwork. Another would be strictly handling the coordination with the animators. There might be yet another for post-production. Since Arthur and Jules, throughout their entire careers, had done everything themselves, when I became supervising producer for them, that's what was expected of me. Only years later did I realise how grossly underpaid I was! I'm joking there. I was very well paid, but I only realised how fortunate I was because they had developed me, and I was very much of their style. So was Masaki, but I wanted to do it all.

'I could get [engrossed] in making a perfect budget and scheduling. I wouldn't allow anyone else to be the liaison with merchandising and publishing and the networks and all that. I was in there directing the actors and producing the orchestra record and working with Peter Lawrence and the head writers. I don't want to sound like I was that great; it's just that that was expected of me. Arthur and Jules never delegated except to me and Masaki, so when they delegated shows 1 to 65 to each of us, I wouldn't have been doing my job if I didn't sign every cheque, and approve every invoice, and review every storyboard and every soundtrack when they were edited, and fly over to Tokyo constantly. I was supervising producer across the board, and everything had to have my stamp of approval. Until I absolutely burnt out much later on, I was too involved. By the middle of the episodes, my younger guys were biting at the bit, and I'd finally say, "Okay Matthew Malach, you want to direct the actors? Take episodes 34 and 35", and I'd be sitting in the booth. But it was time to have that happen, and so it just thrilled me to watch those guys, and I'd be the final stamp of approval and provide notes. We all became a very close family, and I was able to delegate some of that stuff, with Arthur and Jules still knowing that nothing left the office without going past my desk first.'

As previously mentioned, when production on *ThunderCats* was well underway, Rankin/Bass took the decision to make a second syndicated series for the action/adventure genre. *SilverHawks* was produced alongside *ThunderCats* and, with another 65 animated episodes to create, the company needed additional staff.

Though Rankin/Bass continued to operate with only a small team in New York, permanent employees were brought on board to maintain full time 'departments' (thought often comprising of only one person apiece) that could handle editorial, administrative and creative input in-house. 'We all had input,' explains Dannacher. 'Jules and Arthur are the ones who wrote the bible, whether it was for the storylines or how the artwork was going to look, just as they had done for every show they'd ever done. Once they'd set this whole stage and world for us, it was the magical input of everybody. I'd love to take credit for hiring the best production coordinator in the world, Connie Long, or the greatest soundtrack producers like Mike Ungar, but everyone all worked so well and every single one added something, including Matthew Malach, Larry Franke, Tony Giovanniello, John Crenshaw and John Curcio (who did so many of Rankin/Bass's other major productions prior to *ThunderCats*). There was also Chuck Hasegawa, who was an extraordinary asset to the whole thing. There were so many others as well; I definitely don't want to leave anyone out in my praise and extreme gratitude! Over six or seven years I only had to let one person go, and that's extraordinary!'

Another influential figure in the development of *ThunderCats* was script editor Peter Lawrence. While Leonard Starr had overseen the early scripts for the series, it was realised that a full-time writer was needed to commission new talent and fashion the imagination of submissions into a coherent and consistent approach. In addition to Lawrence's writing and editorial duties, he also worked closely with Pacific Animation Corporation in ensuring that writers' descriptions were detailed enough to be realised by the animators.

'Peter Lawrence ran the whole script department,' enthuses Dannacher. 'He was disappointed with more than a few of the writers, but I've never known someone put as much effort into getting the best from a writer as Peter. He shouldn't have had to go through the amount of rewriting that he had to, but it was the schedule. He didn't have the luxury of saying, "Let's have a second draft or third draft," which we could do on the feature films. That's why they've got 15 writers on series like *Law and Order* nowadays. They might have writers coming in, but they do the rewrites. Peter was alone, it was just him; but because Peter is so well rounded, a producer/director in his own right, it was like, "Oh my god, let's also have Peter look at the designs, run them past his desk too," not only because of the inspiration it might give him for future episodes or story ideas, but because Peter's ideas would make the designs better … It's an example of just how much input was had [by everyone involved]. Because Arthur and Jules had told me to comment on everything … I [in turn] was able to let everyone else have that input. Mike Ungar, John Crenshaw or Steve Gruskin, who were hired as episodic producers, could make a comment outside of storyboard comments; it was marvellous, we were open to ideas from anywhere. Ultimately, the enthusiasm kept everyone's morale up. I subsequently learned that's missing from other productions; everyone is very compartmentalised, they're all looking at the clock to see when they can go home. The work ethic [on *ThunderCats*] was amazing, the professionalism of these young people. I realise how young everyone was at the time – it was just remarkable.'

Peter Lawrence recalls that the offices of Rankin/Bass only amounted to the size of the average floor of a house. 'There were two main offices,' he explains. 'Arthur in one, Jules in the other. There were a few other offices – we just expanded into a few more rooms – but we had very little compared with any other production. We had a designer who did secondary character designs, first Bob Camp then Jim Meskimen who was originally an actor. Lee and I had an office side by side, a couple of production staff – one or two were quite good, others weren't people with much initiative or knowledge, they learned on the job. We turned out two, three, four scripts and shows a month, and sometimes more. By the time we were commissioned for the second half of *ThunderCats*, *SilverHawks* was already up and running; you have no idea! I'm saying this because I know Lee won't, and I'm not saying this because she is my friend, but there's no-one in the whole world I've ever met who put in that much work. Without her, it couldn't have happened. She basically destroyed her health for a while, and it just wouldn't have happened without her, period. These were people working unbelievable hours, including the animators, sleeping under their desks … A lot of this wasn't just because we were paid a bit of money to do it, it was because of a combination of friendship, enjoyment and Stockholm Syndrome!'

Asked about the involvement of Bass and Rankin, both Lawrence and Dannacher describe their vast commitment to *ThunderCats*. 'Jules was there five days a week,' recalls Lawrence. 'The same with Arthur,' adds Dannacher. 'They may have disappeared to France or Bermuda for a couple of weeks at a time, but that didn't mean they quit business when they were gone … They played as hard as they worked, and they are very well rounded men. Very interested in life, art, literature, architecture and other cultures. And they brought all of that stimulation back into their work at Rankin/Bass. All the time *ThunderCats* was going on, they were also developing feature films and the next *SilverHawks* idea. So although they weren't upstairs with us on the episodic work, they were there working all the time, and were always there, where possible, if we needed to put our feet on the desk and say, "I need help with this." Both remained involved in the whole of the company.'

The following extracts from Lee Dannacher's personal journal reveal the progression of production on *ThunderCats* and *SilverHawks*:

1984

March – Rankin/Bass got interested in the Cats designs from Stan Weston, so Mike Germakian began artwork, and development started for the characters and show bible. Len Starr began work on the first script(s).
April – Len delivers scripts for one hour special, artwork going back and forth between R/B and Tokyo. Development materials shared with Telepictures, LCI and marketing ideas/toy and merchandising mtgs took place.
May – Bernie Hoffer brought on
June 11 – TPIX gave the green light for 65 episodes
June 12 – Actor auditions
June 19 – Record voice tracks for Shows 1 and 2 (one hour special)
June 26 – Rough music records
July 31 – Peter Lawrence to NY (we had only 10 scripts at this time)
August 14 – Orchestra records (#7 three hour sessions – with

additional week of music overdubs and mixing)

August 27 – Music and vocal sound effects into one hour special soundtrack & shipped to PAC.

September – Up to shows 19 and 20 for voice records

November – Meeting with JB/Stan Weston/Len Starr/Mike Germakian/Peter and Lee to discuss new 'metal character series'

November 25 to December 7 – Lee first trip to Tokyo

December 7 to December 12 – LA, present one hour special (completed) to Telepictures. Plus: presentation of *SilverHawks* art and storylines to TPIX.

1985

Jan 5 – Present *ThunderCats* One Hour Special and *SilverHawks* development presentation at INTV lunch

Jan 11 – Green Light for 65 episodes of *SilverHawks*!

Feb 13 – *ThunderCats* presented at toy fair

March – Schedule began on *SilverHawks* scripts

March 21 – *SilverHawks* actor auditions

April – One Hour script for *SilverHawks* to Bernie Hoffer/music composer

April – Record actors *SilverHawks* one hour special. And mtgs with Kenner (Tom McGrath)

May – PAC artists come to NY for week long mtgs. Covering both *ThunderCats* and *SilverHawks*

May 20 – *SilverHawks* orchestra records/NY

June 5 – Record actors for Show 65 of *ThunderCats* – Lovely celebratory lunch for actors and crew!

June 17 – music demos for *The Comic Strip* (Bernie was furiously busy!)

A Second Season and Beyond

When the first season of *ThunderCats* began airing on 9 September 1985, it was clear to everyone at Rankin/Bass that the show was a huge hit. Amongst its demographic (2-11 year olds), it was rated number one in its time period by all of its broadcasters. A second season of 65 shows was duly commissioned. Supervising producer Lee Dannacher explains how, despite this being a separate commission, there was relatively little downtime between series: 'We never really stopped ... We got into production [on *ThunderCats*] in '84 and were still on about episode 20 in the production pipeline when Telepictures presented the initial one hour special at the NATPE festival out in Los Angeles in early '85. They had such a great reaction, they instantly wanted another show: "Give us another idea!" ... [We then got into] developing *SilverHawks*, and everything went so fast ... We were half way through *ThunderCats*, desperately trying to get ready for the airdate, when we came into production on the first episodes of *SilverHawks*. And if we didn't get a green light on the second series of *ThunderCats* before the first series started airing in '85, we got it soon after. They just wanted more, and saw what a cash cow it was going to be. I shouldn't put it in money terms, but it was obviously going to be great business for everybody '

Several promotional documents were issued by Rankin/Bass over the years that illustrated the commercial success *ThunderCats* was enjoying. The following table was compiled by the company using data from the Cassandra and Apollo industry reports from 1987 and gives a snapshot of some of the local stations that carried *ThunderCats*:

RANK	MARKET	STATION	TIME	SHARE (KIDS 2-11)
#1	New York	WNYW	4.30PM	57
#1	Los Angeles	KTTV	4.30PM	31
#1	Chicago	WFLD	4.30PM	41
#1	Philadelphia	WTAF	3.30PM	39
#1	San Francisco	KTVU	3.00PM	41
#1	Boston	WLVI	3.30PM	23
#1	Dallas	KDAF	4.00PM	10
#1	Washington DC	WTTG	3.30PM	51
#1	Cleveland	WOIO	4.00PM	34
#1	Houston	KRIV	4.00PM	30
#1	Atlanta	WGNX	3.00PM	36
#1	Pittsburgh	WPGH	3.00PM	50
#1	Tampa	WTOG	4.30PM	26
#1	Denver	KWGN	2.30PM	56
#1	Indianapolis	WXIN	4.30PM	22
#1	San Diego	XETV	4.30PM	20
#1	Orlando	WOFL	4.00PM	29
#1	Milwaukee	WCGV	3.30PM	30
#1	New Orleans	WGNO	4.30PM	33
#1	Raleigh	WLFL	5.00PM	18
#1	Columbus, OH	WTTE	3.30PM	34
#1	Grand Rapids	WXMI	2.30PM	52
#1	Birmingham	WTTO	4.00PM	34
#1	San Antonio	KRRT	4.00PM	46
#1	Norfolk	WTVZ	5.30PM	25
#1	Dayton	WRGT	2.30PM	30
#1	Greensboro	WNRW	4.00PM	17
#1	Richmond	WRLH	4.40PM	27
#1	Mobile	WPMI	4.00PM	27
#1	Knoxville	WKCH	4.00PM	24
#1	Fresno	KMPH	3.30PM	54
#1	Toledo	WUPW	4.00PM	27
#1	Des Moines	KDSM	4.00PM	28
#1	Rochester	WUHF	3.30PM	44
#1	Omaha	KPTM	4.00PM	48
#1	Honolulu	KHNL	3.00PM	73
#1	Austin	KBVO	4.30PM	47
#1	Spokane	KAYU	4.00PM	34
#1	Lexington	WTVQ	4.00PM	29
#1	Charleston SC	WTAT	4.00PM	50

#1	Savannah	WTCS	3.00PM	21
#1	Monterey	KCBA	4.00PM	29
#1	Lafayette, LA	KADN	3.30PM	51
#1	Rockford	WORF	4.30PM	50
#1	Harlingen	KGBT	3.30PM	49
#1	Amarillo	KCIT	4.00PM	27
#1	Terre Haute	WBAK	3.30PM	41
#1	Beaumont	KBMT	4.00PM	41
#1	Shoux City	KMEG	4.30PM	38
#1	Eugene	KEZI	3.30PM	47
#1	La Crosse	WLAX	4.30PM	13
#1	Traverse City	WWTV	4.00PM	72
#1	Macon	WGXA	4.00PM	40
#1	Midland Odessa	KPEJ	4.40PM	28
#1	Boise	KTRV	3.30PM	64
#1	Minot	KBMV	4.00PM	48
#1	Lubbock	KJTV	4.00PM	43
#1	Topeka	KTKA	4.00PM	37
#1	Lake Charles	KVHP	4.00PM	25
#1	Biloxi	WXXV	3.00PM	31
#1	Eureka	KIEM	4.30PM	31
#1	Loredo	KLDO	5.00PM	64
#1	Twin Falls	KAZ	4.00PM	68
#1	Portland ME	WPXT	5.00PM	24
#1	Columbia SC	WOLO	4.30PM	42
#1	Huntsville	WZDX	4.00PM	26
#1	Baton Rouge	WRBT	3.30PM	36
#1	Lincoln	KHAS	4.30PM	16
#1	Evansville	WEVV	3.30PM	25
#1	Greenville	WCTI	4.00PM	52
#1	El Paso	KVIA	3.30PM	33
#1	Colorado Springs	KXRM	3.30PM	25
#1	Ft Myers	FTX	4.00PM	45
#1	Peoria	WYZZ	4.00PM	25
#1	Madison	WMSN	3.30PM	58

While production of the first season of *ThunderCats* had been designed to meet a 13-week uninterrupted broadcast run, the second season took a different approach. Beginning in 1987 (with *SilverHawks* having occupied the 1986 season), the 65 new episodes would be aired in batches through to 1989, with repeat showings filling the remaining time slots.

'For the second order, we worked up this formula with Telepictures that they would air only 20 new episodes at a time,' reveals Dannacher. 'Peter Lawrence stayed just as pressured, because we had to stay ahead on the scripts, but in production terms, because we were already heavily committed on *SilverHawks*, we had to shop only 20 at a time. In marketing terms, Telepictures loved it, because it elongated what they could do on the back end. So forget about downtime. When we were finished with *SilverHawks*, which was then a huge success, *The Comic Strip* was then out of development and into production and we were doing the final 65 of *ThunderCats*! Really it was eight years of incredible seven day weeks. At that point, we were so busy with all the other development and the ones we already had in production in various stages, it just felt like, "Yeah, just keep it coming." But all of us fell in love with the concept of *ThunderCats*, and Arthur and Jules felt "This is great".'

Telepictures, fresh from a merger with the television production company Lorimar, would again finance production of the 65 new *ThunderCats* shows. 'Lorimar came in when I was there,' notes Peter Lawrence, 'and they became Lorimar-Telepictures. Later, Warner bought the whole thing. When I was first there, we were still [dealing with] Michael Garin, David Saltzman, Dick Robertson and Michael Soloman. [These] Telepictures [guys] were young and hungry and flying all over the world. They wanted to have their hands in everything, and we worked with them for about a year. They were, at that time, buying individual ideas to amass their own library and go out and sell.'

Dannacher agrees, adding that *ThunderCats* was Telepictures' 'big splash' into the American market: 'The five young guys at Telepictures had made a good business for themselves internationally with old episodes of other shows, but this was their first big foray into the American syndication market. When they became Lorimar-Telepictures, it was still the distribution company that funded the series, and we sat down and created the budget we needed to fully produce the entire series. Not only *ThunderCats*, but *SilverHawks* and *The Comic Strip* as well. We'd submit our budget and they'd tweak it a bit if they needed. I remember a guy calling and saying, "Is this all you need?", which was remarkable, so I thought, "Shall I pad this a little more?" But then they'd approve the budget, and another gold star for Rankin/Bass is that we never went over budget; in fact, I came under budget on the second series of *ThunderCats* and on *The Comic Strip*.

'Telepictures would go and make their deals with the big television syndicates, like Metromedia. When our one hour-long specials were presented out in LA in January, there were a huge number of potential buyers, and if they could get a Metromedia sale and a couple of other sales, we were locked. They'd have enough to cover the production budget they'd given us, and they could spend the next few months selling station to station, like Kansas and Oklahoma; those markets that Metromedia didn't cover. But if they couldn't get a certain percentage of the market sold at that up-front presentation, we wouldn't get a green light and we'd have to stop.'

Asked about specific production budgets for both series of *ThunderCats*, Dannacher describes the difficulties of recalling an accurate per-episode figure with allowance for inflation: 'The way R/B produced television was so different from other companies, who could more easily zero in on an episodic cost. Overall it would be appropriate to say [a series of] *ThunderCats* came in at around $12-$13 million (in 1980 dollars). That would [have been more than some] other production companies were spending at the time, but it was important to us that we have the original music etc. The other guys who were out there were buying overseas shows, buying a library of already-produced music and slapping it on. We were producing all original music. We cut costs [in other ways], because everyone wore more than one hat ... So we definitely saved money in not being so compartmentalised, but we did produce over [the going rate] at the time. It also fluctuated because some of our deals with Pacific Animation were based on the dollar-yen exchange.'

'As far as budgets go, I think that the situation is so different for people reading the book now,' adds Peter Lawrence. 'My memory is that, per episode, we spent roughly, very roughly, somewhere round $150k/$175k. When I came to LA and worked on other shows and learned how much money they had to spend and how much went into the production itself, I realised you could have a per episode budget of $250,000 or $350,000 dollars and still not have the quality that we had! ... Telepictures and Warner should go down on their knees and say thank you, because the money we spent went into the show. It did not go into me and Lee junketing around the world; it did not go into us having 15 assistants. When we went on to do *Peter Pan and the Pirates* for Fox (which was also a fairly contained show), the amount of money that that show had available to do less than we had done on *ThunderCats* was gobsmacking. At one stage on *Peter Pan and the Pirates*, we had five or six editors – not writers, editors. We never had that on *ThunderCats*, ever.'

'It was not a money issue,' notes Dannacher. 'The money was there. It was a time issue. No other animation company in the world has ever produced that many episodes in that timeframe. I remember speaking to the LA guys, and they were flabbergasted that from the time of conception to the time of airing was only a matter of months, and we did it for six years over the three series. The only thing that might have made it a better series was just more time; and that might not have done it either.'

While an exhausting schedule of work was necessary in both America and Japan to deliver Rankin/Bass's output, Peter Lawrence concedes that, serendipitously, it may have been the key to the success of *ThunderCats*: 'I didn't realise it at the time, but looking back, with the way Lee and I worked, there really wasn't any time for anyone to fuck with us. There wasn't really any time for a broadcaster to say, "Oh, well, I don't think we can have a show about Tygra eating magic mushrooms." There was no "development hell" once the show was up and running. Occasionally, Jules would come in after the first few scripts and say, "Too much talk and not enough action," but by and large we went with a single vision. The scriptwriter wrote the script, I edited it, Lee gave notes and it was out – bam! Nowadays, and even some time ago, 15 people would be second-guessing you to keep everyone happy. Everything gets done by committee, so all the edge and any of the humour the actors or sound designers bring to it – and they did bring things to *ThunderCats* – gets lost in this [approach of], "Oh shit, it's the seventh draft, we've got to re-record this and that" You lose a lot of energy that way; it becomes just another bland thing. And nobody can say that about *ThunderCats*. Whatever the faults, whatever may be wrong with it, nobody could say it was bland, or it lacked energy or originality, because no-one had time to knock the shit out of it.

'It would be interesting to [compare] some original scripts and some conformed scripts – ones that came out of the studio. When I write something, I want it to be the way it's written, because I've put so much into it, and I want it to be right. Often people take it away and improvise. My response is, if you're going to improvise, make it better. If you do, you won't hear a word from me. But if you take something and fuck it up because of your ego, I'll be pissed off. I don't remember even once reading a conformed script or listening to a track and thinking, "Lee, Jesus, why did you do that?" That's unbelievable, because in my subsequent career, I've done that a lot of times and made a lot of enemies. Don't change it unless you're going to make it better. We might give Bob Camp a description of a villain and he might come back with something different, and if it's better, it's better!'

'It's a very important point Peter has made,' agrees Dannacher. 'We didn't have that overall monitoring [imposed on us]. I'd also been through many individual shows with the network and working with their broadcast standards department. We had to have big storyboard meetings with the network where they'd have their input, broadcast standards would have to see. I've been in meetings where we've had a three hour discussion on somebody's hair colour. We never had that [on ThunderCats]. During production they had a guy called Jim Moloshok at Telepictures, the head of marketing. He was the most enthusiastic young, extraordinarily talented man; he went on to a really good career after Telepictures. Jim was the only one that we'd funnel scripts through. But it wasn't broadcast standards or anything like that; he never gave notes, just cheery phone calls where he'd say, "I let my kids hear the music and now they're playing it in their cars." We'd get these enthusiastic calls all the time. I don't think we ever got a call from Telepictures asking us to change something, and it was a real timesaver.'

As with the first series before it, the second 65 shows of ThunderCats were passed to Los Angeles in preparation for transmission. From this point on, Telepictures would handle distribution of the master tapes and supply broadcasters with copies suitable for their requirements both domestically and internationally.

'Because we had just this little small townhouse office in New York, we set up post-production in Los Angeles,' recalls Dannacher. 'Masaki would hand in a final print that was cut to time and was already edited, the music was inserted and everything was done. We final mixed it in New York, then we shipped the completed programme with stereo tracks out to Los Angeles. I set up the videotape transfers out there because their tape houses did it just as a business. We hired two great guys who handled all of the final transfers of the film to tape, which I think at that point was 1-inch. Jay Weinman and Mark Saraceni were two very talented men, never losing energy and commitment to the quality of the final tape "product". They continuously solved the myriad of problems that happen in series post work (sync issues/colour correction, etc) without complaint … and always gave me such confidence that our shows would never leave their hands with issues to be dealt with later at the stations themselves. Plus both Jay and Mark were very generous and funny guys, which helped me countless times transcend any jet lag I was suffering when I'd bring materials in for a transfer date at the midnight hour! So Rankin/Bass were still responsible for and had control over that final transfer. Then the 1-inch tape became the master and the 35mm print and all the mix tracks were vaulted.'

Asked about his time spent handling post-production services on ThunderCats, Jay Weinman credits it as his introduction to the world of animation: 'I was to spend the next 15 years working in the industry, and I loved it. Lee Dannacher was a great boss and really brought the best out in everyone. The final answer print [of each episode] was shipped to me at Telepictures and my job was to function as a liaison between Rankin/Bass in New York and the final distribution here in LA.

The 35mm answer print along with the audio for the show (on 35mm 8 track mag stock) was colour corrected during a telecine session on a Rank-Cintel system. This is a film-to-tape transfer that allows you to implement different colour settings at each scene cut point in the film. This means you can balance the colour from scene to scene and maybe enhance some colours that didn't come out in the answer print process. It usually takes about eight hours to colour correct transfer a half-hour cartoon. (Since then, the technology for this process has evolved with the development of a system called the DaVinci. This gives you a lot more control over the colour settings you can achieve. I wish we'd had it then!) At this stage, the film is just colour corrected and put on tape, with about ten seconds between each act.

'After the episode was on tape, we moved into an online edit bay for the assembly process. At the beginning of each season, an answer print containing all the animated episodic title cards and the textless end credit backplate were colour corrected and transferred to tape. During the online session, the end credits were added to the episode electronically using either a Chyron machine or another lettering graphics system called the Infinit. Both systems were in use in the 1980s and it would have depended on which room we assembled the show in, as various rooms had different pieces of equipment.

'The film was transferred to NTSC 1-inch video with stereo audio for distribution in the United States. For foreign distribution, it was transferred to NTSC as well as PAL 1-inch with split track audio (dialogue on channel 1 and music and effects on channel 2). This allowed the country to dub in whatever language translation they chose. Textless title cards and end credit backplates were provided at the end of each tape for the country to type these elements in using their own language. A printed copy of the script as well as the titles and end credits was also provided.

'The post-production facilities were provided by Compact Video in Burbank, California. They did a lot of post-production work for Telepictures on promos and other film-to-tape shows. I worked with Mark Saraceni. He had my job before me and brought me in to replace him when he was promoted. We were both much younger then! The technical challenges in those days for video post-production on animated programming were few. We didn't have the graphics or animation capabilities of Photoshop or digital paint systems like the Inferno, so any fixes had to done on film through retakes. As the graphic capabilities of video post production grew in the 1990s, more of those creative revisions were done in video post, but back in the dark ages of the 1980s, you had to go back to film.'

Administrating *ThunderCats*

Behind the public and creative face of the company, a team of production coordinators and administrators worked diligently to ensure Rankin/Bass operated smoothly. From managing production budgets and salaries, to account handling and dealing with press enquiries, a small but crucial team of employees diligently supported the *ThunderCats* creative team.

As the strain of production increased at Rankin/Bass, additional staff were employed to manage the company's operations. One employee, Peter Bakalian, recounts his experiences: 'I started in the entertainment industry in the area of distribution. I'd heard that Rankin/Bass were hiring; they were looking for what my skills were meant for at that point. *ThunderCats* was in the midst of production – going into the second series – and, at that point, the show was big in terms of administration. There were so many contracts, recordings etc. We were recording with foreign studios in Tokyo and it was a very big logistical challenge. Arthur and Jules were looking for some assistance at that level. Mostly Jules was looking for someone to help him develop new properties and acquire things. I had worked for Home Box Office out of college and then went to Harvard Business School. When I got out I wanted to work in film, more in the production area than distribution. I'd worked in Disney Studios as an intern when I was at school. So when I got out [of Harvard], I came to Rankin/Bass. I knew a little about animation, having worked at Disney, but my strongest points were business and administrative abilities, though my interests were in the creative side, so Rankin/Bass was a good fit.

'Each show had a myriad of contracts to be done. Whether it was recording contracts, music, keeping the production on track. All the elements of the show had to be tracked and kept together. I was working with Lee Dannacher on that. Later at Rankin/Bass, I did some story-editing, but only for a very few shows. Peter Lawrence had really shepherded *ThunderCats*, so I was moving more into that area. I was doing development work and acquiring and evaluating books … I was also dealing with the merchandising side. At that point, LJN were doing the toys, and someone had to deal with them. I was taking care of approvals on that stuff. There was a company called Leisure Concepts that would deal with nitty-gritty day-to-day stuff like putting stuff on a lunch box or disposable cup – we didn't have time to deal with that. But when we were dealing with major characters for the action figures, Leisure Concepts didn't want to be dealing with that directly, it was way too much responsibility.'

In addition to his other tasks, Peter Bakalian also assisted with managing the company's finances. 'They were always, for some reason, in disarray – we never had great accounting. It was nothing that I enjoyed. In general, that kind of stuff would be handled by Lee Dannacher – she had the absolute say, because it was really her show as line producer – but I'd help out with it, shepherd things through … Having a budget that was updated every week, knowing what went into it, dealing with yen conversions for paying Japan – things that are thoroughly uninteresting when watching *ThunderCats* – were, in later life, invaluable. You had to know how to do it. It's like building a house; you bring in freelance people and you shepherd it along. I'd really like to tell you I was a creative force in the show, but not always.

'We knew the show was going well, but at our level – it might have been different for Jules and Arthur – we were just making sure we made our deadlines, turned up on time and got things done. It was a very strenuous situation to produce that kind of stuff, and you're talking pre-internet, a time when there was no e-mail. There were fax machines, which at the time cost $3000 and [used] crappy, miserable paper that always curled up. And that was how we communicated with Japan. No-one was really walking around saying, "We've got the number one show" or anything. Syndication was a different animal to network, at least in the United States. You didn't get the sense you were working on an incredible thing – you were just doing a show.

'Jules and Arthur were always of the mindset of, "What's the next thing we can do?" They were very involved in getting a show on the air and getting the right team together. But when I was on *ThunderCats*, I was thinking, "What's the next thing?" At the same time as *ThunderCats*, we were doing *SilverHawks* and *The Comic Strip*, and it's nothing you'd do in your forties! It wouldn't have hurt to have more people, but as you add people you have to manage them. Everyone knew their jobs and there wasn't much downtime. My guess is that we could probably have done with more Indians than chiefs, but when you're young, in your twenties, you don't think like that, and we were doing things most people didn't get to do and recognised it as an opportunity. If we had been based in LA, I'm sure we would have had far more people involved, but it would have been impossible for a studio over there to do it for the price we did it, because they tended to be over-staffed and protective of "One guy does this, one guy does this". We all cross-specialised every day. No-one said, "That's not my job," we just did it and got it over with. It was tiring and it was hard to look beyond the show itself, because you had so much to do.'

Peter Bakalian was also involved in the preparation and administration of contracts for the personnel involved in the production of *ThunderCats*. Recalling his enjoyment at attending voice recording sessions, he explains how the actors' pay and conditions were negotiated regularly: 'Most of the guys in those sessions were real veterans … Guys like Bob McFadden and Larry Kenney had been in the business since Marconi; they were really fun to listen to and just brilliant. They helped each other during the actual production and you could hear them working off each other. They tended to perform in the same room – like a live radio show – and that had a lot of appeal to it, not only to the guys doing it, but also to those lucky enough to be in the booth (which I was occasionally for contracts that had to be signed). Every time you do these things, the union requires contracts be signed. The actors were forever trying to get a fourth voice to do, because they'd get extra money if they'd played a fourth character. We paid them for every show; it was individually done. Larry was not hired to be Lion-O on a long-term basis. Maybe today you would do that to protect yourself, but we didn't do that stuff, and if you're hired to do those things, you do it. You can always fight your contract on the next show. As any producer will tell you, once you find a crew or a bunch of actors who will do what you want them to do, that understand you, that you can talk shorthand to, you keep them. The actors were paid to do three voices each; whether they did more or less, I think that's what they were paid to do. I believe they were paid by PAC, as it was a film show.

'If you look at a John Wayne or a Clint Eastwood movie, you'll see the same actors time and again. There are so many variables on a production that when there are certain people you can count on, and when people understand you the first time, and time is of the essence, you use them again – it goes for storyboard people, writers etc as well as actors. I use the analogy of building a house: if someone's good at dry-walling, I'll use them every time. It's no different; it's business.'

After his time at Rankin/Bass, Bakalian began writing independently: 'I did situation comedies, and I worked in LA with Dudley Moore on a show. I came back to New York and worked with Gene Wilder on his show. Then Arthur Rankin phoned me and asked me if I wanted to collaborate with him and get the rights to Rodgers and Hammerstein's *King and I*, which we did. There was a show called *Santa Baby* sitting on the shelf of Rankin/Bass for years, and the idea was to have an African-American cast and have soul music in a Christmas special. This was just a few years ago. It was another Rankin/Bass Christmas special and it was sponsored by Coca-Cola. I've worked on stuff for PBS and Universal, I've written animation stuff lately, *Curious George*, *Clifford the Big Red Dog*, and in England, the BBC hired me for a pre-school show called *Big and Small*. It's been pretty steady, and it's the life you live here; pitching a show and getting it made.'

Few employees at Rankin/Bass ever performed only one role during their stay with the company. Because of the varied work undertaken in New York, assistants were expected to engage with every aspect of production, and production coordinator Karen Malach (nee Siegal) was no exception. 'I came to Rankin/Bass in 1986 and started as a coordinator in the writing department,' she recalls. 'I worked closely with Peter Lawrence and Lee Schneider (who were on staff) and of course all of the freelancers. My job consisted mainly of typing scripts – no computers to make life easy. It was actual typing on my IBM Selectric (great typewriter by the way) and doing a lot of cutting and pasting with tape and white out – *not* keystrokes. I enjoyed it very much, a lot of fond memories for sure. I also was in charge of managing, contracting and scheduling the writers.

'I wore many other hats too. Anything from general office work to assisting in the recording studio during voice-over records – that was always a blast. We had an amazing crew at Howard Schwartz Recording Studios, some of the best engineers and editors I've ever worked with. I guess the best thing about being at Rankin/Bass was meeting Matthew Malach, whom I've been married to for many years.'

Another production coordinator to work on *ThunderCats*, Connie Long, is described by supervising producer Lee Dannacher as a 'miracle-worker of a production coordinator'. In addition to her clerical work, Long assisted with American/Japanese communications and oversaw payment to Pacific Animation Corporation. 'I was hired as a receptionist for the company in 1984,' she explains. 'At that time, the only people working in the office were Arthur Rankin Jr, Jules Bass, Lee Dannacher, and Brad Ficken (our part-time accountant from Telepictures). I suppose the *ThunderCats* deal was in the works, but it was still six months away (or so). I had been working for a television commercial production company for a year – the producer there had worked on an R/B production and recommended me to Lee Dannacher. I became the production coordinator on *ThunderCats* at the very beginning of production. I worked in the main office. It began with script development – I went across the street to have the scripts copied. Once we had them finalised, I messengered them to the actors every week. Artists were hired to create the characters, since they wanted to be sure the Japanese animators didn't make the characters look "oriental". I had to keep the drawings organised and periodically ship them to the animation house in Japan. I think I helped with travel arrangements – there was a lot of travel to Japan for Arthur Rankin. The merchandise licensing people would also come in often. Arthur Rankin struck the deal with the animation and I worked with the bank to do the paperwork to pay the animation house periodically.'

Long recalls that corporate shopping was amongst her more unusual duties: 'Each time someone went to [a meeting at the Japanese animation house], it was the custom to take gifts. The first time he went over, Arthur asked me to go shopping at Cartier and Tiffany's to purchase the gifts. It was really fun. Then, the first Christmas, Jules Bass and I went shopping for gifts for the actors. I think we ended up buying crystal champagne glasses and a bottle of Louis Roederer Cristal.

'Our offices were located at 53rd Street and 5th Ave in the building that the Museum of Broadcasting was housed in. It was exciting to work there, because I would unexpectedly see or ride the elevator with famous people who were there in connection with the Museum. My best sightings were Carol Burnett (rode the elevator with her and she was very friendly and chatty) and ... Katherine Hepburn!'

Connie Long lists *ThunderCats* as the highlight of her career: 'I was young, and it was really fun working with this group of people. The work was incredibly busy and I was learning all the time. I was living in New York City, and that was fun and exciting. The offices were in a great part of town. It was exciting when Arthur and Jules sealed the *ThunderCats* deal, and *very busy*. Every day, the "to do" list was endless. Arthur was busy getting the Japanese animation company ramped up and Jules was busy getting production going in New York. Bernie Hoffer was brought in to produce the music library for the series, the actors had to be hired and scriptwriters had to be found. Deals were also made with the merchandising company LJN. I had never worked on a television series before. My job experience was one year of work for a television commercial director. Lee Dannacher was my mentor. Every day she would leave me a list of things to do and be off to the sound studio to do casting or recording. She and the experience taught me how to be organised and efficient. Lee was terrific – very detail orientated and kept a hundred balls up in the air at once. Since leaving the company in 1987, I've moved to New Hampshire, got married and had kids. I worked in corporate marketing communications and hated it. I'm now a school librarian – much better than corporate work!'

A comparison between the on-screen credits for both seasons of *ThunderCats* reveals the additional personnel employed by Rankin/Bass over the course of 130 episodes:

Season One credits transcribed from the series' opening episode, 'Exodus':

Executive Producers
ARTHUR RANKIN JR
&
JULES BASS

Supervising Producer
LEE DANNACHER

Animation By
PACIFIC ANIMATION
CORPORATION

In Charge Of Production
MASAKI IIZUKA

Animation Staff
TSUGU KUBO
MINORU NISHIDA
KATSUHITO AKIYAMA
AKIHIKO TAKAHASHI

YUKIMATSU ITO
YUJI YATABE
TOSHIHIKO SATO
KAZUFUMI NOMURA

Based On Characters Created By
TED WOLF

Project Development
LEISURE CONCEPTS INC.

Head Writer
LEONARD STARR

Music
BERNARD HOFFER

Script Consultant
PETER LAWRENCE

Psychological Consultant
ROBERT KUISIS PhD

Voice Characterisations
ROBERT McFADDEN
EARL HAMMOND
LARRY KENNEY
LYNNE LIPTON
EARLE HYMAN
PETER NEWMAN

Recording Staff
JOHN CURCIO – Dialogue
MICHAEL FARROW – Music
TOM PERKINS – Editorial
LARRY FRANK [misspelling] – Editorial
PETE CANNAROZZI – Effects

Secondary Character Designs
JIM MESKIMEN

Production Staff
TONY GIOVANNIELLO
MATTHEW MALACH
CONNIE LONG
HEATHER WINTERS

HEAR THE ROAR!

Season Two credits transcribed from the final episode of
***ThunderCats*, 'The Book of Omens':**

Executive Producers
ARTHUR RANKIN JR
&
JULES BASS

Supervising Producer
LEE DANNACHER

Animation By
PACIFIC ANIMATION
CORPORATION

In Charge Of Production
MASAKI IIZUKA

Animation Staff
TSUGU KUBO
MINORU NISHIDA
RYO YASUMURA
TAMEO KOHANAWA
YUJI YATABE
SEOK KI KIM

Based On Characters Created By
TED WOLF

Project Development
LEISURE CONCEPTS, INC.

Head Writer
LEONARD STARR

Music
BERNARD HOFFER

Script Consultant
PETER LAWRENCE

Psychological Consultant
ROBERT KUISIS PhD

Voice Characterisations
ROBERT McFADDEN
EARL HAMMOND
LARRY KENNEY
LYNNE LIPTON
EARLE HYMAN
PETER NEWMAN
GERRIANNE RAPHAEL
DOUG PREIS

Recording Staff
JOHN CURCIO – Dialogue
MICHAEL FARROW – Music
LARRY FRANKE – Editorial
MICHAEL UNGAR – Editorial
PETE CANNAROZZI – Effects
JOHN CRENSHAW – Editorial

Secondary Character Designs
JIM MESKIMEN
MICHAEL GERMAKIAN
BOB CAMP
PEPE MORENO

Production Staff
ANTHONY GIOVANNIELLO
MATTHEW MALACH
CONNIE LONG
PETER BAKALIAN
DENNIS J WOODYARD
KAREN SEIGEL
CHARLES HASEGAWA
ELEANOR MUSIOL

Moral Programming

During the 1980s, the resurgence of the action/adventure serial did not go unnoticed by parental groups. Often accused of instilling unnecessary violence into the minds of impressionable viewers, the genre became the target of a vocal band of campaigners. While many argued in defence of this new generation of programming that it was no different from anything seen previously from the genre – including programmes from the dawn of television, such as *The Lone Ranger* and *Flash Gordon* – negative attention was exacerbated by the public perception (in many cases accurate) that cartoons were being driven by toy sales. In effect, cartoons were accused of being nothing more than a huge advertisement for commercial products. Rankin/Bass were keen to pacify the lobbyists with *ThunderCats*.

Most vocal amongst the campaigners gaining ground across America was Peggy Charren. In 1968, Charren had founded the ACT (Action for Children's Television) with a view to reforming television output for youngsters. In a biography from John Vivian's *The Media of Mass Communication* she is quoted as stating:

> 'Violent television teaches children that violence is the solution to problems, that violent behaviour can be fun and funny, that criminals and police make up a larger percentage of the population than they really do, and that violent behaviour is practiced by heroes as well as by villains. But you can't say that there shouldn't be any violence on television. It is the context that is really important. Too often, children are the excuse for banning speech: words and pictures in comic books, movies, classic stories, textbooks and television. But government censorship is not the way to protect children from inappropriate content.'

Ultimately, Charren's actions resulted in the creation of legislation, the Children's Television Act of 1990, designed to safeguard children's programming. Shortly afterwards, in 1992, the ACT was disbanded, Charren's objectives having been achieved.

During the early development of *ThunderCats*, the production team struck a careful balance, injecting the testosterone-fuelled adrenaline necessary to engage young children while at the same time being careful to conform each episode to a moral or life lesson in order to fulfil their self-appointed mandate to produce responsible programming. As Rankin/Bass was synonymous with the gentler, holiday specials market, its new foray into the action/adventure genre was a gamble for the company's prestigious reputation. The safeguards put in place for *ThunderCats* continued a growing trend in the industry, which both placated parental groups and provided an advertising platform in one stroke; Rankin/Bass would employ the services of a child psychologist. In an article from the magazine *Broadcasting* dated 9 September 1985, executive producer Jules Bass gave the following commentary:

> 'In the past [...] somebody had to say: "This show is approved to air."

The network standards department told you what you could and could not do and what values they wanted to see in the show [...] Producing for syndication, however, involves "policing yourself". The idea of using a psychologist evolved when producers were left alone in children's programming; they were somewhat nervous as to how to cope, and we felt somebody besides ourselves should be talking to us. We might as well have a good psychologist.'

Peggy Charren believed these proactive efforts to moderate children's entertainment were welcome, but advised caution, stating in an interview for the same article: 'The use of consultants is not a "bad thing" ... but I hate it when it's used to lobby.'

Dr Robert Kuisis was a psychologist with a doctoral degree in counselling psychology and a postdoctoral certificate in psychoanalysis. Throughout the production of *ThunderCats*, *SilverHawks* and *The Comic Strip*, his services would be engaged to produce a short précis of the educational and social benefits contained within individual episodes. For *ThunderCats*, Kuisis reviewed and analysed all 130 scripts, commenting where necessary and evaluating the episodes for a booklet entitled *Synopses and Morals*. This bound booklet was issued to schools and parenting groups both to advertise the series and to immunise it against criticism. Alongside Kuisis's summary of the moral value of any given story was a short plot synopsis by Rankin/Bass employee Heather Winters.

'My bachelor's degree is in philosophy and I have master's degrees in sociology and theology,' reveals Kuisis. 'At the time I worked on the show, I was directing the office of counselling and student services at New York University's School of Education, Health, Nursing and Arts Professions (now NYU's Steinhardt School of Education). I knew Jules Bass socially and was working on my doctoral dissertation in the early 1980s, parts of which had to do with constructs and concepts like interpersonal problem-solving skills and pro-social behaviour or social competence. As I recall it, groups like Action for Children's Television were monitoring after-school children's programmes in the absence of any network standards, and the question of how children's TV affects behaviour and development was in the public discourse of the time. It was very much on the radar screen, and Congress had hearings on the issue. In surveying research related to my topic, I recall coming across a compendium of research studies on the issue published by NIMH (National Institute of Mental Health).

'Jules had the idea of incorporating pro-social themes in the storylines themselves and using me to review scripts for anything that might negatively influence children, and also to write a moral or lesson based on each script. I met initially with a group of writers so we would know each other personally, but then I was sent complete scripts to work from. I don't recall the specific time frame, but I would periodically get a batch, maybe three to five at a time, and have a few weeks of turnaround time. I recall needing to make very few recommendations for change. The few I did suggest had to do with softening material that could potentially come across as too scary for younger viewers.'

Commenting on the emergence of advisors and psychologists associated with television productions, Kuisis believes the idea wasn't slow to be universally implemented: 'I don't feel qualified to comment with any authority, since I didn't really keep up with specific shows at the time to compare it with. However, I have an article (part of a promotional kit I seem to have kept) which says that, of the 12 animated shows introduced in 1985, half had consultants working to establish pro-social themes. If that is true, I guess we weren't that unique in that regard.

'I wrote a piece for a promotional packet describing the show as including themes that relate to cognitive, emotional, social and moral developmental tasks of childhood. On the whole, its mythic component as a hero myth in which good battles evil helps in the development of personal identity as well as collective values. I was using Joseph Campbell's notion of the hero with a thousand faces as a universal myth found in all cultures. I still think that is as good a characterisation of the show as any. Whether that is what accounts for its lasting power, I don't know. It was also great animation and a great show by artistic standards. My impression is that, today, the American public in general tends to be more conservative than liberal in matters of morality and cultural values. Politically, we are mired in the so-called culture wars in which conservatives characterise media of all kinds as suspect of corrupting the country.'

The 'promotional packet' referenced by Dr Kuisis was a document included as part of the *Synopses and Morals* package distributed by Rankin/Bass. His complete introduction to the educational and moral values of *ThunderCats* is reproduced below:

THE ROLE OF *THUNDERCATS* AS A PRO-SOCIAL PROGRAMME
By Dr Robert Kuisis PhD
Psychological Consultant

The role of television in modern American society is considerable. As summarised in the 1982 report of the National Institute of Mental Health, *Television and Behaviour: Ten Years of Scientific Progress and Implications for the Eighties* (Washington, DC), its influence is pervasive. The report characterises television as an educator whose effect on the aculturation process of children and adults is as powerful as the family, schools, churches and other institutions. Its influence is both positive and negative, and a critical task for parents and teachers is to monitor and balance what is learned by children so that the positive effects outweigh the negative. Unfortunately, parents and educators have little input into planning what shows are created, produced and programmed. Their input, then, is limited to regulating what TV shows children watch and to helping the young viewers reflect on and comprehend in discussion the content of the shows. In carrying out such an educative task, supplementary materials can prove to be an essential aid. The morals in the *Synopses and Morals* book have been assembled to help in this teaching endeavour for the *ThunderCats* show.

The episode synopses and lessons provide the means to help children understand the content of the show. The lessons, which are addressed to the adult mediator, develop the theme of each episode. What can be learned from this show? The themes relate to various tasks of development for children in the cognitive, emotional, social and moral realms. In the cognitive domain, themes involve children's understanding of various kinds of cognitions, such as social groups, friendships, success and failure, concern for the environment, problem-solving, and self-deliberation before acting. In the emotional domain, themes include the recognition of affect, impulse-management, self-control and self-esteem. Social development themes cover topics like responsibility, friendly peer interaction, social sensitivity, caution in dealing with strangers, and pro-social behaviours like altruism and honesty. Finally, in the area of moral development, episodes stress the right judgment of good and evil, the development of conscience and levels of morality, and the value of social responsibility.

In commenting on the show as a whole, the link between its storyline and the development of identity is to be acknowledged. Overall, the show is a fantasy tale with heroes, villains and characters of mythic proportion. As fantasy, it is a morality play in which the forces of good battle the forces of evil. As myth, it provides a means for children to engage in an essential task, the development of personal identity.

Modern man has been characterised as secular man, who is without soul, in that he does not share in a universally shared meaning system that traditional primitive man enjoyed. In earlier eras, myth and ritual provided to man the functions of presenting to him the wonders of the universe, of explaining the forces of nature and ways of containing inner impulses, of validating a specific social and moral order for social communion, and of providing pathways through the stages of life. For Jerome Bruner, the cognitive and developmental psychologist and educationalist, the loss of myth in society has consequences for the development of personal identity. For him, myth is an externalisation of what he calls the vicissitudes of personality and is a way of dealing with our inner impulses. Our discordant impulses are bound and ordered in a set of identities. And myth, in presenting mythic figures to us, is a tutor, a shaper of identities. Bruner cites Joseph Campbell, the chronicler and commentator of myth, who reminds us that individual man is only a fraction of the total image of man, and only in society as a whole can the fullness of the totality be able to be seen. The full picture is seen in a 'mythologically instructed community', which offers a corpus of images, models, and identities to which growth may aspire. Such a community provides its members with a library of scripts upon which the individual may judge the play of his multiple identities. Myth, then, is a criterion for the self-critic in the play of life (Bruner, 1968).

Joseph Campbell, in his book *The Hero with a Thousand Faces* (New York, 1956), traced the universally accepted myth of the hero in its independent presence in all cultures. He saw in this myth a single human quest for identity. But modern man, lacking the guidance of a shared meaning system, must seek individually for identity and choose among a repertoire of identities. Among the sources and repositories of modern mythic identities in our electronic age are films and television in the representations of heroes and the social reality presented there. *ThunderCats* can be viewed as one representation of the hero myth. The ThunderCats, heroes all, have been separated from their home by a catastrophic occurrence and have entered a realm of wonder where they encounter fabulous forces of danger and helping spirits. They penetrate to a source of power, the Eye of Thundera. They do battle with the epitome of evil and its variants. In the midst of their struggle they encounter initiation trials and rites of passage, and they are called upon to maintain a moral code of Truth, Justice, Honour and Loyalty. And ultimately they hope to persist triumphant and attain a boon for mankind, a peaceful, orderly and happy existence. In sum, the show, as a representation of the myth of the hero, may serve a purpose which goes beyond the entertainment of an action-adventure cartoon. For in presenting its viewers with a mythic morality play of good vs evil, it exposes them to a set of heroic identities, the identification of which may provide valuable lessons towards the necessary achievement of a personal identity.

It is hoped that these remarks have served to introduce the pro-social aspect of this series to you. If viewed constructively, *ThunderCats* will be not only a popular form of entertainment, but a positive force in the development of its young viewers as well.

While Robert Kuisis' story notes were both comprehensive and analytical, they seldom resulted in actual changes to content, and he recalls no instances where a script was rejected at his request. Instead, the moral mandate of the series slowly embedded itself into the consciousness of the show's writers. Some writers were reluctant to participate in this, often placing 'risqué' content into their scripts to test the system. Others, however, relished the task, taking it as a challenge to find new moral predicaments to base their adventures upon. 'Some of us thought it corny at first,' recalls Peter Lawrence, 'and a contrived response to the pressure being brought by people like Peggy Charren. However, that underpinning may have been a crucial factor, uniting such diversely created "episodic worlds" into a single coherent show. Imagine reconciling Bill Overgard's astonishing flights of fancy with Len Starr's more "mythological" approach.'

The End and the Beginning

The completion of the second 65 episodes of *ThunderCats* marked the end of production on the series. Though it had enjoyed ratings and marketing success for nearly five years, little or no discussion was given to producing a third season, and the *ThunderCats* franchise lay dormant. 'The ratings weren't dropping, they were climbing,' notes Arthur Rankin. 'That's why we made a second season; 130 of those pictures [in total]. The first 65 did so well we decided to make another 65. By the time we'd done 130, we thought we'd done enough of that and we went on to other things. It became a very popular series – it was number one at the time. It's a commercial business; if something works you do it, if it doesn't you forget it.'

Independent articles and commentary from the 1980s suggests that, while the action/adventure genre in general may well have been in decline, the popularity of *ThunderCats* in particular was still enviable. The following article from *Advertising Age* dated 3 November 1986 reveals the industry's verdict on the series:

ThunderCats success no accident
Written by Larry G Collins

Tracking Shares analyses the performance of syndicated programming based on privately commissioned A C Nielson National Television surveys and A C Nielsen Cassandra reports.

The emergence of Lorimar-Telepictures' *ThunderCats* as a proven winner in its second syndicated season as a daily half-hour animated show is not a surprise or an accident. L-T's approach to competing with the toy-driven animated programmes on Saturday mornings and in daily early-fringe syndication involved a carefully executed programming strategy.

Since the premiere of *Masters of the Universe* in late 1983, a flood of animated shows has hit the marketplace seeking the combustible media/merchandising mix that creates smash hit T-toy combos capable of competing for the overall dollars in the children's marketplaces.

L-T created a six-minute tape featuring its ideas for *ThunderCats* visual concept and its main characters, based on the successful elements L-T executives observed in network and syndicated animated hits. Data from focus groups and an innovative test that placed the concept tape on five or six cable systems around the country – enabling the company to conduct intensive and detailed phone surveys – shaped *ThunderCats* into the kind of show that contains the basic elements shows in this genre need to succeed.

For the last four sweeps periods, *ThunderCats* has been the highest-rated early-fringe animated programme against children ages 2 to 11. The show's combination of strong, tough and resourceful heroes for these tykes, an atmosphere of adventure and fantasy that appeals to teens and positive social values in its storyline, for parents to approve of, provides a formidable, broad-based programming hit.

ThunderCats aired on 109 stations covering 85% of US TV homes in its first season and now airs on 132 stations covering an identical percentage. The show's initial contract, a three-year deal made in September 1985, offers a barter split of 2 ½ national / 3 ½ local minutes per episode in the first, second and third broadcast quarters and a 2 national / 4 local minutes per episode split in the fourth quarter, L-T reports the show is 95% sold at guaranteed cpm[1] of $3.65 against kids 2 to 11, a 12% increase from last season. Participating sponsors include Hasbro, Quaker Oats Co, Kellogg and Mattel.

---

[1] An advertising industry term meaning 'cost per thousand' – the 'm' standing for 'mille', the Latin for thousand.

In addition to high-quality animation, L-T backs its programming while it's still hot with inventive promotional and merchandising support. A two-hour animated prime time movie *ThunderCats Ho!* was provided to stations with all commercial time intact, enabling stations carrying the show to maximise its market impact and promote the 'hub' of their kids' programming blocks. A promotional tie-in with Burger King is reportedly one of the largest in the chain's merchandising history.

Getting to the top has been no accident for *ThunderCats*. With the kind of support L-T is providing, look for it to stay there for a while.

By the end of the original run of *ThunderCats* episodes, Lee Dannacher and Peter Lawrence agree that the market for such action-adventure cartoons was flooded. Rankin/Bass alone had produced 130 episodes of *ThunderCats*, 65 episodes of *SilverHawks* and 65 episodes of *The Comic Strip* (which combined four 'mini' shows: *TigerSharks*, *Street Frogs*, *Karate Kat* and *The Mini-Monsters*). 'By the time the second series of episodes was airing and *SilverHawks* and *The Comic Strip* had come, action-adventure – and the superhero component to it – had kind of come and gone,' admits Lawrence. 'Not only that, but the whole syndicated strip theory was beginning to disintegrate somewhat and we were at the very beginning of what's happened since; the fracturing of the market and the proliferation of outlets.'

'At that time, '88 or '89,' adds Dannacher, 'Telepictures had gone through its own transmogrification. It had sold itself to Warner Brothers, so all of us were under animation contracts with Warner Brothers. Nickelodeon barely existed when we started production in New York, I think they had ten people, but at the end of production they had built up a huge studio. When Warner bought Telepictures, which had us, they thought to themselves, "We want to do this, why are we using Rankin/Bass? We want to build our own studio and produce our own series." The front end of that vertical organisation of Hollywood was beginning, so if Time Warner owned the top of everything, they were going to have Warner Brothers do their animation in-house and not use people like us. So the market changed and so did the business.'

With no further commissions forthcoming, Rankin/Bass began to wind down operations, airing only two new shows in the subsequent two decades. 'After *ThunderCats*, Jules and I had a long holiday,' explains Arthur Rankin. 'We were both exhausted after that. We'd made cel shows for years and we wanted to take a rest. I made a few things after that like *The King and I* by Rogers and Hammerstein for Warner Brothers, and that was cel animation. I'm doing plays now in Bermuda – we have a theatre here that is as good as most Broadway theatres, and occasionally I write a play. This is an English colony, and there is a story about a plane that crashes in the Sahara desert: the first thing the English survivors do is find an oasis, but after that, they form a dramatic society! There's a lot of creative talent over here and I use it.

'Television certainly has changed, the temperament of children has changed. Kids today aren't what they were 30-40 years ago. They are smarter, generally they're more adventuresome, and they're much older than their years. I think kids today, the little ones that come around me, are smarter than I am. The audience of *ThunderCats* today are sitting there with their father who saw it when he was ten years old and he's saying, "Let's look at this together; Daddy saw this when he was your age". With our holiday specials, they sit with Grandma or even Great Grandma, who say they watched them when they were young. It's the same with Disney classics like *Cinderella* or *Bambi*; people remember them from childhood and encourage their children and grandchildren to join them over the holidays and special occasions. That's why those things last. In our business, the wise man said, "Remember this, nobody knows anything". I think that's true; you take your best shot and hope for success. Sometimes it happens, mostly it doesn't. *ThunderCats* is an original idea and it's a good idea. It has enough meat in the characters to keep it going. 130 episodes is a lot of film to keep stories going, introducing a couple of new characters now and then. We worked hard, and very frankly we were very good at that. Our company Rankin/Bass was really good at that.'

After leaving Rankin/Bass, Lee Dannacher found herself moving, briefly, to Los Angeles to continue work in the animation industry. 'It all pales in comparison as far as my animation career after *ThunderCats*,' she admits. 'After Rankin/Bass ... what's a pleasant way of saying "closed"? ... Jules and Arthur went off to their respective villas – though that's not entirely true! After that intensive production schedule, Jules and Arthur decided to disband for a certain time. There was no-one in New York doing what we did. I'd developed some relationships with people at Nickelodeon, but it was a very corporate feel over there. I was spoiled with the kind of autonomy that Rankin/Bass enjoyed, and I knew instinctively that I wouldn't find that anywhere else. I found myself in LA working on a couple of productions. One I did with Peter Lawrence, Fox's *Peter Pan and the Pirates*. Then Masaki Iizuka and I produced several animated specials, re-teaming with Romeo Muller, that we produced independently. *Noel* was one, which was for NBC, and we did a series called *Peppermint Rose* – well, we did a pilot, but it never went to series. I produced many animated specials with Masaki from Pacific Animation Studios. Hanna-Barbera was not a good experience for me!'

'We left New York and came to LA,' adds Peter Lawrence, '... well, separately. It was Lee who got me into *Peter Pan and the Pirates*. It was a very different experience; you had to fight. I remember threatening to throw a network executive out of the window! It just wasn't the same; I was like, "Are you trying to make things difficult?" We brought a certain amount of our *ThunderCats* attitude with us. It was a 52 episode order and we wrote 53. One was thrown away, and it was the best script that we had. It was thrown out because it was based on the "Rime of the Ancient Mariner" and involved killing the Netherbird ... We [were told to tone it down] from that, so that it involved throwing a pin and knocking [the Netherbird] out. [Then we were told to] pull back from that, so that it involved simply scaring it! We sat in a meeting and said, "Wait a minute, this is a show about pirates. Do you know what pirates do? They rape and they murder and they kill." I'm not speaking for Lee, but what may have happened to us is that instead of being fun and light-hearted, you're suddenly thinking that if it's going to be as hard as saving the world or brain surgery, you might as well go and save the world. Hanna-Barbera was just a complete disaster, a bunch of morons running it. I personally made some terrible mistakes.'

Today, Lee Dannacher is committed to her new career working as a Child Protection Investigator. 'That experience just put me off television production,' she reaffirms. 'Continuing in that vein, Masaki and I couldn't get anything into series.

So back in New York, I produced a show direct to video that was *Buster &
Chauncey's Silent Night*, which was fun. But nothing got into development – nothing
went. I had to keep going back and forth between New York and the Mid-West for
personal reasons. I did reunite with Arthur and Jules for a film called *Santa Baby*,
which was just a special for Fox and the Coca Cola company, so it just sounds like
the whole thing petered out.'

With the conclusion of the original run of *ThunderCats* episodes, the series
looked set to recede into the television graveyard of children's programming.
However, while its contemporaries have faded into obscurity, *ThunderCats* survives
in the memories of the generation it first inspired. It has achieved cult status, and
its longevity is testament to the incredible efforts of each and every member of the
production team. And the *ThunderCats* story remains far from over ...

2. THE FORMULA
The Writers' Story

ThunderCats may be best remembered for its dynamic visuals and for pushing the boundaries of television-based animation, but a talented team of writers worked hard to underpin the series with a complex mythology. They imbued the programme with a detailed structure, which supported the innovative and diverse themes explored, and *ThunderCats* seamlessly integrated action, adventure and morality into its 130 broadcast adventures.

Unlike most production departments at Rankin/Bass, the writing team on *ThunderCats* had a complicated – and in some respects contentious – evolution. It began with executive producer Jules Bass. Bass would author only a handful of scripts himself, but his vision for the show and his experience in writing for the animation genre were invaluable in shaping the way *ThunderCats* developed.

Supervising producer Lee Dannacher explains the company's approach to scripting the show: 'Len Starr was the very first call. He'd worked with Arthur and Jules previously on other productions. He and Jules worked one-on-one for three or four weeks. Len came back in and presented a bunch of beginning ideas. Arthur called his best friend, Bill Overgard, and said, "Bill, what do you think of these things?" But Len was still point man as far as being head writer, so he and Jules worked it up, and it's my memory that Jules then sat down and banged out a whole bible for the world itself and who the characters were, but not what future episodes could be about .... I remember them telling me to go down to a comic store and copy down the names of the old comic book writers like Bob Haney and a couple of others [who could be approached to write for the show], because [at that time] there weren't a lot of guys in New York writing action and adventure stories. Rankin/Bass didn't want to go out to LA and call from those markets yet. With Len spearheading it, I remember about eight of us sat round a table – Len and Bill, Jules and Arthur and a few others.'

It was in early 1984 that Leonard Starr was commissioned to provide the opening scripts for *ThunderCats* and to draft the writers' bible – a document that serves as a brief introduction to a series and can be used by a variety of contributors in order to retain a central continuity. Asked how he came to be designated head writer, Starr recalls: 'I suppose it was because my credit should really have been "Developed by ..." and they didn't give it to me. I was due to get participation [in profits], not fully delineated at that point, and perhaps they thought [if they gave me a "Developed by ..." credit] it might entitle me to a bigger piece of the pie. All they had were these posters of various cat people and they didn't know what to do with them. I have absolutely no feel for science fiction or fantasy, but a story is a story whatever the theme, so I concocted this set-up where their home planet was in the process of being destroyed, so they came looking for another place to live, found Third Earth and all that.

'One of the funny things is that I made the bad guys mutants because kids seem to like the word "mutant", and letters came in saying, "If the mutants are the bad guys then what the heck are the *ThunderCats*?" Anyway, we were off and running and it became very popular. We got very funny mail on it. One was a letter from a six year old boy, nicely written so I suspected parental support. Others from Dartmouth or Cornell, one of the New York State Universities. Students would run home from classes to catch the show, because it was on at 4 o'clock in the afternoon in the Northeast. They'd have their *ThunderCats* fix right after they had come out of their trigonometry classes, or whatever it was they were studying.'

In addition to his writing responsibilities, Starr was also charged with editing the early *ThunderCats* scripts: 'Well, that was my job as head writer. I was really an editor.' Starr adds that any script that fell below par would be instantly revised: 'Those were the ones I rewrote. And when I say I rewrote them, I mean I rewrote them pretty much top to bottom. [The original writers still] got paid for them, and we did [one after another] that way. When you work for direct syndication, it's a killer. Mostly you had to cut down dialogue where there was a lot of talk. It had to be kept fairly terse to keep it moving along. Kids don't have a lot of patience, so you had to get into it fast. That was pretty much the traditional short story form where you start in the middle of the action, refer to the beginning just enough to explain what got them to that point, then go off to the ending, which is a punch-line that is hopefully satisfying. So there were some technical things that had to be done, but by then it had become sort of second nature and you didn't even think of it in technical terms.'

Commenting on the input he gave writers, Starr reveals he would rarely intervene at the early stages: 'I don't think I even got outlines from the writers. We got a final script. Maybe the writers talked it over with Jules, but as far as I know there would be just a final script, and there would always be the same faults in the script. If you look at how I did [the newspaper comic strips] *Annie* or *Mary Perkins On Stage*, you will see that I tried very hard to make sure that I had either Annie or Mary in every daily [strip], or at least referred to, since, after all, they were the title characters. And the same thing with *ThunderCats*. [The writers] would have pretty good stories but the ThunderCats were only peripherally involved. The rest of the story would go off in different directions, and I had to keep reminding them that the name of the thing is *ThunderCats* and they should have ThunderCats in it.'

When speaking about the 'parental groups' that lobbied for the abolition of 'violent' programming for children, Starr reveals he thought the show's approach could be restrictive: 'All of the action shows have a lot of violence. The first syndicated series was a show called *He-Man*. It was sort of a model for us, but not really. It would be nice if you could swipe everything, but once you go into it, you find you can't. One of the best regarded stories in *Mary Perkins On Stage* was a rip-off of *Rigoletto*, the opera by Verdi, which is taken from a play by Victor Hugo called *The King Amuses Himself*. I'm an opera buff – I know hundreds of operas – and since the *Rigoletto* rip-off was successful I figured, oh boy, that I could pillage some of the others; but I couldn't find another one that would work. [In *ThunderCats*,] the moral was supposed to take the curse off the violence. "Creative violence" we called it. A lot of mayhem where nobody got killed or even seriously hurt so we'd have no problems with that.

'Robert Kuisis was in on one of the meetings, and we would tack on a moral to begin with, but sometimes we were forcing the moral. Somewhere along the way, I remembered that one of the premises to any kind of writing is that the first sentence should establish what the thing is about. A key example of that is *Moby Dick* where the first line is "Call me Ishmael." It has portent; you know it isn't going to be a love story. A perfect example is *Pride and Prejudice*, where the first sentence is, "Is it a truth universally accepted that a bachelor in possession of a fortune is also in need of a wife." And that's what the whole book is about. I thought that by setting the moral first I could make things go quicker, and possibly even easier, so I started looking at Aesop for morals and books of proverbs that would give me a starting point for a story. One of my favourites was, "Better an honest enemy than a false friend". Wow. The story just writes itself. So it was with many of them. Some, though, you really had to reach for. I had one from a book of Russian proverbs that went, "A flea doesn't know if it's living on a Czar or a Muzhik." Try to make a story out of that! Yet it is still a great proverb. You could just rewrite the characters, but essentially it means that a flea does what a flea does and it doesn't care where it is. It's getting what it wants.'

The following document was handwritten by Leonard Starr and supplied (complete with sketches) as a reference aid for the show's scriptwriters. It describes the primary storytelling objectives for the *ThunderCats* series as envisaged by Starr:

> Goals – That may be stated as valid for the ThunderCats:
>
> Bringing the Universe under control, so that the survival of the many decent and able beings in it may be assured and sustained.
>
> Solving problems related to the stability of the Third Earth itself. Improving the survival of the good inhabitants there.
>
> Re-establishment of the ThunderCats empire – (a fundamentally truthful and honest civilisation based on individual freedom and ability – with an emphasis on exploring the Universe.)
>
> Restoring communication of the many varied peoples (beings) of Third Earth with each other, for the purpose of aligning the planet's population more towards a common agreed-on destiny.
>
> Aiding oppressed or enslaved beings in overcoming their difficulties. (Not like Commie-stuff, just protection of the innocent and downtrodden.)

Writing early episodes of *ThunderCats* was an expansive process with many ideas being heavily edited, revised or removed as the series continued to take shape. Examining Leonard Starr's 4000 word writers' bible, a variety of differences from the televised scripts can be seen, including an early idea for the Lynx God, Maftet, to explain the origins of Third Earth:

> It will be he who explains to the THUNDERCATS that these particular ruins are those of First Earth. They are now living on THIRD EARTH, which is the number of times existing civilisations were destroyed by

global warfare, the inhabitants returning to a primitive state each time, radiation the cause of the strange variegated forms of life now populating the planet. (Other Man-Animal Gods of First Earth's ancient Egypt can be called up as required by the plots.)

While this direct explanation of Starr's atomic devastation idea was removed at the suggestion of the production office, his vision of the planet continued to take root in the series, with a variety of episodes suggesting that the ThunderCats' adopted planet and the Earth were one and the same.

Notable character differences in the writers' bible include the absence of WilyKit, and the naming of the Lord of the ThunderCats as Lion-El, which was subsequently deemed to be too similar to the popular toy train manufacturer Lionel.

Speaking about his work on the writers' bible, Starr contends that less is more: 'I created most of the characters. The bible that I wrote is about six or seven pages long. Most bibles for a show are usually about the size of a phone book, and I guarantee that most writers never read them. But six pages is short enough for a writer to go through and swipe as much as they want, and that's what a bible is for, to set up situations and settings for potential stories.'

Starr's thoroughness was such that he also provided proposals and points of discussion to his fellow writers in an attempt to maintain a high level of character and story development. The following handwritten notes, which supplemented the mandatory guidelines in the writers' bible, contain various story suggestions amongst which the writers could 'pick and choose'. Some ideas, such as Panthro's fear of bats, were realised on screen, yet others, such as the ThunderCats' inherent fear of fire, would remain undeveloped:

> The ThunderCats are tremendously able. If the forces of evil are too inept to develop effective weaponry or techniques, or if they are hindered by lack of materials, then the only way to spice up the game and prolong the contest is to allow the T-Cats specific, individual or group foibles and weaknesses; wherein they may fail occasionally in their attempts to quell the opposition. This would allow, as well, credibility to seep into the show!

> There are few things more human than human error – if we want high audience affinity for the characters, we need to have them communicate a familiar reality, something from the kids' universe that they will recognise & respond to. Who identifies with perfection?

> New Achilles Heels for the ThunderCats:

> Tygra, Cheetara, and Lion-O are all terrified by fire. Panthro, WilyKat/Kit and Snarf are not. (Panthro is not since he has had to control fire in his workshop and knows how it works, Kit/Kat don't because they are too wild to care much – and Snarf isn't because he will be called on to brave the flames for Lion-O and does so gladly.)

Panthro is terrified of bats.

Cheetara can't stand lightning or any unleashed energy bolts. (She is the only one who can't handle this.)

Tygra is still afraid of water. He is, for example, too shaky about it to cross a rope bridge high over a river – not because of the height, but the possibility of coming in contact with lots of water. (He can't swim.) Mumm-Ra could, therefore, foil this ThunderCat by surrounding him with water, making Tygra an island by wizardry.

While he had been responsible for the vast majority of work on the early *ThunderCats'* scripts, Starr's role changed drastically when Peter Lawrence was hired by Rankin/Bass. 'Peter was brought in mostly to help,' says Starr. 'But I think they were already trying to edge me out, because the time was coming where I was supposed to find out what my slice of the pie was going to be, and it was going to be nothing. My contract was a deal memo. I had no idea that a deal memo was legally final. A memo, to me, is a reminder of an intention or necessary action, especially as, in that particular memo, it said "To be decided in a formal contract now in preparation". But none was ever forthcoming. There was never a formal contract. I had done work before with Rankin/Bass, and they had always paid me and I had enjoyed my relationship with them. As far as I was concerned, everything was going to turn out fine. I gave them a winner. *ThunderCats* did better than half a billion dollars, so why would they [not give me a percentage]? I think the reason for that really was that they made so much money. There had been other presentations that they had asked for that [hadn't been successful], and they had been perfectly easy about it. "Well, nice try, on to the next one." The fact that something didn't work or did work was part of the game. Then all of a sudden they were making money hand over fist and they couldn't bear to part with a nickel of it.'

A New Beginning

Peter Lawrence's arrival marked, in effect, a new beginning for the scripting side of the show. 'To Peter Lawrence's credit,' says Lee Dannacher, '[he came in to a situation where] the writing department was in complete disarray. It was the one thing that I now realise just wasn't set up [properly] and couldn't successfully take on 65 half hours. Leonard Starr has to have the credit for co-creating what the world was going to be, the origins of it; but it was not a working writing department, with all of the original creations that were needed, until Peter Lawrence arrived.'

Lawrence explains the problems the company was facing: 'At that point, Jules had cast his net quite widely [for potential writers], and they knew [it was going to be a challenge] finding the quality and volume of work [they needed]. I think (though it's only an impression) Jules probably had tried speaking to a number of [other] writers and nobody had come through. Some of the writers were slow as hell. I don't really remember fully, but when I came in, people were still clinging on, and Jules told me to use them if I could, but he was open to new ideas. When I first met Bill Overgard, I realised that there was gold there. Don't misunderstand me, because in a way we worked out pretty well, but I was kind of stuck with Len Starr. In the beginning, he was kind of passive-aggressive, and I don't blame him. He was given the job of head writer, and we all have particular talents and failings, and I think maybe Len wasn't the guy to be a head writer on a show under that much pressure. I had done a hell of a lot of work in advertising under monumental pressure, so it's different horses for courses. To toot the horn of writers like me, compared to entertainment writers, someone who writes commercially to a deadline is invaluable. I did decide I couldn't work with Len, so we figured out the *modus operandi* that we'd give Len the five-parters to write, or the "go develop this" concepts.'

Steve Perry, who worked under the leadership of both Starr and Lawrence, gives his opinion on the changeover: 'Len Starr was a virtual writing machine, pounding out episode after episode with a quickness the rest of us writers viewed with jaw-dropping awe, and his friendship with Jules Bass went back many years. But the business of television can be cutthroat and stressful, especially when one is talking about vast sums of money. Len's dissatisfaction went a bit deeper than the money, I believe. In the month between my writing "Doomgaze" and beginning "Safari Joe", lots had happened down at the Rankin/Bass offices in New York City. The major thing was the arrival, from England, of a man named Peter Lawrence. Peter had been brought over by Jules Bass. "To help out," as Peter would later say. The truth was that Peter quickly installed himself as the "showrunner", had an office in the Rankin/Bass complex, and after "Safari Joe" was the man all writers submitted ideas to, the man who edited your scripts and the man who saw to it that you got paid. He became, very quickly, my boss. And I had little to do with Len Starr after Peter's arrival. Of course, rumours ran wild, and in subsequent years I believe Len has addressed the subject of just why he and Jules Bass had a falling out. I won't presume to know much more about it, except to say it was obvious there was a bitterness there. Len was ousted, in many ways, and perhaps he wanted it that way – for he thereafter wrote even more of the 65 first season scripts, including the five-part "Anointment" series. It was in this time, also, that Bob Haney disappeared from the scene. I believe he and Len were good friends, and that might have had something to do with it. I recall Peter Lawrence complaining, shortly after his arrival, about "the writers" not doing what he wanted them to do.

'If you check the credits, you will find Peter listed as a script consultant, but let me tell you he was doing far, far more than consulting. The man had assumed complete dominion over all aspects of each show's script, and hammered each one with his own personal stamp. Len Starr had retreated to Connecticut, doing his five-parters. Peter actively re-wrote each script that came across his desk.'

At the time of being invited to work on *ThunderCats*, Lawrence was still enjoying a writing career in his native England. He recalls he was initially wary of accepting Jules Bass's offer: 'I liked Jules at that stage and I'd say we were friends, and at the risk of sounding pig-headed, I could write just about anything. I was working in advertising – I had clients from Ferrari to British Leyland, liquor clients too – and I'd written two novels. Anyway, I went over to New York, and my next question was, "How much are you going to pay?" Jules said, "Two thousand dollars or fifteen hundred a script," and I said, "You must be joking. I'm sitting in a pool in Portugal; you think I'm going to come to New York? You must be crazy". But I went over and he put me to work at the end of '84 or '85, and soon I took the show over; well, it arrived on my lap. Bill and Len were the first people I met and they must have thought, "Who is this British guy coming over and telling me how to write?"'

Asked how he saw Leonard Starr's contribution to *ThunderCats*, Lawrence answers: 'I'm not sure what Len's contract was, but he was allegedly the head writer. I think what happened is that Len, for whatever reason, didn't like Jules – they didn't see eye to eye, and Len could not deliver what Jules wanted. They took him aside and said, "We'll set aside x number of scripts for you and give you head writer credit and you won't have to deal with other writers" (which I think was a great relief to Len). So we got him to write a couple of the five-parters so he could go away and concentrate on that and, in fact, express his vision of the show through the scripts. Len had a very clear idea as to what this show was about. I don't believe that Len really did any editing worth the definition. I think that when he passed the scripts on to Jules – however lightly he had touched them – Jules then worked on them; and that's one reason why Jules realised he needed a full-time editor to replace that part of Len's involvement in the show. But, after a short while, even though we never really warmed to each other, Len and I reached an accommodation, and I greatly respect his career.

'I am vague about the exact timing of the takeover. I know for certain that I did not edit "Exodus" through to "Pumm-Ra", nor did I make any contribution whatsoever to them. I'm fairly certain that I made some contribution to "The Terror of Hammerhand" and "The Tower of Traps" – probably in dialogue and, maybe, clarifying and expanding the action. But I am not 100% certain, by any means. With "The Garden of Delights", my memory is that I did some work on this ... Tygra stoned ... Probably to tone down the stoned-ness! I know I edited "Mandora – The Evil Chaser". It was the start of my great friendship with Bill Overgard – a friendship that thrived, despite his being so pissed at my cuts and additions! From "Lord of the Snows" onwards, I'm certain I had my hands on the wheel – and no-one else (though there was always input from various and sundry ... Lee and Jules first and foremost).

'The first couple of weeks I was there I just wrote scripts. Then I met all the other writers, or rather just Bill and Len and Bob Haney too. The genius of the whole operation was that it was really completely unstructured, so I just found myself beginning to edit other people's work. Jules would throw it onto my desk. Then we had the question of designing the secondary characters. We had a designer in the office, and for some reason I got involved in contributing. Lee and I and the designer worked together, and if we approved a design, it would go over to Jules for final approval. It came down to this: I'd turn up to the office every morning and I'd have two streams of work, one would be my own writing and the other was editing everybody else's work. I'd sit with Jules from time to time and discuss the directions that the show might go in. For example, "Snarf Takes up the Challenge" was specifically an idea where Jules said, "I think we need a script that stars Snarf, because he's the comic foil and he's not getting much play." I said, "I hate him, I can't stand Snarf," but Jules said, "It doesn't matter, we need a show," so I made one where Snarf was the hero. That was the limit of the input. Jules also suggested the idea of "Excalibur". He said, "The Sword of Omens is the best sword in the world, except for maybe Excalibur. Why not have a dual between those two swords?" So there was a certain amount of guidance coming in, not very much, but maybe one in ten scripts was guided by something like that.

'The other element of story editing was working with Robert Kuisis, the psychiatrist, to make sure that we weren't just paying lip-service to that idea and we were actually doing something that had some value. Then, later on, the storyboards started coming back and I would check the storyboards against scripts and put notes on the storyboards. I put notes on the voice recordings too, though I very rarely had anything to say about that, because Lee had a very specific style in which she recorded, and you either liked it or you didn't, and there was nothing more to be said ... Occasionally, I'd be called into the studio to make a comment or work through something that may have been difficult. Not very often, but occasionally. Beyond that, later on, I'd sit and look at the rushes that came back and make comments for retakes, but there were very few, because it was so closely monitored. Most were just technical retakes like hands and lips out of screen.

'That's the day-to-day. I also got dragged into meetings with Lorimar, and into dealing with a woman called Peggy Charren, who was basically running a consumer policing operation designed to ensure that kids' shows weren't too violent or too stupid, a bit like Mary Whitehouse in the UK. But it was very important, because that's why Robert Kuisis became involved. We had to find out what she was doing at the time, because that certainly had an effect on the way in which *ThunderCats* was run and developed creatively. I had to respond to a lot of that stuff; I went to Washington and talked to Jesse Jackson and all that crap. There was a lot of extraneous nonsense, but basically I was the story editor, I was what is now called the showrunner, I ran the back story and the front story. I commissioned the writers and managed them and went through the drafts.'

With Leonard Starr having assumed responsibility for scripting multi-episode serials, Lee Dannacher explains the added benefit this format afforded the series: 'I believe the motivating reason for the five-parters was [to create stories suitable] for home video release. Yet there were so many other areas where it worked well. When they thought about it, they knew it made sense. "Okay, you're going to have a successful run, 13 weeks of the original *ThunderCats*. What's a big way to splash a second season?" [A five-parter could meet that requirement.] Jim Moloshot of Lorimar Television said, "This is a great idea; there are loads of ways I can market these five-parters", because the Monday to Friday market was getting crowded, so he needed a marketing hook to say why *ThunderCats* was coming back for new episodes. It was a great campaign, and perfectly thought through to become available for a home video market that could have its own splash. Also of course (in the case of the second season), it was the way to appropriately introduce a whole new set of characters.'

'It was also done for production reasons,' adds Peter Lawrence, 'so that we could take the pressure off. It was an easier process to collect five stories together, consolidate the design work, the script work and the production work. That's my memory of why we did it. And on the creative side, it got to a point for all of us – Jules, Lee and me – where every single script had a new thing, a new design, this that and the other, and at some stage you think, "Wait a minute, this is not our show." It's very easy for a writer to think, "If I put an elephant's head on a fish's body, I can write a story about that." If you do that, what you're not doing is developing the personality of [regular characters such as] Slithe, Vultureman or Jackalman. You're not digging deeper into the show. Whether it's on *Big Love* or *The Sopranos*, the first tendency of a writer is to come up with his or her version, a new character beyond the boundaries. So the aims we had were to stop the show veering too far off track and to bring it back to the creative mainstream. Two of the many ways to do that were to consolidate a number of shows into one piece and forbid anybody from coming up with another character. [The argument against that is that] when you bring in elephant people with four legs or something, you create an additional plane of interest. That's the Bill Overgard approach, "Fuck the show, I'm going to write about some Harley Davidson queen who rides through space" – and you need that too, because it's a slap in the face.'

Lawrence elaborates on the challenge of finding new writers for *ThunderCats*: 'It was very difficult. To start with there was just Bill and Len and Bob Haney. Before I arrived, those guys tried to tap the whole of the New York comic book scene, and I don't think anyone understood how big this whole area was becoming. When I arrived, neither Jules nor I could get anyone to pay any attention to us. We called all the literary agents and said, "Look, we have a show and we're looking for writers," and they basically ignored us, and I was angry. (I'm still angry at agents. The irony is that I'm looking for an agent now. I've just sold a million dollar screenplay and I can't find an agent! I've had some of the best agents in town, but they've never done a thing for me.) I would literally be given a third assistant wanker [to deal with]. I'd say, "I can't believe you don't have a young writer – though I don't care about the age – that would want to try this," but not one of the major agencies sent anyone. However, I did tap into a woman called Chris Tomasino who worked for an agency called RLR, which was really a sports agency. I got Kimberly Morris, Ken Vose and a couple of other writers through her. Eventually I went to LA and met a few writers. Larry Carroll particularly. I was that desperate, my girlfriend wrote a couple of scripts, and we had Matt Malach, one of the production staff – I'd look anywhere at all. Lee Schneider came in through a friend of a friend of a friend. I would try anything; I put the word out, I didn't care, all I wanted was ideas. At that stage I knew that, given an idea, within 24 hours, certainly 48 hours, I could turn a script around that was okay technically. We just needed good ideas, and it was very hard to find them. I did not take co-writer credits ... I later learnt that so many showrunners take co-writer credits because then they get the royalties.

'Some people found it easier to write than others, so I'm sure that some of the one-episoders just found it too hard, or maybe it wasn't working for them because it wasn't a lot of money. I don't know this, nobody ever said it to my face, but some of them were probably pissed off that they got rewritten. I did get some really awful material from some people, I mean really bad, and I probably didn't ask those people to write again, but I don't want to smear anybody. Generally, if I could work with their material, they kept coming back. Before I arrived there and after, but particularly before the word went out, Jules and Arthur and Len and Bill, they tried to find people, they really tried, a lot of people came out of the woodwork. I had one guy who I commissioned, I don't remember who, he may not have been credited, but I said, "I'm on a really tight schedule, I need you to deliver an outline in a week." This guy went off and started to write, but I didn't hear from him, so I called him again and again and he said, "Oh my boat sank". I said,

"What's that got to do with it?" but he said, "I live on a boat and my typewriter sank and *ThunderCats* sank," so we didn't work with him again.'

As a result of his efforts, and his openness to taking on new talent, Lawrence found himself employing the services of writers of a wide range of ages and levels of experience. He maintains that all he needed was a 'winning idea', and describes what excited him when reviewing writers' contributions: 'When I got stuff from Bill, I was excited to read it, because it would be surprising. I'd say that anything I got that had a twist to it, that was not expected, I would respond to much better than anything else, so I would respond to those kind of things from Bill. Matthew Malach's Vultureman idea was good; I loved the idea that all the characters got switched around. Anything that was slightly surprising, I would respond well to. Anybody who understood the structure of the show – which has to have Lion-O solving the problem with the Sword of Omens – would be good. Anything that added something to a character, or perhaps introduced a new piece of technology or device, would be well-received; anything that opened up the show at all.

'On the other hand, one is always very conscious that this is a show about a hero group and a villain group. It's very tightly structured and you can't mess with that too much. I'm sure from time to time I might have wanted to follow a more adventurous, original path, but it had been drummed into me – and I believe – that kids want to see the same stuff over and over, but just want it to be a bit different. They want to see the Sword and the Eye, they want to see Cheetara's staff, see Panthro and have the standard lines and stuff; but it has to be different enough each time. So anyone who grasped that, we got on well.

'What I didn't get on well with was what I call stupid shit – which is a reason why, when I was done with Rankin/Bass, *Peter Pan* and *Johnny Quest*, I was kind of done with animation, because it turned to stupid shit. I'm just not good with it. If the writers came up with stuff I thought was silly – not funny, but silly – I just didn't like it. I'm also not very sentimental about children, so I didn't respond well to baby shit, and there was some of that. So I had trouble with some writers who I felt talked down to kids, who wrote baby characters. I think kids are really smart if given the opportunity. A lot of people think, "I can write for children. I don't have to have logical structure, I'll just write anything that comes into my head". A lot of kids' shows are like that. But you cheat children that way. Somebody wrote, "Writing for children is just like writing for adults – but harder," and that's right, because you need to respect their intelligence and respect the logic of the show and the internal structures that get you into their corner. But they are kids and you have to have that ADD factor.

'I also wanted scripts that were grammatical and spelt correctly … I was a bit uptight about that, because I felt that writers should have some pride in the craft. I know this sounds pretentious, because it's a kids show, but I still think this is what you do, it's your craft, you use words, you should know more words than people who aren't writers. You should know how to use them and how to spell them. So if a script had errors in it, I responded badly, even though it might have had a good idea.'

Once approached, a *ThunderCats* writer would typically be asked to submit a basic list of story proposals on the basis of which a workable plot would be selected. At this point, the writer would typically be given a fortnight (though the deadline was stretched in certain cases) to write a first draft. While some writers may have preferred to have had first refusal on carrying out any required revisions, Lawrence typically performed rewrites in-house. 'They were contracted to give me an outline, a first draft, a second draft and a polish,' he explains. 'They came up with a premise, and if we liked it, then we would make notes and they'd write an outline. That's when they got paid. Then first draft, second and a polish. Now, I could be wrong, but I'm pretty certain that we rewrote the outlines for them, and when they turned in their first draft, that was basically it and I did everything else. I'm sure I might have sent back some. Chris Trengove told me he has a script covered in notes and held together with tape. With Chris, because he'd worked as an editor, he helped me with the editing. So did Lee Schneider. So they may have written more than one draft, because I knew they would get it and give me what I needed. But some writers don't get it; you're wasting your time, and you might as well write it yourself. The pay was the same for everybody. I would have liked to have paid Bill Overgard double, treble what anyone else got, even though his work is the most controversial. I'd have paid Chris more also.'

As for the input he gave writers prior to the script stage, Lawrence reveals he had a mixed approach: 'I probably gave something between total freedom and complete input. I'd say something like, "I'd like an episode with Cheetara, because she doesn't get enough play." It was easier to write for Panthro and Lion-O and Snarf than it was for Tygra, who was completely superfluous – I don't know why he's in the show. Then we had Pumyra and others, and it's too many characters to deal with. So sometimes I'd say, "Well, let's have an episode that pumps up this character, or maybe an episode with the ThunderTank to add more dimension". It's not just a merchandising thing, but we had a show with stuff like a Thunderclaw and the drawbridge on the castle. If we didn't tell people these things were there, they'd not know they existed. So there was some input, but by and large I just said, "Come to me with your ideas", which is why so many of the scripts centre on a character or a device, because it's relatively easy for a writer to say, "How about a Rock Giant – let's have a story about that, where he comes around and throws rocks." It's much easier to have stories that centre on things like that than say, "Here's your task, write a story that has only our characters, nothing else". And that became one of my jobs and one of my responsibilities to make sure that it wasn't a show about Mandora The Evil Chaser – it's a *ThunderCats* show for god's sake; you can't have the ThunderCats short-changed. You permitted it with people like Bill, because he added so much to the show, but it was my job to ensure Dr Dometone and Mandora, although they were stars, didn't overwhelm the show.'

As Lawrence became more and more confident in his role as script editor, he assumed almost entire autonomy over the writing 'department'. 'I think at the beginning, maybe for the first 20 episodes, Jules had to sign off on everything,' he comments. 'But later on, I don't think so. I think he looked at the storyboards, but even then after a certain level, I don't think so. I think by around script 20, Lee Dannacher and I were completely in control. I imagine from time to time, Jules would pick something up and start screaming, because that was in his nature, but day-to-day, I don't think he had input. He could have had it, it wasn't taken away, but I think, to his credit, he just let it roll. Sometimes, he'd come back to me and say, "What are you doing? This doesn't work", but it wasn't a sign-off in that way. Kuisis, Lee and I had to sign off, and I think that was about it.'

The following memo illustrates Lawrence's correspondence with *ThunderCats'* writers:

MEMO TO:	*ThunderCats* writers
FROM:	Peter Lawrence
Date:	January 11, 1985
Subject:	Scripts #50-65

The first 50 *ThunderCats* scripts have built up a massive cast of characters, a great variety of gadgets and a wide range of settings and backgrounds.

Many of them have been used very fleetingly and most of them are well worth repeat appearances.

We have decided that, for scripts #50 through #65, we will only use these existing elements.

That means:

NO NEW CHARACTERS
NO NEW SETTINGS
NO NEW GADGETS OR PROPS

For these last 15 scripts, we'd like to see simple action plots which concentrate on the main characters – the ThunderCats themselves, Mumm-Ra and the Mutants.

At the beginning of the series, Len Starr established that THE MUTANTS were usually at war with each other and only allied in their search for The Eye of Thundera. Now is the time, perhaps, for that alliance to fragment so that each Mutant can have an episode operating on his own, with or without Mumm-Ra and with or without the knowledge of the other Mutants.

It would also be acceptable for each ThunderCat to have a single, starring episode – always provided that such episodes do not diminish Lion-O.

Certainly, there is no need – ever – to have all the ThunderCats together all the time.

We now have a good collection of scripts with relatively complex plots; for the balance, we want some very direct stories set in the mainstream of the ThunderCat-Mutant-Mumm-Ra 'legend'.

Please don't hesitate to contact me if you have any questions.

While network-produced television series enjoyed the ability to structure episodes over a 'story arc', the syndicated nature of *ThunderCats* meant very little control could be exercised over the transmission sequence on any given channel. Lawrence explains more about the problems of scheduling: 'Apart from the five-parters, you could never run anything consecutively; you couldn't build a story arc over more than one show, because in syndication you have no control over how shows are broadcast – sometimes you do in the first run, but never in the second run. We sent out however many show a month to be animated, but they would not necessarily come back in the order you sent them out in, or be completed in the order they were returned in, so you might have six shows in a row with Mumm-Ra doing the same thing. But I'm sure if you line up the shows, there isn't repetition, other than the repetition you'd expect from the same characters. I think that, because we had so many writers coming in with so many different ideas, perhaps we avoided that.'

To any of the writers who were unhappy about revisions to their work, Lawrence comments: 'Any successful show must have a single voice ... not a committee. That is why so much entertainment writing is crap; it's not the writers, it's the committees. Unfortunately, for anyone complaining, I had to fashion the voice – and wrap it around writers as diverse as Bill Overgard, Len Starr and Lee Schneider. It would have been much easier for me to have hammered them all into a tight box – forced them to write to a very narrow set of parameters – if they wanted to "play" instead. I respected originality and creativity enough to let them run more or less wild – and then took on the task of bringing the wildness and the non-conformity into the main current of the show.'

This correspondence between Peter Lawrence and writer Bruce Smith reveals just how far Lawrence would influence storytelling on *ThunderCats* when he felt a story was worthwhile:

MEMO TO:	Bruce Smith
FROM:	Peter Lawrence
Date:	December 10
Subject:	'LITTLE PEOPLE'

Further to our phone conversations, there follows a story outline which we would find acceptable for *ThunderCats*. If you feel you want to do it and can deliver a first draft to us by January 7th, please sign the enclosed contract. 'LITTLE PEOPLE' is only a working title. We need something more compelling.

1. The ThunderCats realise that much of their valuable equipment is missing. This should go beyond the obvious things like their weapons and needs to be dealt with in an imaginative way. ("Hey! Has anybody seen my nunchuks?" isn't going to be enough!)

2. Dozing in a forest, Lion-O wakes to find himself tied down and helpless (Qv: Gulliver).

3. Lion-O discovers that there is a tribe of little people on Third Earth and that they are angry with the ThunderCats because every time they roar out of the Lair in the ThunderTank, or take on the Mutants, etc, they flatten the little people's villages, fields and generally cause mayhem. (There are several potential problems with this sequence. I'll define the two most severe ones. [First,] set-up must not be covered in dialogue exposition. It needs dramatic and imaginative action sequences, probably in flashback, with minimal explanatory voice-over. And, second, we find it very difficult in this medium to cope

with hordes, swarms, flocks or crowds. Clearly, when dealing with a tribe of tiny people, there is a great temptation to show them all in relationship to Lion-O and the surrounding giant world. We simply have to find a simpler and more imaginative way of doing that. Quite aside from these production considerations, it works better dramatically if we confine things to one or two characters that we get to know. It's not that the ThunderTank smashes whole civilisations, it's that it keeps ruining Uncle Ebeneezer's corn crop – and that means he can't pay for an operation on his old dog's cataracts …)

4. Obviously, it's the little people that have stolen the ThunderCats' vital equipment – in an attempt to protect themselves.

5. They do not trust Lion-O sufficiently to release him, knowing that once he's free he'll be too powerful to control. (There should, in this area of the episode, be material to inject an interesting 'message' or 'learning experience' for our audience.)

6. Without all this vital equipment, the Cats' Lair systems begin to fail.

7. Mumm-Ra and/or the Mutants realise the ThunderCats are vulnerable and launch an all-out assault on the Lair. (If you prefer, they might take advantage of the ThunderCats' vulnerability to do something else dastardly other than attack the Lair. We have done that several times. Part one will probably end at this point.)

8. Snarf finds Lion-O and frees his sword arm.

9. Lion-O tries to summon the ThunderCats ('ThunderCats – Ho!'). The little people prevent anything more.

10. Enmeshed with the Mutants, the ThunderCats cannot help, other than to send Cheetara speeding to him.

11. Despite his pleas – and promises to protect their interests in future – the little people will not free Lion-O. Cheetara displays her ThunderCat superpowers, which awe the little people. Lion-O, however, will not allow her to 'bully' them into freeing him.

12. The impasse is resolved when the Mutants' mayhem affects the little people. (Possibly Skycutters and Nosediver inflicting damage; hopefully something more imaginative.)

13. Lion-O gives his word that he will help the little people if they will free him. They don't trust him and Lion-O has to explain the concept of 'word'. (He might leave Snarf with them as a token of good faith – perhaps even under some deadlined threat. That would give you a good cutaway sequence and a tension – maintaining countdown.)

14. Armed with all the missing ThunderCat equipment, Lion-O puts the Mutants/Mumm-Ra to flight. (i.e.: unravels 7 (above)).

15. He then returns to keep his word …

This is not intended as a rigid, dictatorial storyline but it certainly lays out the 'beats' of a story we know we could use. It also has considerable scope for imaginative action and attention-holding, expanded 'moments'. It also occurs to me that you could start this episode with Lion-O pinioned by the little people. Snarf finds him and frees his sword arm. Lion-O tries to summon the T/Cats. They can't make it because everything's been sabotaged (by the little people, of course). Mumm-Ra/Mutants discover this situation and set out to exploit it. Etcetera…That might be shorter and more dramatic. Just depends on how you handle it.

Towards the beginning of work on the show's second season, a collective decision was made to widen the search for writers into West Coast America. In addition to *ThunderCats*, Rankin/Bass was now in active production on *SilverHawks* and *The Comic Strip*, and a dearth of writers had emerged. Having made agents aware of their quest, Peter Lawrence and Lee Dannacher travelled to Los Angeles to meet with prospective writers.

'I remember it well,' says Dannacher. 'We flew out together. Peter hated the outfit I had on the plane, because it was an orange jumpsuit. We went boot shopping on Rodeo Drive. This is the nice thing about working the way we worked. As I made the budgets, I controlled the budgets. So if Peter and I had to go out there and spend three days interviewing 30 different LA writers in the Beverly Wiltshire Hotel, we were definitely going to do it in style. So we booked adjoining suits and we had the writers come up there and it was all very civilised, very tasteful. We sat on these lovely sofas and they had to come in and present their resumes and their wares. Some came in with a lot of attitude, because they were known Hollywood animation writers, but Peter just treated people so respectfully, it was only after the door closed that he'd say, "That guy isn't worth an episode cost".'

'The main writers I remember using from Hollywood were Larry Carroll and David Carren,' adds Peter. 'I stayed in contact with Sandy Fries for quite some time as well. I think we tried to put a few projects together outside *ThunderCats*. He was a nice guy. But remember that Woody Allen was Mel Brooks' typist and he had to jump on a table to get a word in edge ways. That's how it is in LA; they've got five minutes or ten minutes in which to convince people that they are geniuses and that competitive talking equals "I'm useful". It's just a bunch of people showing off to each other. I know I'm very harsh on them. In reality, it's very hard – it's like acting, it's a cattle call. I've got three minutes to persuade you I'm qualified enough to play a toilet roll on a commercial! Larry and David went on to have substantial careers. We were based in New York and certainly looked down upon by the West Coast creative community initially. I found it impossible to get agents to pay attention to the fact that we desperately needed writers. I couldn't even get my calls returned. Fortunately, there were exceptions to this generalisation and, as mentioned, I met J Larry Carroll, who not only wrote a lot for "my" shows but also shared his great experience. Of course, once *ThunderCats* was a success, everything changed and we were suddenly embraced by the community. I remember one Hollywood hotel doorman effusively asking me how the ThunderCats were doing. How the Hell did he know who I was or what connection I had to the show? Agents called every week, pushing their clients. Too late …'

While Peter would assume absolute responsibility for recruiting writers and delivering production-ready scripts, executive producer Jules Bass would also add his contribution to the show's storylines. In this memo from Bass to Lawrence, Bass's addition to the overall direction of the show becomes evident:

MEMO TO: Peter Lawrence
FROM: Jules Bass
Date: June 24
Subject: Development of new 60 episodes

1. A meeting is held and the ThunderCats agree to build another FORTRESS where the three new ThunderCats will reside (Lynx-O, Pumyra, Ben-Gali).

2. The reason is to extend their surveillance of Third Earth and be in a better position to watch Mumm-Ra and the Mutants.

3. Also, there is not enough room in the Cats' Lair.

4. The new fortress is named the Tower Of Omens, and JAGA lends a hand in giving the Tower special features and powers.

5. It is build around a great EYE and this eye 'sees' much as the sword does. What it 'sees' is transmitted in two ways:

a. Via a special screen; and

b. Via a 'Braille Board' so that LYNX-O can 'feel' what is being projected and then take necessary action.

6. There are other devices build into the Tower to aid LYNX-O.

7. Possibly SNARFER is brought in… for what is a lair of T-Cats without a 'Snarf' to watch over it.

8. The Tower will also need new devices, vehicles, weapons, etc, and a sophisticated communication system with the Cats' Lair.
This gives us a natural extension of the first T-HO episodes and a good reason to introduce new environments.

9. The Bad Guys will also need extensions. The rationale for these

extensions is that they now face a greater force, etc.

10. They build (or Mumm-Ra does) SKYTOMB, which is like a Cleopatra's needle or an enormous Sarcophagus ... along with new vehicles, weapons, etc.

11. Mumm-Ra calls up some creatures from Egyptian mythology to aid him and live in SKYTOMB. These creatures will fit well as bad guys and have a different look from the Mutants.

12. The new characters could be 'Living Mummy Cases' (see scrap). For instance ... an Iron Maiden ... opens – spikes, etc ... special powers that go back to mythology, etc.

13. Finally, what we need is some additional mapping of Third Earth so that we are not back in the same locales. (This does not mean that we cannot use backgrounds from the original series.)

Insofar as plots are concerned ... I feel that we must add some jeopardy and interest so that it is more than Mumm-Ra after the sword.

In effect, we will have added a 'layer' to the show without disturbing the original layer and have separated the characters so that everyone does not have to be 'standing' there all the time.

We will keep the moral posture ... epilogues, etc, as before.

Lee Dannacher explains the working relationship between Lawrence and Bass: 'I think it was really just Peter and Jules going out for a couple of beers and sitting in his office for hours. Before Peter joined, in the beginning, we were explaining to Telepictures what we felt the series could be. Jules came up with, "It's going to be like *Wagon Train*. Every episode ends [with resolving] the jeopardy of that episode, but week after week, the Wagon Train is still moving west." It was perfect for 65 half hours. But Peter complained at the time, because the toy companies were getting a little more pushy; he felt he had to come up with a new toy every time, and that just wasn't where he wanted to go with a whole season's worth of work. So you have to give Peter a whole lot of credit, because he convinced us all there had to be a new approach; a "story is everything" approach. It benefitted everything else.

'We were in the day-to-day, "forest for the trees" situation, whereas Jules, from the overview, could look and plan and plot and see what needed to be done to refresh everything for a whole new set of 65 shows.'

Lawrence agrees: 'That's very true. I would very much doubt there was a week that would go by that we wouldn't go and sit in Jules' and Arthur's office – though it took me longer to get to know Arthur – and put our feet on the desk and shoot the shit, you know?'

The following documents illustrate the far-reaching influence Jules Bass asserted over the series. Though, in some respects, the production team were given a great deal of autonomy, Bass would still suggest story options and, during the beginning of Lawrence's tenure, would still occasionally involve himself in editorial duties.

```
MEMO TO:     Peter Lawrence
FROM:        Jules Bass
Date:        Nov 8 1984
Subject:     Excalibur vs Sword of Omens
```

Mumm-Ra has an idea as to how to do away with Lion-O. He conjures up one of the most famous swords of all times, Excalibur ... With this sword he will tempt Lion-O into a duel ... one in which (by the rules) Lion-O will have to fight without the POWERS of the sword ... using only his sword-skill and strength and agility.

He does this by disguising himself as a knight, complete with armour and a headpiece in which his face cannot be seen. (This is somehow rationalised.) He rides right up to Cats' Lair and asks for food and lodging and, of course, is admitted ...

At every opportunity he puts down Lion-O ... impugning his strength, ability, etc ... This over a period of scenes ... His sword is always in evidence and Lion-O is fascinated by it.

Finally Lion-O breaks and tosses an insult back ... The knight stands and slaps Lion-O across the face with his gauntlet (or whatever) and challenges him to a duel.

The other T-Cats try to talk him out of it ... etc ... but to no avail ... Lion-O will fight. The visitor tells Lion-O that he has heard of his sword and its powers and that it will not be a fair fight unless Lion-O agrees to use the sword in an ordinary fashion. All is agreed. They choose seconds ... Lion-O chooses Snarf (or Panthro) and the knight chooses a Mutant (who is suitably disguised as-blah-blah).

At the crucial moment Lion-O loses his sword ... Mumm-Ra is about to slice his head off but Excalibur stops an inch from his neck ... Merlin appears – seems Excalibur has same problem ... Cannot be used for evil ... Merlin has come to retrieve sword ... Has magic fight with Mumm-Ra and wins ... etc ... etc ...

```
MEMO TO:     Len Starr
FROM:        Jules Bass
Date:        Nov 27 1984
Subject:     TYGRA ANNOINTMENT
```

Len, I would like you to do a second draft on this one in order to clear up some points ...

1. Could we firmly establish in the beginning what the trial is about? It is very difficult to follow and understand ... Initially one feels that LION-O must get to a certain point first (since that's what Panthro says) but that is not the case, at the end. LION-O has a map ... but we never see what is on it and it is confusing. Frankly, after reading the

script I did not know what LION-O was supposed to do ...

2. I think that TYGRA's ability (which he has never used until this episode) is somewhat confusing unless briefly explained ... (especially when these episodes are played and this one seen before a kid sees some other in which Tygra could get out of a situation with Mind Power but doesn't.) How can we rationalise this? Has he been storing all this up for trial? Maybe Jaga should be in this one to help.

3. Page #5 ... Is LION-O supposed to be able to 'see thru' Tygra's mind games or is he supposed to be able to do some of his own? ... Shouldn't TYGRA really be saying something to the effect of 'CAN YOU TELL WHAT IS FROM WHAT IS NOT, etc ...' Here again it is really unclear as to exactly what the trial is to be about.

4. Page #9 ... LION-O says 'Still have a long way to go ...' The audience must be let in on the plot ... It is really getting a bit obscure here.

5. In most instances the cutting back (Page #9) to the Lair contains superfluous information or re-cap stuff and slows us down. Please review.

6. TYGRA has really not done very much to LION-O, nor will he in this half ...Only inadvertently when he creates a blizzard for Mutants ... So far this is a story of Mutants after Lion-O and Tygra working against Mutants ... Loses a bit of focus.

7. Page #16... again... this page in Lair is a re-cap of information we already have and slows us down substantially.

8. Page #17 ... LION-O talks about getting 'past' Tygra, but I don't know (and audience will not) what that means. Tygra hasn't done anything to get past ...

9. Page #22 ... Tygra's line at top makes it seem like this is a simple footrace ... but still Tygra has not interfered with LION-O's progress at all and this is page #22.

10. Page #23 ... again same comment about dialogue in Lair.

11. Be careful (page #27 and elsewhere) of getting too much into the technique of having characters say what they are going to do before they do it ... Action will usually suffice, if it is clear ... (like belt stuff) ... otherwise animation gets bogged down.

12. Len, YOU established (and we recorded) the fact that no one ThunderCat or otherwise could help LION-O ... and here you have

SNOWMEOW helping ... giving him a ride ... You'll have to get rid of that sequence.

13. Page #30 ... The final showdown ... Again ... it is unclear, because of no set up in opening ... as to what has happened. Also it is almost a duplicate of KIT/KAT stuff with pellets ... I think kids are really going to have to absorb much too much information (... 'Power has no effect on animals ...') and that this is going to fall flat. I'm sure you can revise and get Snowmeow out of it and have LION-O reach a conclusion in some other fashion.

14. Please revise Samurai and Ninja coming out of Cauldron to ONE simple thing ... both for animation and continuity with Overgard's show, which had Samurai a good guy and Ninja a bad... how 'bout a simple monster!

15. I think we need a better ending ... The dialogue from Mumm-ra is a bit obscure on Page #32 ...

Len – I know how you have grown to hate the trials ... but there's only one to go ... Hang in there! (By-the-by, have you really figured out how to defeat Mumm-ra and yet keep him in series?) Hope so ... I've grown to like him.

The various writers of *ThunderCats* were based in different locations around the US, and in some cases overseas, but Peter Lawrence attempted to incorporate them all into the production 'family', giving them extensive background material on the series to assist them in their contributions. Each writer would typically receive a copy of the bible written by Jules Bass and Leonard Starr and could also obtain production sketches and artwork. However, while they may have received support from individual production team members at Rankin/Bass, Lawrence believes animation writers were woefully underappreciated at the time, in the industry as a whole:

'I feel very strongly about the way the writers were treated ... If *ThunderCats* had been a Writers' Guild of America-ruled show, with resulting residuals, it was so successful that anyone who wrote a few episodes would have had some support income for life – as they do when they write even the crappiest live action shows. But the WGA at the time sneered at syndicated animation and only later, rather feebly, dabbled their feet. The union was not prepared to fight for this lower echelon of writers – even though, in many respects, to write for a show like *ThunderCats* demands more than any sitcom or live script ... You have no [in-vision] actors to bring their talent, their personalities, even in some cases their magic to the process. It all comes from the writer's imagination, which must in turn inspire the storyboard artists and so on. (Of course, the voice actors do bring their talents to the process, but not in the complete way actors on a live show do.) Believe me, there is no bitterness in this comment. I have had, and have, a wonderful career and working life. No complaints. But there are many writers who have made huge contributions to these shows, and to the gigantic revenues they have spun off, and who are now down and out, working all kinds of menial jobs. And, remember, they were paid peanuts for each script.

'Speaking of which, a confession and a contradiction. From time to time, I would have a problem with a writer demanding more money – which, of course, we did not have. My attitude was, "How long would it take you to earn the same dough digging holes ... or driving a cab?" To which the answer is several weeks, at least. A good writer, on the other hand, supported by the story editor, ought to be able to write a draft in much less than a week ... a second draft in a couple of days ... and a polish in a day. And we rarely asked for second drafts, because we took over the scripts ourselves. So ... yes ... a contradiction.'

Lawrence is unapologetic about his approach to script editing *ThunderCats*, and the vast majority of writers interviewed for this book have nothing but respect for him. 'In one of my shows, "Queen of 8 Legs",' comments Steve Perry, 'you will be struck by the lack of active dialogue in it. I had done this on purpose, trying to tell a story with action and pictures and minimising the spoken word ... This was because Peter had a problem with my ability to write dialogue, or at least write the kind of dialogue he wanted. I tried to write a "silent" show partly out of fear and partly out of an honest creative attempt within a hard structure. Until Peter started bitching about it, I had been very confident in my dialogue – I thought his was awful; simplistic, obvious and rather boring. But Peter was right – clever alliteration, puns and quirky wit had no place [in *ThunderCats*]. Peter Lawrence, I believe, held the firm belief that an American audience of four to seven year old kids needed to be told, in short, concise and plain English, what the hell they were looking at and what was going on. Peter was correct. Otherwise, *ThunderCats* would never have endured nor met with such popularity. Truth be told, the reality of *ThunderCats*, the way the show eventually became, had more to do with Peter Lawrence than with any other single person. There were about 15 shows completed when he came on board, and his hand would fall hard on the remainder of the first season, and *all* of the subsequent season. If anyone deserves the title of Mr ThunderCat, it is Peter Lawrence.

'A new kid on the block had shown up, too, working as an assistant to Peter. His name was Chris Trengove, and he would go on to become one of the series' best, most prolific writers . He worked right there in the offices, at first, as Peter Lawrence's right hand man. Peter wrote more *ThunderCats* shows than anyone, as many shows credited to others – myself included – are more Peter Lawrence re-writes than the credited writer's original.'

Unused Scripts

With *ThunderCats'* scripts being turned around at rapid pace, commissioned episodes were rarely rejected or left unmade. Leonard Starr and later Peter Lawrence preferred to mentor writers into making amendments to bring scripts up to par, and, where that failed, would happily rewrite portions themselves to make material suitable for production.

One of the few unproduced *ThunderCats* scripts was entitled 'Beasts of Doom', later renamed 'The Beasts of Mumm-Ra' before being scrapped entirely. Written by Gerry Matthews, with a script dated 27 July 1984, this would presumably have been intended for the early portion of the first season. Although it features handwritten edits by Starr, the episode was never taken further, for reasons that remain unknown.

'The Beast of Doom' revolves around Mumm-Ra's masters, the Ancient Spirits of Evil, who become animated and wreak havoc on Third Earth. An extract from the script is reproduced below:

MEDIUM FIGURE SHOT – MUTANTS, MUMM-RA

They lean across the bubbling cauldron toward each other.

S-S-SLITHE
Even so – The Eye is still in the hands of the ThunderCats! I can't sssee that *you've* accomplished anymore than *we* have.

MUMM-RA rises up to his full skeletal height.

MUMM-RA
This conversation is over. I shall take the sword and the all powerful eye *myself* and I will rule Third Earth *alone*!

MONKIAN
Ha! That I'd like to see.

S-S-SLITHE (snarls at Monkian)
Quiet, idiot!

CUT TO:

POV from behind MUTANT's heads.
MUMM-RA points his yellow talon at them.

MUMM-RA (drooling)
You may live just long enough to regret that, simian scum.

MUMM-RA spins around to face the four statues, raises up both his hands palm up toward the ceiling.

CUT TO:

FULL FIGURE – MUMM-RA – LOW ANGLE
With MAN/BEAST statues facing him.

MUMM-RA (CONT)
Condawk! Minotaur! Krokdon! Porcinicus Rex!
Come, my beauties!

Lighting crackles from his palms, ricochets about the room and strikes

the statues one at a time. They animate with glowing eyes and
<u>appropriate noises</u>.

CUT TO:

LONG SHOT
The MUTANTS draw back and take defensive attitudes.

S-S-SLITHE
No need to be upset at what thisss ape saysss, Mumm-Ra!

MONKIAN
Hey, whose side are you on, Slithe?

The BEASTS move forward, towards the MUTANTS, but MUMM-RA
spreads his arms to restrain them. They tower over him but obey their
master.

MUMM-RA (amused)
Begone! My beasties don't seem to like you and
they're not easily restrained…

The MAN/BEASTS <u>growl</u> and <u>snort</u>, straining to attack.

Another example of an unproduced screenplay is Kimberly Morris's 'Goodbye Jaga',
an episode that would have originally concluded the first season of *ThunderCats*.
Morris is extremely protective of this script and, consequently, a complete version
has never surfaced. However, the story would have revolved around Lion-O's
relationship with Jaga. Having returned to their home world on New Thundera, Jaga
appears to Lion-O to inform him of his retreat to the spirit world, in the belief that
Lion-O is ready to lead without his input. Lion-O reacts badly and fears he will not be
able to face future challenges without his mentor. With his confidence lost, Lion-O
finds the powers of the Sword have gone, and only when he finds the courage to
confront his fears does the Eye of Thundera return to aid him. Thus we learn that,
rather than Lion-O gaining his powers from the Sword of Omens, the reverse is true.
While script editor Peter Lawrence has no memory of this episode, it can be
presumed that the script was dropped in order to safeguard the character of Jaga for
future plots.

While the examples above are of complete abandoned scripts, unmade portions
or alternative storylines can be found for almost all of the 130 televised episodes of
ThunderCats. In some cases the episodes were condensed for timing reasons, resulting
in material being dropped, and in others the stories were edited to bring in stronger
ideas; such deletions and amendments were commonplace during the editing
process. To try to minimise the editing involved, scriptwriters were required to
provide an initial story outline for each episode, which would have to be approved
prior to development.

An example of this process can be found in the original outline by Ron Goulart
for the story that would later be remounted as 'The Terror of Hammerhand':

THUNDERCATS
Ring Of The Unicorn
Ron Goulart

WILLA and NAYDA are spear fishing along a rocky stretch of coastline. It's a gloomy, fog-shrouded morning, the sea is choppy and slate-coloured. Suddenly through the thick grey mist bursts the prow of a Viking-type ship. The figurehead is a huge skull and the ship's black sail has a skull emblazoned on it. Another ship comes ripping out of the fog, then a third.

'Skullships!' cries NAYDA, tossing aside her spear, sprinting to the place where she's left her bow and arrows. 'It's KILLGAR and the Berserker slave raiders!' Willa, too, rushes to retrieve her weapons. The two Warrior Maidens use sleepgas arrows on the landing raiders. But there are too many Berserkers and it's soon obvious the girls will be overpowered and taken off as slaves.

KILLGAR is a huge bearded man, dressed in Viking style. His ugly horned helmet has been fashioned from the skull of a horned animal. Fighting at his side is an even more frightful raider named HAMMERHAND. His right hand has been replaced by a huge, wicked-looking metal hammer.

LION-O is exploring, alone, a stretch of forest he's never been in before. As he makes his way over a forest pathway he hears a neighing and the sounds of a struggle. He hurries to investigate. Reaching a clearing he finds a snow white unicorn struggling against the clinging arm-like branches of a cannibal tree. Drawing his sword, LION-O frees the unicorn from the clutching branches. He sets the sword aside to attend to the animal's injuries. Then a great dark bird swoops suddenly down, attracted by the gleaming sword. Catching it up in his beak, the bird goes flapping away over the forest.

WILLA and NAYDA have been overcome by KILLGAR's Berserkers. Bound, they are carried aboard a Skullship. The leader plans now to sail further down the coast to loot a fishing village. The three ships sail off, soon swallowed by the swirling fog.

The grateful unicorn makes a melodious sound, nodding at LION-O. He notices now that the animal has a gold ring around its horn at the base. The ring begins to glow and the unicorn indicates he is to take it. Doing so, LION-O guesses this must be a wishing ring. When he suggests this, the unicorn nods positively. Since the thing LION-O most wants at the moment is his sword back, he wishes first for that. Lightning crackles, he is surrounded by pulsing multicoloured light. Then he's gone. An instant later LION-O finds himself riding on the back of the giant bird who's carrying the sword. There is a struggle, he gets back his weapon. As the defeated bird swoops low over a misty stretch of beach, LION-O drops free.

On the beach he encounters several excited Warrior Maidens. They explain to him that NAYDA and WILLA have been carried off by the raiding Berserkers. LION-O wishes himself aboard the Skullship so that he can save the captive young women.

In a cabin aboard KILLGAR's ship WILLA has just about succeeded in freeing herself from the ropes that bind her. NAYDA hasn't done as well.

Suddenly, LION-O materialises before them. He is about to cut away NAYDA's bonds when the door snaps open and in charges KILLGAR, battle axe swinging. They skirmish and the struggle spills out onto the misty deck. The whirring of the mighty sword forces KILLGAR over the side and into the fogbound sea. Watching his opponent fall, LION-O fails to note that HAMMERHAND is charging at his back. But the lethal arm is pinned to a mast by a pronged arrow (the prongs don't touch his flesh, they simply sort of staple the metal hand to the wood). Before he can wrench free, a sleepgas arrow puts him out of commission.

WILLA has freed herself, freed NAYDA. The two, each using a different arrow, have come up on deck to help LION-O. Afraid of the trio, the remaining Berserkers surrender. With WILLA at the helm, the Skullship sails for the shore.

The moral has to do (as illustrated by LION-O's pausing to help the distressed unicorn) with the fact that stopping to help others often ends up helping you, too.

Writers' Profiles

While Peter Lawrence and Leonard Starr had provided a strong and exciting array of *ThunderCats* adventures, it was their selection of writers that gave the series its distinctive variety. Very rarely would two *ThunderCats* episodes be the same, and the refreshing differences between, say, the eccentricity of Bill Overgard's scripts and the more conservative (though no less effective) approach of writers like Kimberly Morris only added to the series' appeal. From famous comic book creators to administration assistants, Rankin/Bass offered many talented writers the opportunity to prove their abilities by generating original ideas. Without this 'relaxed' approach to storytelling, the *ThunderCats* series would surely have suffered.

The profiles below comprise interviews conducted for this book and reveal, for the very first time, the writers' voice.

Leonard Starr
23 episodes: 'Exodus', 'The Unholy Alliance', 'Berbils', 'The Slaves of Castle Plun-Darr', 'The Tower of Traps', 'The Ghost Warrior', 'The Spaceship Beneath the Sands', 'Lion-O's Anointment First Day: The Trial of Strength', 'The Crystal Queen', 'Lion-O's Anointment Second Day: The Trial of Speed', 'Lion-O's Anointment Third Day: The Trial of Cunning', 'Lion-O's Anointment Fourth Day: The Trial of Mind Power', 'Lion-O's Anointment Final Day: The Trial of Evil', 'ThunderCats Ho!' Parts 1-5, 'Mumm-Ra Lives!' Parts 1-5

Head writer Leonard Starr was responsible for more scripted episodes than any other *ThunderCats* contributor. He served as story editor for early scripts, co-wrote the series 'bible' (a 4,000 word document detailing its characters and worlds) and tackled some of the most prominent storylines to be featured in the series.

Starr began drawing and writing for comic books in 1942 and carved out a long and successful career during the 'Golden Age' of the medium, on a variety of titles including *The Sub Mariner* and *Human Torch*. He later diversified into a role in advertising. The highlights of his career include his creation of the comic strip *Mary Perkins On Stage*, which ran for 30 years, and his revival of the *Little Orphan Annie* stories in the 1970s.

'Bill Overgard, a buddy of mine, did the comic strip *Mike Nomad*,' says Starr. 'He had written scripts for [Rankin/Bass], and when they needed writers he introduced me to them. A major attraction was that they were in New York, while most animation studios were in California, as were the writers for this kind of thing. I did a few specials for them. I did *Around the World in 80 Days* and *The Red Baron*, things like that. I don't know who brought *ThunderCats* to them, but the important thing is that they suddenly had a window. A window is available space in the television schedule, and that doesn't happen often. If you don't grab it when it's there, somebody else will, so when one does turn up, you have to move very fast. One day I had a meeting with Jules Bass about *ThunderCats*, did an outline the next day and by the third day we were all ready to go. And it was lucky that it happened that way, because if not, these things can drag out for weeks and months before you finally get them to a place where you can present them to people. Happily this thing went very quickly, and within the week I was writing the first two hours. It was designed so it could be played in half-hour segments, hour segments or a two hour segment. It sounds tougher than it really is. It requires a climax with a semi-cliffhanger at the end of each half hour, each set-up, as steps lead up to the major finale of the second hour.

'So we did that and it was sent to Japan for animation, and the first showing, at least the first that I'm aware of, was in Florida. A close old friend, Dik Browne, the creator of the comic strip *Hagar the Horrible*, who was living in Florida at the time, called me and said that he had seen it at the incredible hour of eight o'clock in the evening. I thought that was the death of it, because who is going to watch an animated science fantasy kids' show at that late hour? But it astonishingly ended up getting terrific ratings somehow, so we were off and running.

'But then, it was one of the earliest of the direct syndication shows, which meant that it went on the air five days a week right off the bat, rather than a whole bunch of the traditional Saturday morning children's shows being piled up to be ultimately played in syndication. It was really hustling, and I was asked to ride "shotgun" on it, because the format was more like a syndicated continuity comic strip, my turf, than it was a Saturday morning series. I wrote about 23 episodes and rewrote a great number of scripts that came in, because there was no time to send them back to the writers, as most writers always wait until the last minute to get them in. Rewriting is easier than facing those blank pages day after day, but I'd been doing that weekly on a daily and Sunday comic strip for a very long time, so I managed. I took no credit for the rewriting, but I got to see a lot of dawn from the wrong end, before we were through with it.'

Prior to his work on the series, Starr had approached Rankin/Bass with a view to developing two of his own projects, involving animated versions of movie legends Charlie Chaplin and W C Fields respectively. While neither was produced,

Starr credits them as his recommendation for *ThunderCats*. 'They had trouble with the estates. Charlie Chaplin's estate was all right with it until the end, when they wanted too much money. But Rankin/Bass paid me for the ideas, and their reaction was, "Well, they didn't work, we'll go on to something else." But the W C Fields show gave me a sort of a lesson. It was supposed to be a comedy show – he's a comedy character and a buffoon – and I don't write comedy, so I watched a lot of W C Field stuff [to try to pick up the style], and somehow I absorbed the character, so when I started to write the thing I wrote it in about a day and a half. Everything just worked. It was the W C Fields script that made Jules call me. He said it was the best script they had ever gotten in house and asked me to come in and see if I had any thoughts about this new thing. They didn't get W C Fields produced but it got me *ThunderCats*.'

Speaking of his writing method, Starr comments, 'We had to have three scripts go out to Japan every week, already recorded with the actors' voices. In Japan they had 600 animators working around the clock. 200 sat down, 200 got up, another 200 sat down, and so forth. They had to have that many to get such good work. I just typed out the scripts. There was no time for me to outline. The thing about writers is they all waited until the last minute to do it. It's an odd thing. What they wanted all their lives was to be writers, and when they got a job they didn't do it until the last minute. So the rewriting would take me well into the night. I still had my regular gig, remember. I went into New York a lot, but a lot of [my scripts] went [to Rankin/Bass in] the mail. Express Mail, I believe, was already in operation by that time, and it was an overnight process. I guess I was in New York about two to three times a week. I wrote on an electric typewriter, an IBM Selectric, so that I could go faster, and even then I had to keep reloading it with paper. But it was easier working on it than it was on a regular manual typewriter. It also had the correcting tape, although I eventually didn't use it that much. I'd correct the script in red pen before I sent it in. I would proof read it quickly and that would be that.

When asked what inspired his storytelling, Starr responds: 'By this point I had been doing a syndicated comic strip for 28 years. I was already working on the comic strip *Annie* [at the same time as *ThunderCats*]. So you can figure that, for all those years, I had been putting stories together with situations, obstacles, cliff hangers and such, so the machinery was already in place. Alas, that kind of machinery rusts like any other. I couldn't do it like that anymore. Now I would have to write a lot of notes and wonder where I was going with the thing.'

While his writing would define Starr's role on the series, he also brought his artistic touch to it: 'I had drawn a map of Third Earth, thinking it might be useful. It was inked by Frank Leonard Bolle, my godson, who at the time was the background artist on *Annie*. Apparently they later used it in the [*ThunderCats*] magazine, and since ours was pretty rough – designed only for the writers' use – they had someone else render it more carefully and in colour, and gave him credit for it!

'To give you an idea of how the writers worked, one writer used everything on that map in one story. I couldn't believe it! My intention for doing the map was that the writers would each take a piece and use it for his or her story. This guy went through the whole map and used all the places and used it all up in one shot! Suffice it to say, that script got a lot of changes. But the map was very useful. It gave the writers a concrete, visual idea of where they were and what was there. Anyone familiar with the show would recognise the hazards indicated on the map. There were unknown territories as well if we ran out. I'd really have liked to have a copy of that map.'

While Starr did not contribute to the design of the principal characters, he did have a hand in a few aspects of the series' visuals: 'One thing that I designed was the sword, and I did a rough sketch of Lion-O holding the sword up to his eyes for the "Sight beyond sight" thing. Maybe a couple of other things like that. But essentially, I did very little drawing for the show. Mostly it was designed by the Japanese. I was very impressed with it and thought they did a terrific job. If you look at the *ThunderCats* line-up that I have on my wall, it's first rate. Very good stuff, and the logo was just terrific.'

In addition to a myriad of Third Earth creatures that would emerge from his creative consciousness (including Berbils, Bolkins, Wollos and many in between), Starr also had a large input into the development of the characters of the ThunderCat team themselves: '[To start with] they had only two characters that I remember. They had the panther man and they had the lion man. So, yes, I created all of the rest of them. They wanted a team, and there are a lot of cats out there. So we had Cheetara after the cheetah, and we had Tygra, which of course derived from the tiger, and Jaga for jaguar, that kind of thing. I named them Lion-L, Jaga-J, Tygra-T and it seemed to be okay, but somebody that we presented it to said that Lion-L sounded too much like it was affiliated to the toy train company Lionel. So Jules Bass changed it to Lion-O and he took the initials off all the rest of them. Mumm-Ra was also mine. I created the whole thing, really. They had the title, poster-sized renderings of two or three cat people and a terrific logo. They had the ThunderTank and something else, maybe the Cats' Lair. The sword was also mine. In fact, I was annoyed when the toys came out. My design had two magnifying lenses in the hilt, so "Sight beyond sight" was really just a telescope or binoculars. I guess it would have been too expensive to make that way, but the toy sword they came up with was pretty dinky. And the animators didn't use the drawing that I made for the sword, with two holes for Lion-O to look through, only a curved hilt for his to look past. So it sort of defeated the "Sight beyond sight" idea. But the Japanese did a terrific job on the series. It was one of the best-looking animated shows on television. Somebody at the time did a *Rambo* animated series and that was such awful animation that I couldn't believe they ever got it on the air. With a big title like that, you would figure that they could have gotten a major company to animate it, but it was just awful.'

Although Starr is delighted to have played such an important part in the history of *ThunderCats*, he is disappointed with how his relationship with Rankin/Bass ended. 'About a year and a half into the show I asked Jules when we would talk about the … promised formal contract. What I wanted were residuals of each show, at least the ones that I wrote, despite it not being standard for animation. I don't know if animation writers have managed to get that abomination changed even yet, but I was sure my deal was unusual. Jules said, "Gee, we can't give residuals on a cheap show like this." So I asked again about the formal contract as stated in the [original deal] memo, and his response was, "Hey, if you want to sue us, sue us. You'll lose." Just like that. So I could see right away that Friendlyville was closing shop.

76

'Arthur Rankin was in Japan through the whole thing. He was involved in only one meeting in the entire time that I worked on the show. So it was mainly Jules that I was working with. One of the things that I told the writers [in my editorial capacity] was that they had 25 minutes [in an episode], so I would like at least four "bumps". A bump is where you take a character to a certain point, meeting an obstacle of some kind that they must surpass, and then move on to the next obstacle, a little more fearsome than the previous one, and finally a bigger one at the end. Just so there are four [story points] with momentum. Otherwise the characters are just walking around talking or fighting or whatever. And it proved to be a pretty good formula.

'Arthur Rankin's credo was that if nobody had ever heard of it, he couldn't sell it. So that's why R/B did *The Red Baron*, *Around the World in Eighty Days* ... even the *Osmonds*, *The Jackson 5ive*, *King Kong*, etc. The fact that they went for an original idea [in *ThunderCats*] was surprising. Plus the fact that they were able to get it off the ground is amazing. Well, that was the benefit of the then existing window, and also I guess their reputation was pretty good by that point. Anyway, as I say, all my relationships with them had been very good, so I had no reason to expect there would be a sour ending, and why should there have been? I gave them a hit. It's hard to even imagine how tough it is to have a hit. How many pilots and series fail? The one lesson from it is that they didn't use me on *SilverHawks*, except for me giving them the title and a couple of scripts that I did. Jules wanted to do it himself, and it pleases me to believe, whether it's true or not, that it's the reason that show went right into the dumper. Another dopey idea was *The Comic Strip*. They had about four different characters for four different shows in the same series and it just didn't work.'

In addition to seeing his scripts on screen, Starr was pleased with how *ThunderCats* translated into merchandising. 'Well, the toys were cute. I never got a collection for myself, but friends would come in and have me autograph boxes for their kids. It was certainly pleasant and it was different for me. I had never been involved in that kind of intense television work. Did I mention that I was supposed to get two percent of the merchandising [royalties]? That was okay, but it was nothing like residuals. I thought I could get some action when the DVDs came out but I didn't even get a piece of that. It's considered a different type of merchandising.

'It was a very interesting period [of my life] that ended poorly. The fact that [the show] is still popular and that someone is still making money from it is nice, but it's not me. I liked the people on *ThunderCats*, the production assistants were all very enjoyable. Just the fact that I was doing something that I wasn't used to doing was the best part of it for me. And the part that it was successful didn't hurt. It was an intense but pleasant period. I'm just sorry that it ended so poorly. When you get lawyers involved, that's called ending poorly.'

Considering whether he preferred the medium of script or comic strip, Starr concludes, 'When I was working, it almost didn't matter; it was all part of the same thing. When I did the comic strips, I wrote the week on Monday morning, then laid it out, then pencilled the figures and set up the backgrounds. The backgrounds were being done pretty much at the same time I was inking. The background men would come in after I had two or three dailies with the characters inked and ready so that there was no time lost. They usually worked two or three days with me; it depended on how long it took them to do it. I thought it was normal for syndicated artists to write their own strip because I was a fan of *Terry and the Pirates* and I knew that Milton Caniff drew and wrote it himself. I had no idea that *Flash Gordon* wasn't written by Alex Raymond. Don't forget that it was 1934 and I was nine. As far as I was concerned, everyone wrote their own stuff, so the first time I illustrated anything by another writer was when I went into comic books.'

The conclusion of his association with Rankin/Bass marked Starr's departure from television writing: 'I did try another series that I created with Bill Overgard called *Wolfmark*. We did some good scripts on it and we were very close to getting it produced. But it never came about, and that sort of broke my heart. Initially we thought about doing it as an animated series, but then we decided to do it live action. We had an Olympic gymnastics champ ready to do it and we would have shot it in Europe. When you do these things, one of the catch phrases is, "Keep it original but familiar". When you take a series idea to a producer, he asks, "What's it like?" And it's such a stupid question. Still, the way to describe *Wolfmark* to people would be that it's like *Prince Valiant* in space. And it would have worked. We could have made a very good series out of it. I planned on doing it in Italy. We had a terrific villain for it, it was a robot, and the act of destroying it would blow it up and kill you as well – that was Bill Overgard's idea – so you had to find some way to destroy the thing without killing yourself in the process.'

Leonard Starr's career boasts a large list of achievements, however he insists it doesn't feel as varied as it may read: 'A varied career would be like going out on location and dealing with a lot of different people. One of the nice things about the *ThunderCats* thing was dealing with a lot of people. You weren't in it alone. It was more communal than working by yourself. I did comic books for a while, and then two comic strips and some television, and that's it.' When reassured that his career is a great deal more expansive than many, Starr replies: 'And less than others. Robert Parker just died. He wrote the Spencer novels among several other series, as well as straight novels, and it's like he wrote a book every 20 minutes. You look at his list and you wonder how he did it. Maybe he had a factory, I don't know. But they were very popular and I'm sure he did well with them.'

Peter Lawrence

22 episodes: 'The Time Capsule', 'Mongor', 'Snarf Takes Up The Challenge', 'Sixth Sense', 'The Astral Prison', 'The Rock Giant', 'Mechanical Plague', 'The Demolisher' (with Bob Haney), 'Excalibur', 'Good and Ugly', 'ThunderCubs' Parts 1-5, 'Chain of Loyalty' (with Bill Ratter), 'The Heritage' (with Bill Ratter), 'Return to Thundera' Parts 1-5

While script editor Peter Lawrence is credited as scripting 22 episodes of *ThunderCats* (an achievement in itself), his input into the series was actually far more extensive. He was hired by Rankin/Bass when executive producer Jules Bass decided a more structured editorial process was needed on *ThunderCats*, after head writer Leonard Starr had overseen the first dozen scripts. Lawrence immediately acquainted himself with the series (then still in the early stages of development) and would shape its course throughout its entire run. In his editorial capacity, he would be responsible for both recruiting writers and shaping storylines – often rewriting many scripts to conform to the show's format.

'When I was at school, I did all the usual things,' explains Peter, '[and did fill in jobs as] a car mechanic, a builder, a construction worker. I ran bricks for an Irish sub-contracting brickie gang and stuff like that. Before university, I had an opportunity through a friend of mine (who had a racing car garage) and we fell into becoming stunt men – my first experience of entertainment! I was going to give up university and become the best stunt man ever. I had a contract for a movie, but it fell through, and I went to university instead. I went to Cambridge and studied law. I had the world's worst university career of all time. "Golden boy" turned into "Dog shit boy" overnight, but I made a lot of friends and it was a good experience. I came out of it without a clue what to do, so I joined British Electric Computers – a leading computer company – and tried to have a career in computers. I hated it; I didn't understand it and only took the job because it was the highest paid graduate job of the year.

'I had always been a writer since the age of 12 or whatever, but the English education system tells you how to criticise Shakespeare, Voltaire and Hemmingway, but says nothing about creative writing, so you're very critical of your own stuff and it never sees the light of day. At British Electric Computers, I got stuck between the engineers who couldn't speak English and the buyers who couldn't speak computer. So I started writing brochures and technical information and realised I could make a career out of writing. All you need is to be paid to write and then you realised, "Maybe I can do this".

'At that point I walked out of the job; it was miserable. I was then working as a lifeguard in a swimming pool in the middle of London, and a friend of mine called me. He said, "I've got a hell of a problem, I'm trying to make a documentary, can you help me overnight?" It was for a bizarre little company who paid you 50 quid to write a treatment and if you sold the film, you got 50 percent of the profits. Suddenly I got one sold, and I became a documentary maker. At that point, I segued into advertising: I made commercials; I made industrial ads. At the same time, I came across a story about an intensive care nurse who was killing her patients and taking bets on when her patients would die. I wrote about it and sold the movie. In conjunction with that, I got called by the same friend who put me into documentaries. He was making a film for Harvey Weinstein, a horror film, and he hated the script, so he called me in and I rewrote it. It was the first Miramax movie that ever got made – it was a horrible experience … This same director got a job for Rankin/Bass making a movie called *The Sins of Dorian Grey* … They had a horrible script, and they called me to New York [to work on it]. I was supposed to be in for seven days, but if I'd known how bad it was, I'd have told them to throw away all the dialogue. By the time I'd write one set of notes, I'd get another. At the time, I got to know Jules Bass pretty well.'

Peter recalls with amusement how he came to be recruited for *ThunderCats*: 'Back in London, I was working with Jerry Mason, a photographer friend of mine. We went out to Portugal with a handful of the most beautiful women you've seen in your life. I'm sitting by the side of the pool in Portugal and the phone rings and it's Jules Bass, and he says to me, "I've got a show; I need you to write some scripts." I said, "What is it?" He said, "It's animation, it's called *ThunderCats*". I said, "I don't know anything about animation, I've never done it in my life. The closest I've ever got is an industrial film for Goodyear showing how tyres are made. And he says, "Just get over here!"'

79

As both a script editor and writer on *ThunderCats*, Peter explains how he decided which episodes to write: 'I think in the beginning, I was paid per episode to write, so it was worth my while to increase the amount of money I earned. But it wasn't the sole motivation. In the beginning, I wrote scripts on my own as part of a learning process, and later on, I wrote them when I thought I had something. 'Good and Ugly' is a good example. I thought a script where the hero is the ugliest fucker you've ever seen and the villain is good-looking was a good idea. 'Excalibur' is another example. Perhaps, post-rationalisation maybe, but once I got the whole thing running and Chris Trengove and Lee Schneider were on board, there was less brutal editing to do. Maybe then I had more time. I'd also, by that time, negotiated an all-in deal, which meant it made no difference whether I wrote or not. If you look at *SilverHawks*, you'll see I'm credited on the script only a couple of times, I think, in fact, I wrote most of it myself – it was so weird that I rewrote and edited so much of it that I literally didn't have time to write my own stuff. That wasn't the case with *ThunderCats*.'

Asked if his editorial experience made writing for the show an easier process, he replies: 'Maybe. I work pretty fast anyway, so I don't know that it did. I hope I was better at it at the end than the beginning, but I don't know it came any faster. Towards the end, I was probably getting a little fed up with writing *ThunderCats*.

'I loved writing Mumm-Ra. I don't know why, but Mumm-Ra to me was the boss, and I loved writing his stuff, so I got better and faster at things like that. I got letters accusing me of being a Satanist, which caused me great amusement. The Mutants, Slithe in particular, I liked because you could do all that "Yesssssssss' stuff. Lion-O was okay, Panthro okay, Tygra was boring. Cheetara was okay because you could actually make her different. I hated WilyKit and Kat, Snarf was okay – I understood why he was there, but he didn't really inspire me.'

Lawrence believes that scripting animation provides a very unique writing experience: 'We didn't have storyboard artists in America – the artists were in Japan – so you wrote everything you wanted to see, *everything*, and that was a problem for some writers. I'd worked as a film editor and a director, so my writing is very visual and is driven by the pictures not the words. So, for me, Jules said, "Remember, everything that's on screen, corner to corner, has to be directed and written by you." If you take a scene at a party, you wouldn't have to say anything about [the background] in a live action script, you'd just list the characters and dialogue. You could say that if you had a storyboard team, that's all you'd write in animation as well. But we had to write the background, because if you didn't write it, it wouldn't appear. That was a big lesson, which had good and bad effects. The good effect was that I had to think much harder about my writing, to describe it, but the negative was that I over-directed later [live action] scripts, and directors think you're treading on their toes. But I think if you're going to buy my script, you can change it, but I'm gonna write how I want. If I write what I'm thinking, then when it comes to acting it out, you know more about it. The detail demanded of *ThunderCats* made me more detailed in my own writing. When you wrote for *ThunderCats*, you weren't only the writer, you were the director. Then you'd pass it to the storyboard guy. Some writers had none of that experience and weren't good about the directing, but give me a good idea and me or one of my guys will sort it.

'When you write parts in animation you have to think of the voice actors, and you try to give them the cadences, the rhythm and the words [suited to their characters]. Mumm-Ra, for instance, would use certain words. I, and I'm sure Chris Trengove and some other writers like Lee Schneider and Matthew Malach (the writers close to the production), would have the character voices in our heads, but writers that were more satellite, maybe including Bill, would not. We completed loads of scripts before we ever heard the actors' tracks, but if you have the character voices in your head, they're inspirational.

'Actors didn't have much input into dialogue tweaks. My memory is that when the conformed scripts came back, the changes weren't extensive. I don't have any great obsession about whether or not the actors change the dialogue – if they do, just make sure it's better than the original.'

Time and again, the *ThunderCats* writers interviewed for this book credit Lawrence for the imaginative path down which he took the series and its storylines, openly admitting how much work he did in revising and improving their scripts. Lawrence is hugely passionate in his belief that young audiences should be respected: '*ThunderCats* was an extremely entertaining show, it was funny, it had action, it had exciting characters, you never knew what was around the corner. But at the same time, there was that comforting repetitious villainy in Mumm-Ra, because people like that. There's a very narrow course to steer between familiarity and boredom. You need to be familiar – you know Mumm-Ra would do a certain thing – but if he does it all the time, you don't want that. Then there's Mandora doing this, that and the other, and you suddenly think, "What's going on?" And it's like a magician, diverting the audience's attention before hitting them with the trick. I'm not saying that was all deliberate, because it wasn't. No-one's that smart. I'm not, for sure. But there was a lot of variety … and we respected the audience.'

Sharing his opinion on why *ThunderCats* was so successful, Lawrence cites a number of factors: 'I think there are some light reasons why *ThunderCats* was successful, like the timing of the show and the fact there wasn't much like it [on TV then]. All sorts of fortuitous stuff that none of us can take credit for. There are also some heavy reasons, like that the show was based on layers of intelligence and real characters that we were forced to think about by Lee, by Kuisis, by Jules and by the actors. There was a strong cast. I wasn't there, but I'd be really surprised if they didn't sometimes say, "Why does Mumm-Ra say this?" I'd be really surprised if we weren't questioned. There's no one thing. But if [I had to say there was a predominant reason], though I don't believe that, it's that we operated completely outside all the norms. We weren't Hollywood; in fact we were somewhat despised by Hollywood. When I first went over there to find writers, they thought we were a load of jokers from New York who didn't know shit from Shinola. It wasn't until we were a success that they'd say, "Hire me, hire me". It wasn't until we were a success that we'd go to the Westwood Hotel and they'd say, "Oh Miss Dannacher, how's *ThunderCats* doing?" And you'd think, "You dick." But we were insulated from all of that. We were our own very individualistic little operation, and whether it was Michael Soloman or Jules or whoever supported us, they didn't fuck with us.

'I must make it clear that I learned a huge amount from these shows. About animation. About writing for animation and about writing in general. About clarity of visual and vision. About improvisation and imagination run riot (thank you, eternally, Bill Overgard). About the disrespect and even scorn that producers and salesmen have for writers, probably because even the best of them couldn't write anything that would hold up against even the worst writers. I learned from Bill, from Len, and on and on. I learned massively from Jules, despite the astonishing and incomprehensible way in which our working relationship and our friendship ended.

'To me, the techniques of writing, of screenwriting, aren't worth shit. The core idea is all that counts, and that's what I took from each writer and attempted – often I'm sure making mistakes, and enemies certainly – to turn into a script that would take the show to new places. Dialogue? Plenty of people can write dialogue. Plenty of people know how to spell. Plenty of people can format a script. *So find me an original idea*! And, if necessary, I'll find the writers who can write dialogue, spell, format, etc. And, if necessary, I'll do all that myself …

'I can never claim – never – that all this was in my head … It was a job. But I do believe we executed it with some degree of integrity and passion. That was all part of the lesson for me; and part of why I look back on *ThunderCats* bemused (so much of my involvement was accidental … coincidental … a twist of fate here … a missed phone call there) but with some pride. It is all these more-or-less indefinable aspects – and the massive talents that went into the animation, the recordings, the sheer hard work of a small but dedicated team – that, I believe, made *ThunderCats* such a success. It was also, I'm sure, a fluke; a wrinkle in time when we were able to be free – or relatively free – and so connect with kids who are, after all, freer than any of us if given the chance. And not just kids but college students and even some adults (though God knows what they were thinking …)

'Warners and the "owners" of *ThunderCats* … even the people who sold and bought the show … had and have no real feeling for any of these subtleties, any of the work, the imagination, the passion, the sheer will that went into the show. And that's why they have no clue what to do with the property now. Ask them and I'm sure they'll tell you they were entirely responsible for the success: their genius sold it, it's all down to them. Bullshit. Sure, without the brains that figured out syndication, stripping, barter etc there would not have been a forum, and for that, these self-proclaimed geniuses should be applauded. But they had nothing without the people who made the show. All those writers who worked for insultingly low fees because they were broke – and they were writers – and now have nothing. RIP Bill Overgard, who left virtually nothing to acknowledge his huge talent. But somehow, *ThunderCats* found a way into our hearts, and we will not let anything detract from that heart-connection.'

Now living in Los Angeles, Peter Lawrence continues his successful career. 'After New York, I came to LA and did all the story editing on *Peter Pan and the Pirates*. That's a smart show, some lovely characters. After that, I did a show called *The Further Adventures of T-Rex*. Then I did *Johnny Quest*, which ended in disaster. After that, I thought I'd had enough of animation. I've always written books and movies, so that carried on in parallel. I wrote *Fishing with Crocodiles* about my time in Africa, and a lot of movies for producers in America and Europe. Basically, I've worked consistently. I still get asked to write for animation from time to time. I wrote for Chris Trengove on *Dennis and Gnasher* and a show called *The Way of the Cat*. I wrote a screenplay for a Finnish film about reindeers, and I've just sold a true crime film for a lot of money.'

William Overgard

14 episodes: 'Mandora – The Evil Chaser', 'The Fireballs of Plun-Darr', 'Mandora and the Pirates', 'Dr Dometone', 'The Thunder-Cutter', 'Sword in a Hole', 'Side Swipe', 'Exile Isle', 'The Jade Dragon', 'The Circus Train', 'Screw Loose', 'Cracker's Revenge', 'Swan Song', 'The Book of Omens'

William Overgard is perhaps the most controversial *ThunderCats* writer amongst the show's fans. With a wildly imaginative approach to storytelling, his 14 episodes include the best and worse examples of *ThunderCats*. When he conformed his ideas to the spirit and tone of the series, his work showcased both his own talents and the programme's potential, yet his tendency to deviate from these confines also resulted in some bizarre and misplaced adventures. Despite this, Bill Overgard was responsible for creating some of the most memorable characters in the ThunderCats universe, and without his contributions, the series would have been notably inferior.

'Bill was ten or 15 years older than me,' says his friend and colleague Peter Lawrence. 'He was a comic strip illustrator who worked for Milton Caniff, one of the greats – it was his inspiration. He went to war as a very young man, about 18, and after that came to New York and met a ballet dancer, Gloria, whom he married. He did a strip called *Rudy Goes to Hollywood*. It's about a talking, dancing chimpanzee, but the drawings and illustrations are out of this world. He and Gloria lived on an ice farm, where you have a big pond that freezes in the winter and you cut the ice and store it and sell it in the summer in New York. They had this beautiful property, the most spectacular house and barn. Gloria was tiny. She worked for the Bronx Zoo, and she'd get up at 5.00 am – she was, literally, the shit shoveller. She had working with her the most bizarre people, but they loved and respected her. While Bill sat in his studio drawing, Gloria would stand at her lectern and read to him. They had an unbelievable relationship. Bill had a successful book, optioned for a lot of money, and they moved to Mexico for this, but things didn't really work out, and Bill wrote loads of Rankin/Bass things and came onto *ThunderCats*.

'I walked into the meeting and here was a guy that looked a little bit English in a way: tweed jacket, a tie, a shirt, very smart – he'd never wear sneakers, he had a phobia about people wearing sneakers. We went out to lunch and he said, "I'll have a Martini," and we drank ourselves stupid on Martinis. From that point on, we were the best of friends, and he was like my older brother. We understood each other; we had the same outlook. He'd get really excited; he was exactly like I used to be – not so much now – but we really connected. I spent a lot of time with him and Gloria socially and became very close to both of them. Bill hated me for rewriting him and he'd get angry, but at the same time there was a respect there. He'd show me other work and ask me to take a look at it and help him sell some work. All I can tell you is that Gloria and Bill were both larger than life in a nice and modest way.'

Lawrence reveals that the wild eccentricity and individuality Overgard brought to the series were every bit as present in his own personality: 'Bill needed a lot of editing to fit in with *ThunderCats*, but it was worth it because he had an inspirational imagination, and when you're a story editor working day in, day out, you cry out for something fresh, and that's what he did. Bill's drawing and craftsmanship were stunning. They had a big conservatory, and in there they had a plant that blossoms once a year for 12 hours, and we happened to be in there one day and it came out – miraculous. Gloria adopted every single animal in the area and she even named the fish in the pond. She fed geese and had a dog, and a one legged crow called Reiter – they'd saved it as a baby and brought it up by hand. It would fly with them on their walks and one day, when they walking with friends, there was a bald man, and the crow got a liking for attacking bald people. That's where all the menagerie of creations came from. Bill said the only animal they never had (and they had racoons) was a possum, because you tried to bond with it and it pretended to be dead.'

Sadly, William Overgard passed away on 25 May 1990, just a year after his final *ThunderCats* script was broadcast. 'I was in LA working on *Peter Pan* and the phone rang,' recalls Lawrence. 'I picked up the receiver and it was Bill's son, Matthew, and I knew instantly that Bill had died. It was like a kick in the gut, and I can honestly tell you I was more affected by his death than my own father's. We were such good friends.'

Stephen Perry
7 episodes: 'The Doomgaze', 'Safari Joe', 'Queen of 8 Legs', 'The Feliner' Parts 1 and 2, 'Tight Squeeze', 'Trapped'

'One day in 1984 I was in the right place at the right time,' comments Steve Perry, whose seven episodes of *ThunderCats* were written under the stewardship of both Leonard Starr and Peter Lawrence. 'Here we are, years later, and you are holding this book. The author has asked me to reminisce about my participation in the creation and writing of an old cartoon series that has shown surprising longevity: *ThunderCats*. I was one of the four original writers who worked on *ThunderCats* from its inception, which to me means before the first script was written. Besides me, the others included Len Starr, Bill Overgard and Bob Haney. Bob Haney, as you no doubt know, worked on *Batman* in 1940; Len Starr, too, had been a part of the Golden Age comics scene, but he is best known for his syndicated strip work for *Little Orphan Annie* and *On Stage*; and Bill was utterly unknown to me – so of them all, it was Bob who struck me with a certain amount of awe, followed closely by Len, who had drawn *The Human Torch* in 1940. I was, after all, writing comics at the time, and had been a comic book collector for my entire life. This might not be an enviable attribute; nonetheless, I was hooked the day I bought *Fantastic Four # 4* off the newsstand for a dime.'

Prior to working on *ThunderCats*, Perry had already carved out a successful career: 'I was living a dream. I was making my living as a freelance writer, writing comic books for Marvel, something I had determined to accomplish shortly after the purchase of that fabled *Fantastic Four # 4* and the discovery, in my Auntie Kay's downstairs closet, of a 1923 Underwood typewriter. The clackey-clack sound of that typewriter mystified and enthralled me, and when it became clear that the gibberish could be made into words, and then the words into sentences and then the sentences into stories … stories about such luminaries as Ben Grimm, Bruce Banner and most of all Donald Blake … I was hooked. And years later, as 1983 became 1984 and then 1985, I found myself living that long-desired dream. I was writing for Marvel. I must have had a certain degree of talent, but I was to learn that everyone I associated with had talent, and lots of it. My friends numbered such people as Steve Bissette, Alan Moore, Rick Veitch, Tom Yeates, John Tottleben and Archie Goodwin and Denny O'Neil. Archie Goodwin, may he rest in peace, had given me a chance at a creator-owned series for Epic Comics. I had finished writing *Timespirits*, and Tom Yeates' beautiful artwork was gracing my stories – I was lucky that way: I had even worked with Steve Ditko, one of my idols, and with the great Al Williamson, whose incomparable line work both influenced and guided Tom Yeates' astronomical talent. Al had just finished drawing a *Timespirits* story, and I was honoured no end that his name stood beside my own. So everyone around me had talent. In fact, they all had much more of it than I; but I had luck, and a lot of it.'

Perry recalls the circumstances that led him to *ThunderCats*: 'I was sitting in the woods of Vermont, in my unique studio beside a beautiful waterfall that emptied into a naked swimming hole, when the phone rang. That I even had a phone was lucky – I had had to run a cord 300 feet to reach the amazing little outbuilding that served as my writing den; a *Cabinet of Dr Caligari*-style tower, three stories high, but only 10 feet wide, built by a man named Robert Dubac, who rented it to me for a pittance of $50 a month. I could look out the huge picture window from three stories high among the tree limbs, toward the swimming hole where a continual parade of beautiful New York and LA artists, visiting the wilds of Vermont and Dubac's studio, would skinny-dip. That the phone even worked that day – for some days it would not – confirmed my luck was holding firm. The call was from Len Starr. I knew of Len's work on *Little Orphan Annie* and *On Stage*, but was not too familiar with it; to me he was a legend for having drawn *The Human Torch* and *Sub-Mariner* in the 1940s, along with his EC and DC work in the 1950s. Len said he had gotten my number from Al Williamson. He said he had asked Al if he knew any good writers. He said Al immediately told him to call me. Len said, "I'm doing this cartoon about cat people for Jules Bass and we need a few scriptwriters. You want to write some cartoons?" "Um, ah … okay," was about all I could manage.

'Len then proceeded to tell me how Jules Bass had given him a day – 24 hours – to come up with a treatment for a cartoon series about a superhero group of cat-people. He had done that, taking bits and pieces of all sorts of things and mashing them together. Jules had a few ideas he absolutely wanted in there. "The main guy has this sword that grows bigger when he gets excited, like a dick," Len said. "They all have names ending in 'O' and are based on cats, you know … like Lion-O, Tiger-O, Cheeta-O, but I changed a bunch of that crap. We got a pretty good bad guy, Mumm-Ra. Ancient mummy who transforms like the Hulk. The characters are all designed – Jules has some toy deal in place to finance the whole thing. I'm working on a series bible. Give me your address, I'll send you all the writers' stuff. You can then get back to me with a bunch of springboards." In the week it took to receive the package from Len, much had been firmed up – they were the *ThunderCats*, Lion-O wielded the Sword of Omens, the planet was Third Earth, Mumm-Ra had a chant we'd use in every show. Suddenly, I was a *ThunderCats* writer. Just like that.

'I was paid $2,500 a script in the beginning, and that was raised to $3,500 a script by the time I wrote a two-parter, the one that introduced Ratar-O and Snarfer – a one-hour special originally called "The Planet of Snarfs". I believe Len Starr was paid better than most everyone – I once heard him bitching that five grand a show was cheap. He expressed this in terms of the total budget for the show. "That's how much they think of writers!" he told me. But I was used to writing comics for 30 to 50 bucks a page – a 22-page Marvel paying around $900. The rate for a *ThunderCats* script was fine by me, to tell you the truth. This would soon evaporate into much more of a struggle with subsequent episodes, as Peter Lawrence exerted his vision and control of the scripts, and as he began to bring in more and more other writers. Unfortunately, one of the attitudes that began to develop was a proprietary dislike of the "new" writers – there were only 65 shows to do, and I wanted as many pay cheques out of that 65 as I could get. Each show assigned to another writer was one I could never do. That, Kind Reader, is nothing more than monetary greed. But it became a part of *ThunderCats* – and not a good part of the creative process.'

In common with many writers, Perry dislikes being asked the eternal question: where do your ideas come from? 'Stephen King hates that question. I think all writers hate that question. For a long time I always answered it, "Wal-Mart." But the truth is that a simple occurrence in real life can often become the germ from which an idea grows. A good example is my *ThunderCats* episode "Queen of 8 Legs". I lived in a beautiful house, a big old Vermont farmhouse, built around the turn of the century – 1800 that is. A great colonial house with nine-pane windows and big, hand-hewn beams and original flooring, drafty as hell. In the back of the house, a huge spider's web appeared, and when my wife got a look at the size of the web, she ordered me to go destroy its builder before it ate one of the children. I reluctantly set about doing as I was told. I went around the house, out back, and examined the massive web. Then, up under the eves of the roof, I spotted the spider. "Spidera" I had called her – a truly enormous black widow. I went and fetched a snow shovel. As I cleared out the web, this giant thing came scuttling down the web and … *attacked*! It attacked the snow shovel! Somehow it lost its footing and it fell. When it hit the hard packed dirt at my feet there was a sound, like a ripe tomato being dropped onto concrete. *Plop*! Loud. The damn thing must have weighed half a pound! I am afraid no matter how large and fearsome this Spidera was, I was no Scott Carey and this was not the great battle of the Incredible Shrinking Man. I stomped on that spider with my big size twelves. There was a cup full of green and white gruel smeared in the dirt and Spidera was no more. I felt … sad. But the wife and children were safe and the menace destroyed; I was a good husband. I never, ever have forgotten that sound … that ripe tomato plopping sound. I knew one day I would have the occasion to write a story about Spidera, and there it was – for a TV show!'

Asked how he gained his successive *ThunderCats* assignments, Perry explains: 'The game was pitching. I had to corner Peter Lawrence and pitch him ideas for more work; for another show, for another pay cheque. It was no doubt around this time that the great Bob Haney, of *Batman* fame, bowed out of his work on *ThunderCats*. Having a stature of such immense proportions, I do not think Bob liked it too much having to get approved on what he wanted to do. If you look at the history of that first season, you will see Bob Haney wrote only a handful of episodes before going on to other things. He did not like to pitch ideas to Peter Lawrence, I think. Someone like Bill Overgard, who had a solid friendship with Peter built on more than just the work, had *carte blanche* on whatever he wanted to do – Peter was that confident in him. Then there was someone like me: I got along very well with Peter (and with Len) but, honestly, was terrified of Jules Bass. I was simply too in awe of him, and often fumbled and flustered and was unable to sound coherent when he was around. I think Jules thought I was a nut case. He liked what I had done, though, because the toy people at LJN liked it, too – they produced a Safari Joe and that made people a lot of money. They produced Ratar-O, too. Same deal. And … I have heard a Feliner nearly went into production. I created all these toys, they sprung from my head, and I gratefully cashed my one pay cheque and accepted that I was giving these creations away, never to see another dime for them. That was the deal.'

Perry remembers that after the success of *ThunderCats*, one of his own creations was put forward to the Rankin/Bass production team: '*SilverHawks* was already in development and Jules Bass, Arthur Rankin and Peter Lawrence wanted to keep the ball rolling; to keep the money flowing, keep the product churning out. Mattel was knocking on the door – the huge powerhouse of the toy business. To hell with LJN, and even Kenner: the Big Boys were knocking. I do not know how many of the original writers of *ThunderCats* were asked – everyone, I suppose. Me for sure, Bill Overgard no doubt, Len Starr and Bob Haney probably and Chris Tengrove most likely … But the question and opportunity were put out there: "What have you got? What do you have for Mattel to turn into a toy line, and for us to turn into a 65 episodic cartoon series?" This is the opportunity of a lifetime for a writer, for a creator. One's own creation. The possibility of a percentage ownership in something big. The offer came through Peter Lawrence, and it just so happened … I had something.

'Steve Bissette, best known for his stunning work on *Swamp Thing*, and I had, in the summer of 1986, or perhaps 1985, co-created a project based on an idea I had. Steve did a bunch of character designs, fleshed out a lot of characters and contributed to a storyline I had mostly worked out. We both loved dinosaurs, and wanted a realistic way to have people and dinosaurs together. We took our mutual love of several different things and mixed them all together: Sergio Leone, time travel, dinosaurs, and plain, outright weirdness. The result was something called *Dinosaur Bill*. I delivered the proposal package to Peter Lawrence and Rankin/Bass in the midst of writing my *SilverHawks* episodes. Jules Bass took a look at it. Other producers, such as Lee Dannacher, took a look at it. A week or so passed. I was in my studio at the waterfall on Broad Brook in Guilford, Vermont. Skinny dippers cavorted outside my window. I was writing a *SilverHawks* episode concerning a gold prospector, sung to the tune of Clementine – that would become the show's title to me, even though it was officially listed as "Limbo Gold Rush". Peter Lawrence called. Everyone … loved *Dinosaur Bill*. Cowboys and dinosaurs, Sergio Leone meets Ray Harryhausen. Remember, this was a full year or more *before* *Jurassic Park* went secretly into pre-production. Even the book *Jurassic Park* was not out yet – I believe it was still on Crichton's typewriter.

'*Dinosaur Bill* was a strong property, realistically getting people and dinosaurs together in an Old West setting, peppered with advanced technology, time travel and science fiction. It had the gritty look of a Leone film, the brilliant character design of Steve Bissette, and was simply a natural toy line – each character had its dinosaur; rider and mount. The saloon girl, Bronto Belle, had her Brontosaurus, the bad guy had his T Rex, the comic "Gabby Hayes" relief had his dino, and on and on. The one-way time travel idea enabled an Old West society to grow up around transplanted time travellers, and Dinosaur Bill himself was the first man born in the Cretaceous period. Simple for kids, good for toys, entertaining for adults, with tons of in-jokes and pop culture reference, *Dinosaur Bill* was going to be a series! A year, perhaps two, *before Jurassic Park* became such a huge hit. And some shark-suited executive says, "Dinosaurs are dead, kids don't care about dinosaurs anymore." It all ground to a sudden stop, was all over, was all done. I finished my last *SilverHawks* script, and no more work came my way. Peter fought for me and got me a potential job writing a *TigerSharks* episode, but when I went to New York, instead of a script assignment he took me out for a beer at 10.00 am. He told me Jules wanted me gone. There was no work for me at Rankin/Bass.'

Perry speaks with great enthusiasm about his time on *ThunderCats*, despite his disappointment with how his association with Rankin/Bass concluded: 'It was and remains an iconic television series. It is fondly remembered by an entire generation. For those of us involved in its creation, it will forever remain a bright spot, and we all are, I am sure, somewhat mystified by the Cats' ongoing popularity and current status as a pop icon. It represents all that was right – and wrong – with cartoons in the 1980s. The rightness is the cartoon itself, the good message born by the ThunderCats, the good talent involved in its realisation, and the message it promoted to children, despite us writers' constant attempts to throw a monkey wrench into it. The rightness is clear, as so many people out there remember *ThunderCats*, remember it with great affection, and over and over recall their childhood through it. But there is a seedy side, a downside – it was a business, lorded over by businessmen. It was all about making a buck. Or a hundred million of them. For me, it all ended on a sour note and with a great disappointment, but that's all in the past, and what is now left is nothing but "Fond Memories" (a *ThunderCats* show written by Lee Schneider in an attempt to use as little new animation as possible; it incorporates a lot of my work – it's almost like I wrote it)!'

Perry is pleased to have collaborated with so many talented writers during his career: 'As one of the original writers on the cartoon series, I had the great fortune to meet many fine, talented people passing in and out of the offices of Rankin/Bass, on 53rd Street, I believe, in New York City. As my home in rural Vermont was five hours outside the metropolis I commuted only when I had to – which would be a couple of times a month for a couple of days. I was also, at the time, writing for Marvel Comics but never managed to get assigned a "top" book – *Hulk, Avengers, Spiderman, X-Men* or any of the other Kirby/Lee anchors. I wrote a couple of inventory jobs for *GI Joe* and *Power Man and Iron Fist*, but they were "mercy" work, and still, undrawn, in a file cabinet somewhere. My take on *Dracula*, messing with poor Marv Wolfman's iconic work with Gene Colan, was more a chance to write for one of my idols, Denny O'Neil. But all that had little to do with *ThunderCats* and the world of cartoon animation. That was my bread and butter.

'I think Peter Lawrence said it best once, way back when. I have always had the highest regard for Peter, and am in awe of his abilities and talent. But he is a creative person too, and although quite good at the business end, he has the heart and soul of a creator. He said once that he absolutely hated the Suits, "who don't have a creative bone in their bodies, telling a writer how to write." I think, being the liaison between the toy people and the creative end, he had to suffer that sort of thing many times. Failure as a writer can be a difficult pill to swallow, and what happened to *Dinosaur Bill* soured me for years on the cartoon business. It is a wrong attitude, I know now, because *ThunderCats* still exists in its pure form: entertainment. Despite the trials and in and outs behind the scenes, *ThunderCats* will forever be a good, wholesome action cartoon, filled with good memories for millions of people, and deserving of its status as a pop culture icon. Most people who were children in the 1980s recall the ThunderCats with the same fondness each generation holds for its own loved characters of animation. Folks my age know the works of Chuck Jones and the unsung Mike Maltese – *Road Runner* and *Wile E Coyote*. Children of the '90s might feel this way about the *Teenage Mutant Ninja Turtles*. Those poor saps of the '70s are stuck with *H R Pufnstuf*. And Johnny Quest ruled the late 1960s. But it is, without question, those of you who grew up in the mid-1980s that know *Transformers, G I Joe, Ghostbusters, Masters of the Universe* and, of course, *ThunderCats*. Ask yourself this, Kind Reader: how many times did you run around your living room yelling "ThunderCats … Hooooo!" Many of you would have rushed home from school to catch, at 4.00 pm, the adventures of Lion-O, Snarf and the others as they paraded about Third Earth thwarting the endless machinations of the evil Mumm-Ra.'

After a period of professional inactivity, Steve Perry had resumed writing shortly before his death in May 2010, aged only 56.

Bob Haney
7 episodes: 'Lord of the Snows', 'All That Glitters', 'Return to Thundera', 'Dimension Doom', 'The Demolisher', 'Secret of the Ice King', 'Mumm-Rana'

Stalwart American comic book writer Bob Haney was invited to work on *ThunderCats* from the very beginning, his experience in the action/adventure world (albeit in pictorial form) making him a natural choice to write for the series.

Ted Steeg, a New York film-maker and lifelong friend of Haney's comments on the man behind the talent: 'If you spent any time in Woodstock in the last half of the 20th Century (yes, that Woodstock), you would surely at some point have run into Bob Haney. In a town of colourful citizens – artists, writers, musicians, actors – he was a glittering rainbow: six foot three, bearded, large-boned, with a rumbly *basso profundo* like James Earl Jones. When he walked into a room, you knew he was there. In warm weather, he could often be found strolling in town, garbed in safari jacket, shorts, calf-length socks – this in honour of his literary hero, Papa Hemingway. He never hunted lions and tigers, but he did fish a lot, in the creeks and rivers around the county. He even called the young women of his acquaintance (of which there were more than a few) "daughter". Many were the times we spent debating the impressive effect of Hemingway's dialogue on modern writing – not to mention the hours together drinking, arguing, driving back and forth from the Big Apple where we both made our living. We even collaborated on a couple of movie scripts. On those, he used the name Robert G Haney. That's also how he signed his Letters to the Editors in the *Woodstock Times*, where we engaged in various epistolary "duals" over civic issues. I used to kid him that I thought the "G" must stand for "gallimaufry", which would irritate him no end. That was in response, of course, to the many X-rated names he was always bestowing on me.'

Asked about the origin of Haney's career, Steeg explains: 'He schooled at Swarthmore, and then Columbia grad, where his thesis was on French literature.

He could give you 15 minutes on Montaigne just as readily as an explication of a Shakespeare plot. The higher learning followed a stint at shipbuilding during World War Two, and then navy duty in the Pacific. All of this informed his first career, writing plots and dialogue for Marvel Comics, and superheroes such as *Batman*, *Superman* and *The Green Lantern*. He was one of the creators of *The Unknown Soldier*, a popular comic book hero of the '50s and '60s, whose general gung-ho attitudes and missions have since been appropriated by the likes of Rambo and his movie brethren. Haney was no one-trick pony, though. To supplement the meagre earnings of those days from the comic book field, he was also a largely self-taught carpenter. This helped support his lovely wife Nancy and the two step-kids, Jency and John. He even designed and built his own home in the woods. That adventure eventually led to a fetching little book, called *Woodstock Handmade Houses*, which was popular enough to go into multiple printings.'

Steeg notes that Haney's recruitment by Rankin/Bass gave his career a new lease of life: 'When the *ThunderCats* people found him, it opened up a whole new career. Animated TV, of course, is sort of a natural progression from comic book panels, and Haney took to it like a superhero to a crisis. He loved working out madcap plots for the various felines, and giving them not only "heart" and "soul", but also hip, spicy lines. And for the first time in his career, he found himself earning paydays commensurate to his talents. Bob was an avid skier, which probably helped inspire episodes like "Lord of the Snow" and "The Ice King". I also remember, about that time, comparing notes with him about the *Star Wars* episode that Irvin Kirshner directed, and commenting on the spectacular use of snowscapes in those visuals. That surely influenced him. When you get right down to it, though, isn't a writer always drawing from many subconscious sources all the time – politics, history, personal life? I remember working on a cartoon script with Bob that had a sneaky comic villain; we modelled him on the disgraced Richard Nixon, not long after Watergate.

'In later years, Bob sometimes flew off to the annual comic book convention in San Diego. To his utter surprise (and secret pride) he found himself lionised by an enthusiastic coterie of fans. The last year of his life, tragically, he was hit by a massive stroke, which put him in a coma. But in a twist worthy of O Henry, he was visited now and then in that sterile military hospital room in southern California by some of those same fans. They would come in and read to his comatose form selections from – get this – his classic comic book stories of the past. What a nice tribute! You know how there are some people in your life that you always feel totally comfortable around? That was ol' Bob to me. He was a guy I could talk with about anything, anytime, anywhere. That's not to say he didn't have a few whopper flaws. But that's okay – what interesting human being doesn't? I do miss him. Oh, and if you wondered, "gallimaufry" (from the French) is a noun meaning an eclectic stew, an olio, a hodge-podge. The talented Robert G Haney was certainly all of that.'

Script editor Peter Lawrence also recalls his memories of working with Bob Haney: 'Bob was a comic book writer who lived in Woodstock, where Lee Dannacher's sister also lived part of the time. Through her and her boyfriend, Lee knew Bob quite well, so when the show was picked up and R/B needed scripts, Lee naturally asked Bob if he wanted some commissions. This was substantially before my time on the show. Bob certainly had the credentials. I believe he was one of the lead writers on *Aquaman*. At that time, Bob was "an older man" and, like Len and – for a heartbeat – Bill Overgard, probably resented the upstart Englishman who appeared out of nowhere to bastardise his golden prose; and that was one of Bob's characteristics – that he thought of himself as a literary writer, not just a comic book or TV cartoon writer. [A difficulty] not helped by the fact that some of his contemporaries, when they knew what he was doing, would talk about "ThunderPussies" and so on.

'Here's one of the tragedies of writing: that many writers suffer some kind of complex that causes them to denigrate the media in which they earn their living. Their mental composition – their psyche, if you like – the very element that drives them to write, to express themselves, to stand out from the crowd, also undermines them. It's the cliché of the insecure writer often hiding behind his beard (which Bob had!) The reality, in my view, is that writing is just another job. I recall Chris Trengove's response to being called a "hack" because he wrote in – and earned money from – so many different genres. "Damn right," he said, "and proud of it. If you can earn a living out of writing, that's an achievement all on its own." (Chris's father, an old-school wheeler dealer, never got beyond the fact that he thought his son was a typist.) The mirror of Chris's view is held by many writers who slave away over novels and scripts that never see the light of day and whose failure to sell becomes the cause of great bitterness (and much extremely tedious, whining, cocktail party conversation). Bob really was a pretty good cartoon writer but he hated being edited because he saw it as an affront to his literary talent. Not at all! It's simply part of the work. It's the story editor/showrunner's responsibility to seize the material and conform it to the show. Sometimes, the editor/showrunner makes mistakes, of course; and sometimes – more often than not – the original writer disagrees with the editing of his golden prose. But, tough, if you're working for the show you have to submit to that process!

'Once we had worked on a couple of scripts and got to know each other somewhat – had a couple of cocktails together – Bob eased up. He was a talent and a good man – and Chevy Chase's uncle, I believe.'

Bob Haney is still most famous for his long association with DC Comics, which lasted three decades and spanned countless comic book titles including the *Teen Titans* and *Super-Sons* series. He was also honoured with the 1968 Alley Award for his work on the title *Track of the Hook*, and a Comic-Con International Inkpot Award presented in 1997. He passed away on 25 November 2004.

C H Trengove
7 episodes: 'Turmagar the Tuska', 'The Wolfrat', 'The Super Power Potion', 'Out of Sight', 'Catfight', 'Hair of the Dog', 'The Mossland Monster'

A British-born writer, Chris Trengove came to the show – his first foray into the world of animation writing – through his long-time friend and collaborator, script editor Peter Lawrence. 'I'd written books with Chris when I was in advertising,' notes Lawrence. 'Chris was working as a mini cab driver and I couldn't find an advertising copywriter, [so I brought him in to do that]. Then, later in New York, I said, "I need someone to help me write scripts," and he came over and wrote a lot of episodes for me.'

Chris Trengove explains, 'I was trained on magazines, and later worked as a journalist, PR agent and advertising copywriter. In the 1970s, I co-wrote two well-received comic novels with long-time friend and writing partner, Peter Lawrence, and in the early 1980s also found success with a biography of Who drummer Keith Moon.'

Trengove recounts his memories of working on *ThunderCats* and the challenges of writing for animation: 'It's crucial to remember it's a visual medium, and that you aren't dealing with actors. Animated characters (at least back in the '80s) had a limited inventory of facial expressions, and you couldn't really do subtlety. So, "terrified" and "ecstatic" equals good, "quizzical" equals bad. I tend to work an "office day" when I'm writing – start around 10.00 am, go on until around 6.00 pm. Now I work on a computer with Final Draft but I wrote all my episodes of *ThunderCats* on a typewriter (generally an IBM Selectric). As they say in Hollywood, "It's all in the re-writes", and writers would generally be required to submit several drafts per script. (In my entire career I've only ever had a handful of first drafts accepted.)

'There was an extensive series bible [for *ThunderCats*]. Anyone who writes for a living is accustomed to following established parameters, and film and TV writing is necessarily a collaborative process. Contrary to some public opinion, anyone who writes for children is aware of the "moral responsibility". Children's TV output – now and then, and on both sides of the Atlantic – generally follows quite a strict set of "compliance" rules, which writers have to stick to. So it wasn't particularly onerous to work within appropriate boundaries. The challenge was to create scripts that were exciting and action-filled, without them containing any actual violence. So a ThunderCat may have had a high-tech weapon, but he wouldn't use it to blow a group of Mutants to smithereens – instead he'd shoot down a chandelier above them, to contain them.'

Trengove is extremely positive about his time on *ThunderCats*: 'It was a great introduction to the nitty-gritty of series screenwriting. Like most writers, I tend to enjoy writing "bad guys", and on a show like *ThunderCats*, you have to make sure you're not building them up to the detriment of the heroes. Mumm-Ra's demented ranting was fun to do. There was a great emphasis on writing lean, pacey scripts (avoid having characters sitting around yakking; show, don't tell; keep it simple.) Writers could always consult with Peter, and Lee Dannacher also had a lot of input. The ultimate arbiter was producer Jules Bass. Many "pitches" would hit the dust for one reason or another, but I never had a script rejected. It shouldn't really happen anyway, as each pre-script stage would have been fully approved, and Peter would pull together any script with serious shortcomings. However, a few writers had only one script commissioned, which probably meant that they didn't quite fit the *ThunderCats* "mould".'

In addition to his writing duties, Trengove also provided editorial support for Peter Lawrence: 'My recollection is that I did bits and bobs as kind of "holiday relief".'

Lawrence concurs: 'With Chris, because he'd worked as an editor, he also helped me with the editing, and so did Lee Schneider. Chris was so reliable. He did not turn in scripts of the wild imagination of Bill Overgard, but they were really crafted, and without scripts like Chris's the show wouldn't have survived – there has to be a main body, and then you can have the wild shit produced by people like Bill.'

Trengove's colleague Lee Schneider remembers how pleased he was to see his creations hit the shelves as part of the *ThunderCats* toy line: 'Chris said it was like "seeing a child of yours go off to college" after he saw one of his characters shrink-wrapped in a store display.'

Trengove remains proud to have been involved in the show, and has since achieved success in a variety of other projects: 'It was fun at the time, and all those involved were committed to producing the best show possible. What we didn't know, of course, was that it would turn out to be a classic. Friends of my son, in their twenties, have been thrilled to "shake the hand of the man who worked on *ThunderCats*!" I've written for animation extensively, and in the '90s was involved in another "classic", *Bob the Builder*. (With the producer, I developed the show and wrote the bible, and scripted numerous episodes.) Also in the '90s, I had a children's book, *Katzers*, published by Bloomsbury. In recent years, I've often worked as a series script editor (for example on *Dennis and Gnasher*, recently broadcast by the BBC) and still collaborate with Peter Lawrence on film screenplays and other projects.'

Kimberly B Morris
6 episodes: 'The Trouble With Thunderkittens', 'The Mad Bubbler', 'Day of the Eclipse', 'The Telepathy Beam', 'The Formula', 'Frogman'

'Writers start writing as soon as they can hold a pencil,' says Kimberly Morris, one of the few female writers to contribute to *ThunderCats*. 'It's figuring out what your writing path is going to be that's a process that can take many years. Professionally, I started writing right out of college. I worked for a small start-up tabloid newspaper in Houston, Texas. I left when I was offered a job in New York City with a company that did a variety of things including producing animated specials for network and syndicated broadcast. Romeo Muller, who wrote so many of the Rankin/Bass holiday classics, was one of the principals of the company. So I was involved with animation long before I began writing it. In New York, I spent three years attending the Lehman Engel BMI Musical Theatre Writers' Workshop – which was wonderful training for writers of anything, because it was all about craft, story, process etc. (The lessons learned in that workshop have applied to everything I've written – animated scripts, short stories, novels and even business proposals.)'

Morris recalls how she came to work on *ThunderCats*: 'Rankin/Bass called the company for which I was working, because they were looking for animation writers in New York City. My boss at the time, Robert L Rosen, very kindly recommended me. I met with Peter Lawrence, and he very kindly hired me to write a script. It was a very exciting opportunity for me – and over the next few years I wrote scripts for *ThunderCats*, *SilverHawks*, *TigerSharks* and *Mini-Monsters*.

Asked about her prior experience of animation, Morris says: 'I had done some editing on a series of animated public service announcements. I had certainly seen the process unfold – watching animated programmes emerge from Romeo Muller's scripts. But I was young and too dumb to know what I didn't know. So I wasn't as intimidated as I should have been. Aside from scene work for theatre pieces, I didn't have any experience with writing for live action, so it was a great education in visualising and then describing the complex visuals you see in your head.

ThunderCats was written many, many years ago and my process has changed dramatically since then. I didn't have as much experience as I do now – it took me much longer to work out the plot points and set up the action sequences. I tended to get very bogged down in back story. As time went on, I learned to get off the mark a little faster.'

During the production of *ThunderCats*, a revolution in electronic media was beginning in America. Morris recalls how she was reluctant to adopt the new technologies available: 'I started before people had computers. I worked on an electric typewriter (electric, not electronic!) You had to pull the ink cartridge out and put the eraser cartridge in when you wanted to correct a typo. So I usually wrote my drafts on a legal pad with a pencil. Then I would cut and paste the stuff I wanted to keep onto scratch paper, and *then* I would begin to type my "professional and polished" (ha ha ha ha) draft on the typewriter. You can't imagine how horrible it looked! Whiteout all over the page. Stuff crossed out. Peter Lawrence was so incredibly nice about it. Looking back, I can't believe he continued to commission me. One day he very gently suggested that when I got a little money ahead, I might consider getting a better typewriter. Word processors came along shortly after I started writing. Like everyone else, I was very resistant. I think I felt like the laborious, exhausting physical struggle of simply producing a readable document was somehow a necessary part of the creative process. Not any more. As soon as I learned to use the word processor, I was sold. If I had to go back to using a typewriter, I would have to find something else to do. Or else I'd have to write really, really short stories. Maybe fortune cookies.

'Another story for you. I was asked to come into the office and help edit some scripts on a tight deadline. When I got there, they put me in an office with an electronic typewriter (which had a bit of computer memory, and there was a delay between pressing keys and hearing the clack). Typewriters are like pianos in that the action feels different from one model to the next. I couldn't get used to the electronic typewriter and the clock was ticking, so they finally had somebody carry that typewriter out and bring in another kind. I couldn't get the feel of that one either. So they made somebody on staff give me their IBM Selectric – which was the Steinway of electric typewriters. Then I hunkered down and slammed out the edits. But I felt like Goldilocks – "This one is too fast. This one is too slow. This one is juuuuust right!" – and they thought I was nuts. They just couldn't believe that I was so behind the technology curve that I could be flummoxed by an electronic typewriter. But I was. And for the record, there will never be anything as satisfying to the hand, brain, ear and eye as an IBM Selectric typewriter. It made a wonderful thundering racket. It was a literary percussion instrument. The insipid "tippy tap tap" of a computer keypad is a very unsatisfying substitute.'

Morris credits the *ThunderCats* creative department with helping her to realise specific characters prior to writing: 'I'm sure I must have got a writers' bible, but I don't remember. When I started, nothing had been animated yet, so I really had no idea how the shows would actually look and "feel". There were a lot of illustrations, a lot of character sketches etc. But somehow the characters felt very real and fully realised as I wrote. I think that was because the main characters were well-delineated and their superpowers were offset with enough vulnerabilities to make real suspense possible. Yes, the good guys always won, but the outcome wasn't a foregone conclusion based on their superpowers alone. They relied on strategy, emotional intelligence and teamwork to figure out solutions.'

Having successfully submitted six episodes of *ThunderCats* to the production team, Morris was initially in contention to write the final episode of the first season. He story, 'Goodbye Jaga', for which she wrote a full script, would have seen a final 'coming of age' for Lion-O as he said farewell to his spirit guide and mentor, Jaga. 'This was not used because they decided to go in a different direction,' recalls Morris. 'They changed their mind about wanting to write Jaga out of the show.' She adds that perhaps Rankin/Bass were keen to retain the character in case further episodes were produced – which of course proved to be the case.

'The '80s was the era of bizarre day-time talk shows,' says Morris. 'Some covered topics of legitimate interest. But a lot were about UFO abductions ... eating disorders ... white supremacists... and my-sister's-boyfriend-slept-with-my-mother's-Aunt Millie-and-discovered-he-was-really-his-own-grandpa-so-who's-the-baby-daddy? Daytime television was an endless parade of wing-nuts and delusional exhibitionists. (Nothing's changed, really, except that now it's night-time television that's an endless parade of wing-nuts and delusional exhibitionists!) A friend called me one day and laughingly said she had no idea I was a Satanist. And could she go with me to the next meeting of the coven? Apparently she had been watching an afternoon show on which the topic was Satanists and their influence on children's programming. According to them, *ThunderCats* was a Satanic TV show full of occult imagery and embedded messages denying God. They firmly believed that the *ThunderCats* writing team was the source of the Satanic content and that we were part of a large conspiracy that met regularly for the purpose of subverting America's children. I told her I had no problem with Satanic conspiring or subverting America's children. But that stuff is very labour intensive. None of us was getting paid that much. And writing backwards while looking in the mirror is harder than you think. Now somewhere out there, somebody is taking this at face value. So just for the record... *that was a joke*! I am not a Satanist. I wish America's children nothing but good health and happiness. But in closing, I do want readers to know that when I do take over the world, every citizen under 14 will be entitled to a pony.'

When asked about her experience of *ThunderCats* (and her extensive career beyond), Morris is amazed at her good luck, and credits Peter Lawrence with helping her learn her craft. 'I wrote for other Rankin/Bass series – *TigerSharks*, *SilverHawks*, and *Mini-Monsters*. I went on to write short stories for the Muppet character groups – *Muppets*, *Muppet Babies*, *Fraggle Rock*. Their creator Jim Henson died very suddenly and my project area was cancelled. My editor there asked me if I thought I could write series novels. I actually had no idea whether or not I could write novels. The idea of writing in that format was pretty daunting, and if hadn't desperately needed the money, I wouldn't have pursued it. But I did, and I went to work writing *Sweet Valley* middle grade novels – and from there, young adult, middle grade, and chapter book novels for a variety of series including *Animorphs*, *Freshman Dorm* and now *Disney Fairies*. I do a lot of speaking and conduct a lot of workshops for students of all ages, adults, and general audiences. I also develop custom publishing projects for corporate and non-profit clients.'

J Larry Carroll
(6 episodes): 'The Sound Stones', 'Hachiman's Honor', 'The Totem of Dera', 'Return of the ThunderCubs', 'The Last Day', 'Leah' (with David Carren)

Arguably one of the most prolific and successful writers to have contributed to *ThunderCats*, Larry Carroll has written and produced hundreds of hours' worth of television programming in a career spanning four decades. He scripted more *ThunderCats* episodes than any other West Coast writer.

Carroll describes his background: 'I wrote and published short stories as an undergraduate at the University of Texas, Austin. Then I began writing scripts for industrial and educational films while still in film school. In 1978 I made my first "professional" script sale; the screenplay for *Tourist Trap* (co-written with David Schmoeller). Author Stephen King, in his book *Danse Macabre*, praised the film as an obscure classic. How's that for flattering?'

As for how he came to work on *ThunderCats*, Carroll recalls: 'My agent set up a meeting with Peter Lawrence, who was in LA interviewing writers for another Rankin/Bass production, *The Comic Strip*. Peter and I hit it off, in large part, no doubt, to the fact that we both had backgrounds in low budget features. (And we were both raising daughters.) My work on *The Comic Strip* led to me being invited to write for *ThunderCats*. Over the years, Peter and I have worked together on a number of other shows including *Peter Pan and the Pirates*. I was on staff at Filmation (*He-Man*, *Shera* etc.) when I first met Peter. Prior to Filmation, I had freelanced on *G I Joe*, *Gobots* and *Smurfs*.'

Carroll believes live action and animation writing are more alike than many would expect. 'Which is not to say there aren't some significant differences,' he clarifies, 'however, both are about storytelling. And to tell a good story, you need compelling premises, characters, dialog etc. That said, you do have to have an understanding of what works for animation and what works for live action. Which, alas, many writers seem unable to do. Actually, in some ways animation scripts are more crucial than those written for live action. Whatever you write, that's probably what is going to be shot – and shot pretty much the way you wrote it. In live action, a director might shoot additional takes, actors can modify lines on the set, the studio might ask for retakes, new scenes etc.'

Carroll describes his working routines: 'I tend to be a morning writer; my writing day might start as early as 4.30 am. Generally I try to reserve the hours between 8:30 am and 12:30 pm as prime writing time. I might extend my writing day if I am on deadline. In terms of "inspiration," a lot depends on whether I'm working on something of my own or an assignment. For the latter, I usually turn to my story files, which currently consist of nine three-ring binders filled with ideas, old pitch notes etc. This is as much for inspiration as ideas. Still, it's always great to find a fit for an old story or story element that I like but never found the right show for. I do all my writing on the computer. One of the happiest days in my life as a writer was liberating myself from typewriters. However, I do have three whiteboards in my office, which I use for brainstorming and roughing out ideas. And from time to time I will pick up pencil and paper to get a start on a difficult scene or sequence.'

Carroll explains his experiences of writing for *ThunderCats* and liaising with the production office: 'Everything came to me through Peter or his fabulous assistant, Karen Malach [nee Siegel] As for the rest of the production team, I was in Santa Monica and Rankin/Bass was in New York. We communicated via mail, FedEx and phone. (This was before everyone had a fax in their office – and the internet was something yet to come.) I didn't even meet anyone else who worked on the show until years later. In television, outlines are *de rigueur*. Studios, stars, production execs, all want to have their input as an episode is being developed. As a result, I nearly always outline. That said, I am currently writing a spec script without an outline. I am curious to see how it turns out – or if it even does. As I recall, on *ThunderCats*, rewrites were almost nonexistent or very light. Usually Peter would call me after the first or second draft and say, "Good job – what do you want to do next?" This is not a common occurrence in my experience as a TV writer.

'I don't recall receiving a *ThunderCats* bible *per se*. The show and characters were pretty well established before I began writing episodes. But there were certainly memos and model sheets detailing new characters and locales. As for working within the bounds of an established continuity, a TV writer's job is to be something of a chameleon; you are expected to write scripts that are the show; scripts that are a seamless fit with its established elements. I've had my share of battles with Standards and Practice, but I am always very aware of the fact that millions of people are inviting me into their living room, where I try not to be rude, or, worse, boring. I don't recall any significant changes to my scripts – certainly nothing that "damaged" the story. There were revisions of course. In television there are always revisions. Sometimes right up to the moment of shooting. And oftentimes it is someone else making those revisions. If that's something that troubles you, then you'd best look for another line of work. Peter is a great story editor. He is clear on what he wants and gives the writer good, specific direction. I always had at least a week for scripts and could take longer if needed. Peter was aware that other things were going on in my life and was very considerate. (Something you really appreciate when raising a three-year-old.) I don't recall anything significant that I came up with not being used. Sure, there were stories I pitched that Peter passed on; but I always understood his reasons for doing so. Again, that's standard operating procedure for writing TV. Some of your ideas will be rejected. Probably most of them actually. As I said, I deal with that by keeping rejected ideas in my story files and reviewing them whenever I'm searching for inspiration.'

Despite his massive success in screenwriting, Carroll remains proud to have been associated with *ThunderCats* and praises the series' high production values: 'Truthfully, the performances and animation probably made my scripts play better than they really were. It was a very good time in my life and my career. I realised that if I stayed on at Filmation, I would probably stagnate and get stuck. But on the other hand, being on staff and having the security of a steady pay cheque … it's hard to walk away from that. *ThunderCats* became the bridge between that "security" and what was to come career-wise. And as my mother would say, I'm tickled to death that after 25 years the show still has fans. I knew the show was popular, of course. But I honestly had no inkling it wouldn't be as ephemeral as most of the other shows I have written for. I once knew a *ThunderCats* fan, she was the mother of one of my daughter's schoolmates. And she had a disturbingly developed fantasy about the ThunderCats' sex lives. It made for some very awkward conversations until I reminded her that it was just a cartoon show … If the characters take off their clothes, there is literally nothing there.

'I liked writing for Lion-O, the ThunderKittens, and Panthro. It took me a while to warm up to Snarf, but in the end I had a lot of fun writing him. Never did find interesting ways to use Tygra and Cheetara. Not that they were bad characters; I just never seemed to come up with stories that made good use of them. The villains were a hoot. Loved writing Mumm-Ra and his crew of villainous minions. I wasn't as enthusiastic about the Lunataks, but still had fun with them.

'I have enjoyed a wildly eclectic career; just look at my IMDb page. After *ThunderCats*, I wrote for a goodly number of other series, both animated and live action. My credits range from *Star Trek: The Next Generation* to *Murder She Wrote* and from *Walker, Texas Ranger* to *Teenage Mutant Ninja Turtles*. I still write animation; in recent years I have written for *Pucca* and *Edgar & Ellen*. I'm currently rewriting an animated feature for an American-Hong Kong production company.'

Bill Ratter (Deborah Goodwin)
6 episodes: 'Runaways', 'Chain of Loyalty' (with Peter Lawrence), 'Locket of Lies', 'Bracelet of Power', 'The Heritage' (with Peter Lawrence), 'The Touch of Amortus'

One of the more unusual pseudonyms to have been used on the production of *ThunderCats* was Bill Ratter, a name created by British-born writer Deborah Goodwin. 'The name Bill Ratter came about because my godmother's husband was called Bill and I was called "Rattie" by a friend of mine. I thought choosing a pen name, particularly a male name, would give me anonymity, and it seemed more suitable for a predominantly male-orientated programme. I became involved in *ThunderCats* as I knew the script editor, Peter Lawrence. We co-wrote six episodes, but for each of those the ideas and storylines were written by me, with Peter and me working together on style and continuity.'

Living in the UK during the production of *ThunderCats*, Goodwin admits to having felt a little detached from the process: 'I have never, even to this day, watched any of the episodes written by me. I was not really aware of the show's success as I lived in the UK at the time, which may, in hindsight, have been a good thing. Perhaps if I'd known that I was writing for such a hit show, I would have felt under pressure and panicked. And for me, with panic, comes a blank sheet of paper that remains blank for some time! It was only when the episodes were being shown on the BBC that it began to dawn on me that the programme was successful and that I should have negotiated a better contract!'

Despite this, Goodwin is pleased to have been part of *ThunderCats*: 'I feel immensely proud. I never thought for one moment that it would be so iconic, and I've met many people who've told me how much they loved it. Believe it or not, only last week I met someone who told me that their boyfriend had watched *ThunderCats* and thought it fantastic … so it lives on. As I lived and worked in the UK, I don't really have many memories/anecdotes of my time working on *ThunderCats*. I did fly out to the USA and meet with some of the production team, but as Deborah rather than Bill Ratter.'

Goodwin had never written for television prior to her *ThunderCats* commission, but continued to work in the industry after the show's completion: 'After working on *ThunderCats*, I worked for Central ITV (in England), later Carlton

Television, as Head of Licensing. This was a fantastic job, licensing rights in its programmes, such as book, merchandising and audio, to third parties. I worked with some wonderfully creative and very nice people. After six years, I decided it was time to see what it was like on the other side and joined the well-respected publisher Andre Deutsch, which had just been sold to Video Collection International, as their Publishing Manager. I was involved in licensing serialisation rights to national newspapers and magazines and acquiring publishing rights in TV programmes including from Granada Television. Seven years later I had a career change to the leisure industry and more recently into education.'

Julian P Gardner (Jules Bass)
4 episodes: 'Trouble With Time' (with Ron Goulart), 'Pumm-Ra', 'The Terror of Hammerhand' (with Ron Goulart), 'The Garden of Delights' (with Barney Cohen)

Julian P Gardner was the pen name chosen by series executive Jules Bass, formed from a variation of his own name coupled with the name of the company in which he began his career: Gardner Advertising. Having used the pseudonym previously when writing a number of holiday specials, he continued to do so on his four *ThunderCats* scripts. Given that his credited co-writers on three of these were generally unaware of his input, it is fair to assume that his credit reflected his editorial work on the scripts. Script editor Peter Lawrence, who did not take up post until after 'Gardner's' episodes were completed, reveals how credits are assigned: 'If you can prove your contribution is up to a certain level, you can put your name on the script. I never did that. I thought, "I'm an editor, that's my job." Even if I rewrote 85%, which people complained I did, that was my job and that was my choice. Maybe I'd have felt differently if there were residuals – I hope not. It was Jules's choice [to take a co-writing credit], and he was perfectly within his rights to do it. Most writers resent that practice and will make a remark like, "He didn't really do anything anyway", but if you look at the scripts page by page, line by line, you'll probably find he did a lot.'

While his contribution to three of his scripts may have been largely editorial, Bass did write one solo adventure, 'Pumm-Ra'. This episode is indicative of how he felt an 'ideal' *ThunderCats* script should run and features all of the writing formulae and devices that would form the backbone of the series.

Despite him having scripted a relatively small number of episodes, Bass's contribution to *ThunderCats* cannot be overstated. Having co-written the series bible and original concept, he also continued to provide advice and guidance throughout the series' development, meeting regularly with Peter Lawrence. 'My view is that Jules isn't necessarily a great writer,' says Lawrence, 'but he is an excellent connoisseur of writing. He's not even a good editor as such, but he can see what's wrong with something immediately and he's extremely articulate, and he taught me a huge amount about animation writing and a huge amount about writing. And that's not by example by his own writing, it's much more by his acuity about writing.'

A series of memos from the production of *ThunderCats* reveal that Bass would constantly inject new material into the *ThunderCats* universe, regularly conceiving new scenarios and format changes that the writers could incorporate. Examples of these changes include the introduction of the 'new' ThunderCats, the Lunataks and the return to the ThunderCats' reformed home world, Thundera, towards the end of the series.

'You should know that Jules wrote a book a couple of years ago that did very well' adds Peter Lawrence. 'It has been bought and is about to me made into a movie. It's a comic novel, and maybe that completely vindicates his writing. I'm serious: maybe in that field, in another area, he's a much better writer than I'm giving him credit for.'

Lee Schneider
4 episodes: 'Divide and Conquer', 'Monkian's Bargain', 'The Transfer' (with Lawrence DuKore), 'Fond Memories'

The second writer to have assisted Peter Lawrence with editorial duties, Lee Schneider, recounts how he came to work on *ThunderCats*: 'My father, an executive at ABC, knew Merrill Grant, who knew Jules Bass. I studied journalism at Antioch College and later became a playwright living in New York. While in New York I directed and produced my plays and I wrote *ThunderCats* and *SilverHawks* for Rankin/Bass. I was familiar with writing for the stage – so I knew about upstage, downstage, and flying things in. Animation was an adventure in many more dimensions. The animators on *ThunderCats* were as talented as they were precise. They wanted us to think through every action, every movement, visualise everything, know how every weapon, tool and mode of transport worked. For me, writing in the "voice" of the character was easy. I knew this from creating characters in the theatre. But writing in the multi-dimensional space of *ThunderCats* was an amazing education in screenwriting and in physics.'

While *ThunderCats* marked Lee Schneider's introduction into animation writing, he credits the genre for inspiring his craft: 'When I was a boy, my parents always worried that I was wasting my time after school watching cartoons. I watched *Bugs Bunny* and other Warner Bros cartoons. There was a live action *Superman* that I was addicted to, and I watched the live action *Batman* on ABC, the network my father worked for. I even met Bruce Wayne [actor Adam West] once in the lobby of the ABC building. When I started writing *ThunderCats*, all the stories I had seen on those shows came back to me and were extremely useful.'

Asked about his writing routine, Schneider comments: 'I was living in Brooklyn with a new wife and a new baby, working at a large roll-top desk in the living room. I wrote at all times of day and night, any time I could. There was no pattern to the timing of my writing process. I wrote every script out by hand on a yellow pad with a particular kind of soft number 1 pencil. Then I typed it up on an IBM Selectric that I had bought on the street from a man who took it from a bloody chicken box and had stolen it from somewhere. But the price was right. I cleaned off the remaining feathers and blood and went to work typing up my script so I could show it to Peter Lawrence in New York. When we revised scripts it was done by typing the changes onto a slip of paper and then taping that over the original pages. Sometimes if there were lots of revisions the script got to be pretty thick and crinkly with tape. There were notes from Peter Lawrence. Sometimes Jules Bass would also have notes. I would then make the revisions. They were very precise in what they were going for. If I couldn't get it right, Peter would do a polish and sometimes Jules Bass worked on some scripts, I'd heard. I don't know if he worked on any of mine.'

Schneider credits *ThunderCats* as being a catalyst for his further career: 'It was a great experience with some of the most talented people I've ever met. I really learned how to write scripts on that show. There was an extensive and well-considered series bible written by Leonard Starr with input also from Jules Bass. It was very easy to work from and sparked many great ideas. Dramatic prime time television shows that I later worked on did not have series bibles as good as *ThunderCats*. We had awesome character designers, including Bob Camp, who went on to draw *The Ren and Stimpy Show*. I remember Bill Overgard sending in some drawings also. I had no idea who Bill was at the time, though now I know he is part of American comics history. The animators were brilliant, detailed and inspired. I felt like I was working on a Martin Scorsese picture, only all the lead characters had fur. Remember also we were in New York and there were Broadway-level actors doing the voices – a high level of talent there.

'I had no idea, whatsoever, how successful *ThunderCats* would be. I remember my (now ex-) mother-in-law saying, "You'll always be known for writing *ThunderCats*". At the time I thought, "She's got to be kidding". Then I returned to journalism. I wrote freelance for *Good Morning America*, became involved with local television news in Los Angeles, became a producer for national news magazines for Fox and NBC and later began directing documentaries.'

Today, Schneider remains in the television industry: 'I'm a documentary director living in Santa Monica, California with my wife Tabby Biddle, a writer and editor. My main focus has been documentaries and journalism for the past 15 years. Along the way there have been detours into other cartoon writing, including a script for *Teenage Mutant Ninja Turtles* affectionately referred to as "the worst ever written" , also some feature film writing and dramatic television scripts.

Matthew Malach
4 episodes: 'The Shifter', 'Key of Thundera', 'Helpless Laughter', 'The Zaxx Factor'

In Peter Lawrence's quest for writers, one obvious avenue to explore was the creative team on staff at Rankin/Bass. One of these was Matthew Malach. In addition to directing recording sessions, making storyboard notes, editing and supervising the final mix, Malach also assisted in the visual direction of many episodes. 'My professional writing career began with *ThunderCats*,' he recounts, 'and I continued to write animation scripts until around 1997. I worked for Warner Brothers, Hanna-Barbera, and others.'

Malach describes how he came to work at Rankin/Bass and the creative constraints of writing for *ThunderCats*: 'I knew Jules Bass's daughter in high school, at which point I met Jules. I stayed in contact with him after I entered the film business. (I'd been making movies since I was ten, and was a graduate of NYU Film School.) I did a day or so of work as a production assistant on a live action TV feature that Rankin/Bass produced in the early '80s, *The Sins of Dorian Grey*. (In fact Peter Lawrence was one of the writers of that tele-film.) Jules later hired me to work on *ThunderCats*. I had no animation experience but had worked in production as an assistant director, coordinator and producer on commercials and low budget productions. Animation requires a full visual description of the action, including detailed descriptions of settings, characters and camera angles. In live action, those details are often left to the director. In the *ThunderCats* days, we had typewriters and cut and pasted scripts. Very primitive. As I was employed full time at Rankin/Bass, I wrote at night and on weekends. After I left Rankin/Bass and became a full time writer, my routine was to write early in the morning around 6.00 am and knock off at about 3.00 pm.'

Malach's extensive experience in the production of *ThunderCats* made certain facets of his writing for the show easier: 'My experience on the production end – running recording sessions, supervising dialogue edits – gave me a pretty clear idea how long a script should be. If I remember correctly we were given brief outlines – beat sheets – that were prepared to explain the action in each act. There were many revisions, but as I recall, Peter did most of them. Since I directed most of the shows I wrote, I was well aware of any changes right away. There were all kinds of changes, but none that I recall having any problem with. Back then, I was just so excited to actually be writing things that ended up on air, I didn't care how many changes were made. I seem to remember having something to do with collecting comments from our psychologist early on in the process. So, when it came to story, I was very much aware of the moral responsibility. On the other hand, *ThunderCats*, much like *He-Man*, was also a marketing tool to get kids to buy toys. There were many who believed that this component was morally reprehensible.'

Malach admits to being somewhat surprised by *ThunderCats'* impact: 'Back then, we were aware of the show's popularity, but these days, when I tell 20-something colleagues that I worked on *ThunderCats*, a look of astonishment comes over them. Many claim the show had a huge impact on them and/or they just loved it. It's gratifying to know that I was part of something that's become a pop culture icon. We knew the show was a success after the first season. My first script, "The Shifter", was among the last scripts of that season. It was pretty clear at that point that this show was a hit.

'I loved Vultureman, and also had a fondness for Mumm-Ra, who as Earl Hammond described him, "had the voice of a bitter, has-been British stage actor from the 1800s". I never liked WilyKit and Kat. They were kids; we couldn't do much with them. No offence of course to Peter Newman and Lynne Lipton who voiced the "children" beautifully.'

Matthew Malach continues to work in the television industry: 'I continued as an animation writer – and sometime dialogue director – after I left Rankin/Bass. Karen Seigel and I moved to California, got married and basically started all over again. Eventually my animation writing career picked up steam and I again worked with Peter Lawrence on a few things, including *Fox's Peter Pan and the Pirates*. Peter was always trying to get work for me, and I'm grateful for his support and friendship. I also remained friendly with Lee Schnieder, who in about 1996 hired me as a writer on a news magazine show about the paranormal, called *Strange Universe*. Lee later also put in the good word for me at E! Entertainment Television, where I was hired as a staff writer. I've been at E! ever since. Currently I'm an executive producer on specials, news specials and other things entertainment related. I have Lee to thank for continuous employment for 12 years straight. I don't write as much as I used to, but I remain fascinated with words, and to this day I'm thrilled to hear something I wrote on the air.'

Sandy Fries
3 episodes: 'Psych Out', 'Time Switch', 'Crystal Canyon'

Sandy Fries contributed three scripts to *ThunderCats'* second season. He has also written for hit shows such as *Star Trek: The Next Generation* and *Quantum Leap*, in addition to having an extensive animation career: 'I've written a lot of animation. I've written for Hanna-Barbera before and after *ThunderCats*, and received an Emmy nomination for my work for them. I wrote for *Spiderman* after *ThunderCats*, and I was story editor at DIC for *Carebears*, which I wrote for, and a show called *Littles* about characters who live in walls and have adventures.

'I really like changing from one genre to another. I'll do, for example, two or three episodes of a sci-fi show then want to switch to a totally different kind of show like comedy or animation. I like variety. But I don't really see sci-fi as [a separate genre]. For my taste, sci-fi is just good writing with all the elements that make up any good writing; compelling characters, a story that connects with the reader, a great theme and a jazzy, powerful, compelling story. The fact that there are futuristic or sci-fi elements, that's just sprinkles on the cupcake. The cupcake itself – to use a bizarre metaphor – is compelling characters that connect from the heart of the writer to the heart of the audience. For my taste, the best *Star Trek: The Next Generation* episode was "The Inner Light" (not one I wrote myself), which was a very character-orientated show that requires family and very universal themes. It gets me, it irritates me, when I see a sci-fi film with phenomenal, eye-popping effects but, "Oh my gosh, we forgot about a good script". The last *Matrix* is a good example of that. The very first *Star Trek* movie is another.

'One thing about writing for TV or movies, which I tell students when I teach writing, is that 50% of your job is being a good diplomat. On *ThunderCats*, I very rarely had changes made. I would submit a script and it would be drawn and animated almost the way I wrote it. Peter Lawrence was a wonderful person to work for. On shows like *Star Trek* and *Quantum Leap*, though, each writer would be given ten sets of notes from different people, … and often they would be different. So you have to be a diplomat to get what you want with the story. Not the case on *ThunderCats*, amazingly, which I think may be why the stories were so good. When Peter gave you notes, and he rarely asked me to change anything major, I would say to myself, "Wow, that was a good idea". On other shows, you'd get notes from the producer and the executive producer and you'd go, "Wow, how in the hell do you make this work?"'

Fries recalls how he came to work on *ThunderCats*: 'If my memory is correct, they gave me a call, and they knew of my other writing credits and wanted me to write for the show. Peter Lawrence and Lee Dannacher came out from New York to Beverly Hills and had a meeting with me at a very impressive, fancy hotel, which I think was the Beverly Wilshire hotel. They'd rented rooms for meetings and I thought, "Wow these guys are impressive. They're spending money at a top notch hotel, we've got tea and coffee and they are very civil, bright and creative." After Lee Dannacher, Peter Lawrence and I met for 45 minutes, just talking and discussing *ThunderCats* and writing in general, I said to myself, "This looks like a classy group of people and I'd love to write for the show." I never had any idea it would be as terrific a show, and as big of a fan favourite as it has become, but I could just tell from meeting Peter and Lee that these were people you'd be excited about working with.'

Fries is full of praise for Lawrence: 'A couple of things I really liked about working with Peter is that, first, he's a really bright guy to work with and, secondly, when he did have ideas, he was always right, and I always said to myself, "Hey that really is an improvement". The other thing I liked was that you got the sense that he was a very well-read literary guy and very talented himself as a writer. On other shows, you had to pitch ten or 15 ideas to get an assignment, but anything I pitched to Peter, he went for. I don't think I ever pitched an idea to him that he didn't buy – that's great for a writer. I think he also did very little rewriting on me. It's terrific to see your writing go from your mind to the screen with very few changes. Also, he wanted me to write for *Tiger Sharks* and *Mini-Monsters*, which I did, and those were, in addition, very enjoyable shows to write for.

'I remember very vividly getting huge amounts of pages of character sketches, character designs and designs of machinery that the ThunderCats drove around in etc. I'd put the pictures all around my workspace and I'd read, several times, the character descriptions Peter would send me by Federal Express, and literally absorb, through my pores and my mind, who these characters were, what their world was about. Having the pictures surrounding you creates that immersion for you.'

Asked what advantages animation provides a writer, Fries replies: 'Anything you can do in your mind, you can do on the screen. Before I write something, I think it though in my mind – that's not the case with live action, it has to be very conscious of budgets and production and special effects costs. I once, as a joke, in a *Star Trek: The Next Generation* script, wrote, "A hundred space creatures attack the *Enterprise*", and I got a nervous call from one of the producers saying, "A hundred with phasers, do you really need that Sandy?" And I said, "Yeah, we need a hundred!" I could see him trying to be diplomatic, but his brain was frying, it was ridiculous. But after a while I cracked up and said, "Just kidding". But you have to be very budget-conscious. The less expensive [your scripts are to realise], the more people like you as a writer. A bottle show is the best, where you use only existing sets, you don't even need to go on location. With animation, though, you can do anything your mind comes up with. As a generalisation, in animation you tend to get your script through intact; with live action, because production budgets are so much higher, you'll literally have ten people putting their ingredients in the stew.'

Fries believes the key to good writing is to take the subject matter seriously: 'Make it a show you care about. If you don't, they won't be your best scripts. Second thing is to immerse yourself in the show. For *ThunderCats*, I'd immerse myself in every nuance I could. I'd watch previous episodes – when I'd eat lunch I'd have the *ThunderCats* show on in the background, so the dialogue and rhythms would absorb into my head. Do your research and study what a character would and wouldn't do. Next step is what I call random brainstorming, where I, for a day or two, think about the episode ideas and jot them down on paper. "Maybe we could do this or that, maybe Lion-O has this experience in this scene, what if Snarf does blah blah blah." I take the pieces of paper, and some ideas make it and some don't. If I like the ideas, I have to make sure that there is a visceral connection between my story and the viewer's life, which is the key thing to a good story that makes it powerful. When I was writing the scripts, I'd try to live it almost to the exclusion of other things. I wouldn't go out to lunch with friends when I was in the script process – if it took a week, I wouldn't read the mail. I wouldn't want things interfering with the script, I'd even screen my phone calls. I used to have a lucky writing shirt, so if it took me a week to write an episode, I'd wear my T-Shirt every day until I finished a script. Now I've written so much TV that it's disintegrated.'

Fries is delighted to note the ongoing popularity of *ThunderCats* – including with many adult fans: 'I know people who are physicians; one is very accomplished and bright, and a *ThunderCats* fan. In addition to writing, I'm an assistant professor at a college in Illinois, and I have students who, without knowing that I wrote for *ThunderCats*, wear *ThunderCats* T-shirts to class. With college students, with physicians and a lot of adults, I know the show has resonance. I think the fact it works for kids and adults alike shows you that one of the keys to its success is that there is a texture to it that has some sophistication, and there's some real guts to it. That comes from the fact that they did deal with real issues, and the dialogue was very clever. That's the best type of kids' show; there's more substance there. If it appeals just to kids, it's not a bad thing, but those shows usually have less guts, less heart and substance and less connection between the writers and the audience.

'I love the fact that *ThunderCats* is still important to people. When I write, I put everything I can into it; I do my best, and you want your work appreciated by the greatest number of people for the greatest amount of time, so I'm delighted and thrilled that people like it as the years progress, and it seems to be a classic in animation. So I'm honoured.

'I was always conscious of the fact that kids have very impressionable minds and you have to have a great responsibility when writing for them. I've always tried with *ThunderCats, Care Bears, The Smurfs* etc to have some kind of lesson in the story, because, for one, it's good karma; number two, it makes the story have a richer texture; and three, if I'm lucky enough to reach millions of kids across the world and make their lives a little better, that is very cool. In addition, you have to be cognitive of that when you're writing for adults. I always try to put a message in there as well, because that message that relates to as many people as possible is an episode's strength – it makes it more powerful. When you find a theme that connects to the viewer, that's either uplifting or teaches you something, that's where the fine texture comes from. My favourite movie ever, *Forest Gump*, has a lot of nice lessons to it and a very entertaining story.

'I thought the *ThunderCats* episodes were wonderful; the animation and the voices. The guy who did Panthro had a remarkable voice. I think that was another reason for the success of *ThunderCats*: the actors matched up to the characters perfectly. I can't think of a better Snarf voice than they used – the same for Panthro, Lion-O and all the voices. I'm hugely grateful to have been a part of this show. It's remarkable that what came out of your mind as a writer reached people across the world. Peter was terrific and remarkable to work with, so thank you Peter. The animation was also incredibly cool and it was great to see your work produced well. I recently bought some *ThunderCats* DVDs and it always gives me charge when my students wear *ThunderCats* T-Shirts. The show is a reflection of the people at Rankin/Bass – wonderful people to work with!

Of his wider career, Fries notes: 'I've done journalism for the *Los Angeles Times* and for travel [publications]. I've travelled to all kind of places: New Zealand, England, France, Venice, all over the world, and I get paid to eat food and visit great places! TV writing I've done. I was a story editor for Paramount for ten *Star Trek* video games. One was called "Star Fleet Academy", which William Shatner starred in. It was a five million dollar production, so at that time it was a big deal. I also story edited other video games for Paramount. There was a *Star Trek* novel, I've written for *Fame*, I've done animation – *Tom and Jerry Kids, Droopy: Master Detective* and *Spiderman* for Fox, *The Smurfs*. Of all my credits, when people ask me what I've written, the huge overpowering reaction always comes from *The Smurfs*. It's, "Wow, you wrote for *The Smurfs*!" You expect them to go, "Wow, *Star Trek*, *Quantum Leap*", but without exception it's *The Smurfs*.

'I just wrote a sci-fi short story, which is probably the best thing I've ever written – I hope I don't sound pompous saying that, but it just flowed from my brain onto the page. I re-read it and was surprised and shocked – I didn't think I could write that well, and I got an Emmy nomination for my writing. Most of the time I love writing; occasionally it's a nuisance, but I'd say 80%-90% of the time, it's a lot of fun and wonderful.'

George Hampton & Mike Moore
3 episodes: 'Ravage Island', 'The Thunderscope', 'Malcar'

'Mike Moore and I first met when we worked at Paramount Pictures in non-theatrical and educational distribution,' explains writer George Hampton. 'I was a member of the Writer's Guild for a Saturday morning pilot I had written, and Mike had written a large collection of songs and poetry. Later, when we worked for Paramount's home video division, Mike found out that Hanna-Barbera was giving a course in animation writing. The course was taught by Bryce Malek, whom we later worked for on *Transformers*. We used our assignments as samples of our work to land our first jobs, which were at DIC, working for Alan Swayze. Before we started working for Rankin/Bass, we had written for *Heathcliff and The Cadillac Cats*, *The Get Along Gang, Dennis The Menace* and a children's live action series called *The Botts*. Mike and I first started working for Rankin/Bass and Peter Lawrence on *The Comic Strip*. After that ended, we started working on *ThunderCats*. We were the envy of our friends, because for two years we wrote for bosses who were three thousand miles away.'

Although Hampton and Moore were based in Los Angeles, Hampton recalls they liaised closely with the New York offices of Rankin/Bass. 'We received a mostly visual "mini bible" comprised of drawings of the characters, props and sets. *ThunderCats* was already on the air by the time we started writing for it, so we gained most of our knowledge of the show by watching it. At first, Mike and I would write everything by hand and then type it up on an old IBM Selectric. Later, we did everything on the computer and sent outlines and scripts to each other by modem. (300 baud. It took a while.) We both worked best late at night. So we didn't talk much while writing. We would start out by writing down as many story ideas (premises) as we could think of and then we would pick out the best, sometimes combining two or three into one story. We would submit at least six story ideas at a time. We always outlined our stories. Mike and I would divide scripts in half and each write one half. We would then merge the two halves and correct any errors and send it off. Our writing styles were so similar no-one noticed that we had each written just half the script. This was a nearly perfect system.

Nearly perfect because in the "Space Menace" episode of *Dennis The Menace*, the character Gina disappears in the second half of the show! (Alien abduction, no doubt.)

Asked if he was aware of how successful *ThunderCats* was becoming, Hampton replies: 'Yes and no. As I said, the show was already on the air when we started writing for it. While we were writing our scripts, the merchandising started to appear in stores (from swords and action figures to pencils and shoelaces). But I think it was a couple of years before I was aware of just how big it was.

'I think the writing was consistent due, primarily, to the efforts of Peter Lawrence. The main character, Lion-O, was a combination of superhero and big kid. I think the animation was great. It was a visually exciting show. I also believe that, despite having a large cast of recurring characters, the fact that nearly every episode had a new character, a new tool or a new location added to the impact of the show.'

Commenting on his experience of *ThunderCats*, Hampton is enthusiastic: 'You are always surprised when you first see your characters, scenes or props portrayed. They never look quite the way you pictured them. However, with *ThunderCats*, it was always a pleasant surprise. I think the animation for this show was great. We particularly liked pairing one of the strong characters with one of the Snarfs. It was the classic matching of heroic adventure with comic relief. We didn't try to avoid any characters; some just didn't fit into the stories we wrote. *ThunderCats* was near the end of our animation careers. Later, we wrote for the animated version of *Police Academy* and *Peter Pan and The Pirates*.

'Mike was an excellent animation writer, but his main artistic passion was music. He wrote lyrics and composed music, and on the weekends sang with his band. One day, we went to what can only be called a "cattle call" for writers. The show that was being presented was about a dog, and was a dog! Five minutes into the presentation, I knew we couldn't write for this show. Mike just sat there quietly looking as if he were paying attention. When we left, Mike started writing feverishly. I couldn't figure out what he could have gotten out of that, that I hadn't. It was a song. While I was sitting there counting ceiling tiles (137), he was writing a song.'

Mike Moore passed away on 6 May 2000. 'Mike had a quiet intensity that some people mistook for unhappiness' says Hampton in tribute to his friend. 'He would beam when his family was around. We shared a strange sense of humour that served us well most of the time and occasionally got us in trouble. Mike passed away, far too young. He was survived by his wife Lynnette and his children Michael, Elizabeth and Jack.'

Ron Goulart
2 episodes: 'Trouble With Time' (with Julian P Gardner), 'The Terror of Hammerhand' (with Julian P Gardner)

'I've been writing professionally for over a century and a half,' jokes Ron Goulart. 'I'm a little unclear on how I came to work on *ThunderCats*. Either [comics writer] Rick Marschall touted me to Leonard Starr or I myself, who knew him, approached him.'

Prior to Peter Lawrence's arrival as script editor, Goulart worked under Starr in developing his scripts: 'I had to come up with the actual plots. I was given a bible and sample scripts and I had a round-table meeting with Rankin/Bass in New York City along with Starr, Howie Post and Bill Overgard. What I did was drop by at Starr's house, which was only few miles from where we were living in Connecticut. We'd go over my proposed ideas and, I believe, decide on which ones I was to develop. I think some kind of synopsis was written up by me and then sent to R/B by Starr. One would be okayed and I'd write that up in script form. For some reason they decided, after I had done two scripts, that they weren't happy with me. Starr, however, liked my stuff, and he had me ghost a couple more scripts, paying me himself. They were accepted. At this point in time, I have no recollection as to what they were about. When I worked on stories directly for Starr we brainstormed, as we used to say in the game, and then I would do the script for the agreed upon notion.'

While both of Ron Goulart's *ThunderCats* episodes credit Julian P Gardener (a pseudonym used by executive producer Jules Bass) as a co-writer, Goulart believes Bass had little or no involvement during the writing stage: 'If Bass had a hand in either of the episodes I wrote, I never knew it. I think I met him twice. I hand-letter my first draft, you know, in comic book style – then type the final draft. In those days, I wrote several hours every day, just about every morning. I still attempt that, but don't always make it. Back when I was turning out 12 to 16 books per year, I often worked afternoons and nights, too.'

While Goulart confesses to having enjoyed writing for *ThunderCats*, he notes: 'It was just one more job. My attitude is that, since I'm a great writer and not some hopeless hack, I always try to do the best job I can do – or that I'm allowed to do. I didn't think *ThunderCats* was going to enjoy such a long shelf life. My idea of interesting animation is the stuff done by Tex Avery, Chuck Jones, Nick Park and my long-gone ad agency associate, Alex Anderson, who created *Crusader Rabbit* and *Bullwinkle*.'

Although Goulart would not contribute any further scripts beyond *ThunderCats'* opening episodes, his characters of Hammerhand and the Beserker pirates would live on, picked up by a myriad of writers across the first and second seasons. Asked if he approved of Hammerhand's design, Goulart replies: 'I don't think I ever saw Hammerhand in the flesh. And since I knew there were no royalties involved, it wasn't that exciting.'

When discussing his long career as a historian and author, Goulart reveals that *ThunderCats* was not his first attempt to sell to an animation market: 'A buddy of mine and I tried to sell scripts to *The Jetsons* when I was residing in Hollywood, many long years ago. Initially they told our agent they liked our stuff, but a couple of weeks later, they told him they realised they had already thought up a similar idea themselves. Had we been of a suspicious nature, we might well have become suspicious.'

Amongst Goulart's prolific achievements are a range of non-fiction books on pop culture subjects, including *Cheap Thrills: An Informal History of the Pulp Magazines* (1972) and *The Adventurous Decade: Comic Strips in the Thirties* (1975). He was also the ghost writer on William Shatner's *TekWar* series of novels. His sixth Groucho Marx humorous mystery novel, *King of the Jungle*, was published in 2005.

Howard Post
2 episodes: 'Spitting Image', 'Return of the Driller'

Another famous contributor to the series, Howard Post had enjoyed a comic book career spanning five decades prior to working on *ThunderCats*. Amongst the titles he had worked on were *Hot Stuff the Little Devil*, *Wendy the Good Little Witch*, *Spooky the Tuff Little Ghost* and, for DC Comics, *Anthro*. He had also become head of Paramount Cartoon Studios in 1964, before creating the popular syndicated newspaper comic strip *The Dropouts*.

Post was amongst the first people invited to write for *ThunderCats*. Supervising producer Lee Dannacher had been given the task of recruiting New York-based comic book writers who understood the dwindling action/adventure genre, and he had seemed a logical choice. Asked how he came up with a 'winning idea', Post explained: 'A good story has an element of suspense in it that keeps the reader wondering. You examine a whole bunch of subjects and see which have the propensity for suspense and entertainment and you follow from there. Characters offer excesses of personality, which make for meaningful plots. The idea is to have fun with the material. Characters have to have fun. Fun would include excesses of character and personality and plot twists. The basic idea is to keep the pot boiling.'

Post's two episodes of *ThunderCats* have a propensity for horror, with 'Spitting Image' being amongst the series' darkest offerings. Asked if he enjoyed adding an element of fear to a story, he answered: 'Not particularly – only when a character or a situation affords that kind of excess. Then I indulge it.'

Considering the inevitable comparisons between animation and comic book writing, Post added: 'A screenplay usually has more plot involvement, and it's a better opportunity for character development. A comic is usually not as profound in its dimensions as a movie or television story.'

After a period of retirement, Post passed away on 21 May 2010, aged 83. His creations and artwork continue to live on and find new audiences and critical appreciation around the world.

Bruce Smith
2 episodes: 'The Micrits', 'Jackalman's Rebellion'

'I earned a degree in journalism and started my career as a newspaper reporter,' reveals Bruce Smith. 'After a dozen years, I went to freelance writing and started doing some advertising and corporate work. Along the way I wrote some short stories and a couple of television scripts with the encouragement of a friend in Hollywood, and although they did not sell, I enjoyed writing them. I also did some comic strip writing, but *ThunderCats* was my first time work in animation.'

Smith explains that his initial commission for the series came through his association with head writer Leonard Starr: 'While working at the *New York Daily News*, I became friendly with some guys working at the [news syndication company] Chicago Tribune New York News Syndicate in the same building on East 42nd Street. They had originally syndicated Harold Gray's *Little Orphan Annie* strip. At the time, the Broadway musical *Annie* (based on the strip) was a smash. Gray's strip was reincarnated in the hands of Leonard

Starr, and a musical film version was planned. At the time, I was working as a reporter in the arts and entertainment department of the *Daily News* and wrote a few articles about the show for the paper. I also came across a trove of original *Little Orphan Annie* archive material in a storeroom in the subbasement of the *News* building. That led to a book deal to write a profile of the *Annie* phenomenon. I interviewed Leonard for the book and we became friends. When he was working on *ThunderCats*, they needed episode writers and Leonard let me try out. He was my mentor, as I learned the techniques of writing for animation.'

Asked about his writing routine, Smith jokes: 'I rise with the sun. When I was freelancing, I worked business hours in my home office. My career has been borne along on the trajectory of text technology, from manual to electronic typewriters, to Wang word processing terminals, to PC to Mac. But for thinking and outlining, nothing beats a number 2 pencil and a blank sheet of paper. When the story is clearly in mind, I move to the manufacturing phase on the computer. On *ThunderCats*, Leonard shared with me his technique of story outlining, which I found worked very well for me. I recall some revising and rewriting on my *ThunderCats* scripts, but not too extensive. When there is a lot of that, it usually means I have a failed story. Both Leonard and Peter Lawrence provided very helpful feedback and guidance from story idea through outline and script drafts.'

In common with many of his colleagues, Smith is proud of his *ThunderCats* output and believes the series deserves its longevity: 'I was delighted to get the chance and enjoyed the work immensely. I knew the show was popular, in large part because of the high quality of the stories and scripts, which was inspiring to me. The show had great characters, outstanding animation, superior cast and direction. Each story had the essential ingredient that sets timeless tales apart from mere entertainment: a moral. Children (of all ages) recognise and respond to a story with a moral at the end, because it helps us make sense of the world and have optimism about the future. I was thrilled to see my stories and hear dialogue I had written on the screen with such liveliness and rhythm. I think that's what set *ThunderCats* apart from most other animated shows of the time. There was literally never a dull moment. I was delighted with how they rendered the Micrits, much better than I had seen them in my mind's eye.'

Smith has retained his original production documentation from the show. 'I received a mini-bible and animator renderings of characters and locales,' he notes. 'I met with Leonard frequently and corresponded with Peter. My first produced episode was broadcast on New York television late afternoon on the day after my son was born. I watched it with my wife in her hospital room. (My son was in the nursery at the time and only later would become a fan of *ThunderCats*.) Changes are inevitable as the actors, directors and production teams work to bring the story to life, but they must have been minor, because I did not notice them in watching the finished episodes.'

Beyond *ThunderCats*, Smith also contributed five episodes of *SilverHawks* for Rankin/Bass. 'I then became engaged in corporate communications and speechwriting work that I continue to this day,' he says. 'My experience writing for *ThunderCats* remains a vivid and gratifying memory.'

Herb Engelhardt
2 episodes: 'Together We Stand', 'Vultureman's Revenge'

'I got into writing in the '80s when a boom in the animation syndication market created a demand for new material,' recounts Herb Engelhardt. 'By 1989, I had pretty much left the field, as work became scarce with an enlarged pool of writers vying for what was available. My first pieces were an episode of *The Jetsons* for Hanna-Barbera. (The original series had only 22 and 65 are required for a 13 week syndication run.) Next was an episode of *Transformers* for Marvel. Both were with a writing partner who had attended film school and showed me the script format.'

Engelhardt explains how he first met the *ThunderCats* production team in Los Angeles: 'I met with Peter Lawrence initially when he came out from New York to meet potential writers for *The Comic Strip* show. I wrote two scripts for the *Street Frogs* segment, which led to the two episodes of *ThunderCats* for the same studio.

'I would typically work during normal day hours, but sometimes into the night as deadlines approached. All of my work was word processed on early versions of the home computer; I had a Kaypro 4 and later an Epson QX10. Almost all of the assignments I got required submission of story premises on spec – less than a page, with beginning, middle and end. When a premise was accepted, the next step was to flesh out the action in prose outline form, usually three to five pages for a 22-minute script. The editor would give notes to be incorporated into the script. I likely got notes on the outline, but did no further work after turning in the scripts. It's likely any rework or polish was done at the studio. I met with the story editor only once about *ThunderCats*, which I had seen only in passing. I believe he suggested the premises.'

Engelhardt reveals that, unusually, he has never seen his episodes of *ThunderCats*: 'Since I was coming into it at the latter part of the second season, I was aware that the show was doing well, but I never saw the finished programmes. It isn't the first show that comes to mind when I tell someone that I used to write animation, but I do mention it. Animation writing is almost exclusively work for hire; unlike live action, there are no residual payments for reruns (the only way to make a living at it, especially if you have a family to support). So you are constantly looking for shows to pitch to get the next assignment.

'Back in those days, we formed a group, the Animation Writers of America (AWA), to share common concerns. The ultimate goal was to get us into the Writers' Guild, which still hasn't happened. Some of the studios were union – I had to join IATSE local screen cartoonists when I got an assistant story editor position for Ruby-Spears. This included Xeroxers, cel painters, etc who worked in all facets of production. Episode writers were not really a natural inclusion, more a hold over from the short cartoon days when the artist figured out three sight gags that the Roadrunner could pull on Wile E Coyote as he story-boarded a short. I recall only one person out of the 60 or so writers in our Association that actually drew; we were writers. The "old timers" in the craft were the (mostly) guys who came from the comic book publishing world (Ker-POW!) and made the natural transition – especially into action shows. Writers with children were a definite minority in this group. Ultimately the demand was satisfied with the spate of productions. And I took up a different line of work – contracting – which I am still doing today.'

Having worked at the heart of the animation boom in the 1980s, Engelhardt is pleased to have tackled some memorable programmes: 'Though I wrote more for action shows, given the nature of market propulsion, my favourite episodes were the comedies. Having seen the original *The Jetsons* series when I was a kid made it fun to work on that story.'

Dennis J Woodyard
2 episodes: 'The Shadowmaster', 'Well of Doubt'

When script editor Peter Lawrence found himself looking for writers amongst the *ThunderCats* production team, one of those he approached was secondary character designer Dennis Woodyard. A talented artist, Woodyard recalls how he came to submit his two scripts: 'The *ThunderCats* scripts were my first professional writing assignments. I was asked to submit story ideas by Peter Lawrence, after he commented that he liked my story sense in response to notes I had made on other story outlines and storyboards. I had been writing stories for my own original comic book characters, so I decided to give it a try. I worked up several *ThunderCats* story ideas and Peter helped me to work them into something usable. My writing routine was simple: I submitted a concept, then an outline, then a first draft, a second draft, then a final. In between each step, the story editor looked the script over and made revisions and changes.'

Woodyard explains the advantages of branching out from production into screenwriting: 'Working on the show helped my writing, because I knew the characters better. But it was still a hard assignment, because of all the back-story available, and the number of characters in the group. Most of the time, you had to devise a way to omit ThunderCats to give an episode a clearer focus. There were tons of changes made to my scripts, and all of them were necessary. I think my first "Shadowmaster" script was 80 pages long – twice as long as it should have been for a half-hour show – but overall, I was happy with the finished product.

'I enjoyed writing for the main characters, Lion-O, and Panthro, but my favourite was Mumm-Ra in his old mummy form. He was like a senile old man living with his dog, Ma-Mutt. It was really funny having him talk to his dog.'

Today, Woodyard continues his career in the creative industries. 'As of now, I've left the LA animation business and relocated with my family to Rochester, New York. I hope to turn to my creative pursuits, under my Dragonfly Entertainment company, established to present and pursue original ideas and properties, including Dragonfly Flipz™ books, my new innovative storytelling print format.'

Barney Cohen
1 episode: 'The Garden of Delights' (with Julian P Gardner)

Barney Cohen has scripted several screenplays for both television and film. Enjoying his notoriety as a 'controversial' writer of children's animation, he also contributed a script for *Masters of the Universe*. Supervising producer Lee Dannacher recalls how he was invited to write for *ThunderCats*: 'Barney is a real character. He was one of these players in New York. He had written something and we'd gone out to lunch a couple of times in the early '80s. He knew a lot of names, producers etc, and he talked a good game, he really did. Before Peter Lawrence [started work on *ThunderCats*], Jules was relying on me to find somebody who could hand something in. Now, Barney did have credits with one of the network shows, the Saturday morning shows, he had animation writing credits, so I introduced them, and Jules gave Barney an episode to write. He asked him, like we asked everyone, to give us five thumbnail ideas – "We'll choose one and you can write a script". We'd meet for lunch and Barney would give me two thumbnail ideas; he was that kind of character to begin with. He did have that one episode – he did hand something in – but I think Jules had to almost completely rewrite it.'

Despite being his only association with the programme, Cohen's 'The Garden of Delights' attracted attention with its obvious allegory for drug-taking and addiction. Despite this, it was passed by both the Rankin/Bass production team and child psychologist Robert Kuisis, who analysed its content as important in teaching children the dangers of seeking immediate gratification.

Since *ThunderCats*, Cohen has found success writing for a variety of television series, including *Sabrina the Teenage Witch* and *Forever Knight* (a series he co-created).

Douglas Bernstein & Denis Markell
1 episode: 'The Evil Harp of Charr-Nin'

'Oddly enough, we have absolutely *no* background in writing for animation or fantasy projects,' says Denis Markell. 'We were, at the time, best known as musical theatre writers who had done comedy writing for television.'

Markell and his long time collaborator and friend, Douglas Bernstein, were introduced to the series because of a desire to explore the talents of comedy writers. 'Our agent called us about the gig,' recalls Bernstein. 'We were told the producers were looking to inject more "comedy" into the series, and thought we would fit the bill. Had it been a humorous kids' show, it might have made more sense. Neither of us were particularly fans of the fantasy genre, either. But there was money – not much in retrospect, but anything was good at the time – and it seemed like a fun thing to do.'

Markell adds: 'It was a real education We read a bunch of scripts, but still it was difficult to realise that we had to create the entire environment – tell the artists what the scene would look like, convey the atmosphere, and be as specific as possible with props etc. Once you understood that you could write almost anything and get it animated (within reason, of course), it became kind of fun.'

Bernstein and Markell both recall their admiration for story editor Peter Lawrence: 'We dealt pretty much exclusively with Peter (if memory serves), with his charming British accent. He had a great sense of humour about the whole thing. You try telling people the *ThunderCats* characters and their personalities and special spells, without cracking up … We remember him repeating Lion-O's mantra to make his sword "grow" and saying "I can't look at you while I say this." I think the Freudian dimension of this particular event was so evident that it was hard to do it without at least a smirk.'

'This was pretty early in the computer age,' recounts Bernstein when asked about how writing duties were divided between the pair. 'We tended to collaborate in a room together. We would meet for maybe three hours and then one of us would take a crack at writing a draft. Then we would send it back and forth, much as we do now, when we write together. Typically, we would write away from the computer screen and transfer it later. (In those days, we'd send scripts via modem. A script of this length could take 45 minutes to transmit, and if you received a call-waiting beep, the transmission was ruined. You had to start from the beginning. Side note: it was in response to this phenomenon that phone companies came up with a way to turn call waiting off.)'

'The *ThunderCats* bible was daunting, to say the least,' adds Markell. 'The only character who had any real chance at humour was Snarf, and that was pretty broad stuff. For the most part the "humour", such as it was, was relegated to lines like "Lion-O: What we need is a plan! Snarf: What I need is a snack!" Ho ho. They showed us sketches and discussed elements of the story they wanted us to play up. (This was specifically a plot featuring the ThunderKittens, so we were limited in what we could propose.)'

While Bernstein and Markell both enjoyed their experience on *ThunderCats*, they were disappointed not to be invited back to the show: 'It was a unique experience and a shame that we got to write only one episode. I think the producers felt we weren't naturals at this sort of work.'

'I don't think we did more than two or three drafts,' recalls Markell. 'We got notes, tried to honour them, and handed the script in. I seem to remember Peter saying "We'll take it from here." Which probably was an indication that they felt it would take less time to simply take what we did and fix it themselves. We basically saw it as another of those *He-Man/She-Ra* type of shows, kind of disposable. From what I remember, the show hadn't aired when we wrote our episode. But that could be wrong. I do know that *no-one* we knew at the time watched it, and it was considered "kids' stuff". It wasn't until years later when I would meet younger people (men mostly, of course) who would look upon me with shining eyes when they heard I'd written a *ThunderCats* episode. Even later, when I typed in "*ThunderCats*" in Amazon.com, I was astounded at the number of comments on the DVDs.'

Asked whether they were satisfied with the production values of their episodes, Bernstein confirms that they were delighted: 'That was certainly the coolest part of the whole thing. Seeing someone you had come up with in sketch form (Charr-Nin), and then in the finals, as well as hearing the voice that was picked for him.'

'We've stayed active in theatre,' concludes Markell, 'working on projects that have been more or less successful, depending on the whims of fate, producers' budgets, directors' lack of vision etc. Our most recent collaboration together was with Joan Rivers on a theatre piece about her life, which played in Los Angeles and London. Doug has also spent quite a bit of time working with the Mayor of New York City, Michael Bloomberg, behind the scenes.'

Danny Peary
1 episode: 'The Mountain'

While the vast majority of writers to have worked on *ThunderCats* list the show as a highlight in their career, Danny Peary is critical of his treatment by the production team: 'My memories of the experience are sketchy, but I think I worked on scripts for two *ThunderCats* and one *SilverHawks*. I think only "The Mountain" was made. I do know that I thought I was writing great, hip stuff, quirky, funny, creative, and the producer was not impressed.

'By the time I worked on *ThunderCats*, I was established as a film critic and pop culture historian. I was writing/editing books and publishing articles and interviews in magazines and newspapers. But I'd dabbled in scriptwriting at USC and was excited when my agent asked me if I wanted to write for an established superhero cartoon series called *ThunderCats* and a new one called *SilverHawks*. She had brought another client to the producer and that was working out well. So I met with a highly-intelligent guy who obviously thought he should be working on something like *Schindler's List* rather than a silly cartoon. Also at the meetings was a male "yes-man" assistant.'

Peary's negative memory of working under script editor Peter Lawrence is rare amongst the writers of *ThunderCats*, but it is certainly true that Lawrence would gladly adapt any script to conform to Rankin/Bass's vision for *ThunderCats*. 'It was a Kafkaesque experience,' says Peary. 'I'd turn in cool stuff and he'd say it was lousy and send me to a script discussion with his assistant to explain to me all the characters and what types of scripts they wanted. Alone with me, the assistant could say nothing, because I was doing nothing wrong. It was very strange. "The Mountain" was meant to be an evergreen, so I told a story that didn't necessarily fit into any chronological progression.'

Kenneth E Vose
1 episode: 'Eye of the Beholder'

Another writer to contribute a sole script to the series was Kenneth Vose. 'I began writing in the late '60s,' he recalls. 'My first book, *Makin' Tracks*, was published in 1975, and I've published nine more since that time. I began writing narration for corporate and documentary films during that period as well. I knew Peter Lawrence, the head writer on *ThunderCats*. He knew my work and asked if I was interested in doing some animation stuff. I was asked to write for the series, and I did. Happily, it led to my work on a number of others as well; my favourite being *Street Frogs*.'

Vose had never written for animation prior to *ThunderCats*, and is pleased to list the series amongst his credits: 'It was great. I was very popular with my friends' children as a conduit to Lion-O. I've had students in my MA/MFA screenwriting course at Wilkes University who grew up watching the series.'

Vose feels his episode may have dated over the last 25 years: 'I have a soon-to-be 16-year-old daughter, Nora, with whom I've watched a fair amount of animation over the years. I find that technical advances make viewing a much more satisfying experience now. The subject matter handled is also far more "advanced" than in the *ThunderCats* era. Nora enjoyed watching it, but I'm not sure how much that had to do with my involvement. And I don't intend to ask.'

Vose has been involved in an impressive array of projects throughout his varied career, having worked in film and television as an editor, writer, producer and director. In addition, he has written for magazines, novels and non-fiction books and for the stage. The highlights of his television writing career include: *Spies* (A&E Network), *The Real Adventures of Jonny Quest* (Cartoon Network), *Peter Pan and the Pirates* (Fox Network) as well as *ThunderCats*, *SilverHawks* and *The Comic*

Strip. He was also the co-writer on the film screenplay for *Greased Lightning*, the story of famed black stock car driver Wendell Scott, for Warner Brothers.

Jeri Craden
1 episode: 'The Mumm-Ra Berbil'

Jerilyn Craden first adapted her writing craft to animation with Rankin/Bass's *SilverHawks*. 'I approached Peter Lawrence to do voice-overs for Rankin/Bass and learned that what they needed were writers – that most of the animation writers were on the West Coast. With my sitcom and live action credits, plus having voiced numerous animation series in Canada, he invited me to try my hand at writing for the show.'

Craden comments that writing for animation was '100 times more challenging' than writing for live action: 'The artists were in Taiwan and everything they were to draw had to be thought up first and described in detail. Also, this was before writing on computers. Every time there was a change to the script, I would have to rewrite the whole thing using carbons. A nightmare to say the least.

'I don't have a set writing routine. When the work is there, the deadline is there, I just go at it. This can mean working around the clock. When working on *ThunderCats*, I had the bible and used it as my template for coming up with storylines that would fit. Peter Lawrence was always helpful as a sounding board. You just go with it. That becomes your reality. The world of the characters and their place in it.'

While Craden contributed only one script to the series, she remains enthusiastic about that time in her career: 'It was a great opportunity. It stretched me as a writer/conceptualiser. I am only now learning how much the show was loved, as I meet adults who watched it as children.

'After *ThunderCats*, I continued to do voice-over work and segued into writing large live events for corporations. Then I wrote my first novel: *Vessie Flamingo Outshining the Moon*. I've also written several plays and numerous short stories.'

Craden also teaches the craft of writing, adding, 'Learning how to structure a story can inspire confidence to share ideas on just about any subject throughout your life.'

Lawrence DuKore
1 episode: 'The Transfer' (with Lee Schneider)

'I began my career as a lyricist, writing for the mass market,' says Lawrence DuKore. 'I worked with some wonderful composers (the late Danny Hurd, who was primarily a big band arranger, and Sid Cooper, who also had a big band background). Although we had wonderful singers recording our songs (Bernadette Peters; Chita Rivera), the Beatles, the Rolling Stones and the rock scene made our songs antiques before their time.'

DuKore explains how he came to write for *ThunderCats*: 'I knew a Brit named Peter Lawrence, because of my background as a film editor. He hired me because he'd seen *Greased Lightning*, a Warner Brothers film that I co-wrote with another *ThunderCats* writer, Kenneth Vose.'

While DuKore's episode, 'The Transfer', is credited as being co-written with Lee Schneider, he reveals it wasn't a collaboration in the conventional sense: 'I think that Lee Schneider took my first draft and did a revision. I had no input. Editing varies from project to project. A first draft is sometimes the longest and then I edit. And there are times when a first draft is too short for a full-length play and I have to ask myself, "Do I have anything more to say?" or "Do I have anything at *all* to say?" There are no easy answers. W Somerset Maugham wrote that a writer has to learn to kill his babies. I'm sure my editors also revered W Somerset Maugham. The final versions were always an improvement.

'There are occasions when a burst of imagination and energy propels me to write an opening scene, after which (after the honeymoon), I pull myself together and try to figure what the hell I'm writing and why I'm writing it. I believe there were guidelines on *ThunderCats*. I had freedom, but of course the parameters were the cartoon characters themselves. Their personalities defined the script and the particular story. That was one of the problems I faced. A successful writer in this genre has to treat his animals as humans – and I don't believe I succeeded in solving that problem.'

DuKore believes that writing for animation and for live action are worlds apart: 'It's a totally different animal. I must confess that I wasn't very good at it, because I stopped reading cartoons when I was eight years old, and although I liked the *Tom and Jerry* cartoons (their violence notwithstanding), it was the writers' job (my job) to initiate the dialogue and the action and *then* animators would go to work. I don't think I gave those animators much to work with. One really must love animation and *know* animation. I didn't.

'Overall, it was fun, and I'd be happy to do it again … if invited. I'm essentially a playwright these days, although occasionally my agent submits a screenplay of mine, along with a prayer. I am prolific. I do have a good imagination. I love to write plays. I write every day, starting early in the morning – and if I can get two hours of good work (as opposed to just typing), then I'm a happy author. During the course of the day, I often take notes in preparation for the following day. I wrote several young adult novels for Bantam and Scholastic. I had to use my middle name, Jesse, so I could pass for a female author, a big sister to my readership, which consisted of pre-teen and teenage girls. Some of my titles included *Never Love a Cowboy*, *Long Distance Love* and *The Boy Barrier* – and my editors at Bantam and Scholastic did not care that I was male, just as long as I could write these romance novels that contained a message. Of course, teenage girls in the 1980s were much like teenage girls of my generation (1950s) … but now we're in the 21st Century, so the novels I wrote then would be scoffed at by today's teens. I might have a readership among the kindergarten set!'

Annabelle Gurwitch & Heather M Winters
1 episode: 'Dream Master'

While Annabelle Gurwitch receives the on-screen writer's credit for the episode 'Dream Master', Rankin/Bass employee Heather Winters recalls that she tackled the majority of the script work. In addition to administrative duties at the company, Winters was not unfamiliar with the writing requirements for *ThunderCats*: 'One of my jobs was to write episode summaries that would later be used, along with episode morals written by the show's psychologist, in a teachers' guide for schools. So I read every *ThunderCats* script and had to condense it down to a few paragraphs.'

Winters is thrilled to have participated in the writing and production of *ThunderCats*: 'I don't think I realised how successful the show was at first, because I was living it day in and day out for years. But I quickly learned how many people watched it. Of course now I am amazed at how popular it was and am very proud to have been a small part of it. When I interviewed my latest assistant, he said he thought it was so cool that I worked on *ThunderCats* – his favourite show when he was a kid! The show's longevity and people's fondness for it are incredible.

'I worked at Rankin/Bass for four years on *ThunderCats*, *SilverHawks* and *The Comic Strip* series. Following that, I was an associate producer for four years, then worked on MTV's *The Real World* before making my first feature film. I produced, creative directed and wrote for corporate, industrial, commercials and feature films, and in 2000 I established my New York-based production company, Studio On Hudson. This specialises in development, production, financing and producers' representation of independent feature films and documentaries. I executive produced Morgan Spurlock's Academy Award-nominated and Sundance-winning documentary *Super Size Me*, Anthony Haney-Jardine's Sundance-winning narrative *Anywhere, USA* (2008 Special Jury Prize, Dramatic Competition) and co-wrote and produced the documentary *Class Act*. I also executive produced A J Schnack's *Convention*, released by IFC Films in May 2010, and served as producer's representative on the social networking documentary *Google Me*, amongst others. I am currently developing projects for television and film and often serve as an industry film consultant, board member, panellist, juror and advisor.'

Co-writer Annabelle Gurwitch has also gone on to find success, as a popular actress, comedienne and social activist, best known as the hostess of TBS's *Dinner and a Movie*.

Romeo Muller
1 episode: 'The Mask of Gorgon'

Most famous for his imaginative stories for Rankin/Bass holiday specials, Romeo Muller also contributed one script for *ThunderCats*. Having written the screenplays for *Rudolph the Red Nosed Reindeer* (1964), *Frosty the Snowman* (1969) and a wealth of other TV specials, he was naturally invited to work on Rankin/Bass' first adventure series.

Supervising producer Lee Dannacher shares her memories of Muller: 'You just had to see the man. He was, in stature and heart, the quintessential Santa Claus – there was not a more gentle giant or talented writer than Romeo Muller for animation. I had no appreciation of [his holiday specials] at the time [they were originally shown]; I didn't grow up with *Rudolph*, I saw them in my twenties. But they *were* Romeo Muller, because it was the first time I understood how you can write for that market with such an open heart and not talk down to kids and not be condescending. *Noel* was one of his brilliant, brilliant storylines, which he did for a radio show long before Masaki Iizuka and I animated it.'

'He was a very nice, soft-spoken guy,' adds Leonard Starr. 'He'd written a play that R/B produced called *A Month of Sundays*. We saw it in a playhouse in

Greenwich Village. It was, as I remember, likeable, very gentle, but it didn't have much of a run.'

While Muller enjoyed working with Rankin/Bass on all of their projects, he did not feel that his softer writing style suited the action-led *ThunderCats*. After only one episode, he moved on to other projects.

Romeo Muller passed away on 30 December 1992 aged 64. His legacy in children's entertainment looks sure to continue as new generations enjoy his legendary Rankin/Bass specials.

James Rose
1 episode: 'Mumm-Rana's Belt'

'I started writing for a labour history show on Pacifica Radio in Berkeley in the mid-1970s,' says James Rose. 'Later I moved to New York and eventually found myself writing all forms of media, i.e. industrials, documentaries, comics, animation and feature films.'

Rose had no animation writing credits prior to *ThunderCats*. He explains how Rankin/Bass came to hire him: 'At the time, I was friends with Bob Camp. He was the main guy on the show: he got me and other friends inside the door. I was given a few [videotapes] of the show to watch, a copy of the show's bible, a pep talk by Peter Lawrence, and then turned loose. And as I recall, I met once with Lee Dannacher over coffee in her office with Peter. It was a low pressure operation, and a pleasant and fun place to work.

'Rankin/Bass followed a "one page equals 30 seconds screen time" formula, which differed from features where the rule is "one page equals one minute screen time". The greatest difference was the demand to precisely imagine all the action that was unfolding. I have always been a night writer. I do my editorial work on the copy during the day, but I find the stillness of the night to be relaxing, and conducive to creative work. Remember *ThunderCats* was all pre-computer. I worked on an IBM Selectric. I loved that baby. Peter Lawrence had some huge, expensive and mysterious machine in his office which he called "a computer". We writers submitted our scripts and Peter transferred them to the computer by manually typing them in. Peter, as story editor, made minor changes in locations and dialogue as he typed my copy into his computer and standardised the script. He did not ask for any revisions, nor a rewrite from me at the time. We are talking about the pre-word processor era. In that time, writers were more careful in the thought process and structuring that preceded the actual typing up of the script – unlike today, where the words and the ideas are in a constant state of flux on the computer screen. Hence writers worked very hard to create a tight first draft. And since a rewrite involved a tremendous amount of work, editors were, it seems, more inclined not to request them.

'I found the work very challenging, and enjoyable. When I wrote for Rankin/Bass, the show was already at the top of the children's daytime TV charts. They had a massive toy line going full boom too. Besides its groundbreaking visuals and action storylines, *ThunderCats* had an overall message about the creative non-violent resolution of conflict, and I was proud of sending that message to the younger generation of its viewers. Things are never quite as the writer imagines, because film and TV production are collective enterprises that involve many people at many different levels, below camera and above, giving their inputs, their creative efforts into making the overall product the best possible – at least, that's how things were done on *ThunderCats*, and the other shows I've worked on. I remember the production people on *ThunderCats* to be friendly and very professional, and the cartoonists to be a wild and nutty and extremely creative bunch.'

While Rose provided only one script for the series itself, that was not his final opportunity to write for the *ThunderCats* franchise. Having been recommended by Peter Lawrence, he wrote many stories for the *ThunderCats* comic series. 'I did the one script for Peter Lawrence at Rankin/Bass,' he explains, 'then he got a call from someone at Marvel looking for a writer for the *ThunderCats* comic line that they had just acquired. I don't remember my comic editor's name, but he was a very good guy. Too many assignments later blur my memory, but I went in and at the first meeting sold two script ideas. With Marvel Comics there were no time frames. You wrote your copy and turned it in to the editor just as quickly or as slowly as you felt. Remember that both these enterprises have an existing pipeline; when your stuff was ready, it went into the creative hopper. I wrote, as I recall, 16 or so *ThunderCats* scripts for Marvel Comics, and they were all published. I recall nothing specific about the work except that it was lucrative fun for me. Rankin/Bass held ultimate approval controls over all my *ThunderCats* scripts at Marvel. Since I knew the show's bible, I knew what the guidelines were. I don't recall that any script was rejected by Rankin/Bass.

'When I worked at Marvel Comics it was before the New Line Cinema takeover. It was still a wild and open operation. There were no guards, no security, I could simply walk in, see my editor, and pitch some story ideas. If he liked them, he'd order a half-page synopsis, for which I got paid $125. When I'd come back with the half-pages, he'd read them then and there. Those he liked, he'd order a script for. I'd go off, get stoned, work two or three non-stop nights and return with the script. He'd accept it on the spot and sign a voucher, which I would take to the cashier and receive my cash payment. The comic scripts were 22-page format, the page rate was $50, so I'd knock back $1,100 for the week, which was a happy sum of money in the '80s. So the main difference between writing for comics and writing feature films was that you got paid immediately for your work.

'It's been a long and winding road for me as a writer since the halcyon days on *ThunderCats*. That was when the money was fast and the living easy. I wrote a couple of feature scripts, one of which came to the attention of Lutz Weidlich, a producer at RTL TV in Cologne, Germany. Lutz began hiring me as story analyst and development guy on a number of movies-of-the-week for his network. Later, when he was promoted to president of CREA TV at the same network, I became one of his "go-to guys". I developed two MOW scripts, the contracts got signed, everything was legal and straight ahead, the money started to flow toward me, and then Lutz's career exploded, he got shoved out at CREA TV, and as is always the case, all the writers in his stable got fired, me included. Financially it was a disaster from which it took me years to recover. Writers, like all artists, are born not made. I've been back in the game for several years now. I have two feature scripts currently making the rounds. One is a police drama called *Signal Hill* and the other a comedy about movie-making in New York City called *Variety*.'

Becky Hartman
1 episode: 'Wild Workout'

'At the time I wrote "The Wild Workout", I was 24, just two years out of college and had never written for television before,' says Becky Hartman. 'I had written on my college newspaper and was taking writing classes at the New School in New York.'

Hartman describes how her *ThunderCats* assignment came about because of her work at Lorimar-Telepictures as a paid intern: 'Because I was an aspiring writer and a former college journalist, one of my responsibilities was to write articles for the Lorimar-Telepictures newsletter. One of my assignments was to write a profile of Peter Lawrence. During the interview, I confessed that I hoped to write for television one day, and he said that writing animation was the best training there was; you were not only the writer, but in many ways the director; you were required to describe the action you were envisioning in great detail, because the laws of gravity and physics didn't necessarily apply. My eyes lit up, and he said that if I were interested in giving it a try, I should write up some ideas for stories. If he liked any of them, he'd give me a shot at writing a script. I don't remember what my other pitches were, but he liked the idea for "The Wild Workout" and hired me to write it.

'Peter was right: the joy of writing animation is that you are not restricted by sets, costumes or the laws of gravity. It was very freeing, but also forced me to be much more specific about setting and action.'

Asked about her writing routine, Hartman recalls that she wrote her scripts at night due to her full-time employment with Lorimar-Telepictures: 'I couldn't have asked for a better introduction into the world of writing for television. I don't remember what season my episode aired in, but the show was already a hit when I wrote my script.

'Writing for *ThunderCats* gave me the confidence to leave Lorimar-Telepictures and become a freelance writer. I wrote for a variety of cable shows in New York before moving to Los Angeles and writing for *In Living Color*. Since then, I've moved from sketch comedy to sitcoms to one-hour dramas. I am currently writing and producing on the NBC series *Parenthood* and have been in Los Angeles writing on sitcoms and one hour series since 1990. Some of my credits include *Sex and the City*, *Larry Sanders* and *American Dreams*.

David Carren
1 episode: 'Leah' (with J Larry Carroll)

A long-time writing partner of Larry Carroll, David Carren collaborated only once on a *ThunderCats* script. 'I started out as a journalist on a newspaper in Texas, then I moved to California to write 200 TV shows over 25 years,' says Carren. 'My writing partner at the time, J Larry Carroll, brought me in to work on a *ThunderCats* script with him. I had already worked on animation for *GI Joe* – four episodes, I think.'

Carren recalls that working with an established *ThunderCats* writer made things easier: 'Larry was already up to speed on the show, so we didn't need a bible or have to wrestle with continuity issues. I write like a drunk on a binge. I'm a binge writer. I sit down and write until I'm done, night and day. I live the script until it's finished. That's how I write TV anyway. Features are a bit more leisurely. Instead of one week, I take three.

'Larry and I structured our script together, then divided up chunks and traded back and forth. We usually did two drafts. Peter Lawrence never abused writers on unpaid or extra drafts. It was fun to write. I was just glad to have the work.'

Since *ThunderCats*, Carren has gone on to achieve huge success with a varied career in television and film. 'I wrote some projects in Texas, like the horror film *Mr. Hell*, which is widely available on DVD. I'm currently an associate professor in film at the University of Texas-Pan American, where I teach screenwriting. But I'm still in the movie game. Just wrote and directed a feature, *The Red Queen*, that starred Valente Rodriquez and Harley Jane Kozak.'

Beth Bornstein
1 episode: 'Ma-Mutt's Confusion'

'I started out writing with Paul Dini in the early 1980s,' says Beth Bornstein, when asked about her introduction to animation writing. 'Paul and I had gone to Emerson College in Boston together and he invited me try my hand at animation writing. Paul was already an established writer in 1981 when I was moving to NYC from Boston to pursue an acting career. My "apprenticeship" with Paul involved working with him on episodes of *Fat Albert* and *Masters of the Universe* for Filmation Studios, and *Scooby Doo* for Hanna-Barbera. You will see my name on one of those *He-Man* episodes, called "To Save Skeletor". I am not credited on a second episode, called "Pawns of the Game Master", and that was a disappointment, as I particularly liked my work on that episode. But I was just at the beginning of my animation career, so something like that could easily happen. After writing with Paul for a while, I went off on my own, writing *Transformers* and *GI Joe* for Sunbow Productions (in association with Marvel). I later wrote for *Jem and the Holograms*, *Doug*, *Batman*, *My Little Pony* and *Tiny Toons*, among others.'

Bornstein recounts how she was invited to submit a script for *ThunderCats*: 'I was hired by Peter Lawrence at Rankin/Bass. He wanted me to write for *The Comic Strip* series and *SilverHawks* in addition to *ThunderCats*. I wrote four episodes of *Street Frogs* and at least one episode of *TigerSharks*. I also wrote two episodes of *SilverHawks*, entitled "Uncle Rattler" and "Switch". My only episode of *ThunderCats* was "Ma-Mutt's Confusion". Now I wish I had written more!'

As regards her writing routine, Bornstein recalls, 'I was writing on a Mac by then. Nothing written by hand at that point, except for notes. I would get up early and start writing in the morning (all on the computer) and would write throughout the day. I tended to write scripts pretty quickly, putting in longer days and turning them early. After the premise was approved – and there were always several premises or story ideas presented – I would then outline the story. There is always input from a story editor, but I think that the idea for "Ma-Mutt's Confusion" was approved very quickly. I had a very good working relationship with Peter Lawrence and he gave me a lot of autonomy in all the writing I did for Rankin/Bass. All of my notes came from him. I do remember that the *ThunderCats* bible was particularly flushed out, so it made it easier to write the episode.

'Working on the series was a lot of fun! Of course, at the time, I don't think any of us had any idea that it would be so popular and have this kind of longevity. I think it was one of the few action shows that tried to teach its young TV viewers a lesson. My episode ends with the ThunderCats telling the ThunderKittens to give Ma-Mutt the benefit of the doubt in terms of what his motivation might have been in leaving Mumm-Ra and going to them – the source of Ma-Mutt's "confusion". I knew that they were concerned with the viewers learning something from what they just watched. I can't think of any other animated series at the time that felt that kind of responsibility to its audience, and now that I am a parent, I really appreciate it. It affected my writing in that I was aware of creating a story where a character went through some kind of change after a series of events. In this case, Mumm-Ra realises that he had been abusive to his dog, and after losing him temporarily to the ThunderCats, he makes a commitment to be a better caregiver to Ma-Mutt. (Kind of an amusing thought, Mumm-Ra as a caring dog owner, but that's what I was going for at the end.)

'I tended, as an animation writer, to always feel that same sense of responsibility to the young viewing audience. During the '80s, I was well aware of being a woman writing in a particularly weapon-orientated era in animation, in terms of toys being associated with the cartoons and the toy companies counting on the series to sell the toys. But I was most interested in writing episodes that used fewer weapons, which was difficult, since the toy companies were involved in everything to do with the animation studios at the time. Many of these series came about simply to sell toys, but that all changed later. During this time, I wrote an episode of *Transformers* that I am particularly proud of, called "The Search for Alpha Trion". Think of it as an Autobot love story! Looking at *ThunderCats* now, almost 25 years later, the quality is not quite as good as I remember it. But it was consistent with the quality of most animation of the time.

'I enjoyed writing Snarf and Snarfer. I also enjoyed writing Mumm-Ra, because he was so evil that it was fun to come up with dialogue for him that had some humour in it. Like "You are a worthless disgrace to all that's evil!" And "Thank the ancient spirits of evil! I thought I lost you, my pet." And of course, it was most fun to write Ma-Mutt! Outside of *ThunderCats*, I loved writing for *Jem*, and particularly enjoyed writing the characters of the wicked Misfits in that series. *Doug* (for Nickelodeon) was fun. Poison Ivy in *Batman* was another personal favourite.'

Bornstein continued to write for animation after her *ThunderCats* script, and still pursues her creative output: 'I was always an actor/singer, too, and I eventually stopped writing for animation, after ten or so years, because I needed to focus on theatre work at that point. I got into animation writing because Paul Dini brought me into that wacky world, and I really enjoyed it and I think I was very good at it. After *ThunderCats*, I wrote for *Tiny Tunes*, *Jem*, *Batman*, *Doug*, and the other assorted series I mentioned. I also created my own series based on a line of Tonka Cupcake toys (they transformed into people!), called *Cupcakeland*. It was my first bible, and I was very happy with both the bible and the script. The series ultimately didn't get picked up (after some serious meetings with Nickelodeon), but it was a great writing exercise for me.'

3. THE GARDEN OF DELIGHTS
The Art of ThunderCats

One of the defining aspects of *ThunderCats* was its ability to overcome production limitations. Rankin/Bass, while successful in its field, was still a relatively small studio, and although *ThunderCats* was not under-funded, it had far from limitless resources. Every dollar invested in the budget had to work hard to further the show's appeal. While every aspect of the production rose to the challenge, it is the art of *ThunderCats* that is remembered as truly groundbreaking in the world of television animation.

Throughout its run, *ThunderCats* was constantly battling to stay on top in the ever-crowded action/adventure serials market. *Masters of the Universe*, with its central He-Man character, had reinvigorated the genre in 1982, and subsequent shows all vied to offer bigger and better production standards. The company behind the He-Man series, Filmation Studios, had established a studio of animators based in California. In line with most other US-based TV animation studios (the biggest of which was Hanna-Barbera), they were responsible for a large output of memorable cartoons. However, budgetary and timing constraints meant the artwork was far removed from the complexity and intricacy achieved by blockbuster motion pictures on offer from Disney. While this had not been a huge hindrance to the studios – indeed, many thrived on their 'simple' and distinctive styles – it was soon realised that, if a more affordable solution was to emerge, a new approach was required.

On *ThunderCats*, Rankin/Bass, funded by Telepictures Corporation, followed the industry trend of using cel-based animation, despite much of its earlier output having used the stop-motion technique. Arthur Rankin explains his rationale for this: 'We had done a lot of cel-based animation prior to *ThunderCats*. For example, on *The Jackson 5ive* and Saturday morning series. We'd also done *Frosty the Snowman* in linear animation. So we'd worked in both mediums always, including in motion pictures. We'd choose our technique based on our subject and how we wanted to produce it … If it was a nice, sweet property like *White Christmas*, a little story about a blind man and a nun, then that was done as stop-motion, because the material [lent itself to that approach].'

Art production for *ThunderCats* began at Rankin/Bass with a small art department based in New York, usually employing no more than one or two full time character designers at any one time. After that, production moved to Japan and neighbouring countries. The show would however remain an American production, and design teams on both sides of the Pacific Ocean would keep in regular contact at all creative stages. This method would prove not only more affordable, but would crucially result in some of the most breathtaking animation that had ever been produced for the television market.

Designing the ThunderCats

During the production of *ThunderCats*, Rankin/Bass expanded its operations in almost all areas. While it would remain a close-knit team working in New York, it was soon realised that, to cope with the massive undertaking involved in production of 65 episodes of *ThunderCats*, it would have to taken on additional staff.

With the newly-founded Pacific Animation Corporation ready to begin the actual animation work in Japan, it fell to US designers to start carving out a visual package to take the show forward. Throughout the evolution of the *ThunderCats* premise, various members of the creative team had put together loose sketches and ideas for how the show might look. Both Ted Wolf, who had suggested the initial concept, and Leonard Starr, who had been charged with creating story ideas, had put forward early drafts, but a dedicated designer was needed to shape the final appearance of the series.

For this input, Rankin/Bass turned to their licensing agents, Leisure Concepts Inc. It had been LCI's president, Stan Weston, who had originally taken the *ThunderCats* concept to the company (courtesy of Ted Wolf), and it was its original artwork that had convinced Rankin/Bass of the show's potential. Weston introduced the show's producers to his long-time friend and collaborator Mike Germakian. Supervising producer Lee Dannacher explains Garmakian's role: 'Mike was working as a freelancer for Stan Weston. They had a long history. With Mike, you'd fall in love with him the minute you'd meet him. He was an extraordinary designer. I'm told his family credit him for a lot of the *ThunderCats* designs; it's a well-deserved credit. At one point we brought him into the office, because so much design had to happen so fast. It was via Stan Weston, because Mike was his designer, but we brought him in and gave him a little office. He'd sit there and pound it out, and he was responsible for great designs.

'Mike took the original designs [as his starting point] and developed them, while Jules [Bass] began working on a bible, and I think he brought Len Starr in at that time. Within three weeks, we had Mike Germakian's designs sent over to Masaki, and then he had Kubo and his people start revising those beautiful designs and adapting them for animation. A lot of people think adapting for animation is just simplifying, not as many lines etc, but sometimes Masaki-san and his team made their job harder, for instance by adding more spots on Cheetara, and then those designs went back to Mike, and it was back and forth between them.'

It fell to Germakian to produce design drawings for all the show's principal characters, including the ThunderCats, Mutants and Mumm-Ra. Additionally, he tackled secondary characters for the early scripts and conceived vehicles and locations. His illustrative style was detailed and evocative and, though his work would be refined and simplified by the Japanese animators, his creative talents shaped the overall look of the show, He also provided the distinctive *ThunderCats* logo.

Germakian's daughter, Nicole Grey, discusses her father's career: 'As a child, my dad loved to draw, doodle, create; it was always in his blood. He attended the School of Visual Arts in NYC. He did brief stints with the Girl Scouts of America and Encyclopedia Britannica in the late '50s to early '60s. He began working for the Comart advertising agency in '62 and stayed for ten years as their art/design director. He left Comart in '72, joining Stan Weston at Leisure Concepts; he was the creative director. Their offices at 116 Central Park South were in a residential building. It was a small group of four guys. In 1982, Al Kahn joined Leisure, the primary benefit of which was a cash infusion. The company was struggling at this time. Mike left shortly after but continued to work with LCI as a contractor. He had started Mike Germakian Design, a business that carried him into retirement in '93.'

Asked about the origins of Mike Germakian's relationship with Stan Weston, Grey recalls that the two met while riding the subway, around 1970: 'They struck up conversation about the toy industry (Stan of *GI Joe* fame ...). They went on to become very good friends and had an excellent working relationship. Stan was the President of LCI – the wheeler and dealer – while Mike was the artist. They vacationed together with their wives and socialised routinely. During the big times with LCI, some of their "properties" were *The Lone Ranger*, *Charlie Chan*, *Farrah Fawcett* (the hair care line) and *Legends of the Superheroes* (*Superman*, *Batman* etc). I would visit their offices and marvel at the walls and walls filled with toys, games and products. It was a sight to see.'

While Germakian's contract for *ThunderCats* no longer exists, his family did retain details of his arrangements with Rankin/Bass for *SilverHawks*. 'Simply put, he received a flat fee of $7,500 to "develop and render characters, sets and concepts for *SilverHawks*",' reveals Grey, adding that the terms for *ThunderCats* had been exactly the same. 'He didn't make much on the design work, but he split the 3% that Leisure Concepts received as a royalty payment with Stan. He loved getting those cheques!

'I recall his working on *the* logo, as does my mom, Alice. He did a tremendous amount of work on the show and invested many man-hours developing an intricate web of characters, descriptions, habitats, concepts, packaging, etc. Much of the rough artwork was tossed after his death, but my mom has a small amount left. It kinda burns me to read that *ThunderCats* is based on characters created by Tobin "Ted" Wolf. I know this is the deal Stan and Mike made with Ted, but simply put, Ted had just a hazy idea about cat people that he discussed with Stan. He received an official credit and the consequent recognition as payout. Mike was the one who was paid as an "employee for hire" by Rankin/Bass. He imagined and developed each and every character to life at his drafting table. The finals, as well as rough artwork, were routinely dragged from his loft-studio at our home, downstairs to the kitchen, dining and living rooms. They were propped up for review and commentary. (Mike loved to show his wife and kids what he was working on. Had great "pride of ownership"!) I remember a time, prior to submission of final work, when he had about 30 perfect, final prototypes sitting in our dining room. As a twentysomething-year-old, I was offended that my dad did all this work and someone else's name was appearing in the credits. Mike would laugh at me and say he preferred receiving the cheques. He loved this time of his life. He was no longer huffing into the city at commuter hours every day. He worked a lot at home after '82 and made his own schedule. He was also enjoying the benefits of payback for this work. He socialised a lot with Stan, who had a place in Garrison, NY, at the time. In the same town was Jules Bass and they often partied together at his place.'

After *ThunderCats*, Germakian continued to work independently with his company, Mike Germakian Design, which was active from 1983 to 1993. A continuing client of his was UPS, for whom he provided illustrations on calendars and newsletters. Germakian passed away aged 74, on 22 October 2001, survived by his wife Alice and children Victor, Nicole and Margo. 'Since Mike's death, almost nine years ago, the great family vibe and feeling we were part of a "hip clan" has waned,' admits Nicole Grey. 'Mike was truly a very cool guy; informed, aware, wise, calm and cutting edge. Every Sunday morning, he would blast through the *New York Times* crossword puzzle in about one to two hours! Try it sometime. It's mind-boggling how much he knew and how low-key he was about it. In our family, we (cousins, kids, grandkids, even boyfriends, son-in-laws, etc) were always keen to spend time with him, know what he thought, listen to his words. He was truly the glue, our nucleus, and it will never be the same without him.'

Having completed countless pieces of artwork for the development of *ThunderCats*, Germakian took a back seat role after the pilot episode had begun production. Later in 1984, he began early discussions about *SilverHawks*, in which he would also participate. Realising that a full time designer would be required to continue 'secondary' character design throughout the remaining run of *ThunderCats* episodes, Rankin/Bass soon turned their attention to a freelance cartoonist and painter named Jim Meskimen.

'I had moved to New York from Madrid, Spain, where I had been studying classic realist painting for several years with a Spanish master,' recalls Meskimen. 'I had worked for a short while as an assistant to storyboard artist Don Rico at Hanna-Barbera under Doug Wildey in 1978. It was on the basis of that very minimal experience that I was able to convince Rankin/Bass that I knew something about storyboarding, which was an exaggeration to say the least. Up to that time, in New York, I had made a modest living doing editorial illustrations for various magazines, and a slew of projects for the King Features Syndicate licensing department under Graham P Halky. I met an artists' rep who got me the interview with Rankin/Bass in 1984 when they were looking for a storyboard artist. At the interview, I told them that the boards they had looked kind of "lean". On the basis of that, and my youthful brass, they hired me. Luckily, I only worked on storyboarding for a few days ... then they took me off storyboards, which I was really struggling with, and put me on character design, which was a dream job for me.

'Basically my job was to take characters that appeared in the scripts and design them if they weren't already designed. So, outside of the original ThunderCats and Mutant leads, I did the initial designs on every new character that wandered in; all of the guest stars. I also did vehicles and weapons when they were peculiar to Third Earth. Then, these sketches, which I did in pen, pencil and brush/markers, were faxed to the Pacific Rim, where the animation team brought them to life. I know they improved on my designs at this point, too, and added colour and all that. I did all the new secondary characters that came along after the pilot episode, beginning with 'Pumm-Ra'. At that time, I was the only visual artist in the studio, the rest being on the other side of the world. I shared space with a girl named Jacquie, who was the accountant, and adjacent to Peter Lawrence, the writer, and Lee Dannacher, the producer. I had my reference books, Syd Mead, *Star Wars*, and others, and a lot of pencils and paper.'

Commenting on the process of interpreting character traits from script to design, Jim reveals that for the most part he just used his imagination: 'I can work that way pretty well, except when a particular species of animal is specified, and then I have to go to a reference. Basically I would get a mental image of what the character might look like, and sketch it out. The drawings were reviewed by Lee and Jules and changes were sometimes suggested. To be honest, I didn't get a lot of feedback, and most of the designs "passed" with little input. This doesn't mean I was the greatest designer, but rather it seems to me that they were depending on the overseas artists to hone the characters and finalise them. The details of the characters were contained in the text of the scripts. Often they were very sketchy and left up to me. Others, like Dr Dometone, were more explicit. It wasn't difficult adapting to the visual style of *ThunderCats*, because it was fairly standard. Sometimes I would have to go back and revise if the producers had their own mental picture of a particular character, and we would discuss it, and sometimes Jules would show me another picture from somewhere that reminded him of the character.'

As with Mike Germakian before him, Jim Meskimen's illustrative style was far more detailed than the final animation model sheets produced in Japan: 'If I did do some extra work on the designs, it was because I love to draw and I didn't have many characters to design at that time. I guess I did do them all in "my style", but that was my attempt at integrating into the existing style of the show. I don't think the extra work of rendering and shading was particularly helpful to the animators overseas, but I thought it was more aesthetic. And I was pretty bored a lot of the time.'

Meskimen recalls the pride he felt when seeing his designs on the toy shelves: 'One character that was totally based on one of my designs was Captain Shiner. He had a weird, melted-looking face. I saw him in a store one time. The fleshy colour of his face made him all the more unpleasant.

'It was sort of lonely being the only cartoonist in the building. I was 24, very new to office life, and also new to New York City. I was taking improvisation classes at the time, and actually got Jules and Lee to come to a couple of shows I performed in. They were very supportive of my acting, and Jules in particular was interested in my ability to improvise songs; he had me down to his private office one time and got out his guitar (he played beautifully) and we improvised a silly song. I think he just wanted to understand the process. I am very happy that I had the experience of working on that show. Although, believe it or not, I never watched it when it was on, it meant a lot to me as a learning and professional experience, that I could hold my own as a pro artist if I had to. During that time I was very near to Matthew Malach, whom I saw every day, and also Steve Gruskin, Lee Dannacher and Jules's assistant Heather Winters, whom I also saw every day. I saw Arthur Rankin only about twice in the whole time I worked there. Peter Lawrence and I would chat every day and complain to one another.'

Though Meskimen's creative talent as an artist was indisputable, his career would later take an entirely different path, although still resulting from his work for Rankin/Bass: 'One day I was doing freelance work in the lovely new studio they built for artists (after I had left their regular employ), and Lee Dannacher invited me to audition [as a voice actor] for a new series they were launching, *The Comic Strip*. I noticed that, next to me on a shelf, were piles of old *ThunderCats* cassettes of the voices, so I loaded them into my Walkman and listened to the style of acting and characters while I was drawing. At the end of the afternoon I went across to their conference room and did an audition of many characters. I found out a few days later, or maybe a week, that they wanted me to play roles in several of the four miniseries that made up *The Comic Strip*. I wound up doing 65 episodes of the show, and never did freelance artwork again. They took a chance on me, and it meant a lot to my career.

'I recall the first day I was invited to a voice recording session on *ThunderCats*, when I was still working on the designs; it was an epiphany. This was up at Howard Schwartz Recording in the Graybar building near Grand Central Station. [The actors included] Earl Hammond, Earle Hyman, Bob McFadden, Larry Kenny, Peter Newman, Lynne Lipton ... it was remarkable, and above all, looked like a lot of fun. And I still think it is one of the most fun jobs going. It was definitely that day that I decided someday I would be in a cast like that.

'I've been a pro actor and voice actor in movies, TV, animation, and now video games for 25 plus years. I also paint and draw, but fine art mainly, in oils. I've worked with director Ron Howard on five films, and Paul Thomas Anderson on two. Sometimes I wonder what my life would have been like if I had continued in animation and design, but I believe I followed my stronger interest.'

Having worked for Rankin/Bass for approaching a year from 1984 to 1985, Meskimen left to pursue other projects, ushering in his eventual replacement, Bob Camp: 'After I left Rankin/Bass formally, they hired me on a day basis to work out designs for *SilverHawks*. I brought in my friend, the infinitely more talented cartoonist Bob Camp, later to gain fame as part of the *Ren & Stimpy* creative team.'

With the role of character designer moving to Bob Camp, art production at Rankin/Bass was gaining momentum. In the three years that Camp worked for the company – 1985 to 1987 – his creative input was required not only on *ThunderCats* but also on *SilverHawks* and *The Comic Strip*. 'In the mid '80s, I lived in a loft in Tribeca with a lot of other cartoonists,' recalls Camp. 'One of my roommates was the cartoonist, actor and comedian Jim Meskimen who, at the time, was working as a character designer on *ThunderCats*. He told me that he was leaving the show and asked if I was interested in taking the job, so I did.

'I started out as a caricature and portrait artist at [amusement park company] Six Flags over in Texas when I was 16. At 18, I worked for the great illustrator Don Ivan Punchatz at the Sketch Pad studio in Arlington. During the late '70s, I studied art and film at the University of Texas at Arlington. I then travelled around the US and Canada drawing people at rodeos and fairs. In the early '80s, I ended up in Provincetown, Massachusetts doing caricatures, where I met ex-*Air Pirate* cartoonist Gary Hallgren, who convinced me to come to NYC, where I started as his assistant doing clean-up and colour work on his *Mustang Sally* sexy cartoon series for *Swank* magazine. He introduced me to Larry Hama and I started working as the movie parody illustrator for *Crazy Magazine*. I also did all the art corrections for all the Marvel titles for a while. I did many covers and pin-ups for various books as well as working on *GI Joe*, *Conan Bizarre Adventures* and *The Nam*. These were all books edited by Larry, who taught me how to tell a story and draw less sucky.'

Camp concedes it is difficult to remember all of the characters he designed for *ThunderCats*: 'I started out as a secondary character designer on the show. I also did lots of props and background drawings. The main characters at that point were all done by Mike Germakian. As new shows were developed, I was more involved with the main design work, especially as the shows went into production. I know I designed the Lunataks. Oh, and I designed the kid versions of the characters. I also did lots of drawings of existing characters in different situations or vehicles. Most of the design concepts came directly from the toy designers. Then I would go over them and make them less toy-like. I would do several different versions of a character, then Arthur or Jules (whichever of them was in charge on that day) would pick one. Then I would clean it up and do turn-arounds.

'They pretty much liked everything I did. I would get a script, then I would go through it and break it down, picking out everything that needed to be designed, and then draw it all. I rarely did colour work unless I was doing presentation work for a series pitch to a network or toy company. I would turn the work in to a production assistant who would pass it on to Arthur or Jules. They were never there at the same time, so it was a little odd to have changing bosses from time to time. I would get the drawings back with notes sometimes, or just an "Okay" to send them for animation. I had total freedom as a designer. When the animators got the drawings, you never knew what they would do to them, as they had total creative control.'

Camp has great memories of his time at Rankin/Bass, including seeing his creations sculpted as toys: 'My toys were mostly made from later shows like *TigerSharks* and *SilverHawks*. It was cool to see the toy versions of my designs. I always wished that I would make some money off the toys as a designer, but that almost never happens. Mike Germakian was the only guy I ever saw that did make money off the toys. The whole experience was pretty nice actually. Mike and I had a nice big studio all to ourselves, with a kitchen that had a fridge that was well stocked. (Beer too!) It was a small outfit, just the head writer, producer, a few production assistants and business people and the bosses. Almost everything else was done overseas. I remember when the Pacific Animation guys would come to visit, the production assistant would have sushi take-out delivered. I told her that they were making faces at the fish, which was clearly inferior to what they were used to. I said they should have brought in steak and some scotch. Anyway, I wanted to make the guys happy, so I rented out a bar in Tribeca called the Racoon Lodge and threw a big party for them. I invited all my cool friends, especially girls, and got the guys all hammered. They loved me after that!

'*ThunderCats* was the first show of its kind, really. Really good writing (thanks to Peter Lawrence), and the animation studio just did great work. I often run into people who are really blown away when they find out I worked on the show. On later shows, we brought in other artists like David Thrasher, who was in charge of storyboards, and Pepe Moreno, the famed comic book artist, and Eric Cartier, a really funny cartoonist from France.'

Beyond *ThunderCats*, Bob Camp's career has gone from strength to strength, and he is best remembered as the director and co-creator of the *Ren & Stimpy Show*: 'Oh, man, I've done lots. I've worked on lots of movies as a story artist since then. I co-directed season two of *Robotboy* for Cartoon Network. I've been doing TV boards for DisneyXD and Cartoon Network in the past year. I'm working at Blue Sky Studios now doing boards for Chris Wedge on his next feature, *Leaf Men*.'

Just prior to Camp's departure from Rankin/Bass in 1987, the role of the character designer was becoming increasingly demanding. The company was now actively developing additional programming, so other artists were brought on board to cope with the workload. During this time, the Spanish-born artist Pepe

Moreno began contributing designs for *ThunderCats* in addition to his existing work on the *SilverHawks* and *The Comic Strip* series. Well known as a comic book writer and artist, Moreno has since worked for DC Comics, including on the graphic novel *Batman: Digital Justice* in 1990.

'I was there with Bob Camp, and I think he brought me in to work at the NYC studio,' reveals Moreno. '*ThunderCats* was just one of the shows we worked on. I came in at the tail end of the show, but I got to design some characters and sets. Mike Germakian, an Italian older guy, was the lead designer. I became the lead designer with Bob on a new show called *TigerSharks*. The job was easy and we would slack off most of the time (especially Bob), but always got it done on time. Bob was quick; it was a total no-brainer for him. I was there for about a year, until I couldn't take it any more. They were great people, and good friends, but most of us couldn't care less about the shows ... The most peculiar thing that we made fun of was the note "NG" sometimes given to us by Rankin (or Bass) ... It meant "No Good", but that was it – no elaboration. We had to figure out what it was that was "No Good" [about that particular design]. I have a mixed bag of memories ... mostly good.

'We did make an effort to design cool stuff, within the parameters of the show's style – but at one point we were designing the shows to fit the toys ... and that was when my interest dropped. I came in on account of starting *TigerSharks*. Some *ThunderCats* stuff came in during the midst of that, and we took care of it as well. We also did some work on *SilverHawks*. We had a great time, that's for sure. Bob was concentrating on characters and I was doing props and sets, but I do remember I designed a girl, though I've seen the character sheets for the show, and none look familiar. I never followed the show in any interested way. I'm happy and pleased that I worked on it and I had a great time, but I went off to do so many far more interesting things after Rankin/Bass that it is just a small anecdote in my career.'

The final employee of Rankin/Bass's art department was designer Dennis Woodyard, who occupied the post for the final 30 episodes of *ThunderCats*. 'I was born in Elizabeth, New Jersey, and studied illustration at the School of Visual Arts in New York City,' explains Woodyard. 'I moved to Manhattan upon graduation to pursue my commercial art career, first in illustration, then animation. In the late '70s, I moved into the animation field, first doing graphic animation and special effects for commercials and TV show openings, including HBO Sports and ABC station IDs. In the '80s, I progressed to animated adventure shows. On my first series, *The Adventures of the Galaxy Rangers*, I designed characters and storyboarded whole episodes. From there I moved to my staff position with Rankin/Bass, working on *ThunderCats*, *SilverHawks* and *The Comic Strip*.'

Commenting on his appointment to Rankin/Bass, Woodyard reveals that he was recommended by a fellow artist on *The Adventures of the Galaxy Rangers*: 'I received a call from Peter Bakalian. He arranged a meeting with R/B producer Lee Dannacher, and soon after that I was offered the job. I worked on the last episodes, including the "Return to Thundera" storyline. As series art director, I reviewed storyboards, work pictures (animation dailies) and final prints. In addition, I designed all the secondary characters for the last 30 shows. All the secondary characters on the *ThunderCats* Season Two – Volume Two DVD set were my character designs. That includes my main characters Jaguara, the Shadow Master,

Torr, Two-Time, Leah, the Mirror Wraith, Screwloose, Malcar, Frogman, Zaxx and many more. I also designed a lot of props and several backgrounds, like Jaguara's underground gyroscope lair. I admit some of the designs look pretty crude by today's standards, but they worked for the show. Again, having a great animation team like PAC made up for any of my shortcomings.

'The first description of the characters came from the written scripts. I would work up rough sketches and present these to the story editor Peter Lawrence and producer Lee Dannacher for notes and suggestions. Since the production of *ThunderCats* was well underway by the time I came aboard, I just had to do tight pencil drawings. Mostly, full figure, front and back views, profile of face and details for transformation or special powers. PAC handled the final design and colouring.'

As noted previously, Woodyard was also invited to contribute two scripts to *ThunderCats*, 'Shadow Master' and 'The Well of Doubt'. Woodyard is grateful to have been given the opportunity to work for Rankin/Bass: 'It was a small office where everyone respected each other and worked great together. It was one of the best working experience in my career. I remain good friends with many of my co-workers. I actually feel very proud to have worked on a classic show that has become so beloved by so many. I had an added kick when DC comics used my Shadow Master character in the re-launch of the *ThunderCats* comic several years ago. I bought one of the original comic pages that featured the Shadow Master. I'm hoping if they ever make a *ThunderCats* movie, the Shadow Master will be included.

'After Rankin/Bass closed up shop, I went back to freelancing assignments. These included being the art director and storyboard artist for a 30-minute animation special that aired on PBS and is now on DVD called *Merlin and the Dragons* for Lightyear Entertainment. After moving to Los Angeles, in 1994, I continued to work on various television animation shows. These included Universal's *Exo-Squad*, Disney TV Animation's *Gargoyles* and Columbia Tri-Star's *Men in Black*. I joined Saban Entertainment in January 1998, where I worked on *Bad Dog* for Fox Family cable network. The following year, I was producer/director on Saban's *Nascar Racers*.

'After leaving Saban in April 2001, I served as consulting animation director for Rankin/Bass's primetime Christmas special *Santa Baby*, which aired in December 2001 on the Fox Network. I also did some storyboarding on direct-to-DVD projects like *Ultimate Avengers 2* and *Dragonlance*. I was also storyboard director on Warner Bros' animated series *Ozzy and Drix* and was nominated for a Daytime Emmy.'

Over the course of five years, the handful of talented creatives detailed above were responsible for thousands of designs that helped bring the world of the *ThunderCats* to life. In addition to the full time employees who handled the bulk of the design work, a number of other individuals also helped shape the visual format of the series. Senior members of the production team, including Arthur Rankin, Jules Bass, Lee Dannacher and Peter Lawrence, contributed too, in that they all reviewed and commented upon prospective design work, and adaptations were regularly made accordingly. Another influence on the design of the series were the designers at work at LJN Toys. Although the content of *ThunderCats* would not be dictated purely by market forces, consideration was given to the appearance of characters and vehicles with a view to maximizing their toy sales potential. To this end, LJN designers like Kevin Mowrer should also be credited for the design work they contributed to the series (see Chapter 8), and creations like the Mad Bubbler emerged solely from the talents of LJN.

With sketches and illustrations authorised by Rankin/Bass, the design work created in New York began its journey across the world, where it would take on a new lease of life. From this point onwards, the conceptual work completed for the series would become the walking and talking inhabitants of Third Earth.

Animating *ThunderCats*

Japanese animation, or anime, has been produced since the early part of the 20th Century, gradually adopting its distinctive visual iconography by the 1960s. Despite countless titles being created over multiple decades for domestic release, Japan for a long time remained relatively inconspicuous on the world stage, overshadowed by US production studios such as Disney. It was during the 1980s, precipitated in large part by productions such as *ThunderCats*, that Japanese animators finally had the opportunity to display their talents to Western audiences.

The name Pacific Animation Corporation (PAC) would become synonymous with the production of *ThunderCats*. It represented the collaboration of several different art studios, all brought together by one man, Japanese-born, Masaki Iizuka. Having worked with Masaki on previous Rankin/Bass productions, executive producer Arthur Rankin was very aware of the effectiveness of Japanese studios and realised they could produce exquisite animated features for television at a more affordable rate than could be achieved in-house in America. For *ThunderCats*, Rankin was crucial in formalising the company's relationships with Asian studios. Thus Pacific Animation Corporation was born, with Masaki assembling some of the best animators and designers in the region to work on the series.

Rankin explains how Rankin/Bass made ties with Masaki and Japan: 'I first went to Japan because I was invited to go by the government. There was a trade organisation in America to anticipate the need for their products and to meet with people who'd like to buy their products. Someone who represented the film industry was searching for the leading animator in America, and he was mistakenly led to me – I certainly wasn't the lead animator. Anyhow, we met and he told me that they had these animation studios. Rankin/Bass did not have our own studios – we were not Hanna-Barbera, and we did not have a building full of animators. The opportunity came to go and see what Japan could produce – and they had some samples with them that were pretty good. So, with their invitation, I went to Japan and I found huge animation studios bigger than anything in America, and they were making a lot of films, but making stories that would have no international appeal – they weren't like European fairy tales. Very obscure titles like *The Monkey King's Revenge* etc. These are Oriental stories which go down very well only in Japan and China. They had the ability to animate and make these pictures, but what they were making was not acceptable or interesting to an American or European audience. But I saw that they had talent, and we began to work with them. The first series we made over there was all in stop-motion, and it was *The New Adventures of Pinocchio* – we made 65 episodes of that and sold that on the market.

'There was a young man in Tokyo called Masaki Iizuka, and he and the other animators were the best in the business in other studios where they'd all contributed in other ways. Masaki arranged to get them all under one roof, and I was very pleased, because we had the cream of the crop then, and it formed Pacific Animation. We were the first studio ever to do business in Japan for years and years, and then Disney hired one of my ex-employees and he asked me if he could come and work in the Orient, because, frankly, we owned the business at that time; everyone wanted to work with us. I said, "Go ahead, there's so much talent out there". But we were the first, and had been the only one for 20 years.'

The process of animating *ThunderCats* would be handled almost exclusively by PAC, including storyboarding, direction, special effects and cel production (cel being short for transparent celluloid – the medium upon which artwork was originally painted). Masaki's first task was to assemble the best team possible to realise 65 episodes of the series in the most cost-effective manner. He started by securing the involvement of Tsugo Kubo and Minoru Nishida, two respected artists who would be hugely influential in the production of *ThunderCats*.

Kubo was a talented designer who systematically took each and every production design from Rankin/Bass and refined it into a workable character sheet for the animators to work from. This entailed producing detailed and annotated model sheets profiling characters from all angles, as well as creating movement and lip-sync sheets to delineate the precise movements of principal characters. Kubo was also a talented animator, responsible for overseeing the creation of key frames (the master drawings showing movements at their departure and arrival points) and directing complex sequences including footage that would be reused throughout the series and was, as such, worthy of special attention.

Nishida lent his skills to the creation of the array of stunning background art featured in the series. Beginning with detailed blueprints for buildings and locations, he personally painted many of the watercolour background plates and revised and added finishing touches to the work of other artists prior to cel photography.

With Masaki's 'inner circle' established, he called upon the talents of hundreds of animators across a range of studios to carry out work on the ongoing production. In addition to using PAC's own facilities based in Tokyo, he also outsourced contracts to studios in Hong Kong, Korea and Taiwan. During all stages of production, all output was carefully reviewed by Masaki and his team in Tokyo prior to being shipped back to New York.

With production in full force on both sides of the Pacific, Rankin/Bass and PAC worked closely to ensure that, while *ThunderCats* episodes would originate in Japan, they would be crafted with a Western audience in mind. 'PAC worked under my direction, and anime was not a part of our technique,' states Arthur Rankin. 'There is just a little bit of it that creeps into the action shows like *ThunderCats* and *SilverHawks* and *The Comic Strip*, but anime, by that time, had not made its mark [in the West]. Everything we did over there looked like it was done in Los Angeles or New York or London. It had very little influence from the Japanese style of anime; it just crept in a few places during the action sequences.

'They were very happy to have American work coming in, because they were paid. We brought money to Japan – we never took anything out of there. We came and paid the animators etc and we had this family relationship We were all very close. If you work in animation, you don't have another life, because no-one comes in and works from nine till five; that's not the style. If you're on a hot streak in a design, you stay until you finish it. You sleep on your storyboard. The same is true in stop-motion … Animation is done in steps. There are the character designers, the inbetweeners [people producing cels that 'fill in' the movements between key frames], the painters, the background people, and they all work as a team. As far as cel painters are concerned, that's another room really. That's the last step before the camera. All the highly creative people are working in teams, and finally it all gets put together and the cels get painted – though now they're done digitally. That was the system, and that's how we made *ThunderCats*.'

Rankin having completed the arrangements for the production of *ThunderCats* with PAC, the day-to-day responsibility of managing production from New York fell to supervising producer Lee Dannacher. She would regularly fly to Tokyo to work personally with Masaki, who remains her close friend. 'Arthur set me up there,' acknowledges Dannacher, 'and if he had not set me up appropriately, I'd have failed in my job. [In Japan] they were not used to women at all in any kind of responsible job like producer. Arthur set me up, and after a few days, with Nishida, Masaki and Kubo, he said, "See this woman, Lee Dannacher, she's the one who can say yes or no, I've got a plane to catch." Without that, it would have been horrible. I had to do all those trips to Japan until Peter Lawrence came on board – thank god. But there was so much going on after *SilverHawks* and, more and more, I took people like Matthew Malach over. We needed someone who could liaise with Tokyo and be a troubleshooting guide and talk Japanese, and Charles Hasegawa [fit that bill]. We never missed an airdate, but there were times when it was very close, and I remember sending Charles over to Kennedy Airport and getting him to fly back with the films, so they didn't have to go through the shipping and customs routine.'

Asked about the purpose of their trips to Japan, Lee Dannacher and Peter Lawrence describe the tasks that awaited them. 'When I first went over,' says Dannacher, 'there would be hours of production meetings with Masaki and his business manager and staff, and then there would be hours of discussions on the creative side of it, with the design guys and the animators, and a lot of heavy drinking involved. I could answer some questions, [for instance about whether or not] a particular storyboard thing worked, but it wasn't until Peter got over there that they had another resource. If Peter could understand, through interpreters, why an animation director was asking a question about a certain character's movement, he could get up and say, "He's the kind of guy who would come into the room like this". They'd look up at him and listen to Peter describing what kind of man was behind the character and they would get it. Peter could give them this whole world that I was not effectively communicating.'

'It's a two way stretch,' confirms Lawrence '[As a writer] you have a particular view of the character in your mind, and you may have three or four dimensions to that character that the animators may not get onto the page. Those attributes usually did get into the [voice] tracks, because Lee would understand what we were trying to get into the script. Lee would tell that to the actors, so you had dimensions to the characters. But when you cross the cultural divide and you're dealing with a different part of the process, you're not a director working with live actors, you're a director working with things that have to be drawn. I effectively [took that role]. You have a hell of a lot of missing information. The animators can figure it out, but maybe they don't figure it out the way you want it.

'[The animators at PAC] were very courteous and respectful and wanted to know our views of why a character moved in a certain way and behaved in a certain way. It wasn't just [a case of telling them], "Do it". These guys were so intensely involved in the character [depiction]. It's like an actor asking their motivation; you can either lose patience and say "You're being paid $50,000 a day, [just] do it" or, depending on the personality, you can say (obviously I'm exaggerating), "This guy was born of an abusive parent," and find the layers that you will never necessarily see on screen but give the actor motivation. The same is true in animation. They'd ask what the colour of a character's shoes should be. What does it matter? We never see the shoes. But to them, if the character wears red shoes, it means one thing; black shoes another. You're essentially conveying information that enables the animators to have a complete picture of the character, and therefore, when you call for a specific shot, they know how to interpret that. Or when they're listening to a track that's not in their native language and they're reading the translation, which may not be a good translation anyway, they have other information and they know who they're dealing with. That's what we had to convey. It's not whether you're any good at it, it's having the body of knowledge. Between me and Lee, we had the knowledge of the scripts. I wrote them, but they all went past Lee, and she might say, "This isn't in character", and we'd either argue and I'd say, "It is", or I'd agree and we'd change it. It's the information we had to give the animation guys in the time and system we had. And the fact they did their own storyboards was another cultural shift.'

With the tiring schedules and huge workload put upon them, the Japanese animators' working conditions were perhaps less than ideal. But Dannacher and Lawrence both believe that, despite the often cramped and difficult conditions they experienced, the staff were extremely enthusiastic about their work. 'First of all, you have to know Tokyo,' notes Lawrence. 'You have families there living in houses smaller than your bathroom. Secondly, I don't think anyone held a gun to anyone's head. I think those animators loved to work on the show, just like we did. They were being reasonably well paid for it and working with the best talent in the country. And just as we were under immense pressure in New York with tracks and scripts, they were under unimaginable pressure to finish the end result. On the other hand, unlike us, they did sleep under their desks. I remember one story that during a rail strike one guy walked home from the studio, and when he got home he started walking straight back, because he'd lost it – he'd cracked. But that wasn't because anyone had them in a workhouse.'

Dannacher agrees, adding that it would be entirely erroneous to have a negative view about PAC: 'Masaki ran a wonderful studio, by getting Kubo and Nishida and the young talent that they attracted. Masaki paid his entire company very well and he made very good deals. When people talk about subcontracting, that wasn't the relationship Rankin/Bass had with Masaki at all. He created that studio when we got the *ThunderCats* deal. He was very much a producer in the old-fashioned sense of the word. The subcontractors are just presidents of their animation studios, which are just factories of work. Masaki built up his studio like we did in New York. The animators came on board because they were so eager to work … When Masaki started, Tokyo produced (and it still does) more animation than anywhere in the world. Now there are Hollywood studios where you go in, punch a time clock and get out at 4.30. You're expected to do a certain number of cels a week. Masaki had a few like that on his crew, but they didn't last long, and they didn't last on our side of the Pacific either. When putting together a film you think, "I'm going to kill myself for two years, but I love it." The people with that attitude are the ones who stayed. I remember coming back to New York, and we were already working ten or 12 hour days, and the crew were complaining, and I told them, "At least I haven't put cots under your desks." That became the running joke, and someone eventually said, "Can we have cots?"'

'I can speak for Lee and myself in saying that we had so much respect for those Japanese guys,' adds Lawrence. 'Lee never worked a ten or 12 hour day. It was more like 14 or 18 hours! A lot of Americans working with foreign studios don't have much respect. We knew Masaki, we liked him, we all socialised with Kubo and Nishida, we respected and liked them. When they asked questions, we listened; we didn't just dismiss them.'

'Going over there, even though it was a tough trip, was like this mutual admiration society, where they couldn't wait to show off all aspects of the production work they'd done,' says Dannacher, 'even down to the ink and paint women's departments. They were just tugging at Peter's sleeve saying, "Come see this, come see that." I came back always enthusiastic and thinking, "Okay, let's keep going."'

Of the huge number of animators who participated in the production of each episode of *ThunderCats*, very few were listed in the show's end credits. Throughout the run of 130 episodes, the only names listed (besides Masaki, Kubo and Nishida) were those of various animation directors who worked on the episodes, both in Tokyo and in sub-contracted studios in Korea, Hong Kong and Taiwan. In recent years, Katshuhito Akiyama has sometimes been cited as 'the director of *ThunderCats*', but he was actually only one of a league of directors to contribute to the show. Others who had a prominent involvement included Kazusuke Yoshihara, who created a large amount of design work for the series, and Norio Yazawa, a storyboard artist.

'Kubo was the key animator,' says Lee Dannacher. 'That's what he was famous for; he had a fan club over in Japan. Nishida was responsible for the key backgrounds. That was true even though they delegated because of the amount of work. On so many of the prior Rankin/Bass two hour movies, whether it was *The Last Unicorn* or *Wind in the Willows* or any of those, they could pretty much handle a lot of it themselves. On a series, they had to delegate; they would hire in maybe three other animation directors. But Kubo would still be ultimately responsible for all of his area, and the same for Nishida for the background designs.'

Rankin/Bass's decision to allow PAC to handle *ThunderCats*' direction and storyboarding, based only on the script and voice recordings they received, was unusual even for an American/Japanese production. To avoid obvious cultural differences, the production office vetted each storyboard in New York prior to animation and appointed Rankin/Bass employee Matthew Malach to monitor the early output from PAC. 'Early on in the series,' recalls Malach, 'I was asked by Lee to review the storyboards from a filmmaker's perspective. I was never an artist, but rather made comments in a typed memo. Every now and then I had to make drawings to explain certain camera angles. I looked for discontinuity of shots, inconsistent screen direction, "breaking the line" – [anything that went against] those sorts of formal film rules (many of which are no longer followed). There was also the issue of cultural differences between us and the Asian artists prepping the storyboards. We'd sometimes see storyboards with the characters giving the "V" sign with their hands, which meant one thing in Asia, and something entirely different in the USA. We had to describe things such as the "Okay" sign, made with the thumb and forefinger – apparently not a common thing overseas. Eventually, for other series, R/B hired *bona fide* artists to [take on that checking role]. And that was a good thing – to this day, I cringe at the primitive stick figures I sent overseas. I hope those atrocities never make it to the internet.'

Communication remained a complication of working so closely with Japanese studios. While Masaki was fluent in English, many of his colleagues (including the many hundreds of animators) had only a basic comprehension of the language and struggled to understand the Rankin/Bass employees. To resolve this issue, Rankin/Bass employed Charles 'Chuck' Hasegawa, who was fluent in both languages. It would be his job to accompany Rankin/Bass employees to Japan, translating where necessary, and also to make independent trips to monitor progress and relay any issues affecting production.

'I graduated from the School of Visual Arts in NYC,' says Hasegawa. 'I studied corporate identity-graphic design (BFA) and I also studied at the University of California, Los Angeles. I grew up in California and Tokyo for my childhood through to college and came from an entertainment family in Japan. All of my family members are Japanese actors. My grandfather is the world-known actor Kazuo Hasegawa. (Several of his Japanese movie titles are available in the US, including *Gate of Hell*.) I started as a designer and an art director at Joseph Messina Inc in New York in the early '80s, and joined Rankin/Bass in 1985 as an art director and associate producer. Rankin/Bass was looking for someone who spoke both Japanese and English and who had an art background. My former employer Joseph Messina and the School of Visual Arts both recommended me, and Arthur Rankin asked me to assist his art production in the US and Asia (Korea, Hong Kong, Taiwan and Japan). I left Rankin/Bass in 1988 and am now more involved in international business worldwide. I am a managing partner at Neotrend Consulting LLC and a director at Proudfoot Japan Inc.'

Hasegawa explains in more detail his involvement in *ThunderCats*: 'I was assisting and coordinating among all production departments – between animation artists, animation directors, scriptwriters, editors in NY and PAC studios. I was also working with a screen director to review the storyboards and give comments and direction back to PAC, approving rough-cut footage and editing it in our NY office. I also explained and described all art direction from Arthur Rankin to PAC animation artists. It was challenging work. Arthur was always very precise about what he wanted to see in the artwork, and was often more educational in film making philosophy, which was hard to understand in Japanese culture. There was so much difference between Japanese film making and American animation. There were always conflicts between budget, time, film making philosophy and art. There were days and nights that we all had to stay up to discuss and exchange ideas among Japanese/American artists, art directors, film directors and screenwriters to find the best way to produce shows. Arthur was always dedicated to all those artists in Japan who were trying to understand the requirements of American art standards. I was always assisting Arthur to ease the tension between Japanese artists and the US art department.'

Commenting on the special relationship achieved between Arthur Rankin and Masaki Iizuka, Hasegawa notes: 'I used to travel back and forth between Japan and New York or the LA office at the time. So I travelled with Arthur Rankin or Matthew Malach, Lee Dannacher or a few other animation directors from the US. Masaki Iizuka and Arthur Rankin had started working together on animation going way back. *Rudolph the Red Nosed Reindeer* and all the Rankin/Bass Christmas specials were created by Arthur with production in Japan. So naturally any Rankin/Bass production was assigned to Masaki Iizuka and his team in Japan. Masaki was hiring Taiwanese, Hong Kong and Korean companies as sub-contractors. Masaki and his team members – Kubo-san, a key animator and animation director, and Nishida-san, who was doing all the background art, the props and any related artwork – were also responsible for giving direction to those Taiwanese, Hong Kong and Korean animation production houses. Kubo and Nishida are two of the most well known artists in Japanese animation history. They were real artists! They only think "art, art, art", "animation, animation, animation", all day long. Arthur's work was visiting all those different animation companies, including in Japan, to supervise and see what was happening out there. Masaki and Arthur had a very special relationship, where they understood each other. Arthur used to tell me that he was the one who brought Masaki into this business, so Masaki almost started from zero. Arthur was very hands-on in teaching Masaki how to do business. Fortunately, Masaki was associated with all those artists in Japan like Kubo-san and Nishida-san, who went on to work on Disney productions after PAC closed down.'

Hasegawa believes the animation work was challenging for all involved: 'Days and nights, seven days a week, I witnessed those people working in tiny studios; sometimes 10 x 7 feet or 5 x 6 feet, little tiny rooms. Ten or 15 animators were packed in these rooms working all day long, all night long. No day off, no break, no time for eating or taking a shower, and that was quite interesting.

'The most [difficult obstacle to overcome] was the differences between animation in Japan and in the US. Arthur had to tell me to explain to Japanese animation artists how to show the expression of a smile, anger, excitement, sadness etc in the way it would be done in American animation. Movement and facial expressions were the most challenging [things to get right]. Japanese animators often had a hard time understanding the differences between Japanese and American expressions. I remember that in the studio in Japan, each animator's desk had a key facial sheet that featured key characters in different angles. Another problem was lip-syncing: the mouth movements are very different between America and Japan, so the animators had a really hard time implementing the American animation drawing style and showing the lip-sync … Also, we often had a hard time asking the Japanese animation directors to put in establishing shots, because in the US, the audiences need to know where the story begins, the locations and environments. They often start with a long wide shot. If it's an ocean, they show the whole ocean. But Japanese filmmakers don't show an establishing shot, they go straight to the action in the water. Differences like that caused a hot discussion between the American and Japanese studios, so Arthur was always an ambassador to try to diplomatically explain what we needed. Japanese artists and directors are surprised why the audience can't figure things like that out. Arthur would say things like, "Us Americans are all dumb, we need it explained". Arthur was very dedicated to art, he spent days and nights with each individual artist in Japan explaining all the differences between American and Japanese audiences.

'Kubo-san and Nishida-san were so dedicated to Arthur. He was treated like a father figure, sometimes like a god. If he asked, they would do it; they'd spend four days without sleep just to produce the artwork Arthur was looking for. It was a hot discussion amongst the artists, and Arthur took precedence. I had a difficult time not making the artists upset when explaining exactly what American audiences were looking for. It was a constant ongoing battle with the Japanese artists, but they always wanted to get the very best results.'

Each episode of *ThunderCats* began production in Japan under the watchful eyes of Masaki, Kubo and Nishida. Once storyboards had been created and approved by Rankin/Bass in New York, animation work started, with more labour-intensive tasks, such as cel painting, often outsourced to Taiwan, Korea and Hong Kong. After the subcontracted studios had completed their work on the episode, packages of sequential cels were either returned to Japan, where they were overseen and photographed by Masaki's team, or processed by the participating studios. 'At the time, Japan was already getting expensive to produce animation,' says Hasegawa. 'Therefore Maski Iizuka and PAC were advised by Arthur Rankin to hire the best animators in Taiwan, Hong Kong and Korea. They were all very well known studios doing work for Hanna-Barbera and lots of clients in California. PAC was just one of their clients; they were also taking clients like Disney. Their animation directors often visited us in New York and met Arthur. Masaki would fly in from Japan to meet them too. But the challenging part was that the individual studios all had their own cultures, and they had to match what Masaki did in Japan, who in turn had to meet American requirements.'

Because of the variety of studios working on each episode, differences did emerge, despite the best efforts to contain them. While outright errors were rare, particular episodes of *ThunderCats* did suffer quality issues, such as poor cel painting and inaccurate likenesses. This was more common in earlier episodes, and by the time of the second season, the consistency of artwork had markedly increased.

'Arthur and I often discussed the differences between the Taiwan, Korea and Hong Kong offices,' admits Hasegawa. 'Sometimes you'd see it in the quality. With the people doing all day inbetween art, there were certainly some artists who were better than others. One artist can't complete all the episodes, so certainly we used to recognise who did this artwork or who didn't. But politically and diplomatically, we were never allowed to mention which worked best. Arthur often told me not to say. It was a sensitive issue; we always had to be careful not to mention this to individual artists, or even Masaki, because he was very protective of artists and participating studios.

'*ThunderCats* was one of the shows on which it was very easy to identify which episodes were better than others. An art expert could instantly recognise how good Lion-O's facial expressions and figure were etc. Some studios had more people to work on it, and again, time management and the skills of all those artists were factors. They were all different in Korea, Hong Kong and Taiwan. But

Masaki-san, Kubo-san and Nishida-san did a very good job to manage the quality and consistency of the artwork.

'I do not remember the names of individual studios. A couple of people visited us from them, and they were well known names in animation studios. Some of them were more well known than those in Masaki's studio, because he was newer in the industry, even though he'd done productions with Arthur. Some of the Taiwanese, Hong Kong and Korean studios had more experience in animation, so there were issues with Masaki and the studios, because they perhaps felt they could do better than Masaki and tried to cut in front of him and talk directly to Arthur. It was always a politically sensitive issue that we, the US office, were not allowed to have any contact or talks without Masaki present. They were just business issues. The other studios had access to other US companies.'

Hasegawa recalls that a tremendous number of artists were involved in creating the *ThunderCats* artwork: 'I believe in Japan, at the headquarter offices of PAC, I used to see probably 30 to 40 artists. Then there was another sub-contracting studio in Japan, so that meant another 40 artists. I'm not sure how many artists were involved in the other countries, but I believe it was 60-100 artists in each country.

'Sometimes, by the time a storyboards arrived in New York and we began reviewing and making changes to them and sending them back to Japan, all the artists had already started work on the artwork, so it was too late. But we always had to get them to correct the film-making and direction. That was a constant battle between the US and Japanese studios, because of the timeframe and the budget. The photography was always done in Japan, I believe, and each script, each show was divided into different countries and different studios. The cels were corrected in Japan and shot in Japan.'

Two examples of studios utilised by Masaki Iizuka were Studio Pierrot, based in Japan, and Wang Film Productions, based in Taiwan. The latter, founded by James Wang in 1978, created four episodes of *ThunderCats* and four episodes of *SilverHawks* from beginning to end. 'I got a teaching assistantship and worked at an animation department while I studied instructional system technology at Indiana University from 1974 to 1976,' explains Wang. 'Before graduation, I had a chance to join the production of *The Adventure of Raggedy Ann and Andy* in New York. After I received my master's degree, I then participated with animation production in Hollywood. Wang Films was established in 1978 in Taipei.

'I knew Mr Arthur Rankin from 1981, when Wang Films produced *Wind in the Willows* for Rankin/Bass. He sent Mr Masaki Iizuka to Taipei around 1985 when Wang Films was doing *ThunderCats*. We undertook four half-hour episodes of *ThunderCats* from layout to finish. Wang Films started with Hanna-Barbera, [animating] 13 episodes of *Laff-A-Lympics* and four episodes of *Godzilla*. Around 30 people were employed at Wang Films, and 15 worked on *ThunderCats*, of which one was an animation director.'

Wang admits that his overriding memory of animating for Rankin/Bass is, 'Everybody was very busy, but there was too much stress.' He adds, though: 'We were all pleased to be working on the show ... There are big differences between American and Japanese animation. American animation is more simple and interesting and Japanese animation has more emphasis on story.'

Wang reveals that his company was supplied with layout and background keys, and that no set 'frame rate' was established for *ThunderCats*, giving the animators the flexibility to devise their own sequences: 'The clients called for retakes after they received the first take, though I don't remember how many times retakes were done on *ThunderCats*. Wang Films did rough edits and sent the finished film to our clients, who then had them sent to their post-production house to mix sounds and effects.'

Chuck Hasegawa recalls that he seldom communicated directly with animators and sub-contractors working on *ThunderCats*: 'Kubo-san and Nishida-san were the only artists that I had a good relationship with. The chain of command situation was that I was not allowed to talk to all the other artists. Even when I said "hello" and had to thank people for their hard work and artwork, or describe quality issues or timing issues etc, I was only allowed to share the information with Masaki-san, Kubo-san and Nishida-san. They were almost like business partners, so we were only allowed to talk to those artists. At the same time as *ThunderCats*, we were also working on other shows, so … it was a quite busy studio – it was amazing. Nishida-san was painting large-sized artwork; the key art backgrounds. Then somebody could copy the style he established and create more. Also the colours, the choice of lines and shape, Nishida-san [established] those in the key art backgrounds. After that, all the individual background artists would implement Nishida's style for each episode. However Nishida-san was always adding his touch to the important backgrounds.'

Although the visual style of the series was tailored to a Western audience, PAC were able to save time and resources by still employing typical anime techniques in their work, including a variable frame rate (the number of cels that compromise one second of film) and a variety of other 'trickery'. For complicated action sequences, the frame rate could be increased to that typical of a feature film production, whereas in simpler sequences it could be decreased so that the image was almost entirely static, in some cases for upwards of ten seconds. In part, PAC were able to disguise such static sequences by employing off-screen dialogue (whereby a character's face is turned away from the viewer or cropped above the mouth) and including blinking and other basic movements. Camera movements such as pans and zooms were also used to add visual interest to otherwise inert drawings. 'Frame rate all depends on the quality of animation you want,' notes Chuck Hasegawa. 'Theatre-released animation requires more cels, but a TV series is very limited, so it's not as smooth – we had to deal with a very limited number of cels in [some shots].' Despite the occasional short-cuts in production, PAC always returned superbly animated episodes, often showcasing their talents by far exceeding script requirements; and almost every episode of *ThunderCats* had at least one action sequence that pushed far beyond the typical animated-TV-show boundaries.

Despite the notable differences between Japanese and American techniques, *ThunderCats* did make use of standard animation production processes. For every shot, a watercolour background, painted typically on cardboard, was placed beneath a 35mm film camera. On top of this base layer was placed a series of artwork images painted onto cellular acetate and perfectly aligned with the background. To save time and money, further transparent cels could be overlaid, including arms, eyes, mouths etc that featured movement independent of the main paintings. This avoided the need for repeat drawing of static elements and negated the trademark 'shudder' associated with cel tracing. Typical cels for *ThunderCats* measured 10¾ inches by 9½ inches, with larger and wider ones sometimes used to facilitate camera movements and pans.

Before each cel was produced by specialist painters, detailed line drawings, sometimes referred to as 'dougas', would be created on paper. These would represent consecutive frames, and the fluidity of movement was ascertained by referring back and forth between them. Unlike in feature film production, the schedule and budget given to *ThunderCats* meant no time was allowed for photographic testing at this stage to check movement and lip-sync; once the drawings were approved by a supervisor, cel inking would begin. This entailed the drawings being traced onto transparent acetates in ink. The acetates were then passed for colouring. Not all areas of colour would be outlined in ink (for instance facial skin tones) and these sections would be suitably notated in the drawings for use by the paint departments. All colours were tested and mixed in Japan and the resulting formulas distributed to participating studios to ensure consistency amongst the principal characters. Once a sequence was complete, the finished set-up was photographed and the resulting film catalogued for editing.

'On the New York side, we never had a chance to see [the initial] pencil [drawings],' recounts Chuck Hasegawa. 'I believe they were all overseen by Kubo-san in Japan, and at the beginning of production they were doing pencil tests, but … they didn't have the budget or the time allowance to do anywhere near the pre-production that [a film company like] Disney would do. Kubo-san was pretty much guessing what everything was going to look like. It was incredible; Kubo-san's skills amazed you … On the Japanese side, they weren't native English speakers; they had to pick through the audio track word by word, sound by sound …Kubo-san told me that it really required special skills to identify the sounds of voices in each script, and they had to reverse-count how many frames they had to create [between consecutive speeches]. So they were amazing skills that they had to evolve for this process.

'We always had to battle with the budget. The budget only allows you to use certain film-making techniques. For instance, we wanted to use a cross-dissolve for certain [scene changes, to avoid] what we call a jump cut. [Sometimes] if [the animators] had artwork problems or timing issues, … they would reuse footage or short-cut it, which meant that it didn't look like a smooth scene change – we even witnessed this [jump cut] sometimes when we couldn't fix it. When Matthew Malach worked on the show and Lee Dannacher, we always got into film-making battles, even between ourselves in New York. We wanted to use different techniques, like we'd want wide-angle shots etc. It was only TV animation, 20-minute shows, so we couldn't replicate a real film-making situation, but *ThunderCats* required lots of realistic film-making techniques, and we thought it created excitement. But again, Japan had a different film-making philosophy. Arthur and other directors in the US used to say that Japanese animation was more sophisticated. American animation is kind of simple, so some of the Japanese directors [went beyond] the script, which described as much as we could. The script editor at the time, Peter Lawrence, knew that we had to put a lot more detail and animation notes in the scripts, so that the Japanese animators could understand what we wanted in a scene. But sometimes, the directors in Japan read too much into something and made it too complicated and the writers didn't get what they wanted from it. Japanese animators tend to make more sophisticated and mature films for their audiences.'

One feature that *ThunderCats* shared with similar productions was the use of certain stock scenes that would be replayed in almost every episode. Besides the introductory credits sequence, which would remain unchanged throughout all 130 episodes, other such scenes included Lion-O's sword call (of which there were several versions), Mumm-Ra's transformation, and minor establishing shots such as Third Earth locations and the ThunderTank being despatched from Cat's Lair. These important sequences were given added scrutiny by Masaki's team and, where possible, were included by the writers in their scripts to reduce the cost of 'new' animation for each episode. Ironically, this short-cut would enhance the appeal of the series to many viewers, who anticipated the familiar scenes with excitement, happy to overlook the fact that this was stock footage.

Unlike some American action/adventure series, *ThunderCats* avoid recycling much material beyond these sequences, although repeated shots did creep in occasionally, sometimes replayed entirely but more often re-photographed with new backgrounds. Because of the scale of production across *ThunderCats*, *SilverHawks* and *The Comic Strip*, PAC were also careful to document and catalogue their existing visual elements, so that items such as backgrounds could be retrieved and reused if appropriate.

Hasegawa recalls that the stock sequences were overseen by Arthur Rankin and occasionally even Jules Bass. 'They were so important,' he insists. 'They were created by Kubo-san and Nishida-san in Japan, so we had to review and evaluate [them as part of] the pilot footage that they [produced] before the actual production began. That was key animation that we spent a lot of money establishing and developing ... We sometimes ran into [situations where] different studios found that the exposure changed, so that in between scenes the lightness of the film changed, so sometimes the reused scenes had to be modified. But cost effectiveness meant that the shots were used over and over, unless there were technical issues requiring a scene to be re-shot.'

Once the entire run of cels and backgrounds had been photographed for any given episode, the resulting footage was edited in PAC's studios in Tokyo. Here, sequences were trimmed to length and a range of visual effects added. Though unobtrusive, these effects were skilfully achieved, enhancing the animation with cutting-edge techniques. Effects used regularly included the beam of light that projected the Eye of Thundera into the skies (the emblem alone was painted on to the cels), lighting effects such as lens flare, and picture overlay effects like Mumm-Ra's cauldron and the 'sight beyond sight' view finder. 'There was a special effects team,' recalls Hasegawa. 'I never met them; they often talked about the effects in the studio, but we weren't allowed access to those areas to see exactly how they achieved them. I'm sure some of it was to do with the confidentiality of each studio; they kept things pretty much to themselves and they didn't want people to copy their techniques. They were conscious of new effects that they would design and create.'

After this, the films were synched with dialogue tracks and 'rough' sound effects were spotted onto the soundtrack, which also included the music selection. Though the audio track would be conformed back in New York (with final effects substituted/added) the 35mm visuals would be sent out as finished copies (subject to review by Rankin/Bass). 'The films PAC sent back to New York were the rough mix versions,' adds Hasegawa, 'so we had to take them to the mixing studios and put in new sound effects and balance all the sound. When you [have a character throwing] a baseball in the US, they'll make a certain sound effect for it; it's like a standard, it's something in American culture. But in Japan, they'd make a totally different choice of sound effect. So we had to change the sound effects to be more accurate for the US. [In Japan] they put in the minimum number of sound effects onto the picture, then we added all the necessary extras. Later on, I'd often be involved when there were so many productions going on. I was also in charge of adding sound effects for certain shows. Here in America, we loved to put a lot of sound effects onto *ThunderCats*, so we were just adding from left to right, and that was quite time consuming.'

Exact timelines for the production of a 'standard' episode of *ThunderCats* are difficult to ascertain as work was proceeding on multiple episodes of *ThunderCats*, *SilverHawks* and *The Comic Strip* simultaneously. 'Everything was overlapping,' confirms Hasegawa. 'But I think from [when voice] recording was done in the US to the episodes being sent out from Japan was maybe about a month and a half to two months. It was pretty fast; it could have been even less.' As previously noted, Hasegawa was sometimes sent to Japan to collect prints, to get them back to the US more quickly than if they went through the usual shipping and customs channels: 'Sometimes, I had to wait at the hotel and at the editing studio in Japan for days and nights, and as soon as the film was ready, I'd put it in a box and go to the airport and bring the film directly back to our studio in New York.'

Episodes did not always come back from Japan in the same order as the audio tracks and scripts had been sent out, as Peter Lawrence explains: 'Apart from the five-parters, we could never run anything consecutively. You couldn't build a story arc over more than one episode, because in syndication you have no control over how episodes are shown. Sometimes in the first run, but never in the second run. We sent out however many shows a month to be animated, but they wouldn't necessarily come back in the order we sent them out in, or be completed in the order they were returned in, so we [might end up] with Mumm-Ra doing the same thing in several shows in a run. I'm sure if you line up the shows, there is repetition, other than the repetition you'd expect from the same characters; but I think that, because we had so many writers coming in with so many different ideas, perhaps we avoided [the worst of] that.'

Although attempts were made to negate the stylistic influence of Japanese anime, various sequences throughout *ThunderCats* do owe a great deal to their origins. Many designs, backgrounds and effects were reminiscent of Japanese art, and helped to showcase, in some way, the efforts of Japanese artists onto a world stage. 'They were not widely accepted at the time by American animation studios,' believes Hasegawa. 'In Taiwan, Hong Kong and Korea, those animation studios were more flexible and could easily implement American film directions. But [the ones in] Japan [did not find] it easy, because Japan has many, many years' history of independent film making. I do [believe] PAC showed American animation companies that they could do something that they had never witnessed before. What Rankin/Bass was doing at the time was quite sensational to many other animation companies in the US, and they had a number one hit show; but at the same time, it was a challenge for the Japanese studios.'

Hasegawa adds that once *ThunderCats* had become an established success, Pacific Animation artists achieved recognition: 'They were like stars at the time. All of the other animation production companies were so jealous of PAC. Kubo-san and Nishida-san became famous; they were so proud that they were the ones that created *ThunderCats*. They took a lot of chances and the results became very successful. Because of Kubo-san's reputation and credibility in the Japanese animation industry, he had access to the best animation directors in Japan at the time. When Kubo-san asked someone to work on an episode, they might not be a PAC employee, but he'd get that person in for a certain episode. The animation directors were all well-credited people in the Japanese animation industry at the time.

'[Japanese-style] comics are very popular in the US now. I think *ThunderCats* was the beginning of that style of animation. It was first introduced in *ThunderCats*. I think that's one of the reasons it became so popular in the US, because it had a flavour of the stylish parts of the Japanese animation style. A lot of the animators at PAC were conscious of that style and implementing it in their work.'

The Japanese animators who worked so diligently to bring *ThunderCats* to TV sets across the globe have a reputation for modesty about their achievements, each deferring their vast individual achievements to the collective group. One animator who fondly recalls his experience of working for PAC on *ThunderCats* is Kitajima Nobuyuki. Born on 11 June 1952 in Tokyo, he began his career as an inbetweener on the 1970 Japanese production *Inakappe Taisho*, progressing to the role of an animation director with *Arabian Nights – The Adventures of Sinbad* in 1975. By 1985, Nobuyuki had forged a strong friendship with fellow *ThunderCats* veteran Katsuhito Akiyama. Today, he remains in the animation industry in the prestigious AIC studios. Translated from his native Japanese courtesy of Nathan Baker, Kitajima Nobuyuki explains how he came to work on *ThunderCats*: 'I was in my thirties and working passionately with my own studio set up. I remember that I was offered work on ten episodes of *ThunderCats* as an animation director after getting some good reviews on my work with Kojika Monogatari and *Lens Man*.

'It was my first time working with director Katsuhito Akiyama, but since then, I've known him for over 20 years. The first time I heard of Tsugo Kubo in the field of character design was for his work in *Tiger Mask* as the director of animation. After that, he had done a wonderful job on projects like *The Hobbit, 20,000 Leagues Under the Sea* and *The Last Unicorn*, but I could never get an opportunity to work with him [until I got the *ThunderCats* commission]. When I first saw the character chart for *ThunderCats*, I honestly thought to myself, "This is going to be tough – will I really be able to pull it off?" But I worked on it devotedly and furiously. I also remember nervously thinking that I'd better not draw poorly or do shameful work, because the opening animation was done beautifully. After finishing ten episodes, we made a Japanese version for promotional purposes, and I remember being thrilled to hear that they chose episode eleven – [one of mine] – as it was done well.'

Nobuyuki recalls with amusement his introduction to Kubo: 'It was when I was working late at night, still feeling very proud that director Akiyama praised my work, when Mr Kubo showed up in my studio without notice, and said to me, "You must be Kitajima? I just came by because I wanted to talk to you. Sorry for showing up unannounced". For about 30 minutes, rather than having a conversation, he one-sidedly talked to me about how animation should be approached, and at the end, he said, "My theory is that there are no skilled fat animators out there, but I changed my mind a little after seeing you" and left my studio. I have no clue why he showed up at my studio that late at night, but every time I think about Mr Kubo, I think about that incident. Indeed, at that time, I was 171 cm tall and fat – I weighed 85 kilos. Afterwards, I was involved in the animation for a few more episodes, but I trained some new animators at the same time. It was probably the period when the work of the veterans was going downhill and it was time for new Japanese animators to take the reins. *ThunderCats*, I think, was sort of a monumental production in that sense.'

After an episode was sent on 35mm film to New York, it generally marked the end of PAC's involvement in the production process on that episode. Retakes, reserved for the most galling production errors, were rare, due to the thorough scrutiny of Masaki and his team in Japan. After the soundtrack had been finalised at Rankin/Bass, the completed film prints began their final journey to a tape house in Los Angeles. Here the story captions and end credits were added and the 35mm film prints were transferred to one-inch NTSC videotapes for distribution to stations across the country. It was also here that fades and idents were inserted for advertising purposes and the final tapes were graded for broadcast. International distribution was also prepared here with conversion to international formats such as PAL, prior to sending.

Despite the incredibly tight production deadlines, episodes of *ThunderCats* were always broadcast on time and on budget. Beginning with a breathtaking introduction sequence, *ThunderCats* burst into the imaginations of youngsters across the world. Offering a standard of animation almost unparalleled in a television action/adventure cartoon at that time, PAC's work would achieve a near-legendary status. As the series continued, the animators never allowed standards to drop and, time and again, the Japanese studios turned out episodes that went beyond anyone's expectations. Where American television animation would often be flat and simplistic, the Japanese animators injected an unparalleled vision into *ThunderCats*. In addition to producing vibrant cel and background paintings, PAC also pushed the boundaries by using sophisticated depth of focus techniques and offering a sublime sense of lighting, affording characters and objects with shadows – all of which contributed enormously to the workload, but also to the finished visuals. That Arthur Rankin's groundbreaking ties to Japan would prove to be so successful provided its own rewards as the series catapulted into first place in its timeslot due, in large part, to the efforts of PAC. *ThunderCats* undoubtedly raised the bar for television animation and set a standard few others would meet for many years to come.

4. SWAN SONG
The Music of ThunderCats

In certain film and television productions, music all too often stands as an afterthought; a homogenous selection of background accompaniment. In rarer cases, it runs at the very heart of the production, flowing through its veins and reinforcing the visuals at every turn. In the case of *ThunderCats*, the latter is surely true.

While using stock library tracks would have been undoubtedly cheaper, the producers of *ThunderCats* believed the series merited a unique series of cues to provide a wider range of musicality. Rankin/Bass quickly sought out the services of Bernard Hoffer, an established composer who had carved out a career in commercial jingles. With his input, *ThunderCats* eschewed the purely electronic, synthesised soundtracks that could be found amongst its contemporaries. Instead, Hoffer referred back to classical scoring techniques to create a timeless body of work.

Supervising producer Lee Dannacher recalls her enjoyment of working with Hoffer: 'Bernie Hoffer and I remain such close friends to this day. I had the pleasure of working with him on previous shows, so I knew him really well by that point. Once we had the writers' bible and had worked out the good guys from the bad guys, he started coming into the office and immersing himself in the whole world of *ThunderCats*. We had this (mostly) out of tune piano, and Bernie would bang out suggestions – we knew his playing well enough that we got the idea. Jules had been producing all of the music for Rankin/Bass for years, and he taught me how to work with composers way back [in 1982] on *The Last Unicorn* with Jimmy Webb. Right after that, he allowed me to work with Maury Laws on producing the music for *The Flight of the Dragon* and the other specials that we did. So when it came time to do *ThunderCats*, I was there the whole way.

'Bernie would bang out his thematic music for everything, and we trusted him … Jules and I sat down and said, "Using the same thematic music, give us two minutes of ThunderCats in trouble, or two minutes of ThunderCats on the run etc". We went through every character and typed through a whole music cue library of what we wanted Bernie to produce. We also had a slew of background loops for Bernie to create, like the "danger" loops and the "tension mounting" loops etc, and then every character has its own theme music, which you will recognise if you're watching the episodes. Cheetara had her theme, for instance, and WilyKit and WilyKat had their subsidiary tracks. Then we would let Bernie go off and compose and do his magic. He worked with an extraordinary man by the name of Siggy Singer, who did all of his orchestrations.

'We would eventually book ourselves [into the recording studio] and plot how long we needed [to record the music] in the studio, and Bernie would book all of the musicians. We decided to splurge and spend the money and do all of the orchestra records there in New York, which was more expensive for us, but it was just wonderful. It was probably two weeks' worth of recording with the orchestra, another week of overdubbing guitars and synthesisers and another week of daily studio work and mixing it down into a 110-minute library of all-original music.'

Composing *ThunderCats*

Bernard Hoffer was born in Zurich, Switzerland on 14 October 1934. His father had been a pharmaceutical research chemist. He held over 40 drug patents, including for the antibiotic Gantrisin, and his achievements included the discovery of a B vitamin and the process of making vitamins soluble for intravenous feeding. In 1941, the company for whom he worked moved its research department, including him and his family, from Basel, Switzerland to New Jersey, USA. Hoffer thus grew up there. His affinity for music began at an early age, and he recalls how his mother, a pianist, must have taught him to write music: 'I had started writing by the age of six. I actually don't know how I learned musical notation, but it seems I always knew it'.

While in grade school, Hoffer began to have formal piano lessons and was sent weekly to Dalcroze School in NYC, where he took classes in various musical techniques. While in high school, he studied composition under the tutelage of Max Wald, a one-time student of the noted French composer Vincent d'Indy, and his counterpoint teacher was Kurt Stone, who later became editor of Universal Music Corporation. Soon, Hoffer began to share his music with others, and a lifetime of musical accomplishments began: 'I wrote compositions for my high school band, chorus and orchestra. I also played piano in swing bands on weekends at church halls and even in clubs, even though I was underage'.

After high school, Hoffer attended Eastman School of Music in Rochester NY, where he majored in composition and studied conducting and theory. He was highly advanced in music theory due to his previous studies, and in 1957 he received a bachelor's degree, followed in 1958 by a master's. 'I don't recall any period in my life up to that time when I wasn't writing music in one form or another,' he states.

Hoffer's association with Rankin/Bass began in the late 1960s when he was a freelance pianist and arranger working at Associated Recording, a studio in New York facilitating demo publishers. From making demos over a period of years, he graduated to playing piano on Maury Laws' sessions for holiday specials, and later ghosted charts for them. 'After a while,' he recalls, 'I got to score all of the action music for *The Return of the King* and some other made-for-TV films like *The Ivory Ape, The Sins of Dorian Gray* and more. I also scored the TV specials *The Easter Bunny is Coming to Town*, with Fred Astaire, and *The Stingiest Man in Town*, with Walter Matthau. After working on and off with Jules Bass (who did the music production) on many projects, I was asked to do the *ThunderCats* series – since I had already established myself as a good writer of action music.'

At the beginning of the 1980s, Hoffer was already among the top writers of music for advertising in New York, having scored hundreds of jingles and TV adverts for all types of products, and was well acquainted with the best musicians in the New York and Toronto recording scene. 'I also had the theme for the most prestigious news programme on television, *The MacNeil/Lehrer Report* on PBS,' he notes.

In 1984, Hoffer, at the age of 49, was officially commissioned to craft the musical score for *ThunderCats*: 'I was given drawings of the characters, as well as a sample script. Also, lyrics for the theme were given to me ahead of time. Cue sheets were also supplied. Jules Bass prepared all of those things. He knew what he was doing, having produced many TV specials prior to *ThunderCats* …

'The theme [had] to delineate the lyrics and create a song that could be easily remembered and also used throughout the show as a unifying structural device. The specifics of each character had been developed prior to my involvement, so all I had to do was to interpret what I saw and felt about them, e.g. Snarf being the comic relief. Also, each character had specific attributes that could be delineated and exploited by the music. Once the style of the music (accessible rock) was determined, it only remained to score each character by his relationship to the story. Cheetara was the fleet one, hence the music ran quickly. Tygra was the senior partner, so his theme was bold. Panthro was the enforcer – dark and powerful – and he drove the ThunderTank – my favourite cue! Of course, Mumm-Ra was the evil leader – the music [for him] had to be mysterious, scary and very dark. The one thing that was most important was that, from the beginning, Jules and I were in complete agreement as to the use of the music. Jules believed in the use of leitmotif – a musical device originated by Richard Wagner in his operas, which establishes a theme for each character and event and recalls that with their reappearance.'

In the days before computer-based music editing became commonplace, all of the music for *ThunderCats* had to be divided into timed sections of various lengths. Therefore, the same key theme would be replayed by the orchestra on multiple occasions. Each time, Hoffer would have to restructure it to allow it to work at the required length – ranging from a short 'sting' or 'ident' to the accompaniment for a long action sequence. 'I am very structural in my musical thinking,' acknowledges Hoffer, 'coming from my classical training. I tried to structure each time segment as if it was a complete piece of music. If this were done today, with the use of Pro-Tools or other digital editing programs, these separate timing segments of each theme would no longer be necessary.'

Hoffer began his work scoring *ThunderCats* by attributing a unique and powerful theme to each of the lead characters: 'The creative process is simple, not mysterious or mystical; you just start to work!' Given three months to write the first set of cues, he was methodical in his approach and tasked himself with writing a set amount of new music each day, despite the fact he was also still heavily involved in other TV advertising work at the time.

Being accomplished at both concert music and television scores, Hoffer was able to skilfully compose a complete work of music for *ThunderCats* that not only complemented the visual action sequences but also enhanced them. 'TV and film music is subservient to the structure and tone of the programme or film,' he says. 'Concert music is structured from indigenous ideas decided upon by the composer or derived from the music itself. Film and TV music always depends on instructions from non-musical sources. It has always been my philosophy when writing TV themes, that if you are in another room and you hear the TV, you should know what programme is on by the sound of the music. Whether it is a film, news show, or just an ad, the principle is the same'.

As Hoffer completed the process of writing his cues direct to manuscript, his music was approved by the production team at Rankin/Bass, of whom he cannot speak too highly: 'I was given sufficient time to do the job right. I was given the choice of the musicians I wanted and I don't think more than two or three cues (out of several hundred) were ever rejected. Working with Rankin/Bass was always a good experience. You couldn't ask for better conditions.'

Recording of the music began in June 1984 at A & R Recording Studios on West 48th Street in New York. Around 20 orchestral musicians were assembled to record the score, and separate sessions were arranged for synthesiser overdubs. Once recording was completed, the finished tracks were handed to the *ThunderCats* editors, and over the next few months, the music was finally placed alongside the stunning animated visuals. The finished results perfectly reflected the tone of the series; and, as desired, every plot twist and turn was foreshadowed and highlighted by the music.

Amongst such a varied body of work, Hoffer finds it difficult to single out favourite pieces. However, he admits to being particularly proud of the ThunderTank music – a combination of powerful electric guitar melodies and an upbeat tempo that surely places it amongst the most powerful and memorable parts of the show's entire musical score. 'The idea of this came from the feel of a song by the group Three Dog Night,' he recalls.

As the series began its broadcast run across the world, Hoffer's memorable theme tune became the language of the playground. Head writer Leonard Starr explains the importance of having a strong theme: 'Jules Bass wrote the lyrics for that, I believe. That's what he really wanted to be: a song lyrics writer. Somehow he got into animation. The theme was very catchy, and a great anthem is one that you can't forget. I recently watched a pop singer singing "Oh, Canada". I couldn't remember a single note of it the minute she finished singing it, and it was long! [By contrast,] you think of "The Marseillaise", "The Star Spangled Banner", "Deutschland Uber Alles"... like them or not as tunes, they're memorable.'

Although the cues recorded for the first series of the show were comprehensive, after 65 episodes, the production team decided to return to Hoffer with a request for additional music. Lee Dannacher describes why this was done: 'For the second 65, I managed to convince Jules to do more. Not that I really thought we needed it, but I wanted to be back in [the recording studio], and Peter Lawrence was creating all these new characters, so I convinced Jules we needed at least another 30 minutes of music for the LunaTaks etc, and we went back in to produce those ... And of course we repeated that on *SilverHawks* and *The Comic Strip*, so a great deal of my life has been spent in recording studios with Bernie Hoffer, and all I can say is, I want more!'

Hoffer was formally commissioned to write 55 additional cues that would complement, rather than replace, the existing music: 'There was a new set of characters [for the second series], and a new cue sheet describing the ideas and length of the cues. The process was the same. All I had to do was follow it. There was no chance for repetition – only remain in the musical style. I believe the second set of cues was recorded at Celebration Studios of MZH&F, a New York ad music house.'

On a personal note, Hoffer recalls his high regard for *ThunderCats*. Aside from the opportunities it presented him with, he is very proud to have played a part in creating countless childhood memories: '*ThunderCats* was one of the most ideal projects a composer could wish for. All of the people involved knew what they were doing with music. Nobody nitpicked; I was given almost complete freedom to write what I pleased after I was given the guidelines. The editors were also hip, imaginative and sensational and had a terrific sense of the use of music.

'Identifying why the series was such a success is impossible. If it were obvious, every television executive and commissioning editor would surely have success after success on their hands. I think *ThunderCats* was a good idea from the beginning and was well executed in all of its elements. Also, the clear definition of good guys versus bad guys (good guys always win) made it clearly identifiable to young people. Many other programmes don't have clearly recognisable elements. The characters were well defined, the animation was well defined, and if I may say so, the music was well defined. Also, the repertory groups of actors were first class. And there were a bunch of young, very hip editors with lots of imagination. Probably what happens with any successful work of art or entertainment is that all the elements come together in just the right manner'.

Hoffer continues to create music to this day. He is involved with several concert projects, both classical and jazz, and currently has three CDs of saxophone music available on the Sons of Sound label: *Variations on a Theme of Stravinsky*, *Suite after Baroque Styles* and *The Toy Chest*.

Musicians

With full orchestral manuscripts in place, the task of recruiting a range of talented performers to match Bernard Hoffer's score fell to experienced musician Sigmund 'Siggy' Singer. 'The musicians were hired individually by my contractor Siggy,' confirms Hoffer, 'who has since sadly passed away. I specified who to hire (if available). At the time, I was very busy writing and recording jingles. All the players were known to me and had worked with me many times. The music was recorded (full band) at once – electronics were added later. The orchestra for both series of *ThunderCats* included four reeds, three trumpets, three trombones, tuba, synthesiser percussion, guitar, piano, bass and drums. The synth parts were written in the score with the other instruments, but we did extra synth-alone dates for effects and specific sounds.'

Hoffer's use of an 'accessible rock' thematic required large sections of electric guitar work throughout the *ThunderCats* score. For the various riffs that would be needed (both scored and improvised), an experienced session guitarist, Craig Snyder, was approached.

Snyder tells his story: 'I'll start with how I got to play guitar. My father's a musician, so I grew up surrounded by musicians, and he was a band leader and owned a music store. My earliest recollection of music is going with my father's band to parties and weddings. I was always around music and, though I went to college as a history major, I always played guitar. I also played drums, but when I was at college, I started playing guitar with a very famous jazz guitarist, Pat Martino, and I fell totally in love with playing guitar. A very close friend of mine was Mike Warren, who happened to teach at my father's store. He left Philadelphia, moved to LA and became a very well-known studio guitar player and a conductor for Helen Reddy. When I was about 18 or 19, I went out there and hung out with him. I fell in love with the whole studio recording thing, and I just wanted to play on records. So, I just geared my playing and my studies to that part of the business. I was going to be a jazz player, but I fell in love with being a studio session player. At one point, I began doing a lot of work in Philadelphia, the Sound of Philadelphia; soul music like Billy Paul. During the disco time, I played for the Village People and many disco albums. I played for Elton John for his only disco album. I also did John Travolta's first albums and worked with many other artists.

'Then I made a choice to move to New York instead of LA. It was, and still is, a place that not only has records but has jingles, sessions for advertising and commercials, and when I first moved to town, one of the first guys I worked for was Bernie Hoffer ... I was his guitar player and I did many, many sessions with him. I was on every *ThunderCats* session, the first year and the second year. Generally speaking, most of the sessions had one guitar player. But back then it was just another session to me. *ThunderCats* didn't even exist as a cartoon yet as the music was done first. I also did *SilverHawks* and all that stuff.'

Asked how closely he followed Hoffer's score, Snyder explains that all of the guitar solos were improvised: 'You would have chord changes and rhythms and then you'd just play; but the ensemble parts with the horn playing and the full orchestra, they were all written out. Listening to the stuff now (I hadn't heard it for 25 years), it's brilliant. It's way ahead of its time. You look at movies now like *Transformers*; Bernie was writing better than that stuff 30 years ago.

'I remember the sessions were really hard. I don't mean not fun; maybe challenging is the word, because you had a whole band sitting in a room and all these cues were put in front of you and you had to really, really play – you didn't get a lot of takes. There were so many cues, but things were put in front of you, run through a couple of times and then you'd record. *ThunderCats* was very challenging, because a lot of the stuff didn't lay on guitar well; some of the intricate ensemble stuff might have been easier on trumpet, but was tricky on guitar. A lot of the solos weren't overdubbed, they were done there and then. I remember the theme tune was overdubbed because I needed to get really loud, and the engineer didn't want my track leaking onto the other microphones. But again it wasn't a case of taking all day, it was like, "We have a couple of minutes, go and do it". But everyone was so excited and loved doing these tracks because it was challenging and you felt you were using all your musical skills. It was original. Bernie didn't say, "I want it to sound like this," because "this" didn't exist. Bernie was making this stuff up from scratch.'

With the use of improvisation, good communication between musician and composer was paramount. Despite this, Hoffer placed a great deal of trust in the hands of his selected musicians. 'There was no discussion as such,' says Snyder. 'He just said, "It's your rock and roll solo." At the time, Van Halen had just come out, so I had that in my mind; I remember hearing "Eruption", where it was super high energy, so I was thinking the solo needed to be as high energy as I could make it. It wasn't a big discussion, it was more like, "Go do it, Craig, then we have to get to the next cue."'

As the *ThunderCats* music score required segments of various different running times, the same complex sequences would often need to be repeated on multiple occasions. 'It's not that difficult to replicate improvised solos,' says Snyder, 'because you're sort of trained to do it. It's really hard to duplicate something like feedback – if you get an accident like a great feedback effect, it never works again –

but we were all used to doing 15 second, 30 second, one minute versions [of the same piece]. It's built into your musicality. It would be more difficult for me now because I'm so used to cutting it in with Pro Tools. We just thought, "Let's go for it live". The musicianship of the band was great – I was always impressed with how good they were. I worked with these guys all the time, but when you get something difficult, you're impressed by your team mates and how lucky you are; the calibre makes you proud to be doing what you do.

'I had two main guitars. One was a '56 Fender Strat. For the other, I remember I'd just got off the road playing guitar for Roberta Flack and Diana Ross, and I'd had Roger Sadowsky, a big guitar maker, make me a guitar that I'd used with those artists, so I brought that along too. [So the playing was split] between my '56 Strat and a red Sadowsky. I had an artist deal with [the Japanese guitar company] Ibanez, and they gave me pedals and stuff, so it was probably Ibanez distortion pedals [I used]. But there wasn't a lot of time to set up, not like now where you take an enormous amount of time getting sounds. We just played it, and things were moving fast.'

Snyder believes Hoffer has never received the appreciation he deserves: 'Everything Bernie wrote was just "Wow, how did you do that?" I'll tell you, I'd always had respect for Bernie, but after these sessions, I thought that, if he'd been in LA, he'd have been as big as John Williams or any of those guys. Bernie, like everyone else, wanted to make sure he got what he wanted, and sessions back then ran from 10.00 am to 1.00 pm, or they might have done a double session, from 2.00 pm to 5.00 pm as well. 10.00 am till 1.00 pm meant you had to get all the work done within those three hours – and if there were musicians who weren't cutting it, they wouldn't be at the next session. That's different now; most sessions are done on Pro Tools.

'I remember doing the theme very well, because I liked the sound of that. Of all the things I've done musically, my kids loved the fact I did *ThunderCats*. I played for all those artists and I have a company with my wife doing music for commercials – a very successful company, which I've done for 15 years – but nothing impresses my children like *ThunderCats*, especially the theme tune. Someone sent me a ring tone of *ThunderCats* on a mono track, and they'd copied my guitar solo on a really cheesy synthesiser and got it note perfect.

'There's a guitar solo at the end of the ThunderTank theme too. We were supposed to keep playing and they were going to fade it out. My last note when we were recording was half a note off, and I wanted to re-record it so badly. The engineer said, "Don't worry, nobody will hear it, we'll fade it out", but I was so into it and improvising that I really wanted to redo it. I also remember a lot of the drum work – I was really impressed with the drummer, he was ripping it up. I just didn't want it all to end. It was challenging and fun, and I wish Bernie had done that – a new season – every year for the last 30 years. I wish on Monday I had another date to play with Bernie. Not to say there aren't great musicians now, but there's a certain level [of musicianship] from the old school where everyone wrote stuff out and people didn't write on sequencers. You don't see that very often anymore; it's just not done that much. All that stuff that Bernie did, none of it was done on sequencers.'

Perhaps the most distinctive 'sound' of the *ThunderCats* cues can be attributed to Snyder's work. From his power solo in the theme tune, to some sublime riffs in a variety of additional pieces, his effortless playing truly captured the mood of the series, imbuing the visuals with power and pace.

Describing his career beyond these recordings, Snyder is delighted to have remained in the music industry: 'I had my own record deal with RCA, and I've done thousands of commercials; produced arranged and played on them. I've played on so many albums and Broadway shows. I was one of the original guitar players in the show *Grease*; the original production. I played on Elton John albums, and one of the most fun albums in the 80s was by Edgar Winter; I did a great album with him. It's funny, when I look back, it's all these great things. I got to produce Spinal Tap for an IBM commercial in the '90s, so I had to fly out to LA, and that was a real ball. They wrote this thing called *Goat Boy*. All these things you do as a musician. I've been really fortunate. I've played some really serious stuff, then some bizarre stuff: *The Brady Bunch* and *ThunderCats*. It's been a great fun ride staying in the music business, being fortunate enough to be successful, raise a family and have a successful business.'

In addition to strong guitar segments, Hoffer's score for *ThunderCats* also made extensive use of percussion and drum sections, featuring the talents of drummer Barry Lazarowitz. Lazarowitz's career includes television, film and album session recordings, including for notable artists such as Leonard Cohen, Dusty Springfield and Judy Collins. His work also involves soundtrack recordings as diverse as the *National Lampoon* films and the 1981 movie *Dressed to Kill*.

'I grew up in New York City, studied drums from a young age and went to Manhattan School of Music (College),' explains Lazarowitz. 'Always wanting to be a studio musician, I pursued that by performing with as many diversified acts and musicians as I could. I met Bernie Hoffer after gaining a foothold in the New York studio scene. Beginning to build a name for myself, I began to play for him on numerous jingles and recording sessions that were a plentiful mainstay in New York in the '70s and '80s. I always loved working with Bernie; his arrangements were always so "right on" for whatever he was writing for. His drum parts were a pleasure to read, at times both complex and hard and at other times smooth and grooving, which was exactly what the *ThunderCats* arrangements were. What I remember of the *ThunderCats* recording sessions is first and foremost how much fun was had and how exciting the music sounded. It was driving and inspiring to play, so well written, the perfect mix of what Bernie wanted, played partly as written (because of orchestral importance) and partly improvised.

'The drum set was a Yamaha studio set, typical for the period. 22" bass, 12", 13" rack toms, and a 16" floor tom, 14" snare, one ride cymbal, and two crashes. As far as I know, I was the only drummer on both seasons. However, there was a percussionist playing tympani etc for the orchestral parts, as part of the orchestra. I do remember how much fun and how exciting it was to play those fight scenes with the percussion and drums exchanging moments. Most of those moments were clearly written, as one would write for percussion ensemble, but Bernie would give me the freedom to play certain specific rhythms on whichever toms I decided to play. I would tune the drums down to sound immense, big and fat and try to rock as hard as possible on the groove sections.'

Lazarowitz remains an active musician and still performs regularly with

Peter Duchin (the son of celebrated American band leader Eddie Duchin) at venues across the world. He remains delighted to have played his part in the production of *ThunderCats'* soundtrack: 'All in all, it was truly a wonderful experience, and it's so exciting to know it is still so greatly appreciated. It was and still is quite a remarkable piece of music, so very well written and arranged, even if it was for a cartoon series. Bernie Hoffer is a class act. No matter what he would write for, be it a jingle or an orchestral piece, he brings everything to the table, he never compromises his musical integrity. If there's one thing I've learned from him, it's to do your best and give the most you can to whatever you're doing, no matter what it is. He's always appeared to do that.'

Though Hoffer's work drew on classical styles, he did not ignore the growing trend in electronic music. But while much 1980s music would be defined by an over-reliance on synthesisers, his subtle use of the latest recording equipment and techniques enhanced the *ThunderCats* score without causing it to sound dated in later years. To perform his synthesiser sequences, Hoffer turned to musician Pete Cannarozzi.

'I'm from Chicago, Illinois,' says Cannarozzi. 'I Moved to NYC in 1979 and soon became a sought-after studio musician because of my synthesiser playing and programming abilities. I met Bernie Hoffer on a jingle session and he asked me to come to the sessions for *ThunderCats* and play synthesiser and create the sounds for the show. I was hired as a synthesiser player and programmer to play parts and create sounds for 65 episodes. We had many recording sessions with Bernie Hoffer and the Rankin/Bass producers in order to create this library, which was used for all the shows.'

Cannarozzi recalls, with amusement, Hoffer's approach to his music: 'In the studio, as I was in the process of creating a sound using a multitude of rack and keyboard synthesisers and digital FX, Bernie would blurt out ... "Don't improve it!" At that point, we would record the part and sound, then order a lot of sushi. It was a true honour to work with Bernie Hoffer and Lee Dannacher, the producer for Rankin/Bass. We worked with the best musicians in NYC, and made great music for television. People still ask me about it to this day.'

Asked about this notorious desire to let his music unfold naturally rather than be 'over-thought', Hoffer recalls that executive producer Jules Bass shared his views: 'Jules would say [the same thing] when a take was good enough. Don't improve it into a disaster.'

Cannarozzi describes the equipment he provided for the sessions: 'I brought in all my own gear and two huge racks of outboard gear, including my own mixer. We very rarely used studio equipment. At the time, I believe I used an Oberheim Eight Voice Modular Synthesiser, a Roland Jupiter 8 keyboard (and rack) and a Roland MSQ 700 Sequencer. There may have been others, but these were my main boards at the time.

'It's really hard to recall those days for me, because I was so busy with other projects. But having listened to the recordings, I believe I recognise my work on a number of cues, including: "Vision through the Sword Hole", "Sword Eye of Thundera", "The Living Ooze" and "The Whirlpool of Infinity". I believe I may have had something to do with "The Roar", but it doesn't sound like it's all me.

'The technique would be to take direction from Bernie, add my own suggestions, then search for and program a sound until we both liked it.

Sometimes it would be a complex combination of multiple synths, sometimes a more simple tone, sometimes a basic patch with a digital effect, and sometimes a "sequence". It was always different depending on the direction and my inspiration. I would play with the orchestra if it was a typical "keyboard" sound and part, but any "SFX" type sounds were always overdubbed later because of the creativity involved.'

In common with his *ThunderCats* musical colleagues, Cannarozzi has had a long and successful career: 'My career was in full throttle at the time. I worked on numerous albums, films and jingles. Currently, I am a music producer for my own music company, Pete Cannarozzi Music (www.cannarozzi.us). Also, I am active as the musical director for Ashford and Simpson concerts, and I am the organist for the NHL's New Jersey Devils at the Prudential Centre in Newark, New Jersey.'

The list below describes the complete orchestral set up that was assembled for both seasons of *ThunderCats* and reveals the many talented musicians who gave life to Hoffer's score:

SEASON ONE

Sessions 1 and 2: 14 August 1984, 11.00 am – 2.00 pm, 3.00 pm - 6.00 pm

Bernard Hoffer	Leader-Orchestrator
Sigmond Singer	Contractor
Barry Lazarowitz	Drums
Jay Leonhart	Bass
Craig Snyder	Guitar
Patrick Rebillot	Piano
David Gilbert	Flute and Piccolo
George Marge	Reeds
Albert Regni	Reeds
John Campo	Low Reeds
Marvin Stamm	Trumpet
David Gale	Trumpet
Robert Millikan	Trumpet
Sharon Moe	Horn
Peter Gordon	Horn
John Clark	Horn
Tony Studd	Trombone
David Bargeron	Trombone
Paul Faulise	Bass Trombone
Tony Price	Tuba
Sigmond Singer	Percussion

Session 3: 15 August 1984, 10.00 am - 1.00 pm

Same personnel as above except:
Joseph Shapley replaces Marvin Stamm   Trumpet

Session 4: 15 August 1984, 2.00 pm - 5.00 pm

Same personnel as above except:
James Pugh replaces David Bargeron   Trombone

Session 5: 16 August 1984, 10.00 am - 1.00 pm

Same personnel as above except:
John Frosk replaces Marvin Stamm   Trumpet
Robert Routch replaces Peter Gordon   Horn
Gregory Williams replaces John Clark   Horn

Session 6: 16 August 1984, 2.00 pm - 5.00 pm

Same personnel as above except:
Jerry Peel replaces Sharon Moe   Horn
James Pugh replaces David Bargeron   Trombone

Session 7: 17 August 1984

Same personnel as above except:
Jerry Peel replaces John Clark   Horn

Sessions 8 and 9: 21 August 1984, 10.00 am - 1.00 pm and 2.00 pm - 5.00 pm
Sessions 10 and 11: 22 August 1984, 10.00 am - 1.00 pm and 2.00 pm - 5.00 pm

Peter Cannarozzi   Synthesisers, electronics

SEASON TWO

Session 1: 25 August 1986, 10.00 am - 1.00 pm

Bernard Hoffer   Leader-Orchestrator
Sigmond Singer   Contractor
Craig Snyder   Guitar
Barry Lazarowitz   Drums
Wayne Pedziwaitr   Bass
Patrick Rebillot   Piano
Raymond Beckenstein   Reeds
Albert Regni   Reeds
Robert Steen   Reeds
John Campo   Reeds

Sharon Moe	Horn
Ronald Sell	Horn
Anthony Miranda	Horn
Marvin Stamm	Trumpet
David Gale	Trumpet
Robert Millikan	Trumpet
Tony Studd	Trombone
John Gale	Trombone
George Flynn	Bass Trombone
Carl Kleinsteuber	Tuba
Sigmond Singer	Percussion
Peter Cannarozzi	Synthesisers

Session 2: 25 August 1986, 2.00 pm - 5.00 pm

Same personnel as above except:

David Tofani replaces Raymond Beckenstein Reeds	
Peter Gordon replaces Ronald Sell	Horn
Wayne Andre replaces John Gale	Trombone
David Taylor replaces George Flynn	Bass Trombone

Session 3: 26 August 1986, 10.00 am - 1.00 pm

Same personnel as above except:

David Tofani replaces Raymond Beckenstein Reeds	
Peter Gordon replaces Ronald Sell	Horn
John Clark replaces Anthony Miranda	Horn
Wayne Andre replaces John Gale	Trombone
David Taylor replaces George Flynn	Bass Trombone

Session 4: 26 August 1986, 2.00 pm - 5.00 pm

Same personnel as above except:

Harvey Estrin replaces Raymond Beckenstein	Reeds
James Pugh replaces Tony Sudd	Trombone
Wayne Andre replaces John Gale	Trombone

The teams of musicians assembled for these sessions provided the orchestral sound Bernard Hoffer had envisaged for his score, but he still had to locate the vocalists who would sing on both the theme tune and its associated stings and idents. For the main vocals, he chose session singers Margaret Dorn and Peter Thom. 'The vocals were dubbed after the music tracks were done,' he explains. 'They were layered so that each of them made several passes.'

'I first met Bernard Hoffer at a jingle session in 1983,' recalls Dorn. 'He recommended that I get in touch with a music house called MZH – owned by Morris Mamorsky, Jack Zimmerman and Tommy Hamm. Bernie had worked with these gentlemen for many years and he brought me into the family there. Everyone was lovely to work with and they took me under their collective wings. It wasn't long before I came to love them all – most especially Bernie.

'I started writing for the house, and one of the perks was singing on almost all the sessions. Over the years, I sang on several Rankin/Bass cartoon theme songs written by Bernie: *Street Frogs*, *Karate Kats* and a couple of others the names of which I don't remember. Of all the themes, my favourite was *ThunderCats*. The fact that I remember it so well speaks to how musical and exciting it was. I watched the show as often as I could – and it was always fun to sing along to the theme. Almost as much fun as we had recording it! Bernie Hoffer's range as a composer is amazing. I became a big fan of his work – from his modern orchestral pieces to his wonderful theme for the *MacNeil-Lehrer NewsHour* (still used today – though [not the original version]) and his commercials. A session with Bernie was always fun, especially on the cartoons, and the stories he told of his experiences in the business were a fascinating look into the life of a gifted musician. I learned so much about writing music from those days – and I owe a great deal to Bernie for sharing his gifts and his wonderful spirit with all of us.'

'I remember Margaret very well,' says Peter Thom. 'I also wrote sporadically for MZH. But by the time I sang this theme [for *ThunderCats*] I was working full time as a jingle singer and my writing was confined to songs for album projects. Bernie's talent was evident via his arrangements for hundreds, maybe thousands of commercials and in his own symphonic creations. As an aside, he and I played chess, and as I well recall, he was a formidable opponent, able to think ahead with ease. We lived in the same neighbourhood and always stopped for long philosophical discussions, sometimes joined in by passing friends of his.'

Of Hoffer's working techniques, Thom says: 'You need to know that the kind of arranging that Bernie did for years gave very little lead time and required many sleepless nights. But he always appeared fresh during those morning sessions. The jingle singers recorded their bits after prior recording of rhythm, string and horn sections. The arrangers were there before anybody else, sometimes receiving the copyist's work and inevitably making corrections. As I recall, the *ThunderCats* sessions were done in the evening, which made sense if Bernie wanted to hire decent singers. Bernie's music was always completely written out, though he allowed for architectural tweaking of harmonic textures and melodic embellishment.'

Asked about the differences between recording albums and screen music, Thom comments: 'Singing for albums is a much more stretched out procedure. In a jingle session, the composer generally played the track or went over the tune on the piano once or twice and then recording began. Most often, the lead singer would scratch out the tune, the backgrounds would be added and the lead would tweak his/her track. All this generally took place in a two to three hour session and was usually the final stage before mixing. The singers would almost never have heard the tune previously. But singers were weeded out if they couldn't be ready for prime time within about five to ten minutes. Singing for albums is, for the lead anyway, a long process. In my case, I'd lived with the tunes for weeks to months. And you had the time to revisit and perfect performances – though some would argue that a bit of rawness was lost through this search for perfection. The bottom line was that time was of the essence in jingle recording. Time constraints were much less for album recording.'

The original cue sheets for *ThunderCats* are reproduced below:

Season One Cue Sheets:

'THUNDERCATS' MAIN TITLE SONG
1   1:15 w/lyric
2   1:15 instrumental Version
END CREDITS
3   0:40 Instrumental of main theme
VOCAL CUE 'A'
4   0:05 First 4 bars w/vocal   WILL BE SHORTER
VOCAL CUE 'B'
5   0:11+ Second 4 bars w/vocal (Time casual)
VOCAL CUE 'C'
6   0:11+ Third 4 bars w/vocal (Time casual)
VOCAL CUE 'D'
7   0:11+ Last 4 bars w/vocal (Time casual)
MAIN TITLE – GENERAL BACKGROUND
8   1:00 Instrumental
9   1:15 Instrumental
10   1:30 Instrumental
11   0:15 Instrumental LITE VERSION
12   0:30 Instrumental LITE VERSION (For epilogues, etc)
13   0:45 Instrumental LITE VERSION
14   1:00 Instrumental LITE VERSION
15   0:15 SPECIAL LEAD-IN before MAIN INSTRUMENTAL
'CHEETARA's THEME'
16   0:30
17   1:30
18   3:00
'PANTHRO's THEME'
19   0:15
20   0:45
21   2:30
'TYGRA's THEME'
22   0:20
23   1:00
24   2:45
'SNARF's THEME'
25   0:20 Moody
26   0:20 Comical *
27   0:20 Jog Along
28   0:20 Meanish
29   0:20 Sad
30   0:30 COMICAL*
31   0:20 Top speed Running
'SWORD ('EYE') OF THUNDERA THEME'
32   0:05

33   0:10

34   0:20

'MUMM-RA's THEME'

36   0:10

37   0:30

38   1:30

39   4:00

'S-S-S-SLITH's THEME'

40   0:10

41   0:30

42   1:30

'CASTLE PLUN-DARR'

43   0:05 Looming in distance – ominous

44   0:10 (loop) for interior use

'THUNDERCATs' LAIR'

45   0:05

46   0:10 (loop)

****<u>MOODS</u> – Ends can loop to tops for endless play ****

     'THE BOTTOMLESS CHASM'

47   0:30

     'THE DESERT OF SINKING SANDS'

48   0:30

     'THE FOREST OF SILENCE'

49   0:30

     'THE GARDEN OF DELIGHTS'

50   0:30

     'THE LIVING OOZE'

51   0:30

     'THE SNOWMEN OF HOOK MOUNTAIN'

52   0:30

     'THE RIVER OF DESPAIR'

53   0:30

     'THE WHILPOOL OF INFINITY'

54   0:30

     'THE SPONGE FOG'

55   0:30

     'THE SERPENT SWAMP'

56   0:30

     'TENSION' General

57   0:10 +

58   1:00

     ANTICIPATION – Danger

59   0:10+

     'UNPLEASANT UNDERCURRENT'

60   0:10 +

****END MOODS ****

'BATTLE' ThunderCats Winning

61   1:00

62   1:30
'BATTLE' ThunderCats losing
63   1:00
'BATTLE' Mutants in control
64   1:00
'BATTLE' Mutants on the run
65   1:00
'BATTLE ACTION' General backgrounds
66   1:00
67   2:00
68   3:00
'IMPACT AND ATTACK' Intense
69   0:30
70   0:45
71   1:00
72   1:30
73   3:00
'THUNDER-TANK CHASE'
74   0:20
75   1:00
76   1:15
77   1:30
'BRAVERY' Brave but withheld – march to destiny
78   0:10
79   0:30
80   0:45
81   1:00
'CAT PROWL' in Jungle
82   0:20 (Loop)
'TEMPO' Movement – very simple rhythm VARIOUS CLICKS
83   0:30   click # Increase clicks
84   0:30   click #
85   0:30   click #
'THE SWORD' Standard Action
86   0:00   Lion-O Holds up arm – outstretched
        0:04   Does "Thunder-call-to-Ho-sword growls
        0:10   Beam into sky
        0:12   Growl out (Symbol in sky animates)
        0:15-0:18
NOTE: We should be able to superimpose the sword cue over a music CUE
'SHORT BATTLES'
87   0:10
88   0:15
89   0:20
'DANGER APPROACHING'
90   0:10 Building to climax
91   0:20 " " "
92   0:30

93   1:00
'VISION THRU SWORD-HOLES'
94   0:05 Loop Magical
'TO THE RESCUE'
95   0:05
96   0:15
97   0:30
'PLAY-INS' ACTION
98   0:03+ Long overhang decaying to nothing
99   0:05 " " " "
'PLAY-INS' DANGER
100   0:03+
101   0:05
 'PLAY INS' SUSPENSE
102   0:03+
103   0:05+
'PLAY INS' Main Theme-Gen
104   0:03+
105   0:05+
'ACT ENDS' ACTION
106   0:03+ w/ending
107   0:05
'ACT ENDS' DANGER
108   0:03+
109   0:05
'ACT ENDS' SUSPENSE
110   0:03
111   0:05
'ACT ENDS' Main Theme-Gen
112   0:03
113   0:05
SHOW END Main Big
114   0:03
115   0:05
116   0:08
'TRANSITIONS'
117   0:03   Danger decay ends   OK to :05+
118   0:03   Suspense   "
119   0:03   Action   "
120   0:03   Comic Snarf   "
'BUMPERS OUT'
121   0:04   "A"
122   0:04   "B"
'BUMPERS IN'
123   0:04   "C"
124   0:04   "D"
MUMM-RA TRANSFORMATION
125   0:00   Incantation-building

126   0:13   Hit
127   0:16   Wild
128   0:20
'JAGA's THEME'
129   0:10
130   0:20
131   1:00
132   1:30
133   2:00
134   2:30
135   0:45   LITE VERSION
GOOD GUY CHASES
136   0:30
137   1:00
138   1:30
BAD GUY CHASES
139   0:30
140   1:00
141   1:30

Season Two Cue Sheets:

LION-O FIGHTS ALONE
142   1:30   (SHADES OF MT-HO!)   MAIN
143   0:30
LYNX-O The STRONG SAGE
144   1:00   JAGA LIKE
145   0:30
PUMYRA – The PARALYZER
146   1:00   LITE
147   0:30
BEN GALI – The BRAVE   HEROIC
148   1:30
149   0:45
MAIN TITLE – BACKGROUND
150   1:30   INST LITE
(w/new feel – somewhere between epilogue & previous generic lite)
151   1:00   INST LITE – DARKER MOOD
THE TOWER OF OMENS
152   0:15   LOOMING IN DISTANCE
153   0:30   LOOP (SHADES OF ABOVE) FOR INTERIOR USE
HOVERCAT + THUNDERCLAW (PANTHRO's NEW VEHICLES)
154   1:30   (CHASE-LIKE TANK)
155   0:30
SNARFER USE SNARF THEME
156   0:20   COMICAL
157   0:20   ON THEIR HEELS!

158	0:20	PETULANT
159	0:05	COMIC BUTTON

THE BESERKERS
160	2:00
161	1:00
162	0:30

MOON DEMONS ARE BACK!
163	1:45
164	0:30

FIST POUNDER – The MUTANT-MOBILE
165	1:00
166	0:30

MUMM-RA LIVES
167	2:00
168	1:00
169	0:15

VULTUREMAN's VENGEANCE
170	1:00
171	0:30

MA-MUTT The HIDEOUS
172	0:15	GROWLS
173	0:05	

SKY TOMB (BAD CASTLE)
174	0:15	LOOMING IN DISTANCE
175	0:30	LOOP (SHADES OF ABOVE) FOR INTERIOR USE

'PLAY – INS'
176	0:05	UNSETTLED
177	0:05	WITH A STING
178	0:05	MAIN- ACTIVE DANGER

'TRANSITION'
179	0:03	TROUBLE AHEAD
180	0:03	TROUBLE BEHIND
181	0:03	ZIP PAN

BATTLE ACTION – GENERAL (DIFFERENT CUES)
182	2:00
183	1:00

IMPACT & ATTACK
184	2:00
185	0:30

BATTLE – TCTS IN CONTROL
186	1:00

BATTLE – TCTS IN TROUBLE
187	1:00

BATTLE – Bad Guys WINNING
188	1:00

BATTLE – Bad Guys LOSING
189	1:00

**** MOOD LOOPS****

'FEASTLAND OF BERBILFRUIT'
190   0:30
'FIREY ROCK MOUNTAIN'
191   0:30
'DARKSIDE – The FORBIDDEN TERRITORY'
192   0:30
'THE FALLS OF INVULNERABILITY'
194   0:30
'UNPLEASANT UNDERCURRENT – 1987'
195   0:30
'THE VILLAGE OF MASKS'
196   0:30
197   LOOP

Recording and Editing

Over the course of two weeks, all of Bernard Hoffer's 165 cues for Series One were recorded at A & R Recording Studios, West 48th Street, New York City. Overseeing recording was audio engineer and musician Michael Farrow.

'I was a music major at Indiana University – trumpet performance,' says Farrow. 'Then I played trumpet professionally in symphony orchestras for 11 years before getting into pro audio. In 1978, I moved to NYC to work at Celebration Recording where I met and worked with Bernie Hoffer on an ongoing basis, with him as the composer and me as the recording engineer. We worked together on hundreds of commercials as well as films, records and TV projects. I was hired by Bernie for *ThunderCats* based on our long-standing studio relationship. We pre-recorded the themes and library for the series – before the animation was done.'

Explaining his responsibilities, Farrow adds: 'Bernie and I would have a pre-production meeting where he would explain to me what the musical style of the recording should be. I would then come up with a studio layout and mic selection that would suit the project. The orchestra rehearsed each cue for roughly ten minutes prior to recording it. I would also make musical comments during the recording about tuning, ensemble, style etc. Once it was recorded, Bernie and I would then mix and edit the material for final delivery. Bernie is a very talented musician and valued expression over perfection. Sometimes when a performance was exciting, but with a technical blemish, he would tell the player "Don't improve it," because Bernie knew that some of the life could be lost while trying to remove the technical flaws. I remember that if Bernie wanted more reverb, he'd ask for the sound to come "from Cleveland".'

Farrow is delighted to have worked on *ThunderCats*: 'Over the years, I have gotten many e-mails from strangers asking about *ThunderCats* and have honestly been amazed. *ThunderCats* was not a show that I personally ever watched, but my children are big fans. At the time, I was pleased to be working on a big project with Bernie. He was always a pleasure to work with.

'I continued working in NYC doing commercials and records. In the mid '80s I started doing more film work at RCA studios and wound up doing a lot of work on *Beauty and the Beast* and *Aladdin*. In 1993, I moved from the NYC area to Los

Angeles to be more involved in the film industry. Since then I have recorded and mixed the scores for many feature films, including *The Blind Side* and *A Serious Man*, both nominees for the Oscar for best picture.'

With a complete library of musical cues recorded, the tracks were handed over to Rankin/Bass for use in the series. They would be edited onto the dialogue tracks by a range of editors, mainly comprising employees and ex-employees of Howard Schwartz Recording Studios – the company hired to record and produce dialogue recordings for *ThunderCats*. This list predominantly included: Larry Franke, Tom Perkins, John Curcio, John Crenshaw, Tony Giovanniello and Michael Ungar.

Having had ultimate responsibility for overseeing the final recordings, supervising producer Lee Dannacher recalls the process: 'We'd record the dialogue tracks and time them like a radio show. Then, the next step on that soundtrack was to have the guys spot the music. We were doing this all without storyboard or pictures – only very rarely did we have a storyboard come to us [enabling us to use it] as inspiration. I was taught by Jules how to do it. For instance, if there was a 30 second gap for an action sequence, I'd spot ten seconds into that 30 second hole – "A tank blows up". With that kind of information, the guys could then decide how to spot the music and how to insert it, and that was then fully reviewed and shipped over to Japan. The animators would have got started [on their work] using the track with just dialogue, and we'd follow it with that same track but with music added to it about three weeks later.'

'The music masters were recorded on two-inch, 24-track tapes,' explains Larry Franke. 'Probably marked AMPEX 456 (tape stock). The cues were then mixed to ¼-inch stereo masters. The first thing we did was make one or two safety copies of the ¼- inch mixed cues. By the time we did the second season of *ThunderCats*, we had two studios running at the same time. Chronologically, things went as follows: year one, the first studio worked on *ThunderCats* season one. Year two, the first studio started on *SilverHawks*. Then, somewhere toward the end of *SilverHawks*, we opened a second studio to do *The Comic Strip*, and then finally the overflow of the second season of *ThunderCats*.

'My role was to record original dialogue with the actors. Then I edited the dialogue according to a "timed" script, slugging in blank leader tape where the action would take place. Then I selected the appropriate [voice] cues to be used for the action going on. That complete dialogue master was laid up to a 24-track blank tape on which many stereo pairs of tracks could be used to add music cues. I mixed this 24-track show master to a Nagra Pilot Tone tape, which was sent to Japan for the animators. This process was the reverse of the normal post-scoring technique, where the animation is done first and the music done afterward. The final show mixes were done to four blank tracks on these 24-track tapes, if I remember correctly – tracks 20, 21, 22 and 23. Track 20 was final dialogue with effects (harmoniser added to Mumm-Ra for example), 21 and 22 stereo music, and 23 any effects we added. Japan added the bulk of the sound effects but we added a few if they were crucial to script timing.'

Franke recalls his days on *ThunderCats* with great warmth: 'My favourite cues were most everything from *ThunderCats*' second season, and all of the *SilverHawks* cues. Bernie is a great and prolific composer who kept all of us musically stimulated for four years.'

Another editor who was deeply involved with music selection was Tom

Perkins. 'Once the editing and pacing of a show were locked in, it was sent to the animators in Japan,' he confirms. 'Then it was months before we'd get to see so much as a pencil test, as this was cel animation, hand drawn. Somewhere within that time period I'd do a music mix, even before the picture was finished ... My favourite cue was Mumm-Ra's theme, ponderous and dangerous with a fabulous gong in it. There were cues for action sequences, soft moods, sad moods, light moods etc. The way it worked was, I'd stripe a two-inch, 24-track tape with sync and transfer the edited voices to that. The voice tape was edited with the proper amount of time left for commercials etc, so the total length was 30 minutes (if it was a half hour show, as most were). I would then slot in appropriate music for whatever was happening; I'd still have the marked script indicating where action and what type of action was to take place.

'I had pretty much full autonomy on music choices, which was great, since I tend to think outside the box when scoring. For instance, after a few shows, I was running out of creative ways to use certain cues, and there were a few moods I felt weren't covered with enough variety. I was feeling adventurous and even threw a few cues in played backwards to create more chaos in some of the action sequences. I had a feeling I'd be overruled and have to redo things to a more strict standard, but I was pleasantly surprised when I got back notes that they loved what I was doing and I should feel free to go further. So I did. I re-edited some of the cues, layered some with others, and frequently used Mumm-Ra's gong backwards. It was a great tension-builder. That kind of creative freedom is one of the things I most enjoy about my work, and I love working with people who aren't afraid to take risks. Once in a great while, I'd get a note about something they didn't feel was working, but that was very rare. I tried to keep each episode fresh and not get into a rut using the same cues all the time for the action sequences. It was hard to keep it fresh, but eminently worth it to put in the extra effort – I think that may be one of the things about the show that's helped it to retain an audience all these years.'

While Hoffer's music was perfectly suited to the style and substance of *ThunderCats*, it was the editors that ensured appropriate cues were selected for any given scene. 'Someone in my past once said that there are four elements to audio production,' says Perkins. 'Voice, music, sound effects, and silence. The least used is silence, and it can be used effectively if done right. Sometimes I found no music under a part was more effective than anything else. I tried all manner of things from drones to stings to abrupt changes or sudden stops. Anything to help advance the story – my one rule was that being creative for creativity's sake is meaningless. You have to advance the story, and I tried always to do that with my part. I worked alone, without supervision, and I valued that trust highly.'

Speaking about the set of additional cues recorded for *ThunderCats* second season, Perkins explains his desire for a new selection of music: 'I do remember making a case for more cues, and seem to recall giving Lee a list of moods and such that would be helpful, and a list of "more like this" kind of things, but I'm totally blanking on how they sounded. I'm pretty sure all of us who were working on the show asked for more music, not just me. I seem to recall that I wasn't as enthused about the newer cues, but there were a few real gems in there that I used a lot for variety. That's not to detract from Bernie's talent, by the way! It was simply a personal preference for the style of the original cues. By the time the second season was underway, I was doing more *SilverHawks*, I think, and less *ThunderCats*. As I was freelancing and doing a lot more work at other studios, I wasn't doing as many *ThunderCats* shows as before. I think Larry Franke was doing more than I by then. But it was good to have new cues and did provide some stimulus and stave off boredom! New things to play backwards ...'

For a generation, the music of *ThunderCats* will never be forgotten. Even now, a legion of fans continue to campaign for an official release of Hoffer's soundtrack. With groundbreaking standards of television animation being produced by PAC, the musicality of Bernard Hoffer delivered an incidental score for *ThunderCats* every bit as exciting, dramatic and enchanting as could ever have been hoped for.

5. OUT OF SIGHT
The Voices Behind the Characters

Modern audiences could be forgiven for thinking that animated features are synonymous with celebrity. With huge, multi-million pound animated productions regularly turning to A-list stars to voice their lead-roles, it is easy to forget that a whole industry of professional voice artists exist. For *ThunderCats*, Rankin/Bass turned to leading talent agencies to provide an ensemble of skilled individuals to handle the many vocal requirements of the series.

Supervising producer Lee Dannacher discusses her search for the *ThunderCats* voice artists: 'We had worked with several casting agencies in New York for the many productions we'd already been through, and Arthur and Jules had done it for a lot longer than when I showed up. I got to know [the agents]. Lester Lewis was one we used a lot; I can't remember the others right now. But, number one, we knew Bob McFadden was on [to be cast]; he was a given. He'd done Rankin/Bass shows for years; an extraordinary talent and a beautiful man. Now I look back at it, he was the only one we just knew, "Bob, just show up, you'll do three or four voices, we'll figure it out when we get there".

'By that time, we had the *ThunderCats* bible and we knew the characters ... In other studios, they'd work with casting directors, and this is how we'd work on feature films, we'd cast for each character. Under the Rankin/Bass method, we called the agents and said, "We're doing a cartoon show, it's action adventure, it's pretty much heroes and villains and over-the-top people – so send us your best people who can do wacky, not cartoon voices, but unusual voices and straight Joe American superhero voices". Then Jules and I went over to a little recording studio, and we were over there two or three days back to back. I think we saw only about 20 people, which is not large at all, but I can remember that we were sitting there in a little booth, and it was just Jules and me and an engineer. One by one, these actors would come in and we'd give them some sides to read – good guy characters and bad guys –and they'd just improvise. We'd give feedback from the booth, "Try this and try that". Bobby McFadden was there to play off of them, but he was a given; he'd sit there and inspire the actors to give us voices.

'I can remember so well when Larry Kenney showed up – he's so much on the money, that guy. Jules said, "Give us Jack Armstrong[2]," and the minute he came out with that one strong, believable voice, Jules looked at me and said, "Okay he's Lion-O". We had him fool around with some more voices, and we

[2] The hero of *Jack Armstrong, the All-American Boy*, a radio adventure serial that ran from 1933 to 1951.

had a chart in front of us, which we'd put tick marks on for Lion-O. The other one who turned up was Earl Hammond, who was a dear friend of mine – they all were, but he was so special. He came in, and he was a big man, six foot something, and he had this extraordinary voice. He'd already come up with something he thought was possible for Mumm-Ra, and that was just it, there was no feedback from me or Jules about that one. [He and Bob McFadden] got us laughing, it was so perfect. We said, "Mr Hammond, can you do anything funny," and he just started on a riff with Bob McFadden. It was unbelievable.'

Structured like a vintage radio-play, the Rankin/Bass recordings required only a select few performers who would, between them, play an entire cast of regular and guest characters. The small cast would record their performances together in one sound booth, forging a 'family' relationship between the team, each performer benefiting from the energy and enthusiasm generated by the others. This method of recording is almost extinct in the industry today, owing to the potential of cross-contamination from microphones and the practicality of assembling the entire cast for each day's recording. On *ThunderCats*, however, it injected a pace and authenticity that meant that lines were always delivered with a collective passion.

'A lot of people accused us of trying to save money by having actors do two or three voices each,' recalls Dannacher, 'but it wasn't that at all, because our budget was very generous – we could almost write our own budget at that time, and if we needed to spend the money it was there. It was simply the experience Jules and Arthur had with casting for voice characters. When you've got a guy like Bob McFadden – a guy with a thousand voices – or Earl Hammond, why would you want others? With the casting of someone like Earle Hyman, we wanted something different; we didn't want a Bob McFadden who could handle anything, like a tiny Berbil in the script in addition to his other two roles that day. Earle might do only one voice, but it was so good, so classical, you couldn't not do it. Earle had never done this kind of work before, he was a stage actor, a theatre actor – he would act Shakespeare in Swedish, because he lived in Sweden or Norway. He was limited, in the early days, because his vocal quality was too similar on each of his characters, but with Mike Ungar and Larry Franke [in charge of sound editing], a little tremolo [could be added] and Earle could have his second part. It was just wonderful to find these people, including Peter Newman and Lynne Lipton, who was the only woman [in the cast] – but she's like a Bob McFadden, she could do so much; comedy or straight. Here we had a group of five or so people playing multiple characters every time, and they just kept giving; there was no reason to bring in people for special roles.'

Robert McFadden and Earl Hammond were well known in the industry, and Larry Kenney had built a career in radio, progressing to become known for his vocal versatility. Lynne Lipton also came to the series with existing acting credits both on-screen and as a voice actor. A less experienced cast member was Peter Newman, who nonetheless proved his worth as a strong performer who could tackle a wide range of accents and characters. Finally, although less experienced than his colleagues in voice-over work, Earle Hyman was one of the most accomplished actors of the group. He had a wide range of credits to his name on both stage and screen, and his career had already spanned five decades by the time he came to work on *ThunderCats*.

With a full cast assembled, dialogue recording began in earnest at the Howard Schwartz Recording Studios in Midtown Manhattan, New York. Larry Kenney explains how the recording sessions were arranged: 'We recorded on Thursdays and Fridays from approximately 9.00 am to 5.00 pm, doing two episodes per day. The first 13 episodes had been written prior to our first session, so we finished those in seven consecutive weeks. Once the series was sold (to TelePictures) there was a break of a month or two to allow the writers to develop new scripts. From then through production of all 130 episodes, we worked only two days per month ... again, Thursdays and Fridays, but sometimes on other days to accommodate holidays etc.'

After discussions between executive producer Jules Bass and supervising producer Lee Dannacher, lead roles were divided between the actors. In addition to one or two regular roles the cast would perform in a typical script, there would also be regular 'try-outs' for guest roles on an episode-by-episode basis. Incredibly, during the course of the entire first series, these six voice artists portrayed hundreds of individual characters, with Bob McFadden alone providing over 40 voices.

After 65 shows, two more performers were added to the cast. Both Gerrianne Raphael and Doug Preis had previously worked in the industry and were able to add to the extraordinary talent already on offer. 'I don't think it would have been too discernable to the kid audience,' says Lee Dannacher, 'but we bought Gerrianne and Doug in because I and the engineers had heard so much from [the original six] actors, and they'd heard so much from each other over 65 shows. We were developing a whole new set of bad guys, the LunaTaks, and a whole new slew of things, and I wanted to do even more, but we thought we'd start with a few new faces in there. It was to spice things up. After 65 shows, everyone's tired, [and it's helpful to have] a new person to bounce a script idea off, or a new character designer to get everyone enthused again, to come in wide-eyed and say, "Isn't this fun, I've got this to offer." It also brings [established] people back to their A game. It's not that the original actors couldn't have continued to surprise us, but it was to develop that whole world.'

Voice Artist Profiles

The profiles below are based on interviews with the *ThunderCats* cast members conducted specially for this book. It should be noted that no official documentation exists stating which characters are attributable to which cast members. The character lists given below are the result of a tireless efforts by fans on internet forums to identify the correct artist in each case. Though the list has been corroborated by the artists themselves, some minor characters (which feature heavily modified or distorted voices) are unsubstantiated.

Larry Kenney
Characters Portrayed: Lion-O, Jackalman, Tug-Mug, Amok, Ratar-O, Claudus, Safari Joe, Ratilla the Terrible, Wizz-Ra, The Inflamer, Kano, Snarf Egbert, Scrape, Merlin, Tor, Charr, Zaxx, Giant Spider Minion ('Queen of 8 Legs'), Vertus Slave Driver ('Sword in the Hole'), Caveman ('Time Capsule'), Spaceship Voice ('The Transfer'), Haunted Boatman ('Anointment Trial Day 5'), Mumm-Ra's Servant ('Totem of Dera'), Thundarian Stone Giant ('Mossland Monster'), Tuska Warrior ('ThunderCats Ho!') SWAN Pilot, Radio Reporter ('Cracker's Revenge')

'I started in radio in 1963 as a disc jockey in Peoria, Illinois,' says Larry Kenney. 'Later, I worked at stations in Ft. Wayne, Cleveland, Chicago, and New York. I Added commercial voice-over work to the mix while in Cleveland in 1970 and became a member of the cast of *Imus in the Morning* in 1973 (until 2008). I also hosted the game show *Bowling for Dollars* on WOR-TV New York from 1976-79.'

Speaking about how he came to be hired by Rankin/Bass, Kenney reveals that his agent arranged the audition: 'I was shown drawings and descriptions of the major characters. I was given a brief synopsis of the overall series, given several minutes to study the material and then asked to read a few lines of any of the characters I wanted to audition for. I believe I read for Lion-O, Tygra, Ratar-O and Mumm-Ra. I felt, as did the producers, that Lion-O's voice should be my own natural voice, slightly dramatised.'

Asked if he was considered for the role of any other lead character, Kenney recalls that he wasn't advised of the initial decision-making process. However, the allocation of secondary characters to cast members took a more collaborative approach: 'Lee Dannacher, the "in-studio" producer, made those decisions. At the beginning of each recording session, she would describe and show pictures of any new characters and either offer us all the opportunity to audition or ask particular actors to read for each part. When she heard what she liked, she assigned the role.

'We usually performed a script from beginning to end. If a particular scene was interrupted by a flashback or something, we might skip the interruption and record the entire scene for continuity of character, etc. Barring illness or other situations (for example, an actor's commitment to another project), the entire cast would be present at each session.'

When a scene called for two of his characters to be in active dialogue, Kenney believes that performing it in 'real time' proved the most effective approach: 'I preferred that method. Others might record all of one character's lines, then all the other character's lines. As time went on, and we each became the voices of more and more characters, it of course became more difficult to develop new, unique voices. When a new one was assigned, the actor could ask to hear bits of any of his previously-recorded voices, and make appropriate adjustments. Lee Dannacher of course was there to catch any similarities with past performances and offer advice, as were the engineers and the other actors. We worked incredibly well together at this.'

Larry Kenney is incredibly enthusiastic about his years spent recording *ThunderCats*, listing the series as one of his greatest professional achievements. 'I wouldn't have changed a thing' he says warmly. 'We had a *lot* of fun. My fondest memory was watching Earl Hammond portray Mumm-Ra, the demonic leader of the Mutants. He visually became the animated character … eyes blazing, arms uplifted, head reared back. As he roared "Ancient Spirits of Evil ..." he actually drooled and spat like his on-screen counterpart. Anytime we got within a paragraph of that trademark Mumm-Ra line, every actor began backing away from Earl's microphone, until no-one was within ten feet of him. Bob McFadden was hilarious, too. He'd often deliver a line as Snarf, look through the glass at Lee Dannacher, and sensing her disapproval of his delivery, mutter "Mother, they hated it!" Bob and Earl were two of the kindest, most generous, lovely people I've ever met. I love and miss them both dearly.'

Regarding the technical requirements of recording dialogue for the show, Kenney acknowledges that retakes were nearly always required: 'On a project like this, you rarely record just one take of a line. Lee Dannacher, the greatest producer on Earth, directed *every* episode. Timing was ultimately important ... and it was all up to Lee Dannacher. It was she who would ask us to speed up or slow down a line, a phrase or a paragraph.'

Comparing *ThunderCats* with his many other career highlights, Kenney believes the most obvious difference was the length of recording time. '130 episodes!' he jokes. 'But the most important aspect was the wonderful people I got to work with. As you know, the series didn't hit the air until a year after we began recording. So we didn't know what we had on our hands until then. Once it had been on TV for a few months, we knew it was huge. I feel extremely proud to have been a part of not only *ThunderCats*, but all of the Rankin/Bass productions. [The show's] success, I think, lies in the talents of *everyone* who worked on it, from the producers to the writers, animators, engineers ... and of course the voice actors. Added to that, of course, was the *love* we all had for the project.'

After the recording of *ThunderCats*, Larry Kenney was also involved in *SilverHawks* (for which he played the character Bluegrass) and *The Comic Strip*. In addition to his accomplishments in entertainment (on screen and radio), he has been heavily involved in the advertising industry, voicing the popular Count Chocula and Sonny the Cookoo Bird characters in a series of commercials.

Earle Hyman
Characters Portrayed: Panthro, Red Eye, Cruncher, Ancient Spirits of Evil (second voice), Nemex, Nemesis Force of Darkness ('Doom Gaze', 'Queen of 8 Legs'), Snarf Oswald, Thundarian Guard ('Return to Thundera'), Penal Planet Guard ('Mandora and The Pirates'), Vertus Pilot ('Sword in a Hole', 'ThunderCats Ho!'), Vertus Guard ('ThunderCats Ho!'), Underdweller 2 ('Anointment Trials Day 3'), Trollog 2 ('Eye of the Beholder'), Malcar's Adoptive Father

'I loved *ThunderCats* – five years of absolute joy!' enthuses Earle Hyman. '[I had not done other] voice-overs except for commercials; maybe a couple. My main career was in the theatre, which I loved and still do. I've done some films and an awful lot of television. I was asked to come in for an audition for a voice-over for this animated series, and when I heard the word "cats" I jumped, because I'm passionate about cats. At the moment, I have four that come in every night to get supper. So with joy I went there and thought, "Standing up in front of a microphone and acting being a cat – wow, what could be more beautiful!" At the same time, I was doing *The Cosby Show* as Bill Cosby's father – it all just seemed too good to be true. But it was wonderful, and I auditioned for *ThunderCats* and found myself being Panthro.'

Hyman boasted a long and varied career in film, television and theatre, and his powerful voice and reputation as a character actor fulfilled Rankin/Bass's criteria effortlessly. '[I remember I went in] and they showed me the drawings of Panthro that were done in Japan and then sent to us for doing the voices,' he explains. 'We looked at and studied the drawings and tried to come up with a voice that we thought belonged to the character. That wonderful woman Lee Dannacher, our director, was heaven, and I read for her, and the next thing I knew they said, "You're Panthro. We'll be in touch for the first recording!"'

Asked about a 'typical' recording session, Hyman reveals the learning curve he encountered adapting his skills to voice acting: 'I'm not sure if I got a script before the recording, but the script was in front of us all the time on music stands when we recorded. The drawings were also there if you wanted to refer to them, but I never looked at them once I'd studied them and got the voices. Then we recorded like an old radio play, except it took me some time to fit into the extraordinary work the rest of the voice cast did. Doing a voice for a cartoon isn't quite the same as acting, and I had to learn. At first, it was a little bit difficult for me. I thought I could just act Panthro, but I realised it didn't sound right. So I studied the work of Larry Kenney, who was Lion-O, and Lynne Lipton, who played all the women and the young girl. They were all brilliant, and I studied them as I did other actors during my career. [Doing voice work] is not fully acting … But when you realise how much is needed for these characters' voices, and not carrying it too far, it seems real. Especially when you put it together with the animation. It took me a little while to adjust to, I have to be honest, but once I adjusted, it was an absolute joy!'

Hyman recalls studying the drawings of Panthro and giving special attention to his nunchucks and shoulder spikes and marvelling at his power and strength. 'Let's say he was the "darker" one of the *ThunderCats*,' he jokes. 'We never said black; no-one was racist about it. But it was obvious he was dark; he was blue. He was the one who could fix anything, and I liked anyone who could fix anything; I had an uncle who could do that. I also looked at my cats. I know them, they are so individual, each one is different. I found the voice and thought, "I have to be really different from all of the other cats". I performed it down to my bass voice. I went there and stayed there!

'I suppose I had to audition for all the other characters I did. I remember Snow-Meow. The others were just occasional, they weren't Panthro – they were easy. I just went up in the register with my voice – up the scale. I'd gone as far down as I could with Panthro – I couldn't go lower than that. One or two were way up there!

'I lived a long time in Norway, and I had a house there. One day I read about a snake, [the country's] only indigenous reptile. I'd never seen one, but I was told that they were preserved by the government; you couldn't kill them. They're 12 inches to 14 inches long. One day I was walking up in the mountain and I heard this loud hissing sound. I looked down, and there one was! The ugliest thing you've ever seen, quite frightening. Their mouths were lined with teeth and they made this hissing sound. But the thing with this snake is, while it is poisonous, not many people have died from being bitten – it makes this terrible noise to make you run. When it came to the voice for the Ancient Spirits of Evil, I used this voice. The snakes are called "biting worms", and that's what became the voice.

'As I said, it was one of the happiest times of my life. I really am passionate about cats, and it was a new field of expression; voices. We had Larry Kenney and Bob McFadden and Earl Hammond, who was the evil one (and we got mixed up all the time, because he was Earl Hammond and I was Earle Hyman). Bob was an absolute genius. He had a wonderful son whom he sent to study with me; I was, at that time, teaching acting on the side when I could, and his son was so gifted too. I thought, here are two geniuses. Bob was incredible – I can't describe. I don't know how he did it. As far as I know, a lot of them haven't done anything much else except voice-overs and animated cartoons. Quite frankly, I don't think they had to do anything else; you can make a fortune! It's a very special art. I'd say everybody on *ThunderCats*, with the exception of me, was a master of this special art. I was in awe of them. We became a family; great friends. I was working a lot in Scandinavia at the time, and sometimes they'd let me record just my lines, only me in the studio, and I'd go to the airport and be gone for months. I always preferred being with the "family" when we recorded, I didn't like doing it alone and having to fit it in. This happened occasionally with the others too – they may have been on other jobs and we'd have to do it without them, and we'd sew it all together in New York.

'I didn't think *ThunderCats* would be a flop, but I envisaged children just watching it and thinking it was nice. I didn't know how I got so much money for doing something that wasn't a strain. It wasn't hard work, if you know what I mean, for all that money. But it was wonderful; they really taught me. Sometimes, I'd ask quite a lot, and they were all wonderful … I think I [must have been] a good boy once in my life, because I was sure rewarded with *The Cosby Show* and *ThunderCats*! I couldn't have asked for more. I've never been greedy for money. I started acting as a job when I was 16 on the radio and I was comfortable, I paid the rent and I could afford to buy anything that I wanted – not rich, but comfortable. But then from nowhere, Bill Cosby and *ThunderCats* came in and money rained in on me, for five years on *ThunderCats* and eight years on *The Cosby Show*. It taught me something: you never know what's around the corner … good or bad!'

Hyman believes the series' scriptwriters were hugely influential in the success of *ThunderCats*: 'I thought the scripts were well written – not only for young children but for everyone. I thought they were excellent. I was thinking of it as a children's TV show; of course it was that and more. In short, it took me a while to grab on to how remarkable that show was, and what great work was being done on both sides of the Pacific Ocean. Where they got their ideas from, I'll never know, but they were a joy to do, and I believed in them. To be very honest with you, I never watched *ThunderCats*, but I did once go with [Keshia Knight Pulliam, who played Rudy,] the youngest child on *The Cosby Show*, to Madison Square Garden, where they had *ThunderCats* as a show – where they skated on roller skates. She saw me, seated not far away, and she said, "Earle, Grandad". [The crowd] recognised her, and everyone went mad for me and *ThunderCats*. Our voices were heard, and Keshia was so thrilled that her on-screen grandfather was Panthro. I'd never told her about that.

'I also remember the last day of recording *ThunderCats*. I couldn't help but laugh through recordings, we were all laughing and smiling, but underneath it was bye-bye time. At least for me. I haven't done any animated recordings since then.

But at the same time, I couldn't just do that, I had to go on to the theatre; that's where I've belonged for 65 years.'

Earle Hyman has remained actively involved in the world of theatre in the years following *ThunderCats*. 'The play I enjoyed doing most was *Driving Miss Daisy* [in the role previously played by] Morgan Freeman,' he says. 'It was in the John Houseman Theatre, a little theatre across the street from where I lived in New York. I remember I'd been talking to Morgan and his girlfriend and said, "I'd love to be in a long running play again – for at least a year". The next thing I knew, I was at a party and someone said, "You got your wish. Morgan is leaving the show and they're going to ask you to take over from him". Imagine going just across the street to do a matinee and all the performances! I played in it for two years, which I loved. Then I went to Denmark and did it in Denmark. I had to play it in Danish, which I understood but had never acted in before. I'd played in Norwegian in Denmark and Sweden. The audiences understood it, because the languages are similar. I'd played in all three [Scandinavian] countries in that. [The plays I did included some] Shakespeare. I always enjoy that. Also some Ibsen – *The Master Builder* twice. [That version of *The Master Builder*] was called a reading, but it was a performance. We carried the book around in our hand, but we had rehearsed it and knew the lines. No sets or costumes, just us, the actors. Then I did it on Broadway with Lynne Redgrave playing my wife and Madeleine Potter playing the girl; that was very exciting! A lot of people didn't like it, but a lot of people say they don't understand [the play].

'I worked continuously until I had my first operation on my back. [I had a problem with] my lumbar region, and that [involved] a series of operations that were a pain in the ass ... or a pain in the back! I'd still do TV and shows. Then I went back to the classics. I did Chekhov, then I did something recently in *The Three Sisters*.'

Asked about his more recent work, Hyman jokes, with more than a touch of frustration: 'Since then I've had another operation, and here I sit dying. Without working, my dear friends, this old man is not alive! But I've been blessed for 66 years. I've played around the world in venues from Greece (where I could see the Parthenon in the background) to London, where I felt at home. I have a physical therapist working with me three times a week, and he grew up with *ThunderCats*. His sister gave him, on his thirtieth birthday, the whole set of *ThunderCats* DVDs, and he just freaked out. I gave him my toy Panthro, which I didn't think I'd give away to anybody. He said, "Oh it was wonderful, I never thought I would meet Panthro!" I get more fan mail from Germany than from any other country in the world. It's amazing – I'm signing all these things. They send the photos and they aren't of me – they are always of Panthro.'

Peter Newman
Characters Portrayed: Tygra, Monkian, Wily Kat, Ben Gali, Hachiman, Ram Bam, Ma-Mutt ('Ma-Mutt's Confusion'), The Wolfrat, The Demolisher, Plutar, The Mirror Wraith, The Shadowmaster, Amortus, Malcar, Unicorn Guardian (male), Hurrick the Bolkin, NEPTUNE, Baron Tass, Retilian Guard ('Fireballs of Plun-Darr'), Oceanic Denizen ('Dr Dometone'), Rhinosauran ('Mandora and The Pirates'), Micrit 2, Tuska Warrior 1 ('Turmagar the Tuska'), Underdweller 3 ('Anointment Trials Day 3')

'Prior to *ThunderCats*, which we started recording in 1984, I had started working in the voice-over business in '77 or '78 so I had been doing it for a few years, but I still felt, to myself, like a newcomer,' admits Peter Newman. 'I didn't have a history in broadcasting or theatre in any real substantial way. I'd tried other things, completely unrelated, so even though I had spent the past seven years or so in voice-overs, ending up with this job was quite a big deal for me. It was the biggest thing that had happened to me, and in many ways, it's the biggest thing that's happened to me in 30 years of doing this, because of the extent of it and the fact it's taken on a life of its own. It's so surprising to me how it's maintained [its popularity] over the years.'

Casting his mind back to the audition process, Newman describes his introduction to the show as 'mundane': 'I had been working in a talent agent's office doing some residual bookkeeping work; keeping track of payments owed to actors in (primarily) commercials, for their work. I was actually signed to another agent, but I was doing this bookkeeping, and they knew me. They called me for an audition, and because I wasn't signed exclusively to the other agent for cartoons, just commercials, it wasn't a conflict of interest.

'They said it was for a pilot for a cartoon, and I thought, "Great, well sure, another audition". So I simply went to the office – it wasn't even a recording studio, it was in the office of Rankin/Bass – and Jules Bass was there and Lee Dannacher. I had an appointed time, and they described something of the series. I don't remember if they had any artwork then, but they spoke in terms of superheroes, ThunderCats – feline characters, but still generic characteristics for the characters. I tried a few different voices, some a little higher, some lower, some more charactery. It wasn't too extensive an interview. I tried to suggest I could do anything, in a humble way of course. That I could do different voices and accents and all kinds of stuff that was true to what I saw as my skills. So I offered some things in response to their requests and a few things of my own, "By the way, I can do this as well" etc. I thought I'd done as well as I could. I don't remember the time frame, whether it was a few days later or weeks later, hearing that I got the job. I thought, this is nice, I'm going to do this pilot thing, but the agent said, "This is big, this is not for just one episode, you're being hired for the series." Then I thought, "Wow, I'm gonna get paid for this" – as it turned out, paid very well. What they did for *ThunderCats* is that they not only paid for the session but also they gave a buyout for the first ten reruns, which was paid up front.

'I was, in some ways, still learning the business, as I didn't have a radio background etc. I'd had some success, but nobody was knocking down the doors to get me. I was a journeyman, happy to be doing what I was doing. But to get *ThunderCats* was a big deal and it turned out, in time, to be even bigger than I imagined. It started with the first run of 65 shows, which evolved into a wonderful time and a terrific experience. Then we did another 65 shows, and it went into *SilverHawks* … It really went beyond my wildest dreams. Not only the job itself, but getting to work with the other people, the talent and the producers. Rankin/Bass were a great company to work for.

'I auditioned for Lion-O and for Tygra. Lion-O was the younger, less experienced leader, and Tygra was, of course, more mature and a steadying influence. So I thought, how does the more mature superhero sound as a prototype? So I pitched it lower, tried to portray a bit more staid and conservative attitude, [to make him] not someone who was prone to flights of emotion. As it went along, they seemed happy with the sound and it seemed to fit the character. When I listened to the first playback and heard Larry doing Lion-O and myself as Tygra, it really was different. Larry had captured the youthful energy of the character – not wanting to be held back – and Tygra sounded much more of a conservative, mature character. So I guess the secret is in the casting, and they did a good job – they got it right!

'It was like auditioning all the time for new characters. It was a friendly competition. Each of us would come up with our own ideas of how people should sound. That's how I came to do Monkian and WilyKat; coming up with my idea and presenting it. Lee would listen to other ideas and then decide. For the first couple of recording sessions, Jules Bass attended, and his guiding hand was there in the beginning, sorting out the initial characters and regulars. Then, not long afterwards, it was Lee who did the directing. After hearing our auditions, she'd say, "Okay, let's go with this one, Larry, Bob, Earl," and she'd make the decision. Many times it would be by acclamation. When someone came up with a voice and it sounded just right, we all just knew that was the voice, "Hold the phones, we have a winner!" It's not as though we wished each other ill. It was great fun to see these talented people coming up with these ideas. With things like Earl's portrayal of Mumm-Ra and Larry's portrayal of Jackalman, when we heard it, we thought, "Wow – that's it. I've got nothing man!" It was thrilling sometimes to hear that and be in a really lively and kinetic environment.'

With each cast member responsible for countless guest characters, consistency between performances was paramount. 'In some ways, that's the job,' explains Newman. 'We did the scripts in order, even if we were doing multiple characters. The hope was that you'd come up with memorable characters that you could swap between. There were times when we'd have to switch and get a little confused and have to stop, laugh and say, "Okay, now let's do it right". Generally it worked out fine. If it was necessary, we could listen back to tracks to see exactly what a character was like. But characters like Hachiman, for instance, were so distinctive [that I had no difficulty recalling the voice]. I was so proud to win the audition for that one, because Earl Hammond had also taken a run at it, and he ended up doing the Snowman. There were other characters where the opportunity was there to listen back to a sample if we needed – but generally it wasn't necessary. Once we'd done a voice for an entire script, it pretty well stuck.

'When you're creating the voice of a character, you're also dealing with their traits. WilyKat is this adolescent, "kids just want to have fun" kind of thing. He always gets into trouble and gets blamed, so not only was it his voice, but it was the character behind the voice. Switching to Tygra, I'm not only changing voices but characters. That also helped the consistency of the voice. Between Tygra and Bengali, it's closer in terms of who they are, but Bengali had a hook – his sound [was like] when you hear a tiger or a smaller cat; that growled, husky sound was Bengali, and even in line readings I used this "grwowwwl sound". Tygra was a straight-down-the-line adult. I don't want to get carried away, I wasn't creating Chekhovian characters, but I wanted to create characters that were important to the show. I have to say that, at times, [listening to voices I've done], I've thought, is that me? I'm not sure? I saw a list of the characters I recorded for *ThunderCats*, and some of them – I don't have a clue. I remember the Demolisher character because it tore up my voice, and when I did it in the audition I got the reaction of, "Wow, are you going to be able to do that for the whole episode?" Fortunately I did, but I then had to recuperate. If it had been a regular character, I'd have had to have been more careful about how I did the voice, because there are things you can do to relax and create the sound without straining your voice. I'd compare it, only tangentially, with a singer who is a theatrical performer and has to sing both a matinee and an evening show. Through technique, you can learn to do that without damaging your voice.'

Newman reveals that between one and three episodes were recorded in a typical week of recording. 'If we did one, we would generally do it in a morning, and that would be it. If we did two, we'd do one in the morning, have a lunch break, and do [the second one] in the afternoon. If we did three, generally it was the very next day [that we did the third one]. I'm sure there were exceptions to that though. It would take about two hours to record an episode. We had retakes pretty much all the time. Even if the first take was really good, we always wanted to have a safety, so if there was something we couldn't quite hear or it wasn't quite as clear a sound as we'd want it to be, there was always an alternate take. Lee Dannacher would have this way … After we'd do a take, no matter what the range of the emotion, there'd be a moment of silence, and Lee would come over the mic from the control room and say, "That is going to be good". It wasn't good yet… So we'd all laugh. It could be a matter of pacing, something she heard or didn't hear. A line reading, or something we didn't understand with special effects or music. Maybe [it needed to be] louder or quieter at some point. So there were always these things to be considered.'

Newman was pleased to see the addition of Doug Preis and Gerrianne Raphael to the cast for the second set of 65 shows – although he jokes that he would have preferred to have done all the voices alone: 'I couldn't have even if I'd wanted to. To have someone else come in who brings a new sound and a fresh perspective, you realise it's really good – it adds to the mix rather than taking work away from you. The six of us initially were great, we were having such a great time and it was such fun doing all these voices. For the second series, with new voices, it was obvious it contributed to the series and expanded the possibilities, because they were talented people and brought a lot to the project, and you recognise it right away.'

Newman describes the input the actors would be given by the production team: 'Pace was something that Lee directed – sometimes she would say that we needed to pick up the pace or slow it down a little – but as time went on we knew by repetition what the pacing should be. We also had to be careful not to step on each other's lines so that, if editing had to be done, the lines were in the clear. It only had to be a fraction of a second but it had to be a clean space. The scripts were very solid – we could ask if we had any questions about the dialogue, but I don't remember any issues. The basic content of the script wasn't subject to our whims – thankfully – but we had some leeway in a character if we felt we could express it in a certain way. I don't remember too much rigidity as long as you didn't change anything of great substance.

'It was a great advantage to record together, in one room, because it allowed us to play off each other, one to respond to the other. Certainly there were sections of script when one character was doing his or her things, so it didn't matter, but frequently it was one character talking, fighting or running with another, and it helped to have the other actor there to talk to. It was fairly rare to do it that way even then. Lots of [other cartoons] were done "wild" – one person would go in and do all their lines in a script. I've done that recently for a newer adult cartoon show, and the director, who was also the writer, would read back to me the intervening lines. It's okay, it works all right, you get out of the studio faster, but it's not as much fun for a performer.

'For the first episodes, there was no animation [completed when we did the voice recording]. That was all to come, and we did it like we were doing radio. We knew we'd been hired to do all the episodes – there would be 65 episodes and the project would be done. Initially, that's all we knew about it, and we carried on. There was no way for us to know in advance how successful or unsuccessful the series would be. I could only assume, given Rankin/Bass's success in the genre at the time, that they thought it would do well. When it first started airing and the ratings came back, we realised it was becoming number one for its category and we were thrilled. I don't remember how soon around that time that we found out there was going to be another series, which was the best news of all. It's the proof of the pudding in the renewal! Clearly [the show remains popular] because it appealed to an audience and then became part of the audience's memory of that time. They had the psychologist approving and reviewing the scripts and working out the moral of the play. I thought there were interesting concepts in the scripts; Tygra going into the cave of time etc. There were definitely some interesting ideas. Good vs evil is always fun, and the people who created it were clever enough to appeal to the younger audience and clocked the zeitgeist. It's also nostalgia, the same way I listen to old rock and roll – it's comfortable.

'ThunderCats is special to me because it was the first such project that I had worked on. It's like your first kiss, you never forget it. Working on SilverHawks afterwards was also great fun – keeping the dream alive. We were able to continue with some additional cast members – having fun doing the recording, while making a living – what more could you ask for? As time went on, we did The Comic Strip, which was a series of shorter cartoons. As I went on and did other projects, it was fine and great fun, but never quite like that first project. I'd have been thrilled if it had continued ten more years!'

Reviewing a list of his many ThunderCats characters, Newman is surprised at the variety of voices he provided: 'WilyKat was fun, doing the voice of an adolescent and carrying it through – I got a real kick out of that. Maybe it's just the ego of the performer being self-satisfied and thinking, "I can do that." I tried to do characters (like Hachiman) in an honest way and not make fun of them. I wanted to do them in a respectful way … We would get to see some sense of what the guest characters would look like, and it does guide you. When you look at a face, the shape, the character, it does dictate what they might sound like. The way you purse your lips etc changes how the sound comes out. It was helpful to see the artwork, because it would move us in a certain direction. We'd look at the picture and so would Lee, so she would also contribute her thoughts as we tried to create the voice. In the end, you want the voice to match the character, and then you hopefully add some of the character traits that would affect how quickly the character might speak, or how haltingly, and how words would flow from their mouth. When we're doing it, nobody is really thinking about that stuff, but analytically, looking at it afterwards, that's what goes into it.'

Newman remembers his time on *ThunderCats* with great warmth: 'It's a process of becoming comfortable with people in a space of time, knowing people won't make fun of you if you try something ridiculous, and being able to share in this creative environment. After a while, you'd come to the sessions and ask people what's going on and how are they doing. It becomes a little temporary community. That's just part of the environment; how it worked. Like most things in life, it comes to an end at some point. Eve when we did three episodes, it would really mean only a day and a half in a week, so it wasn't like a soap opera where the cast are always together, but you got to share some of life's experiences with these people, their families, vacations and other projects they were working on. During that time, I heard a commercial for some pharmaceutical product. Next session, I told Larry, "Congratulations, Lion-O got a commercial", because I recognised Larry's voice. To this day, even though we don't get to see each other that often, when we do cross paths it's always a great pleasure and we have a hug. Lynne and I both had an involvement not too long ago with a memorial celebration for an actor who passed away.

'For someone who didn't start out in the business and who was accepted as a professional, that was just exceptional for me and kept my spirits up. Bob McFadden was very special to me. When I was considering going into the industry, he was very encouraging to me. I met him at the talent agent's office when I was working as a bookkeeper. The first thing I heard him do when he came in was some character's voice; he would frequently [imitate] Paul Lynde, a wonderful character actor who was on television and on Broadway. Bob used [that voice] to express thoughts sometimes. To me, it seems perfectly natural, but I don't know how it seems to people who don't live in this world. Sometimes, the thoughts I have can be expressed in character; that's just the way it works for me, and ideas naturally express themselves through character voices – sometimes, stereotypical things from my imagination. That was very much who Bob was, and I sensed this kindred spirit. The first time we conversed was when he came into the office as a character and I responded to him as a character and he looked at me and he said something like, "Hey that was good – don't ever do it again". But he was very encouraging to me. I'd ask him about the industry and he'd say, "You can do this; you should get out and try this." I was hesitant at first, because I didn't know the reality of it. He was very generous with his advice and I got to work with him even before *ThunderCats*, and I'd see him at auditions. When I saw him on *ThunderCats*, it was the icing on the cake. Bob had a wonderful baritone sound – he was a singer with a rich voice.

'I didn't know Earl Hammond before this, and he was a larger than life character. He knew Marlon Brando and did stage work from that period when Brando was coming up, and he had this wild side to him – he'd tell us stories of his younger days and who he was. Behind the mic, he was as wacky and crazy as everyone else. Seeing Mumm-Ra bursting out of this character with demonic laughter was great. To be able to connect with these kinds of creative characters in a very permissive environment, where it was okay to make a fool of yourself, where there were other experienced actors doing the same thing, was a great, existential experience.'

After *ThunderCats*, Newman continued to build on his career as a voice artist. 'I got older,' he jokes, commenting on his life beyond the series. 'I had the opportunity to do all sorts of projects. Every so often I get to do an "on camera" advert. Sometimes I do industrials; it might be a doctor talking to a patient about a medical condition and you have to speak the jargon, which is sometimes pretty challenging. For a few years, I was the narrator for a TV program called *Extreme Makeover* – not the home edition, it was the predecessor for that. I talked the audience though what was happening and told the story behind the scenes. Also, I've done lots of commercials of all types using regular voice, character voice and accents for lots of different companies. In life in general, my wife and I have always enjoyed travelling, and life goes on, and still repairs have to be done around the house.'

Lynne Lipton

Characters Portrayed: Cheetara, WilyKit, Luna, Willa, Nayda, Mandora, Mumm-Rana (1st Voice), Ta-She, Queen Luna, Queen Tartara, Unicorn Guardian (female), Alien Spaceship ('Sixth Sense'), Ro-Bear Belle, Leah, Maiden from Arthur Story ('Excalibur'), Members of Tor's Family ('Return to Thundera')

For the first 65 episodes of *ThunderCats*, New York actress Lynne Lipton was the only female voice actor to work on the series. She provided a large number of distinctive vocal performances, though one role in particular would earn her a place in the affections of a generation of adolescents.

'Cheetara is deeper than my speaking voice,' acknowledges Lipton. 'She had a real body to her voice. It was really Lee Dannacher's decision, because when I went in to the audition, and they showed me a picture of Cheetara, and she said that whoever got the job would have to do two ongoing characters, Cheetara and WilyKit. WilyKit was a snap, and when we looked at Cheetara we said, "No, she's deeper, she's sexier". So it was Lee's direction that got me the job – I'm an actor and I did it, I always say that to her. She was just great. I've worked with other directors, and most times you are voicing to picture – they've done it already – but [that wasn't the case here]. Lee was just amazing, and she directed you in such a way that she always got what she needed. She was perfect and she made us all feel good.

'I guess I was more of a theatre actress. I come from Second City, which is an improvisational theatre in Chicago. I was born in New York and did a lot of off-Broadway before I [went to] Chicago in the '70s. Then I went to California and did television. I did a lot of series, and also worked in a theatre called The Committee. Then I came back and did Broadway. That's what you did to make a living. You did shows and you did commercials. *ThunderCats* was just this gift that everyone was given. My agent called me to audition and I had no idea what it was, and I just went in, like any audition, and it was great. I thought, "Okay, what do I do now?" I was the only girl with all of these amazing men. This is what they *did* – a lot of them. Larry was working on *Imus in the Morning* at the time, but Bob McFadden and Earl Hammond were masters at doing it. Basically, I learnt on the job; they paid you to have fun. There was a wonderful man named Earle Hyman; he was doing *Othello* in Scandinavia. He was doing *The Cosby Show* as well. He would bring me back these little pieces of Scandinavia, and he is probably one of the nicest people I've met in my entire life … a dear, dear man. I loved him a lot. I loved all of them, but he was so special. They were so nice to me. I'd done commercials and was known to be able to do characters, but this was different, it was doing it every week, three shows a week, and it was constantly coming up with new characters. We'd all audition for the same characters. I'd always say, "This isn't fair – you guys are so much better than I am". A man's voice has a different kind of range; a greater range.

'After the first 65 shows, I recommended Gerianne, and I also recommended Doug Preis. Doug always made me laugh, because he does the best James Mason [impression] in the world, and I loved James Mason. He only had to say "Hello" in that voice and I was dead. There was a guy called Jim Meskimen who came in and did some drawings for Rankin/Bass and then came and did some voices on later shows. He was very nice and extremely talented. Lee Dannacher is a dear friend, and it was a great time we had!'

Lipton is adamant that the best results in recording a show stem from approaching the subject matter in as natural a manner as possible, including assembling an entire cast: 'It's a pleasure doing a whole script from beginning to end. It's a story, and we have much more fun doing it that way. Many years ago, when I was 18 in LA, I got a job to do a movie – providing the voice of a dog. It was before *ThunderCats*. They told me Richard Burton was in it. I was so excited and I got all dressed up and went to the studio and he wasn't there. I was so disappointed. I think people make a mistake doing it separately. I think if you get people all together, you get an energy. We're professional enough not to overlap when they don't want us to.'

Lipton adds that, when her characters were required to talk to each other, both she and Lee Dannacher preferred recording in real time: 'It was easy for me, because they were two different characters I knew so well. Bob McFadden always said, "You've got to do them together, otherwise they're not talking to each other." Lee is such a good producer that she'd always have the track up when we came in and she'd say, "Oh, it's Mandora again"'.

Lipton recalls the inspirations for her most memorable voices on the show: 'I remember for Mandora, Bob McFadden said, "She looks like John Wayne". Bob could give you a personality for wind. He was a genius. They would all start doing John Wayne impressions – they would give it to me. Bobby was very funny; he had this filing cabinet in his brain and would remember every voice he'd ever heard. He'd say, "Put a little Joan Crawford into that". That's how the voices came about, because [for me], being an actor, it's always about the character and not about the voice, and they approached it that way too. Earl Hammond was amazing. He always complained he would lose his voice, but he never, ever did. I'd done some [voice work] for an animated film called *The Little Red Pony*, and for a few minutes, I was friends with [its star] Mia Farrow. That's where Willa came from; Mia Farrow doing an impression of an English accent. Luna was fun. My nephew, Noah, who is now ten, loves the *Redwall* series of books, and Luna comes up when I do voices when I'm reading him stories. I also remember that I was riding Doug Preis's back, as he voiced the Amok character. Nayda was Katherine Hepburn and was suggested by the guys. Earl Hammond would suggest some obscure things that were way before my time, like "Do Al Jolson". I knew the name, but I'd be like, "What the hell did he sound like?" And he'd do an impression.

'The character picture would be in front of you. The only leg-up I had was Lee saying, "This is for a woman, so only McFadden can try out for this with Lynne" – because he could do anything. It was a group thing that found the characters. Most especially Bob and Earl, though Earl was more like, "Do it this way, higher or lower". They loved to make fun of me, because I used to bring a camera in and record some of the sessions, because it was so fun watching these guys work. They were the giants. I knew, because I'd done my homework, who they were, and I had great admiration and respect for them. They could have said "She's terrible" and I'd have been gone. It was a great opportunity.'

Asked about the inherent difficulties of performing every female lead in the first season of *ThunderCats*, Lipton modestly replies: 'It was wonderful – just perfect. I remember having lunch with Lee, and by the end, I'd suggested bringing in Gerrianne Raphael, not because I couldn't do it, but because the timbre of my voice is a whole lot different from Gerrianne's and I think it made it more interesting. But it was like going to the theatre, watching these guys work. They could do anything. Larry is one of the funniest guys in the world … He is extraordinarily generous and he makes the atmosphere very fun. We laughed a lot. I can't fault anybody – even the engineers. We should really have a reunion. There was something very pure about *ThunderCats*. Lee was such a perfectionist. The joke about Lee was always that somebody could do a perfect take and she'd still say, "That was fabulous, but can we have a safety on it?" She was amazing; she always covered it. She worked 28 hours a day doing this stuff. As I get older, I appreciate more what she did – she was the show.

'I like to do volunteer work, and I'd take *ThunderCats* scripts up to schools in Harlem or homeless shelters and have the kids read them. That was the only time I sensed [how popular the show was], because they knew exactly what to do and they were so excited and thrilled. The kids would run out to the streets with their Sword of Omens. But we didn't feel it at the time; we were doing the show and our other work. I was doing commercial voice-overs at the time and everyone had something to balance [their *ThunderCats* work]. We were working actors in New York. We never thought about it. We just loved doing it, every week; it was like this little family. We knew each other very well – how often do you get this wonderful situation where everyone likes each other?'

Lipton recounts some of her fondest memories: 'Larry was always falling asleep in the studio and we'd have to kick him to wake him up. Once a year, we'd all go out to dinner and Lee would give us a wonderful gift. A great time was had by all, but Lee almost killed herself. My favourite thing was that, when we knew it was the last show, I made a videotape of the last recording session, and they quite liked it. It was especially important when the big guys later passed away, which was really sad to me, but I suppose it happens to all of us. I love making little films, because it's a great memory. I think it's important to know whose shoulders you've been standing on in your life. I knew who'd come before me and who helped me, and doing this show was just a gift.

'I started out as a waitress-actress, which you all did until you became an actress-waitress – when you were working more than you were waitressing. I'd always just walk through Tiffanies, because I couldn't afford to buy anything, but one year, I went in and got a money clip for each of the guys with their character name on it. I think Earle Hyman and Peter Newman had said to me this was the best job many of us had ever had, financially and in many other ways. So, I thought a silver money clip from Tiffanies would be great. Peter tells me he still has his and uses it! It was a great time, and we got paid to overact! I think, as in my case, it was one of Peter's first animation shows. He's quite wonderful, and he got better and bigger. We used to laugh because he used to swim a lot and consequently he had really good lung power. He's probably one of the nicest people you'll meet. I saw him grow. It wasn't that we were both new to the business or recording, but we hadn't done much animation. We were like brother and sister there. Especially as we did WilyKit and WilyKat. It was such fun. If someone had a birthday, we had a cake. Earl Hammond would tell me problems he was going through and I'd listen, and people don't know how good a guy Larry was. I can't imagine what it was to be as committed as Earle Hyman; he was doing Shakespeare, and there was a great humility to him. It was the people. Though all of us weren't intimate friends, we were a family.

'I think *ThunderCats'* longevity has to do with Rankin/Bass and Lee Dannacher and their level of excellence. The animation was extraordinary for that time; beautiful and full, with a great attention to detail. The scripts weren't about violence, they were about a story with a lesson, which great literature has. I'm not saying *ThunderCats* was great literature, but it was a learning tool for kids. It was like the great myths. At the time, I was reading the *Mahabharata*, an Indian text that is really the philosophical history of Indian culture. You read that and you realise it's the same in all cultures. There are the good guys and the bad guys and there is morality – not that there is any in our world today! – but there is a sense of what is just, and that's what *ThunderCats* had. It was great for kids, and I wish there was more of it around.'

Lynne Lipton remains a working actress in New York and her extensive career includes a swathe of theatre work as well as television credits as diverse as *Law and Order* and *My Little Pony*. 'I've also been cut out of a lot of movies, that's for sure!' she jokes. 'I'm on the cutting room floor of *Precious*, which is a strange movie. I've done a lot of television and films. About five years ago, I had a bad accident and I was off my feet for about a year, but now I'm fine, and I did voice work during that time because you can't stop working. It gets slower as you get older, but I just did a reading for a wonderful play called *Let Me Go*, and they're hoping to get a production out of that. It's just being an actor in New York. I volunteered for a couple of months for Barack Obama when he was running for President. The world has changed – it's not that innocent world of *ThunderCats* any more, unfortunately. It's a different time. I live in Manhattan, and when the *Star Wars* prequels came out, there were people sleeping on the street for weeks in the queue to see them at the Ziegfeld [cinema]. So I went around the neighbourhood and made sure they got food. The kids called me line mum. This was a mission – I wanted to make sure they were okay. When they found out I was Cheetara, they had heart attacks and ran screaming down the street. I gave one fan my doll of Cheetara, which Lee had given me. They'd put my name into the internet and found out who I was. I think anybody I run into, including producers of a certain age, get crazy for *ThunderCats* and Cheetara. I think she was a fantasy to many, and I hope I don't disappoint!'

Earl Hammond
Characters Portrayed: Mumm-Ra, Vultureman (2nd voice), Jaga the Wise, Hammerhand, Snowman of Hook Mountain, Captain Cracker, Turmagar, Quick Pick, Ninja Warrior, Spidera, Ro-Bear Bill, Ro-Bear Bert, Ro-Bear Bob, Other Ro-Bear Berbils, Wollo Elder, Bundun The Bolkin, Melchior the Tabbot, Kymera Leader, Samurai Automaton ('Hachiman's Honour'), Frogman, The Ecology Inspector, Mr. Grubber, Moleman 1, Thundarian Guard ('Return to Thundera'), Giant Thundarian Scorpion ('Return to Thundera'), Oceanic Denizen ('Dr Dometone'), Tartara's Guards, Micrit Leader, Underdweller 1 ('Anointment Trials Day 3'), Trollog 1 ('Eye of the Beholder'), Incubi ('Anointment Trial Day 5'), Intro Voice-Over ('Exodus, Feliner', 'Thundercubs', 'Return to Thundera')

A talented performer both on and off screen, the late Earl Hammond had an extensive career spanning five decades, concluding with a role in the 1999 blockbuster *The Mummy*. More familiar to *ThunderCats* fans is his faultless performance as the ThunderCats' arch nemesis, Mumm-Ra, a role he believed was his '*Sgt Pepper's*'.

Hammond's son Eric shares his memories of his father: 'My dad had been in the acting business since he was an adolescent. Lots of stage and radio work. I believe he heard about the *ThunderCats* audition through his agent, J Michael Bloom. My dad just loved to make up voices … Since I can remember, whenever he told me and my sister stories he would do it in character. I remember him trying always to imitate the *Looney Tunes* voices for us … Mel Blanc was one person he admired greatly.'

Eric recalls how proud his father was to be associated with *ThunderCats*: 'He said on more than one occasion that this was the best cartoon on the air and he had the most fun doing it ever in his acting career. He was always telling random people that he played Mumm-Ra and giving them a little sample of it by saying a few words in character. It was a happy time in his life. He was making a good living doing what he loved. He mentioned to me on several occasions that he did not consider the success of the work because he was having so much fun. He knew that *ThunderCats* was groundbreaking. I did also. To this day, I see people wearing *ThunderCats* T-shirts and see *ThunderCats* bumper stickers and car window decals. My son knows about the show because we have the DVD collection, *but* his friends who are all in the third grade also know about it, so I think it is safe to assume that it has crossed generations like other great cartoons.'

Asked how his family felt about Hammond's association with Mumm-Ra, he speaks with great pride: 'It was always kind of cool, but what I enjoyed more was trying to pick his voice out in other characters that I didn't know he did on the show. After *ThunderCats*, he continued to do voices and acting until his health and mind started to fail. One notable thing he did was provide various voices for the feature film *The Mummy*. Fitting, isn't it?'

Earl Hammond's only recorded comments on *ThunderCats* appear in video footage recorded by Lynne Lipton during the final recording session for show 130, 'The Book of Omens'. Asked about how he felt about the show, he responded simply: 'Best job I ever had in my life. More fun … everything – the definitive experience … really. That's all I've got to say, because I'm not good at interviews.'

Hammond's enormous talent gave the *ThunderCats* series some of its most memorable characters. His range was such that he was able to swap seamlessly between the ranting monologues of Mumm-Ra and the gentle, aged tones of Jaga the Wise. His many colleagues remember, with great fondness, the animated and wholehearted performance he would give at every one of the recording sessions. His delivery of Mumm-Ra, in particular, has achieved legendary status amongst his peers. After a lifetime of achievements, Earl Hammond passed away on 1 May 2002.

Robert McFadden

Characters Portrayed: Snarf, Slithe, Lynx-O, Snarfer, Grune the Destroyer, The Driller, Captain Shiner, Top Spinner, Mongor, Molemaster, Char-Nin, Burn Out, Two Time, Guardian of the Book of Omens, Vultureman (1st Voice), Dr Dometone, Mule, Captain Bragg, Polly, The Mad Bubbler, The Terrator, Brodo the Wizard, The Ice King, Baron Carnor (recording), Carnor's Gargoyle Thieves, Screw Loose, Hammerhand's Right Hand Man ('The Terror of Hammerhand'), The Living Ooze, Dirge, Maftat, Tree Monster ('The Terror of Hammerhand'), Moleman 2, Creatures in Neitherwitch's Cave, Tartara's Guards, Vertus Communicator/Cry for Help ('Sword in a Hole'), Micrit 1, Tuska Warrior 2 ('Turmagar the Tuska'), Storyteller in Mumm-Ra Cauldron ('Excalibur'), Fog Demon ('Anointment Trial Day 5'), Reptilian Guard ('Trouble with Thunderkittens'), Vertus Guard ('ThunderCats Ho!'), Spirit of Nishida ('ThunderCats Ho!'), Intro Voice-Over ('ThunderCats Ho!', 'Mumm-Ra Lives'), Frogman's Laughing Lillypads, Thundarian Shuttle Pilot ('Well of Doubt')

One of the most prolific and versatile actors to work on *ThunderCats*, and one of the first to be cast, was established voice artist and performer, the late Bob McFadden. His skills as an impersonator and character actor were extraordinary, often leaving his colleagues in awe. He had been in the industry for three decades prior to *ThunderCats*. His working life began in the US Navy during the Second World War, and an affinity with singing and impersonations began as he spent his shore-leave performing at a variety of venues where he was stationed. During the 1960s, he began regular voice-over work for commercials and television serials.

McFadden's son Brian describes his passion for performing: 'My father was a stand up comic for years. He always had a talent for voices and characters and he was always a wizard with impressions – which he used to do in his stand up act. He did a lot of gigs in hotels and stuff like that. As a young guy, he came to New York City, and he was doing stand up, and his agent got a call for him to do a mad scientist voice. My father did a great Bela Lugosi or Boris Karloff voice, and he realised, "Wow this is really good, I could make a lot of money from this, and I'm very good at it". My father used to say, "In nightclubs, you had to battle against the drunks", which of course you didn't get with voice-overs. He became one of the top voice artists and got a lot of work. He had an incredible back catalogue of voices he could do. Voices nobody could remember, actors and people from Vaudeville, and he could do perfect impressions of them.

'Over the years, he worked with the guys at Rankin/Bass, and they did *A Year Without Santa Claus* and *Frosty the Snowman* and *Rudolph the Red Nosed Reindeer*. Then they got *ThunderCats* and they got my dad in to do voices for it. When I was young, I was also doing voice work on commercials and voice-overs, and I went up for the *ThunderCats* audition, [as did my brother]. They called up my father's agent, and my father was told "They can't use your boys". Obviously we didn't have what they were looking for, or we weren't ready or skilled enough. But my father misunderstood them and thought they'd said "They can't use your *voice*, because there wasn't enough experience". My father said, "I've been doing this for 30 years. I don't understand, I have such a long track record!" His agent said, "What are you talking about, Bob?" He said, "They don't want to use my *voice*?" "No," they said, "they don't want to use your *boys*, but they want to use you." And that's how they came to my father, because they knew he had a tremendous amount of vocal versatility.'

Brian recalls his father's enthusiasm for the series: 'He loved working on the show because he got to work with all those guys, Earl, Peter, Lynne Lipton and Larry, and he loved the joy of going there and being creative and doing what he wanted within the show. I went to one or two of the recording sessions when I was a kid, and he loved being able to play and do that. It was a steady job, a steady gig – it was recording all the time. He had no idea it would become as big as it did at the time, but he always looked forward. He loved being a voice actor. If you saw him in the studio, he really got animated, he enjoyed playing other characters and really got into them.

'*ThunderCats* is something that was such a big part of a lot of kids' lives. It became a huge phenomenon and it lives on to this day. I walk down the street and see the *ThunderCats* insignia on people's T-shirts all the time. Kids grew up with that show. At the time, you don't know the effect it's having. My father lived a somewhat quiet life in suburbia and he didn't recognise that this was something kids came home to watch every day. A whole generation of kids grew up with memories attached to a particular entertainment thing – which is how we spend our time. Our lives get attached to music or a film we watched with someone we met. After school, kids watched *ThunderCats*. For some reason the show struck a chord with them and left an impression on them, and a lot of them maintain their memories to this day, and they keep the thing alive with T-shirts and things like that.

'My father was really good at voices. Whenever he [auditioned for] a cartoon, they'd show him a picture of the character and my father would throw seven different voices at them. If it was a cat, he'd base the voice on the sound of the animal. Snarf is kind of a small cat, so he based the voice on a meow; he took it and thought, "What would this animal sound like if he spoke English?" The one character that worried about stuff was Snarf, and he was surrounded by all these other characters, and it provided a counterpoint. The paradox being that my father also did the voice of Slithe, which was the total opposite of Snarf. My father loved that about it – he got to play all ends of the vocal spectrum ... He had certain voices that he'd repeatedly do. He'd always stick Richard Nixon in things. I'm not sure if that ended up in Slithe, but if you take Nixon's sleazy vocal tonality and muddy it up a little, you get that kind of character. He'd take a celebrity and add a grovel or growl or a vocal tick to get the voice. There were some times when he'd do voices that were straight impersonations – although I'm not sure he did that in *ThunderCats*. He did "Cool the Cool, Super Agent", which was just Jack Benny; and he did one of the best impersonations of him! He would do him dead on, and I learnt how to do it from him. He did a cartoon show called *Fearless Fly*, in which he did Walley Cox, a straight impersonation; "Without my glasses, I'm helpless". He did a great Boris Karloff, so he was the voice of Franken Berry cereals, one of his most popular adverts, which he did for about 15 years – and a lot of people remember that. He was also in the movie *Annie Hall*, but he was cut out of it, and it was a big regret, because he never got a copy of his scene with Woody Allen. In it, he played a typical game show host on TV. Woody Allen starts yelling at the TV screen and my father yells back and says, "Why are you watching if it's so crap?' Woody replies, "This is just terrible". My father says, "Well, change the channel then. Why are you watching?"'

Brian McFadden has followed in his father's footsteps and carved out a career as a performer and comic. He believes his father was a vocal genius: 'When I was doing voice-overs, I'd say, "Dad, I've got this character, what do I do?" He'd [suggest an actor whose voice I could imitate]. I wouldn't even know who it was. I voiced a football coach once, and he said, "Do Eddie Mayhoff", and said, using his accent, "He had a voice like this – we're gonna go in and hit 'em hard and hit 'em low, we're gonna fight fight fight and go go go!" My father had such an advantage over other actors, because he was such a student of other actors and picking up vocal inflections and being able to do impressions. He gave me an advantage too, because no other actor knows Eddie Mayhoff, and I was a young guy doing these impressions. As far as being a creative guy, he was very gregarious, everyone loved working with him, he was very spontaneously funny. He really lived to do the kind of work that he was called to do in this realm. He was so good at it during a time when there were not a lot of people doing that type of work – he was like a lesser-known Mel Blanc and Dog Butler. My father was way up there, but he's not as well known, because some of his work didn't have such a high profile. Now if you watch animated movies, the voices are done by celebrities. But back in Disney's time and my father's time, they were done by actors like Frank Whelper, who were well-known voice actors – who were so fantastic! Now they pay Cameron Diaz millions of dollars to do *Shrek* and you could take her out of the movie and no-one would notice.

'My father had an insecurity about himself that he would hide. His talent was his salvation in some ways. He used his voices as a kind of buffer between himself and other people; he was a bit of a loner and didn't always, I think, know who he was. That's why he enjoyed working so much, because he could inhabit these characters. He was beloved in the industry, because he could do anything: he could do sound effects, animals, bad guys, good guys and any dialect or accent. Everybody loved my dad. He was not somebody who was super-social, but when he was working with people he always got along with everyone. He loved working and cracking up with funny people like Larry Kenney, who was somewhat bawdier than my father. If you listen to some of the *ThunderCats* outtakes, my father is never cursing, but Larry Kenney is. My father loved working with other talented people with whom he could do his thing and luxuriate in their creativity and just watch and laugh and enjoy it. My father just loved working, especially on something like *ThunderCats* that continued and became a hit and had a nice really long run, which a lot of cartoons don't.

'No-one knows what my father really sounded like, including his family! I'm partially kidding, but the truth is that my father was never very comfortable speaking in his own voice in shows. He was very rarely the guy who got the commercial where he'd say, "Go down to Burger King". He'd always play the part of the burger going, "Hey everyone, check me out, I'm delicious, I've got pickles and ketchup". Larry Kenney does a lot of that straight stuff. My father could do that and did do that on the show, the bumpers etc, but it wasn't his forte. He could do it when asked, but they'd call him when they didn't want to say the name of the product, they wanted the sponge or the stain.'

After a long and distinguished career, Robert McFadden sadly passed away on 7 January 2000. His enormous contribution to the *ThunderCats* series saw him playing more unique characters than any other performer, from the comic characterisation of Snarf to the menacing portrayal of a host of villains. He remains one of the most talented performers to have ever entered the industry.

Gerrianne Raphael
Characters Portrayed: Pumyra, Chilla, Jaguara, Mumm-Rana (2nd Voice), Sondora, Kudi, Space Tanker Pilot 2 ('Exile Isle'), Members of Tor's Family ('Return to Thundera')

For any actor or actress, the idea of joining an established cast is daunting. The first 65 episodes of *ThunderCats* had been recorded using only six voice artists, and for the second 65, the addition of Gerrianne Raphael, an experienced performer of Broadway, television and commercials, was a logical progression. Lynne Lipton had previously voiced every female character on the show, and the arrival of Raphael allowed for greater variety. Her principal role would be Pumyra, one of three 'new' ThunderCats added to the team for the second season.

'My agent got me the audition,' explains Raphael. 'I was already doing a show for them – part of *The Comic Strip* called *Karate Kat*, in which my main character was Big Mama . They just offered me *ThunderCats*. I tried several voices for Pumyra and they said, "*That* one!"'

As Raphael recalls, she had no difficulty integrating with her fellow cast members, most of whom she already knew: 'I had no problem joining the original group. The size of the cast was perfect. Much fun, lots of joking, laughter ... A great time, and they always paid for lunch! It was the most fun, as we were all in the room together. On other series that I have done, I have been completely alone in the studio doing each line separately, with no co-actors present.'

Raphael says that the recording schedule on the show was stepped up for later episodes: 'We almost exclusively recorded at Howard Schwartz Recording. Days of the week always varied, and we did five shows at a time. Two full days for four shows and another half day for the fifth.'

Of the process of voicing guest characters, Raphael notes: 'We auditioned in front of each other on a break while recording. We usually had no need to listen to tracks.

'I remembered my [established] voices pretty well ... but if we needed them, they had them all ready for us to hear. Timing was never a problem. We'd sometimes be told "Pick it up" or "Stretch" – whatever was called for.'

She adds that, unlike some of her colleagues, she rarely had to voice multiple characters in 'real time': 'I never had to talk to myself, and the characters were, vocally, quite far way from each other. Pumyra was of course my noble character. I loved doing Chilla because she blew blue breath on everyone – I figured out that I was, of course, unable to say my line after blowing the "blue breath", so I devised a way to make a great hissing sound that sounded like I was blowing out, but in reality I was "zooping in" and then had plenty of breath for the line that followed!'

Gerrianne Raphael is delighted to have worked on *ThunderCats*. 'I had no idea it was such a success,' she acknowledges. 'I have a huge list of credits, but people are always most knocked out when they read that I was on *ThunderCats*. I think Bob McFadden was incredible ... He would go into "Jack Benny" and a variety of other celebs, which he did perfectly, at the drop of a hat ... Earl Hammond was larger than life, very funny, and the whole workplace was a joy. We were making great money and having a ball doing it.'

With career highlights including parts in *Law & Order*, *As the World Turns* and *A Little Curious* for television and *Hallelujah Baby*, *King of Hearts* and *Seventh Heaven* for Broadway, Raphael's resume is brimming with achievements. Still actively working in the industry, she continues to look for exciting projects that utilise her many skills as a vocal performer.

Doug Preis
Characters Portrayed: Alluro, Ancient Spirits of Evil (1st Voice; 'Thundercubs'), Crownan, Char ('Return to Thundera'), Space Tanker Pilot – British ('Exile Isle')

'I was an actor and voice-over performer working on radio and TV commercials,' explains Doug Preis, who joined the series alongside Gerrianne Raphael during its second season. 'I did narration, movie and network promotion and animated series. I honestly can't recall whether I had to audition for *ThunderCats* or whether they called me in, as the show was already in production when I began working on it. I think the basic reason I was added to the cast was that the other actors had pretty much exhausted their "other" voices, and the show needed new voices that didn't sound similar. Since this show was recorded in New York and I had been working in the business for many years, joining an established team was no problem, as I already knew all the cast from other jobs and work situations.'

Though he concedes the specifics of recording are a bit of a 'distant memory', Peis does recall that usually two episodes were recorded at a time, and two hours were allowed to record each episode. 'Before and after that time, I was running around New York on other jobs and auditions,' he adds. 'We recorded episodes straight through from beginning to end. All cast members in the particular episode being recorded were present at the session, and everything was recorded in real time.'

Preis's preference was not to voice two roles in active dialogue: 'If there was a scene with two characters voiced by the same actor ... one character's line would be read ... and then the second character's lines would be read ... and the editor had to integrate the dialogue after the fact.

'For guest characters, most of the time the voice was established after offering a few different options, then the favourite was decided by the producers. As in any television project, the final decisions are always made by the producers at the session. Similarly, the parts were assigned by the producers. I didn't find it difficult to maintain consistency of a voice, as that's pretty much a requirement of the profession. I don't recall ever listening back to tracks during a recording session.

Timing is always important when recording dialogue. It's especially important for a half-hour animated show. I think you just fall into a certain pace and rhythm, and if it's not moving fast enough, the director will let you know soon enough. Retakes were really kept to a minimum, unless there was a flub ... or someone cracked up ... or choked during one of the *long* speeches by Mumm-Ra. From my standpoint, I enjoyed doing lots of characters ... as that's what I do. The more ... the merrier.

'I don't think anyone was all that aware of the success of *ThunderCats* at the time of the recordings. It was kind of just another job for everyone. A great job ... but still just a job at the time.'

Asked about the atmosphere at recording sessions, Preis reveals the joy felt by cast members and recording staff alike: 'Aside from basically having a lot of fun during the recording process ... and trying desperately not to crack up at some of the crazy dialogue we had to recite, I remember that Larry Kenny had a crazy schedule, having worked on an early morning radio show every day. So between episodes, he would sneak a nap on the couch. I did a great impression of Larry ... and while he was napping, I used to interpret "Larry's dreams" in his voice. It seemed funny at the time. Bob McFadden and Earl Hammond were great, funny and talented performers ... and a lot of fun to work with. Extremely professional ... and exceedingly silly at the same time. Since it was recorded like an old radio show ... with everyone present ... it was a lot of fun. I have worked on other series where the dialogue was recorded to the picture ... and also recorded separately with just one actor doing all of his characters at a session.

'I wish there was more opportunity for this animation to take place in New York again. It's still amazing to me that sometimes I can work with a new producer on a new project ... and they seem so intrigued by the fact that I worked on *ThunderCats* ... as it was so long ago for me. The interesting thing is to see how my kids will react to it, as I have some of the series I worked on that have come out on DVD.'

Preis remains committed to the industry, working as an announcer and voice-over artist for radio and television. His distinct talents can also be heard in a variety of commercials including Lucky the Leprechaun for Lucky Charms and the Vlasic Pickle Stork. In his personal life, he has a huge passion for the famed ventriloquist Edgar Bergen and is the leading historian and archivist for the entertainer's double act with Charlie McCarthy. Additionally, he is committed to his family and has high hopes that his young children will follow in his footsteps.

Engineering *ThunderCats*

Behind the scenes, a crew of talented engineers and directors worked tirelessly to choreograph the finished tracks for *ThunderCats*. Unlike many other animated productions, the show relied hugely on having a precisely finalised soundtrack for each episode, because the entire animation process took place after the recording sessions were completed. Therefore, the visuals returned from Japan would be tailored to the style and pace dictated by the directors and dialogue editors. If a 15-second silence was inserted into the tapes, that precise length of animation would be returned from PAC as the action sequence. The editorial team would be required to select and structure the best takes from the dialogue sessions, 'time' action sequences (structuring the episodes accordingly) and select sound effects and music from the show's library.

Although there were many set technical specifications for the series (including modulation for a variety of character voices), the team would rarely even be given a storyboard prior to recording. The only vision for finished episodes of *ThunderCats* existed in the creative minds of the editorial team, and the part they played in the success of the series cannot be overlooked. Leading the recording sessions was supervising producer Lee Dannacher, who for the most part directed dialogue and worked closely with the technical team to execute the perfect soundtracks for delivery to Japan. Her assembled crew of engineers mostly originated from the studios used to record the series. These included Tony Giovanniello, Larry Franke, Tom Perkins, John Curcio, John Crenshaw and Michael Ungar. Also present at the studios in the early days was executive producer Jules Bass, although once production was more established he took a back seat role. Additionally, other Rankin/Bass employees would assist with recording and, towards the end of the show's second season, Dannacher would begin to delegate certain episodes to alternative directors, including Matthew Malach.

While the final dialogue sessions for the show were recorded at RCA records on 1311, 6th Avenue, New York, the majority of recording for both seasons took place at Howard Schwartz Recording (HSR). Established in 1975 by Howard M Schwartz, these soon became synonymous with high-quality sound services for television, radio and film. Schwartz assembled a dedicated studio specifically for Rankin/Bass productions, and built two additional ones over the course of recording, located on the nineteenth floor of the Greybar building on 44th Street in New York City.

Recording engineer Larry Franke explains the studio set-up for *ThunderCats*: 'The scripts were recorded using four or five AKG 414 and/or Nueman U87 microphones arranged in a star pattern with music stands below to hold the scripts. Dialogue was recorded to a master and a back-up safety ¼-inch mono tape machine, and then edited by me, John Curcio, Mike Ungar and later John Crenshaw. Blank leader was slugged into the mono dialogue reel to allow for action time according to the scripts. The mono dialogue master was then laid up to a two-inch 24-track tape. We then added the music from the library. I generally used four stereo pairs of tracks for music, a few for mono dialogue tracks, and a few for effects. This was then mixed down to a four-track "fullcoat" 35mm and Nagra ¼-inch pilot-tone for sync, and sent to Japan for animation. Kind of backwards to the way it's commonly done. All shows got final approval by Lee Dannacher. As *ThunderCats* became successful, Mike Ungar and John Crenshaw were brought in. Tom Perkins was also involved at the very beginning, until I officially left A & R Recording and moved over to HSR.

'There's a reason awards are now given out for work on the technical end of our business, and our work on *ThunderCats* would surely be a candidate for the Audio for Cartoon Animation category. This was a team effort, and when I listen to the shows today, they stand up wonderfully. I used skills I had acquired recording music and applied them to the dialogue recording and mixing of *ThunderCats*. I'm very proud of our work on this series.'

Speaking about his colleagues, Franke acknowledges the huge talent of the entire team: 'I knew Lee Dannacher from the Rankin/Bass days at A & R Recording pre-*ThunderCats*. I received her vote of confidence when I was offered the opportunity to work on the show, and constant support thereafter. She was always professional and demanded the highest standards for our recording and mixing. She set the bar high from the beginning. John Curcio was a mentor of mine from A & R Recording. We worked on many record projects and jingles together. He also gave Rankin/Bass the nod when it came to me getting the *ThunderCats* gig, as he had recorded all their hour-long specials like *Frosty the Snowman* and *Rudolph the Red Nosed Reindeer*. Tony Giovanniello was a great producer whose patience was limitless when it came to the tediously painstaking process of putting these shows together. Tony wound up contributing many creative ideas to the shows, along with Matthew Malach, as well as producing the final product. Matthew Malach was an amazing and hilarious force behind the shows. He was incredibly fun to work with and contributed much in the editing process as well as producing dialogue in the studio. Finally, John Crenshaw, a great musician and singer (brother of Marshall Crenshaw of rock and roll fame), was an editor along with me and Mike Ungar. We did many rock and roll side projects during these years and it was John and I to whom Bob McFadden gave his "personal side shows" for post-scoring. These were little vignettes he did at home in his many different voices on his reel-to-reel. John and I spent countless hours on Bob's projects for the love of it.

'I began my career as an audio engineer in 1979 at A & R Recording under the tutelage of Phil Ramone and Eliot Scheiner. I worked with Billy Joel, Steely Dan, John Lennon, Joe Jackson, Laurie Anderson and Christine McVie. I also worked on a couple of *Sesame Street* projects, singing backgrounds and engineering. Rankin/Bass was a regular client of A & R Recording. When they had the idea for *ThunderCats*, John Curcio was busy with other projects and I was offered the gig. After some deliberation about leaving the music world, I made the move to HSR, where we set up shop for the new series. Once a script was approved by Lee Dannacher, Matthew Malach and the R/B writers, the dialog was recorded by John Curcio, Tom Perkins and me, with producers Tony Giovanniello and Steve Gruskin.'

Having worked on *ThunderCats* from 1984 until 1988, Franke acknowledges the great affection he had for the job: 'I think it's a great show. I think all Rankin/Bass work had a humanity and warmth that other shows don't, and I think that must be credited to Jules, Arthur and Lee. The years doing *ThunderCats* were the kind of time you look back on and realise you'll probably never have an experience quite the same. It was a time of camaraderie between us, learning, excitement and of course success. For me, this was a magical time in my life and career, and what made it so was the constant creativity that went into making the shows, the antics and humour of the actors, and the camaraderie we developed between one another over the years.

'I remember when we got the word that *ThunderCats* had overtaken [*Masters of the Universe* in the ratings]. We all felt elated and enthusiastic to produce better and better shows both story-wise, and in my case, on the audio side. I was challenged to constantly come up with different sound processing for characters. For example, Earl Hammond could only make his voice go so low for Mumm-Ra, so I helped bring it down to a more menacing sound with a harmoniser. Of course, this meant that all Mumm-Ra's lines had to be harmonised the same way. I did this on the 24-track tape in an additional step. Harmonising and pitch-shifting were common practice in creating different and interesting dialogue quality of many of the characters. Others I can remember where processing was key were Grune the Destroyer, the Berbils, Monkian and the Wolfrat. Somewhere, in my journal, I still have all the settings for the outboard gear we used for the voices.

'There were many cast parties over the years, weddings etc. The show's final episodes were recorded at RCA Records when we moved out of HSR. It was there in Studio B that we all said our final goodbyes. This was combined with a birthday party for Earl Hammond. Parting was indeed sweet, sweet sorrow! After *ThunderCats* ended, I got a call from a friend at Saatchi and Saatchi who offered me a job as a music producer. The timing was perfect, and I have been in the ad business ever since.'

One of the first recording engineers to work on *ThunderCats* was Tom Perkins, who was already working for Howard Schwartz with a multitude of other clients. 'I grew up in rural Connecticut in the '50s and '60s,' recounts Perkins. 'My town was, at that time, mostly a summer community for people from New York. I was always interested in music; my mother used to tell how, even at age two or so, I'd be in front of the record player bouncing to the beat of some song or other. I taught myself drums and guitar and got into bands through my teen years. My grandfather had a tape recorder that fascinated me. He showed me how to use it, and it was a natural understanding for me; the whole process of recording. I went to college and majored in broadcast journalism in Boston, but soon changed my major to production. I got into a band there and we got a recording contract, so my first experience in a professional recording studio was that. Every second I wasn't in the studio singing or playing, I was in the control room watching the engineer. Again, most of what I observed, I simply understood at a molecular level – it was a natural fit. Any questions I had, he answered, and it all fell into place. I decided then and there that I was better suited to the technical than the performing. After college, I attended a course in New York at the Institute of Audio Research, which at the time was the only place of its kind, educating people on the technology of the recording studio. After that, I sought employment and got a job back in Boston making tape copies and doing assistant work at a studio there. They had a film division, so I learned about location sound as well; a fellow named Bill Wangerin was my mentor. I owe him so much, I can never repay his kindness and patience with me. He remains a dear friend.'

Commenting on his introduction to Rankin/Bass serials, Perkins recalls that he joined HSR in 1980, after several jobs at other studios: 'I began there as a tech, wiring a room and doing tape deck alignments and such. Clients I had had in Boston were using HSR to do jingles and recording people from the NY talent pool, and they began requesting me for sessions. Once I'd shown Howie [Schwartz] that I was indeed a mixer and editor, I began building a client base there. When Rankin/Bass started talking to Howie about *ThunderCats*, he asked if I'd be interested in doing it. The upside was that it was a very different and fun project. The downside was that it would consume a lot of time that I'd not be able to spend working with other clients. I thought the trade-off worth it, so I said yes.

'I worked on the show from the very first recordings until somewhere in 1986 or '87, I think. I really don't remember when I stopped! I recorded and edited the original recordings for the pilot and most of the first season's episodes. Unlike many of today's animated shows, we recorded with the entire cast in the booth, each on his or her own mic, and we did the script in page order. Most animated shows I've worked on since then have been recorded out of sequence and frequently one character at a time, in order to get the tightest possible sound. Personally, I think this is a mistake, as there's an energy among a group of actors that transcends whatever mic-to-mic leakage you may have. The same tight-mic disease plagues most music today too. There's no openness, no energy flow, things tend to sound like a series of parts instead of an organic whole. *ThunderCats* was different that way; the actors were all into it, playing off each other, joking between takes, and taking cues from each other. It made my job a little harder, as I had to ride levels and open and close mics, but the end result was a superior performance. The performance, I think, is far more important than nitpicking a little mic leakage that'll be buried under a mountain of battle SFX and music. Lee Dannacher was a great director and got great performances out of the cast.

'In the early stages, Jules Bass came to sessions as well, but he pretty much left the directing to Lee. There seemed to be a trust there that, once we got into a rhythm, he felt she didn't need monitoring. She and I had one difference of opinion, however. I used limiters to keep from overloading the tape. (Remember this was before computers!) I never used them as a crutch like some people do; I used them to actually control peaks far faster than I could, so that a little distortion wouldn't ruin a perfectly good take. And there were many occasions where the actors would be *really* loud, especially Earl Hammond as Mumm-Ra. Anyway, Lee said to me one day, "Well, (name of an engineer) *never* uses limiters; he doesn't need them". I told her it was pretty much impossible to record such dynamic voices without that protection, but I acquiesced and did without. There were a lot of blown takes due to overloads, but we got through. After a few months, I began to get requests from other clients, and I was having a harder time doing all the *ThunderCats* recordings. Lee managed to get the aforementioned limiter-less engineer to come in and record the tracks. Guess what? First thing he did was set up a bunch of DBX 160 limiters in his recording chain. (I'd been using LA-3As.) I pointed this out to Lee. For some reason, it was okay for him to use limiting, I guess, but not for me. That is the only thing about that project that still ticks me off – that she wouldn't see that he *was* doing exactly what she said he *wasn't* doing. He didn't really do anything differently from the way I did, but for whatever reason it was more acceptable from the guy she was more familiar with. That was the first instance of something like that in my career. Since, there've been a few others. It's still irritating.'

Commenting on the amount of editing required to create a finished track, Perkins reveals his 'rule of thumb' was a 3:1 ratio: for every one hour of recorded dialogue, three would be required in post-production. 'As I recall, we'd record actors about once a week at first. Many times we'd do more than one episode in a session. There was a *lot* of editing. That was in the days of tape, physically cutting and splicing. Today, using Pro Tools and such, you can go a bit quicker. Of course, it all depends on how many retakes there are in a given script! But on a show like *ThunderCats*, every break between sentences, every back-and-forth conversation, every breath or p-pop had to be edited to a fare-thee-well. It was very detailed editing, which I happen to enjoy and am good at.

'We would always run a safety tape in the unlikely event something got cut that shouldn't have been, so we had two first-generation master recordings. All editing was performed on one of those to preserve quality. After recording, I'd edit out the bad takes and make a rough edit with no real pacing, make a copy and send it to [Rankin/Bass]. Then Lee would take the script and they'd mark it with places where they'd want space for action sequences. For instance, it might come back with a note saying "22 sec battle" or something like that. I'd then go back and put the proper amount of leader tape in where required and would edit the show to length. Maximum was 22 minutes for a half hour episode. Once timing and spacing were locked in, we'd make a tape with 60 Hz sync on it for the animators to transfer. The sync was so that the mag stock would be recorded and played back at the proper speed; once you had timing locked in, it was vital that there be no deviation in speed. There were going to be a lot of generations of sound after that point and it had to be right.

'Finally, I would mix a music and voice track in several variations. I did the mix internally on the 24-track tape so there were no sync issues. As I recall, there were a mono mix, a stereo mix, and a split mix where the voice and stereo music were balanced to each other, but on separate tracks in case adjustments were needed later in the process. Once I finished those mixes, my part was pretty much done. It was still long before the picture was ready, and my tracks were given to someone else who added the SFX and did the final mix; I don't remember who that was. It might have been Larry Franke. A ¼" tape with a mix was also sent to the animators to make any adjustments to the picture that might benefit from being keyed to the music hits.'

Tom Perkins remains passionate about his work on *ThunderCats* and the collaborative atmosphere he observed during recording: 'I need to say that the cast we had, every one of them, were and are the best. I still see Larry, Lynne, Peter and Doug Preis regularly. Earle Hyman was on *The Cosby Show* playing Bill's dad. I'd worked with all of them before *ThunderCats*, of course. They're top NY talent. Bob McFadden was one of the funniest men I've ever met, and the range of voices he could do was nothing short of astonishing. He is sorely missed. The sessions, though hard work, were also a hell of a lot of fun, given the personalities involved. There was, of course, a lot of fooling around, and some of the outtakes – oh my!

'After a time, I left Howard Schwartz to freelance elsewhere, but Rankin/Bass wanted to keep me as part of the show. I'd go to Howie's at night and work alone doing the music mixes; that went on for a long time. I also did the same work on *SilverHawks* when that show debuted. Tony Giovanniello had been an assistant engineer at Howard Schwartz, but then went to work for Rankin/Bass directly. I enjoyed a friendship and great working relationship with him; it was a little strange at first with him going from associate to client, but he's such a gentleman and overall good guy that any bumps in the road quickly smoothed out. That particular period of time happened to be a great time to be in pro audio, too. Analogue technology was reaching a pinnacle and Howie was always at the forefront of new technology. He wanted and demanded the best from vendors and is still that way. He had a crack tech staff and the machines were always maintained in perfect working order. It was rare when something would break, and if it did, it was fixed immediately. We were very busy, with advertising mostly, and Howie's was the premier place in the city. We did jingles, too, and there was a regular stream of top NY session players in every week, along with the best voice-over talent and celebrities. Mixing with timecode to lock picture and sound was becoming a regular occurrence; many places continued using mag dubbers well into the '90s'.

Continuing to make his living as a freelancer, Perkins has been able to take the experience gained from his analogue roots and thrive in the digital age: 'My career has continued apace since then. I've worked on a lot of other animated series. The new ones all seem to be [recorded] one character at a time, which I don't think is conducive to the best performances. I've recorded voices for several Nickelodeon series such as: *Spongebob Squarepants*; *Avatar: The Last Airbender*; *The Mighty B*; *The X's*; *Ni Hao, Kai Lan*; *Fatherhood*; *Ren & Stimpy*; and many others. My work consists of radio and TV commercials, industrials, audiobooks, TV series, films and music. The most recent music I did was Peter Criss's album *One for All*; I recorded and mixed that record. I've been doing a great deal of ADR[3] for movies, working with Harvey Keitel, Ally Sheedy, Keri Russell, Hugh Jackman, David Duchovny, Jim Gandolfini and many, many others. A documentary I mixed for Planet Grande Pictures won an Emmy award, and promos I've done have won a total of 16 Emmys. I've a number of Clio awards to go with all that; it's been a great ride so far. I've mixed reality shows including: *Whose Wedding is it Anyway*; *She's Moving In*; *Perfect Partner*; and others. Last year I mixed a documentary in Dolby 5.1 for the Smithsonian on John Cohen, an American musical treasure. I've edited the nomination packages for the Grammy Awards – and let me tell you, when your work will be heard by the best ears in the business, along with nearly a billion people worldwide, it gets your attention in a hurry. Since summer 2009, I've been freelancing and have added narrating to my repertoire. I'm becoming proficient in Final Cut Pro and hoping to develop a base in editing visuals.

'There's not much else I'd have wanted to do with my life; audio has always been my passion. If anything, I'd have loved to have done more music, but there's still plenty of time for that. All in all, the experience I've gained, the knowledge I've accumulated, the technology I've been privileged to operate, but most of all the people I've worked with, have made my life more rewarding than I could ever have dreamed as a kid from rural Connecticut. I've worked with the biggest stars in the world on a regular basis; I've worked on advertising seen by hundreds of millions of people; I've made friends with some of the best talent in the world – the New York talent pool, who are the finest, most professional people, and I'm proud to call many of them friends.'

Another member of the team, Tony Giovanniello, acted as a producer and supervisor. In addition to facilitating the technical requirements of the series' audio, he was also responsible for reading finished scripts and deducing the precise timings needed for action sequences. He also performed directorial duties on occasional episodes and was responsible for reviewing the finished output from the team of editors. 'Working on the production of *ThunderCats* was probably the best university I could attend for animation production,' says Giovanniello. 'As an associate producer at the beginning and then supervisory producer, I got to engage in almost every job short of drawing the animation. My engineers, Larry Franke and Michael Unger, would dread my listening to the first cut of the voice-overs, as I was a stickler for a "mouth noise free" clean track. I also selected music from an

---

[3] Additional dialogue recording.

extensive music library composed by Bernie Hoffer and reviewed the rough-cut animation we received from Pacific Animation Corporation in Tokyo. I also supervised music/voice-over mixing and final audio mix to video. I had my hand in so much of the day-to-day production that, even today, when I watch the DVDs of the show, I can tell which ones I produced.

'I began my career in audio/video production in the late 1970s in New York. In the beginning, I apprenticed at various musical instruments and recording gear retail stores and recording studios. I finally landed a full time paid position at Howard Schwartz Recording Studio (HSR). HSR was, at the time, a multi-service facility i.e. audio recording, voice-over, music recording and, in its later days, audio for video. Today the studio is still going strong. It was a fantastic place to really begin a career, as there was much opportunity to experience everything about the audio business. Lots of great engineers and producers to learn from, and the quality of the work was world class. I spent a few years there, off and on, and eventually became an engineer and then studio manager. I remember these days fondly; lots of hard work but a great education. I have made lifelong friends through my association with Howard Schwartz the man (yes there really is a Howard Schwartz) and the studio.

'I left HSR in late 1983 to pursue an opportunity at a New York City music-recording studio. Although the studio was a fantastic facility, it just wasn't the right fit for me. After about six months there, I called up my friend Howard Schwartz. We had lunch at his office, I told him I was looking for something new and challenging and asked if he would "keep his ears open" for me. As I left his office, I passed an attractive young woman in the hallway. We smiled briefly in passing and I was on my way. She was Lee Dannacher of Rankin/Bass. R/B was using HSR for their voice-over recording and production of *ThunderCats*. Lee walked into Howard's office and asked him if he could recommend someone who she could hire as an associate producer on the show. The show was just in the pre-production mode, gearing up for episode one. Howard said he did know someone, and he just walked out the door! I had a message from Howard waiting for me when I got back to work. Being a recording engineer is one of the best ways to learn all aspects of production and "get your feet wet" as a producer, as you are working with different producers every day. And having "good engineering ears" (and hopefully good taste) gives you an added advantage. I believe that, at that time, many engineers wanted to eventually move into production in their careers and so did I. Well, as the saying goes, "the rest is history".'

Having worked on the series from the pilot, 'Exodus', through to the show's finale, 'The Book of Omens', Giovanniello insists he looked forward to going to work every day: 'The staff was also a fun bunch of people to work with. Every day, John Crenshaw would show up with his "over the top" pompadour haircut and tell us about his escapades the night before, in a ThunderCat voice. Most all of the recording staff were musicians, so there was lots of commonality. We would all go out after work, sometimes hang out on the weekends, and have a blast at the company holiday parties. The whole staff knew at the time that *ThunderCats* would be a hit show. There was a certain magical element to these ThunderCats from Thundera. The actors were an amazing bunch, all veteran voice-over actors on the New York scene. You would hear commercials on TV when you got home at night and know it was Cheetara or Lion-O. You could watch *The Cosby Show* and see

Panthro playing Bill Cosby's father. It was quite hilarious when some of them would flub a voice-over line and curse in a ThunderCat voice. There was an outtake reel to prove it. I am honoured to have had the opportunity to be part of such a wonderful production. The concept was dynamic, the writing was superb and the production was top notch. I have since changed careers, but when I am asked by someone in their thirties what I did before, they are ecstatic when I say I worked on *ThunderCats*. Sometimes, they even jokingly bow in respect. It is pretty amazing the impact that *ThunderCats* has had on pop culture worldwide.'

When completed recordings were sent to Japan, they consisted, as previously mentioned, of final dialogue edits, precise timings (to facilitate the animation) and a loosely assembled music and effects track that would be conformed in post-production scoring. To make a workable review print, editors at PAC would place their own sound effects onto the 35mm prints that were returned. 'They put some wild and sometimes overblown sound effects on the soundtrack,' says Giovanniello. 'In their defence, I think that was because most Japanese animation companies were working on mostly anime at the time, which didn't have a big budget for the actual animation (necessitating fewer cels per second, as that brings costs way down), so they would over-compensate by putting in lots of big sound effects (explosions, synthesiser sound effects etc). We in New York would add something maybe more appropriate at the final mixing-to-picture stage. We might have tried to lower, or fully edit out, an effect from Japan and replace it with something in the library of the Mix Place, where we would do the final mixing. We would also maybe add some echo effects where we thought they were needed, like ThunderCats entering Mumm-Ra's pyramid or a cave etc.

'I had the privilege to work with all the actors and the entire production staff in New York and even some of the technical and production staff at Lorimar in California. It was also great to meet some of the lead animators from Japan as they came to New York on occasion. It was a great group of people and some are still very close friends.'

Unlike many of his colleagues, Tony Giovanniello has relinquished the world of television and film production to pursue his vocational interests in international healthcare: 'After *ThunderCats*, I took some time off. I had the opportunity to move to Los Angeles and continue working in the business, but at the time, I wasn't sure if LA was the place I wanted to live. I travelled with my friend and *ThunderCats* art director/ Japan liaison Chuck Hasegawa to Hawaii for a bit of rest and relaxation for one month and stayed for six years. I have always had a love of Asia – its culture and history – and was looking for an opportunity to work and play there. We formed IVY and Associates, a consulting firm with its headquarters in Tokyo and an office in Kona, Hawaii. IVY guided an international clientele of entertainers, bankers, corporate CEOs and individuals in East–West corporate branding and US investment and mergers. In 2000, I went back to college and earned my Master's degree in Science and Acupuncture with a specialty in stress, anxiety, depression and post-traumatic stress disorder (PTSD). I am currently practicing in New York City, with an eye for establishing an international practice. In 2008, I founded the non-profit Acupuncture Ambassadors. Its mission is to travel, teach and treat with acupuncture in areas of the world that have little or no healthcare. We have a focus on treating PTSD in the refugee and conflict victim communities worldwide. We have been in Vietnam, Cambodia, the Navajo Reservation in Arizona and most recently in Nepal and Senegal, West Africa.'

Two further members of the team, Michael Ungar and John Curcio, recall the energy of working on *ThunderCats*, *SilverHawks* and *The Comic Strip*. 'The spirit of collaboration and friendly competition amongst all of us post-production guys helped to explore the creative process for ourselves too!' says Ungar. 'It made me a much better engineer, mixer, music editor and producer by working alongside people who wanted each and every show to turn out better than the last. It gave me a blueprint as to how to conduct my professional life, and I am friends with many of the people I worked with 25 years ago.' Curcio agrees, adding that Rankin/Bass were a 'class act': 'Jules was great to work with; he was a pro, and we had a lot of fun. He handled the soundtrack and Arthur Rankin dealt with the animation, so I worked with Jules more than Arthur. Arthur was the epitome of a gentleman and I always enjoyed his visits when we were in session in the studio. The longevity of their holiday specials is well-deserved. I look forward to seeing them air every year and hear comments from all generations about how much they are loved.'

'Recording of the characters was done in an ensemble fashion,' confirms Ungar. 'Four to six mics set up in a star pattern in a fairly large room for maximum isolation (which often was not much, because everybody played pretty full voiced characters). This made for a challenging dialogue edit on occasion, but more importantly gave the show a sense of timing and togetherness that other shows lacked. Most of the cast were in the room at the same time, giving outlandish performances that encouraged everyone to really take it to another level. Most other shows recorded actors one or two at a time doing line readings. This tended to make them more stilted reads and completely relied on the dialogue director to create consistency within the story. After all, it is not so much about the dialogue as it is about the line reads. Rankin/Bass insisted on ensemble work whenever possible, and those characters truly filled the room with their presence, not to mention the camaraderie it created between the group.'

Curcio expresses the admiration he felt for his colleagues: 'The cast loved Lee Dannacher and she was really on top of tweaking the script and making it the best it could be. Larry Kenney, the voice of Lion-O, was always clowning around, and his signature "ThunderCats Ho!" was his constant refrain. People who knew I worked on the show would ask me to ask Larry to record a customised "ThunderCats Ho" for them, such as, "Hi Billy, this is Lion-O. Have a great day and remember – ThunderCats, ThunderCats Ho!" – and he never turned me down. Earl Hammond, as the Mumm-Ra character, would end up hoarse from screaming his intense lines. He really went at it one hundred percent. Bob McFadden would always light up the room – what a talented guy he was. Everyone loved and respected Bob. The talents of Lynne Lipton, Peter Newman, Doug Preis and Earle Hyman all helped make this show a hit. The technical staff were excellent; they were so much fun and turned out some great-sounding shows. I was very fortunate to have had the opportunity to work on *ThunderCats*, and I was very glad to have been a part of that wonderful experience.'

Curcio began his career at A & R Recording Studios in 1969: 'It was one of the hottest studios in New York at the time. Phil Ramone was one of the principal owners and I worked with him on many projects. A & R had a talented group of staff engineers and they were instrumental in helping me learn my craft. The studio had a very diverse clientele list. I was very lucky to be able to get involved in just about every aspect of recording projects – jingles, records, movie scores, Broadway cast albums, radio etc. Don Hahn was one of the staff engineers that I worked with quite often. I was his assistant when he recorded the music scores for some of the Rankin/Bass holiday specials. When it came time to record the actors, edit and mix these specials, Jules Bass offered me the opportunity to do it. Prior to *ThunderCats*, I was involved with many of his holiday shows. We started recording *ThunderCats* in 1984 and I worked on it from the beginning through both seasons. It was very popular at the time. I recorded the actors for the shows and I had a great time with the cast. There was never a dull moment from the time the characters' voices were created, to the time we laid down the scripts.'

Asked to account for the longevity of *ThunderCats*, Ungar believes the show was more esoteric than its rivals: 'In all the other shows of this ilk, including *Galaxy Rangers* and even the immensely popular [*Masters of the Universe*], the goal of the characters was to accomplish some great task – either catch a criminal or foil a plot to destroy the world (again) or whatever your standard storyline was. To that end, these superheroes were not that super. They rarely if ever caught their nemesis. After all, where would the show go if you kept catching all the criminals? No more bad guys after a while, and certainly not ones that you could repeat or could use to become popular. It was always at the last minute that they stopped the world from ending, and it usually meant major collateral damage, if not to life, at least to property. I always thought it was cool that if you were a ThunderCat, due to your circumstance, all you had to do was to survive, to win. That forces were aligned against you daily, but all you needed to do was make it through the day, and that was a victory. Rings a bit more true than the other cartoons, I always thought.'

Both still earning their living from audio production, Michael Ungar and John Curcio continue to put their many skills to good use in a variety of projects. Ungar is Senior Vice President of Broadway Sound, a division of Broadway Video Inc. Curcio, meanwhile, is employed by HBO. 'I decided to work there when I saw that the studio and music scene were leaving New York and moving out to LA,' explains Curcio. 'I have been with HBO for a number of years now and I'm into a variety of work – audio, graphics, quality control etc. It's not as exciting as the A & R days, but it has its own rewards.'

As well as adding two further cast members to the recording team, the second season of *ThunderCats* also saw the introduction of additional technical staff, including sound designer John Crenshaw. 'I was a touring musician with my brother, Marshall Crenshaw,' he recounts. 'After life on the road got to be too much, I got a job as a messenger at Howard Schwartz Recording. I worked there for about eight years. [During that time], I began to assist on sessions, taking editing notes and changing reels of tape. I began working on *ThunderCats* at the beginning of the second season. I took it upon myself to start making suggestions to the dialogue director, Lee Danacher. I then became a full time assistant for *ThunderCats*. We all wore many hats, as the saying goes. I started as assistant and then became a dialogue editor. Sometimes, I would do voices on the show; really more like vocal sound effects such as grunts and laughs and that sort of thing. We would all end up doing each other's jobs from time to time. If something needed to be done, whoever was around did it. It was an exciting time. We would work ridiculous hours, living and breathing *ThunderCats*! We also had a great time, and as long as things got done, we were left to our own devices. There were always ridiculous deadlines, but it was never really daunting, because the people I worked with were all fantastic and R/B were appreciative of all the hours and hard work.'

While Crenshaw no longer sees many of his former colleagues, he still feels a strong bond with them: 'It's like we went through something really big and important together. To me, it was about growing up and learning things from a small group of incredibly talented people. Larry Franke was/is a brilliant music engineer, and a lot of what I learned came from watching Larry at work. It's funny, I knew at the time that *ThunderCats* was an extremely popular show, but I never realised how huge it was until I began working with people who were kids at the height of its popularity. I think it is still looked upon fondly because it wasn't just trying to beat the bad guys. It was about survival on a new planet and trying to re-establish the culture of a destroyed planet; kind of deep actually! During *ThunderCats*, another series came along called *SilverHawks*. I worked on that show as well as another series for R/B called *The Comic Strip*. Somewhere during *SilverHawks*, I left Howard Schwartz and was hired by Rankin/Bass. I was still editing dialogue, but was also directing the actors, supervising final mixes, going over storyboards with the animators via fax machine (as there was no internet, which is hard to imagine now). I believe that Lee Dannacher, Peter Bakalian and I were the last employees of Rankin/Bass when they closed the doors of their offices in the Museum of Television and Radio. After R/B, I was once again hired by Howard Schwartz and worked there with fellow *ThunderCats* veteran Michael Ungar. I worked there until 1994 when Michael and Ralph Kelsey opened Broadway Sound, the audio division of Broadway Video owned by Lorne Michaels, the creator of *Saturday Night Live*. I have worked there since then, primarily mixing interstitial breaks on Showtime. I have also written music for commercials and have just completed four songs for a movie in production called *Losers Take All*, about the mid 1980s punk scene in the US.'

One final name must be noted when discussing the *ThunderCats* recording sessions: Rankin/Bass employee Matthew Malach regularly attended the sessions and, in his capacity as an episodic director (both on some dialogue sessions and reviewing storyboards from Japan), earned the respect of his fellow team members, contributing to a wide range of production processes. 'Production didn't kick in until the script was written and approved,' explains Malach. 'After the show was recorded, the audio cutting began. Besides the dialogue itself, we would have to add time for "action sequences" and/or pauses between talking characters. It's an interesting practice: one must imagine how long it would take for, say, Lion-O to jump out of the ThunderTank, unsheathe his sword and lay into Mumm-Ra. In the audio edit bay, action time was added next to the dialogue in the form of blank tape. We would trim sequences in order to get the show to the exact time, which was something like 21.02". We would then add music from the library – wonderfully composed by Bernie Hoffer. None of this was done to picture, but based on script and eventually the storyboard. Finally, the finished product would come from Asia and we would mix the show – rarely making any other audio changes. There was no post-show picture editing here in the US; everything was cut exactly to time and the show remained locked that way throughout the production. It's a wonderfully efficient and cheap way to control content. In the beginning, Lee Dannacher was doing all of this herself, a remarkable work output. Eventually, I began directing recording sessions, made storyboard notes, added time, supervised edits and supervised the final mix (as did Tony Giovanniello and Steve Gruskin). Near the end of the first season, I offline edited the *ThunderCats* one hour movie for video and some other projects like that as well.'

Uniquely, Matthew divided his professional responsibilities between the recording studios and the Rankin/Bass offices, ably 'swapping hats' between scriptwriter, administrator, director and sound designer. He says there was a marked contrast between his places of work: 'There were two environments in the *ThunderCats* production: the office, which was somewhat staid; and the studio, which to me was like a funhouse. To this day, I haven't had as many good times as I had working with the folks in the studio. My time spent with Larry Franke, Michael Unger and John Crenshaw was hilarious. We made so much noise and had such a blast. Part of the fun was when Larry and Michael would put together outtake reels, some of which are now legendary on the internet.'

The overall impression one gets from speaking with the cast and crew who painstakingly recorded each episode of *ThunderCats* is of a great passion and enthusiasm for their work. None of these talented individuals recalls their time on the show simply as a mark on their resume, instead telling of the deep enjoyment they gained. This must surely have played its part in creating the energy and dynamism seen – and heard – on screen; from the beautiful delivery of dialogue from the voice artists, to the imaginative use of music and pacing brought from the recording engineers. The many sessions committed to tape at Howard Schwartz Recording ensured that *ThunderCats* could never be anything short of revolutionary. The unique atmosphere described by so many of the cast and crew is testament to how proud each and every member of the team was to be involved. The longevity of *ThunderCats* is a befitting result of their contributions.

PART TWO
EPISODE GUIDE

6. BOOK OF OMENS
The Complete Story Guide

In the following comprehensive story guide, each *ThunderCats* episode is given a rating (out of five stars) and reviewed by this author. A short commentary from the screenwriters and/or production personnel involved is also provided. This is intended to serve as a companion to the series' official DVD releases and, as such, the episodes have been listed in accordance with their broadcast order. For season one, this differs slightly from the order in which the episodes were written and produced – due in large part to the animation schedules, which often returned completed programmes out of sequence. Below each episode's title, airdate information has been provided both for the domestic American run and for the BBC1 transmission of the show in the UK. The aim here has been to give the first broadcast date for each country. While this may seem a simple task, research into the broadcast history of the second season has proved remarkably difficult due to the series' nature as a syndicated show. While the first season airdates are recorded in detail, neither Rankin/Bass nor Warner Brothers collated or retained paperwork giving the exact transmission dates for the second season. Compounding the problem, contemporary TV listings merely list the series title, not the individual episode title. Because of this, it is entirely possible that completely reliable first broadcast data no longer exists for the second season episodes. Some of the dates given below have thus had to be estimated, using production documentation and station correspondence that gives a good indication of the relevant broadcasting periods with only a small margin of error. In these cases, the dates have been marked with an asterisk.

SEASON ONE
1985

1. Exodus (4.5 stars)
Written by: Leonard Starr
US Broadcast Date: 23 January 1985
UK Broadcast Date: 2 January 1987

The ThunderCats' debut adventure is a fast-paced epic penned by series stalwart Leonard Starr and, as a screenplay, lacks no ambition. Written in the style of a Hollywood blockbuster, it depicts the destruction of an entire civilisation and the near extinction of an alien race – despite having only 20 minutes in which to do this. It is testament to the pacing of Starr's script that it achieves so much in so little screen time.

If any small criticism can be levelled at 'Exodus', it is the challenge it poses the audience to take stock of proceedings in so short a time frame. It is no surprise that the movie-length pilot, which combined 'Exodus' and the next episode, 'The Unholy Alliance', runs at a slightly improved pace. An additional handful of scenes were included in the compiled pilot and several short scenes were excised from the episodic version to fit the time slot. Whilst the missing scenes do not affect the core storyline, they do give the viewer very little time to absorb the information provided. Another unintentional consequence of this episodic re-edit is the occasionally poor splicing of scenes and background music.

Poor edits notwithstanding, the standard of animation on display in 'Exodus' is impressive. From the opening title sequence that introduced the world to the ThunderCats, through to a range of superbly realised and directed scenes, the episode is a showreel for the quality of programming *ThunderCats* would offer. The royal flagship crashing through the atmosphere into Third Earth is a visual triumph, and the revolutionary techniques of depth, lighting and visual effects all set the scene for what would become a pioneering television serial.

To those familiar with *ThunderCats*, it is apparent that 'Exodus' has a darker tone than later episodes. In particular, it has several scenes of dialogue without background music, which gives it a sombre feel. Equally, the voice actors, new to their roles, portray their characters a little differently from how they would later develop.

The decision to have Lion-O transform from a small boy to adulthood during the pilot episode was a brave one. In children's programming generally, it is far more commonplace for the lead protagonist to be a youngster, yet *ThunderCats* cleverly rejects this formula by reflecting the notion that children strive to be considered equals by their mentors, rather than embrace their vulnerability. The maturation process that Lion-O begins in 'Exodus' was one every child could empathise with, and the show may well have been decidedly inferior should Lion-O have remained a child throughout.

Finally, 'Exodus' is notable for its lead character. Considering Jaga's role would be relatively minor in subsequent episodes, it is interesting that he is presented here with such prominence. For fans re-watching the episode, it offers a unique experience to see Jaga participating in a story beyond his typical 'advisory' capacity, and he is presented as a stern and not altogether likeable character who, nonetheless, performs the ultimate sacrifice in a death somewhat derivative of *Star Wars*.

A pilot script must surely be one of the most difficult to write. In many shows, the pilot falls short of the quality of later episodes – or, conversely, establishes a standard that cannot continue to be met as a series progresses. With 'Exodus', Leonard Starr strikes the right balance and, while the idea of introducing over a dozen characters and a mass exodus from a dying planet may seem ambitious, the episode succeeds in its mandate to introduce the world to the ThunderCats and set up a show that would thrive for decades to come.

Writer's Commentary from Leonard Starr:

The first story was written in such a way that it could be played as a two hour show or an hour show or four half-hour shows – depending on where it was being broadcast. Each separate station could decide for itself.

We left Thundera, because putting the ThunderCats in a circumstance familiar to the viewer (Earth – albeit an alternative version) would be easier, and a villain being a mummy would be advantageous for the kids. Subsequent stories would follow a traditional form – there was an obstacle that had to be overcome in order to reach a resolution. We made Lion-O a child initially because it was children's show. For Lion-O to start as a boy and grow into manhood would help the development of the show, and I could get some wisdom imparted into him through Jaga. We showed what was called 'creative violence'; in other words, a lot of stuff happened but nobody died.

2. The Unholy Alliance (4 stars)
Written by: Leonard Starr
US Broadcast Date: 23 January 1985
UK Broadcast Date: 2 January 1987

The *ThunderCats* saga continues with the second half of the series pilot. 'The Unholy Alliance' effectively expands the characterisation of the ThunderCats introduced in 'Exodus', while giving their arch-nemesis his own introductory episode. Right from the outset, this episode unfolds at a much more relaxed pace and we can at last take stock of the situation the ThunderCats find themselves in.

Once again Leonard Starr takes a successful gamble, by dedicating the majority of the second instalment of *ThunderCats* to both Mumm-Ra and the Mutants. This quickly establishes the formula for subsequent episodes that villains will be given equal screen time to the core characters.

The character of Mumm-Ra has clearly been given much consideration by the show's creators. Unlike other contemporary animated series, *ThunderCats* adds depth to its lead villain as well as its heroes, by hinting at his own backstory; and viewers of the time must have been truly shocked as the articulate, decaying mummy becomes a raging giant that proves a genuine menace for the ThunderCats.

The relationship between Mumm-Ra and the ThunderCats is instantly fascinating. Whilst Mumm-Ra's initial motivation revolves around the desire to possess the source of the ThunderCats' power, the Eye of Thundera, the ThunderCats are, from his point of view, an invading force. From this point on, much of Mumm-Ra's impetus lies in his desire to protect his perceived kingdom, a device that adds far greater dimensions to his aggression than simply being a 'figure of evil'.

Mumm-Ra's revelation that he had been around since the planet was still known as 'First Earth' is suitably vague, and while this may be an alternative version of our own world, this is left to the viewer to decide.

The parallel between the ThunderCats and the Mutants – both stranded and trying to survive – resonates with the viewer, and Mumm-Ra's introduction is memorable. Once again, the animators excel, and Mumm-Ra's transformation is no less impressive for being repeated so often in later episodes.

'The Unholy Alliance' may not be the most dynamic *ThunderCats* episode, but it does give the viewer all the background needed to progress through the series. The reciprocal understanding between Mumm-Ra and the Mutants is full of clever and witty dialogue, and the principal characters of Slithe, Monkian and Jackalman all make their mark as more than standard villains, each with distinctive and developed personality traits.

In 'The Unholy Alliance', Lion-O continues his unwilling transformation from child to adult. He is presented here as a petulant youth, at first reluctant to participate in chores for the betterment of the group and later showing contempt for the 'gentle creatures' of Third Earth. This imaginative writing balances the inherent likeability of the series' protagonist, whilst illustrating that he has a long way to go before he will be a fitting leader of the team. That he is no match for Mumm-Ra, at this early stage, is an important concept for the series and establishes the ThunderCats' morality – that only through teamwork can they survive on their new home

Perhaps the only real disappointment of this episode is the climax to Mumm-Ra's attack against Lion-O. The method of defeating Mumm-Ra via the reflection of 'his own evil' seems somewhat unoriginal, and his potential is a little diminished because of it. Despite this, 'The Unholy Alliance' feels much more like a 'familiar' *ThunderCats* episode than 'Exodus'. The formula of Mumm-Ra attacking the ThunderCats, only to be repelled via his "Achilles heel", would be reused many times later on, but this ultimately tiresome repetition should not count against its impact at the beginning of the series.

Ultimately, the introduction of Mumm-Ra would prove to be as crucial to the series as the ThunderCats themselves, and 'The Unholy Alliance' maintains the standard of imaginative writing and production values as the viewer begins to invest interest in the unfolding serial.

Writer's Commentary from Leonard Starr:

One thing that I had written was that Third Earth was Earth after a big atomic conflagration, but they took that out because they thought that would be too scary for kids. It didn't matter; it was still Third Earth, however that happened to come about. It was the cycle after Mankind was done on the planet. It was not inhabited by human beings as we know them. All we did was eliminate the references to how it came about.

I tried to remember what I liked when I was a kid and what kids still like, and they like mummies. They've redone the original mummy film now several times and done sequels and everything else. It was the same reasoning. What did I call him – the Everliving? The fact he could transform into various shapes was because kids like things like *Transformers*. There really wasn't a hell of a lot of original stuff in there.

3. Berbils (3 stars)
Written by: Leonard Starr
US Broadcast Date: 11 September 1985
UK Broadcast Date: 8 January 1987

The third instalment of *ThunderCats* represents a slight dip in the level of adrenaline-fuelled excitement. 'Berbils' can best be described as a simple story, competently executed.

The introduction of the Ro-Bear Berbils is welcome. While their design may initially lead the viewer to believe that *ThunderCats* has taken a turn towards the bizarre, their dialogue and morality prevent them being represented as mere comic relief. And although 'Berbils' isn't a particularly memorable episode in its own right – possibly because the eponymous characters would become so familiar later on – it does move the 'story arc' along, and we see the first appearance of the famed ThunderTank and the beginnings of the Cats' Lair (courtesy of blueprints created by Tygra). 'Berbils' also indicates how the ThunderCats are going to be able to survive on the planet, progressing from being alone and vulnerable to securing a food source, allies and a (willing) workforce. In fairness to Leonard Starr, these early episodes still have to lay the foundations of the show, and this inevitably restricts the amount of other story material that can be included.

'Berbils' continues the trend of having the ThunderCats face multiple attacks in quick succession. In 'Exodus' they fought off attacks by the Mutants both on board their ship and on Third Earth. 'The Unholy Alliance' presented further attacks, first by the Mutants and then by Mumm-Ra. Now the ThunderCats face threats from both the Trollogs and the locust. In time, this practice would be discontinued in favour of each episode having one, more considered plot, giving time for greater development of characters and storytelling.

There are some nice moments in 'Berbils', and the comic pairing of Snarf and Lion-O begins to work very well as they exchange some genuinely witty dialogue. ('I think they're called Berbils,' says Lion-O. 'That's not what I've been calling them!' replies Snarf.)

Despite the (relatively) straightforward nature of this script, Leonard Starr does throw in some interesting story threads: Lion-O's character is clearly continuing to evolve, and he feels much more like the man he is destined to become in later episodes. Starr also cleverly misleads the audience, leading us to believe that Lion-O is so enraged by the Trollogs' attack on the Berbils that a Trollog massacre is bound to follow. However, Lion-O reigns in his anger (through his own accord) and merely defends his new allies. At the end of the episode, Mumm-Ra's reaction to defeat is once again unexpected: rather than his more usual self-chastisement, he simply retreats to his sarcophagus with almost a smile on his face; Mumm-Ra is enjoying the fight just as much as any victory – yet another character asset that sets this protagonist above standard cartoon villainy.

Even if 'Berbils' isn't quite good enough to 'stand out', there's more than enough to make it successfully 'fit in'.

Writer's Commentary from Leonard Starr

Where did we get our ideas from? Stories just came out of thin air really. We'd been [writing] for so long they sometimes manufactured themselves at some point.

The trouble with the Berbils was the voices they got for them – you couldn't understand them. That was the fault there. I guess [it was my fault] that I [introduced] these robots. But I wasn't responsible for the voices, although I did make suggestions occasionally. I never liked the voice of Snarf either. I wanted him to be like one of the dummies of Edgar Bergen[4]. The voice they had for him never pleased me. But there's no wrong way to have a hit, so it all sort of worked.

4. The Slaves of Castle Plun-Darr (3 stars)
Written by: Leonard Starr
US Broadcast Date: 12 September 1985
UK Broadcast Date: 15 January 1987

The introduction to the world of *ThunderCats*, as written by Leonard Starr, concludes with 'The Slaves of Castle Plun-Darr', a stand-alone episode that nonetheless serves as the fourth and concluding part of the initial story arc.

This is a showcase episode, serving as a reminder of the elements that have been introduced over the previous three. When viewed from this perspective, it achieves its mandate admirably. It is arguably a showreel for the *ThunderCats* format, and shamelessly displays the best parts of the show, tied together with a simple but effective plot.

It must not be forgotten that while Leonard Starr had been given the honour of creating the opening episodes of *ThunderCats* (an opportunity nearly all of the series' writers would have jumped at), it did not come without a heavy responsibility. This episode is a good example of a script being put together to serve a specific purpose, rather than giving Starr carte-blanche to indulge his creativity. In this instance, it falls to 'The Slaves of Castle Plun-Darr' to introduce the newly-completed homes of the ThunderCats and the Mutants – Cats' Lair and Castle Plun-Darr respectively.

While the ever-friendly and resourceful ThunderCats have recruited a

---

[4] A noted American ventriloquist.

willing band of labourers, the Mutants have taken a more aggressive route, having enslaved a peace-loving race native to Third Earth. The contrasts between ThunderCats and Mutants continue to be explored in this episode, and the story offers a direct comparison between the opposing forces.

The episode starts with a high-paced chase through the forest with the ThunderKittens, then each of the main characters is given a share of the airtime, allowing for his or her skills and attributes to be displayed to the viewer. Cheetara shows her speed and agility in a battle with Jackalman; Tygra dodges an attack by an armed Monkian; and Panthro faces the Mutants' leader, Slithe. And as each of the principal ThunderCats is spotlighted in turn, Bernard Hoffer's music score is given ample time to play out that character's 'leitmotif'. Even the ThunderTank is given another outing to prove its worth.

Once again, we see that the Mutants are no real match for the ThunderCats, as each in turn is defeated. Panthro's eagerness to face Slithe without weaponry illustrates both the bravery and that integrity that the ThunderCats possess. Lion-O too takes centre stage and, for the first time, there is almost no show of immaturity. To the casual viewer tuning in for the first time, there is little to suggest that Lion-O is not the rightful Lord of the ThunderCats in both body and mind. His resolve to face the Brutemen at the end of the episode draws criticism from his fellow ThunderCats, but the hypocrisy of this is not lost on the viewer, given that nearly all of them are equally guilty of standing their ground when faced with a challenge. If anything, Lion-O beings to show a penchant for leadership that will later earn him respect amongst his peers.

The episode isn't without minor niggles. For instance, Slithe's exposition in Castle Plun-Darr, where he explains both the plot and his plans to the audience, seems a little lazy and unnecessary (something that probably wouldn't have made it past the editing desk of script editor Peter Lawrence in later episodes). But these shortcomings are small enough to go unnoticed when watching the episode.

A highlight of the episode is the moment when Lion-O calls to the ThunderCats: 'Will the Eye of Thundera penetrate even stone? We'll soon know.' This presages a great visual treat, as the beam emanates from the sword and battles the twists and turns of Castle Plun-Darr before emerging from the tip of the building – using it as an aerial. Additionally, Leonard Starr once again proves adept at judging when it is necessary to omit Mumm-Ra, and his exclusion from proceedings allows more pressing storylines to be resolved.

Writer's Commentary from Leonard Starr:

All adventure stories depend on an interesting villain. If you've got a dull villain, you've got a dull story. The idea was to make the Mutants as interesting as possible so they'd have a greater obstacle to overcome to reach the end of the story. It's all basic storytelling.

By that time, I'd been doing a syndicated strip for 25/30 years, so pacing and progressing a series were natural to me. You need an idea that is capable of infinite projection, and it's the same with the *ThunderCats*. That was the point of the Third Earth map I drew, that they had this new terrain to deal with. By that time I had an instinct for pacing things across episodes, and I tried to instil it in the other writers. Sometimes things work, sometimes they don't. Some episodes are always better than others.

We just hoped to God that the story would work and that someone would watch it. Three stories went to Japan each week, so you can imagine how much work went into that. We had an elderly British woman [in the team] and she said it was like London during the Blitz! Everybody was just in there and doing it and hoping to God that they survived.

5. Pumm-Ra (3 stars)
Written by: Julian P Gardner
US Broadcast Date: 13 September 1985
UK Broadcast Date: 29 January 1987

The first episode of *ThunderCats* to come from the pen of a writer other than Leonard Starr is this charming and effective entry from executive producer Jules Bass (using the pseudonym Julian P Gardner) – his one and only solo script contribution. Given that Bass was one of the principal instigators of *ThunderCats*, it provides an interesting indication of his personal take on the series.

While the episode features a relatively pedestrian 'Mumm-Ra infiltrates'-style plot, it does contain a few nice touches. With the reintroduction of Mumm-Ra, we get to see the first encounter between Lion-O's fellow ThunderCats and their principal adversary, and his exploration of the newly constructed Cats' Lair provides a perfect opportunity for the viewer to see its interior.

Where 'Pumm-Ra' is most effective is in its dialogue. Bass displays great skill at handling this, and there are some incredibly sincere exchanges, including Mumm-Ra's impassioned monologue, which somehow manages to evoke empathy from the audience: 'I am not the intruder, it is you that has disturbed my rest!' Bass also succeeds in painting a detailed picture of life on Third Earth and providing a brief look at ThunderCat domesticity in the Lair. Simple touches such as the provision of cooking and sleeping areas really give an added credibility to the series, and this attention to detail instantly places *ThunderCats* in a league above its contemporaries. We also learn that the ThunderCats are intent on rebuilding their way of life, and their council meeting (where Tygra has been placed in charge) is an interesting glance at Thunderian democracy in action.

Lion-O seems to have regressed a little in this episode, showing much of the petulance of the initial adventures, yet his vulnerability and predisposition to revert to childlike ways seems in keeping with the character and reminds us that he has far to go in persuading his peers that he deserves the title of Lord of the ThunderCats.

Sadly, Mumm-Ra's disguise as Pumm-Ra is not particularly well developed and we get precious little time to see his counterpart in action before the mummy reverts to his natural form. However, overall, 'Pumm-Ra' is a welcome addition to the first batch of *ThunderCats* episodes, and its central premise – that the *ThunderCats* are alone and desperate to find other survivors from their past life – is suitably profound, affording Mumm-Ra one of his most cunning endeavours. If nothing else, we also learn that Cheetara can cover a mile on Third Earth in 30 seconds!

Head Writer's Commentary from Leonard Starr:

Producers don't write. Producers are people who say, 'Boy if I only had the time, I could write it better'. Jules Bass did write one story, 'Pumm-Ra', and it was terrible. Really, really terrible. I didn't know that Jules had written it; he wrote it under a pseudonym, Julian Gardner. I told him, 'We can't use this guy,' and Jules said, 'No it's all right, it's okay.' It was really bad. He just didn't understand the whole thing. I think that's what sunk *SilverHawks*. They could have had an entire new series going, but he had to do it his way and it was going to be great, and it wasn't.

6. The Terror of Hammerhand (2 stars)
Written by: Ron Goulart & Julian P Gardner
US Broadcast Date: 16 September 1985
UK Broadcast Date: 5 February 1987

One of the reasons for the continued success and longevity of *ThunderCats* must surely be its high animation standards and production values. Uncompromising in its approach to visual storytelling, *ThunderCats* at its best outshone nearly all of its 1980s rivals. It is this expectation of excellence that regrettably makes the slightly disappointing 'The Terror of Hammerhand' stand out from its neighbouring episodes.

It is true to say that the *ThunderCats* production team and Masaki Iizuka's Pacific Animation Corporation were still 'finding their feet' during the early run of episodes. Because of the intense workload, many elements, and indeed some entire episodes, were outsourced to various animation studios across Japan, Taiwan, Hong Kong and Korea. While all final elements were overseen by Masaki, Nishida and Kubo (production executive, background artist and key animator respectively), standards did sometimes vary. While the majority of early episodes feature occasional 'awkward' sequences, 'The Terror of Hammerhand' is peculiarly 'experimental' in its direction, and individual cels are, at times, poorly realised – featuring character likenesses that fall far from the mark. Nonetheless, the episode is not without redemption, and the beautifully hand-painted backgrounds (overseen by Nishida), offer an outstanding standard of artistry. In particular, scenes set in the forests of Third Earth and on board the Berserkers' ship are perfectly executed. There are also some stylised sequences (including the one-to-one combat between Lion-O and Hammerhand) that are extremely effective.

Unfortunately, to compound the episode's occasional visual shortcomings, 'The Terror of Hammerhand' also features a confusing plot. The introduction of Hammerhand is welcome, and he is immediately memorable as a guest villain. However, the Berserkers (who would later be redesigned by LJN toy designer Kevin Mowrer for 'ThunderCats Ho!') fail to make much of an impact here, and the depiction of humanoid characters in a landscape full of a myriad of weird and wonderful creatures seems a little unremarkable.

While the script isn't without merit, it does feel a little like ' *ThunderCats* by numbers' and one can't help but feel it could have been more engaging. Sadly, key story elements struggle to combine to form much of a plot, and concepts such as the Unicorn Keeper's ring (with its 'magical powers') seem utterly superfluous given the presence of the Sword of Omens. The episode also begins poorly with a random battle between Lion-O and a tree, before the ThunderCat inexplicably takes flight courtesy of a giant crow. These unnecessary diversions slow down the action and prevent adequate time being spent in developing the guest villains.

The final point of note is Bob McFadden's vocal delivery of Snarf. Once again, the 'settling in' period is evident, and his portrayal of the character, though effective, seems at odds with his usual performance; pitching Snarf an octave or two above his usual range.

The above notwithstanding, 'The Terror of Hammerhand' redeems itself with a small selection of notable scenes including the Unicorn Keeper's speech about Third Earth becoming an altogether more dangerous place since the arrival of the ThunderCats and, perhaps most importantly, the introduction of Ron Goulart's excellent creation Hammerhand. The irascible pirate would continue to be used in subsequent episodes and prove to be a memorable addition to the series. Ultimately, although the production standards of 'The Terror of Hammerhand' may be below par, its original audience would doubtless have been none the wiser, and it is perhaps true to say that the episode simply had a greater potential than was realised on screen.

Writer's Commentary from Ron Goulart:

Since I once wrote a science fiction novel called *Clockwork's Pirates*, I can admit that I have always been moderately interested in the topic. And in my youth they were making a lot of pirate movies – *The Sea Hawk*, *The Pirate* etc. I know I made up the name for Hammerhand, so I must've had some input into the inventing of the story. I would have had a thrill from adding a character had I have been handed a bonus or an honorarium every time Hammerhand lumbered onto the show. But such was not the case.

7. Trouble With Time (3 Stars)
Written by: Ron Goulart & Julian P Gardner
US Broadcast Date: 17 September 1985
UK Broadcast Date: 22 January 1987

The second and final contribution from writer Ron Goulart is a vast improvement on his previous episode. 'The Trouble with Time' offers a brilliant premise, revolving around the quest for a power source to fuel the ThunderTank. This provides both the writers and, in fictional terms, the ThunderCats with the perfect opportunity to explore their new terrain, and effectively 'takes the ThunderCats to trouble' rather than the more usual approach of 'trouble finding the ThunderCats'.

The scenes at the beginning of the episode where Lion-O is seen 'joyriding' the ThunderTank are both enjoyable and amusing, and the balance of 'downtime' versus 'action' is handled well. Another welcome addition aspect is the introduction of Willa and the Warrior Maidens. Given that both the ThunderCats and the other Third Earth natives are mostly male, the addition of an 'Amazonian' race of warrior women is ingenious and balances the show's appeal to a female audience. The fact that the Warrior Maidens are initially so suspicious of the ThunderCats makes their encounter all the more exciting and, for the first time, the ThunderCats need to work hard to forge an ongoing relationship with a group of Third Earth natives.

It is nice to see a writer making good use of Tygra (all too often neglected in later episodes), and credit should be given both to the character designers and to voice artist Peter Newman, who give the 'aged' Tygra a believable and highly effective presence in the episode.

The episode isn't without niggles. The Lizathon attack scene near the beginning is just as random as the 'hungry tree' scene in 'The Terror of Hammerhand', and one wonders if this 'padding' may have been included at co-writer Jules Bass's behest. Equally, Monkian's comment that Slithe is a 'chauvinist reptile' seems a little contrived, given his persona as a male Mutant with less than scrupulous intentions.

Fortunately, the series' normal impeccably high standards of animation make a welcome return here, and some scenes, including Lion-O raising the Sword upon reaching the geyser of life, are nothing short of stunning – ably illustrating how Pacific Animation Corporation continued to push the boundaries of what could be achieved with only a 'television animation' budget.

Writer's Commentary from Ron Goulart:

I must admit that, at this point in time, my memories of my time working on *ThunderCats* are dim rather than crystal clear. Plus, writing for the show was not a high point of my career, and outside of watching the initial broadcasts of the two or three shows I was involved with, I haven't looked at an episode since.

I have no idea who invented the Warrior Maidens. I know I've written several stories and a couple of novels about bands of tough ladies. So it's possible I did think them up. Since *ThunderCats* was the only animated cartoon show I ever wrote for, I can't say that creating new characters for a show was a policy of mine. I hate to sound crass, but I've been a professional writer since I was 22, and the main thrills have always come from my work, with my name prominently attached, getting recognition and bringing in an income.

8. The Tower of Traps (4 Stars)
Written by: Leonard Starr
US Broadcast Date: 18 September 1985
UK Broadcast Date: 12 February 1987

Leonard Starr returns to *ThunderCats* with a beautifully crafted script that pulls the series firmly away from a predictable formula and showcases how easily it could offer the unexpected. 'The Tower of Traps' displays just how comfortable and adept Starr was with writing the early episodes, and the script seems to flow perfectly from scene to scene.

The sight of a topless Lion-O bathing in the early scenes is amusing and illustrates the importance that Starr placed on small details. While a writer like

Bill Overgard may not have thought twice about, say, showing cats breathing in space, Starr's episodes seem to have a thoroughness that belies their origin in a children's fantasy series. The recognition that Lion-O simply wouldn't swim with his clothes and boots on seems inconsequential, but the failure to take account of such things was something that compromised many of the show's contemporary rivals, which gave little or no regard to the intelligence of their audience. Starr's thoroughness never fails to enhance his episodes with an edge of credibility.

More than anything, 'The Tower of Traps' is a genuinely menacing episode. Not only are its many traps (like the impassable staircase) enticing and often disturbing, but the episode ends with the discovery of its antagonist, Baron Karnor, in the form of a rotting corpse on full display. The fact that Starr challenges children to confront frightening ideas is a credit to the episode and endows the story with a 'darker' theme that sets it apart from those around it. Skilfully, Starr also offsets the negative with a positive: a subplot featuring the plight of a Wollo, whose specially-crafted wedding gift has been stolen *en route* to his daughter's wedding. When the ThunderCats return the item, a much needed 'feel good factor' is injected into the story.

Starr also proves his effectiveness at writing dialogue, and WilyKit's summation of the bond she shares with her brother is touching: 'I wouldn't ask you to do this for me,' she comments, 'but I know you'd do it anyway'.

While the previous episode showed a return to form for the programme's production values, 'The Tower of Traps' positively basks in glory, with stunning background scenery and exciting direction (including when the Sword of Omens is impaled on the ceiling). Anyone watching this episode as an introduction to *ThunderCats* would have surely been hooked! All in all, this is *ThunderCats* at close to its very best, and Starr's skill as a storyteller shines through with ease.

Writer's Commentary from Leonard Starr:

Sometimes a villain can be [an aspect of] nature or a construction that Lion-O has to fight. The same rules apply; he has to fight it on its own. It's like dealing with a guerrilla; there's no recourse. You can't use your intellect or anything else, you just have to be as clever as you can to avoid it and survive it. It's the same with hurricanes and earthquakes and that kind of thing. It's just another obstacle.

The idea was to have as interesting an episode as is possible, and we did whatever we could to achieve that. Children like to be frightened. We did have frightening elements from time to time, but we had to be very careful, because there was a code in children's programming that you couldn't go too far in those directions.

9. The Garden of Delights (2 Stars)
Written by: Barney Cohen & Julian P Gardner
US Broadcast Date: 19 September 1985
UK Broadcast Date: 19 February 1987

'The Garden of Delights' is somewhat of an oddity. Commissioned before script editor Peter Lawrence was established in the role, it raised more than a few eyebrows amongst the cast and crew, given its obvious use of an allegory for taking drugs – specifically, hallucinogenic substances.

While the episode has some redeeming features (and a very effective sub-plot), the scenes with Tygra 'flying' in his addicted state are rather silly, and it seems as though scriptwriter Barney Cohen was more interested in shocking the various parental concern groups of America during the 1980s than in effective storytelling. While one of the undeniable strengths of *ThunderCats* was its mandate never to patronise children, 'The Garden of Delights' feels more gratuitous than revolutionary. That said, given that the drug references were subtle enough to slip past the series' psychologist Robert Kuisis (and indeed the network censors), it is likely few children would have been aware of any such subtext or inference, and therefore the episode's integrity as a piece of children's television remains reasonably intact.

Tygra's addiction to the hallucinogenic fruit is not only the most contentious aspect of the script, but also the least necessary and least believable. As Tygra is always portrayed as the most responsible ThunderCat (even given the title of 'Head of the ThunderCat Council' by Jaga in a previous episode) it seems odd that he would be so easily seduced by 'Silky'.

'The Garden of Delights' does, though, offer some enjoyable moments. Willa makes a welcome return – providing an opportunity to learn more about the Warrior Maidens and their growing trust and support of the ThunderCats – and it is rewarding to see Mumm-Ra and the Mutants finally get their hands on the Sword of Omens (albeit briefly). Mumm-Ra is also well written in this episode, with a portrayal that leans firmly towards a more threatening persona. The scenes where he rants at Willa in the Black Pyramid give him a well deserved air of menace and, while his plan is not without holes (chiefly that his attempted corruption of the 'pure' Willa would surely make her just as evil as him – and therefore useless to command the Sword), it all adds up to some enjoyable action.

Additionally, there is a great 'ThunderCats Ho!' call from Lion-O in the episode, and, on the whole, the art direction continues to improve (aside from in a short scene where Tygra 'eats' the fruit, despite his mouth going nowhere near it).

Incidentally, this is the final script to be co-written by executive producer Jules Bass, and while his contributions may well have been more editorial than original, his input resulted in some of the core foundations that shaped the series.

Writer's Commentary from Barney Cohen:

I've only written two animated episodes of anything ever. One was the episode of *Masters of the Universe* called 'Evilseed', in which Skeletor and He-Man team up. The other was *ThunderCats*' 'The Garden of Delights'. Both of them caused tongues to wag, and I'm very proud of that ...

Script Editor's Commentary from Peter Lawrence:

Tygra's drug-taking episode ... More, as Kuisis wrote, about instant gratification. I didn't edit this episode, but my memory is that no-one thought much about the drug-taking analogy until the script was finalised and went into recording. The sound guys and actors, of course, riffed on it instantly, as did the audience. My view? Drug-taking or not ... not a bad message for the audience, and one that no show, now, would ever address. Tygra was always enigmatic (and a spare part, in my view).

Don't forget that Jules Bass put his own pseudonym on this script. I'm not sure how much of it he actually wrote. Somewhere, there's a shadow of a memory that Jules wanted me to work with Barney but it was just too difficult.

10. Mandora – The Evil Chaser (3 Stars)
Written by: William Overgard
US Broadcast Date: 20 September 1985
UK Broadcast Date: 26 February 1987

Writer William Overgard bursts into the world of *ThunderCats* with an episode that aptly showcases his eccentricity. He must in all fairness be credited as one of the most original, creative and imaginative writers ever to have practised his craft on *ThunderCats*; but, at the same time, it must be acknowledged that he was responsible for not only some of the best but also some of the worst aspects of the series' output.

While storylines and characters clearly came easily to an experienced writer like Overgard, the viewer can't help but feel, during some of his episodes, that he would have preferred to have been writing his own show instead of being 'lumbered' with the established concepts and mythology. But when he gets the balance between original and existing creations right, he is nearly unbeatable as a *ThunderCats* scriptwriter; and, if nothing else, his episodes can never be accused of being bland.

'Mandora – The Evil Chaser' shows, once again, that *ThunderCats* is anything but conventional. It's an episode that just about manages to feel like standard *ThunderCats* fare, while trailing the introduction of some more outlandish concepts. While the previous episodes had painted a picture of isolation (having shown the ThunderCats stranded, with only the natives of the mysterious Third Earth for company), this one informs us that there is free space travel between worlds and an interplanetary police force to supervise criminal activity. It is these concepts that make 'Mandora – The Evil Chaser' an acquired taste, and Overgard's unique styles of dialogue and characterisation are in abundance throughout the episode. Anyone who has seen even a handful of *ThunderCats* adventures should easily recognise this as an Overgard script; and it adds a welcome sense of variety to the show.

Overall, the episode works relatively well. It features some nice interplay between Snarf and Lion-O, and Mandora is perfectly painted and comes across as highly engaging. The idea of Lion-O stumbling upon (and accidentally opening) a prison ship is well conceived, and the pacing is good. In the context of *ThunderCats* as a whole, the episode would have fitted better in the programme's second season, and by its placement alongside far more conservative offerings, it inevitably stands in greater contrast.

The episode also features a few production oddities, the most noticeable of which is in the voice acting and direction: Bob McFadden, the man of literally hundreds of voices, performs both the River Ooze and Burnout characters using a voice nearly identical to that of lead Mutant Slithe (although thankfully he doesn't make an appearance in the episode). Given the normally meticulous direction of supervising producer Lee Dannacher, this seems to be a strange error to slip through, and is a little distracting to the viewer. It also has to be mentioned that Lynne Lipton's performance of Mandora is perilously close to that of Cheetara, though her additional enunciation and lower pitch just about succeed in audibly separating the two.

These reservations aside, 'Mandora – The Evil Chaser' represents a crucial turning point in the history of the series. From this point on, a 'typical' *ThunderCats* episode would become an ever rarer thing.

Script Editor's Commentary from Peter Lawrence:

Bill [Overgard] excites a lot of conflicting views, it seems – and always did. Those who were obsessive or controlling about the nature of the show hated that he basically threw away the main characters and played with his own creations. I loved the fact that he brought so much novelty and so much imagination to the table, and I believe that one reason for the show's success and longevity is that it was never predictable. If Len [Starr] or I or anyone else had written everything … if there had been no place for Bill … there would certainly have been far fewer surprises and far fewer captivating supporting characters.

Mandora is a great figure, smart, sassy and sexy, and let no one deny that a lot of boys watching the show loved the women. I wish I had a dollar for every now-adult fan who has told me that he fell in love with Cheetara. That's not something I quite understand, but if it worked for them …

The Interplanetary Control Force – who could resist that organisation? – especially if it employed sassy babes on space Harleys, babes who rose above the babe stereotype by being witty, intelligent and tough.

The problem with any Bill Overgard script was to bring in the main characters – and to give them, or at least Lion-O, a significant role. Bill tended to pay for a 'Matt Damon' and then relegate him to a doorman in a couple of unimportant scenes. In the end, I stopped asking Bill to remember he was writing for *ThunderCats* and to please employ the cast we had created; I encouraged him to deliver whatever came to mind, and then got out the shoehorn and jammed in the main characters myself …

Another wonderful aspect of Bill's writing was his dialogue. ('An ancient formula. It used to be called soap.') He had written some great books, *Pieces of a Hero* and *A Few Good Men* to mention just two. *Pieces Of A Hero* almost made him an A-list Hollywood writer. It was due to be made into a major motion picture starring Lee Marvin but, as I understand it, at the last moment Marvin opted for *Emperor of the North* instead. Bill did, of course, write several other produced screenplays, but perhaps he was too idiosyncratic for a conventional screenwriter's career.

That idiosyncrasy is what appealed to me – and it made a huge contribution to the show.

11. The Ghost Warrior (5 Stars)
Written by: Leonard Starr
US Broadcast Date: 23 September 1985
UK Broadcast Date: 5 March 1987

If an episode of *ThunderCats* can achieve perfection, 'The Ghost Warrior' must surely come close. As with any piece of animated television, many individuals and disciplines are required to come together to form the finished output. Because of this, it is not uncommon for one production element to outshine another. With 'The Ghost Warrior', every single facet of production is on top form. The script is exciting and enticing, the animation and direction superb, the performances subtle, and the music selection sublime. Everything comes together here to reveal *ThunderCats* at its best.

First, Leonard Starr once again shows his writing proficiency by mining the very mythology that he helped to create for the series' inception. We see our first glimpse of Thundera since the series' pilot episode; and the return of Jaga, in a predominant role, would surely have excited its audience (also representing a rare occasion when Jaga can be seen by anyone other than Lion-O). Starr's sense of humour is also on top form, with some great dialogue (like Panthro's response to the invisible hands of Grune the Destroyer, 'I'll do more than budge them!') He continues to imbue the series and its characters with added layers of personality, and we learn that Cheetara has a unique gift as a visionary.

The standard of animation in 'The Ghost Warrior' is also impeccable. The subtle lighting effects throughout are spectacular. These include Grune's reveal in the Cats' Lair and the reflection of fireworks on the ThunderCats' faces during Jaga's battle with Grune – each unparalleled in cartoon animation. Even the editors seem on top form, with some great use of the music and effects library, and there are some brilliant vocal performances that show how skilled the small team of actors really were.

The idea of a rogue ThunderCat is inspired, and every twist and turn of the plot, from Grune's discovery by the terrified Bolkins to his epic battle with Jaga, are perfectly paced. As a further bonus, there are even flashbacks, and the rich backstory of Thundera (which sits at the core of the series) is never utilised better than by Leonard Starr. If any episode could be guaranteed to solidify *ThunderCats* in the daily consciousness of young children, it is undoubtedly 'The Ghost Warrior'.

Writer's Commentary from Leonard Starr:

A lesson had to be taught in each episode of *ThunderCats* and I finally decided that attaching a moral to a story once it was written was too tough, so I would start with the moral and write the story around it. One of my favourites was 'an honest enemy is better than a false friend'. There you go – you've got a story there already. So I did the episode from that point of view.

Having a backstory is important in storytelling – the thought that the ThunderCats came from somewhere, that they didn't just spring out of the ground as ThunderCats. Most characters have a backstory and sometimes it's just implied, but sometimes you go in and have flashbacks and that kind of thing.

12. The Doomgaze (3.5 Stars)
Written by: Stephen Perry
US Broadcast Date: 24 September 1985
UK Broadcast Date: 12 March 1987

Steve Perry's debut episode of *ThunderCats* is an enjoyable look at the darker side of Mumm-Ra and his quest to rid his home-world of the ThunderCats. It's an ominous offering that features some genuinely chilling moments, showing that Perry is adept at writing for the horror genre. Given some menacing lines and incantations, Mumm-Ra escapes his all-to-often caricature treatment and is finally imbued with dialogue and a plotline he warrants.

Sadly, the introduction of Ta-She is too underdeveloped to really appraise her character. Largely due to the short running time of a *ThunderCats* episode, no sooner has she appeared than she is once again banished to the Timewarp Prison. This is probably the episode's greatest failing: it's a promising premise that feels like it comes to an abrupt end before we see the antagonist's full potential. Nonetheless, the character's power of control over minds (specifically male minds) is a great concept and fits perfectly into the world of *ThunderCats*. It also provides an opportunity for Cheetara to shine, and her reaction to Ta-She is sublime. 'You may mesmerise men with your evil beauty,' insists Cheetara, 'but I am a woman. You hold no mystery to me!'

While they have been seen looming over Mumm-Ra's tomb since the second episode of the series, the Ancient Spirits of Evil make their first 'appearance' here, sounding suspiciously like Panthro. While Earle Hyman is a great character actor and performer, his voice is a little too distinctive to provide a range of characters in quite the same way as his colleagues, and the vocal similarity becomes a little distracting at times.

There is, however, some beautiful art on display in 'The Doomgaze', most notably Ta-She's vessel flying through the clouds (watch how the oars of the ship are visible only at each flash of lightning). Unusually, there is also a shot of Tygra taken from the opening credits (albeit with a new background) as he responds to Lion-O's summoning. Mumm-Ra's transformation shot is also given a new, 'on location' background, showing how cel sequences were often re-photographed with new background paintings.

Overall, 'The Doomgaze' is an enjoyable adventure and its 'girl power' theme, while unintended by the writer, is a good indicator of why the series was so popular with children of both sexes.

Writer's Commentary from Steve Perry:

I had pitched several ideas over the phone to Leonard Starr, and he liked 'The Doomgaze' best, and told me to do that. I wrote a first draft in three days, express mailed it down to Len in Connecticut, and he called me with rewrites and tightening up ideas.

Len shared a studio with the artist Stan Drake, and as we were talking about Ta-She and the story content of what would become show #12, 'The Doomgaze', Len decided we needed to name the Egyptian barge Ta-She rode around on, because he thought it had toy potential. 'The whole show is one big ad for the toys,' he would say. 'We've got to name everything.'

If you recall this episode, and the Egyptian barge of Ta-She, you will recall it is crewed by a bunch of crocodile men. As we were shooting names for the ship back and forth, Stan Drake piped up in the background: 'How about calling it the Crock-a-Ship!' After we stopped laughing, we gave up trying to name it. It could never be anything except ... 'the Crock-a-Ship'.

Some people have pointed out to me that this was considered to be a 'girl power' *ThunderCats* episode, and as such a rare show. This is something I was completely unaware of and had never heard, and there was no conscious effect by me or anyone to make it a pro-feminist episode. I think that's a classic case of people reading in attributes that were not put there on purpose, but I sort of see how one might come to that point of view about 'The Doomgaze'.

I wrote my *ThunderCats* show in an idyllic studio on the Broad Brook in Guilford, Vermont. It was an amazing studio on a waterfall and skinny-dipping hole, surrounded by a constant flow of famous, semi-famous and unknown artists, sculptors, actors, writers and the like – a real community of creative people. I was often considered to be one of them, until they found out I worked on 'cartoons', and that made me 'not a serious artist'. It was that snobby So-Ho attitude.

13. Lord of the Snows (4 Stars)
Written by: Bob Haney
US Broadcast Date: 25 September 1985
UK Broadcast Date: 19 March 1987

Bob Haney's participation in *ThunderCats* had been guaranteed since the earliest days of production when Lee Dannacher had been given the task of recruiting comic book writers who understood the action/adventure genre. In 'Lord of the Snows', this innovative approach to recruitment pays dividends, and one of *ThunderCats* most skilled contributors is given his first chance to shine.

Haney's origins as a strip cartoon writer are clearly evident, and the episode is structured accordingly. The action never wanes, and one can imagine every scene being conceived as a striking visual in Haney's mind (not least, Lion-O's journey to Hook Mountain, which manifests itself on screen beautifully). Although he uses dialogue sparingly, Haney's talents in that direction are no less defined, and his characters deliver some wonderful exchanges. Lion-O's declaration that he cannot leave the Snowman to die is suitably heroic, and Haney rounds off the scene with the wonderful line, 'I cannot make the friend of a dead man.'

Pacific Animation Corporation deliver a visual treat every bit as exciting as Haney's script and, from the very first shot (a gorgeous pan shot), they throw everything they have into the production, showing that the 'settling in' period of animation glitches is long behind them. Shots such as the reflection of the charging steed in the Sword's blade really give us a glimpse into the creative talent of the storyboard artists, and the art directors are also on fine form, inserting a three-cut camera zoom as the snow breaks away from Hook Mountain towards Lion-O and Snarf – adding a sense of drama to proceedings.

In introducing two new characters in 'Lord of the Snows', Haney adds a recurring villain and a popular ThunderCat ally simultaneously. The gentle giant

Snowman and his loyal companion Snowmeow are welcome additions to *ThunderCats* lore, and the perhaps inevitable discovery of a snowscape on Third Earth is executed perfectly; Snowman's home in particular is superbly realised. Vultureman – or more specifically his people, the Vulturemen – had first been referenced by Leonard Starr in his initial outline of the series, but his debut appearance has been significantly delayed relative to those of his counterparts. Because of this, he (and indeed his 'flying machine') appears an odd inclusion, coming without any backstory or apparent explanation. However, his character would become one of the most enduring and popular villains in the series, enjoying a plethora of character-specific episodes. It should also be noted that the voice used for Vultureman's first appearances, courtesy of Bob McFadden, is somewhat different from his more familiar tones as depicted by Earl Hammond in later episodes.

In short, Bob Haney could hardly have provided a better debut story to showcase his craft, and given his impressive reputation as the creator of a range of memorable comic strips, his inclusion in the scriptwriting line-up is an honour for *ThunderCats*.

Script Editor's Commentary from Peter Lawrence:

This is a mainstream *ThunderCats* story that features new characters that are very comic-book and animation-friendly, as you would expect from someone of Bob Haney's experience. The script also demonstrates most writers' desire to invent their own characters rather than work with the [established elements of the] show. It's often much easier to come up with a new character, new settings, new villains, weapons and vehicles, than it is to bring your own ideas into the mainstream of a developed show. My inexperience with animation and series writing and story editing meant that I allowed more of this 're-invention' than many other story editors – until we got to the point that we had such a gigantic cast of guest stars that it was blindingly obvious, for story and for production processes, that we needed to pull back and concentrate on our core group.

This was Vultureman's first appearance (or perhaps his first starring role). He was a character that I particularly liked and later developed, with Matthew Malach, into a villain who was both funny and threatening. I'm not sure about SnowMeow! Perhaps if I had had my feet under the desk longer, I would have insisted on a grander name. Bob wrote Lion-O pretty well. He had the 'kid in a man's body' down pat, and it comes across strongly in this episode.

14. The Spaceship Beneath the Sands (3 Stars)
Written by: Leonard Starr
US Broadcast Date: 26 September 1985
UK Broadcast Date: 26 March 1987

Leonard Starr's seventh broadcast episode of *ThunderCats* is a reasonably effective affair, although, as with many episodes of the era, it suffers from having to advance the series as a whole. Starr's writing seems undeniably better when he is given a blank canvas on which to work. The decision to reintroduce the Mutants' technology and weaponry is a welcome one, but it restricts the episode to a reasonably simple plot.

The idea of rebalancing power between the ThunderCats (who had initially been able to salvage all of their ship's equipment) and the Mutants (who had remained beholden to Mumm-Ra) is a great one, opening up new storytelling possibilities for future writers. Indeed, the preceding adventure, 'Lord of the Snows', had clearly encountered the problem of how to move the Mutants around Third Earth and had therefore had to utilise both Vultureman and his flying machine. The revelation of the Sky Cutter and Nose Diver serves to bolster the Mutants' cause considerably, and the timing of this reintroduction gives the series an added boost.

Although the remaining plot is reasonably thin, there are some nice individual scenes. Starr's narrative regarding the trapped Sequine is touching, and Panthro's speech shows that, while the series could occasionally step too far into purposeful morality, its messages could equally be achieved in a far more subtle manner. 'We can always replace the ThunderTank,' says Panthro. 'No way we can ever replace a life.'

Finally, it must be mentioned how well Leonard Starr's episodes are integrated into the series. If viewed back to back, they pretty much tell the entire progression of the series and, on every occasion, Starr manages to add something new. In many ways, each of his episodes acts as a sequel to the last, and 'The Spaceship Beneath the Sands' is very much a continuation of the opening episodes of *ThunderCats*. From the exodus from Thundera, through to the slow introduction of the many races of Third Earth, the Anointment Trials and even the introduction of the 'new' *ThunderCats* and villains in the second season, Starr's evolution of the series is extremely well constructed. That his episodes are distributed evenly throughout the first season is fortuitous, and for those children who paid attention to the writers' credits, the prospect of a 'Leonard Starr episode' must have been an exciting one.

Writer's Commentary from Leonard Starr:

It's been 30 years, and we did them all so fast, so it's very hard to remember which ones I did. I'm telling you about a job; it was what we did for a living. Some of it pleased me, some of it did not. We don't sit down to create something that gives us pleasure.

I have no feelings for science fiction whatsoever, and I approached the whole thing from a point of view of storytelling. I'd have villains and heroes, and when I was editing, I'd tell the writers that I'd want four 'bumps' in every episode that would work with the commercial breaks. Each one should signify more danger for the ThunderCats in the story, and finally there should be a climax that would … end the story in an area you would least expect it. Some of the writers complied, some didn't, and it just went on that way.

15. The Time Capsule (3.5 Stars)
Written by: Peter Lawrence
US Broadcast Date: 27 September 1985
UK Broadcast Date: 2 April 1987

'The Time Capsule' may not be a revolutionary *ThunderCats* episode, but the fact that it marks Peter Lawrence's debut script contribution secures its significance in the show's history. As script editor, he would go on to write and rewrite countless episodes, and many attribute the show's signature style directly to his influence.

During the course of the episode, it feels as though Lawrence is finding his feet in writing for the world of *ThunderCats*. The plot and pacing are pleasing, and there are many glimpses of the style Lawrence would adopt in later episodes.

The first and most welcome addition is a flashback sequence revisiting scenes depicted in the show's opening episode, 'Exodus'. Later, Lawrence would often refer to the ThunderCats' past history and display his capability at adding further layers to Leonard Starr's origin stories.

'The Time Capsule' is, essentially, a 'many perils of Third Earth' adventure, as Lion-O explores his new world in search of a time capsule that will reveal more about his childhood home. To explore Lion-O's homesickness is a strong storytelling move, and marks Lawrence's attention to characterisation as much as action. The more successful episodes of *ThunderCats* need a strong motivating factor to propel the protagonists – and any viewer can empathise with Lion-O's frustration.

Minor niggles in 'The Time Capsule' include Lion-O's propensity for summoning his fellow ThunderCats, which becomes somewhat tiresome after a while. But the episode's greatest flaw is that, after the viewer has sat through the quest for the time capsule, the story is resolved without the device's potential having been explored. (Fortunately, this will be rectified in the later episode 'Return to Thundera', but the fact that Lawrence did not choose to pen that episode is strange, given that it's almost a sequel to this one.)

A small yet important development in this episode is the introduction of the ThunderKittens' vehicles, the Space Boards, which will prove to be a catalyst for many future stories featuring the duo. As the series progressed, many writers would tend to avoid using the Kittens in favour of the more senior ThunderCats, and in an effort to give all the characters equal footing, Lawrence's device helps the Kittens achieve independence from the team.

The animation and direction are once again superb, and the lighting and detail during Lion-O's arm wrestle are truly memorable: proof of how well the animators had settled into the production process, with results almost unrecognisable from their work on episodes like 'The Terror of Hammerhand'.

While Lawrence's best work on the series was still to come, there is more than enough in 'The Time Capsule' to reassure viewers that the series was in safe hands.

Writer's Commentary from Peter Lawrence:

I liked the Jaga figure and the relationship with Lion-O, and although it's by no means original, I liked the fact that Lion-O was a child in a man's body and therefore had a lot to learn. At the same time, he had the strength and physical maturity for real adventure. As a writer, you did not have to mollycoddle him.

In 'The Time Capsule', we could combine Lion-O's immaturity with a real physical adventure – all guided by the ghostly but absent Jaga. What better quest for a kid than to discover his past, his family's past, and be big and bad enough to face down villains … all the while guided by the wise and greatly-loved Jaga! And think of this – a father figure who had no power to enforce his advice! Isn't that the best of all worlds?

Until I read the summary, I had forgotten about the action involving the other ThunderCats – essentially a sub-plot that keep the clock ticking and the tension ratchetting up all the time. At least, that was the intention. One other aspect of this script – a story editor's point of view, really: the writers often liked to concentrate on one or another, or perhaps two, of the hero group, but we needed them all to feature, to build their personalities, their interactions and the whole 'family world' of *ThunderCats*. If I had not been faced with that need and direction, I might have preferred this to be a solo story for Lion-O.

16. The Fireballs of Plun-Darr (3.5 Stars)
Written by: William Overgard
US Broadcast Date: 30 September 1985
UK Broadcast Date: 9 April 1987

Perhaps the most obvious comment to make about 'The Fireballs of Plun-Darr' is how very tame it feels considering its origins as a Bill Overgard script. While his contributions would usually embellish the *ThunderCats* world with weird and wonderful devices and characters, this outing is remarkably conservative in comparison.

On paper, the plot seems pretty straightforward, and from the first few scenes viewers could have been forgiven for thinking it may have been a rather dull instalment. However, Overgard proves that less can sometimes be more. With the cast stripped down to Tygra and Willa for the majority of the episode, there is plenty of opportunity to explore the Mutants' homes and personalities. This must surely have been the writer's intention, and he succeeds admirably. For the first time in the series, we get a detailed look at the workings of Castle Plun-Darr, and the Mutants are for once presented as a relatively menacing threat. We are also, once again, provided a profound insight into the impact on Third Earth and its residents of the warring parties.

The torture device inflicted upon Tygra is remarkably brutal and, as 'ticking bomb' storylines go, the threat of a senior ThunderCat being ripped limb from limb provides more than enough motivation for his fellow team members to rescue him.

'The Fireballs of Plun-Darr' proves just how versatile Bill Overgard was when writing for *ThunderCats* and illustrates that, while it wasn't always easy, his imagination could be confined to work within the boundaries of the series. There are, however, still enough Overgardian touches to identify with – watch out for a great scene where Snarf tries (unsuccessfully) to predict the coordinates needed for the ThunderTank's mission while Panthro impatiently proceeds using his instincts alone.

The final scene of the episode is a nice touch, as Panthro is revealed to be terrified of 'Bushy' the spider. From this point on, the series would begin to introduce ever more cringe-worthy puns to conclude each episode. That the majority of these tag scenes would feature a certain amount of imaginative wordplay means the producers can just about be forgiven for letting them through. After all, the humorous content of the show would become one of its most memorable features.

Script Editor's Commentary from Peter Lawrence:

A rather ordinary episode by Bill's standards – and that's what happens when you try to corral a wild talent. Here, we tried to get him to write 'the show' and feature our main characters. He did – and made a pretty good fist of the Mutants. Sure, he couldn't help himself and incorporated the Warrior Maidens, but by and large, this is a straight-ahead, linear *ThunderCats* story, and one that does not draw much on Bill's imagination and talent.

If it's one of the duller of Bill's pieces, the production – and I – have to take the blame.

17. All That Glitters (4 Stars)
Written by: Bob Haney
US Broadcast Date: 1 October 1985
UK Broadcast Date: 16 April 1987

Bob Haney's second *ThunderCats* script acts as a sequel to his debut episode, 'Lord of the Snows'. In this instalment, the ThunderCats must act to refine and utilise the Thundrillium-rich meteorite that they fought so hard to recover previously.

At first, this episode may seem to be a much poorer effort than its predecessor, and the first few scenes lack a little focus. Furthermore, the rather childish moniker 'Grygory Grygion' only adds to the viewer's reservations. However, Haney's script quickly recovers ground as we see Lion-O and Tygra unwittingly attempt to destroy one another.

From this point onwards, Haney provides an enticing and engaging storyline as the consequences of Lion-O's and Tygra's hastiness become apparent. The idea of destroying the Sword is a brilliant one and raises the stakes significantly (something one can only imagine children would have found tremendously exciting). Jaga's scolding (and perhaps overly harsh) attack on Lion-O also makes for brilliant watching: 'Yes Lion-O, gone forever – because of you!'

Once again, Haney proves his experience as a writer. The episode is not only structured perfectly, but the early set-up of Cheetara retaining the 'worthless' gold is nicely planted to be used at the story's resolution. While many *ThunderCats* writers could be accused of breaking the 'Chekhov's Gun' rule (whereby any device or plot point mentioned early on in a story must be resolved by its finale), this cannot be levelled at Haney. By introducing the means to the story's climax at the very beginning, he creates a much more believable and satisfying end to an exciting *ThunderCats* adventure.

Another refreshing approach is Haney's telling of the story from the protagonist's point of view. While most episodes would begin with Mumm-Ra and the Mutants explaining their 'dastardly' plan to the audience, here we are kept entirely in the dark about their trap for the ThunderCats. The fact that *we* aren't expecting the events that follow – any more than Tygra or Lion-O are – gives the episode an added resonance and involvement.

A myriad of other enjoyable sequences include a nice 'focus swap' as Lion-O and Snarf arrive at the caves, the 'sexy' scene of Lion-O scooping up Cheetara at the story's end, and the plot twist of the Inflamer double-crossing the ThunderCats. There is also an unusual music arrangement, whereby Lion-O's call to the ThunderCats is mixed with a continuing incidental music score.

While the episode doesn't quite reach 'legendary' status – it comes very close.

Script Editor's Commentary from Peter Lawrence:

Bob Haney was somewhat literary, and this story seems to me to have some classical themes. Friend turning on friend – an Othello and Iago moment. The Inflamer – the sword forger – could also easily be a figure from Greek or Roman (or Japanese) mythology; he is not a straightforward blacksmith but represents something more.

Of course, I'm perfectly aware that a lot of readers will see this view of Bob's script as pretentious. After all, we're discussing a relatively lightweight kids show. Or is it? It certainly seems to have touched an awful lot of people and stayed with them into adulthood. One reason, perhaps, is that it does draw on some wonderful archetypes and myths, courtesy of writers like Bob Haney.

And the fact is that all writers draw on all kinds of myths, memories and archetypes even when we're writing 'lite'. Bob, at least, went back to the source; he had read his materials, unlike a lot of contemporary writers whose experience of life and literature is confined to the TV screen …

A personality like Bob could not help digging into literature – and more power to him. I think this is one of the best-written first season scripts, even if it is a bit pompous here and there – plus Bob really exploits the world of the show, its characters and locations. He does not fall back on outside elements to create his drama and interest.

18. Spitting Image (3.5 Stars)
Written by: Howard Post
US Broadcast Date: 2 October 1985
UK Broadcast Date: 23 April 1987

The first of two *ThunderCats* episodes to be provided by writer Howard Post, 'Spitting Image' is a rare venture into the world of the horror genre.

Nearly every science fiction serial will, at one time or another, explore the concept of an 'evil twin' or clone. While the idea may not be an original one, it is executed well in this episode and certainly provides a scare-fest for young children. (Watch out for the scene where the clone Panthro's skin 'burns' inside the fires.)

The episode begins with a nice scene inside Mumm-Ra's Black Pyramid. The fact that his vaults are crammed full of rare gems and riches is incredibly befitting, and one can readily imagine they are the results of many centuries of pillaging his dominion of Third Earth. The episode is notable in introducing a recurring villain – the Driller – although his contribution is woefully short and it would, perhaps, have been nice to have seen his origins expanded upon. His motivation in obtaining diamonds to sharpen his drill points is a unique one, and the set-up of Mumm-Ra capturing and cloning Panthro is well established.

It has to be said that the reintroduction of Hammerhand (albeit in ghost form) is rather unnecessary, and aside from a line or two (whereby the clone Panthro emulates his vocal patterns, e.g. 'Evil, evil, evil'), there is little or no reason for his presence. His scene at the end of the episode, where he destroys the cloning mould, is equally bizarre, and the audience can't help but feel they must have missed a vital part of the plot!

The scenes of 'evil' Panthro ravaging Third Earth are wonderfully scripted and animated, and Pacific Animation Corporation's use of special effects (namely the fire effect burning through the forest) is first-rate. The episode cannot resist the obligatory scenes of the real Panthro fighting the clone, however these are depicted well and feature plenty of nunchuk action.

Aside from being a journey in pure action/adventure, 'Spitting Image' also has a nice emotional subtext, and Panthro's scenes doubting his involvement in proceedings are incredibly touching. 'I couldn't have done it, could I? … You must believe me – I did not do any of those things!' We also get a rare chance to see a ThunderCat (namely Panthro) out of his uniform, wearing only his belt from 'Exodus'.

If anybody harboured doubts that *ThunderCats* would push the boundaries of horror in children's television, this episode is surely the antidote.

Head Writer's Commentary from Leonard Starr:

Howie Post was one of my oldest, closest friends. We both attended the High School of Music and Art, though Howie transferred to a different school in his senior year, so we lost touch until I ran into him at DC in, I guess, the late '40s. His forte was humour. He wrote and drew his own stuff, though I can't remember any specific characters, and did well. Later on he became Head of Animation for Paramount Pictures. Eventually came the time when I needed writers for *ThunderCats*. Rankin/Bass was New York-based and most of the animation writers were in California, so writers had to be found locally, and Howie was one of the writers I called.

19. Mongor (3.5 Stars)
Written by: Peter Lawrence
US Broadcast Date: 3 October 1985
UK Broadcast Date: 30 April 1987

In much the same vein as 'The Ghost Warrior', 'Mongor' deals with the aftermath of a previously-extinct menace being inadvertently released from his tomb. Unlike the former episode, the villain is not a ThunderCat gone bad, but rather a creature that seems to be a cross between a horned ram and the grim reaper.

Peter Lawrence injects a welcome pace to the episode by beginning the story half-way through events. As well as being a novel way to structure the script, this also has the benefit of opening with the dramatic scene of Mongor ravaging the planet.

The design of Mongor (the 'eternal face of fear') is not hugely terrifying during his introduction scenes, however, in fairness to all concerned, WilyKit does indeed pick him up on this with her comment, 'You don't seem very frightening to me!' And as the episode progresses (and he replenishes his energy) his form become more sinister in keeping with the story. Indeed, his transformation throughout the episode becomes one of its most distinctive features.

Mongor's decision to pick off the ThunderCats one by one also enhances the episode, and Lion-O's call to the ThunderCats (where nobody is able to respond) is a high-point. Other highlights include Panthro's shoulder armour being used to anchor him into the ground and an obvious nod to Perseus from Greek legend as Lion-O defeats Mongor's reflection in his claw shield. That the climax of the episode is seeded in the inscriptions on Mongor's tomb provides a strong message: The answers to present day issues can often be found in history. Additionally, it makes for a more convincing resolution than simple sword trickery.

'Mongor' also affords an interesting illustration of Lion-O's changing role in the series. By this point in the run, he is seen leading the ThunderCats in chastising the ThunderKittens for their irresponsibility. That the ThunderCats endorse this (and the Kittens accept it) illustrates that his maturation (at least in the eyes of his peers) is almost complete. The final scene, where the Kittens reveal they were more scared of their mentors' reactions than of Mongor himself, is witty, and it's a situation every child could surely recognise.

It has to be said that this point in the *ThunderCats* series is somewhat of a 'golden era'. There are very few exceptions throughout this block of scripts, with almost every episode seemingly offering the viewer something unexpected or new. Where Peter Lawrence marks himself out as a writer is in his use of dialogue. His strengths in this area are apparent, and his script work is never dull. A great example is Lion-O's delivery of the 'final blow' to Mongor: 'For Thundera, for Jaga and for the ThunderCats – strike down this power of fear!' With lines like that, even the most mundane sequences are injected with spine-tingling excitement – something *ThunderCats* would always deliver in abundance.

Writer's Commentary from Peter Lawrence:

Pretty straightforward. Kids have to find their way through fear in order to release the greater power of their adult friends and family.

From time to time, people have mocked the role that Dr Kuisis played in the *ThunderCats* script process and the seriousness with which we took the need for each story to have a moral; a moral that was fundamental to the story and not simply tacked on. I'd say that out of the 130 screenplays, perhaps five didn't genuinely incorporate a 'morality theme' or a lesson into their structure. Kuisis himself, from time to time, suggested themes we might explore, and this one, fear and how to overcome it, may have been prompted by the doc.

It's quite self-evident, isn't it?: fail to confront fear and you empower it. It grows until perhaps you cannot confront it. That's the entire basis of this story.

20. Return to Thundera (5 Stars)
Written by: Bob Haney
US Broadcast Date: 4 October 1985
UK Broadcast Date: 7 May 1987

In a series like *ThunderCats*, there are certain episodes that, with their title alone, alert everyone to prepare for a classic instalment. That this episode would see a 'Return to Thundera' is reason enough to watch, and the opportunity to see more of the ThunderCats' home planet would always have been utterly compelling. Completing a hat-trick of superb episodes, Bob Haney delivers everything any school boy (or girl) could possibly have hoped for, and this stands amongst the series' very best adventures.

Picking up from the events of Peter Lawrence's 'The Time Capsule', the episode tells two separate tales that converge in the climax. While it is perhaps disappointing that more screen time is not allocated to Thundera, it is understandable given the series' focus on the present-day struggle on Third Earth rather than previous encounters. To see the Thunderian capital and meet Lion-O's father Claudus (and pet Kano) is wonderful, and the scenes' tender execution makes them truly memorable. Lion-O's emotional response to seeing his father once again is subtle and understated, but resonates nonetheless, and Claudus's final speech is beautifully crafted: 'May my son, Lion-O, grow up to be as brave and noble as you'. We are also given new information about the ThunderCats' exodus from their planet; and Claudus's sacrifice on Thundera goes some way to explaining Jaga's stewardship of the team in the opening episode.

Meanwhile, having crafted a secondary plot based on Third Earth, Bob Haney embellishes this section of the script with just as many bells and whistles. Great scenes include the head of Cats' Lair being ripped off and the near abandonment of the ThunderCats' home. Once again Haney proves that, to have an effective resolution of a story, plot points must be seeded early on; and besides being a nice scene in its own right, the 'visit' of Slithe and Vultureman to Claudus sets the wheels in motion. The unexpected result of the Mutants' defeat is that, at last, they have not been utterly humiliated. They could not possibly have known that the ThunderCats would obtain plans for the Warbot, and their failure was more bad luck than poor judgement.

Ultimately, 'Return to Thundera' sums up everything that was distinctive about *ThunderCats*. For action, adventure, tension and an underlying emotional gravitas, the viewer need look no further.

Script Editor's Commentary from Peter Lawrence:

An interesting and challenging idea, but the critics are quite right: there's no reasonable explanation for the fact that Lion-O ends up on Thundera on exactly the right day for this story to unfold … It's hard for me to accept that we missed that glaring error.

With hindsight, this episode sees Bob moving out of his natural territory with the use of the Warbot. As I have said elsewhere, he was more inclined to classics and grand character, literary themes. In fact, he was rather a grand old hippy, with longish grey hair and that 'peace and love' demeanour, though perhaps a touch bitter at his lack of worldwide recognition! He would have liked to have lived as a novelist or mainstream playwright and, for all I know, may have written books and plays but, like many, many writers – some immensely talented – he never got his break. I'm not sure, either, of [the extent of] his output, his body of work. I recall that, at least on his own material, he worked rather slowly. As a sidebar, he was related to Chevy Chase –may have been his uncle – and Chevy was always encouraging and supportive. Even with that connection, Bob never made the jump into a bigger league. A great shame. He was a nice man.

The reunion, in this story, of Lion-O with Claudus and Kano is very much in Bob's style, and there's an odd marriage between these quite archetypal themes and the more sci-fi Warbot/absorber disc elements. Depending on your 'purism', this marriage either gives you an interesting and eclectic story or is a bit muddled.

21. Dr Dometone (3 Stars)
Written by: William Overgard
US Broadcast Date: 7 October 1985
UK Broadcast Date: 24 September 1987

Although a bizarre episode when viewed in context as an instalment of *ThunderCats*, 'Dr Dometone' is nonetheless enjoyable.

Bill Overgard once again demonstrates his vision that the ThunderCats themselves are more background accompaniment than star players. Having said that, he (and script editor Peter Lawrence) just about manage to shoehorn Lion-O and the team into the plot, and while it still feels 'odd' amongst its neighbouring episodes, it just about gets away with it.

On the plus side, Overgard creates another set of interesting characters, notably the eponymous Dr Dometone, and the episode's premise is an interesting one. It is fascinating to see what can only be described as 'humanity' still having a small presence on 'Third' Earth. If we follow Leonard Starr's premise that the planet is our Earth at some future point, then the information that the Great Oceanic Plug was installed seventeen centuries previously opens up some new timelines for fans to speculate upon.

There is very little in the episode that doesn't seem wholly enjoyable, and it is littered with highlights, including the 'compressed air bubble' climax, which is certainly one of the show's more technical and sophisticated resolutions. Also we are given a glimpse of the ThunderCats' dining room; and there is an amusing scene where Scrape gives the research team a warning to abandon ship and, seconds later, we see all of the emergency evacuation pods launching.

The episode's greatest failing is that it simply feels *too* different. Many of the scenes would seem more at home in a Gerry Anderson production (notably *Stingray*), and even the shark disguise idea was explored previously in the popular *Tintin* cartoon adventure 'Red Rackham's Treasure'.

Nevertheless, Overgard's imaginative introduction of alternative elements to the show delivered as many triumphs as it did disasters. 'Dr Dometone' may not feel like standard *ThunderCats* fare, but I'm sure if you were to ask any child watching it for the first time, they would say they enjoyed it.

Script Editor's Commentary from Peter Lawrence:

I remember having a lot of difficulty editing this episode. In truth, it really didn't need the ThunderCats at all (and in the original draft they were barely present).

Plus, the world of Dr D was hardly Third Earth. It's true that Dr D travelled to the Lair to ask for help ... but did he really need it? There's not much to be said about this story – the originality of which I love ... The Great Oceanic Plug? ... Scrape? – except that if you like the more conventional episodes, this one is probably not for you. If you like the wilder side, then it is. I had to fight for some of Bill's ideas, and they were absolutely worth fighting for.

22. The Astral Prison (3.5 Stars)
Written by: Peter Lawrence
US Broadcast Date: 8 October 1985
UK Broadcast Date: 1 October 1987

Given the fleeting nature of his appearances throughout the series, Jaga-led episodes are always welcome. To see him in his 'true' form (rather than his more common ghostly apparition) is simply a bonus.

'The Astral Prison' showcases the imagination of writer Peter Lawrence and his ethos that *ThunderCats* scripts must have a strong idea behind them (admitting that dialogue and direction could always be improved – but only with an exciting concept in place). His idea certainly hits the mark here, and the opportunity to have Lion-O and Jaga fighting side by side is too good to miss.

It is fitting that Lion-O should finally be able to repay his debt to Jaga, and the fact that it is Jaga who is in need of help really makes the episode resonate. That Lion-O would gladly surrender his own existence to free his mentor speaks volumes of his personality, and these emotional signatures (in which Lawrence excels) are threaded throughout the episode.

The story is quite surreal, and the disembodied hands and eyes in the Netherwitch's cave are genuinely strange. It is a pity that more screen time isn't given over to exploring the Astral Realm – although, as in the case of 'Return to Thundera', we must remember the series is anchored primarily in the events of Third Earth. In contrast to the surreal aspects, there is also a healthy dose of humour throughout the episode, including an amusing, if fleeting, scene where Jackalman allows a wheel to roll over Monkian's foot.

Towards the end of the episode, Pacific Animation Corporation once again rise to the occasion and provide an exciting showcase of the ThunderCats themselves. Beginning with Lion-O repelling Vultureman (look out for the X-ray effect of the Sword's power), there are some great character drawings and angles in the climax. For the more attentive viewer, there is also a cel-mispaint to watch out for during Lion-O's fall: his insignia colours are inverted.

The scene where Lion-O disappears slowly from Third Earth (as he sees Mumm-Ra's transformation) is cleverly executed, and his subsequent rematerialisation at the end of the episode (where the Cat's eye appears from an apparent nothingness) is equally exciting. Additionally, look out for the one and only appearance by the Astral Moat Monster, who would later become a toy in the LJN *ThunderCats* line.

'The Astral Prison' isn't perfect, and the Bridge of Slime is nearly identical to the Bridge of Light in Lawrence's earlier episode 'The Time Capsule', but it's a definite highlight from this era. Once again, Lawrence's superlative dialogue is effortless, not least in Jaga's exchange with Lion-O: 'So now we're even, Lord of the ThunderCats!'

Writer's Commentary from Peter Lawrence:

This was only the second animated script I had written from start to finish, and I had never worked on a big series before. I had a lot to learn, and the script demonstrates a couple of both 'good' and 'bad' lessons. One is that I went directly to the writer's 'safe room' – inventing my own characters and situations rather than doing the harder work of staying within the show. When in doubt, throw in Nemex! Oh, Nemex isn't enough? Well how about Brodo? Oh … and there's not enough to work with on Third Earth – then let's invent an Astral World. All examples of Hitchcock's theory of McGuffins. A very different style from the linear dictates of the Hero's Quest. So this makes for a huge amount of extra production, and delays the further development, in depth, of the show's main characters and world. Its upside is that it does give the show a greater variety and the audience is never sure what weird, wild or woolly McGuffin will turn up next.

I always liked the Jaga figure and the in-the-shadows relationship with Lion-O. Personally, too, I'm fascinated by parallel dimensions, astral planes, and so on. I've never been fortunate enough to experience any kind of supernatural, supernormal phenomenon but would give my eye teeth for that! (And, incidentally, that was one of the bases of *The Real Adventures of Johnny Quest* … long before *The X-Files* owned that territory.) Writing this kind of 'other world' for a young audience is liberating. It has to be clearly expressed and understandable, which makes the writer think more deeply and clearly, too.

23. The Crystal Queen (3.5)
Written by: Leonard Starr
US Broadcast Date: 9 October 1985
UK Broadcast Date: 28 May 1987

In a series awash with contributions from Bill Overgard, 'The Crystal Queen' may seem to be a relatively 'normal' episode. However, considering this is a contribution from Leonard Starr, who nearly always wrote more conservatively, it is perhaps more significant. As mentioned previously, many of Starr's episodes had a remit to advance key elements within the *ThunderCats* series as a whole. This time, we see him 'unleashed' from these responsibilities and given free rein over an episode. The result isn't perfect, but it's amongst the more quirky examples of his work.

The central theme that Lion-O will strive tirelessly to protect each and every one of the inhabitants of Third Earth, however small, is an admirable one, and the episode has enough fun and adventure to sustain its running time. (It is interesting that Starr recalls that the adventure was originally conceived to run for two parts, as it's hard to imagine there would have been enough potential to expand such a relatively basic premise.)

Highlights include the story twist that, rather than Lion-O freeing the Arietta bird (as intended), it is the bird that frees Lion-O. The sub-theme that Snarf is getting old also helps to move the story along, and we can't help but feel sorry for Lion-O's faithful companion. That Snarf's integrity is restored at the end of the episode is pleasing, and it makes for some humorous lines throughout the show, including Snarf's evident distain when eating the food he has prepared.

Starr also plays around with the format of the show and delivers a humiliating blow to Lion-O, having the young leader encased in glass mid-call to his friends. It is often simple moments such as this that keep the audience on their toes, reminding them that stories won't always turn out as they may predict!

'The Crystal Queen' is a simple yet quaint story that broadens the scope of the series. While the ThunderCats would more commonly be engaged in a battle to the death, sometimes the noble pursuit of decency would be more than enough to rouse them. It is also a story of loyalty. Through thick and thin, Snarf will never abandon his young charge, even if his own capabilities are in doubt. In the words of Snarf himself, 'See, old Snarf – just gets better with age!'

Writer's Commentary from Leonard Starr:

This story just kept going and going. It was about an Ice Queen, and had a quasi-Russian theme, lots of snow and ice, and it was actually a two-parter to start with, but Jules Bass cut the hell out of it and made it into a one-parter. It was really stupid of Jules considering how frantic we were for scripts. And that also cut out a fee for me for a whole script.

I believe I gave the Queen a Russian name. The only thing I remember about it is that someone sits down on an icy hump, which shakes free, and it's Snarf underneath the ice. It was full of that kind of thing.

24. Safari Joe (4 Stars)
Written by: Stephen Perry
US Broadcast Date: 10 October 1985
UK Broadcast Date: 4 June 1987

An inspired *ThunderCats* entry, 'Safari Joe' not only offers a hugely original premise, but delivers an episode worthy of the concept. The idea that an intergalactic big game hunter has arrived on Third Earth to obtain his latest catch, introduces not only a brilliant idea, but a truly disquieting thought for children. Safari Joe is determined to hunt down and murder our heroes for nothing more than 'fun' ('I'm a Sportsman') – one of the most disturbing concepts ever explored in the series.

The episode is full of great moments, including the eerie sight of Safari Joe's empty cages, all with name badges labelling their intended victims. Steve Perry's summary of each of the ThunderCats' strengths and weaknesses is also outstanding, and we learn for the first time that Cheetara can't maintain her extreme speed and (perhaps more bizarrely) Tygra can't swim when visible. There is also an amusing scene where Lion-O avoids his trap by upending the Sword and using it as an improvised periscope.

Not only does Perry deliver on ideas, but the character of Safari Joe is perfectly crafted. Not only is he well conceived but he is given dialogue befitting the character, with amusing lines such as 'Nice kitty, or I'll turn your tiger friend into a rug!' We even get a great catch-phrase – 'Safari Joe does it again' – which only helps distinguish him from other guest villains.

The climax of the episode is engaging, and the lethal game of cat and mouse between Lion-O and Safari Joe throughout Cats' Lair raises the stakes for our hero. It is perhaps a shame that Safari Joe would make only one fleeting return in the series, as his dark humour surely warranted further return appearances.

Perhaps the only factor that detracts from the episode is Safari Joe's rather disappointing defeat. While it is an important component of the story that he shows his true colours as a coward, it all happens extremely quickly, and some of the earlier menace is therefore negated. Despite that, this instalment of *ThunderCats* is amongst its best offerings, and the idea that an enemy may be rehabilitated rather than banished or destroyed is another novel inclusion. Though his appearances would be brief, Safari Joe would rightly take his place as one of the series' greatest villains.

Writer's Commentary from Steve Perry:

Of all the *ThunderCats* episodes I wrote, 'Safari Joe' is my favourite. It was the second springboard accepted by Len Starr, the head writer, and the first show managed by Peter Lawrence, the new showrunner. It had taken me three weeks to write my first episode, 'The Doomgaze', and there was perhaps a week or two in between the final rewrite of that and the go-ahead on 'Safari Joe'.

Safari Joe was, for me, very dear. He was a no-brainer character, and while I was shocked by and did not like his character design (I had described and written someone who looked quite different), I have come to accept it. You see, I used that character in other work – most notably in the *Timespirits* [comic book] story drawn by Al Williamson. He was called Rex Tandem in that story, but Safari Joe *is* Rex Tandem. Rex is how I wanted Joe to look. They even have the same tag line: 'Rex Tandem does it again!' It is a case of me ripping off myself and getting as much mileage out of something as a writer possibly can. It's … cheating.

But during the writing of the script for 'Safari Joe', I knew I had a good episode. It flowed out of me quick and easy, and the finished script was sent to animation nearly untouched. Peter Lawrence might have changed one or two lines, but that was about it.

The great Jim Meskimen, who has gone on to such a fabulous acting career since then, was the secondary character designer, and he designed the Mule, Safari Joe's robot. Jim made the Mule a train – this was completely Jim's doing. My version of Safari Joe's Mule was very, very different – if I remember correctly, I had envisioned a Robbie the Robot type. I believe Jim's train Mule is a case where an improvement was made. And while my Safari Joe description spoke of a handsome, Jungle Jim sort of guy, the bald, British final form of him does speak 'bad guy' a lot louder than my version.

'Safari Joe' was the easiest for me to write, and I very much enjoy the fact he was a major toy in the LJN line. I recently bought a loose Safari Joe figure at a flea market, and could not resist blurting out to the flea market dealer that I had created that character. They looked at me as if I was some pathological liar from that

Saturday Night Live skit about the Liars Club.

I would write, hotly, for two or three hour stretches, and then rush out of my studio, strip naked, and throw myself into the swimming hole. Often I was yelling, 'Safari Joe does it again!' When others were present, they looked at me as if I had gone off my rocker. But I didn't care. I was so into the writing of 'Safari Joe', and it was coming to me so quick and easy, and I was excited about this to such an extent that I seemed to be living on Third Earth. Much of the dialogue spoken by Safari Joe in that episode is lines I would yell to the waterfall. I was crazy.

25. Snarf Takes Up the Challenge (4 Stars)
Written by: Peter Lawrence
US Broadcast Date: 11 October 1985
UK Broadcast Date: 14 May 1987

The most surprising thing about 'Snarf Takes up the Challenge' is how enjoyable it is. While Snarf certainly earned his place in the *ThunderCats* series (providing necessary comic relief), an episode with him in a starring role may have been destined for mediocrity. Confounding this expectation, Peter Lawrence delivers a wonderfully exciting episode, fully justifying Snarf's place in the ThunderCats team.

The episode begins with a lonely scene of Cats' Lair, as Snarf tries in vain to locate his fellow ThunderCats. This eerie image sets the tone perfectly, and it must surely be any child's greatest nightmare that one day, their parents will be gone and they will be left alone. As with one of his previous episodes, 'Mongor', Lawrence cleverly opens the action half-way through the adventure, making the most of the short running time. His flashback scenes feature imaginative traps as, one by one, the ThunderCats are snared. With each scenario, the adage 'curiosity killed the cat' comes into play, as each member falls foul of his or her inquisitive nature.

As with many of Lawrence's episodes, the script feels effortless and flows at a perfect pace. There are plenty of novel moments, including the Mutants' ingenious use of an Eye of Thundera projector. From the production side, look out for some unusual scene transitions (such as interlocking triangles during the ThunderCat traps), and a determined battle between Mumm-Ra and Lion-O in the Black Pyramid that utilises re-photographed cels of Lion-O from the opening credits.

Where the episode really excels is in the surprise revelation of the mummified ThunderCats entombed with Mumm-Ra. Lion-O's eyes alone tell the story, watching Mumm-Ra's every move with terror, and this narrative choice is a touch of genius from Lawrence, who once again displays his prowess with dialogue. 'We'll bully the Berbils, we'll terrorise the Talbots, whip the Wollos, smash the Snowmen,' declare the Mutants.

The episode's climax, where Snarf's new-found friend spins a web around Mumm-Ra's sarcophagus, is cleverly conceived, and the ThunderCats bursting out of their wrappings as they praise Snarf ('You underestimated the seventh ThunderCat') is exhilarating. While Mumm-Ra's weakness (the reflection of his own evil) has never been particularly imaginative, it can just about be justified when used sparingly.

'Snarf Takes up the Challenge' is, in many ways, an allegory for the challenge that script editor Peter Lawrence was facing; to integrate a sometimes unpopular 'minor' character and utilise him as the lead protagonist. His success in this endeavour is evident.

Writer's Commentary from Peter Lawrence:

I never much liked Snarf, who seemed to me to be the obligatory comic character (and who, incidentally, was originally drawn with a little arsehole dot, so that in shots where he was walking from camera, there was that dot; instantly censored). Perhaps, by script #25, and in view of my bias, he wasn't getting enough air time, and so, I believe, Jules asked me to write a show starring him. I wanted to make him more than a token 'Ha-ha-ha' figure, the constant nay-sayer too, and therefore challenged him to be heroic. It added another dimension to his character.

26. Sixth Sense (3.5 Stars)
Written by: Peter Lawrence
US Broadcast Date: 28 October 1985
UK Broadcast Date: 17 September 1987

Featuring Cheetara as its central character, 'Sixth Sense' is an interesting investigation into her psychic abilities. This premise is handled well and the darker side of her 'gift' is explored, leading to some disturbing scenes as she becomes possessed.

The nature of the mysterious craft that crashes into the atmosphere of Third Earth is cleverly concealed throughout the episode. Not only does this add considerably to the suspense, but it also allows the episode to concentrate not on the ship, but on its effect on Cheetara.

'Sixth Sense' is cleverly constructed and, with the personal jeopardy of a lead character, offers a very real sense of danger that the ThunderCats must overcome. That this isn't the result of a villainous plot makes the story even more original.

We also begin to see some dissention amongst the Mutants here, as Monkian ignores Vultureman's 'order' to leave the ship unharmed ('Nothing attacks Monkian and gets away free!'). Vultureman's scorn of his companions proves his role as an intellectual superior, and some fascinating subtext is touched upon regarding the Mutants' compulsion to destroy anything that is not fully understood.

Some witty moments are littered throughout the episode. Snarf's comment that he's 'too close to the ground to enjoy snow' raises a smile, and Peter Lawrence playfully explores the relationship between Lion-O and Cheetara (one it would seem the alien craft is keen to encourage).

While Cheetara's psychic abilities had previously been only marginally explored, 'Sixth Sense' showcases her character, and the fact that she is shown to remain strong and resolute (even as she nears her 'end') is testament to the scriptwriting. Cheetara would never be a stereotypical female heroine, and this episode proves to be no exception.

Writer's Commentary from Peter Lawrence:

Lee Dannacher always felt that the male-dominated writing and production team gave Cheetara short shrift, and she was right. As a side issue, we tried to recruit female writers, but it was difficult. Kim Morris was a success for us, and a pleasure to work with – a very dry wit and a tough audience, she made me think hard about her work, and that challenge is always a pleasure for an editor. In general, however, we didn't have much luck in balancing the team, perhaps because *ThunderCats* was perceived as a boys' show and a lot of the women writers in kids animation were writing shows like *My Little Pony*. If that's a stereotype, it's no less true for being stereotypical – and I wonder, no more than curiosity, how many guys were on the staff of *My Little Pony, Berenstain Bears*, etc. (If the answer to that is 'lots', then that's an even more powerful indictment of sexism in the industry!) So, Lee pressed me to further develop Cheetara's character, to use her powers and to feature her more prominently – and this episode is one result.

I've always felt that a lot of writers shy away from working with the self-evident truth that women are different from men. Intimidated by the potential accusation of stereotyping or sexism, they prefer to simply make the female hero (and they don't even like to use the word 'heroine', which, they say, offends some feminists) a guy in a dress. Not a cross-dresser, of course; simply a player that looks like a woman but is actually male in character. I think it's possible, even in this genre, to build a character that is essentially female but uses her 'feminine' persona and power in a superheroic way. That is, her femininity does not diminish her, it enhances her. So, here, we see Cheetara behaving in selfless, supportive and caring – heroic – ways that, perhaps, the male characters would not have chosen. It's interesting that S-S-S-Slithe's ultimate solution is to blast the alien ship to pieces. Perhaps, if there had been a female Mutant villain, she would have found a more 'feminine' way to unleash the ship's powers.

Sure, all this sounds pretentious and even politically correct, but we weren't motivated by PC. It's that simple. See *The Real Adventures of Johnny Quest*. We developed Jessie similarly – to be a real woman as well as a heroic figure. Interesting that once we had left the show, the ensuing writers and producers put her in a fucking pink dress. So I'm told. I was so disgusted by various events there that I never watched that version of the show. I always hope that writers, whatever their social or political persuasions, will show some insight and courage – break moulds and stand up to the crasser demands of their producers, the merchandisers, the market – but it's often a vain hope. The pay cheque is everything – and never more so than now. I'm sure I've sold out too, many times, along the way. But, to return to the essentials: this was an attempt to develop Cheetara further, to make her more interesting and more powerful and so guarantee her roles in future episodes.

27. The Thunder-Cutter (4.5 Stars)
Written by: William Overgard
US Broadcast Date: 29 October 1985
UK Broadcast Date: 22 October 1990

A triumph of storytelling, Bill Overgard's Oriental tale proves unequivocally the many benefits the writer brought to *ThunderCats*. While he would often overstep the mark, 'The Thunder-Cutter' perfectly balances the introduction of engaging and original characters and the successful utilisation of the established characters and the world they inhabit.

Hachiman, as a character, is perfectly formed, touching upon the very adult concept of honour that lies at his heart. Given that Mumm-Ra's main purpose in summoning him is to obtain a rival blade to the Sword of Omens, the Samurai could easily have been a faceless sword-wielder, but what emerges is far more original. The way in which Mumm-Ra cleverly 'spins' his version of Lion-O as an aggressor is brilliant, and great moments keep coming in abundance as the episode progresses.

Overgard's dialogue is on top form, with some magical moments including Lion-O's polite address to Hachiman: 'Pardon me sir, but as I started to cross first, I ask you please to back off.' 'It is good manners if a boy gets out of the way for a man!' replies the Samurai. The childish battle of one-upmanship that follows also leads to the great line from Lion-O, 'I am not a boy and that is not my little sister!'

It is impossible to list all of the highlights from the episode, but notable elements include: the ruins of Third Earth, which give a brief but tantalising glimpse into the history of the planet; the eerie 'Ninja', with his figure seen in almost complete silhouette, who is sinister and appealing and proves the perfect foil for Hachiman; a fun moment where Lion-O and his team improvise a catapult from a tree; and the flash of resourcefulness Lion-O shows in improvising a ledge for the plummeting Nayda.

As mentioned, the episode touches on some adult subject matter, and the concept of negotiation is chief amongst this. The idea of Slithe's capture being used as a bargaining counter is unusual for the series, and Mumm-Ra's declaration 'Never do what your enemy expects' takes proceedings in an unpredictable direction.

A special note should also be given both to voice actor Peter Newman and to the *ThunderCats* character designers who realised Hachiman with every bit of grace and imagination as described in the script.

The episode falls just short of perfection, incorporating a bizarre and unnecessary declaration that the (wonderfully realised) Treetop Kingdom is a three day journey from Cats' Lair (despite the small shortcut that the Warrior Maiden's provide). Not only does this contradict previous episodes (not entirely problematic or uncommon in itself), but it somewhat undermines the climax of the episode, where the *ThunderCats* respond to Lion-O's signal in a matter of moments. Nonetheless, this does not spoil a wonderful adventure and, from this point on, the return of Hachiman could only ever have been mandatory.

Script Editor's Commentary from Peter Lawrence:

I don't know what it is, exactly, but swords have a fascination. One only has to think of the role they play in *Star Wars* where swordplay is, you would think, both incongruous and anachronistic but nonetheless works perfectly. The latest *Alice in Wonderland* [movie] features a legendary sword and, surprisingly, it works.

Since we – Lion-O – had the most powerful sword ever known, it was inevitable that other swords would be created to confront it. Hence the

ThunderCutter.

Bill Overgard was a great student of Japanese and Samurai culture and had written a movie called *Bushido Blade* for Arthur Rankin. He drew on that knowledge – and the sense of fun that he had developed around the subject – for this episode, and for the invention of Hachiman.

For many of us on the show, [the involvement of] Masaki Iizuka, Arthur's longstanding love of Japan, the coming of anime and the growing interest in Japanese animation were inspirational. We wanted to know more. We had read or watched *Shogun*. Some of us went to Japan to meet with the animators, to discuss and develop the show. I hope that our respect for that world carries through, even to this cartoon show for the younger audience ...

28. The Wolfrat (3.5 Stars)
Written by: C H Trengove
US Broadcast Date: 30 October 1985
UK Broadcast Date: 17 December 1990

Perhaps the most notable aspect of 'The Wolfrat' is that it introduces long-term writer and editor Chris Trengove to the series. While it isn't his finest episode, it's still an enjoyable foray into the world of miniaturisation – a concept that crops up at one point or another in most fantasy/sci-fi programmes.

The greatest detractor for this strong concept is the episode's short running time. With only some 20 minutes to work with, a screenwriter must carefully balance pace. Unfortunately, no sooner are the ThunderCats miniaturised, they are reinstated.

'The Wolfrat' does, however, offer many redeeming features. The eponymous, transforming character is cleverly realised, and his various disguises add a real touch of originality to proceedings. Lion-O holding a 'giant' Sword is also an iconic moment and there are some inspired animation sequences as the ThunderCats shrink, coupled with some great angles as they look up at their environment.

Trengove also proves his affinity with humour, and the 'Snarf MK1 Charger' provides an amusing resolution to the episode. Snarf's 'gigantic' ending is perhaps a little silly, but it facilitates some fun dialogue and provides the (by now standard) closing gag.

'The Wolfrat' would surely have benefitted from being expanded into a two part serial, with the first episode concentrating on the Wolfrat's impregnation of the ThunderCats' fortress and the second allowing more time to explore the many challenges of being miniaturised. Despite this, 'The Wolfrat' is surely one of the more memorable episodes of *ThunderCats* to emerge from the first season, and it's a fitting homage to a range of literary sources, such as Mary Norton's *The Borrowers*.

Writer's Commentary from Chris Trengove:

Hmm ... more combining of existing creatures! (Let's think – what two animals are vaguely menacing? Ah yes, a wolf! And a rat!) This episode also made use of the idea of reducing characters in size (which is okay in animation – it gives you 'kind of' new characters, without involving any extra design work).

This was the first episode I wrote featuring Mumm-Ra, a character all the writers liked, I think. Always cool when he did his transformation into an ancient Egyptian bodybuilder. However, you had to watch out that you weren't making the 'bad guys' more interesting than the 'good guys', and it was drummed into us that the 'Cats were always the heroes and should occupy the majority of the screen time.

It was fun to have Snarf 'saving the day.' He was another character that all the writers liked, and it was nice to have him step out of his 'lovable buffoon' role for a little while.

29 & 30. Feliner – Parts One and Two (5 Stars)
Written by: Stephen Perry
US Broadcast Date: 31 October and 1 November 1985
UK Broadcast Date: 12 and 19 November 1990

The series' first (and only) two part serial ranks amongst its finest offerings. Writer Steve Perry successfully combines three exciting story strands: the introduction of the villainous Ratar-O; a Planet of Snarfs; and the ThunderCats' new space craft, the Feliner. Doubling the screen time facilitates an expansion of storytelling opportunities and, for once, an 'epic' tale isn't destined for disappointment due to a rushed ending.

By far the most beneficial addition to the series is Ratar-O. Not only is the character perfectly conceived, but he is also given great dialogue, not least in his scolding of Slithe and the other Mutants: 'A sitting target and you bungled it … Call yourself a gunner – you'd do better back as a cook!' For the first time in the series, we see the Mutants as a viable threat. Under the command of Ratar-O and his RatStar, the Mutants' interplay with their 'master' produces some memorable scenes, and their dissenting nature is explored to great effect.

The episode opens with a tantalising sequence and, within a few seconds, we see a new Planet of Snarfs (numbering 43 in total), an alien spacecraft and a new Mutant, deliberately confusing the viewer and setting the perfect tone for the episode, one that will push the series in a new direction. It's also interesting to see that the ThunderCats have now progressed their salvaged technology to the point that space travel could once again be possible. This would give the series' writers new storytelling opportunities and prove vital in future episodes.

'Feliner' offers an array of highlights. The scene where Snarf (now revealed to be named, Osbert) stumbles upon his cousin Snarfer outside Cats' Lair is an emotional reunion, and his speech, 'But you were just a baby – I must be getting old', is perfectly judged.

At the close of episode one it would, perhaps, have been nice to see the series' first cliffhanger. However, the story seems to have been paced so that both episodes can be viewed in isolation. Fortunately, this works within the context of the episode and the idea that the ThunderCats will 'steal' the Mutants' Hyperspace Mega Condenser (thereby making their spacecraft operational) is an ingenious one.

The opening scenes of the second episode boast some wonderful background art as we see the wreckage of the RatStar. Once again, the episode regains pace, and Ratar-O's angry display of power to his fellow Mutants is beautifully realised. His cold, unresponsive stare before blasting them with his weaponry is truly menacing, and Vultureman begging for his colleagues' lives is sublime.

There is a strange yet effective repeat of the climax to episode one played out over seven minutes into the second episode, but this only serves to illustrate the attention to pacing given in these episodes. 'Feliner' also features some superb direction from Pacific Animation Corporation, and the scenes where the ThunderTank and Mutank do battle are bursting with energy.

As mentioned, this episode succeeds where others have failed, by littering the narrative with sub-plots that actually have time to play out. While Mumm-Ra's appearance may be a little unwarranted, his meddling does add to proceedings, and his motivation in simply wanting to disrupt the ThunderCats really sums up his character. Lion-O attaching a hook line to Mumm-Ra as he is dragged through the sky is also a nice touch, although it's a shame that Mumm-Ra seems to abandon his quest with relative ease.

Overall, 'Feliner' is a *ThunderCats* classic. Ratar-O, the 'new' Snarfs and the Feliner would all live on in the show, making countless return appearances, and this is a testament to Steve Perry's writing. Snarf's declaration that he would leave the ThunderCats in the concluding moments of the show is surprisingly touching (the tears in Lion-O's and Snarf's eyes being a nice touch) and even the least enthusiastic supporters of the Snarf character must surely have been glad to see his return. 'What in Thundera would you do without me!'

Writer's Commentary from Steve Perry:

Although I was aware [that Len Starr was writing a] five-part story, I was very surprised when Peter Lawrence suggested that I combine a couple of my ideas into a two-part story. These were 'The Planet of Snarfs' (Snarf's home planet and extensive family is revealed – new characters include Snarfer) and 'Rats' (a new evil Mutant based on a rat is introduced to organise Slithe and the others and make them more menacing). Since it meant a double assignment, and two pay cheques in the bag, I was all for it. I believe I had pitched 'The Planet of Snarfs' as the title, but that was changed.

Jim Meskimen did a lot of the secondary character design, and the hour-long show came out quite well, if you ask me. I particularly like the opening of the first part, and the music. The music written for that first part opening sequence was used in many other shows, too. It was a big show, introducing lots of potential ancillary merchandise. We had Ratar-O, his spaceship, the RatStar; we had a new bunch of Snarfs; and we had the Feliner. For one story idea, Rankin/Bass was getting a lot; so was LJN. They liked the whole thing so much they gave me more money to write. I got a raise! I wrote the two shows in the space of three weeks, and Peter Lawrence did his rewrite. Now, all of this points right to the true nature of what cartoons in the 1980s were all about: commercials for toys. We cannot get around that simple fact – the thing was all built around the success or failure of a line of plastic toys. I do not know how successful the LJN line of *ThunderCats* toys was, but I'll bet they did better than *SilverHawks* did for Kenner.

Ratar-O was completely my idea, and I think it was another one of those no-brainers. Cats and mice. Mice are not so threatening, but everyone hates rats. Mutant rat guy. A no-brainer. I distinctly recall a conversation with Peter about the Mutants. Jules wanted them used, and all the writers bitched about it, because they were obviously ineffective, they could never win, and if you saw them in a show you knew from the get-go they would fuck up, they would fail, they would screw everything up, they would lose. It sort of made any suspense impossible. Just a glimpse of Slithe and one knew the Mutants were bound to fail. By the time I wrote 'The Planet of Snarfs' (to me it will always be titled that) the evil Mutants were sort of a joke – we called them the Three Stooges. They were, to rob from *Blackadder*, 'about as menacing as a little bunny with the word "boo" written on its forehead.'

The character design of Ratar-O was quite different from what I had envisioned. I had seen much more of a Splinter character (from the *Teenage Mutant Ninja Turtles*) in Ratar-O, an older Oriental, but still a Mongol. Either Jim Meskimen or Bob Camp latched right onto the Gengis Kahn take for Ratar-O and definitely went that route as opposed to Japanese or Chinese. I had called him a Mongol-like warlord, but actually described a Japanese-type sensei. I certainly approved of the final Ratar-O, though. It's a good example of how collective cartoons are: yes, Ratar-O sprang from my head, but the finished product was a result of other people's input, ideas and revisions.

I was talking to Peter about new toys for the line. I had suggested the Feliner – everyone loved the name; again, a right-on no-brainer. How do we introduce it? Well, there's a problem with the Mutants, they need to be upgraded somehow. I told Peter on the phone that I had a character in mind, Ratar-O. To tell you the truth, I named him Ratan. Peter suggested Ratar-O. 'You know … Lion-O. Rat-*tar*-O!' It made perfect sense, and I was dumb not to have thought of it. I had him using the two sais because I was ripping off *myself*. I had written a comic book, a proposed series, that never went anywhere, never got published or drawn, or even out of the proposal stages, for Marvel. It was called *Turbo-Sai* and was about a character who used high powered sais, in explosive hand to hand combat. The comic had the two sais, and the functions you see in the show – such as crossing them and firing an X-beam, and a beam that could capture people – were all in my comic book proposal. When I created Ratan (later Ratar-O), he had the sais and used those weapon tricks.

Snarfer and all the other Snarfs – Snarf-Oswold, Snarf-Bert, Snarf-Ernie, all that sort of hyphenated name thing going on – was all Peter Lawrence's idea. He named our Snarf Osbert. (It's a British thing, I think – no-one in America liked it or thought it as funny as he did.) I had a 'planet full of Snarfs' in mind for one simple reason – you could add tons of different characters and have them all look the same, look like Snarf. Same toy mould, a dozen different characters – just change the lettering on the blister pack.

31. Mandora and the Pirates (2.5 Stars)
Written by: William Overgard
US Broadcast Date: 4 November 1985
UK Broadcast Date: 21 May 1987

Controversial writer Bill Overgard always walked a fine line between enhancing the series with his vivid imagination and obscuring its key elements. Unfortunately, 'Mandora and the Pirates' represents the first time he fell the wrong side of that line.

Perhaps the most noticeable difference between this outing and a standard *ThunderCats* episode is that it's set in deep space. Without the regular landmarks of

Third Earth, Cats' Lair or indeed any prominently featured ThunderCats besides Lion-O, the episode seems out of place and, as such, uncomfortable. This need not be a fatal flaw in itself. Indeed it could be argued that 'Mandora and the Pirates' is very similar to Overgard's subsequent and greatly superior adventure 'Sword in a Hole'. Even the plots of the two are similar – the ThunderCats being attracted into space by a deception and encountering a space menace. However, while 'Sword in a Hole' will feature a credible pathway to space (in the shape of the Feliner spacecraft), this episode's method of Lion-O riding into space on the back of Mandora's Electracharger is nonsensical and ludicrous. Overgard's usual talent for character development also seems to desert him here, and Captain Cracker falls into the category of a 'generic pirate'. Given that the series had already featured a renegade pirate in the form of Hammerhand, it has to be said Cracker is the inferior of the two in terms of characterisation.

Even the plot isn't Overgard's finest, with many scenes seeming to lack direction. Ultimately, this is the story of an interplanetary police officer pursuing a criminal in space. The ThunderCats (i.e. Lion-O) really have no place in the story and, as such, it would perhaps have been more suited to *SilverHawks*.

Despite this, the episode isn't without merit. Overgard's trademark device of disposing of the Sword of Omens throughout the episode (so that it can't always be relied upon to resolve the plot) has to be commended. Lion-O walking a space plank is an original idea, and Mandora's fate (hanging over a pot of boiling oil) is particularly gruesome. The reappearance of the Quick-Pik character (albeit rehabilitated) is also welcome, and Cracker's trap to attract Mandora with a series of traffic offences is ingenious.

Ultimately, episodes like 'Doctor Dometone' prove that Overgard could deliver a script that stood in contrast to those of his fellow writers and still get away with it. However, to do this successfully, the story had be a strong one. On this occasion, it wasn't.

Script Editor's Commentary from Peter Lawrence:

Producing a show like this, on a very tight schedule and with a much, much smaller crew than competing shows, we worked hard to exploit existing elements – designs, concepts, secondary characters and so on. Bringing back Mandora was a pretty easy decision, and rekindling her fiery relationship with Lion-O equally obvious. My memory is that in the first draft their exchanges were hotter and more suggestive. Nothing distasteful, but witty and sharp. I was asked to cut them back and did so, but without much enthusiasm for the task.

The episode demonstrates Bill's great sci-fi/sci-fantasy imagination, with its space milieu, the autonomous Harley, the prison itself (which, I now realise, might have sparked the prison from which Mon*star escaped to kick off *Silverhawks*). The Orbit Brake? What a great cartoon/animation idea. And then, just when the story seems to be rolling along conventionally, Bill throws in Lion-O's walking the plank.

I completely understand why so many of the 'straighter line' fans did not – and do not – care for Bill's flights of fancy. Many viewers want their stories and their characters to be somewhat predictable – the drama and the surprise contained within a known world. The ThunderCats always behave in a certain way. Mumm-Ra has his MO. And so on. But every show needs a shake-up and Bill Overgard's stories play that role to perfection.

32. Return of the Driller (3 Stars)
Written by: Howard Post
US Broadcast Date: 5 November 1985
UK Broadcast Date: 11 June 1987

In his second (and final) episode of *ThunderCats*, Howard Post was unable to recapture the originality of the first appearance of his character the Driller in 'Spitting Image'. Unfortunately, while the Driller seems an interesting adversary, his appearance here is just as brief as in his debut, and the viewer is still left wanting more. Bizarrely, the few scenes that do feature the title character are almost identical to those in his previous story, as he once again visits Mumm-Ra's treasure chamber.

The idea of an acid lake flowing underground and ebbing ever closer to Cats' Lair is an interesting one, and it's a nice device. Sadly, Post's background as a comic strip writer comes through here, and an abundance of inconsequential subplots are littered throughout the episode. These include attacks by Rockmen, Mechanosects and a Giant Worm. While this type of plotting suits the nature of an episodic comic strip, it seems a bit 'choppy' in a series like *ThunderCats*. Other ideas, like the Spongefog used to 'plug the hole', are a little silly, and the thin plot is stretched to its limits. There are admittedly plenty of exciting moments – they just don't fuse together as well as the viewer might like.

It's nice to see *ThunderCats* tackle an 'environmental' subject, and the idea that nature can be every bit as devastating as Mumm-Ra and the Mutants works well in the series. Post also creates some effective dialogue and cleverly uses Mumm-Ra to great effect. 'How very charming – what a tranquil scene!' he rants. 'The ThunderCats romp and play unmolested on my planet. I shall soon put an end to this frivolity – be gone, foul image!'

'Spitting Image' certainly stands out as Post's best contribution to *ThunderCats*, and it feels as though an opportunity to develop the character of the Driller was missed here. Nonetheless, an unintended consequence is that the character would become one of the most mysterious villains ever to grace the series.

Head Writer's Commentary from Leonard Starr:

don't remember why Howie Post did only two episodes of *ThunderCats*, and I don't remember what he did for work up until his final illness. His death was a terrible shock. He attended my retirement party years back. He'd written a poem for the occasion and read it when we cut the cake.

33. Dimension Doom (4 Stars)
Written by: Bob Haney
US Broadcast Date: 6 November 1985
UK Broadcast Date: 15 October 1987

Another strong contribution from Bob Haney, 'Dimension Doom' is packed with excitement. The opening scenes explore a little of Mumm-Ra's backstory (something that is extremely welcome, as most of the show's flashbacks feature the ThunderCats), and the depiction of him at the height of his powers (sailing through the skies on a barge emblazoned with his iconic twisted snake icon) is beautifully realised on screen. There is a tantalising glimpse of a Sphinx on the planet, which reinforces the origins of Third Earth, and the heart of the story concerns a wizard defeated long ago by Mumm-Ra. The idea that the gateway to his dimension was inadvertently covered by Cats' Lair is inspired, and the story moves along at speed. In fact, Mumm-Ra is well used throughout the episode (he even wears the Enchanted Helmet with style), and we also learn the name of the Vultureking, one of his mysterious masters, the Ancient Spirits of Evil.

Although it isn't a hugely original concept, it's still interesting to see the ThunderCats fall under the influence of the helmet's powers. Cheetara's simple yet clever trick to move the statue, thus deceiving Mumm-Ra, resolves the story effectively. The episode's title, 'Dimension Doom' doesn't, perhaps, strike the right note; however, tiny niggles aside, this episodes stands as a highlight of the first season.

In short, Bob Haney delivers his usual standard of script – always exciting his audience along the way, and using the world of the ThunderCats to best effect.

Script Editor's Commentary from Peter Lawrence:

This is much more in Bob's comfort zone: the character of Wizz-Ra; Cheetara's reluctance to ask for help for fear of ridicule – a nice touch for a superhero; the Wizz-Ra/Mumm-Ra backstory; the Seventh Dimension; the Sphinx; and on and on. There's probably too much here. Do we really need the Golden Helmet of Mind Control?

But, often, writers and story editors lose confidence in simplicity. We forget that making the dramatic most of each moment is often more than enough, and so we throw in the kitchen sink for our own security.

'Dimension Doom' is classic, mainline *ThunderCats* – the exact opposite of an Overgard story. Was the show such a success on account of these classic episodes? Or was the huge variety – the exploration of the wilder shores – its secret? Don't ask me. I was only the story editor … More seriously, I do like the eccentricity of the show, but the wilder shores would not have worked without the solidity of the mainstream.

34. Queen of 8 Legs (3 Stars)
Written by: Stephen Perry
US Broadcast Date: 7 November 1985
UK Broadcast Date: 8 October 1987

'Queen of 8 Legs' opens with a spectacular panoramic shot of the Kingdom of Webs that sets the tone for a beautifully designed episode of *ThunderCats*. Regrettably, it isn't one of Steve Perry's finest scripts, however there are some very strong concepts explored, and the idea of giant spiders works really well within the fantasy theme of the series.

Where the episode doesn't fare as well is in its interrupted plot. Only a relatively small portion of the episode involves the ThunderCats interacting with the spiders, and Mumm-Ra simply wasn't needed. His ultimate appearance, as a bizarrely designed diamond fly, is certainly the weakest element.

There is nothing hugely wrong with 'Queen of 8 Legs', it simply lacks the spark of brilliance it could easily have had. During the second half, the pace definitely picks up and things start to turn around, but the earlier scenes are a little dull and could have been lost in favour of expanding later scenes.

The episode does, however, have many positives, and chief amongst them is the spectacular art design and direction from Pacific Animation Corporation. The standard of background work and cel painting is superb and, in every scene, the figures of Lion-O and his counterparts are perfectly executed. As *ThunderCats* was often outsourced to various animation houses, one can't help but think that the studios responsible for this episode were, by far, the its greatest artistic asset. There are many showcase sequences, like one where the ThunderCats leaving Cats' Lair – bumping the ThunderTank along the way – and one where the Sword beam bursts through the ground. Perry's sense of humour is also evident with a few funny scenes involving Snarf: 'Lion-O's not the only one with muscles around here!'

Once again, Earle Hyman struggles to disguise his voice as Nemesis and, consequently, the character sounds almost identical to his portrayal of Panthro and the Ancient Spirits of Evil.

This episode could surely have been a classic, and the Kingdom of Webs is certainly memorable – it simply doesn't quite hit the mark in the way that Perry's best work always did.

Writer's Commentary from Steve Perry:

Of all the [writing I did for] *ThunderCats*, the creation of Spidera in 'Queen of 8 Legs' was the most enjoyable … and the most disappointing. I had always been a big fan of 1950s atomic mutation movies, and wonderful films like *Tarantula* had a special place in my heart. In a way, 'Queen of 8 Legs' was my response to that movie and countless others that had big spiders in them, right up to that William Shatner [disaster] where they dressed up a VW Bug with legs and drove it along a hill line horizon. I was also affecting the great Ray Harryhausen – and Spidera, my version of Spidera at least, was not some pug- or chow-faced blob of a spider. She was something else entirely, and an obvious tip of the hat to *Jason and the Argonauts*.

Robert Kuisis PhD was in full bloom by then, and every script had to run by him for his stamp of approval, his brief synopsis, and his sometimes strained paragraphs wherein he sought the positive moral value of the story, so Rankin/Bass could point and say to various parents' groups and PTAs and other narrow-minded fuddy-duddies: 'See, this is not violent, escapist fare – these are action-filled morality tales teaching a positive moral outlook to children.' As a writer who loved sleaze and violence and a Joe Bob Briggs drive-in approach to my film fare, I know I was always trying to sneak in as twisted a thing as possible, just to see what the good doctor would make of it, and how on earth he could find some positive moral value there. When I finished my draft of 'Queen of 8 Legs' I said to myself, 'There, let's see what the good doctor can make of this!' I wrote Spidera as having a nude woman's upper torso. I had just watched *Jason and the*

Argonauts, and Medusa was fresh in my mind. My Spidera was to look like Medusa, except with a spider's body, not a rattlesnake. It really was a very twisted image. My wife at the time, who feared spiders quite a bit, was horrified at my description and sketches of Spidera. 'You can't have that in a kid's show,' she complained. 'They'll change it.'

The episode was partly disappointing because of the character design of the main menace – Spidera was simply not frightening! And there was one other thing that was in my script but got cut – a big disappointment there. If you recall, a bunch of smaller spiders steal the Sword of Omens. Once of them seems to chew and spit bubble gum, and this was the Bubble Gum Spider. There was another smaller spider that I had labelled the Yip Yap Spider. It was supposed to bark like an obnoxious little ankle-biter dog, continuously, as it nipped at … well, at Lion-O's ankles. I was always disappointed the Yip Yap Spider was missing. I had some good friends who owned six or seven of those little kinds of dogs – often no bigger than a small cat – and the Yip Yap Spider was a little homage to Rob and Glenda. Rob was a very famous guitarist, had a number one hit song – 'Voices Carry' – with a band called Til Tuesday. Glenda had been the girlfriend of Joe Perry (no-relation) – you know, of Aerosmith – before she left him when she met Rob. Glenda adorns the cover of an early Aerosmith LP. They loved their little, obnoxious dogs, and I had told them about the Yip Yap Spider being inspired by their … well, yip-yapping pack.

But I still view 'Queen of 8 Legs' with satisfaction: the Kingdom of Webs was finely realised, and the show had a creepy feel to it. If it scared some small kid into nightmares about spiders … then I'll always be happy.

35. Sword in a Hole (5 Stars)
Written by: William Overgard
US Broadcast Date: 8 November 1985
UK Broadcast Date: 10 December 1990

Any suggestion that William Overgard was not capable of greatness is banished here, as 'Sword in a Hole' must rank as one of the series' greatest offerings. Everything in it is perfectly judged and, though it features Overgard's usual quirkiness, this works only to the benefit of the programme.

The basic story set-up sees the Feliner receiving a distress signal. In true benevolent form, Lion-O responds, and is ensnared by the beautifully-crafted Captain Shiner. Yet again, Overgard gifts the show another perfectly rounded villain (complete with great dialogue, wonderfully realised by Bob McFadden). The beauty of Shiner is the introduction of a mercenary into the series; a far less clear-cut notion than a 'good' or 'evil' character, which really treats the young viewer with a great deal of respect.

Again, Pacific Animation Corporation deliver spectacular visuals, and the episode really feels like a feature film. The Vertus spacecraft conveys a great scale compared with the Feliner (which flies alongside it) and an eerie scene accompanies Lion-O when he boards the abandoned space vessel – finding no trace of crew or passengers.

The episode progresses at breakneck speed, with no exposition to slow it down. It's never predictable, and during the theatrical 'Ceremony of Expulsion' one really has to wonder how the ThunderCats will be able to turn this situation around. Overgard's dialogue is also on top form, with some perfectly delivered lines. 'I am a mercenary, I did it for the money ...' explains Shiner. 'And I paid the money,' adds Mumm-Ra, materialising into view. As the lights go dark and the crew experience the strange sensation of passing through a black hole, the tension mounts and it really is story telling of the highest degree. 'You're directing me back to the black hole?' pleads Shiner. 'Not back to it,' explain the ThunderCats, 'into it!'

Cheetara's determination to believe in the ThunderCats' wellbeing is admirable and the scenes set inside the Neptune power station are the highlight of the episode. With all seemingly lost, Jaga's timely appearance to Lion-O (and his subsequent retrieval of the Sword) is tremendously realised. 'Sealed or not, the eye sleeps only until needed.' Music, dialogue and animation all come together to create one of the most magical moments of the series as the Eye of Thundera illuminates the entire area, bathing it in red light as the Sword bursts towards Lion-O's hand. Shiner's disbelief is fitting indeed, and the scenes from here on are bursting with energy.

Some may quibble about Bill Overgard's cavalier failure to write in breathing equipment for the ThunderCats but, while it would have been a nice addition, it doesn't detract from one of the series' highlights. As the episode closes with Shiner's 'resurrection' we look forward to his return.

ThunderCats was always made to compete in the lucrative action/adventure genre and, in 'Sword in a Hole' it fulfils that purpose with style.

Script Editor's Commentary from Peter Lawrence:

In truth, I don't recall much about working on this episode. Captain Shiner demonstrates, once again, as if it were needed, Bill Overgard's preference to work with his own character creations, and Shiner is a perfect Overgard creation. Prussian? A space mercenary?

I seem to recall that Mumm-Ra did not feature – at all – in the first draft. His appearance does seem quite fortuitous and even redundant. Lee Dannacher always insisted that Cheetara should see her fair share of the action. Some of the writers were quite reluctant to feature a heroine – and/or weren't sure how to write her. Here, I think Bill did a pretty good job.

36. The Evil Harp of Charr-Nin (4 Stars)
Written by: Douglas Bernstein & Denis Markell
US Broadcast Date: 11 November 1985
UK Broadcast Date: 2 February 1991

'The Evil Harp of Charr-Nin' features the ThunderKittens in a leading role and, unlike similar episodes, uses them to great effect, making this a surprisingly good episode of *ThunderCats*.

Originally included in the character line-up to represent the child audience, Wilykit and Kat were not always popular with scriptwriters, often being reduced to background accompaniment. In an attempt to give them greater airtime, Denis Markell and Doug Bernstein (comedy writers by trade) create a story that, while not hugely original, is entirely effective.

Featuring a clever take on the genie in the lamp fable, the episode is not the first in which the ThunderKittens have been seen to explore their new world and unwittingly release an ancient evil. Where it works well is that the Kittens are directly pulled in to Charr-Nin's deception, and their obvious guilt and terror when Lion-O disappears makes for great television. That the genie turns out to be a villain is a clever twist on the typical Aladdin tale, and the episode is a story of temptation – of the Kittens, Lion-O and even Mumm-Ra.

Other highlights include the dialogue given to Wilykit and Kat: 'We thought you were our friend … Why are you doing this?' There is also an unusually feral and masculine battle cry from Lion-O as he breaks free from his bonds ('And I have something for you!'). A scene where Char-Nin dispatches the ThunderCats with relative ease is refreshing, and it's a nice device to have the double-cross between Mumm-Ra and Char-Nin.

'The Evil Harp of Charr-Nin' works so well because it is timed perfectly. The plot moves along well and just as it looks like there is to be a 'typical' episode resolution (i.e. the ThunderCats responding to Lion-O and 'saving the day') the tables are turned and Charr-Nin proves himself to be a genuine menace. He effectively defeats the ThunderCats, and their ultimate victory is only the result of in-fighting between Char-Nin and Mumm-Ra.

This is a perfect example of writing for the younger members of the ThunderCats team and proves that, given the right script, every character can be afforded a unique and effective episode. Ending with an extremely sinister return from Mumm-Ra (complete with an unusually disturbing cackle), Earl Hammond delivers a brilliant performance and concludes the story on an unusually dramatic note, somewhat different from the closing gags we've come to expect.

Writers' Commentary from Denis Markell and Doug Bernstein:

Markell: We were kind of stumped to come up with something that would fit into this world and still play to our strength as comedy writers/songwriters. Ultimately, we settled on a magic harp, as it seemed to be peripherally involved with music.

The name for the genie was a shout out to our good friend and mentor Martin Charnin, the man who created, directed and wrote the lyrics for the classic musical *Annie*. We were working with him on a project when the opportunity came our way to work on *ThunderCats*. We were a little ambivalent about doing it but he said, 'You must! And you *have* to put a tape recorder on during your story sessions to record the fights about things like "Panthro *has* to ride the rocket sled!" Or "Don't be an idiot! Snarf would *never* say anything like that!"' In appreciation for convincing us to take the job, we were able to use his name in the episode!

Seeing as the script we worked on wasn't exactly *Citizen Kane* (or *The Simpsons*, for that matter) the style of performance for Charr-Nin (from the voice actors) was totally appropriate for the writing. The animation was on the whole on a par with what we'd come to expect from the earlier episodes we'd watched. The only acting that seemed to be chewing the scenery to a greater extent was Mumm-Ra, especially at the end of the episode when he kept on repeating 'Mumm-Ra lives! HaHaHaHa!'

Bernstein: There were plenty of revisions to what we handed in. The only one

I remember specifically was where we had the genie open his hand and a butterfly flew out. It was changed in the script to a 'spacebird.' That's when we realised that we really weren't all that clued into the fantasy genre! More notably, we noticed what *hadn't* been changed. The 'mystic words' that Charr-Nin intones when he casts his spells ('Baba Ka-Lad-Noor') were actually a shout out to our friend David Kalodner (now a successful theatre agent at William Morris). The fact that they kept it in meant more to us than anything.

It was incredibly fascinating to me what was allowed and what wasn't. I think it was an accepted limitation that you could not impale or shoot anyone (seeing bullets actually go through a body), which meant that the violence or fighting was pretty much confined to pushing, punching, and a *lot* of restraint. The 'magical bonds' that trapped the characters in our episode were pretty much par for the course – I had the fleeting thought that we were producing a generation of young boys who would be into bondage later in life and have no idea why.

To be honest, most of the characters were pretty much on the same level in terms of their personalities and qualities. Perhaps writing for Mumm-Ra was the most fun, as a good villain is always a great lark – how often does one get to write 'He laughs maniacally!'?

37. Lion-O's Anointment First Day: The Trial of Strength (5 Stars)
Written by: Leonard Starr
US Broadcast Date: 12 November 1985
UK Broadcast Date: 10 September 1990

Leonard Starr created some of the very best episodes of *ThunderCats*, and his five-part Anointment Trials mini-series must surely be his greatest contribution. It's a perfectly conceived concept, and each of the five episodes delivers hit after hit. Pacific Animation Corporation also push the boundaries further than ever before, delivering some of the most beautifully designed episodes the series would ever see. The lighting and background art in these episodes are nothing short of stunning, and each scene is carefully differentiated from the next with a subtle use of colour and artistic prowess to show the progression of time and location.

Leonard Starr is a master of story structure. Though the idea of a 'coming of age' serial is original and exciting, it still has to be maintained and expanded throughout five episodes, with Lion-O's inexperience triumphing over each of his team mates in turn. Not only this, but soundbites like 'faster than Cheetara' and 'stronger than Panthro' have to form the basis of entire episodes. Starr rises to each of these challenges, and turns in some of the very best *ThunderCats* episodes of the entire run.

Offering a great opportunity to develop Lion-O's character, the Anointment Trials show his willingness to participate in Thunderian tradition (despite occasional second thoughts) and illustrate how far he has progressed since the show's first instalment, 'Exodus'. Also, though his appearance is relatively brief, Panthro is given some great material. His attempt to goad Lion-O to fight him is suitably epic and superbly handled – his motivation being duty rather than relish – and similarly his rejection of protocol as Lion-O is threatened in the ravine is nicely in keeping with his character.

The script work throughout the episode is first class, and the discussions between Lion-O and Panthro are a highlight. As he realises their impact, Lion-O rejects the Trials. 'Well then, if it means fighting a friend, then I don't have what it takes.' he concedes. Panthro's reply is pitched perfectly: 'That is what we're here to find out ... Fight!' Upon his victory, Lion-O's concession to Panthro is also wonderfully delivered: in response to Panthro's 'You're very strong Lion-O', he acknowledges, 'Because of you, Panthro!'

Bernie Hoffer's music score is also used brilliantly here, and the editors show their proficiency at using his library of cues to best effect. A great example is the scene where a bird approaches Lion-O's trap, the initial silence being followed by a powerful sting of music that finishes the scene perfectly.

The direction of the episode is faultless, with some inspired sequences including Lion-O's battle against the Vortex. The climax is the perfect end to the story, and Panthro's reluctance to jeopardise the Wollos' village is a nice reminder of his integrity and gentleness (despite his muscular physique). The glowing sword that tells the ThunderCats of Lion-O's victory is a lovely touch and gives an added 'feel-good factor', as does the ceremonial 'handing over' of the ThunderCats' insignias one by one. 'You've done it Lion-O, you're stronger than I am!'

Each episode ends with a teaser to the next and there could not have been a single viewer who would not have counted down the hours before Lion-O would have to 'be faster than Cheetara'.

Writer's Commentary from Leonard Starr:
One of the series that I did – I don't recall if I was asked to do it or I suggested it – was the Trials of Lion-O. It seemed like a good idea that now that he'd reached his maturity it was ThunderCat tradition that he establish himself as the rightful Lord of the ThunderCats. So he had to deal with every one of the ThunderCats and their special skills; Panthro's strength, Cheetara's speed, Tygra's wisdom etc. I don't remember having any trouble with it at all. It sounds daunting but I had no problems writing it and I think it went well. All I remember is typing. It was non-stop typing, typing, typing. And I'm not a fast typist.

When they did *ThunderCats* on DVD, they didn't have them in order, so I don't know what the hell happened there – most of the production stuff was out of my hands.

38. The Demolisher (4.5 Stars)
Written by: Bob Haney and Peter Lawrence
US Broadcast Date: 13 November 1985
UK Broadcast Date: 5 November 1990

A joint effort from writers Peter Lawrence and Bob Haney, 'The Demolisher' represents the best of both worlds, showcasing the latter's action/adventure proficiency and the wonderful dialogue and humour of the former. It is somewhat of a variant of 'Safari Joe' – however, rather than simply retreading the 'galactic sportsman' theme, it succeeds in offering a tale just as exciting as Steve Perry's epic.

The character of the Demolisher himself is well conceived and, while his design and characterisation are handled satisfactorily, it's his voice and mannerisms that make him far more interesting. Peter Newman does an outstanding job of voicing the character and deserves great credit – his vocal chords must still be recovering!

The approach to storytelling here is refreshingly simple. Given a tight plot, there is no need to over-embellish a script, and this is aptly displayed here. That the Demolisher's first 'victim' is Mumm-Ra is a brilliant stroke of genius, and the Everliving's subsequent attempt to turn this defeat to his advantage (by goading the Demolisher into a fight with Lion-O), is both cunning and apt. The fight between Mumm-Ra and the Demolisher is also effectively executed, and Mumm-Ra's many defences (including his strange new ability to materialise body armour) are hugely entertaining. The vignette Mumm-Ra displays in his cauldron features an array of Lion-O's past battles (featuring clips from previous episodes) and this is a nice recap of his highlights.

Like 'Safari Joe', the episode touches upon the remarkably sinister concept of a villain (symbolic of a bully) who searches the stars, challenging and destroying what he finds, with 'fun' or 'sport' as his sole motivation. Nothing Lion-O or the ThunderCats can do will dissuade the Demolisher from his firm resolution. While this might seem inexplicable to young children, it makes the character extremely menacing, and his variety of weaponry and cunning facilitates some exciting battle scenes. While it could be argued that the Demolisher is a rather simplistic villain, the brief snippets of information we are presented with (including past victories) suggest a far more interesting nemesis than is seen on screen. It is the dialogue and sentiment of the episode that really make it stand out, and Lion-O's lack of comprehension regarding the Demolisher's motivation is handled brilliantly: 'Why are you fighting me? What have I done to harm you?' The Demolisher's simple response gives us a great glimpse into his character: 'I fight you because you exist!'

What really helps this episode is its concentration on the personal conflict between the Demolisher and Lion-O – the two 'champions'. Each has his own comic squire (creating the episode's only share of amusement – notably when Snarf snaps the Dirge's drumsticks) and it really is a 'fight to the death'. As the battle reaches its climax, the episode looks in urgent danger of disappointing the audience with the usual concoction of Lion-O calling his friends who dispatch the villain with ease. However, the writers play with this expectation, and Lion-O's triumphant victory proves the viewer wrong: 'I'm no coward, Demolisher. I called my friends to save you, not to save me … Force me to fight on and I will surely destroy you!' The retreat of the Demolisher, who remains unequivocally determined to pursue 'all that he knows', is a fitting end and more in keeping with his character than the somewhat undermining exit given to Safari Joe.

Writer's Commentary from Peter Lawrence:

I don't recall why my name is on this script. Generally, even when I almost entirely rewrite a script, I don't share the credit – at least, I did not on *ThunderCats*. Perhaps it was an absolutely end-to-end rewrite. Or perhaps Bob sent in an outline and then, for some reason, couldn't complete the script. In any event, we tried to make the character of the Demolisher heroic even in his violence or nihilism. And we tried to avoid the obvious solution – that the ThunderCats simply blast him into oblivion. There's something of the old-fashioned Western gunfighter in this: a man who is driven to be the fastest gun in the West until, inevitably, probably as he ages, he is killed – pointlessly –z by someone faster.

There were a combo of reasons for this show ... probably with some Robert Kuisis input ... [the idea being] how to feature and debunk an entirely negative character. I do remember that Masaki used a new subcontractor for this show and it came back horrible. In one sequence, the critter's jaws were detached from his head and floating about the screen like a limbo dental demo. This was not one of our production's finest animation hours, in design or animation. Perhaps the script didn't deserve any better!

39. Monkian's Bargain (4 Stars)
Written by: Lee Schneider
US Broadcast Date: 14 November 1985
UK Broadcast Date: 18 February 1991

At some point in the run of *ThunderCats*, every major character, both good and evil, typically received an episode dedicated to them. In this case, it is the previously underused Monkian who gets his 15 minutes of fame. Mutants like Slithe and Vultureman would typically feature more heavily in the show, and 'Monkian's Bargain' provides a welcome opportunity to see the eponymous character in a more substantial role.

The script successfully utilises only existing characters from the *ThunderCats* universe and, considering Monkian's previous form as a somewhat dumb 'henchman', writer Lee Schneider succeeds in transforming him into a surprisingly menacing adversary who comes closer than many to overwhelming the ThunderCats. The scenes where a giant Monkian smashes his fist through the eye sockets of Cats' Lair (and the ensuing 'grabbing' from within) particularly raises the tension. The washed up figures of Lion-O and Snarf, unconscious in Monkian's palm, is also a remarkably effective image.

The pact between Monkian and Mumm-Ra is cleverly explored, and Monkian's lust for power is in keeping with his established character traits. In previous episodes, he has been willing to challenge his fellow Mutants, and this one sees the natural progression of that restlessness. One has to wonder why, as ever, Mumm-Ra chooses to bestow his Orbs of Power to Monkian (rather than use them himself), however it can be presumed that he would rather his minions put themselves in harm's way. Incidentally, Mumm-Ra's map of Third Earth (which he uses to lure Monkian) is taken from Leonard Starr's hand-drawn map originally created to help the show's writers utilise the landscape of the planet!

As events turn and the ThunderCats regain control, the action continues with a series of exciting challenges in Mumm-Ra's tomb. Lion-O goading Monkian into pursuing yet more power (and thus alienating Mumm-Ra) is a clever touch from Schneider, and Monkian's 'price for power' gives the episode a fitting climax as he must face an eternity of imprisonment, his dominion ruled from afar. There are some great scenes during these sequences, including the ever-erecting walls in Mumm-Ra's tomb and Snarf being frazzled during the conflict between Lion-O and Mumm-Ra. The ThunderKittens' interruption of Mumm-Ra's transformation mid-chant is also a unique addition to the episode.

'Monkian's Bargain' may well feature one of the simpler plots to grace the series, yet it delivers on its premise in abundance. It would perhaps have been nice to see a contribution from Monkian's fellow Mutants – as it would have been fitting to see Monkian put Slithe in his place. Despite this, Monkian's near-victory helps the viewer see the character from a new perspective – and one more threatening than previously realised.

Writer's Commentary from Lee Schneider:

Faust comes to Thundera in this story, and it proves that there are no new stories, just new audiences. It also shows that you can strike a resonant chord with characters like the ThunderCats. They were only cartoons, but they had a lot of personality. The so-called 'Faustian bargain' – in which a man sells his soul to the devil in exchange for knowledge – is a classic German legend going back to 1587 or something like that, and Johann Wolfgang von Goethe had a good time with it in a play he called 'Faust', published around 1808. But enough of this – it's crazy pretentious to use the words Goethe and *ThunderCats* in the same sentence.

I picked Monkian for this story because he seemed the most gullible and most likely to go for a bargain offered by the devilish Mumm-Ra. And we all know that power is intoxicating to monkeys.

40. Tight Squeeze (4 Stars)
Written by: Stephen Perry
US Broadcast Date: 15 November 1985
UK Broadcast Date: 11 February 1991

'Tight Squeeze' opens as it means to go on, full of action, with the story well into the latest Mutant scheme to defeat the ThunderCats. Steve Perry cleverly turns this set of events into an unexpected tirade of abuse from Vultureman towards his fellow Mutants, as he destroys their arsenal of weaponry and equipment.

As Slithe's relatively simple attack on Lion-O is thwarted, we see a great moment where Lion-O chooses to save the reptilian despite being double-crossed for his troubles. The moment Vultureman operates the self-destruct switch is well directed and there are plenty of similarly effective scenes throughout the episode, including the unusually feral snarls from Panthro and Cheetara as they become imprisoned in Castle Plun-Darr. The pace of the episode really works to its advantage and no time is wasted in unnecessary exposition. Indeed, even Mumm-Ra's first appearance occurs straight into his transformation sequence.

The episode features, at its heart, the very simple concept of distancing the ThunderCats from their technology, as even the standard *deux-ex-machina* device of calling the Sword to Lion-O's hand fails to give them access to their weapons. Though simple, this proves a remarkably effective idea, and the decision to send Snarf through the ventilation shafts is both novel and reminiscent of prison escape movies. The scenes of Snarf squeezing through the shafts, pursued by Jackalman, are beautifully conceived and work really well on screen, providing a great sense of claustrophobia and heightening the tension.

The episode ends with the spontaneous release of Panthro and Cheetara after Lion-O regains control of the Sword. While this sort of thing occurred quite often in the series, it poses an interesting question – do the ThunderCats gain additional strength from the Eye of Thundera or does it simply provide extra motivation? The standard of script work both here and in adjacent episodes of the period is extremely high. By this point, the entire scriptwriting team are on top form, and the series continues to go from strength to strength.

Writer's Commentary from Steve Perry:

I cannot recall 'Tight Squeeze'. I know I have seen it, but it was one of the last things I wrote for the show, and I do recall I was not into it very much by then, moving onto other things. I was more absorbed in the bible for *SilverHawks*; I would feed Peter Lawrence page after page of characters, ideas, locations and settings and he would hammer it all into a bible format.

When one tried to get a new episode assignment, it would begin with a phone call to Peter. If you caught him in a good mood, on a good day, you could pitch five or so ideas at him on the phone: a story about Snarf; a show that features Tygra; a show where the Mutants almost win; a show where Mumm-Ra does this or that ... And if anything caught Peter's attention, or several ideas seemed to work, he would say, 'send me a bunch of springboards.' And on and on like that. After Peter had gotten the page, you'd call him, and he would either tell you to go ahead with one of the springboards, or that none of them worked and to send him more. Fortunately, I always seemed to have at least one springboard that went on to become an episode.

A lot of discussion was often about how to make more with less, and Peter was the driver behind this. It was always a part of *ThunderCats* – Mumm-Ra's transformation, the Sword getting bigger with the Ho! thing. These 'bits', along with Sight Beyond Sight were *required* to be in every episode for the simple reason that the animation was already done, and they added up to at least a minute or two (out of the 22-minute script) that would not need to be animated. I am sure they had a figure on this - it cost so much per minute of show (probably thousands and thousands of dollars) that every second one could save was well worthwhile. The fact that these little 'bits' worked, and became 'catches' and iconic parts of the show, became evident right away. How many kids ran around yelling 'Thunder ... Thunder ... Thunder ... ThunderCats Hooooooo!'?

41. The Micrits (4 Stars)
Written by: Bruce Smith
US Broadcast Date: 18 November 1985
UK Broadcast Date: 21 January 1991

The first of two contributions from scriptwriter Bruce Smith, 'The Micrits' is a strong and surprisingly engaging episode of *ThunderCats*. The story concerns a group of 'tiny people' whose lives are being unwittingly affected by the ThunderCats. It's a nice idea to turn the tables on the ThunderCats, presenting them, for the first time, as the aggressors (albeit unintentionally). The resulting backlash from the Micrits is original and leads to some successful sabotage attempts that prove 'size isn't everything'. Their attempt to disrupt the ThunderCats' operations is remarkably successful, and the jeopardy caused by the Mutants' opportunistic attack on Cats' Lair leads to some great action scenes.

'The Micrits' is a quaint episode that doesn't take itself too seriously, and there is a nice sense of humour threaded throughout. ('I don't see anyone', 'That's the problem!') Despite this, the episode presents its fair share of action, and the scenes where the Mutants bombard Cats' Lair are extremely effective. What really marks out the story are the ThunderCats' reactions to the invasion of their fortress. Without weaponry and Lion-O to protect them, there is a deep sense of impending defeat, summed up by Panthro's retreat to the sword chamber with only a spanner for defence: 'I guess this is as good a place as any to make a final stand!' This is as close as the Mutants will ever come to defeating the ThunderCats, and the unexpected twist that Lion-O reaches his team mates despite having already called them to his aid is welcome.

Ultimately, the episode is about trust, and more specifically Lion-O's efforts to persuade the Micrits that he can be trusted (using Snarf as bait). The closing scenes of Snarf playing chess with the Micrits is a nice conclusion, and it is certainly a sentimental outing for the ThunderCats. It becomes a little preachy at times about the importance of protecting one's neighbours, but none of this gets in the way of 20 minutes of good-natured fun.

Writer's Commentary from Bruce Smith:

The obvious inspiration was *Gulliver's Travels*. Given that the ThunderCats were relatively new arrivals on Third Earth, I thought it would be interesting to introduce them to some of the lesser-known inhabitants. The story is really about ignorance that can lead cultures to collide. The chess match near the end between Snarf and the Micrits' chief with living Micrits as chess pieces – I think I had seen something similar on one of the original episodes of the *Star Trek* TV series. The physical scale of the Micrits made that an easy leap.

42. Lion-O's Anointment Second Day: The Trial of Speed (5 Stars)
Written by: Leonard Starr
US Broadcast Date: 19 November 1985
UK Broadcast Date: 17 September 1990

A brilliant continuation of the Anointment Trials, Cheetara's outing as chief antagonist takes Lion-O right to the edge of defeat in his 'coming of age' mini-series. Adding the Mutants into the mix, Leonard Starr presents yet more jeopardy to stand in Lion-O's way and prevent him justifying his title as Lord of the ThunderCats. Again, the writing and animation are spectacularly on-form, and yet more weird and wonderful Third Earth locations are explored to great effect.

Once more needing to expand the basic contest between Lion-O and Cheetara into a full episode, Starr cleverly chooses to give Lion-O the wisdom to take the quicker, albeit more dangerous, route to the finish line. The great thing about this simple concept is that it is not only useful in storytelling terms but also leads the viewer to believe Lion-O's only chance is to navigate this terrain faster than Cheetara does her own route. When we see Cheetara has made equal progress near the end of the episode, and therefore presumably a simple race will take place, it appears Lion-O is doomed. This leads to some of the greatest character moments for Lion-O ever seen in the series, and his determination (against the predictions of his fellow *ThunderCats*) leads to a thrilling race. 'I may lose, but it won't be because

I gave up,' he declares. The beads of sweat on both ThunderCats' faces only add to the tension in one of the most beautifully crafted sequences of the entire programme. If children learned only one thing from watching the series, the perseverance shown by Lion-O towards life's challenges should be chief amongst them.

The race being displayed on the console at Cats' Lair with the protagonists being represented by two dots – one red, one green – is a nice idea and really helps keep things in context. The Mutants' involvement in the episode is relatively small (and thankfully so), though it sets the scene for further mischief in the next trials. It does, however, lead to a great moment when, in response to Monkian's claim that his information is fed from a source in a tree, Jackalman states, 'She sounds a little out of her tree to me', adding a little comic relief to the tense proceedings.

'Second Day' ably picks up the reigns from the previous Trials episode, and the story once again ends in anticipation of the next contest. 'I'll do my best', says Lion-O, 'but I'll never forget that you are my friends – everything I am … I owe to you!'

Writer's Commentary from Leonard Starr:

I wanted to have all of the ThunderCats represented in every episode to some degree. You couldn't do stories in 25 minutes using all of the ThunderCats except for specific types of stories. It was very funny that the writers would come in with what were pretty good plots but they wouldn't have the ThunderCats in them. They would go so far off-field. Keeping the title characters in there became very important.

43. The Rock Giant (3 Stars)
Written by: Peter Lawrence
US Broadcast Date: 20 November 1985
UK Broadcast Date: 15 October 1990

A rather perfunctory contribution from Peter Lawrence, 'The Rock Giant' is reasonably enjoyable, but not as dynamic as neighbouring episodes from this era. There is nothing inherently wrong with it (indeed it is far better than certain episodes from the second season), nor is it particularly controversial, it simply comes across as somewhat of a 'filler' – a relatively simple idea expanded to fill the schedule.

The episode isn't without merit, however, and highlights include the character design for the Rock Giant himself, which works well. There are also a series of enjoyable scenes, including the ThunderTank clawing its way, vertically, out of the ravine; Lion-O and Panthro almost inadvertently blasting the ThunderKittens to oblivion; and a wonderful long-shot of Cat's Lair as the Tank races home pursued by the Giant.

Where 'monster' episodes sometimes suffer is the lack of a perceived villain. While the Rock Giant is presented as a viable threat, and his size and presence certainly make him memorable, the ThunderCats cannot interact or converse with him and, as such, he can only ever be a one-dimensional menace. The episode also suffers from a slow set-up, with Mumm-Ra, yet again, unnecessarily involved in proceedings and arguably slowing things down. However, the second half definitely picks up pace and works much better. There is a nice scene with Jaga in which he bestows his advice to combat the Rock Giant, and the moment when Lion-O slices a boulder in two gives an added flavour. The climax is also relatively well executed as the Rock Giant plunges to his doom.

The episode's most successful aspect is the atmosphere created. The storm is well presented on screen and there is a distinct sense of impending doom throughout, as the show continues to display the many strange and wonderful creatures of Third Earth.

Writer's Commentary from Peter Lawrence:

To be truthful, I remember almost nothing about the genesis of this episode and, reading the synopsis and the morals, it all seems to me to be a bit of a stretch! I believe that the Rock Giant was one of those characters proposed by Len early on in the development of the show, before I arrived. I could be wrong about that, but this isn't a character that, typically, I would create. I think it's more in Len's style and, if that's true, I imagine that Jules or perhaps even LJN asked to see a story built around it.

Once you begin to work with 'animated rock', you're probably automatically led to physics, volcanics, the properties of granite and other rocks … and on and on … which is how the fire and ice solution would have come about.

44. Jackalman's Rebellion (3 Stars)
Written by: Bruce Smith
US Broadcast Date: 21 November 1985
UK Broadcast Date: 14 March 1991

'Jackalman's Rebellion' is an inoffensive yet basic offering. Like 'Monkian's Bargain' and 'The Super Power Potion', it is one of those episodes that spotlights and expands on a particular character. Whether or not such episodes succeed depends on the writer. Unfortunately, 'Jackalman's Rebellion' has none of the flare of 'Monkian's Bargain'; and whereas that episode succeeded in showing Monkian as a viable threat, this one seems to be played for laughs and, if anything, reinforces the belief that Jackalman is a bungling oaf.

As ever, there are redeeming features. There is a strong opening where we see Jackalman having inexplicably stolen Vultureman's flying machine: 'Bye, bye Mutants – this time I'm going solo'. In an interesting reversal, it is the ThunderCats who, for once, get in the way of Mutant activity, as Slithe and his band pursue their renegade. It is also nice to see previously underdeveloped villains like Driller and Mole Master return, yet, in his third *ThunderCats* appearance, the poor Driller is still relegated to simply drilling holes!

Mutiny within any faction is always an enjoyable concept and ripe for development by any writer. Unfortunately, this episode is certainly the weaker of Bruce Smith's two contributions and, as mentioned, the comic approach overwhelms its dramatic possibilities. While Jackalman's self-appointed mantle as 'General' is twee at first, it becomes a little staid, and we learn precious little about his character. One welcome note, however, is a reference back to the events of

'Feliner' as Jackalman reveals he squirreled away Ratar-O's VeriCannon, leading us to the conclusion that Jackalman has harboured thoughts of dissension for some time. Other enjoyable touches include Cheetara being challenged to catch Molemaster, to which she replies, 'Gentlemen, place your bets!' Sadly, these endearing moments are short-lived and the episode drags along in places.

Further quirks include the ThunderCats' perplexing new ability to spy on Castle Plun-Darr, which surely would have been exploited previously had it existed. There is also a great example of hyperbole as the dramatic declaration that there is 'trouble in sector ten' turns out to refer to a Unicorn tied to a tree.

This is far from the worst of *ThunderCats*, it's simply an enjoyable 'filler' that doesn't quite live up to its potential.

Writer's Commentary from Bruce Smith:

Jackalman is the classic organisation man with the fatal combination of small talents and large ambition. I thought it would be interesting to plunge the Mutants into crisis and show how thin were the bonds that held them together. It was also an opportunity for the ThunderCats to ponder their own team culture and contrast their loyalty based on mutual respect against the Mutants' culture of convenience and opportunism. Looking at the episode now, I think it was too 'talky' and did not put the ThunderCats into sufficient jeopardy. I was trying to make the point that unvarnished personal ambition is a terribly limiting trait that can wreak havoc on any organisation.

45. Turmagar the Tuska (3 Stars)
Written by: C H Trengove
US Broadcast Date: 22 November 1985
UK Broadcast Date: 10 September 1987

'Turmagar the Tuska' is a difficult episode to analyse. On the one hand, the complex animation on display throughout is a visual triumph. On the other, it departs a little too far from the show's usual style to feel comfortable. A clear example of *ThunderCats* animation being outsourced to various studios, the episode feels largely out of place.

The background art, while beautiful (especially the sunset glow as the Tuska's city is attacked), is obviously influenced by anime. While all episodes of the series were animated in Japan, Hong Kong and Korea, this native art form was generally subdued in favour of a more Western presentation. 'Turmagar the Tuska' represents the closest the series ever got to true anime, and the Mermaid, in particular, is straight out of Japanese culture, as is the well-designed Technopede. At times, indeed, one can hardly recognise this episode as *ThunderCats*. It is the visual equivalent of a Bill Overgard script, where a huge creative change leads the viewer to question its merits.

Visuals aside, Chris Trengove's script is rather thin and the story lacks focus. There is a nice opening sequence where the ThunderCats' alarm systems go crazy at the arrival of Turmagar, and the eponymous character is definitely the highlight of the episode, representing a worthy new ally for the ThunderCats. In common with several episodes of a similar ilk, it is the first half that lets it down. The underwater scenes with the ThunderTank are rambling and dull, and while Tygra (once again) succumbs to temptation (this time in the form of a vampire), the whole scene seems a little out of place and a strange diversion from the main events.

Where the episode succeeds is in its subtler touches. The World War I-inspired design of Turmaga and the Gomblin works well, and there is a great sense that we have explored some further areas of Third Earth, the perception of distance really adding to the story. The Giant Technopede is a great creation, and the fact we never learn his origins somehow adds to his appeal.

'Turmagar the Tuska' is a story with an environmental message but variable appeal. It's difficult to pinpoint quite why it stands out from its neighbouring episodes, but and the closing scene with a hyperactive Snarf bathing in the stream possibly summarises its qualities: quirky, strange and perhaps a step too far.

Writer's Commentary from Chris Trengove:

Although I'd been a freelance writer for a decade, this was the first half-hour TV script – and the first animation script – I'd ever written. My first draft was all over the place, my inexperience manifesting itself in the breaking of all sorts of animation 'rules', and script editor Peter Lawrence had his work cut out to hack it into shape.

Looking at the script again now, it still seems a little simplistic – someone asks for help, ThunderCats give help, end – and I obviously got stuck on inventing creatures by combining two existing ones (human and walrus, shark and spider). Having said that, preserving water as a means of sustaining life did turn out to be an eerily prophetic theme (not that I had such 'green' issues in mind when I was struggling through draft after draft!)

On the upside, the character I created, Turmagar, was used in several later episodes, and later chosen to be a toy (and I have one in the attic, still in its box, and undoubtedly worth good money to collectors!) I was also very happy with his design – exactly as I imagined him!

46. Lion-O's Anointment Third Day: The Trial of Cunning (5 Stars)
Written by: Leonard Starr
US Broadcast Date: 25 November 1985
UK Broadcast Date: 24 September 1990

The third instalment of Lion-O's quest to fulfil the traditions of his people continues with a battle of cunning against the junior members of the ThunderCats' team.

While this episode may be considered the weakest of the five that comprise the Anointment Trials, Starr's writing is still on top form. Its shortcomings can be attributed simply to the fact that, whereas besting Panthro or Cheetara seemed an almost impossible task, few would believe the Kittens could actually defeat Lion-O, even using the many ingenious tests they have set for him. To some degree, Starr addresses this by making the Mutants' involvement in the Trials ever more present. In this context, their devious attempt to disrupt proceedings does help expand the episode into its time slot and provide a greater test for Lion-O, as he must deflect not only his fellow ThunderCats but also prevent the Mutants from achieving their aims.

Starr also uses viewer expectations to his advantage by providing a great opportunity for WilyKit and WilyKat to shine. The very fact that the odds are stacked against them gives them free reign to try every trick in their arsenal. Indeed, what child wouldn't want the opportunity to prove his or her worth? Another stroke of genius from Starr is to take the 'battleground' of the Trials to a new location. Setting events in the mysterious Maze of Infinity is inspired and, consequently, this doesn't feel like any other episode of *ThunderCats*. The Under Earth people are also a welcome addition and, as Third Earth races go, are amongst the most unusual! The idea that they have been driven underground by the ancestors of Third Earth (too afraid of their learning) is a nice aside, and their affection for reading is subtle but touching.

Throughout the episode, the ThunderKittens do conduct themselves with integrity, and their various traps and plans are executed well. The scenario also provides an opportunity to test Lion-O's abilities to think his way out of a problem, rather than rely on his physical assets. In addition, there is an eerie atmosphere in play throughout the story (including when the Kittens laugh hauntingly as Lion O must choose the correct entrance to the caves).

It has to be admitted that there are a few negatives too, including an unusual production problem: during the episode's opening scenes, the conversation between Monkian and Jackalman aboard Sky Cutters is conducted against a poorly looped background. Every few frames, the clouds snap back to their original location – a minor point, but an obvious error by the usually fastidious Pacific Animation Corporation. Finally, it could be argued that Starr does rely on Third Earth's many 'monsters' (usually in the form of dinosaur-like creatures) a little too heavily in the Anointment Trials, and a more original obstacle might have been welcome in their place.

However, nothing can detract from a hugely enjoyable continuation of the anointment saga. Given that, on paper, this instalment should be the weakest, it is testament to Starr's craft that it ably maintains the high standards achieved for this mini-series, and it's hard to imagine how the ThunderKittens' trial could have been handled better.

Writer's Commentary from Leonard Starr:

I wanted Lion-O to reach his maturity, and the fact that he had to fight each of the ThunderCats at their own specialty was an appealing idea, I thought. And it was not easy. How did you get faster than Cheetara, stronger than Panthro and all of that stuff?

Every story has its limitations. On my syndicated strips I had to tell a story in 90 seconds' reading time every day and then hook it into the previous episode and [trail] the next day's. It becomes a technique, and somehow it becomes automatic after a while.

47. The Mumm-Ra Berbil (4 Stars)
Written by: Jeri Craden
US Broadcast Date: 26 November 1985
UK Broadcast Date: 25 March 1991

'The Mumm-Ra Berbil' marks the arrival of the first of a number of new writers for the series. In this instance, Jeri Craden crafts a remarkably enjoyable adventure, the worst aspect of which is possibly its rather uninspiring title. It's an 'enemy within' plot that sees Mumm-Ra infiltrate Cats' Lair in one of his many disguises. There is absolutely nothing original in the premise, yet Craden's articulate and inspired script turns this from being a retread of a standard *ThunderCats* episode into something altogether better.

Whereas he more commonly uses the Mutants to do his bidding, 'The Mumm-Ra Berbil' shows Mumm-Ra attempting his own ambitious scheme to destroy the *ThunderCats* – a scheme that comes perilously close to succeeding. Where the episode really comes to life is in the large dose of horror littered throughout. In scenes reminiscent of *Village of the Damned*, the ThunderCats not only become hypnotised to Mumm-Ra's will – but enjoy themselves along the way. The sinister smiles on display after they have been 'transformed' are extremely disturbing and, coupled with their piercing red eyes and devious intentions, really take the series down a dark path. Even Snarf falls prey to Mumm-Ra's scheme, and any scene that features an evil (and particularly feral) Snarf attacking Lion-O has to be worth watching.

Every so often, a *ThunderCats* script would restore Mumm-Ra from being a particularly ineffective and 'camp' villain to a genuine threat. Jeri Craden's debut does this in abundance. There are also some nice touches throughout, including our first glimpse of Cheetara's wardrobe – which, humorously, features multiple copies of her standard leotard. There is also cause for a collective cheer as Mumm-Ra reveals he has learnt from his mistakes and is now (courtesy of some fetching eyewear) impregnable to the threat of his own reflection.

The only aspect preventing 'The Mumm-Ra Berbil' from achieving true-classic status is its simple (and unbefitting) resolution. The reversal of fortunes for the ThunderCats simply because of Lion-O's sword call is rather uninspiring. Earl Hammond's portrayal of Mumm-Ra in the early scenes is also a little 'off the mark' – sounding more like Jaga in certain scenes. However, given the simple ideas it presents, the episode really succeeds, while using only existing characters from the series. The scene of Mumm-Ra pinned down by the Kittens is effective and there is some nice dialogue from him to conclude the show: 'This is not a failure, ThunderCats, merely a setback, and each time we meet, I learn more – one day, I'll prevail!'

Writer's Commentary from Jeri Craden

Watching this episode again reminds me of the extraordinary team involved in the production of *ThunderCats*. Peter Lawrence, script consultant, who gave me the opportunity of writing for the series, was never at a loss for fresh ideas and encouragement. Evil Mumm-Ra, who takes the form of a teddy bear-looking Berbil, is a poignant metaphor for many things in life that appear to be harmless, claim support and best intentions, but whose only aim proves to be the attainment of power. The camera angles and incredible hand drawings of the characters – powerful and larger than life – inspire the imagination and heighten the already high stakes. And when all seems lost and Lion-O is the only one left to either destroy or save his ThunderCat friends, now under the spell of Mumm-Ra, he chooses not only to save them, but to connect them once again to their true selves.

It was fun writing Snarf and the ThunderKittens. My son was young at the time so it felt natural writing the softer elements of the story. So I would say some of my inspiration came from him. I wrote into the episode a playful thing I liked to do as a child and sometimes did with my son when he was little, which was to create a make-shift tepee with a blanket.

Incidentally, if you had asked me about *SilverHawks*, I would have said my favourite characters to write for were Zero the Memory Thief and Seymour, the taxi driver.

48. Mechanical Plague (3 Stars)
Written by: Peter Lawrence
US Broadcast Date: 27 November 1985
UK Broadcast Date: 29 October 1990

In any long-running series, there is always a need for 'filler' episodes to complete the schedules. 'Mechanical Plague' certainly falls into this category, with a rather thin plot and the return of existing villains. But while the plot is relatively unmemorable, the episode is at least saved from irrelevance by Peter Lawrence's quirky and unique writing.

As the episode opens, we see that the ThunderCats each have a holographic recording device following them to compile a record of life on Third Earth for future generations. While this is not crucial to the plot, it does enhance the episode, and the strange Big Brother allegory works well. Indeed, some of the best sequences of the episode are when the ThunderCats each 'show off' to the camera – none more so than Lion-O, who sets the heavens alight with some impressive swordsmanship (utilising animation from the show's opening titles).

Sadly, the episode's main premise doesn't work nearly as well. In his capacity as script editor, Lawrence was a great believer in reusing existing elements from the series (to try to negate new writers' tendency always to create their own characters and environments). 'Mechanical Plague' shows him practicing what he preached, yet it isn't as imaginative as his usual outings. The central villains have little presence in their return appearances and, short of a few nice action sequences, the plot fails to really develop. The episode also features the standard resolution of Lion-O calling the ThunderCats to 'save the day'.

Unfortunately, the episode's animation doesn't help matters as, once again, the bulk of the work seems to have been done by a less experienced studio. Look, for example, at the background painting in Mumm-Ra's tomb, which is nowhere near as detailed as usual – although the standard does improve as the episode progresses, and there is a nice scene of the ThunderTank, ThunderKittens and Cheetara all racing to Lion-O in line with one another! We also see our first glimpse of an elevator that services Cats' Lair in another example of the thoroughness Lawrence gave to each of his scripts.

With any Lawrence script, whether perfectly-crafted (like 'Excalibur') or underwhelming (like 'Mechanical Plague'), there is always a great sense of fun, and it's his small but distinctive touches that, in part, rescue this episode from oblivion.

Writer's Commentary from Peter Lawrence:

Fan criticisms have it dead right. This is a poor episode. It was written as a direct request from Jules Bass and there were several reasons for that request. One, we were behind the schedule and needed to find a way to re-use existing animation. Two, it was a nod toward an MTV-style of episode. And, three … that's about it. I tried to get some fun out of it – or put some fun into it – but really … quite poor.

49. Trapped (3.5 Stars)
Written by: Stephen Perry
US Broadcast Date: 28 November 1985
UK Broadcast Date: 22 April 1991

A quaint final contribution from writer Steve Perry, 'Trapped' doesn't represent his most imaginative work for the series, but it's still an enjoyable ride.

There are two distinct strands to this story, one concerning the plight of the Feliner coming in to land, the other the ThunderKittens' impromptu imprisonment in their old suspension capsules. Both of these elements work really well and, from the opening sequence, which is beautifully animated, there is a great sense of impending danger. Even better is that Perry achieves this pervading atmosphere by using the darker forces of nature – a refreshing change amongst the myriad of Mumm-Ra- and Mutant-inspired plots.

The Feliner component of the story is handled brilliantly, and Lion-O's and Panthro's efforts to bring the ship home safely are well scripted with some effective dialogue. This includes Lion-O's query as to whether the other team members can 'talk them in', to which Panthro replies, 'Frankly Lion-O, the book says no – but I never read that book!' As all other options fail, Lion-O's decision to use the Eye of Thundera to guide the ship home works brilliantly, and all aspects of these scenes (including the animation, script work and music choice) combine to heighten the excitement. The music in particular is well selected throughout the episode and really benefits the adventure. There is even an unusual use of the theme tune (albeit an instrumental version) towards the end.

Where the episode fares less well is in the resolution of the ThunderKittens' saga, and Mumm-Ra's deflection is particularly disappointing given the momentum 'Trapped' has built. Nonetheless, while it drops the ball in the final act, the episode is full of enjoyable attributes, including the obvious link back to the show's debut episode through the suspension capsules, and Perry's reuse of the idea of Lion-O attaching a claw line to Mumm-Ra's cloak (last seen in 'Feliner'). Perry's imaginative writing would be missed as the series progressed.

Writer's Commentary from Steve Perry:

'Trapped' came about as a result of Peter Lawrence saying, 'We need a show about the kids'. It is a unique episode for me. I have never, ever seen it. I do not remember it in the slightest. I know I wrote it, but I have never seen the finished cartoon, and long ago threw away the script. I honestly have no idea what the show is about … at all! I am pretty sure that if I ever see it, it will all flood back to me, and there is a reason for this block. The reason is *SilverHawks*. I was pulled off *ThunderCats* toward the end of the first season to work on *SilverHawks* right from its inception.

I am quite unfamiliar with the second series of *ThunderCats*, or rather the second and third years. I have only recently gotten the DVDs for the second year, and Jesus, do not recognise any of those new cats. I was completely absorbed in *SilverHawks*, and then *Dinosaur Bill* (an unproduced animated series), while that was being put together. All I can remember is that 'Trapped' was about the ThunderKittens – oh, yeah, they got locked in a capsule of some sort, right? I am blank. That's how memorable they are, I guess. I suppose I saw the writing on the wall then; I was done with *ThunderCats*. I was stumbling around the Galaxy of Limbo then.

50. Lion-O's Anointment Fourth Day: The Trial of Mind Power (5 Stars)
Written by: Leonard Starr
US Broadcast Date: 29 November 1985
UK Broadcast Date: 1 October 1990

The fourth chapter of Lion-O's 'coming of age' mini-series presented a problem for writer Leonard Starr. Whereas the other four episodes offered him a logical premise for a challenge (strength for Panthro, speed for Cheetara and cunning for the Kittens), Tygra's main special ability had so far been his powers of invisibility. Realising that this would be a visually ineffective basis for a contest, Starr chose to expand Tygra's character by revealing that he also has powers of mind control. This leads to another beautifully crafted episodes of *ThunderCats* as Lion-O faces, arguably, his toughest challenge.

While it may seem overly convenient for Tygra to reveal a 'new' ability just for the purposes of the trial, his sensibilities and personality (as the staunch 'second in command') do lend themselves to this – despite his penchant for falling victim to various temptations along the way. Starr also confronts the issue head-on by having the ThunderCats asking the very same question about Tygra's gift. The reply is satisfactory, as we learn that it places a 'terrible strain' on him if used too often.

Once again, the location moves, this time to the snow plains of Third Earth, ably distinguishing this from other 'Anointment' episodes and leading to some interesting physical challenges for Lion-O, as well as facilitating the return of the much-loved Snowmeow.

In many ways, Tygra's episode is the most sinister of Lion-O's trials, and Tygra is determined to succeed against his lord. The moment Lion-O is transported back to Thundera is superb, but shows how far Tygra will go to fulfil the traditions of his people. It's an incredibly psychedelic sequence and provides the perfect end to the episode, giving a small hint at the lasting damage Lion-O has suffered from witnessing the death of his home world at such a young age: 'My greatest fear is that I'll be afraid again'.

The only detractor from the episode is that it stands out amongst its fellow trials as having animation that was clearly outsourced to a lesser studio. The standard of artwork is inferior to that in the other episodes that surround it, and some of the figures and animation cycles are a little crude. Despite this, the ThunderCat portion of the trial concludes in style, leaving the much anticipated final battle about to commence.

Writer's Commentary from Leonard Starr:

Essentially for me, *ThunderCats* was a nice change, and it was more money, so I did it with that in mind. You always want a success, and in our case, we got one.

I was a professional and I knew what I was doing. Sometimes one character would have characteristics that I would feature so that he or she would be more prominent in the story. But generally I tried to use every ThunderCat in every story in a greater or lesser degree, and that was sort of tough, because you only had 25 minutes to do it. With the characters you have to be careful not to lose the threat.

51. Excalibur (5 Stars)
Written by: Peter Lawrence
US Broadcast Date: 2 December 1985
UK Broadcast Date: 26 November 1990

One of a group of *ThunderCats* classics, 'Excalibur' is thoroughly enjoyable from start to finish. While it is actually quite bizarre and something of a departure in terms of subject matter, the Arthurian legends sits perfectly in the fantasy-led *ThunderCats* series, and Peter Lawrence hits his stride with this episode.

Opening with a nice summary of previous victories by Lion-O (and his Sword), there is some wonderful art on display as Mumm-Ra stands at his cauldron pondering his latest scheme. The scenes covering Arthur's reign are beautifully crafted, and the idea of a battle between two famous swords is inspired.

The episode is near faultless, and Mumm-Ra's infiltration of Cats' Lair is one of his most exciting schemes. Where he would usually camouflage himself with forced niceties, Mumm-Ra (in the guise of Arthur) is hugely provocative, and his goading of Lion-O (including Arthur's medieval slap) is great to behold. Credit should also be given to Earl Hammond, whose voice for Arthur is a softer (yet just as sinister) version of Mumm-Ra's.

This is a story about pride, specifically Lion-O's, and its culmination in a joust is perfectly judged. That climactic sequence is well created, featuring some unusual freeze frames and some great direction, including the triple zoom as Lion-O arrives on his steed. Cheetara's lack of comprehension towards Lion-O's actions adds to the drama and all of the main characters are given some great dialogue. 'The whole thing is ridiculous,' says Cheetara, 'he's fighting for his pride … He could have walked away. He's just lowering himself to that madman's level!'

It's a great idea to have the swords take the fight to the skies, and the moment the legendary Eye of Thundera is pierced as the ThunderCats collapse, has to rank amongst the all-time best scenes from the series. The resolution is every bit as exciting as the rest of the episode. Merlin's presence in *ThunderCats* should be a step too far, but instead it reinforces everything that is great about the series – its ability to adapt to various forms of storytelling. 'Excalibur' is Peter Lawrence at his best, and his ability at building suspense is shown here, as is his sublime dialogue. 'Fool, did you really think that the greatest sword of all time would serve your evil purposes?' asks Merlin, scolding Mumm-Ra. 'Your brief moment of glory is over – get back to your dark sarcophagus.'

Writer's Commentary from Peter Lawrence:

Jules suggested to me that we should write a show about the two greatest swords in the history of the world – Excalibur and the Sword of Omens. Excellent idea, and one I should have thought of myself. Once I decided to tell it through the medium of Mumm-Ra as an Arthurian, it wrote itself – particularly as I knew the Arthurian legend inside out, loved Mallory's *Morte d'Arthur*, and always got a great kick out of writing Mumm-Ra. (And, ashamed to admit, re-writing everyone else's Mumm-Ra dialogue. Perhaps that's why I received letters accusing me of being a Satanist.) From the beginning of my involvement with *ThunderCats* – and remember I had never written any animation before, except for a Goodyear tyre demo! – it was drummed into me that we had to keep the images rolling. Act don't talk. Simplify, simplify. Therefore, the first draft of this script was slam-bang action. To his credit, Jules suggested that I throw out a lot of the action and build the character and dialogue, which is why this script is probably slower, more thoughtful and even more characterful than many others – all leading to the spectacular battle between the swords themselves, with Lion-O and Mumm-Ra no more than bystanders at that point. At least, that's how I recall it.

52. Secret of the Ice King (4.5 Stars)
Written by: Bob Haney
US Broadcast Date: 3 December 1985
UK Broadcast Date: 3 December 1990

To have a 'love story' within a *ThunderCats* episode is a strange concept for the series. It does, however, work extremely well, because it is confined to a unique twist at the end of the episode. For the most part, the eponymous and misunderstood 'villain' is a great addition to the series and provides a welcome opportunity for Bob Haney to revisit his creations of the Snowman and Hook Mountain. As usual for a script by Haney, the episode is brimming with originality and the pacing is perfect. There is a particularly beautiful beginning to 'Secret of the Ice King', as a long-since perished Third Earth menace is revived from his sleep in the ice.

What makes this episode stand out is the visually effective weapon of the Ice King; the ability to freeze his victims. As he systematically encases each ThunderCat, the tension rises, and the ThunderTank's fate, in particular, is incredibly engaging. As the episode gets under way, the Snowman's 'final words' to Snowmeow, 'Fetch help, fetch the ThunderCats at once,' provide the perfect set-up for the events that follow. The avalanche from Hook Mountain that covers Third Earth lends itself perfectly to animation and, despite the sheer quantity of snow being a little unbelievable, these scenes are hugely effective. Perhaps the only criticism one could have about Haney's script is his occasional lack of active dialogue. Because of his lineage as a comic writer, monologues do creep into his scripts at times, an example here being early scenes with Lion-O 'explaining' events to himself. However, Haney's ability to 'show' rather than 'tell' more than makes up for any shortcomings, and 'Lord of the Snows' is a novel script that, arguably, outshines his first outing in 'The Snowmen of Hook Mountain'.

Cheetara's resourceful placement of the Sword of Omens in Lion-O's hand (chipping away the ice to reach it) is a satisfactory climax given its handling, and it is accompanied by a great music selection throughout. The episode's 'secret weapon' is its final scenes, as we realise that the Ice King is merely searching for the last remnant of his past – the princess he has vowed to rejoin in death. The sombre melting of the Ice King as he is reunited with his past is sentimental indeed for *ThunderCats*, but only proves how flexible the series could be in the pursuit of solid storytelling. Snarf's closing sentiments succinctly summarise the emotion of the episode as he realises that he has, inexplicably, turned down a lifetime of happiness, riches and a large family. 'Oh well,' muses Snarf, 'I'm already happy, my riches are my friends, and a better family a Snarf couldn't wish for!'

Script Editor's Commentary from Peter Lawrence:

Another mainstream Haney and a mainstream *ThunderCats* story, very well executed. In fact, it plays much better than I remember it, coming alive on screen in a way one might not have seen on paper. It has, too, a touching emotional core that perhaps appealed to those in the audience who had their first crushes, their first boyfriends – or girlfriends. I suppose one might observe that, emotionally, the ThunderCats weren't really involved or essential to this story – but that's common to a lot of episodes, and perhaps the show, overall, benefited from the fact that quite often stories simply played out within the ThunderCats' field of vision rather than within their grasp.

53. Good And Ugly (5 Stars)
Written by: Peter Lawrence
US Broadcast Date: 4 December 1985
UK Broadcast Date: 7 January 1991

'Good and Ugly' is a superb offering from Peter Lawrence. While it is undeniably conceived around a moral (namely not to judge a book by its cover), Lawrence avoids it becoming too preachy and delivers an amazing 20 minutes of non-stop action.

Where the episode triumphs is in Lawrence's decision to remove from the equation all of the core characters besides Lion-O and Snarf. This creates an intimacy that works incredibly well from the very first scenes, as we see both characters relaxing on Third Earth. Rather than the other ThunderCats having minor roles that slow the action, we're left with a cast of only four characters for the majority of the episode, which concentrates events. This really highlights the differences between the first and second seasons of *ThunderCats*. Broadly speaking, the series would gain more and more characters as it went on, with storylines becoming ever more complicated and elaborate for their short screen time (though there are, of course, exceptions). 'Good and Ugly' strips away the unnecessary and crafts a *ThunderCats* classic.

The core storyline revolves around Lion-O's poor judgement when two alien vessels arrive on Third Earth. Though we empathise with his actions, Lion-O's realisation that the Terator has been 'attacked' unnecessarily is a beautiful character moment and a potent image. 'It was right Snarf, it didn't attack us, I attacked it,' says Lion-O. Snarf's unusually ruthless response accentuates the emotional weight of the episode: 'What does it matter, Lion-O? Just be glad it's gone!'

There are some wonderfully animated sequences throughout, including the spacecraft battles and the triumphant moment when the Cat's Eye penetrates through Third Earth's atmosphere and into deep space. The Terator and Kymera are both designed brilliantly and the 'two sides to every story' idea is a stroke of genius as Lion-O realises both stories are identical. The powerful defence mounted by the Terator in the first act is well conceived, as he effects a block on Lion-O's signals and even the Sword. The Kymera's attack is sinister indeed, as he turns on the ThunderCats. The action reaches new heights when the creature uses Cats' Lair's defences against Lion-O. Lawrences's dialogue is also on typically good form, with some excellent lines from Lion-O: 'I should have known the Terator didn't mean us any harm when the Sword of Omens didn't obey me, and anyway, it was just plain stupid to assume it must be bad, just because it was ugly!'

Though it might seem to epitomise a morality tale for children, 'Good and Ugly' also features some very 'adult' concepts regarding trust and character flaws. The fact that the Terator must assimilate 'English' throughout the episode (at first speaking his native tongue) is unusual for *ThunderCats* and lends some credibility to the universes depicted in the series. It also hints at the difficulties of language barriers that lead, in part, to Lion-O's conflict with the Terator – another more advanced allegory for world events and the importance of communication.

Writer's Commentary from Peter Lawrence:

A quite simplistic story 'inspired' (if that's not too pretentious a word) by the moral of the piece: good-looking is not necessarily good; and ugly is not necessarily evil. A decent lesson to teach and, hopefully, in this script, not too preachy. We were pretty serious about [paying attention to] Robert Kuisis and the morals of each story, but from time to time the writers would rebel – somewhat – and, under the pressure of the schedule, we'd backslide. The ideal way to accomplish the built-in moral would be to start the outline with the lesson in mind, but that rarely happened. 'Good and Ugly' is one of those stories that really did begin with the moral – the simplest of all lessons: do *not* judge by appearances. From that point on, it more or less wrote itself. Lion-O, the big kid, would see an ugly (and it was supposed to be truly monstrous and revolting … see *District 9* for a much better illustration) creature or object and automatically assume it was bad. Just as something handsome is assumed to be good … This is such a simple premise and moral that there's really not much more to be said!

54. The Transfer (3 Stars)
Written by: Lawrence Dukore & Lee Schneider
US Broadcast Date: 5 December 1985
UK Broadcast Date: N/A

Somewhat of a meandering episode of *ThunderCats*, 'The Transfer' covers the dangers of radioactivity and is, presumably, an allegory for nuclear power and bombs. The idea is solid enough, and it's a 'countdown to destruction'-style script featuring a race to contain the latest threat to Third Earth inhabitants. The early scenes are reasonably effective and there is a chilling realisation that Mumm-Ra would gladly sacrifice every living creature on Third Earth in his quest for utter domination (Mumm-Ra being the only survivor of a fallout from the ensuing threat). There is a nicely animated sequence outside Cats' Lair as the lightning flashes upon the monotone forms of Mumm-Ra and Slithe, concealed beside the Lair. Furthermore, Jackalman stowing aboard the Feliner is a nice touch.

Unfortunately, beyond this, the story fails to really engage the viewer. It slows down and becomes increasingly familiar in its similarity to so many other Mumm-Ra-based episodes.

Mumm-Ra climbing his pyramid is a strong idea, well realised on screen (especially when he reaches the summit as he deflects an attack by the Flying Machine). However, the resolution to the episode is poor, representing one of the worst uses of the over-relied-upon weakness of Mumm-Ra – the reflection of his own evil. Even Panthro has to comment on Mumm-Ra's declaration that 'next time' he will triumph. 'Yeah, we've heard that one before, mummy!' he replies. The safe detonation of the ship in space ends that plot thread somewhat more satisfactorily, but the episode is still a little disappointing overall.

It should be mentioned that the mysterious ship that precipitates events in 'The Transfer' looks a little similar to both the Kymera's ship in 'Good and Ugly' and the source of Cheetara's troubles in 'Sixth Sense' – clearly a case of certain design influences being reused. 'The Transfer' is reasonably enjoyable, but if originality is expected, there is little in play here.

Writer's Commentary from Lawrence DuKore:

The only thing I can remember about this episode has to do with my own personal conflict. My background was as a peace activist and a 'ban the bomb' New Yorker who supported the UK's March to Alderston. I had also been on the staff of the American Friends Service Committee (the Quakers) and was active in the early days of the peace movement in New York and Washington. The above notwithstanding, I was and am a realist. On one hand I saw the necessity of intercepting the bad guys (diplomacy was never part of this series), and yet there was something about this episode and the entire series that made me feel like I was working for the Department of Defence – so I don't know that I put my heart and soul into my writing. I'm sure I didn't. I think that Lee Schneider took my first draft and did a revision. I had no input.

55. Divide and Conquer (3.5 Stars)
Written by: Lee Schneider
US Broadcast Date: 6 December 1985
UK Broadcast Date: 14 January 1991

'Divide and Conquer' is a novel instalment of *ThunderCats* with a clever idea that exploits the ease with which voices in an animated series can be interchanged. Lee Schneider injects a required dose of humour, especially in the dialogue between Mutants. 'That voice imitator is the best idea I've ever had,' declares Slithe. 'Your idea? I invented it!' asserts Vultureman!

The plot of the episode is essentially true to its title. Each ThunderCat is singled out and snared by Vultureman's latest invention. This leads to probably the strongest and the weakest aspects, as Cheetara's trap (imprisoned in a giant beehive) is particularly intriguing, yet Tygra's and some of the others are incredibly underwhelming by contrast.

There are plenty of exciting moments to drive the plot forward, and a giant bee bringing the ThunderCats to the heart of the action works really well. The ThunderKittens' inexperienced (though effective) command of the ThunderTank is also a highlight. In fact, 'Divide and Conquer' is led by the action sequences and is relatively light on dialogue. This isn't necessarily a bad thing, but further development could possibly have been given to the central premise and the traps made more intricate. Indeed, the episode's best part comes in the closing scenes when the ThunderCats gain control of the voice imitator. Here, Lion-O carefully calculates the Mutants' coordinates, causing them to crash. This sophisticated writing displays the damage both sides could have caused by maximising their impersonations. Sadly, the preceding scenes are more pedestrian, with some ThunderCats simply falling straight into their traps.

Writer's Commentary from Lee Schneider:

The fun part of this script was realising that I could exploit a technical, production matter that was ready to be manipulated. At the time I wrote this episode of *ThunderCats*, I was writing for the theatre mostly, a place where an actor came equipped with a voice that remained inseparable from his or her body. But, as I soon discovered, in animation the voices are recorded first and the pictures are created later to fit. An out-of-body experience! That made it easy to switch around the voices for the different characters.

Isolating the storylines into threads was a good way to emphasise the 'moral' of this particular episode. When they worked alone, the *ThunderCats* got into trouble. Banding together and relying on each other made it possible for them to beat the Mutants. We could intercut each story, and then as the episode reached its climax blend the stories together, so structurally it helped accelerate the tempo. It's likely that I put way too much thought into this script since I have managed to write two whole paragraphs about it here.

56. Dream Master (3 Stars)
Written by: Heather M Winters & Annabelle Gurwitch
US Broadcast Date: 9 December 1985
UK Broadcast Date: 13 May 1991

This sole contribution from Heather Winters and Anabelle Gurwitch is a creepy affair. From the music cue selection (which utilises eerie, atmospheric loops) to the disturbing image of lifeless ThunderCats floating away from Cats' Lair, 'Dream Master' offers an ingenious scheme from Mumm-Ra to target the protagonists' dream selves.

While the idea is a nice one, it doesn't have sufficient merit to be expanded to comfortably fill an entire episode. What starts as ingenious and engaging quickly turns predictable as Mumm-Ra commands each ThunderCat to appear before him. By the turn of the ThunderKittens, this device has been overused, and from this point on the episode follows the standard *ThunderCats* model, offering very little originality.

There are a few enticing moments. Panthro's ThunderTank crash is well devised and Lion-O's reaction is unmissable. 'What happened?' asks Panthro. 'You fell asleep!' snarls Lion-O, full of scolding. There are also some nice visual sequences, including Mumm-Ra's sleep pots being hooked, one by one, on to the Sword of Omens.

This is a simple concept that feels at home in a run of episodes struggling to maintain originality as the first season comes to a close. It's a 'bread and butter' entry that isn't quite strong enough to stand out and is not helped by a poor climax as, yet again, a call to the ThunderCats rights all wrongs.

Writer's Commentary from Heather Winters:

I had never written a screenplay before, which was painfully clear to the head writer! Somewhere in the middle of the first season I started wondering if it might be fun to have an episode that was more cerebral and less action packed. I'd always been interested in dark, dream states and other states of consciousness and I was wondering if it might be possible to write a script about Mumm-Ra stealing the ThunderCats' dreams.

I was at lunch with a friend of mine, actress Annabelle Gurwitch, and we bounced some ideas around. She's a talented writer, so I asked her if she wanted to write it with me; and I did the majority of the writing once I fleshed out the story. I asked the head writer if I could have a shot at it and he said yes. Many, many, many drafts and months later they finally accepted the script. It was one of the last scripts for the first season, so I barely made it in. I was very lucky to have that opportunity and it was the beginning of my writing professionally. It was one of the happiest moments of my life and I still have a Xerox copy of the cheque.

I was thrilled to *finally* see the script I wrote as a finished episode. It was the first thing I had ever written and sold and I was grateful to have been allowed as a staff member to contribute to the series and be part of a show written primarily by seasoned veterans.

57. Out of Sight (3.5 Stars)
Written by: C H Trengove
US Broadcast Date: 10 December 1985
UK Broadcast Date: 25 February 1991

'Out of Sight' begins well with a particularly brutal attack on the Warrior Maidens by the Mutants. There are some lovely art backgrounds depicting the Maidens' kingdom, and the threat of fire to their homes is a simple but terrifying concept. Equally, there is some nice exploration of Castle Plun-Darr and its grounds as Tygra and Nayda infiltrate the Mutants' fortress.

This is a relatively simple premise that facilitates the reuse of existing characters and locations for the final group of first season episodes. Within this mandate, it works well and there is plenty to entertain the viewer. Tygra's taunting of Jackalman (with a levitating skull) is an amusing scene and his insistence that this 'ghost' is responsible for events runs throughout the episode to comic effect. 'I'm telling you, I was attacked by a ghost,' insists Jackalman. 'Ghost my beak, never heard such nonsense. You two fools let her escape,' retorts Vultureman.

The episode really begins to move forward when Tygra and Nayda realise they cannot regain visibility. This is a great story device and adds a welcome sense of jeopardy to proceedings. Indeed, it leads to the best scene of the episode as Lion-O uses the Sword to reverse their predicament, and this is animated wonderfully, with some superb lighting and direction.

Although 'Out of Sight' is enjoyable, the end of the first season does begin to feel a little tired. While it was a noble effort to try to give added development to existing characters, the show does begin to miss the involvement of 'outside influences', specifically new villains to inject variety.

Writer's Commentary from Chris Trengove:

Writers sometimes tended to give Tygra less attention than the others, probably because he couldn't help being something of a 'second banana', caught between Lion-O (the boss) and Cheetara (the wonder girl). So, step forward Tygra, I thought, and who can we team you up with? Well, everyone loves a Warrior Maiden …

Almost all of the *ThunderCats* episodes finished with the team relaxing and summing-up, the script being topped with an 'ending joke.' Many of these jokes were verging on the excruciating, but I have to admit that this episode supplied one of the worst: Tygra: 'Invisibility has its uses, but as a way of life …' Nayda: 'I just can't see it!'

58. The Mountain (5 Stars)
Written by: Danny Peary
US Broadcast Date: 11 December 1985
UK Broadcast Date: 11 March 1991

'The Mountain' is the only script that Danny Peary contributed to *ThunderCats*. While, by his own admission, much of the dialogue was courtesy of script editor Peter Lawrence, the resulting episode is a brilliant addition to the series. Not only is it original and engaging, but it manages this despite the fact that it features only the ThunderCats and Mutants with no new characters or significant devices (besides the Mutants' new Thundrillium weapon). While other episodes around this time were struggling to find new adventures for the core characters, Peary's script demonstrates that exciting adventures could still be crafted from even the most basic of plots.

In the spirit of the very beginning of television drama, 'The Mountain' concentrates the action into one 'set': in this case, encasing the ThunderCats and Mutants in a confined space. Not only does this require the dialogue to work incredibly hard (with the absence of action sequences to disguise any shortcomings), it also necessitates the collaboration of both sets of characters to survive. Pacific Animation Corporation deliver some brilliant animation throughout the episode, which does ample justice to the script. There are some spectacular sequences, including Lion-O's mountain fall – his glove shield bursting into shot to save him.

There are many strands to this story and all work equally well. Lion-O's tussle with Jackalman makes for great viewing, and Jackalman's tenacity is admirable. Mumm-Ra is also used perfectly here. Although featuring little in the episode, he raises the stakes by providing the Mutants an added incentive – obtain the Sword or suffer the consequences. This 'last chance' ultimatum seems to really give the Mutants a much-needed motivation. Jackalman, in particular, simply won't let go of the Sword, and we can't help but feel that Mumm-Ra's threat played some part in this determination. 'So long Jackalman,' declares Lion-O, before realising that his moral code prevents him from leaving the Mutant to his fate. 'Oh heck,' he utters.

The end of this battle results in the disturbing vision of a lifeless Lion-O washed up in the stream. Other iconic scenes include the Mutants' attack on the Eye of Thundera, projected in the skies. Again, it is small details like this that take the expected *ThunderCats* story devices and give them an added twist. This far into the run of episodes, anything original, however small, is welcome.

The dialogue in 'The Mountain' is also noteworthy. Jackalman's triumphant call, holding the Sword aloft, is amusing. 'Plun-Darr, Plun-Darr, Plun-Darr, Jackalman, Ho!' This isn't the only humour in the episode, and it's all judged perfectly. 'You'll be in big trouble when Jackalman gets us out of here,' declares Slithe, not quite believing his own threat. There are also some more sinister moments, and Jackalman in particular is handled far more credibly than in his antics in 'Jackalman's Rebellion'. 'Never do a favour for a favour,' he tells Lion-O. 'One step closer and I'll finish you with your own Sword!' Watch out for a brilliant growl from Lion-O in response to this before he regains the Sword and ultimately frees Tygra, Panthro, Monkian and Slithe, who are close to death, their oxygen exhausted. This scene is the perfect culmination to the episode as the Sword penetrates the rock 'just in time'.

In essence, 'The Mountain' is an unexpected surprise, refreshing the latter part of the first season and giving us faith that a second was not only worthwhile, but mandatory.

Writer's Commentary from Danny Peary:

I liked the idea of a journey from one place to another, which gives the story an episodic epic quality, and I had to have a rescue, so that's in there too. I turned in that script and my other story ideas, and possibly a *SilverHawks* script, and parted company with the producer, feeling like there was an opportunity lost. I turned on the TV one day to show my daughter the show I had worked on, and unbelievably it was 'The Mountain' episode. I wasn't surprised they had jettisoned all my nifty dialogue. I think they did it out of spite. The story remained intact, but it was hard to say joyfully, 'That is my script.' I never saw it or the show again.

I'm glad it's a popular episode but I'm reluctant to take sole credit – or blame – for it, because my unwanted 'co-writer' – the story editor who got rid of my dialogue – is equally responsible for what was produced. It would have been better if he had left the script I wrote alone. I do think that the story was left pretty much intact. I think some of the best action films, from Westerns to gangster films, are about characters (often best friends) who choose to be good or evil and are two sides of one coin. Those who choose evil usually feel connected to the good guys who took the right path, and somewhere within them good hibernates. I like the idea that the Mutants, in one small space, have to tone down their baser instincts and join with our heroes in a task so they can all stay alive. And the good guys have to trust the Mutants to a degree and not think of them as enemies. If these characters can get along for a few minutes despite their differences, then of course, there can be peace in our world. It works well, I think, because they're all trapped inside the Earth, and the surface world doesn't matter. In regard to Lion-O, he is a genuine hero, because he will save everyone in trouble, even enemies. Every living creature matters. Probably if I'd have stayed with the show, I'd have wanted to reveal that even Jackalman has a heart! They wouldn't have wanted that.

59. The Superpower Potion (3.5 Stars)
Written by: C H Trengove
US Broadcast Date: 12 December 1985
UK Broadcast Date: 28 January 1991

Every character must have his/her moment in the limelight, and 'The Super Power Potion' is Vultureman's moment to shine. The episode opens with a beautiful backlit establishing shot of Castle Plun-Darr, which sets the scene for some wonderful animation throughout, including a very high standard of cel painting and character likenesses. Events move straight in to the middle of the action (which is to be commended) and, within seconds, we see Vultureman transformed into a muscular and threatening opponent.

The various abilities the potion bestows upon Vultureman are impressive and work well visually. He can see the invisible, shoot laser beams from his eyes and inflict a state of suspended animation on his victims. Add to this his newfound ability to fly and Vultureman has truly ascended the ranks of cartoon villainy.

The episode is an enjoyable romp for Vultureman and races by, rarely decelerating the action. The scenes where Vultureman taunts Mumm-Ra are amongst the best moments of the episode, and his threatening treatment of the mummy, including pinning him to his sarcophagus, is chilling. The resulting battle of wills between the two characters is spectacular. Vultureman's quest for everlasting life is a clever prelude to his dealings with Mumm-Ra, and crucially there is an enjoyable scene where he proves his powers to his fellow Mutants.

Slithe's resulting 'zombie' state is also an inspired touch.

There is relatively little contribution from the ThunderCats here. Besides it falling to them to resolve matters, 'The Super Power Potion' revolves predominantly around Vultureman's fellow villains. It is a relatively simple episode. Given its standard dramatic premise – of a 'magic potion' and the effects it has on a lead character – it delivers all that is expected of it. It falls somewhere between the quality of the similar episodes 'Monkian's Bargain' and 'Jackalman's Rebellion', without the camp 'lightness' of the latter, but without the dynamic originality of the former.

Writer's Commentary from Chris Trengove:

The 'magic potion' is of course another classic SF/fantasy plot device that offers up all sorts of possibilities – particularly when taken by a character with something of a 'chip on his shoulder' like Vultureman. As a flying 'supervultureman', he takes centre stage, his pantomime villain antics making for a slightly more comic episode than usual. I have a soft spot for this episode, as I later played a video of it to a potential agent and she signed me forthwith. (I'm still with her 20 odd years on, so thank you Vultureman!)

60. Eye of the Beholder (4 Stars)
Written by: Kenneth E Vose
US Broadcast Date: 13 December 1985
UK Broadcast Date: 18 March 1991

Unusually, 'Eye of the Beholder' presents a scenario where Mumm-Ra and the Mutants are effectively provoked into action against the ThunderCats. The episode revolves around a practical joke that Lion-O decides to play against his enemies based upon Snarf's request for a replica Sword. This idea is executed extremely capably when the inevitable backfire occurs and Snarf is ensnared.

While the ThunderCats do bring the ensuing pandemonium upon themselves, the suggestion that even they have character flaws is endearing and somehow lends added credibility to the series. The plot is well thought through, including the ThunderKittens' information 'leak' to overhearing Trollogs. There is also a sense of extreme detail in Ken Vose's script, which gives every story element due attention (including assurances that the ThunderTank will arrive 'in 30 minutes'). While some writers take minor elements like this for granted, 'Eye of the Beholder' is a well-choreographed affair.

There is also some nice Mutant disharmony on display in 'Eye of the Beholder'. Monkian and Jackalman are happy to leave Slithe out of proceedings. 'We'll put Slithe back in the kitchens where he belongs,' they decree in a reference to the two-part 'Feliner' episodes. In turn, Slithe then pursues his own dealings with Mumm-Ra in a scene that accelerates proceedings as an unusually menacing Mumm-Ra puts the Mutant in his place.

Where the episode is most successful is in its portrayal of Lion-O, who is quick to atone for his misjudgements. Though he has reservations, he concedes to follow Panthro's suggestion to call the other ThunderCats, despite his embarrassment about his actions. His affection for Snarf is also touching as he determines to save his faithful companion: 'I swear by the Eye of Thundera, I'll tear Plun-Darr apart with my bare hands if they've harmed one hair on Snarf's head!'

Unusually, there are times where the story seems to be 'played for laughs' by the production team, most notably in the strange and inappropriate sound effects accompanying Snarf's movements in Mumm-Ra's pyramid and in Slithe's stooge-like fall as he narrowly avoids the ThunderTank storming towards him. There is also a somewhat disappointing climax, with the much-abused 'Mumm-Ra's reflection' device being dragged back into proceedings – although at least on this occasion it is redeemed a little by the purposeful introduction of a mirror into the faux-Sword.

Overall, the episode is a highlight of the latter part of the first season and, though it resolves around a practical joke, it proves itself anything but laughable.

Writer's Commentary from Ken Vose:

I wanted to do a story that 'starred' Snarf, which I did and thoroughly enjoyed. It's strange, but looking at the episode now, for the first time since it was broadcast, fails to trigger much in the way of interesting background or gossip dealing with the series etc. The only thing it brings back is a reminder of a pattern I seemed to follow on all of the animated series I worked on: to try to find something unusual or different to focus the story on. With *ThunderCats* it was as simple as giving Snarf his own episode; in *Peter Pan and the Pirates* the episode was built around baseball; in *Jonny Quest* it was about what really happened to Amelia Earhart; and with *Street Frogs* an episode about the life of a cartoon writer, and another about racing where a girl frog wins the race. (Maybe seen by a very young Danica Patrick?[5]) There were probably others, but I can't dredge them up.

Did the production do the script justice? I see no reason to think that it didn't, and don't recall any such feelings at the time. No laughter here in front of my PC, but I did enjoy seeing Snarf again. The moral in the tale was to be careful what you wish for, because you just might get it; which was, I think, effective without sounding too preachy …

As for any 'professional appraisal', I'd have to say that the series was one of the better ones for the era in which it was made. I'm both amazed and gratified that it's still able to find an audience in today's *Avatar* world.

61. Lion-O's Anointment Final Day: The Trial of Evil (5 Stars)
Written by: Leonard Starr
US Broadcast Date: 16 December 1985
UK Broadcast Date: 8 October 1990

The perfect end to a perfect mini-serial, the 'Final Day' lives up to expectations as proceedings reach new heights. The episode opens with an enjoyable recap of the past Anointment Trials, and it's a brilliant choice to conclude the mini-series by having Lion-O combating Mumm-Ra (and far more enjoyable than the only other alternative – a showdown with Snarf!) Alone and without the Sword, it seems

---

[5] Danica Patrick is a famous female American racing car driver.

Lion-O will have a huge battle to overthrow Mumm-Ra. Fortunately, a huge battle is exactly what Leonard Starr delivers in one of the darkest episodes of the series.

Jaga's appearance in the Trials is welcome, and Lion-O politely but firmly declining his help marks a turning point for the character. Jaga's apparent distain for his charge is also a nice touch. The opening scenes take place in the ruins of 'First Earth' that surround the Black Pyramid. Moving underground, Lion-O's interaction with Maftet (a character, incidentally, that featured in Starr's original writing bible for the show) works well, and the latter's weakness, due to a lack of active worshipers in thousands of years, is a subtle but effective idea. As he closes in on his final destination, Lion-O's many challenges navigating the River of Doom are extremely eerie, and the faceless boatman sets the scene for Mumm-Ra's many obstacles.

However interesting the journey, Lion-O's penetration of Mumm-Ra's tomb chamber is where the episode has been leading, and where the viewer know it will live or die. Having confronted each other many times before, Mumm-Ra and Lion-O could well have had a rather uninspiring face-off. Instead, it really is a fight to the death, executed and animated wonderfully as Mumm-Ra's tomb chamber crumbles around them. Even one of the four Ancient Spirits of Evil is victim to the fighting, as his head is ripped away. Lion-O's accurate summation that the key to Mumm-Ra's power lies in his sarcophagus is inspired, and entirely logical given the mummy's continued reliance on the crypt. The resulting destruction of the sarcophagus and the disintegration of Mumm-Ra are spectacular; the perfect end to a perfect episode!

Lion-O's triumph in successfully surviving his Trials is given due acknowledgment and the ceremony he enjoys is brilliantly conceived – a huge audience of well-wishers from Third Earth surrounding Cats' Lair as Lion-O raises his Sword in victory. The inevitable end to the 'Final Day' is Mumm-Ra's cackling return from the depths of destruction. While it may take some credibility away from the episode, the series would not have been the same without its chief antagonist and, though he would return, it still surely ranks as his greatest defeat.

Ultimately this episode marks the end of Starr's journey for Lion-O from a boy to a man – the journey that began in 'Exodus' – and Lion-O will have to prove himself no more.

Writer's Commentary from Leonard Starr:

The final trial was against Mumm-Ra. He's a mummy that lives forever. There is practically nothing original in the entire thing. Mummies and such have been turning kids on forever. I'm surprised that I didn't have a vampire in it, except that vampires mean nothing to me. I've never seen a vampire movie, from Bela Lugosi's onwards, that didn't bore me, except for the television movie with Darren McGavin where they had a vampire in Las Vegas. It was called *The Night Stalker*, and I was surprised to find that I enjoyed it. Another reason why I'm not a multi-millionaire.

62. The Trouble With ThunderKittens (3.5 Stars)
Written by: Kimberly B Morris
US Broadcast Date: 17 December 1985
UK Broadcast Date: 8 April 1991

The debut contribution from Kimberly Morris displays in abundance her skills and background as a children's writer. Featuring the ThunderKittens would often prove difficult for fellow writers, and all too commonly the characters were relegated to background fodder. Dedicating an entire story to the eponymous characters, Morris writes extremely well for the youngsters, with realistic dialogue and a deep sense of empathy for a childish game that goes wrong. Though the world of *ThunderCats* would often feature the weird and the wonderful, 'Trouble with ThunderKittens' is a story about children pushing the boundaries and the consequences of doing so. This added realism is both commendable and necessary for the series' longevity, acting as a moderating counterbalance to more outlandish episodes from writers such as Bill Overgard.

Morris shows a talent for comedy throughout the episode and, even as the action intensifies, still manages to include a sense of humour into proceedings (including Monkian admiring himself with his nunchakuin a mirror). Additionally, 'Trouble with ThunderKittens' explores Castle Plun-Darr in perhaps more depth than any other episode from the series, and it's enjoyable to see our villain's lair as the ThunderCats navigate the building in search of their lost weaponry.

There are production issues that affect the episode at times, including some unusually 'choppy' editing, leading to jump cuts and ridiculously short sequences. This may be the result of some 'short cuts' from Pacific Animation Corporation with the reuse of existing scenes for minor shots such as close-ups etc. This is achieved particularly badly during Lion-O's battle with the Mutants, where a stock clip of Lion-O is used, complete with a leafy meadow background, despite events taking place in Castle Plun-Darr.

While the episode is undeniably enjoyable, it's a simple adventure for the ThunderCats and is resolved with relative ease, courtesy of laughter gas. Where it succeeds is in its capable execution. It's the small touches that make the show memorable, and none more so than Lion-O's decision to conceal the Kittens' actions from his fellow ThunderCats. Throughout, Lion-O is incredibly protective of the Kittens, and it's this interaction that stands out in the episode. With Lion-O and the Kittens having been of approximate ages when Thundera was destroyed, it's a unique relationship between the three characters. Through the course of the season, it has developed to a point of absolute respect from the Kittens towards their leader and a reciprocal tolerance from Lion-O when they invariably step out of line.

Writer's Commentary from Kimberly Morris

This was the first script I wrote, and I met with Peter Lawrence periodically during the process. He was a good teacher and by the time I finished that script, I felt like I'd had an education in writing for animation. I approached the subsequent assignments with much more confidence. I was also reminded of what I already knew; when writing for animation, always s keep in mind why and how the medium is different from live action – and write accordingly. If you are writing scenes that could just as easily be filmed in live action, there is no reason to animate.

However … live action special effects have come so far over the last 20 years, it's become hard to think of things that could be done only with animation. So I suppose the mandate now will be for animation to evolve in new and creative ways.

63. Mumm-Rana (4 Stars)
Written by: Bob Haney
US Broadcast Date: 18 December 1985
UK Broadcast Date: 15 April 1991

'Mumm-Rana' marks the swansong of Bob Haney, one of the most creative and able writers to ever grace the series. As was now standard for his scripts, it is both imaginative and effortlessly constructed. Though it isn't his finest contribution, it is still amongst the most memorable episodes of *ThunderCats*, and the obvious parallel between Mumm-Rana and Mumm-Ra must have been simply too enjoyable a concept to resist.

As usual, Haney's script races along, opening with a surprise reappearance by the RatStar, though no explanation is given for the omission of Ratar-O. After the ship is damaged (although presumably not utterly destroyed, given its later appearances), the scenes featuring the Mutants' escape pods drifting into Third Earth's atmosphere are wonderfully conceived, and Mumm-Rana's tomb is beautifully designed. Each design element mirrors its equivalent in Mumm-Ra's Black Pyramid. Pacific Animation Corporation also continue to be on top form here, with some beautiful background art of the wrecked Cats' Lair as Lion-O and Tygra hang from the Lair's 'eyes'.

The parallels in play throughout the story are appealing for children, and the age-old conflict between good and evil is explored in detail here. Mumm-Rana is an effectively realised character, despite the obvious danger that she may become only a parody of the demon priest himself. Mumm-Ra too is written well in the episode, with some chilling dialogue, including his declaration that Mumm-Rana must first 'be tamed' before he bursts into a disturbing cackle. As events proceed, highlights include the Mutants clasping the ThunderCats in chains, Mumm-Ra and Mumm-Rana sitting side by side on their thrones and the eventual battle between the two as Lion-O helps the latter to regain her mind courtesy of a welcome appearance from Jaga.

Unfortunately, though it is a hugely enjoyable episode, 'Mumm-Rana' does lack the thoroughness of Haney's previous scripts. Though they aren't many, a few minor niggles do detract from the episode, including the random appearance by Mumm-Ra in Mumm-Rana's pyramid at the beginning of the episode and more notably the preposterous 'exile' scene. 'ThunderCats, you are condemned to wander in exile for all eternity,' declares Mumm-Rana, only for it to transpire that the place of exile is in fact close to Castle Plun-Darr. The use of the tired 'Mumm-Ra's reflection' device also seems uncharacteristically unimaginative for a writer of Haney's calibre. Nonetheless, there is plenty to entertain here, and the shear originality of the idea makes it a highlight of the final episodes from the first season. It is also nice to see the damage to Cats' Lair (which often occurs without apparent consequence) being restored in the final scenes as its head is satisfactorily winched into place.

Script Editor's Commentary from Peter Lawrence:

In another time and another place, I would have developed Mumm-Rana as a recurring character torn between her innate good and her Mumm-Ra-induced evil. I'd have given her a lot more free will in her decisions – made her quite conflicted – and I'd have worked with the Ancient Spirits of Good. However, by the time this story came along, we were too far into the show to introduce such fundamental themes and changes. We had our hands full with the world that had developed and sprawled across the production landscape. It was all we could do to bring some sense of order to it, without going off into yet another story dimension.

I realise now that Bob was a better writer than I gave him credit for and I wonder why we didn't use him more often. I do recall that he was rather slow and sometimes a little awkward to work with. That's not intended as a criticism or a mean sideswipe. Often, talented writers with strong views are awkward to work with – but worth it for the ideas they bring. Unfortunately, when the production schedule is insane, they are sometimes not given the time and consideration they need to produce their best work.

64. The Shifter (4 Stars)
Written by: Matthew Malach
US Broadcast Date: 19th December 1985
UK Broadcast Date: 29th April 1991

Matthew Malach's debut script for *ThunderCats* is a strong opening gambit, full of humour, action and a clever use of the 'swapped bodies' device commonly found in children's drama. While similar to the earlier episode 'Divide and Conquer', 'The Shifter' narrowly outperforms it, utilising the concept to better effect, with clever use of parallels throughout the episode. It is no coincidence that Panthro and Snarf are the chosen candidates for transformation, offering as they do the greatest potential for differences in both temperament and physique, which are explored well. The same is true of Slithe's 'body swap' with Jackalman. Both examples work nicely, and the idea is exploited brilliantly with scenes including Snarf (in Panthro's body) driving the ThunderTank and Panthro (in Snarf's body) using nun-chucks and karate kicks.

This really is a visual episode, and the 'shift sequences' are well designed and executed. Effort has also been given to subtle manipulation of the standard character designs. For instance, all four principal characters have modified facial expressions, including a frowning Snarf and a vulnerable-looking Panthro. Pacific Animation Corporation deliver another faultless example of their animation prowess and, coming near the end of the season, this reminds us how far their talents have come since the variable quality of the opening episodes.

The dialogue and characterisation on display in 'The Shifter' are remarkably acute given Malach's lack of experience. His one-liners serve the episode well, including Vultureman's harsh appraisal of the situation: 'All Panthro's skills in

Snarf's useless carcass.' It is also nice to have the Mutants revealed to be responsible for the device only after the ThunderCats have already fallen foul of its effects, and the tempo of the episode is well judged.

The situation is resolved well, and the Sword's inability to distinguish Lion-O from WilyKat is a really nice touch. Not only does this give us the unique scene of WilyKat trying (unsuccessfully) to call the ThunderCats, but it facilitates Malach's clever idea to require both ThunderCats to complete the task.

'The Shifter' is a fun and engaging episode. Though they never detract from the drama of the situation, Malach's humour and imagination will be prove him to be a welcome addition to the series' writing team.

Writer's Commentary from Matthew Malach:

'The Shifter' was the first script I ever wrote and got paid for. It was a test run of sorts, given to me thanks to the generosity of Peter Lawrence, whom I look upon as a mentor. Peter taught me a great deal about writing and I'll always look up to him and his work. 'The Shifter' was my attempt at humour – the idea of Snarf and Panthro switching bodies was irresistible to me, and of course not exactly an original concept. At first, I wanted to call the show 'Shifting Salts', but Peter said the title sounded too much like the name of a laxative. I have to agree.

When I thought of the idea of 'The Shifter', the first characters that came to my mind were Panthro and Snarf. They are complete opposites. At first they are horrified at the switch, but they learn to respect and eventually deftly use their new bodies. The accidental swapping of Slithe with Jackalman was just an introduction to this idea; the smarter Slithe being saddled with the body of a lowly jackal is the ultimate insult. As for the 'somoflange line', I have to admit, that probably came from Peter. He was a big fan of adding technical nonsense to dialogue, and in fact was the king of that when we were on *Peter Pan and the Pirates*. That show made heavy use of pirate slang, which though authentic, was unintelligible to nearly anyone who watched the show, pirates excluded.

65. Fond Memories (4 Stars)
Written by: Lee Schneider
US Broadcast Date: 20 December 1985
UK Broadcast Date: 20 May 1991

The closing instalment of *ThunderCats'* debut series is a mixed bag. While it is far from the best episode, it does successfully recap both what the show had represented up to this point and feature some memorable villains. It is a story of vanity and, in this case, Lion-O's belief that his actions could be commemorated by the people of Third Earth. This is an incredibly strong concept, which isn't really examined to maximum effect. Instead, the action overwhelms the episode a little, with the majority of the running time comprising of fight sequences.

Old enemies such as Ratar-O, Safari Joe and Spidera make a welcome return, and highlights include the 'monster' portraits dotted throughout the cave and Lion-O's reaction to the warp gas (scuttling, cat like, into a hole in the cave wall).

The most memorable and enjoyable aspect of 'Fond Memories' is Mumm-Ra's disguise as an 'evil' Lion-O (complete with fetching red attire). The ensuing battle between the two is spectacular and works well on screen. Lee Schneider also offers some enjoyable dialogue throughout, including Mumm-Ra's scathing attack on Lion-O: 'Did you really think that the miserable creatures of this planet would go to the trouble of building a museum just for you?' Lion-O's staggered reaction is well judged and speaks volumes.

Essentially, 'Fond Memories' is something of a recap of the events and formulas of the first 65 episodes of *ThunderCats*. To this end, it works well, and it's a worthwhile opportunity to use this approach one final time, before things are given a re-shuffle as the ThunderCats return for their second season. 'After all that, I'm all in!' suggests Snarf in the closing moments, and *ThunderCats* would indeed take a short break before it returned to take off in a new direction.

Writer's Commentary from Lee Schneider:

This script started out in a purely mercantile way. I pitched all my own ideas to the producers. Since I knew we were reaching episode 65, I wanted to find something they would buy without hesitation, because we all believed that *ThunderCats* would end with episode 65, would instantly be forgotten, and we would all be looking for new jobs. It would be cool, I thought, to have written the final episode of the series – 65 was something of a magic number in the animation world. (Even sitcom seasons back then only went to 22 episodes or so.) Hoping for a successful sale of the idea, my first thought was to see if I could save the producers money by re-purposing, recycling and thereby showcasing previous episodes. Not only would it provide an honourable way to end the first series, but it would also give the viewers a retrospective of the best set and character designs. 'Fond Memories' takes place in a museum, and I'm dead certain I ripped this off from an old movie I saw but can't remember now. Anyway, the thrifty strategy worked and the producers liked the idea.

As I started working from my outline I realised that I had an opportunity to use a very human trait of Lion-O's very feline character: Heroes are subject to vanity. Lion-O would want to defeat villains he'd defeated before, something like an athlete trying to break all his old records. Just in time, of course, Lion-O realises that his vanity isn't going to defeat the villains. He's got to call in the rest of the ThunderCats, thereby reinforcing the ThunderCats' Code of Conduct. By the way, having Lion-O fight his 'evil twin' in this episode is another science fiction conceit that simply had to be exploited or else I would have had my poetic licence revoked. I don't think there's ever been a science fiction or fantasy series that did not use the evil twin conceit somehow, and I wanted to be sure that *ThunderCats* wasn't going to be the exception to that rule.

SEASON TWO
1986-1989

66-70. ThunderCats-Ho! Parts One – Five (5 Stars)
Written by: Leonard Starr
US Broadcast Date: *27-31 October 1986
UK Broadcast Date: N/A

ThunderCats returns to our screens with a 'movie' special. 'ThunderCats Ho!' was designed to run episodically over the course of one week as well as be edited into a compilation for home video release. There is plenty on offer in all five parts of the story to sustain and build interest, though the compilation version is marginally superior, with some of the slower scenes excised.

The show's standard introductory sequence remains unchanged for the second season and, while it works fine here, it will become less and less relevant as the episodes progress and new characters and locations dominate proceedings. Therefore, a revised montage might have been better and more dynamic.

One element that has been amended for season two is Bernard Hoffer's music score. Full credit has to be given to the editors here as, rather than use the new cues exclusively (which would have made the season feel too different from its predecessor), they drip-feed them into the episodes alongside a majority of previously-heard music, giving only the occasional hint of what's to come. As ever, Hoffer's music is brilliantly written and performed, and scores for the new ThunderCat vehicles add a fresh burst of energy.

The opening scene of the story is perfectly judged. Taking events right back to the ThunderCats' beginnings on Thundera, it acts both as a recap of the pilot episode and as a welcome opportunity to expand on the show's mythology. Here we learn that Lion-O witnessed the apparent deaths of three Thunderians on the Flag Ship's flight from Thundera (yet more reason for his nightmares about the events revealed in his Anointment Trial against Tygra). Once again, he is disturbed as the events return in the form of dreams. This is an effective device, as slowly the story of the Thunderians' journey beyond Thundera is revealed. The scene where a teary-eyed Lion-O must accept Jaga's decision to leave his countrymen is touching. 'One day, as Lord of the ThunderCats, you will have to make many hard decisions, Lion-O,' says Jaga. 'This is but the first of them.'

Where the five episodes feel a little different from those of season one is in their use of linking cliffhangers and recaps. Some cliffhangers are notably better than others, however this added dimension of storytelling helps distinguish the mini-series and creates a short story arc. Time is also afforded to this serial, and events are nowhere near as rushed as in previous adventures. Arguably, this does lead to some padding around the middle acts, but some nice ideas are explored because of the flexibility given to the format.

The serial sees the return of many friends and villains from the first season, but rather than simply retread previous adventures, Leonard Starr proves his ability at handling other writers' creations. Hammerhand, for example, is given his best story by far, outshining his previous appearances and becoming a much more engaging character in the process. The scenes featuring the Beserkers are some of the most original and engaging of the story, and these new versions of the characters (conceived by the show's toy licencees) are far superior to their predecessors. Other villains handled with ease include Ratar-O and Captain Shiner.

Another highlight of the serial is Snarf's stealthy performance when imprisoned by Ratar-O. His shock when Lion-O plummets from the RatStar is also touching. 'You've served your master well, fuzz face,' says Ratar-O. 'What have I done? What have I done?' pleads Snarf. Starr is equally capable of breathing new life into the various ThunderCat allies seen throughout the episodes. Snowman returns with Snowmeow, complete with some great lines: 'Lord Lion-O, and he is wrong colour – not supposed to be blue!' The episodes set around Hook Mountain are extremely enjoyable, and Lion-O's apparent surrender in the ice is a great scene.

'ThunderCats Ho!' is amongst the series' most action-packed stories. Notable examples of this include Tygra's near-obliteration of Lion-O, when the latter is riding a Sky Cutter; the scenes featuring the Fist Pounder (clearly a toy invention); and those of Panthro trapped under the burning ThunderTank – 'If the fire reaches the fuel tank, he's finished,' summarises Cheetara.

Remarkably, given that the plot revolves around them, the three 'new' ThunderCats, Bengali, Lynx-O and Pumyra, are afforded relatively little screen time. However, what we do see bodes well for their future appearances, with each given adequate development that nicely distinguishes him from the existing ThunderCats' line-up. While the first season had offered some of the best episodes, by far, of the entire *ThunderCats* run, the formula had been beginning to wane by the final episodes. Here, the show is rebooted, with the three newcomers injected to revitalise interest.

Lynx-O is possibly the most interesting of the three new characters, and his blindness is both a brave and purposeful move from the show's writers. Pumyra's agility and naivety are well handled, and Bengali's forceful nature reminds us of Lion-O's impetuousness before his ultimate maturation. All three characters enjoy a strong bond and are extremely protective of Lynx-O (demonstrated in the scene where Slithe declares Lynx-O's blindness will make him 'easier to handle').

Mumm-Ra is also a key component in the action unfolding on Third Earth, complete with his new pet Ma-Mutt. His manipulation of events throughout the story is integral to proceedings and, though he is not involved with it directly, Lion-O's challenge within the Black Pyramid is one of the best components of all five episodes. 'Who would these guys be? Mumm-Ra's ancestors?' asks Lion-O. 'No, Lion-O, they are my prisoners for eternity, as you will soon be,' replies Mumm-Ra. The slow mummification of Lion-O is brilliantly envisaged and animated and is perhaps the best cliffhanger of the serial.

Given the many plot strands within 'ThunderCats Ho!', the climax is reasonably handled, and the fifth episode really hikes up the pace. The scenes featuring the Vertus thrust into space are well directed, and the on-screen countdown is a small but effective touch. In a story that reflects on the best of the *ThunderCats* series, an appearance from Jaga is mandatory, and it's great to see a rematch between the ThunderCat and his old enemy, Grune. Their battle for the Star of Thundera serves as a brilliant climax, as does Mumm-Ra's apparent destruction in his quest for power. Given their prominence in the episodes, the Thunderians' ascension is handled rather quickly. It is still effective, though, and leads to some brilliant scenes, including Lynx-O's speech to Lion-O recalling Claudus. Finally, Lion-O declares his plans for the trio: 'Well, you've handled yourself like ThunderCats and, once I've anointed you, you'll be true ThunderCats!'

The story isn't without a few negative points. There are some continuity issues throughout all five episodes, including the unexplained appearances from Hammerhand (who perished in his first adventure, later revived as a ghost). There is also a perplexing resolution to Lion-O's quest to infiltrate Mumm-Ra's tomb as, after experiencing near-mummification, he randomly decides to abandon his task in favour of a new approach. Hachiman's aggression towards Lion-O is also a little unbelievable, given his previous dealings with Mumm-Ra, and a little out of character. (Incidentally, Great Uncle Nishida is a reference to one of the show's lead animators.) Overall, though, 'ThunderCats Ho!' is a classic instalment of the series and sets the second season on track to continue the standard of the first 65 episodes. It sustains interest for over 100 minutes and must be given credit accordingly.

Three new ThunderCats will now have to be integrated into the series, and things are set to change still further.

Writer's Commentary from Leonard Starr:

This was just purely commercial. They had toys there and they had used up the basic set of characters, so we kept introducing things to give them other things to market. It was a business really, and I had nothing to do with that. They wanted some extra characters, so I gave them some extra characters.

Where did the phrase 'ThunderCats Ho!' originate? It may have come from the sub-basement of my memory bank, having read Charles Kingsley's *Westward, Ho!* in my early teens, my 'Captain Blood' days. It's a terrific adventure story set during the Elizabeth I period. Anyway, there was no wrenching executive conference regarding it. We needed a call, 'ThunderCats Ho!' came to mind, I wrote it into the bible (I think) and that was it. And why not 'Ho!'? 'Hi-Yo Silver!' Or, if you prefer, 'Up, up and *awaaaaaaay!*'

71-75. Mumm-Ra Lives! Parts I – V (3.5 Stars)
Written by: Leonard Starr
US Broadcast Date: * 7-11 September 1987
UK Broadcast Date: N/A

Leonard Starr's tenure on *ThunderCats* comes to an end with a less-than-inspiring five part adventure that fails to capture the magic of his previous and vast contributions to the series.

Unlike 'ThunderCats Ho!', 'Mumm-Ra Lives!' fails to maintain suspense for its entire duration. There is a wafer-thin premise, namely the introduction of the Lunataks, which could have easily been realised in only one episode.

Three new ThunderCats having been introduced in the previous adventure, it seems a sensible choice to bring in a new generation of villains as well. However, the new antagonists, though made out to be superior to the much-maligned Mutants, are soon revealed to be equally inept. While the Mutants may never have been successful in their many plans, they did always inject some humour into proceedings, something sorely lacking from the Lunataks.

The central characters are revived at the behest of Mumm-Ra, who is convalescing following his encounter with the Star of Thundera in the previous adventure. Courtesy of some nice backstory, we are told that the Lunataks encountered Mumm-Ra previously in their quest to dominate Third Earth and, presumably during the height of his powers, were defeated and imprisoned. The Lunataks consist of a self-appointed leader, Luna, her loyal steed Amok, the ice queen Chilla, the hypnotic Alluru, Tug-Mug and Red-Eye (voiced by Earle Hyman, who finally distances himself from his performance as Panthro). These characters (like the Mutants) all originate from the many moons of the planet Plun-Darr, and are gifted with powers relevant to their home worlds. This is a strong concept and is intended to provide additional difficulties for the ThunderCats to resolve. Aluro and Chilla are, arguably, the most interesting additions. Luna is the most aggravating; unfortunately, both her character design and voice acting stand as an annoying parody of cartoon villainy.

Beyond the introduction of the Lunataks, the story stalls, with no clear direction to drive it. The ThunderCats and Lunataks wander aimlessly trying to foil each other's plans, despite it being clear that the battle between them will never be resolved, and this simply isn't enough to give structure to the storyline, which meanders from episode to episode.

However, there are positive points. The second season continues to mark its territory as being different from the first, not simply a retelling. The newly-commissioned music library steps up a gear, with more and more new tracks being heard, and the 'feel' of the show begins to change and redefine itself. A highly enjoyable moment from the serial includes the navigation of the Forest of Mists with Lynx-O's Braille Board. While it may be technologically implausible, this device is a nice way to include Lynx-O in various adventures. The Lunataks' territory in Darkside is beautifully realised, making it one of the most disturbing regions of Third Earth ever seen in the series. The revelation of the Lunataks, still encased in lava, is handled well and there is a nice reference to 'The Slaves of Castle Plun-Darr' as the poor Brutemen are once again called upon to work on the villains' lair (which, in a clever twist, is mobile). The Lunataks' initial bombardment of the ThunderCats makes for some wonderful scenes, and Tug-Mug's effortless destruction of the Sword of Omens really heightens tension. There's also a conscious effort from Starr to give each of the central characters a reasonable amount of screen time, and he constantly pairs the new ThunderCats with existing team members, helping to solidify and integrate the new line-up. Best of all, Mumm-Ra is given a new transformation sequence that breaks away from the predictability of the previous series.

Two further additions to the series are Snarfer and Ma-Mutt. Though Ma-Mutt was first seen in the previous adventure and Snarfer in the two-part 'Feliner' story, 'Mumm-Ra Lives!' elevates them to central characters. Both additions are questionable. Snarfer is a sweet and humorous character and his interplay with his uncle does lead to some enjoyable scenes. However, in an already crowded line-up, the addition of a second Snarf seems unnecessary. Meanwhile, while Ma-Mutt alone is inoffensive, Mumm-Ra's somewhat camp dialogue with his hound is another concession to the youngest demographic. Ma-Mutt's narrative purpose is at least clear – giving Mumm-Ra a figure to explain his plans to, avoiding the need for the monologues of the first season – but Snarfer's role is less clear.

The serial resolves itself well, considering there is relatively little to resolve, and it's refreshing to see that Mumm-Ra is no longer susceptible to his own reflection.

Leonard Starr undoubtedly played a huge role in the evolution of *ThunderCats* and was one of the series' best-loved writers. However, towards the end of his contribution, he became unhappy with the terms of his work for Rankin/Bass, and regrettably it begins to show through in these scripts. The writer's falling interest manifests itself throughout 'Mumm-Ra Lives!' and, while it's a competent offering, it falls short of his earlier work.

Writer's Commentary from Leonard Starr:

I did a story about the death of Mumm-Ra, and Jules said to me, 'We can't lose Mumm-Ra, we'd have no villain'. My response was that Frankenstein has come back at least six times from the grave and so has Dracula. He's a villain, so he gets to come back to life, because he's a main money-maker. So Jules said, 'Oh'. And that was that. So he came back to life. That's the kind of thing the comic book writers would get really flaky about. They'd have a character really stuck in a cave with a poisonous snake at the airhole, an avalanche blocking the entrance or something, but absolutely no way to get out. They'd worry it and worry it until finally, if they couldn't figure a way for him or her to escape and the deadline loomed, they'd write, 'Once out of his predicament' … and move on.

MEMO TO:	Len Starr
FROM:	Peter Lawrence
Date:	July 30, 1986
Subject:	ThunderCats – MUMM-RA LIVES!

I enclose notes on this morning's meetings for your information.

The next stage in the production of MUMM-RA LIVES! Will be for you to develop the new Bad Guy characters based on your notes and today's discussions – with particular emphasis on the 'nemesis element' of each new Bad Guy.

Once we have all agreed that the characters are right, we will move on to an outline of MUMM-RA LIVES!, which will be constructed like THUNDERCATS-HO! – five scripts with cliff-hangers and recaps, which can also play as a 'movie'.

From the outline we will move directly to scripting, with a delivery date (for all five scripts) of September 15. Please do contact me if I can help with anything.

76. Catfight (4 Stars)
Written by: Chris Trengove
US Broadcast Date: * 14th September 1987
UK Broadcast Date: N/A

Coming so soon after the introduction of the 'new' ThunderCats, Chris Trengove's 'Catfight' is the perfect exploration of how fragile the trust between new and old can be. The episode is remarkably well conceived, with a large range of enjoyable components. Mumm-Ra's guise as Jaga is well-judged, given Lion-O's natural reliance on Jaga's advice, and it's interesting to consider that Jaga has not previously passed judgment on Lion-O's appointment of Lynx-O, Bengali and Pumyra. Therefore, the episode succeeds because it has the air of plausibility.

In an example of a writer returning to his own creations, Chris Trengove brings Turmaga (albeit a Mumm-Ra disguise) back for another outing. Mumm-Ra's attack on the ThunderTank is a clever device to inadvertently cause a civil war between the ThunderCats. While Lion-O and his original team may have attacked one another previously, while under various influences, they would never have doubted each other's integrity. This episode proves the newcomers have some distance to travel before they are fully accepted.

There are some great moments, none more so than the battle between the ThunderCats – the fight between Cheetara and Pumyra, in particular, is a highlight. Perhaps the only serious criticism that could be levelled at the episode is that more could have been made of the central premise. Another negative is that it inexplicably begins with a summary of the entire adventure in Mumm-Ra's cauldron, which somewhat negates the need to watch further. The Lunataks also complete their descent from being a vague threat in their introductory episodes to being almost entirely inept – while lacking the comic value of their counterparts, the Mutants.

Overall, 'Catfight' takes an enjoyable look at the relationships between the key protagonists, achieved with Trengove's usual sense of humour – including in Snarf's aggressive reaction to his nephew's apparent treachery: 'If I find out that Snarfer's up to something, I'll teach him a lesson he'll never forget!' The end scene is also a nice touch, with Tygra and the ThunderKittens returning from their 'field trips' (in effect a way of temporarily removing some of the large cast of characters). 'We didn't miss anything, did we?' asks WilyKit. 'Oh, nothing much,' says Pumyra, 'just a civil war between the ThunderCats!'

Writer's Commentary from Chris Trengove:

'Catfight' is notable (to me) for another appearance by Turmagar the Tuska, although he's actually Mumm-Ra in disguise. We're now up to show 76 (out of 130) and there are a lot of subsidiary characters to keep up with, including the 'Cats second team, Pumyra, Lynx-O, Ben-Gali and Snarfer.

In most long-running TV series, animated or not, extra characters are introduced as the episodes pile up (and in animation there may be demands related to toy marketing too). It's fun to work with 'newbies' of course, but you have to remember who the series is basically about, and not to allow new characters to overshadow the original team.

77. Psych Out! (4 Stars)
Written by: Sandy Fries
US Broadcast Date: * 15 September 1987
UK Broadcast Date: N/A

Following in the traditions of the first series, 'Psych Out!' turns the spotlight on one lead character. Here, it is the Lunatak Aluro who takes centre stage in a story reminiscent of previous adventures like 'Monkian's Bargain' where Mumm-Ra bestows powers on his minions. The episode is notable for some wonderful animation during Aluro's hypnotic sequences, complete with some incredible cel shading techniques and brilliant special effects that surpass anything seen in rival cartoons of the period.

Aluro is certainly one of the more interesting Lunataks and it's appropriate that he is given top billing here. His perseverance in inflicting his will on his victims is disturbing as he succeeds in dominating the ThunderCats. 'He's right,' exclaims Lion-O, 'I don't stand a chance'. 'Psych Out!' is also praiseworthy for being the first of several episodes to show Lynx-O's disability in a positive light. 'Maybe I'm the one person who can get that blasted talisman away from Aluro,' he proudly declares.

The high point of the episode is the moment the ThunderCats capitulate to their predicament. Only Snarf is left to persuade them to fight on. The following scenes of him bravely taking every conceivable weapon to avenge his comrades are both touching and highly amusing, and the clever revelation that his courage was self-derived is a nice twist. More amusement is provided by Lion-O's call to the ThunderCats, which on this occasion seems to be motivated purely by his unwillingness to travel the short distance to meet them – instead favouring them coming to him!

While this period of *ThunderCats* marks a run of generally rather uninspiring episodes, there are highlights, and 'Psych Out!' is chief among them.

Writer's Commentary from Sandy Fries:

There was a good deal of Snarf in 'Psych Out!' and I always liked the character because he was funny and cute. I liked it on the TV when I heard the actor do his 'Snarf, Snarf' dialogue. He was fun to write for and relatively easy. It was a lot easier to write for Snarf than for Tygra in 'Crystal Canyon'. There was a nice, uplifting message in this episode, which was important to me. I liked Aluro and the new villains. I liked the title 'Psych Out!', which was cool. Sometimes a title can excite you. I do remember it being a little difficult with the Aluro character, because I remember saying to myself, 'Okay, he controls minds and clouds people's minds, how do you break that?' There was some hesitation towards him as a character. Clouding minds is a nice idea, but in animation, how do you show the effects of that? It's not the most visual of things.

I like the Snarf stuff a lot and the message. I love the opening titles for *ThunderCats*, it was so cool then and still so cool today. A nice idea I had back then was to show Lynx-O's blindness making him resistant to Aluro, taking what seems to be a difficulty, but turning it into a positive. It's like the saying, 'When life gives you lemons, make lemonade'. It's a phenomenal thing for kids to learn. A child's mind is more open to ideas than adults' minds are. If it's a good idea, it might stick with them throughout their lives. Adults are mostly calcified; you can't have that much effect on them. I remember things as a kid that affected me. I remember watching *Frosty the Snowman*, another Rankin/Bass show, and it moved me when he melted but, hey, he came back. The bottom line is that you can have the opportunity to impact children's lives!

78. The Mask of Gorgon (5 Stars)
Written by: Romeo Muller
US Broadcast Date: * 16 September 1987
UK Broadcast Date: N/A

If 'Psych Out!' bucked the trend in a run of stilted episodes, 'The Mask of Gorgon' is even better, offering one of the most exciting episodes of the entire second season. Writer Romeo Muller was a Rankin/Bass stalwart, but this represented a huge change of audience for him, as he typically wrote the company's holiday specials, aimed at much younger children. Ironically, though he reportedly didn't enjoy the transition, he delivered one of the series' most sophisticated and well-scripted offerings.

The episode thrusts the viewer into the centre of the action as Lynx-O has, apparently, become crazed and Pumyra and Bengali rush to Lion-O in a bid to help him. Another nice device is a book containing the secrets of Third Earth and uncovered by Mumm-Ra, which leads to the discovery of the mysterious Mask of Gorgon. This successful twist on the Gorgon tale is used to great effect as a succession of characters are turned to stone. (Kudos to the design team who realised the characters' clothes would remain unaffected.)

There is some brilliant scriptwriting throughout, in both plot construction and dialogue. The episode is riddled with clues, mysteries and anagrams and builds momentum until the Hills of Elshimar are revealed to be a sleeping giant.

It's an eerie instalment of *ThunderCats* and moves at breakneck speed. Even the climax is well considered, and Lynx-O's intuitive plan to disable the creature (by flying into his ear canal) has to rank amongst the most intelligent resolutions to any episode of the series. Sadly, 'The Mask of Gorgon' would be Muller's only contribution to *ThunderCats*, leaving viewers to ponder what else he could have gifted the series.

Script Editor's Commentary from Peter Lawrence:

Romeo was already a fixture at Rankin/Bass, so he was somewhat willed on me. He's a much gentler, softer writer than I am, and personality, and he's very, very good at that ... not necessarily pre-school, but that softer-edge material. My recollection is that he wasn't very good with *ThunderCats* and he didn't enjoy the direction he got from us, but I don't think it ended badly.

Supervising Producer's Commentary from Lee Dannacher:

As far as Romeo on *ThunderCats* is concerned, he didn't want to write for that show, it wasn't what he was, it wasn't what he did. I'm sure Jules just said, 'We're doing this new show, let me send you something. See what you can do with the script.' I'm sure he just said, 'I'll give it a shot', and it just wasn't something that was him. He might have enjoyed it just as an exercise, but if it was anybody's decision not to continue, it was Romeo's. He was such a polite and beautiful man, he'd have never quit. So probably, after one script, the next conversation would have been to do with the next type of show that he'd want to write.

79. The Mad Bubbler (4 Stars)
Written by: Kimberly Morris
US Broadcast Date: * 17 September 1987
UK Broadcast Date: N/A

Considering her brief was to incorporate an LJN toy bubble machine (ultimately unproduced) into an episode of *ThunderCats*, Kimberly Morris does a great job of crafting a remarkably effective storyline.

The Mad Bubbler himself is played by Bob McFadden, and unusually for him, his performance is a little too similar to (indeed a cross between) his voices for Lynx-O and Slithe. The character's chosen weapon, namely the ability to draw out the latent evil within everyone, is an original flourish in a much-exploited genre of 'good turns bad' episodes. Marks should also be given for making the Lunataks equally susceptible to the Bubbler's powers. The victims' demonic red eyes are a nice touch and, added to the beautiful design of the abandoned mine, the scenes of the ThunderCats stalking each other on the platforms are wonderfully macabre.

Other benefits of the episode include the Feliner extinguishing the burning forests, the 'neutron converter' freezing the Ice Lake mid-flow (we can overlook techno-babble when it's this much fun) and the comfortable addition of the Snowman. There is also a poignant speech from Jaga, which touches upon some mature concepts with the realisation that evil resides in even the ThunderCats. 'In all of us there is the capacity for good and evil,' explains Jaga. 'It is a choice!'

The conclusion of 'The Mad Bubbler' wraps things up nicely – even though it stretches credulity that the only species incapable of evil thought is the Snarf (despite the fact that we have already seen 'our' Snarf fall foul of evil forces in the series). Nonetheless, it works within the context of the episode and rounds off a strong effort from Morris.

Writer's Commentary from Kimberly Morris

I think this character already existed or was suggested by Peter Lawrence. The Mad Bubbler sounds like it would have made a great toy! Too bad it wasn't produced. I would have bought one for sure. It absolutely could have been a toy-maker's creation. Most animated programming is conceived in conjunction and/or partnership with a toy company. In my experience working with Rankin/Bass (later Lorimar/Telepictures), the writers were often given characters to introduce or integrate into stories, but those tasks were creative challenges that were fun. Never were they allowed to compromise the storytelling.

Snarf was a 'nanny/yenta' personality: 'Drink your milk. Put on a jacket! Why the long face? Be careful with that Sword.' He was a nurturer entrusted with the care of Lion-O during his period of maturation. It just made sense to me that the reason he would be entrusted with that role was that he was somehow incorruptible. Incapable of evil in thought or deed. Also, it's always fun when the least likely 'hero' of the group saves the day.

80. Together We Stand (3.5 Stars)
Written by: Herb Engelhardt
US Broadcast Date: * 18 September 1987
UK Broadcast Date: N/A

The first of two submissions from Herb Engelhardt, 'Together We Stand' is an unremarkable, though entertaining, episode of *ThunderCats*. It features the return of the Beserkers, who once again outshine the new 'central' villains the Lunataks, and who, courtesy of Mumm-Ra, have obtained Thundranium-coated armour.

The positive aspects of the episode include a stunning standard of animation from PAC throughout. It's clear they have perfected the art of delivering faultless episodes by this point in the run, and by and large it is now impossible to discern which studios have contributed to any given episode. There are also a few exciting elements, including the ThunderCats' cunning plan to remove the Beserkers' Thundranium by flying the ThunderStrike and HoverCat simultaneously to create a vortex. Whatever the technical folly here, it's highly entertaining.

Things really get going when the Tower of Omens attempts to communicate with Cats' Lair, only for Aluro to appear before the ThunderCats. Thus begins the ingenious plan by Tygra and Lion-O to mimic being under Aluro's control. Things wrap up rather quickly with the reveal that the ThunderCats resisted the Lunataks' powers courtesy of some ear plugs. Corny in the extreme, but still largely engaging, and the Lunataks' trail of destruction at Cats' Lair is an amusing note on which to end proceedings.

Writer's Commentary from Herb Engelhardt:

Peter Lawrence actually suggested the character groups for my two episodes. I was unaware of the propensity of the other writers for adding new villains to the cast. I don't recall speaking with any others in LA that were working on the show, and I had no contact with the East Coast other than Peter. Creating new characters is a lot of work for the art department, and I would guess Peter was urged by the production team to make more use of some of the ones that had already gone through the design and modelling process. Besides, they were all new to me as I was only vaguely familiar with the show before taking on the assignments.

Pivotal moments can be good spots for humorous lines, something I always tried to incorporate. In fact, I think that most of the best lines are the funny ones. Too-serious characters can easily become 'talking heads' – an industry bane. Lines need to be short and to the point. Especially in fantasy, which can become linguistically stodgy or biblical.

It was a bit difficult coming in cold to write episodes for *ThunderCats*, which I hadn't seen previously. Beyond the obvious (age, gender, the traits of their animal counterparts, etc) I didn't feel the ThunderCat characters' individual personalities. Their lines were pretty much dictated by the situations and almost interchangeable. Some of the villains, notably Chilla, the Berserkers and

Vultureman, had more obvious potential, but their sheer numbers in each episode was also a limiting factor.

81. Ravage Island (4.5 Stars)
Written by: George Hampton & Mike Moore
US Broadcast Date: * 21 September 1987
UK Broadcast Date: N/A

'Ravage Island' sees the welcome homecoming of the Mutants in a fiendish plot from Mumm-Ra. It opens with Lion-O and Snarf engaging in a spot of joy-riding, and Lion-O soon becomes aware of the Beacon of Ravage Island. The Beacon itself is beautifully designed and painted, with a huge broken glass dome that once encased the machine at the heart of the story. The artwork throughout the episode is wonderfully macabre and full of stormy clouds and angry skies.

Along with the Mutants, we have a return to the humorous interplay between the villains, much missed with the Lunataks. The Mutants are back on top form. 'No-one can control my mind!' insists Slithe. 'Not even Slithe can control his mind,' jokes Jackalman.

ThunderCats scripts can typically be divided between those featuring new characters and those featuring new contraptions. Obviously falling into the latter category, the Beacon of Ravage Island is imaginative; and, while mind control has been explored many times before in the series, it's originally handled here – particularly in the form of the 'imaginary' prison that contains the ThunderCats. Better still is the revelation that its effects continue even after the destruction of the beam.

The episode presents another opportunity for Lynx-O to prevail because of his disability. This sets a wonderful example for children and helps prove the show's diverse and enlightened approach to storytelling. Mike Moore and George Hampton are clearly skilled at writing for *ThunderCats*, and their dialogue and plotting are spot-on. There are some great exchanges, including the witty retort from Panthro to Vultureman: 'I'll give you "submit quietly", you mutated macaw!' There is also a brilliant scene where Lion-O almost hands over the Sword of Omens to Mumm-Ra before, with huge will-power, he tosses it aside. 'You will never have the Sword of Omens as long as I have breath in my body,' challenges Lion-O. 'In that case, the Sword will soon be mine,' replies the mummy, 'for you are not long for Third Earth'.

Writer's Commentary from George Hampton:

I guess the inspiration for this episode was one of those spinning disks with the lines spiralling into the centre, supposedly used to hypnotise people. To update that, we made it a beam. The Snarfs weren't affected by beams because they couldn't concentrate on anything (other than food) long enough to become hypnotised. I can't think of another animated series where a blind character saves the day.

This was our first episode, and the first episode is always the hardest to write. Our problem was getting used to the visual freedom of *ThunderCats*. At first we were 'restraining ourselves'. Because of what we had been told on previous shows, we were thinking of production costs instead of possibilities.

In our premise for 'Ravage Island', we had Mumm-Ra grabbing the Sword of Omens. It was explained to us that the Sword could do no evil or be used by evil. We discussed our story ideas with Peter Lawrence before we wrote the outline and then discussed the outline before we wrote the script. Peter wrote very detailed notes.

82. Time Switch (3.5 Stars)
Written by: Sandy Fries
US Broadcast Date: * 22 September 1987
UK Broadcast Date: N/A

Larry Kenney's vocal chords are stretched to breaking point in a light-hearted adventure that takes Lion-O back to his days as a kitten. 'Time Switch' is a somewhat bizarre and unusual entry for the series, yet it succeeds in its aims. While it isn't the most profound of episodes, it is strangely engaging, and the viewer can't help but anticipate what form the rejuvenating Lion-O will take next.

The story begins with an enjoyable reference back to the very first episode of the series as the ThunderCats decide to belatedly tidy up the wreckage from their initial crash on Third Earth. Using a strangely Earth-like crane (rather than a more obvious piece of ThunderCat machinery such as the Hovercat or Thunderstrike), Lion-O falls foul of the escaped contents of the Time Suspension Capsule, causing his age to wind back periodically.

The concept is a novel one, and we're treated to the antics of a particularly mischievous Lord of the ThunderCats as he causes havoc around Cats' Lair. There is a well-crafted sense of jeopardy throughout as we learn that, if left untreated, Lion-O's condition will cause his very existence to be nullified. Kenney does a brilliant job of presenting a recognisable voice for Lion-O, raising an octave higher each time his age recedes. The character designers also ably present ingenious versions of the youngster. (Watch out for the humorous folds in Lion-O's clothes as they no longer fit.)

The climax to the episode is well seeded as we return to the Cave of Time, first seen in the season one adventure 'Trouble with Time'. Snarf's brainwave to lure baby Lion-O into the cave with a biscuit is twee, but suits the mood perfectly. Moments to look out for include the blatant inclusion of the LJN toy Tongue-A-Saurus and Pacific Animation Corporation's brilliant decision to craft a bespoke 'ThunderCats Ho!' sequence for the young Lion-O. The scene of Tygra passing Lion-O through the prison bars is also inspired. 'Wanna give it a try, little fella?' asks Tygra. 'Lion-O ThunderCat' squeals the infant.

Writer's Commentary from Sandy Fries:

I really enjoyed 'Time Switch'. Great animation, and I just like the idea of this big, brave, strong and noble character reverting back and back and back to a tiny little baby, and we get to see him being a little awkward and nervous. If you're going to do that to a character, make it the strongest character, because that makes it the most interesting. It wouldn't have worked with Snarf, because he's kind of like a kid anyway. So I was intrigued by the idea of pulling a character back in time.

I liked the title 'Time Switch'. Certain words together sound cool, and I was proud of that. I remember there was a thing called the Cave of Time that Lion-O crawled into, and I think they lured him in there with a biscuit. I liked the idea of luring this little kid in there who would grow older, and thought it would be cool visually. Also, at the beginning of the episode, there's a crane uncovering the capsule, and I like to start an episode with a strong visual. You don't want an animated episode to be a bunch of talking heads.

It was kind of fun to write dialogue for Lion-O as a young kid and a baby, and I remember saying to myself, 'Let's put him in a place that would really change his character'. What you always try to do is to take a character and throw him into a really big dilemma, and this big character faces a heck of a dilemma when he's a leader of a large bunch of cat people.

I thought the voice work on my episodes was excellent. I like the way they regressed the Lion-O character vocally – that was terrific – and the Snarf voice was great to write dialogue for.

83. The Sound Stones (3 Stars)
Written by: J Larry Carroll
US Broadcast Date: * 23 September 1987
UK Broadcast Date: N/A

There is precious little original material to be seen in 'The Sound Stones' and, though it has its redeeming features, it epitomises the stagnant repetition of the early episodes of season two. The main problem is a lack of new characters to inject some excitement into proceedings. During this run of episodes, we merely see constant battles between the ThunderCats and their established foes. In short, the series feels as though it needs a new direction.

'For the last time Vultureman, no!' screams Slithe, in one of the series' best opening lines. For a moment, the episode seems reminiscent of a first season entry featuring a 'Vultureman's weapon of the week'-style plot. Even less originality is on show when events descend into the usual fracas involving the Lunataks. One of the other failings of 'The Sound Stones' is the poor characterisation of Vultureman. Gone are his previous cunning and arrogance; instead, the Mutant genius is reduced to a parody of his former self, prancing across Darkside. Other plot points are poorly explained, such as Snarfer's knowledge of Third Earth legend, despite him having lived on the planet for only a short time. (Perhaps his research is extremely comprehensive …?) Furthermore, the use of Snarfer to explain events seems an unfortunate choice.

While in previous episodes steps had clearly been taken to try to integrate the 'old' and 'new' ThunderCats, here starts a growing trend for placing the original cats in their Lair and Bengali, Lynx-O and Pumyra in the Tower of Omens. This brings to mind Lion-O's stirring speech in 'ThunderCats Ho! Part V' where he invited the Thunderian newcomers to live amongst his team. While their separation facilitates the expansion of operations on Third Earth, it does little for ThunderCat morale!

Lynx-O once again takes centre stage here, proving that he is, by far, the most interesting and engaging character amongst the newcomers, a fact clearly not going unnoticed by the scriptwriters. In the episode's favour, there is a brief, but effective, attack on the HoverCat, and utter mediocrity is avoided by the appealing inclusion of Sondora and the Darkside ruins in which she resides. Her prophetic summary that the ThunderCats will one day succeed in ridding the planet of evil is well placed and ends proceedings on a positive note.

Writer's Commentary from J Larry Carroll:

I'm not sure where the idea for 'The Sound Stones' originated. I know writing Vultureman was a draw for me. It was my first *ThunderCats* script and I really wanted to write for the 'original' villains, even though the Lunataks had taken over the villain franchise by this point. I don't think it's my best work on the show; I wasn't quite in the zone yet.

I liked writing for Lion-O, the ThunderKittens and Panthro. It took me a while to warm up to Snarf, but in the end I had a lot of fun writing him. Never did find interesting ways to use Tygra and Cheetara. Not that they were 'bad' characters; I just never seemed to come up with stories that made good use of them.

The villains were a hoot. Loved writing Mumm-Ra and his crew of villainous minions. I wasn't as enthusiastic about the Lunataks, but still had fun with them.

84. Day of the Eclipse (4 Stars)
Written by: Kimberly Morris
US Broadcast Date: * 24 September 1987
UK Broadcast Date: N/A

'Day of the Eclipse' is another strong offering from Kimberly Morris, featuring a plan from Mumm-Ra to cause maximum difficulties for the ThunderCats, or, in Mumm-Ra's own words: 'Cause stone to crumble, and steel to corrode, systems to fail and friends to quarrel'. In the difficult task of trying to inject originality into one of Mumm-Ra's many plans, this 'Day of Decay' hits the right note, and the idea that the effects of the curse will last until the next eclipse (a once-in-a-hundred-years event) adds a much-needed timeline to count down to the climax of the episode.

The scenes covering the demise of the ThunderCats' Lair and equipment are brilliantly written and animated. From Panthro's discovery of faults at the Lair, to the out-of-control ThunderTank ploughing through the Berbil field, there is plenty in 'Day of the Eclipse' to entertain. The success of the episode is directly attributable to Morris's script and, in a run of generally lacklustre adventures, she resurrects a much needed sense of anticipation and jeopardy by precise plotting and a good understanding of timing. Further highlights include Cheetara's fire-fighting in Cats' Lair and the moment that the Lair, quite literally, crumbles to dust.

The episode's conclusion isn't perhaps its strongest virtue, however the eclipse that Lion-O generates from the Sword (thus cancelling Mumm-Ra's magic) is just about clever enough to give a satisfactory end to an exciting adventure.

Writer's Commentary from Kimberly Morris

There probably was an eclipse the week I wrote this episode and it gave me a hook to hang a story on. I pull ideas from everywhere – newspapers, weather reports, conversations I overhear on the bus. You name it. But eclipses also have an iconic and atavistic significance. Ancient peoples were terrified by them. For that matter, present-day people still read all sorts of 'the-end-is-near' meanings into weather and planetary events. An eclipse 'resonates' as something that signals a sinister shift in reality. From a technical perspective, an eclipse is just a good plot device to use instead of a ticking clock.

I think the whole landscape of the show had a sort of ancient look that suggested decay – so I extrapolated from there. When writing animation, I visualised far more vividly than I do when writing novels. You have to do that when writing animation, because you are really writing like a director. With animation, if you cannot visualise it, then you cannot tell your story. So first you must visualise, then you must develop a facility for describing complex visuals.

85. Sideswipe (1.5 Stars)
Written by: William Overgard
US Broadcast Date: * 25th September 1987
UK Broadcast Date: N/A

Ranking amongst the very poorest episodes of *ThunderCats*, 'Side Swipe' is almost without redemption. It is simply a step too far away from the confines of the series and, along with other bizarre instalments, gives life to writer Bill Overgard's divided reputation.

All time lows from the episode include Snarfer flying to get a Mexican take-out from the Berbils' Taco stand (the less said about that, the better), Chilla's 'hit and run' with Snarfer, and the constant 'cop' references as Mandora gives chase. 'Side Swipe' lumbers from nonsense to parody and has virtually nothing in common with other episodes of *ThunderCats*.

There are still touches of Overgard's usual thoroughness – the clever, though out-of-place, use of chilli to 'defrost' Mandora is a nice touch – but the episode is a little boring by the writer's standards. The scenes with Lynx-O's disappearing Braille Board are just ludicrous and poorly explained. 'Are you telling me, what I was holding in my hands was an idea?' asks Luna, who clearly has a better grasp of this absurdity than the audience. Further assaults on the series' integrity include Vultureman reclining as he reads a newspaper, and an overuse of humour, not assisted by the helpful 'punchline drum' as Snarfer delivers his gags. Perhaps the episode's only redeeming features are the disturbing design work and the use of the Lunataks' mind machine on Lynx-O.

'Side Swipe' would, fortunately, be one of only a handful of episodes that perhaps should have been culled prior to production. However, for every disaster like 'Side Swipe', Bill Overgard produced a lot of classics of the calibre of 'Sword in a Hole'. Overall, his legacy to the series remains safely intact.

Script Editor's Commentary from Peter Lawrence:

When we get deep into the second season reviews and comments, my memory isn't as reliable. I know the first season characters, arcs and locations far more intimately. Perhaps this late into the second season my hands were full with *SilverHawks* and even the early stages of *The Comic Strip*, which was a nightmare to develop: four shows in one, and Jules Bass was particularly difficult.

'side Swipe' is a strange combo of Bill's wilder ideas – such as the inclusion of Mexican food – and a straighter *ThunderCats* plot involving the Lunataks. It also reflects our direction to reuse characters with whom both the audience and the animators were familiar. Nonetheless, Bill just can't help himself – the Braille Board. You can almost hear him arguing with himself, veering between the wild and the conventional, then finally using a classic Sword of Omens *deus ex machina* to bring the story to an end.

On a personal note: by this time, we simply had too many characters; particularly, too many heroes. I'm sure that was the result of Leisure Concepts/LJN pressure. I firmly believe that it's impossible to wield this many heroes convincingly – at least in dramatic terms – and to do justice to their personalities and abilities. I had that problem even with the core group and was always looking for a way to drop one or two off on a paid vacation. A lot of writers simply split the group up so that one bunch was off on one mission and another on another – then intercut between the jeopardy and perhaps tie it together by working it so that one group has to resolve its jeopardy in order to help the other. But, for me, that becomes very formulaic, and I think the show began to suffer from these and related problems.

86. Mumm-Rana's Belt (3.5 Stars)
Written by: James Rose
US Broadcast Date: * 28th September 1987
UK Broadcast Date: N/A

Bob Haney's character Mumm-Rana is resurrected in a sequel from writer James Rose. Here, she is revealed to have defeated Luna's grandmother generations previously and retained her powerful belt. Her return to the series is welcome, though it is does raise the question why she did not wear the belt in her previous appearance in season one, given how fiercely she guards it now. The scenes featuring the near-destruction of Mumm-Rana's pyramid are distressing, yet the character participates little in the episode beyond this and is reduced to a supporting role.

The episode begins with the somewhat contrived scene of Luna inadvertently overhearing some Third Earth folklore, 'So that's what happened to Grandmother's belt!' she declares. As the action progresses, we finally get to see a little more of Pumyra, and it's nice to see she can run at super speeds like Cheetara. The rather annoying Luna is also used at her best here. Her 'full sized' form is far more competent and menacing than her usual one and, as such, the character seems much more endearing.

The episode's set-up and resolution revolve around Luna's poor handling of her steed, Amok. Having treated him with contempt throughout the episode, she meets her downfall through him exacting his 'revenge'. It's a nice enough sentiment, and the episode has sufficient content to sustain its duration, though it falls a little short of being particularly spectacular. Though it was admirable to attempt to give the young and inexperienced Pumyra a chance to shine, this chance is somewhat squandered, and an opportunity for added characterisation may have been missed.

However, there are plenty of enjoyable aspects to 'Mumm-Rana's Belt', and the Mutants' small but engaging appearance helps considerably. The scene of Monkian and Slithe playing cards in Castle Plun-Darr (and not wishing to be disturbed) is a small, yet incredibly astute commentary from James Rose. While Mumm-Ra and the Lunataks are motivated by the need to obliterate the ThunderCats, one gets the impression the Mutants would prefer a quieter existence. They are constantly urged into battle by Mumm-Ra, rather than having any personal ambition to wreak havoc themselves.

Writer's Commentary from James Rose:

I am surprised how the visual style of animation has radicalised since *ThunderCats* was made. The episode now appears almost quaint to me.

Rankin/Bass was a well-oiled machine and Peter Lawrence was one of the best in the business as story editor. Indeed he remains a major talent in the industry today. I wrote one of the last set of episodes for the show. I handed in my script to Peter and he ran with it. It's really too many years ago to say which parts are mine and which Peter changed. For this writer, it's all thousands of pages ago. Memory fades or gets whited out with time. What I can offer is that [the production team] were a great bunch to work with, and many went on from that show to have fabulous careers in the industry, but I was not one of them so blessed. They were friendly and very professional, and I remember the cartoonists to have been a wild and nutty and extremely creative bunch.

87. Hachiman's Honor (3.5 Stars)
Written by: J Larry Carroll
US Broadcast Date: * 29 September 1987
UK Broadcast Date: N/A

'Hachiman's Honor' isn't the best episode to feature the ThunderCats' samurai ally, although his characterisation is spot on and Larry Carroll does a good job of breathing life to him.

By far the most exciting component of the episode is the Automoton, who sports a great design. It's an ingenious concept that, being a machine, the Automoton is neither good nor evil and, as such, can circumvent the ThunderCutter's in-built defence that, like the Sword of Omens, it won't respond to evil. Sadly, these scenes are a little brief and could easily have been expanded to make a more engaging adventure.

The episode begins promisingly, and the 'good Samaritan' scenes of Hachiman assisting Luna work well. Other highlights include the beautiful ruins where much of the episode takes place, and these set the perfect tone for proceedings. The mysterious and tenacious chains that emerge from the ground and pursue our heroes are also an inspired addition.

Overall, 'Hachiman's Honor' is a competent offering, however Luna's mysterious ability to appear in the clouds is a little bemusing, and the episode diverts its attention in too many directions, rather than concentrating on the more unique element, Automoton, that lies at its heart.

Writer's Commentary from J Larry Carroll:

I liked Hachiman and wanted to use him in a story. Plus I had directed a film (*Ghost Warrior*) several years earlier that was about the trials and tribulations of a 400–year-old frozen samurai brought to life in modern LA. So I felt I could bring a special point of view to the story. It was fun to write and I was pleased with the way it turned out. (Much better than *Ghost Warrior*, by the way.) The only disappointment was the chains. Which is as much my fault as anyone's. They just didn't animate well.

88. Runaways (4 Stars)
Written by: Bill Ratter
US Broadcast Date: * 30 September 1987
UK Broadcast Date: N/A

Episodes revolving around WilyKit and WilyKat are an acquired taste. However, while the pair may not always have been involved in the most action-packed stories, they were essential to the construction of the series, and it was necessary for the writers to work them into plots to prevent them falling into the background.

Here, Deborah Goodwin (writing under her Bill Ratter pseudonym) brilliantly crafts a story around the ThunderKittens' perception that they are ignored by the adult ThunderCat group. With the threat of 'running away' being ever-present in most households, this show would have really resonated with its target audience, who would have been able to empathise easily with the Kittens' predicament. Just as Kimberly Morris did in 'Trouble with ThunderKittens', Goodwin writes perfectly for the two characters, and the scenes showing the effects of the poisonous berries are deeply worrying. Arguably the episode's weakness is the character of Kudi, who is a little nauseating and sports a deeply strange design. However, this does have the advantage that Mumm-Ra's impersonation of the character really gives the overtly friendly creature a sinister edge.

Mumm-Ra's 'infiltration schemes' are becoming a little tired by the eighty-eighth episode, but this one is handled pretty well and is not a huge component of the plot. Sealing the ThunderCats into the Lair is a nice touch, and the cat leaping from the sword and forcibly ejecting Mumm-Ra really injects a great dose of originality into events.

If one views carefully, a noticeable animation error can be seen from Pacific Animation Corporation – WilyKit's dialogue is spoken by WilyKat as the Kittens explain the events of the episode to the 'real' Kudi at the conclusion.

Overall, 'Runaways' is a pleasing member second season episode. One of its strengths is undoubtedly Goodwin's dialogue, and there is some well-judged character interplay, especially when the ThunderCats debate whether or not Kudi can visit the Lair. 'Half the time we have to stay home and miss the action anyway,' accuses WilyKat. 'You just make us feel like kids!' asserts WilyKit.

Writer's Commentary from Deborah Goodwin (Bill Ratter):

I lived in England when I wrote *ThunderCats* so I didn't meet the production team. The brief was very limited if not non- existent. I remember reading about someone who got lost in the outback, or perhaps it was the jungle, who managed to survive, just, on eating, amongst other things, berries. I decided that rather than use the berries as a survival tool in this script, I would use them negatively and build a story from that point.

I was aware of the moral responsibility a writer faced when writing for the show. It did affect my writing because it had to contain a moral, which I hope I achieved. However, I didn't realise that they hired a child psychologist to review scripts.

89. Hair of the Dog (3 Stars)
Written by: Chris Trengove
US Broadcast Date: * 1 October 1987
UK Broadcast Date: N/A

'Hair of the Dog' is, at best, a strange *ThunderCats* episode. To give Chris Trengove credit, the script is well constructed. In the opening moments, those ThunderCats who are not central to the plot are effectively written out – sent on an apparent space mission. While this may seem a simple touch, it is surprising how many similar stories simply omit members of the vast cast of characters altogether with no explanation.

The main gist of the story revolves around the transposition of Snarf with Ma-Mutt. This results in some humorous sequences, and Ma-Mutt speaking through Snarf (complete with growls) is a highlight. Bernard Hoffer's second season compositions are also used well here; there is a beautiful piece heard as Snarfer wakes up and tells the crew of the Tower of Omens about his concerns for his uncle.

The principal weakness of 'Hair of the Dog' lies in Mumm-Ra's poorly-conceived plan. Though Ma-Mutt succeeds in poisoning Lion-O, Mumm-Ra then simply waits for the latter to recover, rather than utilising his opportunity. Things are resolved by Snarf's resourceful use of the Ancient Spirits of Evil. Though the idea of him recanting Mumm-Ra's spell is ingenious, one has to wonder if the Spirits would really grant him his wish; and the notion of Snarf-Ra the Everliving (complete with a heavily electronically-modified voice) is a little silly. However, 'Hair of the Dog' is full of originality and has to be given credit for that. The 'giant Snarf' is reminiscent of Chris Trengove's season one adventure 'The Wolf Rat', but it does help the episode stand out, given its essentially run-of-the-mill premise.

Writer's Commentary from Chris Trengove:

Snarf-Ra the Ever-Living – love it! (Nuts and bolts dept: I have the original typewritten script of this episode, and it's a mess of crossings-out, Tippex and Sellotape. Hey kids, that's how we did it before computers …)

'Hair of the Dog' is a snappy title, which prompted someone to ask which I generally came up with first, the title or the idea. The answer is 'always the idea' – the title would generally be the last thing you'd worry about.

90. Vultureman's Revenge (3 Stars)
Written by: Herb Engelhardt
US Broadcast Date: * 2 October 1987
UK Broadcast Date: N/A

There are precious few new ideas explored in 'Vultureman's Revenge', which adheres to the 'Vultureman's wacky invention of the week' formula from the first season.

On this occasion, we see a less-than-spectacular plan from Vultureman to construct a Thundranium weapon to destroy the protagonists. The story really doesn't delve any deeper than that most basic of ideas, and things roll along slowly as the Mutant's 'revenge' represents a pretty poor effort.

One nice touch is that Vultureman allies himself with the Lunataks rather than the Mutants. There are also some interesting snippets of action and dialogue, including Vultureman's declaration that he hates the phrase 'Two birds with one stone'. Additionally, the scene with the Wollo playing the melody from the *ThunderCats* theme tune on his instrument is a fun stroke of genius, and the music fits perfectly to the background cue.

The story's resolution gives Bengali an unusual moment to shine, and it's nice to see the return of Jaga (being seen less and less as the series progresses) to advise Lion-O to use the Sword's powers to restore the Wollo's frozen village (which is well illustrated by the animators). Overall, the episode simply suffers from a severe case of *deja vu*.

Writer's Commentary from Herb Engelhardt:

I felt the opening titles of *ThunderCats* had better animation than the episodes – not uncommon in heavily-merchandised shows.

Dramatically it would have been more interesting to see the villains exploit character flaws in the ThunderCats rather than just use Thundranium to weaken them (as happens in both of my episodes). And *vice-versa*, a villain with a glimmer of redeeming quality would have had more potential for better storytelling. Of course this would have required more time than the production schedule allowed. It would have been nice to offer a chance for development of characters with more depth and opportunity for growth, perhaps for a more mature audience. Disney did pretty well in that vein, which is why the product had so much cross-generational appeal.

Overall, I think I might have had a better chance to take some of my own advice if I had been involved earlier in the show, had the character bible to work with etc. And of course more time.

91-95. ThunderCubs Parts I-V (4 Stars)
Written by: Peter Lawrence
US Broadcast Date: * 5-9 September 1988
UK Broadcast Date: N/A

It's all change for *ThunderCats*, with an epic five-part serial from script editor Peter Lawrence. Without doubt, the early second season episodes had seen various plotlines become stagnant and repetitive. Though there were notable exceptions, the series had the feeling of being tired and in need of a shake-up. Fortunately, this is exactly what Lawrence provides here, and in one feature-length adventure we see the reformation of Thundera, the subjugation of Third Earth by the Lunataks, a new and more terrifying guise for Mumm-Ra and much more besides.

'ThunderCubs' begins the slow return of the ThunderCats to their home planet. This is an incredibly astute move by the programme-makers, as part of the problem with the preceding adventures was the change in the spirit of the series. The ThunderCats were originally introduced as survivors of a dying world. They had to survive the many perils thrown at them on Third Earth, and this was the driving force of the stories. As the show progressed, the ThunderCats were able to not only survive but thrive on their new world. New bases and characters were introduced and the antagonists' plans became ever more far-fetched. In essence, a status quo had been achieved, the ThunderCats having proven their ability to survive anything Mumm-Ra and his cohorts could throw at them. By taking the main characters back to Thundera, this whole process is renewed. Once again the ThunderCats are plummeted into a difficult situation, and it opens the doors for original storytelling.

As shrewd as the reformation of Thundera was, the way it is explained in this serial leaves something to be desired. The revelation that chunks of the planet are rejoining together raises no scientific problems, but the idea that people, races and even architecture have survived on small chunks of the planet (with no atmosphere, gravity or natural resources etc) is just plain silly. While we can easily overlook this brief explanation, it would have been more palatable had Thundera's return been the result of the Sword of Omens' powers or similar 'magic'. Grounding it in science (and a flawed science) feels like a misstep.

Nonetheless, the first episode of the serial begins proceedings in earnest. We are given a tantalising glimpse of the history of Thundera as we see Ratilla and a young Jaga engage in combat. Here, Lawrence hits us with a wonderful explanation for the events of the very first episode of *ThunderCats*: the destruction of Thundera was inadvertently caused by Jaga casting the powerful Sword of Plun-Darr into the core of the planet to contain its magic. As an explanation, this is far more enticing than a freak earthquake, which had previously been assumed responsible.

As ever with a Lawrence script, certain aspects can be relied upon to shine. The dialogue and characterisation are perfect, a great example being Mumm-Ra's plea to his superiors: 'Ancient Spirits of Evil, grant me, Mumm-Ra, your venomous bootlicker, the disguise of Snarfer' (incidentally a character brilliantly portrayed in his evil guise by Bob McFadden). Lion-O's self doubt in the fourth episode is also a touching moment in the character's development. 'The real problem is that I've made all the wrong decisions,' Lion-O admits to Snarf. 'Maybe I shouldn't be Lord of the ThunderCats'. Fortunately, Jaga is on hand to reassure him: 'You can't expect everything you do to be an instant success, Lion-O!'

The pace of the five-part serial is also well judged. Aside from the usual slight lull in the middle acts, the adventure races along, and the eponymous ThunderCubs don't even appear until half way through the penultimate episode. Perhaps this indicates that the naming of the story is a little ill-judged. The ThunderCub element is actually amongst its weakest attributes – the exploration of

Thundera being a far more interesting and engaging story strand.

'ThunderCubs' is a high-octane adventure drama and other highlights include some great traps for Lion-O and Panthro in Mumm-Ra's pyramid in episode one. (Watch out for the humorously blue-tinted stock footage of Lion-O calling his friends as the pair are trapped underwater.) The heavily modified 'intergalactic' Feliner is a nice idea, and the craft plummeting through the atmosphere with its crew frozen is a great sequence in episode two.

The serial is also a visual masterpiece, not just in the animation from Pacific Animation Corporation but also in the scripted placement of numerous small, almost insignificant shots that really help to set the tone. Lawrence is an expert at writing for animation and really maximises the impact of his script directions. The chain-ganged Snarfs are a perfect example of an incredibly sinister image in the story, as we see hundreds of imprisoned Snarfs on Thundera. Even minor scenes featuring the ThunderCats camping in their sleeping bags paint a picture of intense vulnerability. The character designers and art team also do a superb job of bringing these five episodes to screen. Mumm-Ra's redesign is astonishingly powerful, and the moment he creeps up on Lion-O in the final episode is incredibly effective. The various new accessories and clothing (such as the thermal protection suits) are well designed and really help this serial seem new and refreshing. The ThunderCubs are also an interesting visual addition. The young Tygra and Cheetara are designed well, but Panthro's younger self actually looks more like an older and frailer version of the character (though Earle Hyman's more youthful voice for him is surprisingly effective given his deep vocal range). Mumm-Ra's 'new' pyramid is, fortunately, distinguished from his original on Third Earth and features a modified Sarcophagus chamber and octagonal cauldron. Only the presentation of the Canyon of Youth is perhaps a little questionable, its overly colourful landscape being somewhat twee.

The new Thundera, as referenced in the story, is indeed a strange place. Effort has clearly gone into distinguishing it from Third Earth with the use of colourful skies and a different colour palette. While the looming moons in the skyscape make for an interesting visual, the explanation of the planet being under the influence of the moons of Plun-Darr seems a little like technobabble. However, within the context of the series, it's just about strange enough to work.

The conclusion of the mini-series features some brilliantly executed battle scenes between Lion-O and the newly-modified Mumm-Ra. The manifestation of the Ancient Spirits of Evil is an original touch, and the new Mumm-Ra is genuinely chilling! The 'freeze frame' effect used during the battle is perhaps misplaced and, though we have seen this 'crayon' effect in previous cliffhangers, it doesn't work as well here and dates the episode. The return to the Cave of Time is a little repetitive, though it works well enough, and all of the strands of the story are adequately resolved. The placement of the magical flute earlier in the story works well in helping Lion-O to return to Third Earth courtesy of Mumm-Ra's time and space machine, although the latter craft seems a stretch too far for Mumm-Ra's powers.

Ultimately, 'ThunderCubs' ushers in a new era for the series and, from this point on, things will never be quite the same.

Writer's Commentary from Peter Lawrence:

One reason for the development of the five-parters was to consolidate them into full-length movies; but, of course, they also had to work as stand-alone episodes, because the second run broadcast schedules couldn't guarantee consecutive airings. This explains why, despite the fact that there are so many parallel stories going on in each episode, they are not effectively linked throughout the five-parter. There is, in fact, an element of the kitchen sink at play here – throw everything in and see if it works. In this particular five-parter, the consensus seems to be that it does, perhaps because there's such a wide range of villains in play; because Snarf and Snarfer get to star; and because, for once, Mumm-Ra gets to have some extended success!

I honestly cannot say why we returned to Thundera. I don't even recall if it was a Jules directive. Perhaps we felt we had tapped Third Earth's potential to its fullest extent. (Though why would we believe that? If we wanted new locations and scenarios, we could simply have added them.) Maybe there was an element of 'returning home' … and the possibilities of all the 'stuff' that had been left behind.

96. Totem of Dera (3 Stars)
Written by: J Larry Carroll
US Broadcast Date: * 12 September 1988
UK Broadcast Date: N/A

The most noticeable attribute of 'The Totem of Dera' is that, after the events of the previous five-part serial (which saw the storytelling possibilities of the series expanded enormously), things have reset, temporarily, to how they were before. In fact, this episode has more in common with early season one adventures. It's a typical ThunderCats vs Mutants and Mumm-Ra set-up and remains faithful to the early series formula. Lion-O's battle with the generic swamp demon, in particular, is extremely reminiscent of days gone by.

'The Totem of Dera' isn't a particularly remarkable story, though it features some interesting ideas. The Totem's special ability, namely to heal, works well and stands in contrast to the usual 'gadgets' seen in the series, which are more commonly used to destroy than to revive. The idea that the device can go beyond restoration and actually give life to inanimate objects is just about credible too.

Larry Carroll takes the brave decision to give Snarfer top billing here. The scenes with Jaga trying to communicate with him are by far the best of the episode, and it's an original idea to have Jaga forced to communicate with a member of the team other than Lion-O. It's also nice to see Snarfer given added characterisation, rather than always being his uncle's stooge. A touch of welcome humour is brought to proceedings with the following Mutant exchange: 'Are we gonna let him talk to us like that?' asks Monkian, after they have been called a 'bunch of cowards' by Lion-O. 'Yes,' replies Vultureman, before scuttling away!

The drawbacks of the episode include the rather improbable revelation that the ThunderClaw, despite its size, cannot hold three people (even more incredible given the team comprises of WilyKit and Snarfer); and Lion-O's poisoning, though a decent scene in itself, is effected a little too easily.

Overall, while 'The Totem of Dera' is a reasonably enjoyable *ThunderCats* adventure, it's an anti-climax for those waiting to see the fate of New Thundera unfold.

Writer's Commentary from J Larry Carroll:

I was drawn to the idea of Snarfer and Jaga working together (albeit Snarfer was unaware they were) to save Lion-O. And I liked writing a story in which an outmatched Snarfer takes on the Mutants. I think this was also the only time I wrote a script that featured Snarfer. (Truthfully, I never understood why Snarfer was in the series; it's always been a bit confusing to me, the whole Snarf-Snarfer thing.)

97. Chain of Loyalty (3 Stars)
Written by: Bill Ratter & Peter Lawrence
US Broadcast Date: * 13 September 1988
UK Broadcast Date: N/A

The story arc of New Thundera resumes here as the ThunderCats return to the planet in the first of many missions to recover the Treasure of Thundera. The episode opens with a nicely-placed scene of Lion-O frustratedly trying to decipher the Book of Omens. Upon noticing the Chain of Loyalty, Jaga bids him retrieve the object lest some dire consequences befall the team.

The episode's greatest failing is the poorly-judged idea of a device being responsible for keeping the peace amongst the ThunderCats. While it's certainly an original notion, the unwelcome inference is that the ThunderCats' allegiance to each other stems from compulsion. This seems to stands at odds with the morality of the series and is a particularly cynical take on their team arrangement. During their many adventures, the ThunderCats have shown loyalty through their desire to honour the traditions of Thundera and through genuine friendship. The suggestion that, upon the destruction of an artifact, they will revert to savages intent on destroying one another discredits their integrity in the extreme. It is a little surprising that this negative connotation was not excised from the scripts by the production team. Another misstep comes when we get one of the most overt and misplaced moral messages of the entire series. To have Panthro finding a drinks can on Thundera is unsubtle enough, but the immortal line that follows is cringeworthy in the extreme: 'So, even on Thundera, people leave their litter all over the place – a very nasty habit!'

Nonetheless, 'The Chain of Loyalty' has plenty on offer to entertain. Though the aforementioned 'fight' scenes are the episode's downfall, they also provide its saving grace: as the ThunderCats fight Lion-O one by one, his attempts to protect his friends, despite their deeds, are admirable. 'I didn't want to do this,' he says, forced to use the Sword against them.

Writer's Commentary from Deborah Goodwin (Bill Ratter):

My inspiration for this came from a conversation I had with someone about teamwork, and how loyalty and trust in each other play a big part in making a good working team but also how fragile and easily that trust and loyalty could be broken. This was particularly on my mind, as I was writing the scripts in the UK and didn't really feel part of a team.

I remember a number of revisions to my *ThunderCats* scripts and, at times, script editor Peter Lawrence would be at the end of the phone telling me that so-and-so wouldn't say that, or so-and-so wouldn't do that, so re-write!

98. Crystal Canyon (5 Stars)
Written by: Sandy Fries
US Broadcast Date: * 14 September 1988
UK Broadcast Date: N/A

'Crystal Canyon' is a rare second-season example of a near-perfect episode. It has an abundance of action to provide the visual excitement needed for a truly classic adventure, but additionally is led by some superb character development. Not only that, but the character in question is the underused Tygra, which makes Sandy Fries' achievements in this script all the more commendable.

The story revolves around an energising crystal that clouds the mind of whoever possesses it. In this case, it is Tygra who becomes addicted to the powers contained within. This concept fits perfectly with Tygra's previous form in being susceptible to addiction in adventures such as 'The Garden of Delights' and 'Turmagar the Tuska'. What follow are some of the best-scripted character moments of the entire series, beginning with a brutal exchange between Tygra and Snarf. 'I might have expected you to side with Lion-O,' snaps Tygra. 'I didn't mean anything bad,' whimpers Snarf. Tygra then journeys back to Cats' Lair where, in turn, his teammates visit him, all greeted as though they mean to attack him. Tygra's power trip culminates with a beautiful glimpse into the character's reserved nature: 'Ever since I was a kid, I was shy – but with the keystone I feel self-confident. For the first time in my life, I feel like I could do anything!' Tygra's accusation that Lion-O relies on the powers of the Sword of Omens in a similar fashion offers food for thought; and the scenes of Tygra frustrated and seated at his drafting table also add to the texture of the episode.

The depth and writing finesse in 'Crystal Canyon' stand in stark contrast to their lack in 'The Garden of Delights', which used addiction gratuitously. Where this adventure succeeds so well is in tackling the space between the 'black and white' of children's storytelling. While *ThunderCats* usually shows characters as either purely good or purely evil, Tygra's transformation places him somewhere between these two extremes. Unlike on previous occasions when the ThunderCats have fallen foul of outside influences, causing them to switch completely from good to evil, in 'Crystal Canyon', aspects of Tygra's character remain unchanged, leading to a much more intriguing dilemma.

Outside of the core premise, the other story components shine in equal measure. The Canyon itself is perfectly conceived and animated, and Pacific Animation Corporation show their usual thoroughness by painting a reflection of the ThunderStrike in the crystals. Though a small flourish, this kind of detail really adds depth to the visuals and is unusual in cartoons of that era. As the ThunderStrike crashes, we see the stark and powerful imagery of a lifeless Lion-O and Snarf slumped out of the vehicle. The scenes that follow deal with death in a more head-on way than is usual for the series, with the declaration that Lion-O's 'pulse is growing weaker by the moment'. Because of its target audience, the series would often talk in terms of 'destruction' and 'obliteration' rather than death and, at times, a sense of real danger was lost. 'Crystal Canyon' increases the potential jeopardy by showing the characters' contemplation that Lion-O is not immortal, as explained by Lynx-O, who tells Snarf that the Sword of Omens is no guarantee of his survival.

The episode's ending resolves the events of 'Crystal Canyon' nicely, and another brilliant touch from the series' art team is Tygra's subtle reduction in muscle tone throughout the story (causing his clothing to become increasingly baggy) before he 'reinflates' as he regains his strength. As if anything else were needed, the episode even finishes with one of the show's better 'end gags' as Panthro returns from a mission to Thundera, complete with the gift of a crystal. 'Do you have anything in wood,' jokes Tygra.

Writer's Commentary from Sandy Fries:

On *ThunderCats*, I tried to deal with issues that people might have a problem with. Back then and still, young people, whether kids or teenagers, viewed addiction as a big thing, so we had an addiction episode. It was an addiction to crystals in *ThunderCats*, however that's a metaphor for anything: an addiction to drugs; a bad habit you develop that you do at school that you shouldn't be doing; an addiction to alcohol; and so on. So I remember saying, 'Great, I've got a theme here that can connect to a lot of people in the audience; not everyone, but a lot.'

I was proud of 'Crystal Canyon', because it had a very strong lesson to it, which is that you've got to have the ability to overcome bad habits and addictions. There were also some cool visuals that I thought up, including the Canyons themselves. I remember thinking, what has *ThunderCats* not done that could be a cool message? When I hit on that I thought, 'I'll call Peter Lawrence'. The production was very well done on it.

One of the reasons I used Tygra, who generally wasn't used as much as other characters, was that story editors and producers usually like that. An easier way to sell a story idea is to think of a character that's not used as much as the others and come up with an idea for him. The producer then sees the value of showing that character in a more prominent way than before. It's usually a selling point – unless it's a character that's unused because it's not a good character. On *ThunderCats*, the easy characters to write for were Snarf, because he was funny, Lion-O and Panthro. Tackling something that other writers hadn't tackled made it an easier sell for me – that's my mercenary side.

I do remember looking at what had been done before and thinking, 'What's some new territory I can work on that hasn't been explored?' The Mumm-Ra character was very cool, very visual, but nothing really occurred to me to spark me to think, 'Oh boy, that's a new direction'.

99. The Telepathy Beam (5 Stars)
Written by: Kimberly Morris
US Broadcast Date: * 15 September 1988
UK Broadcast Date: N/A

Unbelievably, two second season episodes in a row take the standard of storytelling to new heights. 'Telepathy Beam' works in the same way as its immediate predecessor, 'Crystal Canyon', in delivering some brilliant characterisation, this time for ThunderCat, Cheetara.

Cheetara's 'sixth sense' having been a mainstay of the series, writer Kimberly Morris cleverly plays with this notion and has Vultureman construct a device that can manufacture visions and place them in Cheetara's mind. Not only is this a return to form for the ingenious Vultureman (who has appeared in a run of terrible episodes lately), but it also facilitates exploring Cheetara's character traits in great detail. The teaming of Vultureman (as an inventor) and the Lunatak Aluro (with his mind control skills) is inspired, and the pair put together a competent plan to combat the ThunderCats. 'Soon her sixth sense won't be worth two cents,' jokes Vultureman.

After a run of 'inaccurate' manufactured predictions, Cheetara conceals her premonition of Panthro's fate for fear of embarrassment. This is a brilliantly astute response from the proud Cheetara and, when Panthro is found to be missing, Vultureman projects images of the ThunderCat trapped on Hook Mountain, imprisoned in Castle Plun-Darr and at the mercy of Mumm-Ra.

The episode races along and is beautifully paced, unfolding with perfection. Other highlights include Lion-O's visit to the Black Pyramid, where he falls foul of a trap courtesy of some unusual help from the Ancient Spirits of Evil, who come to life and pin him down. There is a strange absence of Mumm-Ra here, with only a cackle emanating from his sarcophagus, which is strangely pleasing and effective.

As with 'Crystal Canyon', the emotional depth of 'Telepathy Beam' makes it a truly classic *ThunderCats* adventure. Cheetara's journey from confidence to defeat to regained resolve is brilliant to watch. As she sits demoralised at one point, Lynx-O's advice that she should listen to her instincts results in a great monologue from the character. 'I am Cheetara,' she declares, in a psychedelic but astonishingly powerful animated sequence. 'In my heart, I know I am the strongest of my kind – the pride of my people. I am unique in this universe – and I will not be defeated!' This really represents the best aspects of *ThunderCats*: great writing, performances, animation and music.

With Cheetara's inner strength regained, the character realises that she has innate telekinetic abilities as well as telepathic powers; feeding back her emotions to destroy Vultureman's device and restore the *ThunderCats*. Though she is unsure if she can reuse this new power, she is confident she has now mastered her visions and declares they will no longer weaken her as they have in the past. This represents some great character progression for her, and is testament to Morris's acuity as a writer.

Writer's Commentary from Kimberly Morris

Cheetara's sixth sense had become something of gun on the wall that never got fired. (There's an old writing rule that stipulates that if there's a gun on the wall in Act I, somebody needs to get shot in Act II.) It was time to shoot somebody. Cheetara needed a story in which her sixth sense played a significant role.

I think male writers tend to think of female characters as foils for hyper-masculine heroes. Cheetara was certainly a great character, but I thought the 'sixth sense' thing was really just stereotypical 'female intuition' repackaged as a 'super-power.' But then I thought, well, why not? That's a pretty good super-power to have. Having said that, I think the reason the show appealed to girls as well as boys was that Lion-O and Snarf were highly empathetic and clearly capable of affection – traditionally 'feminine' traits. In that regard, I think the show had a sophisticated emotional subtext for its time. But I don't think it was intentional. It was probably a reflection of the ongoing national conversation about male and female roles, traits, etc.

Sadly, I'm not sure either sex has achieved much lasting progress in the 'super-hero' world. The tone and tenor of the genre today strike me as unrelentingly dystopian. The 'super-heroes' are often as violent and sociopathic as the villains. The female super-heroes might as well be men with enormous breasts. This, too, is probably not intentional, but a reflection of what is going on in the national psyche. America (indeed, much of the West) is in the midst of an identity crisis. We cannot find an identity that suits us. We used to think of ourselves as a super-heroic culture. Then we became a super-power harnessed to endeavours of dubious merit and political morality. Are we super-heroes? Or just super-powers? Are we good guys? Or bullies? Are we using our powers for good or evil? When we can't answer those questions, our default posture is: 'Who cares?' or 'What's the difference?' All of this socio-political confusion is reflected in the subtext of our popular culture.

100. Exile Isle (2.5 Stars)
Written by: William Overgard
US Broadcast Date: * 16 September 1988
UK Broadcast Date: N/A

'Exile Isle' marks a return for Captain Cracker amid a weak plot filled with the usual eccentricities of writer Bill Overgard. Events begin with a would-be attack from the Lunataks that proves to be the last straw for Lion-O and the ThunderCats. They assemble both a courtroom (beautifully decorated with a looming insignia and wooden booths) and a jury (courtesy of the many resident species of Third Earth), and judgment is duly passed to exile the Lunataks. On face value, this is a nice scene and a powerful indicator of the Code of Thundera gaining ground on Third Earth. However, no backstory is provided for the court or the overreaching technology required to 'teleport' the villains across the galaxy, which begs the question: why have the ThunderCats never used these prior to the events of 'Exile Isle'? It certainly is not through a lack of provocation.

As the episode progresses, things get stranger still. The weird creatures piloting the space tanker *Xlam Queen* seem more in keeping with *SilverHawks* than *ThunderCats*, and the script is simply too full of outrageous concepts for a single episode. While Overgard's ideas here are ingenious (e.g. killer palm trees), their execution is often too far-fetched (e.g. the bellows of Exile Isle concealing an entire 'shoal' planet). As Overgard penned more and more scripts for the series, a downward trend in the suitability of his work became evident. While his first season scripts pushed the show's boundaries, his second season offerings disregarded the boundaries entirely. Continuity is also thrown out of the window, and the ThunderStrike has now become an intergalactic space vehicle!

As a stand-alone adventure, 'Exile Isle' is entertaining. Highlights include the court scenes referenced above, and WilyKat whispering the location of the ThunderStrike to the Lunataks, pointing upwards as the vehicle descends. Lion-O calling the Sword remotely is also a brilliant moment as it growls into life contained in the claw shield. Removing the Sword from proceedings compels Lion-O to utilise some quirky defences against the Lunataks, combating Chilla with rock salt, giving candy to Amok and coming armed with a 'lie translator' for Aluro. The latter leads to one of the most unintentionally funny lines of the series, courtesy of Aluro: 'Just as soon as Lion-O's guard is down, I'll bash him with the psych club!'

Script Editor's Commentary from Peter Lawrence:

Yeah. Not one of the best. This could have been written by one of the less imaginative or more conventional writers (not to demean any of them; every writer has his or her strengths and every show needs the 'calmer' minds that take the 'quieter' routes). I hate to repeat myself in these notes, but at this point we were working hard to use familiar characters and locations. We had too many heroes to allow us to invent yet more characters that the audience would have to grow to love (or hate), and, as important, we were on a horrendous production schedule. The studios were working flat out. If they could re-use or adapt even a few backgrounds, and work with characters they already knew how to animate and so did not have to develop and re-develop, it would help. And that explains the familiarity of this episode.

By this time, I really needed writers I could rely on to deliver, and – as everyone knows – I loved Bill's work. Also enjoyed working with him. And when a story editor is under pressure, he or she will almost always revert to writers he likes and can enjoy working with. The last thing you need is any kind of personal incompatibilities. That, of course, is a shame in some respects – because often conflict and argument result in more interesting material and surprising directions.

101. Key to Thundera (4 Stars)
Written by: Matthew Malach
US Broadcast Date: * 19 September 1988
UK Broadcast Date: N/A

'Key to Thundera' is a strong entry from Matthew Malach and introduces viewers to the mysterious chambers of the Book of Omens and its Guardian. It opens with a wonderfully powerful image of Lion-O being dragged into the Book, and the episode hits every beat as it progresses.

Malach's penchant for humour is ever-evident, and Mumm-Ra's reaction to his companion's odour is notable: 'You know Ma-Mutt, we really must do something about your breath'. (That said, Mumm-Ra's relationship with his dog does, at times throughout this era, become a little tiresome, and his comic exchanges can diminish his villainy). The mummification of Lion-O and Snarf is a highlight of the episode, and it's a great idea to send Mumm-Ra into the Book of Omens. Lion-O's decision to save his foe from his dire fate is a noble gesture and is well suited to his character.

'Key to Thundera' is, at times, a strange adventure, and it works better when viewed as a prelude to the series' final instalment, 'The Book of Omens'. From this point on, the countdown to the end of *ThunderCats* would begin, but not without additional changes to the format ...

Writer's Commentary from Matthew Malach:

Of the four episodes I wrote, this is my favourite. I was happy to do something different with Lion-O's Sword and the Eye of Thundera, which until that point, had been nothing but a glorified skywriter. Here the Eye sucks people through its vortex and into a book. There's a running joke in the show, where the keeper of the Book asks Lion-O, 'Do you have the key?' His response is, 'Key? What key?' Eventually, whenever the key is mentioned, the response is the same: 'Key? What key?' It's my homage to the film *Marathon Man*, where Laurence Oliver repeatedly asks Dustin Hoffman, 'Is it safe?'

When I wrote 'Key to Thundera', I believe I had already moved to LA and was no longer a member of the production team. So I wasn't privy to the future of the show. If I remember properly, the Book of Omens was created without any real direction, they just asked me to come up with a story. I can take credit for the concept of the Sword acting as a portal into the Book, and so I was pleased when Bill Overgard (who I admired greatly) took the idea and ran with it.

102. Return of the Thundercubs (3.5 Stars)
Written by: J Larry Carroll
US Broadcast Date: * 20 September 1988
UK Broadcast Date: N/A

Coming only seven episodes after the conclusion of the 'ThunderCubs' five part mini-series, a 'return' to the premise may seem a little premature. In many ways, Larry Carroll's attempt to use the characters is just as competent as Peter Lawrence's original, but neither makes the ThunderCubs particularly relevant or useful to the plot.

The episode begins, unusually, with Mumm-Ra experiencing a disturbing dream and being scolded by the Ancient Spirits of Evil. The temporary home they erect for him on Thundera works well, and the composite of cave, sarcophagus, statues and cauldron recreates the feel of his home nicely.

Further welcome story points include the visit by Lion-O and Snarf to Castle Plun-Darr carrying a white flag and appealing to the Mutants for use of their spaceship, the RatStar, in return for money. It's an appealing proposition for the Mutants, who hope to ambush the ThunderCats, and it's a touch of originality from Carroll that works well in the context of the episode. Mumm-Ra in the disguise of Lion-O represents the best aspect of 'Return of the ThunderCubs', and 'evil' Lion-O, complete with fangs, is given some great lines. 'Just do it, you little brat,' he snaps to Cheetara! Other snippets of sublime dialogue include Vultureman's reaction to his spacecraft rolling out of control, 'We're upside down,' he squawks. 'Thank you Sherlock Holmes,' replies Slithe (a reference perhaps out of place in the world of *ThunderCats*, but humorous nonetheless). The end gag is also engineered well, as the Mutants squeeze themselves into the Feliner's luggage hold.

Other interesting additions to the adventure include the adult reflections of the ThunderCubs in the Mirror of Truth and the return of Mumm-Ra's ever-more-demonic form (complete with the Sword of Plun-Darr). What really lets the episode down is its poor conclusion. Mumm-Ra is defeated with ease and the situation is simply reversed (though at least the Cave of Time isn't used again). While 'Return of the ThunderCubs' doesn't quite come together as a whole, its many parts are entertaining. Snarf's appeal to Lion-O to shoot down Mumm-Ra is thought-provoking and, when he refuses, his comment is rather poetic: 'Revenge is the delight of a mean spirit'.

Writer's Commentary from J Larry Carroll:

When I found out Rankin/Bass was looking for a way to bring the ThunderCubs back, I quickly developed and pitched this story. They also needed a story to exploit the lost Treasure of Thundera, so this became a two-for-one deal. I loved the subplot of Lion-O and Snarf having to enlist the aid of the Mutants – who everyone knew would double-cross them at some point. It worked well because it kept both Lion-O and Snarf alive while providing comic relief.

103. The Formula (3.5 Stars)
Written by: Kimberly Morris
US Broadcast Date: * 21 September 1988
UK Broadcast Date: N/A

Aluro's 'Multi-Octane, High-Potential, Maximum-Velocity Fuel Formula' is the subject of Kimberly Morris's 'The Formula'. The story is incredibly imaginative, the concept is original, and the animation beautifully depicts all the strange and wonderful creatures and vegetation that spring from Third Earth. A discernible allegory regarding environmental concerns is present, but it isn't forced, and the premise works brilliantly. There are also a lot of welcome touches that help drive the episode along, including the small mouse that is saved by Snarf and later repays the favour when he grows to giant proportions.

The only criticism that could be levelled is that action prevails at the expense of dialogue (unusually so for a Morris script). This makes the episode repetitive at times as the ThunderCats battle to control the undergrowth. There is, in particular, a marked lull in proceedings during the middle act.

'The Formula' isn't a remarkable episode of the second season, but credit should certainly be given for its sheer originality and visual splendour.

Writer's Commentary from Kimberly Morris

The Lunataks were (to me) more fun to write for than the original cast of villains. They were more diverse, prone to in-fighting, and offered more comedic possibilities. They were also more cerebral in their approach to evil. So the fun of this script was in the set-up and the scheming.

Usually, once you set up a show's premise, you thin out the number of characters, because you only have a half-hour to work with. You want to tell a clear story and you don't want to have to keep cutting away to follow eight characters. This one, however, was thickly populated. Blocking it was a bit like blocking stage farce. Lots of timing issues. Needing to have characters in the right place at the right time to play their parts. So yes, it was tricky. But that's what made it fun to write.

Oddly enough, I do remember there was some worry that this story might be interpreted as an environmental screed – which in a way, it was. But I don't think anyone ever did object. Or if they did, Peter Lawrence probably took care of it. I think he did a good job of keeping the firewall up between the writers and the merchandisers/sponsors.

I don't have a preference for revolving stories around new characters or new devices – either one is fine. I like being given a content mandate. It becomes a creative challenge. A puzzle. An interesting set of creative problems to solve.

104. Locket of Lies (4 Stars)
Written by: Bill Ratter
US Broadcast Date: * 22 September 1988
UK Broadcast Date: N/A

Deborah Goodwin's pseudonymous script for 'Locket of Lies' has an inspired premise. Following the series arc of recovering the Treasures of Thundera, a scheme by Mumm-Ra to plant a false object in the treasure trove is an incredibly simple idea, but also surprisingly effective. Finally, Mumm-Ra is given a reasonably cunning scheme and, though it is naturally destined to fail, it does at least have an outside chance of success (compared with comparable escapades).

Things get even better as the episode progresses and we're treated to some one-upmanship from the ThunderCats, Cheetara, Tygra, Panthro and Lion-O all trying to outdo the others as they jump across the rocks on Thundera. Courtesy of some brilliant animation and a great script, their showmanship is highly entertaining. (Panthro's shoulder roll, in particular, is sublime.) 'I've never seen three worse show-offs in my life, so get this!' says Lion-O as he displays his sword powers.

The pinnacle of 'Locket of Lies' is the abandoned palace to which Mumm-Ra lures the ThunderCats. Not only is this a spectacular background painting, but the events that follow almost raise this episode to classic status. 'Ding, dong, dell – kitten's in the well – who put him in? Little Mumm-Ra,' teases the Demon Priest as he captures his pray. The ThunderCats' realisation that any attempt to escape their prison closes the walls around them adds to the jeopardy of proceedings, and these scenes are highly entertaining. There is also a great sub-plot including Snarf Oswold and Snarf Egbert. These quirky scenes really work well due to some highly amusing dialogue by Goodwin, including a heated debate about the Great Tebbit Wally and the Lesser Kinnock Wally (an obvious allusion to two prominent UK politicians).

Sadly, 'Locket of Lies' falls just short of perfection, featuring a disappointing resolution to events. The ThunderCats' escape from the well does not do the episode justice, and the Sword becomes a *deux ex machina* yet again. Nonetheless, the ingenuity on display in 'Locket of Lies' makes it a highlight of the season.

Writer's Commentary from Deborah Goodwin (Bill Ratter):

Part of the idea for this script came about through getting totally lost with a girlfriend one day in her car, despite being given directions. We spent an hour driving around, only to find ourselves at the same road junction an hour later! I took this as the basis for this script, and I used a locket as a 'homing device' as lockets were fashionable items of jewellery at the time.

I did receive a series bible for *ThunderCats* but it wasn't difficult to infuse my ideas into an established continuity. In many respects I found it easier to work within the boundaries set than perhaps I would have done had I been given a blank canvas.

105. Bracelet of Power (3 Stars)
Written by: Bill Ratter
US Broadcast Date: * 23 September 1988
UK Broadcast Date: N/A

'The Bracelet of Power' is simply a re-hash of many different storylines and elements from the *ThunderCats* universe. While there is nothing terribly wrong with Deborah Goodwin's script, it feels too much like *deja vu*, and the theme of mind control begins to seem overused around this point in the season.

It's helpful that Snarf is the first to wield the power of the latest artifact from the treasure hoard of Thundera, and there are plenty of light-hearted and comical scenes around his domination of his friends. Other touches of originality include the 'Mumm-Ra' fly that, rather brilliantly, walks across the mummy's face nonchalantly before giving Mumm-Ra his latest guise (note the brilliant redesign of the fly complete with Mumm-Ra's facial features and bandages). There's also a nice quad split-screen technique used to show the subservience of Lion-O, Cheetara, Tygra and Panthro to Mumm-Ra. Additionally, Goodwin once again proves herself adept at dialogue, and there are some brilliant exchanges, including Mumm-Ra's command to Ma-Mutt to 'Go outside and chase some Berbils'. Even better is Snarf's appeal to Mumm-Ra, 'Forgive me exalted one – my old war wound is acting up'. 'War wound? What war?' demands Mumm-Ra. 'The Great Snarf Rebellion, '42 to '47,' replies Snarf. 'I was a commando, you know. My hands are lethal weapons.' Special mention should be made here of Earl Hammond's sterling vocal performance!

As with many of its neighbouring second season adventures, 'Bracelet of Power' contains some nice scenes, but overall lacks an original plot and fails to bring something new to the series.

Writer's Commentary from Deborah Goodwin (Bill Ratter):

I thought it would be interesting, rather than to have Snarf serving the ThunderCats, for him to have power over the ThunderCats, at least for a while. It allowed me to give Snarf unusual dialogue for a servant of the ThunderCats and also allowed the ThunderCats to have subservient dialogue. This came about through wondering what it would be like saying things that are totally out of character, and what the response would be from the unsuspecting recipients of that uncharacteristic behaviour.

I didn't time my scripts, although I did have other writers' scripts around me and reckoned that if I worked roughly to the number of pages they'd written I'd produce a script of about the right length.

106. The Wild Workout (3.5 Stars)
Written by: Becky Hartman
US Broadcast Date: * 26 September 1988
UK Broadcast Date: N/A

With a script by one-off contributor Becky Hartman, 'Wild Workout' has a relatively eccentric premise, but it's strange enough to actually work within the context of the episode. The story revolves around the Lunataks' attempts to revive Sky Tomb's motors by manually generating power courtesy of some gym equipment. While this may seem bizarre, it is given added credibility by the thoroughness of Hartman's script. She makes a great effort to explain each and every component of the plot, and the resulting adventure is fun and refreshing.

There are plenty of enjoyable moments throughout, including Lion-O being turned into a block of ice while trying to use the Sword of Omens (with the superb scene of the ice block collapsing). Additionally, the Sword calling all the way from Thundera to the ThunderCats based on Third Earth is a nice touch.

As the episode progresses, the Lunataks decide to harness the physical abilities of the ThunderCats to assist in jump-starting their ship. As things look bleak for the felines, Cheetara decides to try to overload the generator by leading her fellow detainees in some serious exercise. The events on Third Earth run parallel to a Thundera sub-plot that is equally engaging, and the scenes featuring Mumm-Ra's mirror reflections are beautifully realised as Lion-O must find which panel contains his nemesis. Overall, 'The Wild Workout' is a good example of a *ThunderCats* adventure that maximises its potential. Though episodes of this kind are never destined to be classics, they achieve all they set out to, and add to the eclectic variation of the show's storytelling.

Writer's Commentary from Becky Hartman:

My inspiration for this episode came from a few different aspects of my life. I had just joined a gym and was working out quite a bit. My apartment had a very temperamental radiator, so I was often freezing. And finally, as a feminist, I wanted one of the female characters to save the day. I was very fond of Cheetara, which is why I focused on her in my episode.

At the time, I was using a first generation Macintosh word processor. It made revising the script easier than if had I done it on a typewriter, but when a document became too large, you couldn't print it or save it. I had pulled an all-nighter to get my draft done and was preparing to print it out when I discovered, much to my horror, that it was too long to either print or save. I had to handwrite about ten pages of it, then delete them and print out the rest of the document; then save that partial script onto a disk, delete it from my computer and re-type the ten pages I had deleted, and then print them. It was then a mad scramble to get from my apartment on 110th Street to mid-town where the Rankin/Bass offices were to get my script in on time. That script printing fiasco is my most vivid memory of that experience.

The one thing I remember was that Peter Lawrence's notes on my first draft mostly consisted of, 'It needs more fights. It needs more explosions.' I did a second draft and maybe a third. I think my inability to write really exciting fight sequences may have hurt my chances for more scripts.

107. The Thunderscope (4 Stars)
Written by: George Hampton & Mike Moore
US Broadcast Date: * 27th September 1988
UK Broadcast Date: N/A

One of the most poignant moments of the entire *ThunderCats* series is provided in the opening segment of 'The Thunderscope'. After the show's credits roll, we see Snarf and Lion-O reminiscing about Thundera. They are sat beside the ruined backdrop of their flagship that first brought them to Third Earth 106 episodes previously, and this is a beautiful link to the series' roots. We are then treated to a brilliant montage of Lion-O's expectations of his homecoming as a touching smile appears on his face. 'We'll all be going back to Thundera very soon, Snarf, very soon,' he tells his companion. 'We'll rebuild our city, reunite our people, share the knowledge we've gained all these years apart.' The visuals accompanying this monologue are equally striking, and we are treated to the sight of a ruined vision of the ThunderCats' citadel.

Fortunately, the episode continues to deliver an equally engaging plot, revolving around a device capable of identifying people and objects associated with Thundera (thus providing a tidy way of regaining the remaining treasures of Thundera). Upon Snarf's discovery of the Thunderscope, we are presented with a riddle regarding the object's purpose, and Mumm-Ra soon involves himself in trying to possess the device. The mummy's disguise as Lynx-O is particularly creepy, and his lifeless, elevating body is chilling.

Other superb moments include the savage use of Ma-Mutt, who becomes significantly more threatening than usual as he chases Snarf, complete with razor sharp teeth. Equally exciting is the moment when Lion-O's insignia goes blank after the Eye of Thundera burns itself out after it hits the Thunderscope.

Ultimately, it's the mythical component of 'The Thunderscope' that makes it so enjoyable. Not only do we return to the programme's own on-screen history, but we also get a glimpse of the very origins of the ThunderCat people as we are told, by Lynx-O, that the Thunderscope was created during the 'Great Migration' that, apparently, led to the ThunderCats' settlement on Thundera.

Writer's Commentary from George Hampton:

The Thunderscope was originally going to be able to see through things like mountains, trees and caves. It evolved into a device that could make things from Thundera glow, thus helping the ThunderCats find parts of the Treasure Of

Thundera. The scope could also find lost Thunderians.

The *ThunderCats* production team worked closely with us, especially regarding the action scenes. But they gave us input on all aspects of the script. The title was originally called 'The Lens'. Peter had written in our notes, 'We should come up with a good name for the telescope. ThunDERscope … or something.'

We were asked to use the Lunataks, featuring Tug-Mug and Chilla because their 'actions animate very well', in Mumm-Ra's climactic attack on the Tower Of Omens. This script fit into the overall storyline perfectly, though we didn't know it when we submitted the idea. Three episodes later, the entire Treasure was retrieved.

108. The Jade Dragon (3.5 Stars)
Written by: William Overgard
US Broadcast Date: * 28 September 1988
UK Broadcast Date: N/A

Bill Overgard delivers a particularly tame screenplay with 'The Jade Dragon'. However, though it's not a spectacular adventure, the opportunity to see a little more of the popular Hachiman is enticing.

We learn that the samurai hails from the Planet of the Red Sun and, while some aspects of the story are a little fantastical (even by *ThunderCats* standards), it is considerably more grounded than the previous second season episodes penned by Overgard. With the absence of some of the more contentious aspects of his storytelling, we are once again able to marvel at his ingenuity and imagination. Great examples include Hachiman's mechanical horse (a brilliant idea, designed beautifully) and a rare intervention from the Ancient Spirits of Evil, who attempt to attack Hachiman. Other enjoyable moments include the chaos and destruction inside the Black Pyramid, and Hachiman's skilful splicing of the Jade Dragon artifact (which contains the ThunderCats).

As in many other Overgard adventures, the ThunderCats themselves play only a minor role in 'The Jade Dragon'. The episode predominantly revolves around Hachiman and Mumm-Ra. Ironically, its only shortcoming is a lacklustre plot. While some of Overgard's scripts fail because they are too fanciful, 'The Jade Dragon' is, if anything, a little dull at times, reinforcing the notion that his genius trod a fine line. However, credit should be given for trying to include some of the series' own mythology into events and, though the continuity of these scenes is somewhat questionable, it's nice to see a young Jaga making an appearance at the beginning.

Script Editor's Commentary from Peter Lawrence:

Personally, I think this is one of Bill's best. Clearly, he's keeping to the mainstream of the show – using Mumm-Ra as the lead villain, for example. He's also sticking to the directive to re-use characters. At the same time, he's building an 'Overgardian' MacGuffin* – the Double Headed Dragon of Doom – to drive the story. Again, a personal note, I like Hachiman. He reflects Bill's great love of Japanese culture and his deep knowledge of Bushido. So, all in all, an interesting combination of elements go to make this an episode that really does work.

*MacGuffin ... Lord knows if anyone remembers Alfred Hitchcock. When I started out, even I hated being referred to this great 'master' whose films I didn't much like. He seemed entirely of a different and passé era. Nonetheless, apparently, he coined this word to describes the device that drives a plot and, once I began to write episodically (or, more specifically, edit and story-direct a lot of shows in a very short time), I realised the value of the MacGuffin.

109. The Circus Train (2 Stars)
Written by: William Overgard
US Broadcast Date: * 29 September 1988
UK Broadcast Date: N/A

It's 'all change' in a bizarre episode that provides the final catalyst for the ThunderCats' decision to leave their adopted home of Third Earth. On face value, providing a script writer with the opportunity to write nearly all of the series' regular villains out of a programme should be a gift. While each episode usually had to reset itself before the events of the next, 'The Circus Train', in theory, should have been liberated from this by being free to provide a suitable exit for so many popular characters. Unfortunately, it proves to be anything but a fitting exit for stalwarts like the Mutants and the Lunataks. Though it wouldn't actually mark their final appearance (as is suggested in the episode), it did mark their departure from the regular texture of the series, and much more could have been achieved with this.

'The Circus Train' embodies all of the eccentricities associated with its writer and sits at the nonsensical end of his creativity. Its lowest moments include the cringeworthy attempts by WilyKat to decipher Captain Bragg's controls, Vultureman's ridiculous umbrella being used as a parachute (a la *Mary Poppins*), and frankly the entire premise of the adventure.

Because of its obvious shortcomings, its few redeeming features are relatively easy to identify. Captain Bragg is a reasonably interesting character, and his personality and interaction with WilyKat (especially the strange ventriloquism scene) are well crafted. It's also exciting to see the downfall of the Lunataks, who had become increasingly stagnant characters as the season progressed. The destruction of their weapons and abilities at least provides a fitting end for them. There are also some nice visual sequences, including Lion-O's 'ThunderCats Ho!' battle cry aboard the front of the Circus Train, as it races into view.

'The Circus Train' isn't the lowest point of the series, although it comes close. Fortunately, this adventure sets in motion a revitalisation and breaks the occasional monotony of its immediate predecessors.

Script Editor's Commentary from Peter Lawrence:

When I looked back on *ThunderCats* in detail – something I almost never do; the show was a big item in my past but, as they say, the past is past and not to be dwelled upon – and, in particular, when I was asked to review the late, great Bill Overgard's work, I must admit that I confused Safari Joe with Captain Bragg. And here, perhaps, is an interesting comparison: Steve Perry with Bill Overgard. It had never before occurred to me that they had a lot in common and, perhaps, if I had developed as close a working relationship with Steve as I did with Bill, it might have been a lot more productive. *ThunderCats* might have had some wilder episodes. However, I'm not sure that Steve had Bill's great facility with character and dialogue. Note that I say 'not sure'. In my experience, his work did not jump off the page like Bill's. Plus, of course, there's always the question of personality. People gell, or not, and I never got to know Steve as well as I knew Bill. My loss, I'm sure.

So … Captain Bragg – not Safari Joe! Surprising that we allowed an entirely new character, and all his accoutrements, at this late stage. Perhaps I wasn't paying attention – or, more likely, I simply liked the premise and outline too much and discarded the producers' directives, which, anyway, were beginning to grate on me. Hence an episode that, in many ways, has nothing to do with the ThunderCats aside from Lion-O and WilyKit racing in at the last moment to save the day. If you think about it, Captain Bragg certainly had the personality, the nous and the equipment to handle Luna and Amok but, after all, the show's title was *ThunderCats*, so at least one ThunderCat (in this case one and a half) had to save the day …

110. The Last Day (5 Stars)
Written by: J Larry Carroll
US Broadcast Date: * 30 September 1988
UK Broadcast Date: N/A

'The Last Day' is a superb offering from Larry Carroll and rounds off the latest round of second season episodes perfectly. The episode is built around the simple premise that Mumm-Ra has one final day to rid Third Earth of the ThunderCats. Having lost his allies, the Mutants and Lunataks, the Ancient Spirits of Evil have become terminally impatient with Mumm-Ra and give him one final opportunity to appease them. In a bid to do just that, he unleashes chaos on Third Earth through a series of geological incidents that threaten the very existence of the planet.

'The Last Day' represents one long and intense confrontation between Lion-O and Mumm-Ra. It feels like the culmination of their many battles over the course of the series, and it is perhaps their most effective encounter since Lion-O's Anointment Trials. Everything about this episode feels epic, and it has an ambitious and filmic quality to it, which offers brilliant pacing – achieving an awful lot, without seeming rushed.

The adventure also ties up a lot of loose ends. In many ways, 'The Last Day' resolves the original concept for *ThunderCats*, with the central characters having not only survived on Third Earth, but having also flourished. The second season story arc also becomes more relevant here as we return, once again, to the Book of Omens. The Treasure of Thundera is also utilised, and the scenes of Snarf taking every conceivable object that has been recovered from Thundera into the Book is amusing. 'And if that's not enough for you to tell us how to defeat Mumm-Ra, then I don't know what is,' he declares.

There's also the touch of magic and mysticism that defines the series on display throughout the entire story, and Jaga's appearance is the 'icing on the cake'.

Placing the ThunderCats in 'limbo', creates a mood that is both disturbing and surreal, and the resolution to the episode (with the ThunderCats emerging from the Sword) is incredibly exciting, as is the magnificent visual of 'super Mumm-Ra' crumbing to dust. 'The Last Day' surely marks the end of an era and the beginning of something quite different ...

Writer's Commentary from J Larry Carroll:

As I recall, Peter asked me to come up with a story ... that would incorporate various elements from previous episodes. But as I developed it into an outline, he told me they wanted to end the episode with the (apparent) demise of Mumm-Ra. (There may have been some thought of writing Mumm-Ra out of the show, but that's all it ever was – a thought.) Like the fans, I was a bit concerned that it would come off too much like a series finale. (Actually, I was a little concerned that it might be the end of the series.) But with apologies to Edward G Robinson, no way was I going to pass up the chance to write: 'Ancient Spirits of Evil... is this the end of Mumm-Ra?'[6]

111-115. Return to Thundera! Parts I-V (4 Stars)
Written by: Peter Lawrence
US Broadcast Date: * 4-8 September 1989
UK Broadcast Date: N/A

In the knowledge that *ThunderCats* would not return for a third season, the programme-makers took the ambitious decision to redefine the show for its final 20 episodes and explore a new direction. This was an astute move, and, taken in isolation, this final run of episodes represent some of the most original of the second season.

Prior to the ThunderCats' return to Thundera, the show had certainly begun to seem repetitive and, while brilliant instalments would still make their way through, there was also a tendency towards recycling story ideas. 'Return to Thundera' (unhelpfully given the same title as Bob Haney's season one adventure) offers something new by providing the ThunderCats with a new mandate. Where the first season had built momentum around the ThunderCats' battle to survive following their exodus from their home world, the second season had struggled, at times, to find its purpose, as the villains proved they were no match for heroes. In effect, the ThunderCats had brought peace to Third Earth, and a new 'mission statement' was needed. Now, the ThunderCats face an even greater struggle, to rebuild their civilisation and return their people to their homeland. This really refreshes the series and, because the ideas contained within this five part serial are so strong, the episodes are both engaging and move quickly to build the plot, without the lull that is common in the middle acts of multi-episode adventures.

Reinforcing the show's new direction, 'Return to Thundera Part I' opens with the symbolic detonation of Mumm-Ra's pyramid on Third Earth. We are then

---

[6] In the 1931 movie *Little Caesar*, Robinson has the parting line, 'Mother of mercy, is this the end of Rico?'

introduced to the League of Third Earth, which comprises: Mandora, Willa, Nayda, Snowman, Snowmeow and Berbils Belle and Bill. This is a nice idea and, having followed the characters throughout the series, it's rewarding to see them granted peace on their planet. Another, less welcome, change is the removal of stalwart Tygra and relative newcomer Pumyra from the series, condemned to stay on duty on Third Earth. Although they will make guest appearances beyond this episode, it seems particularly harsh for these characters to be left behind (especially as they won't even be inhabiting the same building). Given the flight time between Thundera and Third Earth (which has been treated as practically insignificant as the series has progressed) this comes across as a blatant attempt to remove some characters from the mix to benefit the scriptwriters, rather than a logical precaution for the ThunderCats to enact.

Throughout 'Return to Thundera', we see the first tantalising glimpses of the new Cats' Lair being constructed on New Thundera. The inclusion of small touches like ladders and scaffolding really marks out *ThunderCats* from its competition, and it's this attention to detail that Pacific Animation Corporation prided themselves upon. Without the aid of the Berbils, Cats' Lair mark two is constructed by an army of Snarfs, who, it should be noted, are particularly slow on the uptake in continuing to rebuild the Lair every time Mumm-Ra effects its destruction. This leads to the adventure's central plot concerning a gyroscope that holds the planet's gravity in balance. While this concept is typically over-the-top, it has the air of authenticity, and Jaguara and the Great Beneath are all great additions to the series' mythology.

To fill all five parts of the adventure, we have a range of guest villains and allies, however, rather than a repeat of the 'greatest hits' formula of previous five-parters, we're treated to many new characters. These include Charr, who proves to be a formidable addition (and full marks for having Charr reforge the Sword of Omens rather than taking the more predictable path of having Bengali repair it for a second time). Incidentally, it might have been better for the animators to have shown Charr reforge only the Sword's blade, rather than turn the whole object into a melted puddle, which seems bizarre.

Another brilliant character to emerge from 'Return to Thundera' is Two Time, who sports an inventive design (complete with a brilliant flip/walk) and some good dialogue, with a great vocal performance. We're also treated to a new vehicle, the Whisker, which is as effective as its predecessors in facilitating the ThunderCats' movements, after they leave the majority of their equipment on Third Earth.

Highlights from the serial include, both from 'Part III', Mumm-Ra's alternation between his frail and Everliving forms when defeated by Lion-O, and a challenge to the false Jaga from Panthro: 'If we are false and you are true, use the Sword of Omens to destroy us'. 'Part IV' places Snarf in danger as Cats' Lair collapses, and Lion-O's determination to free his friend is touching. Mumm-Ra's climactic battle with the Lord of the ThunderCats in 'Part V' is also impressive, being reminiscent of *Star Wars*, as the combatants engage in a sword battle. Mumm-Ra's dialogue is perfect, and Peter Lawrence's fondness for writing the character is evident throughout these scenes.

Any weaknesses on show in this serial are few and far between. Grune's appearance is a little lacklustre, and so too is the idea of the Mutants being reprieved only to be reincarcerated aboard the Circus Train after their 'bit part' is resolved. This only really serves to undermine their exit and adds relatively little to proceedings. The Ancient Spirits of Evil also display a questionable motive in forcing Mumm-Ra to pursue the ThunderCats to New Thundera. Since the opening episode of the series, Mumm-Ra has merely wanted the ThunderCats removed from Third Earth (once he realised the powers of the Eye of Thundera would never do his bidding). As such, his decision to follow them seems counterproductive. Nonetheless, 'Return to Thundera' is a fine collection of *ThunderCats* episodes. It does, at times, play too heavily to the magical properties of the Eye of Thundera and, indeed, the Sword of Omens can now do practically anything, which can be an outlet for sloppy writing. Overall, however, Peter Lawrence crafts a memorable adventure, which ranks as superior to its fellow multi-part stories 'Mumm-Ra Lives!' and 'ThunderCubs'.

Writer's Commentary from Peter Lawrence:

Reviewing these five-parters, I've made an interesting (to me, at least) discovery. It's difficult to ascribe a single point of motive to them, because they have such an intense and multi-plotted structure, with many characters from past and present. It's easy to explain the genesis of (or point to) a story like 'Good and Ugly': don't be deceived by appearances. But these five-parters? Other than that they were designed to play both as individual episodes and as full length 'movies', there's not really a lot one can say.

Obviously, we tried to involve a lot of existing characters, for two reasons. First, the audience knew them and, we believed, wanted to see them in action again. Secondly, the animators knew the characters – and the more an animator gets to know a character, the more he or she can bring to it, even in limited animation. And so, for example, we see Mandora developing, not just on paper but in the way she moves and 'acts'. I think it's interesting, too, to meld the very different characters that, say, Bill Overgard and Len Starr dreamed up into one storyline. I do believe that one of the reasons for the show's massive success was its great variety of characters and 'worlds'. For some reason, instead of it being a mess of incongruous pieces, it all seemed to work together. I can't claim that was deliberate and I'm not sure exactly why it worked – and continues to work. Perhaps the sheer strength of the hero group – and the overarching character of Mumm-Ra – was strong enough to embrace all these weird and wild differences. I note that we had the same kind of differences of character and worlds of *SilverHawks* but that they did not work as well together, or were not as warmly embraced by the audience. Perhaps that's because, with the notable exception of Commander Stargazer, the *SilverHawks* heroes were simply not that interesting or powerful a group (in terms of character).

By the time we got to this story, we had way too many characters, and the new or additional characters weren't that interesting. Let's face it, once you have a hero group of more than four or five, you've more or less run the gamut of personalities and abilities – unless you're prepared to explore the dark sides of your heroes (qv *The Dirty Dozen*, if anyone remembers that; or any of the *Oceans 11* saga). For me, Tygra was the weakest of the characters – though I did like the bolos! – and I didn't really care for his 'voice'. That's not a dig at the actor or at the voice direction. It's more a comment on his personality, which is, perhaps, a dig at the writers – myself included. However, by the time I began to work, we were pretty much hemmed in. Not a lot of places we could go, unless, as I say, we could find some darker corner of his psyche and use that. Another reason to leave a unit back on Third Earth was to allow for parallel stories and 'ticking clock' scenarios in both locations … intercutting action and tension. Fairly standard stuff and, in this case, probably not necessary since there were so many parallel stories even with the group on Thundera.

116. Leah (5 Stars)
Written by: J Larry Carroll & David Carren
US Broadcast Date: * 11 September 1989
UK Broadcast Date: N/A

'Leah' offers a brilliant start to the ThunderCats' adventures on New Thundera. With a newly completed Cats' Lair (suitably different from its predecessor), the ThunderCats must turn their attention to recovering some Thunderian citizens who are lost in space. The first of these to be drawn into the planet's atmosphere is the eponymous star of the episode, a Thunderian youngster named Leah.

There's an emotional resonance throughout the episode, and it's a great idea to centre events around an abandoned youngster. Once Leah is invited into Cats' Lair, this gives us an opportunity to explore the ThunderCats' new home. There's also some brilliant backstory, courtesy of some recordings retrieved by Panthro that show the Thunderian refugees falling foul of a meteor shower. As well as having plenty of action sequences, it's the desire to reunite Leah with her parents that proves to be the underlying driving force of the adventure.

The guest villain is the sinister Mirror Wraith, who conceals himself, rather eerily, as a child's doll. The Wraith's design is well conceived and is reminiscent of a muscular gargoyle. The idea of a creature that exists between mirrors is beautifully original, as is the episode's brilliant climax. Snarf's cunning plan to 'seal' the Mirror Wraith inside the void he occupies is superb, and the Wraith's panicked attempts to move from mirror to mirror as Snarf extinguishes them one by one is, perhaps, one of the most well-considered story resolutions in the series' history.

'Leah' is extremely clever in offering a story set in a new location, with new characters, but still managing to feel surprisingly familiar. It is, in fact, remarkably similar in tone to the early season one adventures, with even the music cues mostly comprising of tracks from the first season library. One wonders how much of this was a deliberate decision, to reassure casual viewers that they were still watching the same series, however much things may have changed.

As desired, the final scenes provide a reunion for Leah and her parents and, for the first time in many episodes, a notable moral emerges, warning us of the perils of keeping destructive secrets to ourselves.

Writer's Commentary from J Larry Carroll and David Carren:

Carroll: I have mixed feelings about this episode. I think the fun part of the story was stifled by the rather grim (albeit worthy) moral that, for a child, a secret you can't tell your parents or other adults is a bad thing. It's nearly always a mistake in TV to have a guest character who is at the centre of things like Leah was. Also, I think the Wraith's rampage in the climax became too hectic; a jumble of action that was difficult to follow. Nobody to blame about any of this except myself.

Carren: I don't remember which of us came up with the central character but I can say we were fascinated with children and parenting in our films, or how one affects the other. All through our career, we did stories along those lines. A lonely alien child looking for a dad in *Future Imperfect*, our *Star Trek*. A lead character in *Beyond Reality* trying to reunite with a father who fought in World War II. And the features I've done recently are almost always about kids of one kind or another. The feature I just wrote and directed, *The Red Queen*, is about a daughter searching for the truth about her mother. Even a horror film I wrote, *Mr Hell*, focuses on a girl who is grieving over her lost father. Call it an obsession, but it has been a satisfying and successful one.

117. Frogman (3.5 Stars)
Written by: Kimberly Morris
US Broadcast Date: * 12 September 1989
UK Broadcast Date: N/A

The ThunderCats turn their attention to the practicalities of survival in their new environment in a final contribution to the series by Kimberly Morris. 'Frogman' is not her finest work, but her scripts are always enjoyable, and this is no exception. The eponymous star of the show could perhaps have sported a more fearsome name, but his characterisation is engaging and he has some original attributes, including the ability to camouflage himself and call upon an arsenal of weapons in the shape of lily pads. It's also a nice touch that Frogman's history is littered with prior encounters with the ThunderCats. In fact, it's the flashback sequences featuring the characters imprisonment by Jaga (after a failed attempt to dominate New Thundera by harnessing the power of water) that save this episode from mediocrity.

Having only recently completed the new Cats' Lair, the ThunderCats find it almost entirely submerged, and while the landscapes and buildings are new (helped by a purple-tinted skyline to differentiate the planet from Third Earth), we soon find that our heroes are susceptible to the same forms of danger. Leading the events of 'Frogman' are WilyKit and WilyKat, and Morris's confidence in handling material for the ThunderKittens pays off by imbuing the Frogman with a menacing mandate to destroy the ThunderCat youngsters.

The climax is successful and is clearly well considered. It's good to see Jaguara return to aid the ThunderCats and, once the flood waters recede, we're left with the superb imagery of Cats' Lair covered in mud and grime. To top things off (in true *ThunderCats* style) we have a clear moral, that we must learn to trust our instincts.

Writer's Commentary from Kimberly Morris

Originally I called this character Bogman – but Peter Lawrence said I had to change it, because in England, bog is slang for toilet. I'd never heard the term before. He said calling somebody 'Bogman' was like calling them 'Poopman'. I thought it was hilarious and lobbied to stick with Bogman. Alas, Peter was adamant, and the character's name was changed.

Writing backstory is always a tricky issue with a series – whether it's a television series or a book series. Ideally, you'd like a viewer, or a reader, to be able to watch one episode, or read one book, at random, and understand the entire world that you are presenting. But at some point, that's not possible. You just have to decide that not every viewer will understand every allusion or get every inside joke. If you have done a good enough job with your main story, it won't matter. They will enjoy it anyway. If they like what they see or read, then one hopes they will be intrigued enough to watch or read additional episodes and find out what they missed.

118. The Heritage (3.5 Stars)
Written by: Bill Ratter & Peter Lawrence
US Broadcast Date: * 13 September 1989
UK Broadcast Date: N/A

The scrap metal collector Charr returns to *ThunderCats* in a lacklustre pseudonymous episode from Deborah Goodwin. There's nothing intrinsically missing from the formula used to construct the plot; it's all pretty standard fare from Mumm-Ra. But the episode fails to capitalise on the series' renewed impetus. Instead, it merely rehashes previous tried-and-tested ideas. The first half is its weakest act, revolving around the quest to posses the mysterious Golden Sphere of Setti, which like countless other artifacts seen in the series bestows great powers upon its owners (in this case increasing Mumm-Ra's powers by a factor of four). Unfortunately, as in nearly all these cases, the Sphere emits a mesmerising influence, and deception and trickery soon follow.

Fortunately, beyond a dull opening, the episode does build momentum, and an injection of originality comes in the form of the Ancient Spirits of Evil. Goodwin cleverly plots a rebellion by Mumm-Ra, whereby (in the knowledge that the Sphere of Setti will prove his salvation) he casts his masters aside, hurling the insult that they are 'useless relics of a bygone era'. Predictably, this does not end well for the demon priest, as the Spirits remove the Sphere and deny him his powers. The scenes of Mumm-Ra locked out of his pyramid (given the impossible choice between his home or the Sphere) show a rare glimpse into the vulnerability of the character, and should be commended.

'The Heritage' is a collection of good and bad, resulting in an interesting adventure, but failing to move the season forward. On one hand, moments like the ThunderKittens' impromptu skydive engage the viewer; on the other, the rehashing of ideas (like the Sword of Omens being broken yet again) fails to do the story justice. This is a pity, especially as Goodwin includes some brilliant dialogue, not least from Mumm-Ra. 'Don't worry about Charr, ThunderCats,' he declares. 'He's just stunned. If you want to worry, worry about me, for I have the Golden Sphere of Setti.'

Writer's Commentary from Deborah Goodwin (Bill Ratter):

I've always had a bit of an interest in England's heritage, and coming up with the idea of the Golden Sphere gave me the opportunity of explaining that whilst it may be great to find something of value, whether historical, financial, or both, keeping it for yourself may not be the best course of action to take.

I suppose that on average I wrote two to three drafts each for my *ThunderCats* episodes. I don't recall how long I was given to write an episode. What I do know is that I would normally write a script in around three to eight days.

119. Screwloose (4 Stars)
Written by: William Overgard
US Broadcast Date: * 14 September 1989
UK Broadcast Date: N/A

While his other script contributions from this period were mostly terrible, Bill Overgard proves once again that he is the master of contrast, delivering here a great episode that puts his imagination to best use. The idea to bring a gyroscope engineer to New Thundera is inspired, and the brilliant character Screw Loose could only have come from the mind of a writer like Overgard. He is given some wonderful dialogue, and his interaction with other characters is a huge benefit to the episode. His introductory sequence is also good fun, with Bengali delivering the news, via intercom, to Lion-O that 'parts of him' are present, but 'parts of him aren't'.

The character is enormously likeable, and the plot revolves around a classic 'robot gone bad' story device that feels highly original in *ThunderCats*. From being an engaging yet gentle character delivering great one-liners ('Nothing lasts these days, they just don't make me like they used to'), Screw Loose takes on a more sinister persona when Mumm-Ra swaps his circuitry and corrupts him. The poor SAP (Self Acting Phenomenon – robots, we are told are decidedly inferior creations) puts up a sterling effort to resist the mummy's instructions, and this internal conflict of allegiance lies at the heart of the episode. His occasional bursts of villainy are wonderfully amusing. 'What do you take me for, you old hag – a moron?' he asks Jaguara. 'I've forgotten more about gyroscopes than you'll ever know'.

This really is a very strong entry in the final group of *ThunderCats* episodes, and the viewer feels a tinge of frustration that Bill Overgard couldn't deliver scripts like this more often in the second season. 'Screwloose' proves that his eccentricity and imagination can still deliver distinctive episodes while nevertheless working within the house style of the series.

Script Editor's Commentary from Peter Lawrence:

It was very Bill, who had an old-fashioned streak to him about women*, that he would choose Jaguara to have problems with New Thundera's gyro – whatever in the name of Jaga that might have been. For the rest of it, the story is quite conventional – at least for this writer.

Screw Loose, his personality (I suppose he is a 'he') and role, are particularly

Overgard, as is the gyro. We should have written a story at the very end, where every doomsday device and scenario falls into Mumm-Ra's hands. He presses each of these buttons and, finally, blows the entire *ThunderCats* universe (and his own) to hell. Now that would have been a grand finale.

* I don't know how much detail is too much detail but ... Bill married Gloria when they were both 19, in New York, both having arrived there to seek their fortunes, she as a ballet dancer and he as an artist. Gloria was tiny and indomitable, a power behind the throne. The pond and grounds of their house harboured many refugee animals, each of which had a name. A Canadian Goose with two broken wings, hence unable to migrate, named Wide Load. A one-legged crow that used to accompany them on walks until it started to attack their friends. (It then lived in the house.) A mentally defective Doberman. Even the fish had names (two of them, Jules and Sylvia Bass). All this will tell you what a remarkable, strong and wonderful woman Gloria was – but even that did not quite obliterate Bill's sometimes old-fashioned social values ... one of which was the sundown Martini, which we all loved.

120. Malcar (3.5 Stars)
Written by: George Hampton & Mike Moore
US Broadcast Date: * 15 September 1989
UK Broadcast Date: N/A

'Malcar' features an ingenious plan by Mumm-Ra to enlist the services of an ancient alchemist to convert the ThunderCats' fuel source, Thundrillium, into the one substance they cannot repel, Thundranium. Both the plot and the central character of Malcar seem refreshingly original and, while it's not the writers' best work for the series, it fares well alongside its neighbouring episodes.

At the beginning, the return of Thunderian refugees once again provides the catalyst for the events that follow, and the ThunderCats must travel into deep space (thus depleting their stocks of Thundrillium) to retrieve their countrymen. There are two distinct threads to this story: one involves Malcar and the other concerns the fate of Bengali and Snarfer, who become trapped in an old mine. The latter aspect slows things down considerably and should perhaps have been jettisoned to concentrate on the primary plot. It certainly doesn't create the same sense of jeopardy as similar encounters such as the one in 'The Mountain'. This is especially true because the character of Malcar is not given adequate development or screentime to realise his potential.

The idea to play around with Malcar's age works brilliantly for the medium and, from being a young and powerful alchemist in Mumm-Ra's projection, he is dragged to Third Earth as an old man. From there, he returns to the pinnacle of his powers before regressing to infancy in a brilliant climax to events. Jaga's intervention in the story is welcome; it's nice to see him actively participating rather than, as is more often the case, simply advising Lion-O to use the powers of the Eye of Thundera. Jaga's battle with Mumm-Ra is really the highlight of 'Malcar', and it's exciting to see the character appear in the Black Pyramid. 'I will destroy you,' insists Mumm-Ra. 'In another life, perhaps, Mumm-Ra,' retorts Jaga, 'but on New Thundera – never!' Coupled with Malcar's regression, this provides a brilliant resolution, and it's good to see Malcar being adopted in the closing scenes. 'Do me a favour,' Lion-O asks of Malcar's new family. 'Don't teach him any magic!'

Writer's Commentary from George Hampton:

This episode was originally entitled 'Malcar the Alchemist'. Malcar's orb is of course the 'philosopher's stone'. The character designers did a great job of drawing Malcar at three different ages. Due to the illness of another writer, our due date on this script was moved up a week, which is why we almost submitted this script with the inappropriate dialogue below.

If Mike or I were stumped for a line or a description while writing our half of the script, we would write something absurd in a red font and hope that the other would think of something to put in the final version. In 'Malcar', when Lion-O and Snarf break through the rubble to save Panthro (later Bengali), Snarfer, Egbert and Oswald, I couldn't think of a line so I wrote:

> LION-O
> Panthro, where are the Snarfs?
>
> ANGLE ON PANTHRO
>
> COUGHING UP SNARF FUR
>
> PANTHRO
> What (cough) Snarfs?

Somehow this came out in black and not red. Fortunately, Mike caught it in time and wrote back, 'Did you mean to put this in red?' If we had sent this in, we might have found out about the child psychologist.

Soon after we submitted our final drafts we received recording scripts, which were exactly like the filmed version of the episode. The only change I can think of that stood out to us was where we had Panthro trapped in the Thundrillium mine/cave with Snarfer, Egbert and Oswald. The Panthro character was changed to Bengali.

121. Helpless Laughter (4 Stars)
Written by: Matthew Malach
US Broadcast Date: * 18 September 1989
UK Broadcast Date: N/A

If one were to judge 'Helpless Laughter' based on its synopsis alone, one could be forgiven for expecting a less than enthralling adventure. Fortunately, Matthew Malach turns an unpromising premise into an exciting episode and carefully balances the potential absurdity of proceedings.

It's a twee but rewarding episode about a lunar eclipse of the five moons of Plun-Darr that results in a drought far more dangerous than any adversary. As the inhabitants of the planet feel the effects of the water shortage, the ThunderCats encounter Eezuka, the Water Serpent of Dreary Canal, who attacks our heroes with a strange, string-like substance and is a worthy addition to the list of strange creatures and monsters that have graced the series. While his actions are hostile, he's merely fighting for survival, and the environmental subtext of the episode is reinforced.

Humour plays an important role here, and Malach threads his comic versatility into the narrative effortlessly. The exploits of Snarf and Panthro under the influence of the mysterious swamp waters are genuinely amusing. Credit should be given to Earle Hyman, Bob McFadden and Earl Hammond, who all perform with perfection their characters crippled with laughter. There's also some great dialogue when the characters are 'under the influence', including Bengali's conversation with Panthro. 'Do you read?' asks Bengali. 'Yes I read,' answers Panthro, '...novels mostly!' As the story progresses, there's a nice plot reversal that sees the ThunderCats encounter a tidal wave.

Some lazy storytelling detracts a little from the episode's potential. Using the Sword of Omens to create rain is a particularly predictable solution. Jaga is also, once again, relegated to simply telling Lion-O to rely on the powers of the Eye of Thundera. (One would have hoped he would have began using them already by this point.) Nonetheless, Malach prevents the episode falling into farce, and a strong story emerges. Thankfully, the 'laughter' aspect is restricted to only three central characters, and we can grant Malach the indulgence of plunging Mumm-Ra into the water, simply so we can hear the immortal line, 'Mummy overboard!'

Writer's Commentary from Matthew Malach:

What better way to defeat Mumm-Ra than by having him laugh himself to death? It's another common dramatic device, and it was a hoot to record with the cast.

Why humour, in most of my shows? The entire *ThunderCats* ethos was so bloody serious it begged to be toyed with. To me it's natural to combat fear with humour. Since the ThunderCats were constantly imperilled, it only made sense that humour would easily come out of those situations. Also, generally on television, when an otherwise dramatic series toys with humour, it's often memorable. For instance, take the original *Star Trek*. The funny shows such as 'The Trouble with Tribbles' and 'A Piece of the Action' were out of character for the series, and that sticks out. I suppose I wanted to stick out a bit from the crowd, and humour often does the trick.

122. Cracker's Revenge (1.5 Stars)
Written by: William Overgard
US Broadcast Date: * 19 September 1989
UK Broadcast Date: N/A

In the endless debate as to the merits of Bill Overgard's unpredictable work on *ThunderCats*, few could deny that 'Cracker's Revenge' falls amongst his absolute worst offerings. It joins 'Side Swipe' in taking the show to its lowest point.

The character Captain Cracker – who failed to elicit much excitement in his season one debut, seeming decidedly inferior to his pirate rival, Hammerhand – returns for another hapless performance. There's precious little of merit to redeem this episode. Low points include Snarfer flying a pizza run to Third Earth and the

Lunataks being pointlessly reintroduced only to be banished again at the conclusion. The internal chronology of Overgard's episodes continues to gain momentum here, and the usual suspects of Exile Isle, Mandora and the Circus Train are needlessly thrown into the mix, only serving to confuse whatever weak plot lies at the episode's heart.

If we overlook the fact that 'Cracker's Revenge' is relatively nonsensical, some small shoots of Overgard's enormous talent can be seen in Snarfer's plan to contact Mandora by attracting a speeding ticket. Snarfer disguised as a Berbil is also quite funny, and the way Mandora reaches for her weapon is a great homage to Westerns. Aside from the above elements, and perhaps a welcome return to Third Earth, 'Cracker's Revenge' is an incredibly poor advert for the series, and one can't help but feel that anyone returning to the show for the first time since season one would have found it almost unrecognisable.

Script Editor's Commentary from Peter Lawrence:

It has been suggested that if you assembled all of Bill's episodes you'd have a show of its own: that it's almost as if Bill was writing a separate narrative interrupted by other *ThunderCats* writers. This episode is a good example of the point – the reappearance of many of Overgard's characters, locations, inventions and themes.

This particular story is, I think, a mess. It has some wonderful moments and ideas but, overall, does not hang together. I should certainly have either reworked it or sent it back to Bill for a complete rewrite, to simplify it and to make it a *ThunderCats* story and not just a paramilitary expedition through Bill's imagination.

I can't explain why I didn't do that, because I often edited Bill quite savagely – so much so that on a later show (Fox's *Peter Pan and the Pirates*), he called me and threatened to resign. I made my point that, rightly or wrongly, I was the single mind hired to bring a single dramatic vision to the show (an interpretation and synthesis, of course, of all the other producers', artists' and network executives' views) and he accepted that. I think he just wanted to vent. I undoubtedly gave him a lot of leeway, because his work was so much fun to read and work on. I always looked forward to a new Overgard script, no matter how whacked out and off-show it was. Some of the other writers' on-show pieces were simply too ho-hum for me. Even those who knew the show well and wrote perfectly okay.

So, this one? Lunataks on the rise and then on the wane and so on … with Overgard characters woven in and out and the ThunderCats playing supporting roles. If they were human, I'm sure they would have been counting their lines and asking the director who on Thundera the stars were supposed to be …

123. The Mossland Monster (3.5 Stars)
Written by: Chris Trengove
US Broadcast Date: * 20 September 1989
UK Broadcast Date: N/A

'The Mossland Monster' offers an incredibly simple storyline, much the same as series one adventures such as 'The Rock Giant'. In essence, it features a generic monster (given no apparent backstory or explanation) who silently terrorises and pursues the ThunderCats, this time turning his foes to moss (rather than fire, ice or rock as seen in previous adventures).

While this might seem the formula for a particularly lacklustre show, 'The Mossland Monster' doesn't feel as undeveloped as it first appears. It's certainly an episode for the lover of action, which predominates over dialogue, but is enjoyable and certainly fares no worse than its first season equivalents. It's arguably another example of 'ThunderCats by numbers', but there seems always a place for that kind of episode in the series, and Chris Trengove offers enough flourishes on top of the basic premise to engage the viewer. Most notably, it's the return of Tygra that proves the highlight.

On his way to New Thundera (no doubt to relieve the interminable boredom of standing guard in the Tower of Omens), Tygra decides to ignore the advice of his colleagues and plough straight through a meteor shower. Though he survives intact, his diversion takes him to the Mosslands of New Thundera, which introduce the ThunderCats to their latest villain. What saves the episode is undoubtedly this appearance by Tygra and, moreover, his guilt and atonement for placing the ThunderCats in danger (cue our life lesson that we should listen to our elders – or, in Tygra's case, youngers).

The introduction of the eponymous monster is incredibly exciting, and it's only in his subsequent scenes that there is a noticeable lull. The reappearance of the Stone Giants remedies this, and the scenes of them fighting with the Sword of Omens are brilliant. In fact, these sequences feature an unusual degree of violence for the show, as the Giants not only slice off the Mossland Monster's arms but melt him to the accompaniment of an agonised scream. Perhaps this is why the Monster, as a character, was so undeveloped compared with previous adversaries like Frogman, to make him feel more like a wild beast than a sophisticated villain.

Writer's Commentary from Chris Trengove:

Among the last ever episodes. If I remember rightly, there was some 'mossy' background design going begging, and as with characters, it's always a good idea to reuse designs if possible, if only from the economic point of view. Seriously, I can't really remember! I'm extrapolating. But if there was a Mossland Monster, I suspect it would have come out of there being mossland …

In any event, I was given a 'moss' theme to work up into an episode, and the Mossland Monster is surely one of the weirdest of the ThunderCats' 'bad guys'. (He's made of moss – and he turns things into moss!)

124. Ma-Mutt's Confusion (2.5 Stars)
Written by: Beth Bornstein
US Broadcast Date: * 21 September 1989
UK Broadcast Date: N/A

Beth Bornstein's one and only contribution to ThunderCats has a nice central premise but lacks enough structure to turn it into a stronger entry in the second season line-up. Ma-Mutt's defection to the ThunderCats after years of abuse at the hands of Mumm-Ra is a brilliantly simple idea, but Mumm-Ra's behaviour is at odds with his usual persona and only serves to undermine it.

The Babylonian Barbarian Boiler appears every bit as ludicrous as its name, though its purpose – to liquefy the ThunderCats – is suitably grand, and the attack on Cats' Lair is pretty well handled. However, while the exterior of Cats' Lair melting is an iconic image, it seems to have perplexingly little effect on the interior (or indeed the ThunderCats trapped within), which only confuses matters.

Bornstein seems to have targeted her story at a younger audience than usual for *ThunderCats*. It gives the impression of having been written as a cartoon of the *Tom and Jerry* ilk. The scenes of Mumm-Ra running after Ma-Mutt (after the dog drinks Cauldron juice) set the wrong tone from the outset, and the adventure can't quite connect with the series' established formula. Things aren't helped by Mumm-Ra's reduced status (just compare his antics here with his debut in 'The Unholy Alliance'), and any authority from the character is lost. Sadly, he is reduced to delivering awful lines such as, 'Goodie, goodie goo drops. Everything I dreamed is coming true'.

The best part of the episode is undoubtedly its handling of Ma-Mutt. It is nice to see his personality explored, and fitting that he should be granted an episode of his own. The idea to build a device to transcribe the dog's thoughts is also an excellent one, and Bornstein gives him the default 'name, rank and serial number' response of a prisoner of war once he becomes influenced by Mumm-Ra: 'My name is Ma-Mutt. Adjutant to Mumm-Ra the Everliving. Dog license: 3462'.

Overall, 'Ma-Mutt's Confusion' is a competent offering, but no more. Bornstein's extensive experience as an animation writer proves her proficiency with the craft, but one can't help but feel the demographic of the series must have been miscommunicated to her, as the episode seems to have written without its target market in mind.

Writer's Commentary from Beth Bornstein:

In this episode, I wanted to focus on the relationship between Mumm-Ra and Ma-Mutt, showing the humour, frustration and attachment of the dog owner (albeit evil dog owner!) and his pet. Years before, I had worked with Paul Dini on an episode of *Scooby Doo*, and I remember what fun we had with Scooby's dialogue, so here it was again, the opportunity to let the dog speak! And even with all of his powers, Ma-Mutt, like any feisty pet, occasionally gets into trouble when he misbehaves. In this case, Ma-Mutt drinks from the cauldron while Mumm-Ra is working on yet another ThunderCats-thwarting invention: the Barbarian Babylonian Boiler, intended to liquidate the Cats' Lair – and hyped up in a sort of magical/mad sugar rush, Ma-Mutt runs around trashing the Pyramid. This prompts Mumm-Ra to banish his dog. I remember sitting at the computer laughing, thinking of all the ways in which Ma-Mutt could potentially annoy Mumm-Ra: wrapping him in bandages and causing him to fall, licking his nose, drinking from the cauldron and then burping loudly, knocking things down when he runs around, nuzzling up to Mumm-Ra after he admonishes him, etc. What any dog might do, right?

Later, Ma-Mutt almost betrays his master by spilling the beans about the Babylonian Boiler, through use of the translation device. What I liked about writing the translation device was that it was an opportunity to let Snarfer come up with the invention himself when the ThunderCats were too busy thwarting off Mumm-Ra's attack. A good lesson for the kids, I thought: if your parents or older siblings can't help you solve something in the moment, see what you can come up with on your own.

When Ma-Mutt finally returns to Mumm-Ra, and the Babylonian Boiler backfires on the Pyramid after the ThunderCats successfully ward off the attack, Mumm-Ra panics when he can't find his pet. At that moment he realises how much he missed Ma-Mutt, and upon finding him says, 'Ma-Mutt! Thank the Ancient Spirits of evil! I thought I'd lost you, my pet. From now on, I'm going to do everything I can to make you the most horrible, happy hound in the universe!' It was nice to write this softer side of our villain, when he begs his dog for forgiveness for having been abusive. (Funny, he never does that with the *ThunderCats*!) Another good lesson for the kids comes at the end of the episode when Snarf questions Mumm-Mutt's motive for going with the ThunderCats in the first place, saying that it was probably an elaborate trap. Lion-O responds with, 'Come on Snarf, you can't live your entire life suspecting the worst of everyone. You have to give them the benefit of the doubt sometimes!' I really enjoyed writing an episode of *ThunderCats* that focused on Ma-Mutt/Mumm-Ra and the ThunderKittens.

I remember laughing with Peter Lawrence about the owner/dog relationship between Mumm-Ra and Ma-Mutt. That anybody with a dog could relate to the kind of trouble Ma-Mutt was getting into with Mumm-Ra. I think there were a few changes from Peter. I know my writing voice, and in watching the episode, I hear a few things that might have been changed later. Like Mumm-Ra calling Ma-Mutt a 'cursed, craven, canine creature.' I love the alliteration of that, but I don't think I've ever used the word 'craven' in my life, let alone writing it into a script! Although it was a long time ago; I certainly could have written it. I did have a thesaurus and I used it often!

125. Shadowmaster (5 Stars)
Written by: Dennis J Woodyard
US Broadcast Date: * 22 September 1989
UK Broadcast Date: N/A

'Shadowmaster' is a superb episode of *ThunderCats*. It represents everything that the series stands for and delivers (in abundance) action, adventure and mythology. Crafted by newcomer Dennis Woodyard (a character designer working for Rankin/Bass), this episode introduces Claudus to his grown-up son Lion-O – he having been unaware of the identity of the 'stranger' in his previous appearance in 'Return to Thundera'. For a children's cartoon, this proves to be a particularly emotional reunion.

The story begins well, with the Shadowmaster's appeal to the Ancient Spirits of Evil to free him from his exile. This provides a perfect excuse to explain the character's origins (courtesy of some brilliant flashbacks) and shows just how closely Jaga and Claudus worked together to protect Thundera during the reign of Claudus. Here starts a brilliant subplot – that Mumm-Ra actively works against the Spirits' wishes, for fear of becoming redundant. These machinations add a great story thread to proceedings, and it is refreshing to see the character acting independently rather than always in deference to his masters (particularly given his pathetic characterisation in the preceding adventure).

As we learn that Claudus did not perish upon the destruction of Thundera, and instead was imprisoned by the Shadowmaster, Lion-O is taunted via his dreams to travel to the Shadow Realm and effect a rescue for his father. When he achieves this (courtesy of some advice from Jaga), he nobly offers to switch places with his father, and a great battle of wills ensues. The character of the Shadowmaster is capably written, but there's not too much time to learn anything more about him than the basics. He proves he's a competent adversary, and, but for the timely intervention of Ma-Mutt, his plan would presumably have succeeded.

The real heart of the episode comes at the climax when Lion-O regains the Sword and calls his father. It's enormously rewarding to see father and son fighting side by side, both grasping the Sword, and these scenes have an excitement factor of ten! Upon their escape from the Shadowmaster's clutches, Claudus declares that his time on Thundera has passed. 'Farewell Lion-O, Lord of the ThunderCats, you've made your father a proud man,' he declares. The former Lord could never have been permanently reintroduced to the series without undermining Lion-O's journey through adolescence, but this is a wonderfully apt conclusion and, we get to see Claudus and Jaga standing side by side in the Shadow Realm (in a scene inspired by *Star Wars*).

Writer's Commentary from Dennis J Woodyard:

The concept for 'Shadowmaster' started with the idea of a magic cloak. I had submitted a story idea where the ThunderKittens found this and got into trouble using it. That idea was turned down, but, still liking the idea of the magic cloak, I came up with the Shadowmaster. I had reviewed an early show that featured Lion-O's dad, Claudus, showing how he stayed behind when Thundera was destroyed. Since no death scene of him was presented, I thought it might be cool to use him again. Luckily, the 'Shadowmaster' idea worked without too much backstory. I hope the Shadowmaster makes a reappearance in any future *ThunderCats* projects. His appearance was too brief to really flesh out his character and the creatures he could project from the cloak. He did appear in the re-launch of the *ThunderCats* comics, which picked up from the end of the series. That was a real treat for me. I hope people get my salute to *Star Wars* at the very end of the story, where the ghost images of Claudus and Jaga appear, just like Anakin and Ben in *Return of the Jedi*.

126. Swan Song (4 Stars)
Written by: William Overgard
US Broadcast Date: * 25 September 1989
UK Broadcast Date: N/A

There is no room for criticism of Bill Overgard here as, in a return to form, he delivers a sublime episode. While it's true that 'Swan Song' features all of his usual flourishes, he appears to take the episode far more seriously than other recent offerings, and the result balances the weird with the wonderful.

Two new characters introduced in the serial include the Ecology Inspector (a wonderfully strange concept) and his Pilot, who are both well conceived; and Overgard even manages to revive the character of Two-Time (fleetingly seen in

'Return to Thundera'). The idea of Dome-Down stealing whole environments is certainly far-fetched, but is leant an air of authenticity by the detail and tone of the script. It's a sensible episode and, as with 'Sword in a Hole', the concept behind the technology is more interesting than its physical execution.

It's nice to see the original Feliner (without its second season modifications), and there's a great emergency landing scene for the vehicle. The removal of Cats' Lair by Dome-Down is also one of the greatest moments of 'Swan Song', and concepts like this simply weren't seen anywhere else in the series; it's just hard to reconcile this as originating from the same author as the terrible 'Cracker's Revenge'!

Other highlights include some beautiful animation and direction throughout, with Pacific Animation Corporation exploring some new ideas (including some brilliant lighting during Lion-O's rescue of Snarf and Snarfer). The environmental message of the episode isn't too preachy and, upon the defeat of Two-Time, the decision to reuse Dome-Down to distribute interplanetary resources is inspired. In short, it's brilliant to see Bill Overgard in fine form.

Script Editor's Commentary from Peter Lawrence:

Imagine an Ecology Inspector in 1986 … and in a kids' show to boot. Not a lot to be said about this episode, which is right in the mainstream of Bill's work. Either he or I throttled it back, at least to the point where the solution is firmly in Lion-O's (and the Sword of Omens') hands. Personally, I love larger-than-life ideas (like the Cats' Lair being contained in Dome-Down). Until I worked on *ThunderCats*, I was always rather constrained by logic. Everything had to work. My long-time collaborator Chris Trengove will confirm that. I used to drive him crazy when I became a script's 'logic cop'. I had little time for dramatic licence. *ThunderCats* changed that – and I have some of the *ThunderCats* writers to thank for the change. 'Swan Song' is a great triumph of drama over logic (even given that the 'logic' of a show like *ThunderCats* is quite malleable).

127. Touch of Amortus (4 Stars)
Written by: Bill Ratter
US Broadcast Date: * 26 September 1989
UK Broadcast Date: N/A

Deborah Goodwin introduces us to a strange 'guest villain' in the form of Amortus, an old enemy of Thundera with a tentacle in lieu of a right arm. The episode has a fairly straightforward plot, but Goodwin adds some extra interest by providing a backstory for Amortus and details of a prior encounter with Mumm-Ra. There's also a novel exploration of Amortus's powers that are used against Lynx-O – arguably one of the series' most vulnerable characters. There's an emotional strength to this episode, and the viewer really empathises with Lynx-O's exploitation. Using Cheetara to comfort him (by use of her telepathic abilities) is also an original flourish.

Amortus's powers lie in his ability to turn opponents to stone. Rather than this being an instant effect, we're shown a slow transformation of victims as flesh gradually turns to stone, limb by limb. The revelation that ancient Thunderians lie scattered around Amortus's dominion is chilling, and it's brilliant to see them resurrected to aid the ThunderCats when called upon by Lion-O.

The only area for improvement in 'Touch of Amortus' is in the vocal performance of its eponymous character. His over-the-top ranting has become rather annoying by the episode's climax, and his voice could have been far more sinister, in keeping with the dark tone of the adventure.

'Touch of Amortus' really is a simple tale, but it's still remarkably enjoyable. Yet again, a writer hits upon the perfect formula for *ThunderCats* and adds action, adventure and mythology in equal measure. Nothing in the episode is necessarily original or breathtaking, but it offers the 'magic' of *ThunderCats*, which was so easily omitted from other episodes.

Writer's Commentary from Deborah Goodwin (Bill Ratter):

I can't really remember the inspiration for this, but I do recall that I was in America when I wrote it and was looking forward to returning to the UK, so it's possible this may unconsciously have had a bearing on the script.

I would normally write in the mornings. I'd probably spend a couple of hours outlining a storyline, changing it, thinking through the moral of the story, until I felt I had something that would produce an exciting episode. I always handwrote the outlines as I really enjoyed the freedom of being able to lavishly mark the pages with red lines and arrows, until I felt I'd reached a structured order. I'd then type it out and send to the script editor for his approval before getting stuck in to the writing.

128. The Zaxx Factor (3 Stars)
Written by: Matthew Malach
US Broadcast Date: * 27 September 1989
UK Broadcast Date: N/A

Matthew Malach's final script for the series is not the most robust of *ThunderCats* adventures, and it's probably the weakest of the writer's four episodes. Perhaps its greatest failing is in the poor characterisation of its central character, Zaxx, who only serves as a superficial adversary. Things aren't helped by a poor choice of accent (broad New Yorker) for the character, and Zaxx fails to elicit much response from the viewer.

'The Zaxx Factor' sticks rigidly to a tried and tested *ThunderCats* formula; and by this point in the series, plots featuring omnipotent objects and ancient enemies of Mumm-Ra seem tired. Nonetheless, the episode sees the welcome return of Vultureman, and it's only fitting that a Mutant (albeit one who wasn't present in the pilot episode) should make an appearance at the end of the series.

The plot concerns Vultureman's apprehension of the Interplanetary Book Mobile in an effort to escape his imprisonment. The ship is an enigmatic, but enjoyable, part of the story, and the *Ancient Third Earth History* disc discovered by Vultureman provides a brilliant way to bring the viewer up to speed with the events of the episode. The 'Saga of Mumm-Ra and Zaxx' informs us that, at one point in time, Third Earth's rule was divided between Zaxx's dominion in the Southern Hemisphere and Mumm-Ra's in the North. Unsurprisingly, both tyrants were engaged in a constant battle to overthrow the other.

While the basic plot behind 'The Zaxx Factor' is largely unoriginal, Malach does add some touches that aid it in standing out from similar adventures. For instance, it's a great idea that Zaxx's medallion gradually removes its wearer's personality to facilitate the villain's own existence; and it's even better that Vultureman, in his excitement, misses this vital information. Other highlights include the Whisker's crash scenes (with Panthro injured and Snarf, apparently, 'lost') and the perfectly-executed characterisation of Mumm-Ra, who regains some of the menace lost in recent encounters. Furthermore, it's a brilliant thought to have Snarf wear Zaxx's medallion, leading to a great line from Mumm-Ra. 'Oh how terrifying,' he mocks, just before Snarf sprouts two new arms.

Unfortunately, at the conclusion we are given yet another false ending for Mumm-Ra (who appears, yet again, to have been utterly destroyed – only to pop up in his pyramid moments later), and these scenes could have easily been avoided. Had it appeared in the first season of *ThunderCats*, 'The Zaxx Factor' might have been viewed more favourably; however, so late in the show's run, it simply feels like a reworking of previous scripts.

Writer's Commentary from Matthew Malach:

A bizarre show, featuring one of my favourite mutants, Vultureman. It's a very surreal episode: the story includes a spaceship bookmobile actually shaped like a book. Ridiculous! I think we were trying to put the point across that Vultureman was actually quite a literate fellow. By the way, you'll have to ask Peter Lawrence to verify this, but to me, it seemed that Vultureman was clearly gay, and in fact the only gay Mutant in the bunch.

I also wrote this episode as a freelancer, so I can't really address what the thinking was regarding the general direction of the series. But clearly, story ideas were growing thin. As I mentioned, this was such a strange show, it was nothing like my previous scripts.

129. Well of Doubt (4 Stars)
Written by: Dennis J Woodyard
US Broadcast Date: * 28 September 1989
UK Broadcast Date: N/A

The penultimate episode of *ThunderCats* takes the series into unchartered waters. Dennis Woodyard offers a unique storytelling style, and the result brilliantly summarises the evolution of the series and, more importantly, provides a tantalising glimpse of the domestic challenges the ThunderCats will certainly face during the revivification of Thundera.

The opening of 'Well of Doubt' sees the ThunderCats visiting an impressive Thunderian settlement. With shiploads of Thunderian countrymen returning day by day, it's clear that the ThunderCats are no longer just the survivors of a doomed race, but are now the custodians of peace and rule on the planet. The latest intergalactic spacecraft (clearly inspired by 20th Century space and aircraft) sees the return of a Thunderian 'businessman' named Baron Tass and his assistant Mr Grubber. Tass had been heavily involved in the trading of slaves on Thundera, and his dubious interests are at once quashed by Lion-O's new regime. 'They haven't changed at all,' explains the ThunderCats' new ally, Torr. 'Maybe not,' declares Lion-O, 'but Thundera has changed and, by Jaga, his shady dealings will not be allowed here any more.' The music and direction of this scene perfectly reflect the sentiment, and Lion-O's authority, courage and integrity show how he has developed since he was a young boy who escaped the planet in its dying days.

The tone and substance of 'Well of Doubt' are remarkably mature, and it's a brave gamble by the show's producers to conclude the series in a manner that far surpasses its original mandate. While a duplicitous trader and his tax accountant may seem pedestrian villains to feature, this has the consequence of preparing the series for its resolution; the viewer can be safe in the knowledge that Thunderian civilisation is firmly on the road to recovery. It's also refreshing to see that not all Thunderians have noble intentions, and this adds some credibility to their culture. Having offered a complex opening premise, the episode also later appeases action-lovers by ramping up the energy-stakes during the closing half, courtesy of Tass's resurrected warriors.

The Well of Doubt itself is relatively self-explanatory; an ancient well rediscovered by Baron Tass to wreak revenge on the ThunderCats. We're promptly told, 'The more you drink, the more you sink into the depths of self doubt'. Lion-O does, indeed, succumb to this, and his collapse of confidence at the Whisker's controls is a highlight of the adventure. Additionally, we have a welcome appearance from Jaguara, who proves instrumental in aiding Lion-O's recovery (as Panthro, Snarfer and Torr combine through the Sword to override the effects of the Well's waters). There's even a nice end gag. 'All's well that ends well,' jokes Snarfer, to which Jaguara comments, 'For that remark, you can walk back!'

Writer's Commentary from Dennis J Woodyard:

The main inspiration for the 'Well of Doubt' story was the pictures of the Toltec heads in Mexico and thousands of terracotta warriors discovered in China. Those images fired my imagination. Again, my first idea was to use the ThunderKittens. WilyKit, the girl, finds an ancient headdress that awakens these Stone Giant Guardians, who mistake her for their long-dead princess. They cause all kind of chaos on New Thundera before Lion-O destroys them in a thunderstorm. Again, the original idea was rejected, but I reworked it to keep the Stone Giants in it. Like 'Shadowmaster', 'Well of Doubt' features characters I created in writing, and designed as art director. So, it was a lot of fun seeing my characters come to life.

130. Book of Omens (5 Stars)
Written by: William Overgard
US Broadcast Date: * 29 September 1989
UK Broadcast Date: N/A

The final instalment of any television series must surely be just as difficult to craft as any pilot episode. While a series' opening adventure may present commercial challenges, the decision to end a series carries with it the weight of expectations of a legion of fans (in this case a whole generation of children) who must be placated while every loose end is successfully resolved.

Bill Overgard's 'Book of Omens' was the script chosen to complete the 130 adventures of the ThunderCats and, in short, it performs admirably. While many may have had fears about this assignment being entrusted to a writer as unpredictable as Overgard, these prove completely unfounded. Overgard's enormous creativity is coupled with an obvious collaborative input from the production office (given the importance of the episode) and the result functions brilliantly as both the series finale, and an exciting adventure in its own right.

From the fading title caption, the viewer is thrust into proceedings, and the action never diminishes as this epic races along at breakneck speed. We learn that Thundera is once again being racked by geological instability, and Lion-O and Panthro turn to the Book of Omens to learn its fate. Here they are instructed by the Guardian to complete a series of tasks in precise order, at an exact time, lest the planet and the ThunderCats should be lost forever. It's a classic 'ticking clock' storyline, and it's perfectly judged for this episode. A tile from a fountain must be returned to the Caverns of Cold, a Golden Oar to the Baleful Swamp and a Gem Light to the Mountains of the Moon, and an ancient *ThunderCats* flag must fly once more in the Iron Forest. If these tasks are successfully accomplished by the ThunderCats, these regions of the planet will be restored to their former glory. Lion-O, meanwhile, must battle Mumm-Ra in the Book of Omens for possession of the Key of Thundera, which must be presented to the Guardian at the anointed hour.

From this point, Overgard's experience as a scriptwriter bears fruit, and at the close of the first act we are treated to a dramatic recap of the ThunderCats' predicament, which really builds tension and excitement. Beyond this, the ThunderCats are frozen in time, and the remainder of the episode concentrates on the central conflict underlying the entire series: Lion-O vs Mumm-Ra. For the first time, we see the mortal enemies engaging in hand to hand combat and, though Lion-O could always have been guaranteed to emerge the victor, we're treated to some brilliant interaction between the characters. Lion-O dedicates his actions to 'Justice, truth, honour and loyalty,' to which Mumm-Ra replies, 'For evil, greed and falsity. I will twist off your Lion's head.' Lion-O, undeterred, has the final word: 'It will take more than the feeble arms of a mummy!' This sublime dialogue is maintained throughout the episode, culminating in the battle every viewer had waited two seasons to witness.

Mumm-Ra, as a character, is handled wonderfully throughout the events of 'Book of Omens', and it's incredibly liberating to see him stand up to the Ancient Spirits of Evil, rejecting their instruction and declaring, 'I am in command here'. Mumm-Ra is, of course, inevitably defeated, along with the Ancient Spirits' ultimate champion, Pyron, who is despatched in a last-ditch attempt to thwart the forces of good. With his task completed, Lion-O declares the ThunderCats victorious and, for the first time in the series, we see the iconic *ThunderCats* emblem manifest itself as a three-dimensional black cat that travels across Thundera, freeing the ThunderCats. With this, the treacherous territories of Thundera transform into beautiful panoramas, and a new age on Thundera begins.

While every possible wish for the series finale could never have been realised (for instance, it would have been nice to have seen Tygra, Pumyra and Third Earth featured), Book of Omens achieves an incredible amount in its short screen time. While it may not be the best episode ever, it fulfils its purpose effortlessly and represents everything that made *ThunderCats* memorable. The final postscript to the series takes place outside Cats' Lair as the ThunderCats join hands, declaring who they are and what they stand for against the background of a setting sun. Finally the series finishes as it began, with a shot of Thundera, sitting amongst the stars; once again the proud home of the ThunderCats.

Script Editor's Commentary from Peter Lawrence:

I wish I could remember how focused we were on the final episode. Or even if we knew it would be a final episode. I'm sure we knew it was the end of this particular order and, personally, I'm sure I'd had enough of the show (and maybe of Rankin/Bass).

No doubt I chose Bill to script it as much for personal reasons – my enjoyment of his writing, our friendship and his need for work – as for professional reasons. But I'm not sure who else I could have contracted. Len Starr was somewhat out of the picture and not happy with Rankin/Bass. Lee Schneider and Chris Trengove were working full bore on *SilverHawks* and/or *The Comic Strip* development. Larry Carroll was off in a new direction. And most of the other writers – most, not all! – were a bit iffy. I'm sure that I did not want to have a massive edit/rewrite on my hands, felt that I could trust Bill and, at the very least, knew he'd bring something wild to what is a fairly middle-of-the-road *ThunderCats* story.

I'm sure we developed the story as much in house as left it in Bill's hands. The idea that there were once beautiful locations that became dangerous locations has an in-house ring to it, and the process of entering a book is a story device I've always loved. Not original, I know – but then what is, in the final analysis? And the point is not the originality of the idea but its expression and dramatic interpretation. Separating the Ancient Spirits of Evil from Mumm-Ra is a theme I wish we'd explored further. Where, exactly, did their powers come from and why did they confer them on Mumm-Ra? I did try to explore some of these ideas and was accused by some viewers – their parents, more particularly – of being a Satanist!

I think it a terrible mistake – looking back – to have allowed Mumm-Ra to be defeated entirely and, worse, to be overshadowed by Pyron, but I do think it dead-on the *ThunderCats'* overall storyline for Lion-O to be able to control the dragons that fried him. I suspect that, if I'd been paying more attention – or had a little more time – I would not have permitted this dilution of Mumm-Ra's power and, for sure, Mumm-Ra himself would have found a way to neutralise the dragons!

There is a purity in the conflict between Lion-O and Mumm-Ra. Of course Mumm-Ra cheats. And of course Lion-O does not. And, of course, Lion-O wins. If we were writing the show now, today's zeitgeist might demand that Lion-O cheat too … but we were far too white hat/black hat for that. It will be interesting to see if the new *ThunderCats* series is as unambiguous when it comes to heroes and villains. I also particularly like the black puma. (Was it a puma or a panther?) A different way to use the *ThunderCats* symbol, which by this time was a little careworn. All in all, I think this episode shows the production team and Bill Overgard working at their collaborative best – a relatively conventional *ThunderCats* story brought to life and greatly enhanced by Bill's imagination; yet, that imagination reined in and kept 'on-show'.

PART THREE
CHARACTER PROFILES

7. GOOD AND UGLY
An A-Z of the ThunderCats *Universe*

ThunderCats introduced us to an abundance of weird and wonderful worlds and creatures. Over the course of two seasons, the ThunderCats journeyed from Thundera to Third Earth and back again, interacting with a myriad of heroes and villains. The series' scriptwriters, character designers and voice artists worked tirelessly to expand the its universe, and the list that follows is a non-exhaustive overlook at the most memorable worlds and characters they created. It features excerpts from the writers' bible, production notes, animators' drawings, scripts and psychologist Robert Kuisis's moral summaries.

ThunderCats

Bengali

A blacksmith on his home world of Thundera, Bengali was not destined to be a ThunderCat, yet the destruction of his planet led him to take shelter on Third Earth alongside his comrades, Lynx-O and Pumyra. After they showed great courage in their ordeals with Mumm-Ra, Lion-O decided to anoint the trio as ThunderCats. Bengali's 41 appearances in the series began with his season two debut, 'ThunderCats Ho! Part I'. His character design sheets made the following observations: 'He is Tygra's albino brother i.e. belongs to the same tribe. He is younger than Tygra. He acts as a leader among the three Thunderians. He is more muscular than Lynx-O. His nose is a little wider than Tygra's. His chin is square. His hair should not be too wild or long. His eyes are typically Thunderian; long and narrow. Costume: His toes are visible. The bands are fastened crisscross on his back.' Bengali's temperament would eventually become more docile than his initial description suggested, with only occasional bouts of impetuousness. Of the three 'new' ThunderCats, it would be Lynx-O who would emerge as the more natural leader.

Cheetara

Originally intended to be named Cheet-A, the series' leading female protagonist appeared in 117 episodes. A central member of the original *ThunderCats* team to leave Thundera in 'Exodus', she played a crucial role team and was famed for her incredible speed, agility and telepathy. Though her abilities to see visions through her 'sixth sense' were indistinct early in the series, she slowly began to exert a greater control over them in the show's second season. 'Her special trait is speed,' explained Leonard Starr in early show notes. 'In action she is virtually a blur except when slow motion is desired. In these cases her antagonists can be shown in extreme slow motion while her movements can seem to be at normal speed. Her voice should be very feminine, with an element of purring in it, somewhat like Eartha Kitt.'

The animators' design sheets for Cheetara are notated with the following comments: 'Her weapon is a magic staff. She takes off the staff, which is attached to her left arm with a magnet; it is no larger than her fist. However, when she flexes her hand, it telescopes into a long, multipurpose weapon. She can fight with it, pole vault with it or use it as a spear. Her specialty is that she can throw it by spinning it, and it flies into the legs of her enemies and trips them. When her use for it is complete, she need only flex her fist again and it reduces back to its original size.'

Jaga

Jaga's first appearance, in 'Exodus', was also his last in the realm of the ThunderCats. However, having made the ultimate sacrifice to save the ThunderCats by piloting their flagship, unprotected from the ravages of time, to Third Earth, this noble knight of Thundera soon returned to Lion-O from the astral realm, guiding him through his many adventures. 'He should wear a helmet,' instructed Leonard Starr's original character notes. 'His voice should be deep and dignified, somewhat like Alexander Scourby. When he reappears as a ghost it should be slightly reverberant, sepulchral.'

He was given the preliminary production name Jagu-R, and the writers' bible entry for him stated: 'For wisdom, the spirit of JAGA can be summoned. The spirit of JAGA hovers over [the scene] and his spectral voice booms out: "Pay heed, for this is the 'Eye of ThunDERa', the source of the THUNDERCATS' power!" LION-EL stares at the spirit awestruck … he seems to remember … he touches the sword tentatively … and it virtually comes alive in his hand, the "Eye" glowing fiercely.'

Throughout his time on Thundera, Jaga had been the loyal friend of Lion-O's father, Claudus, and in a notable battle with the Plun-Darrian Ratilla, he had cast the legendary Sword of Plun-Darr into the core of Thundera, inadvertently causing its eventual destruction. Though ever-present in the series' fabric, Jaga appeared in only 39 episodes.

Lion-O

Lion-O was originally named both Lion-L and Lion-EL in Leonard Starr's early story notes. The son of Claudus, he was first seen as a young boy in the series' opening adventure, 'Exodus'. His journey to adulthood was then fraught with obstacles as he assumed his rightful place as Lord of the ThunderCats. His intergalactic voyage from Thundera to Third Earth had resulted in an enigma; while he had physically reached adulthood, he had missed the life experiences and maturation of adolescence. His emotional transition would be the lynch-pin of the series as he proved, beyond doubt, his capability, integrity and credentials to lead. He was the only character from the *ThunderCats* saga to appear in all 130 episodes.

Addressing unused designs from toy manufacturer LJN Toys, head writer Leonard Starr noted: 'The physical description in LJN's notes are fine. The Sword as shown in the drawing should work, since it is slung on a diagonal. He-Man's sword, though never shown from the back, seems to be slung perfectly vertically. If the handle is constantly shown as in the drawing, except possibly over the left shoulder as Lion-O is right-handed, and the diagonal is emphasised even more, there shouldn't be any conflict. I like the glove.'

Starr also specified his preference for the Lion-O's voice: 'His voice should be baritone and manly while still maintaining a youthful quality as he is (especially in the early episodes) emotionally immature. This will probably have to be done by inflection rather than by choice of voice. In combat, in common with the other ThunderCats, he snarls, spits, growls, roars.'

In his writers' bible, Starr described the backstory for the character: 'LION-EL will become an adult without having gone through the process of growing up. The years of 10 to 18 were spent in the suspension capsules and raced by in a matter of weeks, so there's a great deal that he won't know. Some things he will discover for himself and others will be explained to him by the older and wiser THUNDERCATS. Herein lies our opportunity for both humour and the passing along of a message about growing up to our young audiences.'

In the character design sheets created to assist the show's animators, Lion-O is listed as: 'The largest and most perfectly-proportioned character. A 6' 9" body-builder type. Lion-O also carries a large, metal lion's claw glove/shield, which he wears on his left arm during battle.'

Lynx-O

The oldest member of the ThunderCats' team, Lynx-O was amongst three Thunderians who were saved by the Ro-Bear-Berbils during the destruction of Thundera. 'ThunderCats Ho! Part I' reveals that he was blinded shortly before his rescue and, ever since, his other senses have been attuned to compensate. Upon his ascension to ThunderCat status, Lynx-O quickly becomes an invaluable member of the team, having utilised the technology of a Braille Board to interpret events on Third Earth from his base in the Tower of Omens. He has a deep respect for Lion-O, and in return his leader looks upon him for wisdom.

'After he is blinded during the exodus from the exploding Thundera, his other senses become extremely sharp,' summarise Lynx-O's character design notes. 'His ears twitch and rotate as he tries to catch sound. He has a muscular body. He has an ability to defeat his enemy in an instant by concentrating all his spiritual forces. He emits ultrasonic waves from his mouth, which can destroy small objects. His costume is Oriental even after he becomes a ThunderCat. After he is blinded in Part A, his eyes are usually closed. So, he is usually assisted by Pumyra or Ben-gali when they are with him, and when [he] is alone he uses all his other senses with concentration to move or act by himself i.e. his actions should look different from others' who can see things, although he should not frown or look nervous. He should act naturally.'

In common with his comrade, Bengali, Lynx-O made 41 appearances.

Panthro

Present in 124 episodes, Panthro provided not only the 'muscle' of the series, but also an incredible talent for engineering. 'I like the bit about his being too strong for his own good, but those episodes should be confined to instances where he loses his temper,' stated Leonard Starr in his production notes from the 1980s. 'As the engineer of the ThunderCats he must be capable of delicate work and so he can't be inadvertently crushing and tearing things. It is good for him to be short-tempered though, and to go on periodic rampages. His voice should be deep and dignified while suggesting the black culture.'

First appearing as part of the ThunderCat convoy leaving Thundera in 'Exodus', Panthro (originally to have been named Panth-R) had a range of abilities that were expanded upon in the writers' bible: 'PANTHRO is the nightfighter, possessing exceptional acrobatic ability and martial arts skills. PANTHRO is the THUNDERCAT with advanced engineering skills. He can salvage enough equipment from the wreck of the spaceship to provide them with some weapons, and even some vehicles. They will not need a new source of power for a while. Fortunately, the anti-matter module that powered their spaceship is intact.'

The character's design drawings explain: 'Panthro is a martial arts expert and carries a set of nun-chucks as a weapon. When he's not using them, he either slings them around his neck or stashes them in his belt, not visible.'

Pumyra

Pumyra is the youngest of the new ThunderCats. Her 32 appearances in the second season were fewer than those of her fellow teammates, and her timid nature led to her being overshadowed by more prominent ThunderCats. Her defining characteristics are her agility and tenacity when faced with danger. Her most notable adventure came in the episode 'Mumm-Rana's Belt', in which she single-handedly attempted to thwart a scheme by Luna. Pumyra's character design sheet gave the following information: 'There is a colour tracing line on her ear like Panthro. Her eyes are rather round, unlike other Thunderians. She is younger than Cheetara. She is a charming Thunderian female and not as muscular as Cheetara. Her tail-like belt is tied at her left waist. She can jump highest of the three and moves very quickly like a leopard when she beats her enemy. When she acts, she is light and nimble.'

Having debuted in 'ThunderCats Ho! Part I', Pumyra elected to remain on Third Earth to protect the many citizens of the planet while the ThunderCats returned to New Thundera to rebuild their civilisation.

Snarf (Osbert)

Lion-O's faithful companion Snarf was present in the ThunderCats' line-up from the show's opening adventure 'Exodus', and he assisted his fellows in 124 episodes. Snarfs and ThunderCats have had a long association on Thundera, and Osbert (who is fiercely protective of anyone using his real name) was enlisted to be Lion-O's childhood nursemaid. 'In appearance [he is] somewhere between a sheepdog and a small bear,' read Leonard Starr's original notes. 'He can operate on his hind legs and use his front paws as hands, but for speed he resorts to all fours. He was LION-O's nanny and now still serves him, persisting in thinking of LION-O as still a little boy, much to LION-O's annoyance. He feels unappreciated, is long-suffering, and invariably predicts disaster as the outcome of the ThunderCats' adventures. His voice should be that of a gloomy Mortimer Snerd with a slight lisp.'

Snarf's writers' bible entry is similarly descriptive: 'Next to LION-EL's capsule is his nursemaid or nanny. It is somewhat like a sheepdog, but with space creature characteristics (horns, scaly feet, etc). Its name is SNARF and it persists in thinking of LION-EL as a child even when he has become a fully grown superhero, worrying about his going out in bad weather, making him finish his food, clumsily trying to pull him out of harm's way, thereby occasionally messing him up. He can also be fierce when pressed, overcoming his natural gentleness when LION-EL is in danger.'

Tygra

Tygra was Jaga's first choice to oversee Lion-O's development, ensuring their new lord made decisions wisely. Bestowed with the power of invisibility as well as elements of mind control, Tygra (or Tige-R as originally conceived) was wise and reserved, yet prone to temptation with aspects of an addictive personality. 'Except when JAGA makes his ghostly appearances, TYGRA is the titular head of the ThunderCats,' instructed Leonard Starr. 'He is also the architect among them, and it is he who will design and supervise the construction of Cat's Lair. His bearing is thus especially noble and tolerant. It will be for him to deal with LION-O's impetuousness and rashness, PANTHRO's tantrums, WILYKAT's and WILYKIT's mischief, etc. His voice is authoritative but warm, as much like the radio voice of the Lone Ranger as possible.'

Starr's comments on initial design drawings for Tygra reveal the evolution of the ThunderCats' weapon: 'I think the whip as such is a bit mundane. Maybe we could have a weighted ball at the end of it so that it could be used something like a bolo, pinioning arms, wrapping itself around ankles, pulling opponents' feet out from under them, etc.'

Tygra's story was further expanded on in the writers' bible: 'Tygra is the master of camouflage, capable of merging with any background. The THUNDERCATS are now much like the settlers of the early American West. They must build temporary shelter with the wreckage of their spaceship and whatever natural materials they can find in their new environment. Until they are able to determine what is edible from their surrounding vegetation, they must depend upon what remains of the supplies they had stocked aboard the ship for their journey. They know that they must build a fortress or be at the mercy of hostile forces, the MUTANTS for certain, and others whose number and strength are not yet known to them. TYGRA is the architect among the THUNDERCATS. The mountains nearby could be quarried for the stone needed to build "THE CATS' LAIR", but they are few in number. Construction will take a very long time. Can they survive that period unprotected? It is questionable.'

Having first been seen in the series' pilot story 'Exodus', Tygra went to make 102 appearances throughout both seasons of ThunderCats. Alongside Pumyra, he was destined to remain dutifully on Third Earth as his colleagues returned to their home world.

WilyKit and WilyKat

The inseparable twins WilyKit and WilyKat are the junior members of the

ThunderCats' team. Wildly adventurous and prone to mischief, they often feel excluded from their elders' adventures. They appeared in 103 *ThunderCats* episodes (each appearing only once without the other).

Debuting in the opening adventure 'Exodus', the ThunderKittens were originally envisaged as only one character, named Wildcat (and later Wiley-KT). In his first descriptions of the character, Leonard Starr wrote: 'Wiley-KT is mischievous and a troublemaker, unable to resist pranks, often fouling up the activities of the others who then have to pull his fat out of the fire. (Unlike the drawing of Wildcat, he should be smaller, a feline Dead End Kid).'[7]

Explaining the evolution of the character in his original notes, Starr added: 'In the original artist's renderings, WILDCAT was depicted as an adult. Because of the disparity in size between a wildcat and the larger cats, I converted him to WILYKAT, an adolescent. When Jules Bass felt we needed another female character I gave him a sibling, WILYKIT.'

Additional comments from Starr to LJN toys noted: 'Although their ages are never established, they behave much like unruly teenagers. They are mischievous, disrespectful to the older ThunderCats, and though often brought up short by them, are never totally repentant. They stand about chest high to the other ThunderCats. They usually wear crafty expressions but can often be surly. In combat, however, they are as effective as the other ThunderCats, but in their own way. They wear cartridge-type belts containing powders of various sorts. Some produce smokescreens, others contain sneezing and itching powders. Others crystallise into sharp-pointed tacks shaped like children's jacks ... They release [them] by spinning in place, the loop of the lariat sometimes whirling up above their heads, sometimes down towards their feet so that they have to step out of the loop, depending upon whether their target is high or low. Their voices should sound like teenagers. WILYKAT does a lot of snickering; WILYKIT giggles.'

Forces for Good

Berbils

One of the first groups of Third Earth residents to befriend the ThunderCats are the Ro-Bear Berbils. Making their debut in the series' third episode, 'Berbils', the friendly creatures provide the workforce to build Cats' Lair and help the ThunderCats secure food reserves such as Berbilfruit. Led by Ro-Bear Bill, the Berbils originate from the planet Robear, a world too small to house their entire population, thus they travel to other planets to survive. A small group of Berbils was responsible for saving the 'new' ThunderCats, Pumyra, Lynx-O and Bengali, from the destruction of Thundera.

Leonard Starr's writers' bible made the following observations about Ro-Bear Bill (originally named Coo-Ber) and his people: 'LION-EL is hoisted up out of the pit and finds himself surrounded by small furry creatures called BERBILS. They

---

[7] The Dead End Kids were a group of young characters who first appeared in the Broadway play *Dead End* in 1935.

jabber at him, their speech punctuated with sound effects as they gleefully recreate for each other the way LION-EL crashed through their trap and thudded down to the bottom, imitating the sounds precisely. LION-EL doesn't find it all that funny, and SNARF is embarrassed by his capture. They struggle against their ropes as they are pulled along. They are taken to the Berbil village, a loosely arranged group of mushroom-shaped huts. The BERBILS are farmers, and the fields of Berbilfruit are cultivated in rows according to colour, one colour being Meatfruit, another Breadfruit, others various Vegefruits, Candyfruits, etc. The leader, an elderly BERBIL named COO-BER, shows LION-EL a stand of trees. Crude spigots protrude from the trunks. They are Tingo trees, and the BERBILS milk the sap as a beverage. COO-BER pours a cup for LION-EL. To celebrate their victory, the BERBILS throw a feast for the THUNDERCATS, who in turn find the BERBILS, though rustic in appearance, to be clever, gracious and highly amusing in their antics. Furthermore, the BERBILS will help to build their stronghold, "THE CATS' LAIR", in return for their protection. It is agreed and a toast is drunk to friendship.'

Bolkins

The Bolkins are a peaceful yet mischievous race native to Third Earth. They first encounter the ThunderCats in 'The Ghost Warrior', where their actions inadvertently freed Grune the Destroyer. Their initial character description can be seen in Leonard Starr's script for the episode: 'The BOLKINS are about chest high to humans, with spindly legs and muscular upper bodies, their faces hairless but fringed with hair of uniform length so that it looks as though they are peering through a wreath. They are dressed in rough medieval garb and are not threatening in appearance.'

Brodo

A once-powerful wizard of Third Earth, Brodo was banished to the Astral World by Mumm-Ra. He meets Lion-O when the Lord of the ThunderCats travels to that realm to free his mentor Jaga, who has become the prisoner of Nemex. Brodo is able to return Lion-O to Third Earth in return for his good deed in freeing him. Peter Lawrence's script for 'The Astral Prison' reveals the original description for the character: 'BRODO's voice is extremely old and quavering [...] JAGA and LION-O look into the cell. THEY SEE: an ancient, wizened creature with long red hair [realised as white in the finished show] and a red, grizzled beard. He has only one eye – and that is dim and rheumy. But it twinkles as BRODO looks up at JAGA and LION-O.'

Brutemen

Although they appear brutal, the Brutemen are a docile and peaceful race native to Third Earth. They first appear in 'The Slaves of Castle Plun-Darr', where they are enslaved by the Mutants to build their fortress. The Brutemen are later enlisted by the Lunataks to assist with the reconstruction of Sky Tomb. 'These are misshapen creatures not resembling any particular animals, so as to distinguish them from the THUNDERCATS and the MUTANTS' stated the writers' bible. '[The Mutants] have no compunctions about enslaving them and forcing them to build their TOWER OF EVIL.'

Leonard Starr's script for 'The Slaves of Castle Plun-Darr' gave the following early description of the creatures: 'The BRUTEMEN are slightly larger than normal human size, muscular in an undefined sort of way. They have no neck to speak of, odd patches of hair sprout from their bodies willy nilly, and though their colour is predominantly grey, the colour of their hair varies. Their faces look as though features had begun to be sculpted out of putty but never completed. There is something pitiable about them. Two or more of them carry large blocks of rough black stone, as they move up a jungle trail in a ragged file. They grunt and groan.'

Captain Bragg and Crownan

Captain Bragg is the pilot of the Circus Train, an intergalactic vehicle that served as a base for his former operations as a bounty hunter. With his feathered companion Crownan, Bragg travelled the galaxy looking for paid work. After an encounter with the ThunderCats in the second season episode 'The Circus Train', he renounced his former ways and agreed to detain both the Lunataks and the Mutants in a bid to prevent their sinister antics on Third Earth.

Charr

Charr is an irascible scrap metal dealer who first appears in the season two adventure 'Return to Thundera Part II' and returns in 'The Heritage'. He twice repairs the Sword of Omens, but his allegiances are difficult to ascertain. While he predominantly acts out of self-interest, he reluctantly assists the ThunderCats. His nature is best described in Peter Lawrence's script for 'Return to Thundera': 'CHARR is a mobile wrecker and scrap metal dealer who cruises the galaxy in his Flying Furnace, salvaging scrap. He is a neutral character, neither good nor bad. He will work for anyone who will hire him.'

Claudus

Claudus was the former Lord of the ThunderCats prior to the destruction of Thundera and is Lion-O's father. In his youth, he was a much-beloved ruler of the ThunderCats' home world and, together with his loyal friend and warrior Jaga, defended the planet with the aid of the Sword of Omens. Claudus was blinded in an attack with the Plun-Darrian Mutants and was later willing to sacrifice himself to oversee the launch of the spaceship that would take his son and the ThunderCat nobles to safety under the protection of Jaga.

Claudus debuts in the season one adventure 'Return to Thundera', when Lion-O is able to travel back in time and meet his father. After the destruction of their planet, it was presumed Claudus had perished; however, the second season episode 'Shadowmaster' reveals that he had survived as the prisoner of the titular character. Travelling to the Shadow Realm, Lion-O frees his father, who ascends to the Astral World where Jaga resides.

In his script for 'Return to Thundera', Bob Haney described Lion-O's first view of Claudus: 'LION-O's father, a THUNDERCAT of noble LEONINE type, middle-aged, powerful, but blind [...] An older carbon copy of LION-O. We SEE now his noble sightless eyes, staring OFF.'

Doctor Dometone

Making his debut appearance in an eponymous episode, Doctor Dometone is a scientist and guardian of the Great Oceanic Plug that protects Third Earth. Bill Overgard's script for 'Doctor Dometone' described him as having: 'A smooth, bald head and a heart-shaped face, brush moustache and most arresting glasses. These operate like small binoculars. As the head turns, the lenses zoom in and out automatically, adjusting for proper focus. The face gives the impression of delicacy and intelligence.'

Gomplin

The Gomplin is the brave flying companion of the Tuskas. 'The GOMPLIN is like a cross between a feathered DRAGON and a WORLD WAR I biplane,' revealed Chris Trengove's script for his debut appearance in 'Turmagar the Tuska'. 'It is a creature, rather than a machine, but it has been modified mechanically to serve the TUSKAS' purposes.' The Gomplin also plays an important role in thwarting the Beserkers in 'ThunderCats Ho! Part IV'.

Guardian of the Book of Omens

First appearing in the second season adventure 'Key of Thundera', the Guardian of the Book of Omens is a mysterious figure, only heard, and never seen. He fiercely protects the secrets of the ThunderCats from anyone who enters the Book without the desired credentials. The Guardian is featured in several episodes during this period, culminating in the final instalment of the series, 'The Book of Omens', where he commands the ThunderCats to save Thundera and return it to its former glory. Matthew Malach's script for 'Key of Thundera' described the Guardian's chamber as: 'An ancient room with a grey slate floor, rather large with four dark walls. Each wall is adorned with a huge DRAGON HEAD, made of grey stone (total of four dragon heads). These are fierce, evil looking dragon heads, with huge gaping mouths, which are wide, open and baring long teeth, which seem to be made of ivory.'

Hachiman

A true friend to the ThunderCats, the samurai Hachiman lives his life by the Code of Bushido and will honour his friends to the death. He is introduced in the first season story 'The Thunder-Cutter', where Mumm-Ra brings him to Third Earth and tricks him into fighting Lion-O. Hachiman carries his famed sword, the Thunder-Cutter, which, like the Sword of Omens, possesses great powers and will not respond to evil. Hachiman makes several subsequent appearances, aiding the ThunderCats in their quest to free Third Earth from evil.

Dr Robert Kuisis made the following analysis of Hachiman for his moral commentary on 'The Thunder-Cutter': 'Honour is excellence of character, aspects of which include dignity, integrity, courage and pride. In this episode, Lion-O, who lives by the Code of Thundera, meets the samurai, Hachiman, who also lives by a code that includes honour. The honour of Hachiman, however, is almost subverted by the deception of Mumm-Ra, who attempts to have him and his sword fight on the side of evil against Lion-O and the Code of Thundera. During the course of their encounter, Lion-O and Hachiman, blinded by a false bravado, lose their perspective and engage in a duel. Neither claims he can back down and maintain respect and honour. But true honour is not a confrontation, which ignores the rightness, justice, and truth of one's actions. In a stand-off in which these principles are ignored, no-one wins. Were it not for the practical good sense of Nayda, both Lion-O and Hachiman would have perished for a distorted notion of honour. They are brought to their senses by the power of their swords, which are unable to be used for evil purposes. Reminded of true honour, they join forces and persevere against Mumm-Ra, the Mutants and the honourless Ninja. In our lives, we must be careful to learn the real definition of honour, which involves reference to rightness, justice and truth. We must be on guard so that we do not fall victim to a false bravado, which ignores judgements about the purposes of our actions.'

Ice King

The Ice King made only one appearance, in the episode 'Secret of the Ice King'. Inadvertently freed from his long sleep, he fights the Snowman of Hook Mountain for the apparent possession of his castle. At first he is presumed to be a legendary threat, but it is soon realised that he desires only to be reunited with his lost love and recover the last remnant of their existence on Third Earth, a thousand years previously.

Dr Kuisis' notes on 'Secret of the Ice King' advocated the need for empathy: 'The Ice King is driven by a primal urge, and the intensity of his drive compels Lion-O and the Snow Knight to recognise it as justified and positive. They decide to help him rather than block his intent and, creating a truce, they help him attain the egg he seeks. Gratified by the blissful vision he sees in the egg and by the memory of his past love, the Ice King expires, fulfilled in his quest. Sometimes our ability to empathise with others results in the acknowledgment that their needs and goals at a particular time are very important and necessary to them. In some instances, it is a worthwhile choice to set aside our own preoccupations and help them attain what they need.'

Jaguara

Jaguara is an ancient Thunderian sorceress. She is the guardian of the mighty gyroscope of New Thundera, located in the Great Beneath. The device is responsible for maintaining the new planet's gravity, and is actively sabotaged by Mumm-Ra in 'Return to Thundera'. Jaguara debuts in the first episode of that five-part serial, where she falls under the influence of Mumm-Ra before aiding the ThunderCats in restoring stability to New Thundera. She makes several subsequent appearances and later invites the engineer Screw Loose to the planet to assist her in the maintenance of the gyroscope.

Kano

Kano was Lion-O's loyal companion and pet during his childhood on Thundera. He is introduced in 'Return to Thundera', but his fate beyond the destruction of Thundera is unknown. The following description of Kano is sourced from the original script for 'Return to Thundera': 'ANGLE ON A PILE OF RUBBLE. A shaggy BEAST crouches behind it. It is similar to a massive DOG but has large SABRE TEETH projecting from its jaw and a ridge of razor-sharp bone growing down its back.'

King Arthur

King Arthur is a legendary king whose form and lineage are impersonated by Mumm-Ra in the first season story 'Excalibur'. The Ancient Spirits of Evil summarise the King Arthur legend to convince the demon priest to seek to obtain Excalibur. The script for the episode gave the following character description: 'KING ARTHUR, armoured, but without his helmet, rides out on a magnificent, armoured charger. He carries a shield emblazoned with a gilded coat of arms, and a royal pennant flies from the tip of his lance. EXCALIBUR is at his side.'

Kudi

The second season adventure 'Runaways' marks the only appearance of Kudi. Having saved the ThunderKittens from poisonous berries, she is impersonated by Mumm-Ra, who uses her image to infiltrate Cats' Lair. Deborah Goodwin's (aka Bill Ratter's) script for 'Runaways' offered the follow notes: 'Suddenly, a strange face pokes into the cave and SEES THE THUNDERKITTENS – reacting in some surprise. (NOTE: This is KUDI, a benevolent-looking, female, creature with a cat-like face – huge eyes – and a body structure somewhat like an ostrich.)'

Leah

The star of an eponymous second season adventure, Leah is a Thunderian refugee who becomes separated from her parents during their intergalactic return to Thundera. Upon landing on Third Earth, she first encounters Mumm-Ra, who gifts her a doll containing the sinister Mirror Wraith. When found by the ThunderCats, Leah inadvertently brings the Wraith to Cats' Lair, where it wreaks havoc before being defeated. At the conclusion of the episode, Leah's parents are located and returned safely to New Thundera. The script for 'Leah' offers the following character brief description: 'As the pod's hatch HISSES open ... A YOUNG THUNDERIAN GIRL appears. Wide-eyed and frightened. Her name is LEAH and she is about seven years old.'

Maftet

The Lynx God Maftet's only appearance in the series comes in 'Lion-O's Anointment Final Day: The Trial of Evil' by Leonard Starr. During Lion-O's quest to defeat the demon-priest Mumm-Ra, he stumbles upon Maftet's treasure chamber. Though Maftet is initially aggressive (fearing Lion-O is a thief), he soon relents and admits his power has waned due to a dearth of worshipers. Maftet was originally conceived to play a greater role in the series' opening episodes and would have explained the origins of Third Earth to Lion-O. The writers' bible contained an early, unused description of the character: 'The Lynx God, MAFTET, guards the Treasure of the Pharaohs in the ruins of an ancient Egyptian civilisation. Unlike the THUNDERCATS, in whom human and animal characteristics are more or less blended, MAFTET's body is wholly human, his head wholly that of a Lynx.'

Mandora

Mandora, The Evil Chaser plays an integral role in the adventures of the ThunderCats on Third Earth. She is an intergalactic law enforcer determined to rid the galaxy of law-breakers, a role she affects with gusto. She first appears in Bill Overgard's first season adventure 'Mandora The Evil Chaser', the script of which describes her as follows: 'Astride the ELECTRA-CHASER. She's boring in STRAIGHT AT THE CAMERA. The streamlined faring of her space bike blazing with flashing lights, the wailing of a siren, double-whip aerials singing. Every gaudy extra ever made is on the bike; chrome guards, saddle bags, radio, radar, sissy bar and buddy seat. The wheels form fiery pin-wheels, leaving a shower of sparks in her stellar wake. (Note: For design – use basic concept – but make it original.)'

Mandora's appearances in the series continue well into the second season, and she is appointed one of the 'League of Third Earth' who vow to protect the planet upon the ThunderCats' departure to New Thundera. Her final appearance comes in episode 122, 'Cracker's Revenge'.

Merlin

The ancient wizard Merlin appears in Peter Lawrence's first season adventure 'Excalibur'. He assists Lion-O in defeating Mumm-Ra, who has taken the guise of King Arthur in an effort to obtain his legendary sword.

Micrits

The Micrits are the eponymous stars of a first season episode. They are a miniature race of Third Earth natives who imprison Lion-O in a bid to cease the inadvertent destruction of their settlements. They later release the Lord of the ThunderCats after reassurances are given about their safe cohabitation on the planet. Bruce Smith's script for 'The Micrits' described the moment Lion-O first encounters the species: 'Atop the THUNDERCAT emblem on [Lion-O's] belt stands a tiny creature, a MICRIT. No taller than a thumbnail, he is a thin, bearded creature garbed in sturdy work clothing and boots. The MICRIT studies LION-O.'

Mumm-Rana

Appearing twice in the *ThunderCats* saga, Mumm-Rana represents the antithesis of Mumm-Ra and gains her power from the Ancient Spirits of Goodness. Residing in a White Pyramid, she is similar to her counterpart in that she is ancient and weak when rested, but returns to her past form when using her magical powers. In her opening story, 'Mumm-Rana', she is temporarily transformed by Mumm-Ra into a force for evil, before regaining her freedom and assisting the ThunderCats in foiling Mumm-Ra's plans. She next appears in the second series episode 'Mumm-Rana's Belt', which revealed that she defeated Luna's grandmother, Queen Luna, generations previously and became the guardian of her magic belt.

Dr Robert Kuisis addressed the comparisons between Mumm-Ra and Mumm-Rana in his analysis of her opening adventure: 'Good and evil are indeed opposites, and Mumm-Rana and Mumm-Ra represent their characteristics in this episode. The peace and serenity of Mumm-Rana contrast with the estrangement and self-hatred of Mumm-Ra. Evil may at times seem more powerful than good, because it is ruthless and plays by its own rules and not the accepted rules of a moral code. It may even set aside goodness for a time. But in the overall scheme of reality, good is stronger and its effects more powerful. Human nature has a basic propensity for wholeness and to be in peace and harmony with itself, rather than fragmented and alienated. When it responds to goodness, our nature is strong and secure, full of the power that comes from self-respect. This sense of wholeness and fulfilment is a stronger attraction ultimately than the effects of evil, which breeds only disrespect. We should commit ourselves, like Lion-O and Mumm-Rana, to alignment with the course of goodness. In doing so, we will receive the highest reward, self-respect.'

Quick-Pic

Quick-Pic debuts in the first season episode 'Mandora – The Evil Chaser'. He first encounters Lion-O on escaping from a prison term for pick-pocketing. Although initially a character of dubious intent, he redeems himself in his subsequent appearance in 'Mandora and the Pirates', when he assists Lion-O in defeating Captain Cracker.

Analysing the moral themes in 'Mandora and the Pirates', Dr Kuisis made the following observations: 'Both Lion-O and Mandora stand-up for Quick-Pic in seeking a pardon for him. He has earned their support by his reform and the good deeds he performed in assisting them in combat against Cracker and the prisoners. Friends are worthy of support and assistance, and when we interact with them, we feel a camaraderie and closeness. Sometimes, however, like Quick-Pic, when we do something wrong that we are ashamed of we are isolated from friends. We must never feel that we cannot change or make amends or that we must always be an outsider. When we do something with good intentions to make up with our friends for what we've done wrong, we will be accepted back into their friendship.'

Quick-Pick's initial character description is revealed in Bill Overgard's script for 'Mandora – The Evil Chaser': 'In the silence that follows, QUICKPIC slithers out. Tall, thin, muscular, and wiry – he's dressed in a space version of Puck's costume; Phrygian cap, voluminous sleeves and striped pants. Helping LION-O and SNARF to their feet, he brushes them off, hands moving rapidly, smoothing, rearranging, tucking. Then, tipping his hat, he saunters off.'

Scooper

Scooper is a robotic canine companion of the ThunderKittens. Built by the Berbils and gifted to WilyKit and WilyKat, he first appears in Bill Overgard's second season adventure 'Exile Isle'. He communicates with the ThunderCats via an inbuilt computer terminal and is capable of flight.

Sondora

The Guardian of the Sound Stones, Sondora, debuts in Larry Carroll's second season story 'The Sound Stones'. Sworn to protect the powerful Sound Stones from all who seek to harness their powers for evil, he assists Lion-O in foiling Vultureman's scheme to dominate Third Earth using a sonic device powered by the Stones.

Snarfer/Snarfs

Lion-O's loyal nanny, Snarf, is a core component of the series from the show's opening story. However, it is Steve Perry's two-part serial 'Feliner' that marks the introduction of further members of his species. It reveals that after the destruction of Thundera (and a long and close association between ThunderCats and Snarfs), 43 Snarfs survived and colonised another planet. One of these refugees was Snarf's nephew Snarfer, who becomes a regular member of the ThunderCats team in the second season, appearing in a total of 33 adventures. Upon the ThunderCats' return to Thundera, the Snarfs assist the ThunderCats in constructing the new Cats' Lair after being liberated from their subjugation by Mumm-Ra. Other notable members of the race include Snarfs Oswold and Egbert, whose tumultuous friendship is explored in the episode 'Locket of Lies'.

Snowman and Snowmeow

The Snowman of Hook Mountain and his faithful steed Snowmeow are trusted allies of the ThunderCats. Debuting in Bob Haney's first season adventure 'Lord of the Snows', the Snowman appears regularly throughout the series, and is invited to become a member of the League of Third Earth upon the ThunderCats' return to Thundera. His final appearance is in Larry Carroll's second season episode 'The Last Day'. Although fearsome in appearance, Snowman is loyal to the death, and his bravery aids the ThunderCats on numerous occasions. His original character description can be found in the script for 'Lord of the Snows': 'Out of the CASTLE comes a SNOWMAN, a fearsome giant YETI-type, covered in fur and wearing medieval armour. He is armed with an ice lance, sword and mace. His shield is made of glittering ice crystals and an ice visor covers his face, which heightens the sinister effect. He is mounted on a SNOWCAT, a large, muscular, white creature based on a LYNX. The SNOWCAT seems only half-tamed, snarling and rearing, its eyes flashing fire and ice. The SNOWCAT's name is SNOWMEOW.'

Terator

The Terator debuts in Peter Lawrence's first season adventure 'Good and Ugly'. Arriving on Third Earth during a space battle with his fierce nemesis, the Kymera, he is presumed hostile due to his unconventional appearance. Having realised this lapse of judgment, Lion-O assists the Terator in destroying the Kymera menace.

Child psychologist Dr Robert Kuisis made the following observations about the character in his moral analysis of the episode: 'Because [the ThunderCats] have never encountered a spaceship or creature like the Terator, and because its looks, mannerisms, and sounds are ugly and foreign to them, they consider it hostile and seek to defend themselves by attacking it ... Often our assumptions about others are based on peripheral in-characteristics rather than essential ones. Because some persons may be handsome or pretty, we judge them to be good, and because other persons are not pleasing in appearance, we view them to be bad.'

Thunderians

The peace-loving inhabitants of Thundera appear periodically throughout the series. While all ThunderCats are Thunderians, not all Thunderians are ThunderCats; a title reserved for the noble rulers of the planet. The ancient Thunderian race (possessing both humanoid and feline characteristics) are hugely varied in their appearance, each owing their lineage to different species of cats. The vast majority of Thunderians were presumed lost in the devastation of Thundera, however a large number of survivors return to the planet after its reformation in the second season to rebuild their civilisation.

Torr

The Thunderian countryman Torr is an ally of the ThunderCats who first appears in Peter Lawrence's second season episode 'Return to Thundera Part III'. A refugee returning to his homeland of New Thundera, he is initially captured by Two-Time along with his family.

Peter Lawrence's script for the episode initially credited the character only by the name 'Thunderian Refugee': 'ANGLE OF A SMALL CORRAL (metallic, like everything else in DomeDown) in which the THUNDERIAN REFUGEES are penned. The group comprises an OLD WOMAN, a YOUNG COUPLE and a SMALL CHILD. They look like the THUNDERCATS did before JAGA gave them their special clothes.'

Turmagar and the Tuskas

The many allies of the ThunderCats include the Tuskas of Third Earth. Led by Turmagar, this gentle race debuts in the first season episode 'Turmagar the Tuska'. Subsequent appearances solidify their role in aiding the ThunderCats to rid the planet of evil. Turmagar is impersonated by Mumm-Ra in the second series adventure 'Catfight', which almost triggers a civil war amongst the ThunderCats.

An extract from Chris Trengove's script for 'Turmagar the Tuska' reveals the initial description for Turmagar's species: 'The TUSKA is a humanoid with a head and upper body that resembles a WALRUS. Most of the time, it gives the appearance of sad resignation – but, when aroused, its whiskers bristle, its huge tusks threaten and it growls fearsomely.'

Under-Earth People

During 'Lion-O's Anointment Third Day: The Trial of Cunning' by Leonard Starr, the Lord of the ThunderCats encounters a race of cave dwellers known only as the Under-Earth People. Though they are fiercely protective of their treasured library of books, years spent underground have robbed them of their vision. They are at first hostile towards Lion-O, fearing he means them harm. However, after being shielded from a Mutant attack, they are assured of the ThunderCat's intentions. In return for Lion-O's good deed, they assisted him in rescuing the ThunderKittens from the perils of the caves.

Unicorn Keepers

The Unicorn Keepers are a humanoid duo who guard the gentle Unicorns of Third Earth. Their debut is in the season one adventure 'The Terror of Hammerhand', the script for which noted: '[There is] an OLD MAN who looks somewhat like Father Time ... very ethereal – with a long white beard touching the ground and a long wooden staff. A Gandalf. The OTHER KEEPER is a female version of this character. The forest has an ethereal magical look, as well.'

Another notable appearance for the duo comes in 'Snarf Takes up the Challenge', where the female Unicorn Keeper proves instrumental in assisting Snarf.

Warrior Maidens

The Warrior Maidens of Third Earth are a race of female warriors who reside in the Treetop Kingdom. They first appear in the season one episode 'Trouble with Time' and are initially cautious of Lion-O and his team. However, in time, the Warrior Maidens became one of the ThunderCats' greatest allies. The Maidens are led by Queen Willa, who is usually in the company of her younger sister, Nayda.

The Warrior Maidens were first referenced in Leonard Star's writers' bible, which revealed an undeveloped bond between Willa and Lion-O: 'They live in the treetops of their Forest Kingdom and are wary of any threat to their domination of their area, but WILLA is perplexed by inexplicably strong feelings for LION-EL, which she tries to suppress, not always successfully. LION-EL is impressed only with her prowess with bow and arrow, spear and knife. He is not aware of her as a girl. Although the THUNDERCATS as a group are occasionally [a help] to WILLA and her tribe, in personal encounters it is usually WILLA who helps LION-EL out of scrapes rather than the other way around, because of her familiarity of her native terrain. In situations of extreme danger, however, it is LION-EL's brawn that is the deciding factor.'

Wizz-Ra

The sorcerer Wizz-Ra is an ancient enemy of Mumm-Ra and appears in the first season of *ThunderCats* during the events of 'Dimension Doom'. Exiled to the Seventh Dimension, he can return but once every 7,000 years, and brings with him a powerful helmet that Mumm-Ra attempts to utilise in vanquishing the ThunderCats. Having defeated his old enemy, Wizz-Ra returns to the Seventh Dimension.

Bob Haney's script conveyed the following description of Wizz-Ra: 'WIZZ-RA is a tall, handsome, noble-looking Egyptian wizard of the ancient dynastic period. He wears a toga of the period, his muscular arms and legs showing bare. On his head he wears a shining gold helmet of the ancient Pharonic style with formalised bird wings on its either side, and a low profile crest. The helmet gives off an aura of golden light. CAMERA COMES IN SLOWLY ON WIZZ-RA. He peers out of a mirror in an anxious way.'

Wollos

The Wollos are a peace-loving race of Third Earth villagers who regularly encounter the ThunderCats and support their efforts to free the planet from evil. Their debut appearance comes in Leonard Starr's 'The Tower of Traps', the script for which reads: 'The TRAVELLER is an elderly WOLLO, short tan fur, white circles of fur around his eyes, bearded. He's dressed in simple medieval garb and rides a donkey-type creature. His ASSAILANTS are hideous (they will turn out to be GARGOYLES come to life) but for now WE ONLY GET FLEETING GLIMPSES of their faces, which are grey, as are their clothes. There are TWO of them. ONE is pulling the TRAVELLER off the rearing donkey, while the OTHER snatches a purse ... attached to the TRAVELLER's belt.'

Mumm-Ra and his Cohorts

Aluro

Aluro is one of the most competent Lunataks of Plun-Darr, possessing powers of mind control and an incredible strength of will. The following extract from Leonard Starr's second season script for 'Mumm-Ra Lives! Part II' contains the initial description for Aluro: 'A male whose weapon is his voice. He can screech – and paralyse people – but, more important than that, he can psych opponents out. He will say, very quietly: "You don't stand a chance, ThunderCat! Give in!" and the words "Give in" will echo in THE THUNDERCAT's mind ... repeating until THE THUNDERCAT's own voice begins to repeat it ... and THE THUNDERCAT does, indeed, give in. He has a PSYCH-GUN that can fire a paralysing sound beam or ... entrap an opponent within a visible forcefield. As long as he remains entrapped within that forcefield, ALURO's opponent remains too scared to act.'

Having appeared in 22 episodes of the series, Aluro becomes a perpetual prisoner of the reformed mercenary Captain Bragg and is last seen in Bill Overgard's second season episode 'Cracker's Revenge'.

Amok

Luna's loyal steed, Amok, provides the Lunatak leader's transport. Amok rarely speaks (aside from grunting approval or dissent) and is fiercely loyal towards Luna. His most prominent appearance comes in the season two adventure 'Mumm-Rana's Belt', when he mounts a short-lived rebellion against Luna in response to her poor treatment towards him.

An extract from Leonard Starr's script for 'Mumm-Ra Lives! Part II' reveals the first depiction of the character: '[AMOK] carries LUNA with him wherever he goes. AMOK has almost no ability to think but has formidable physical powers. So together LUNA and AMOK are almost invincible but separated they are useless.'

Amok's 23 appearances in the series culminate in Bill Overgard's 'Cracker's Revenge'.

Chilla

Able to freeze her opponents at will, the Lunatak Chilla is a dominant force amongst her colleagues. Gifted with her own vehicle, the Ice Runner, she is an independent force, often concocting her own plans and prone to challenging Luna's leadership.

Leonard Starr's 'Mumm-Ra Lives! Part II' script reveals: '[CHILLA is] a female whose body temperature is absolute zero. She can touch and freeze any object – and she can freeze opponents with her vaporous breath. This is particularly effective against LION-O because she can freeze his vocal chords (preventing him from summoning help via THE SWORD) and she can freeze over THE EYE OF THUNDERA, so that LION-O cannot use SIGHT BEYOND SIGHT. She can also generate a heat beam with one hand – which can unfreeze her victims. All her abilities and weapons revolve around her powers to change the temperature of her opponents and their weapons.'

Having featured in 22 episodes, Chilla is incarcerated alongside her fellow Lunataks aboard the Circus Train in Bill Overgard's 'Cracker's Revenge'.

Jackalman

Jackalman is a central member of the Mutant assembly on Third Earth, first introduced in the series' pilot episode 'Exodus'. Though he is typically cowardly in action, he is extremely tenacious, and he harbours a lust for power. He features in 57 episodes, and his most notable exploits include attempting to steal the Sword of Omens in Danny Peary's 'The Mountain' and leading a mutiny in Bruce Smith's 'Jackalman's Rebellion', both from the first season. Leonard Starr's early correspondence for the series described the Jackalmens' speech as having, 'a staccato quality, slightly throaty, suggesting dogs barking. Their laughs are hyena-like. They yelp if hurt'.

Jackalman is imprisoned on board the Circus Train in Bill Overgard's adventure of the same name and makes his final appearance is in Peter Lawrence's 'Return to Thundera Part IV'.

Luna

Luna is the vocal and overbearing leader of the Lunataks. She is almost entirely dependent on her steed, Amok, but her small stature is more than compensated for by her forceful will. Leonard Starr's script for 'Mumm-Ra Lives! Part II' introduced her as: 'A tiny female genius almost incapable of movement. She never underestimates an opponent and she has a symbiotic relationship with Amok.'

Luna often struggles to maintain her leadership due to the rebellious and squabbling nature of her fellow Lunataks, however her dominance and strategic abilities gain the reluctant respect of her comrades. Luna is also notable for her high-pitched and screeching voice (ably performed by Lynne Lipton). Though the current Lunataks arrived from the Moons of Plun-Darr, the second season story 'Mumm-Rana's Belt' reveals that Luna's ancestors originated on Third Earth. Having recovered her grandmother's magical belt, Luna is able to grow to full height and is endowed with the powers contained within it. However, she underestimates her partner, Amok, who proves her downfall, and normality is restored.

Luna features in 23 episodes and, as with all the Lunataks, her final appearance comes in 'Cracker's Revenge'.

Ma-Mutt

Debuting in Leonard Starr's second season opener 'ThunderCats Ho!', Ma-Mutt is the loyal canine companion of Mumm-Ra. He aids his ever-living master across 42 episodes and is the only creature in existence to garner the affections of the demon priest. He soon proves indispensable to Mumm-Ra, routinely assisting him in a variety of tasks. His most notable appearance comes in 'Ma-Mutt's Confusion'. Here, he briefly defects to the ThunderCats after being berated by Mumm-Ra for his mischievous nature. At Cats' Lair, the ThunderCats are able to communicate with Ma-Mutt via a translator, and he reveals his role is as 'adjutant to Mumm-Ra the Everliving' and that his dog license number is '3462'. Mumm-Ra quickly returns Ma-Mutt to his rightful home at the Black Pyramid.

Monkian

Monkian is a strong-willed if impulsive Mutant of Plun-Darr. Arriving with his fellow team members in the series' first episode, 'Exodus', he makes 55 appearances altogether. He is aggressive and irritable by nature and at times must be restrained from acting in haste. He reluctantly takes orders from Slithe, though, like many of the Mutants, he desires to assert himself as leader. Monkian's most prominent adventure is Lee Schneider's first season tale 'Monkian's Bargain', which sees a pact formed between Monkian and Mumm-Ra. Courtesy of some powerful orbs, Monkian is briefly granted omnipotence over Third Earth, but on learning the price of his new abilities (that he must perpetually remain in Mumm-Ra's pyramid), he relinquishes his powers. He is later imprisoned by Captain Bragg aboard the Circus Train and bows out in the season two episode 'Return to Thundera Part IV'.

Leonard Starr's early correspondence referenced Monkians as speaking 'very

fast, suggesting chattering. Their laughs are particularly monkey-like. They screech if hurt.'
Notes accompanying Monkian's character design sheets reveal his people are 'very powerful and quite large. Their weapons are also medieval. Our lead Monkian carries a flail and a shield. They have very long ape-like arms that drag on the ground.'

Mumm-Ra

Having debuted in the series' second episode, 'The Unholy Alliance', Mumm-Ra is one of the most recognisable characters in the *ThunderCats* saga. The demon priest has existed for generations – since a time when Third Earth was still First Earth – prior to meeting the ThunderCats. Residing in his Black Pyramid, the Everliving relies upon the powers of the Ancient Spirits of Evil to restore him to his previous powerful malevolence. Mumm-Ra sees the ThunderCats as an invading force on Third Earth and, through a myriad of failed plans, tries everything he can to gain possession of the Sword of Omens and subjugate them. With his loyal hound Ma-Mutt at his side, he even travels to New Thundera to pursue Lion-O when the ThunderCats return to their homeworld.
Mumm-Ra's initial character design drawings noted: 'He will transform his feeble bandaged mummified form into a masculine warrior form. This very form is his previous form. He transforms his form saying the usual magic spell ANCIENT SPIRIT[S] OF EVIL TRANSORM THIS DECAYED FORM TO MUMM-RA [later given the addition of ...THE EVERLIVING]. In Mumm-Ra's ancient previous life, he was called Poisonous, Python, Mumm-Ra. He is surviving in a sarcophagus in the black pyramid. He came to know the existence of the Eye of Thun-Dera by the power of the pyramid. He will be given a new life by possessing it.'
Unused ideas for the character are recorded in Leonard Starr's early show notes: 'The Egyptian tombs were called the "Everlasting House" and the deceased had a "Ka" or double, which could leave the tomb, but which had to return to the mummy or perish. This suggests the Dracula/coffin shtick and could be useful in explaining why he must use the Mutants as his delegates. He is reluctant to leave his mummy unattended: if it is destroyed, he too perishes. From time to time, in one or another of his incarnations, he does chance it however. He should also be heavily muscled, unlike LJN's suggestion that he be tall and lean. Or maybe he grows the muscles when he assumes his other guises. Anyway, the kids can't get enough of muscles [...] The five-headed serpent is also MUMM-RA's insignia, invisible on his chest until it glows from within, behind the bandages, possibly pulsing. He has a bass voice, but raspy, like George Macready, and reverberant, befitting his environment.'
Mumm-Ra's introduction to the series was described in Starr's finalised writers' bible: 'A part of the onyx wall dissolves and MUMM-RA's voice says, "ENTER", and continues as the MUTANTS pass through various treasure chambers. "I AM AWARE OF THE "Eye of ThunDERa". I DISCOVERED IT DURING MY FIRST LIFE SEVEN THOUSAND YEARS AGO WHILE CHARTING THE HEAVENS. I KNOW OF ITS POWER AND MEAN TO POSSESS IT!" The MUTANTS are incredulous. MUMM-RA has lived for seven thousand years? They are now in the burial chamber proper. An ornate mummy case stands against the

wall. The lid now flies open and MUMM-RA stands revealed, his muscular body wrapped in decaying bandages, wearing a cape and helmet in the Egyptian style. Through a gap in his bandages his terrible eyes are seen as he fixes the MUTANTS with a malevolent gaze. "AS LONG AS MEN OF EVIL EXIST, MUMM-RA <u>LIVES</u>!" An uneasy alliance is struck. The MUTANTS need MUMM-RA's magic. MUMM-RA, confined to his tomb, needs the MUTANTS' ability to move about. Each secretly believes that they will destroy the other once the Eye of ThunDERa has been wrested from the THUNDERCATS.'

After being featuring in 88 episodes, Mumm-Ra is last seen in Bill Overgard's series finale 'The Book of Omens', where he engages Lion-O in hand-to-hand combat and is ultimately defeated.

Red-Eye

Red-Eye is a member of the Lunataks team with special optical powers. Like his comrades, he is revived from his imprisonment in lava in the five-part 'Mumm-Ra Lives!' serial. He is huge in stature and fierce in battle. Leonard Starr's script for 'Mumm-Ra Lives! Part II' stated: '[Hi is] a male whose optical abilities stem from his ability to "read" heat masses. He thus has a very characteristic POV – similar to the robot cowboy in WESTWORLD. Any object that gives off heat is visible to RED-EYE, who can, therefore, see TYGRA even when he goes invisible. On the other hand, it is possible to blind RED-EYE by overloading his "eyes" with heat. RED-EYE then whites out ... loses all his sight. He also has a heat-seeking weapon – THE SIDEWINDER – which he can hurl at an enemy and which returns to him once it has done its damage.'

Red-Eye is perhaps the least prominent member of Luna's team and is rarely integral to the Lunataks' plans throughout his 19 appearances. He becomes a perpetual prisoner of Captain Bragg in 'The Circus Train' and makes a final appearance in 'Cracker's Revenge'.

Tug-Mug

The final member of the Lunataks is Tug-Mug. With his weapon, the Gravity Carbine, he is a formidable character. Leonard Starr's script for 'Mumm-Ra Lives! Part II' introduced him thus: '[Tug-Mug is] a male with massive strength that stems from the fact that he lived on a PLUNDARRIAN MOON that had enormously powerful gravitation pull. On THIRD EARTH, therefore, TUG-MUG can leap nearly a hundred feet straight up in the air. He can move faster than CHEETARA and is her nemesis. His weapon is a gravity carbine that affects the weight of its targets, making them too heavy to hold – or too light to remain on the ground. The carbine can make an opponent's body so heavy that he is immobilised.'

Having made 21 appearances in the series, Tug-Mug is last seen as a prisoner aboard the Circus Train in 'Cracker's Revenge'.

S-S-Slithe

Slithe is the duplicitous leader of the Mutants. Across 59 adventures, he crafts a variety of plots in a bid to appease Mumm-Ra and destroy the ThunderCats. His debut comes in the series' pilot episode, 'Exodus' and, like his comrades, he is finally imprisoned aboard Captain Bragg's Circus Train, making a final appearance in 'Cracker's Revenge'. Because of the Mutants' inherent desire to usurp him as leader, he maintains strict discipline and is not afraid to chastise his colleagues for failure. He has a dry sense of humour and his arrogance often proves his downfall.

In Steve Perry's two part adventure 'Feliner', it is revealed (by Ratar-O) that Slithe's former occupation was as a cook, before he asserted himself as leader of his people, the Reptilians. Leonard Starr's early notes to production departments recorded: 'The Reptilians' speech has a hissing quality to it, the sibilants being accentuated and held slightly.' Slithe's design drawings noted: 'They wear [a] dumpy, prehistoric costume with metal leg bands. The leader carries a large battle axe and a shield. This is also a shield shooter.'

Vultureman

The evil genius and inventor Vultureman was conceived as a member of the Mutants' team from the very beginning of the series. However, while his colleagues debut in the pilot episode, his first appearance his held back until the subsequent adventure 'Lord of the Snows'. Having been responsible for creating and reinventing the majority of the Mutants' arsenal, Vultureman spends the majority of the series plotting intricate plans to destroy the ThunderCats, enjoying a tumultuous relationship with the Mutant leader, Slithe, who regards his schemes with scepticism. While his fellow Mutants typically work together, Vultureman is happy to 'freelance' his skills to likeminded villains including Ratar-O and the Lunataks, and he famously pilots his vehicle, the Flying Machine.

Leonard Starr's early show notes contained the following information about Vultureman's species: 'Vulturemen should have less costume as it would encumber them when they fly. They should also have a kind of helmet to go with their beaky (but also recognisably human) faces. Their necks, however, are long, and capable of the kind of mobility that long-necked birds have. They are scruffy looking with the kind of feathery collars that vultures have. Their wings, rather than sticking out of their backs the way angels' wings are usually depicted, are folded across their bodies when not in flight, the way real birds' do. They carry lances of a crude medieval design and possibly a variation on the other Mutants' shields. The Vulturemen speak with a croak. Their laugh resembles the crows' CawCawCaw. They squawk if hurt.'

Vultureman appears in 40 episodes and is the last Mutant to be featured, outlasting his teammates with a final appearance in the series' antepenultimate instalment, Matthew Malach's 'The Zaxx Factor'.

Forces of Evil

Amortus

Amortus is an ancient enemy of Thundera who has the ability to turn his victims to stone. He appears in Bill Ratter's second season adventure 'The Touch of Amortus', where he appeals to Mumm-Ra for help in retrieving him from exile in the Land of

No Return. After a failed attempt to exact his revenge upon the ThunderCats, Amortus is banished to the Netherworld by Mumm-Ra, who is fearful of his treacherous nature.

Ancient Spirits of Evil

The four statues looming over Mumm-Ra's cauldron in the Black Pyramid are the mysterious Ancient Spirits of Evil. They represent the source of Mumm-Ra's powers, and he enjoys a tumultuous relationship with them; at times their slave, and occasionally their master. Mumm-Ra must appeal to the Ancient Spirits of Evil to allow him to transform to his former self, and they also periodically grant him additional powers, including the ability to impersonate others.

In one of Leonard Starr's original and unused concepts for the series, the Spirits would originally have had a fifth member and would have appeared in a different form: '[Mumm-Ra's] sarcophagus stands upright against the wall of his tomb, the Black Onyx Pyramid. The murals on this wall depict the five Man/Beast Gods, all ominous in their appearance, that MUMM-RA is able to transmogrify himself into by means of his staff, the top of which is a five-headed serpent, all heads wiggling. By touching one or the other of the heads, MUMM-RA expands in size, and amid smoke and flashes of light, is seen wearing helmets depicting the Beast God summoned. MUMM-RA's glowing eyes should be seen through the helmet's eye-holes but a bit of his mummy face should be seen beneath the helmet. The Beast Gods are: HOR-RA the Destroyer (hawk-headed helmet), SMYE the Devourer (crocodile-headed helmet), BAT-TAR the Dreadnought (bull-headed helmet), GRUN-TAH the Defiler (boar-headed helmet), SCREE-CHAH the Deceptor (baboon-headed helmet). These helmets should all have Egyptian decorative characteristics, but should be much more massive and ominous. (The actual Egyptian designs are somewhat benign.)' Although this extract provides names for the Ancient Spirits of Evil, contradictory evidence can be found in a commissioned but ultimately unproduced season one script entitled 'The Beasts of Mumm-Ra' by Gerry Matthews. In this, Mathews named the creatures Condawk, Minotaur, Krokdon and Porcinicus Rex, and depicted them coming to life and terrorising the ThunderCats. On screen, only one member of the Ancient Spirits of Evil was ever named: given the moniker of the Vulture King in the season one adventure 'Dimension Doom'.

Baron Karnor

Baron Karnor has the dubious distinction of being one of the ThunderCats' only adversaries to threaten them from beyond the grave. His one and only appearance comes in Leonard Starr's season one adventure 'The Tower of Traps'. After a lifetime of pillaging the treasures of Third Earth, he has equipped his fortress to prevent the theft of his vast collection. Lion-O and the ThunderKittens find his Earthly remains after navigating his many traps.

The character is best described in Leonard Starr's script for the episode: 'The BARON, a large figure, is seated in a high-backed chair facing the door. In his hand is a large sword and he wears a helmet with a crest on its front bearing the large letter "K". The chair seems to be in the middle of a mound of gold coins, trinkets, chalices etc, so that some spill over his feet, some are sprinkled on his lap. He is top-lit, the light hitting the top of his helmet, the sword, the tops of his thighs. His face is in total darkness as is his chest, except for a heraldic "K" SEEN DIMLY on his chest armour. He doesn't move.'

Baron Tass and Mr Grubber

Baron Tass and his accountant Mr Grubber are Thunderian citizens who return to their home world in the penultimate episode, 'Well of Doubt', written by Dennis Woodyard. In his former life on Thundera, Tass was notorious for his duplicitous dealings and was linked with enlisting less fortunate citizens into slavery. Upon his return to the planet, Lion-O declares that New Thundera is no place for the duo's criminal dealings. In response, Tass seeks the Well of Doubt in an effort to bring down the new regime. He and Mr Grubber are thwarted by the ThunderCats and face judgment at the new Thunderian settlement.

Burnout

Appearing in 'Mandora – The Evil Chaser', Burnout is an intergalactic criminal who briefly escapes incarceration. He is returned to Mandora to serve out his punishment after a brief encounter with the ThunderCats. His character description, as crafted by writer Bill Overgard, was as follows: 'His appearance is announced by the supersonic sound of a powerful engine, the squeal of tyres and the noisy shifting of gears. Physically, he resembles a large, ugly warthog, with a crew haircut and tiny, mean eyes. His powerful body, armoured in old automobile parts, IS A CROSS BETWEEN MAN AND MACHINE. Although he runs, he gives every appearance of a fast-moving car, his FEET ending in a blur.'

Captain Cracker

The robot pirate Captain Cracker is an untrustworthy adversary of the ThunderCats who appears in numerous episodes. His debut comes in the first season story 'Mandora and the Pirates', while his final outing is the second season adventure 'Cracker's Revenge', both penned by series veteran Bill Overgard. In the script for his debut story, he is described as: 'A robot of ancient manufacture. Every part in his "body" has been replaced many times, some with makeshift spares of a different model. Hence, he has an uneven, patched appearance. His left "eye", apparently not replaceable, has been covered with a black steel plate screwed in place. His face, lively with the stamp of the old rascal, has a cunning about it. A droopy "moustache" of irregular filament wires completes his antique look.'

Captain Shiner

Captain Shiner is the mercenary of the *ThunderCats* universe. Piloting his huge space vessel, the *Vertus*, he has a large crew at his disposal and travels the universe looking for paid missions. Neither truly good nor evil, he proves to be a notable ThunderCat foe in their first encounter in Bill Overgard's season one adventure 'Sword in a Hole'. Overgard offered the following script description of the character: 'CAMERA PANS UP (HOLDING SNARF's VIEWPOINT), taking in a towering FIGURE in a WWI Prussian officer's uniform. Most arrestingly, he wears a mirror of a monocle. As he turns his head down toward SNARF, the monocle sends out a blinding flash of light for one numbing second. This is CAPTAIN SHINER.'

Having been commissioned by Mumm-Ra to lure the ThunderCats to the *Vertus* in his debut adventure, Shiner is forced to enter a black hole and companion the ThunderCats in their quest to escape its clutches. Having jettisoned himself from the wrecked *Vertus* in an escape vehicle, he presumably rebuilt the vessel by the time of his subsequent appearance in 'ThunderCats Ho!', where he was utilised by Mumm-Ra to transport Thunderian slaves to Fire Rock Mountain.

Charr-Nin

The season one episode 'The Evil Harp of Charr-Nin' by Douglas Bernstein and Denis Markell introduces the mysterious genie Charr-Nin. Emerging from his magical harp, he ensnares his victims with the offer to grant wishes. He first reveals himself to the ThunderKittens and later imprisons them along with Lion-O. His downfall comes in a battle with Mumm-Ra, after the mummy fails to set him free from his imprisonment in the harp.

Driller

The Driller is a mercenary who is memorably utilised by both Mumm-Ra and Jackalman in a bid to defeat the ThunderCats. The Driller must obtain diamonds to sharpen his drill points, and it is in return for these gems that the he will work for hire. His debut comes in Howard Post's season one episode 'Spitting Image'. The following description of the character is taken from that script: 'A sand devil (dust spiral) swirls violently on the desert sands. A sink hole appears beneath it and the sand devil is sucked down into the desert. Now THE DRILLER emerges, spinning fast as it rises up from beneath the sand's surface. THE DRILLER is at least as big as a THUNDERCAT. It has a screw-thread, pointed head and a mean, mantis-like face. It has powerful pincer arms folded across its thorax (chest) and, like an insect, its abdomen (lower body) is tapered to a point – patterned like a wood screw.'

Demolisher and Dirge

The Demolisher travels to Third Earth in an eponymous adventure with his squire, Dirge. Seeking Mumm-Ra (for an unprovoked duel), he instead finds himself battling Lion-O, who brings his unbeaten record of conquests to an end. Dr Robert Kuisis made the following observations about the character in his moral analysis of the 'The Demolisher': '[He is] a mercenary, who seeks violence for violence's sake, and fights without regard for any principles. He has no beliefs and fights not for a cause, but merely as an exercise in strength. As a result, he appears out of control and is a victim of his own disorder and confusion. Whenever we allow our own physical impulses to be expressed without moderation and without regard for purpose, we too are subject to disorder and confusion. Any expression of force must be linked with a rational purpose and must be appropriate to an end.

Behaviour must always be consonant with moral standards.'

Giantors

The Giantors of Third Earth are a brutal, towering race who first appear in the series' third episode, 'Berbils'. They are briefly mentioned in the writers' bible in the following context: 'The BERBILS are jubilant, [and] gather around LION-EL happily. It is the first time the TROLLERS [later renamed Trollogs] have ever been repelled. But now heavy footsteps are heard thudding through the forest. The GIGANTORS, ordinarily too lazy to raid the BERBILS themselves, have come to teach the upstart warrior, who cheated them out of their booty, a lesson. There are three of them – each roughly twice the size of LION-EL. He reaches for his sword – prepared to fight – but SNARF tells him that he will be no match for them and that he should call for reinforcements and not be a show-off.' The unwitting slaves of the Giantors are the similarly menacing Trollogs, who are enlisted to perform their masters' wicked conquests.

Grune

Grune the Destroyer is a renegade ThunderCat who first appears in Leonard Starr's season one adventure 'The Ghost Warrior'. He is a close ally of Jaga's and fought side by side with him in defending Thundera. Regrettably, he succumbed to the temptations of power and turned against the code of Thundera. His subsequent appearances see him seeking revenge upon his former order. The script for 'The Ghost Warrior' described him as: 'A fierce MARTIAL FIGURE, helmeted, wearing armour. One sabre-tooth protrudes from his upper lip on the right side. (Note: He is a RENEGADE THUNDERCAT, SABRETOOTHED TIGER variety, and should be designed accordingly.)'

Hammerhand and the Berserkers

The ruthless pirate Hammerhand is introduced in Ron Goulart's first season episode 'The Terror of Hammerhand'. Named after his brutish metal limb, he sails the seas of Third Earth wreaking terror with his band of Berserkers. Though his ship and crew are apparently lost in their debut adventure, he returns on subsequent occasions and is notably enlisted by Mumm-Ra to capture Bengali, Lynx-O and Pumyra in the five-part serial 'ThunderCats Ho!' Here Hammerhand's associates are named as Cruncher, Ram-Bam and Top-Spinner.

Goulart's script for 'The Terror of Hammerhand' gave the following early description of Hammerhand: 'Two mean characters look at the shore. They are the BERSERKERS and they speak as if "berserk" ... They shake their heads and are very very uptight about everything. They are dressed in somewhat of a Viking style and have beards. The very big guy is HAMMERHAND ... his left hand formed in the shape of a HAMMER (a la a James Bond-type character). The other – shorter and fat – ... is his #1 man. Although we assume there are other BERSERKERS (rowing the ship etc) WE SEE them only in passing – in the background ... doing things pertaining only to the running of the ship.'

Inflamer

The Inflamer's first encounter with the ThunderCats comes in the season one episode 'All that Glitters' by Bob Haney. His services are called upon to reforge the Sword of Omens in the heart of a volcano. However, rather than aid the ThunderCats, he turns against them. The creature's initial description is revealed in his debut script: 'SNARF moves to a kind of stone chair on which a weird lumpish FORM sprawls. Some grey smoke rises from BEING. CUT TO: SNARF approaching weird form on stone chair. A sooty, ashy black and grey face IS SEEN on the BEING, which resembles a burned pile of bones and rags.' Once restored to his former glory, the Inflamer is later described as: 'A completely different being. Thirty feet tall, a fiery red and yellow sleek form, hair all yellow flame, demonic face and upper powerful torso all red flame, lower body tapering to a kind of funnel-shaped point, which now dances over the ground like a tornado of fire.'

The Inflamer returns as an obstacle to Lion-O's confrontation with Mumm-Ra in the ThunderCat's final trial, 'The Trial of Evil'.

Kaymera

The Kaymera are an aggressive race engaged in an unending war with the Terator's people. A Kaymera attacks Lion-O during the events of Peter Lawrence's first season adventure 'Good and Ugly' and attempts to convince the Lord of the ThunderCats (who presumed their gentle appearance reflective of their personality) that his intentions are true. Having realised the error of his ways, Lion-O destroys the Kaymera's space craft, thus saving the Terator.

Dr Robert Kuisis made the following observations about the Kaymera in his moral summary of 'Good and Ugly': 'Because the Kymera is handsome and pleasing, they assume it is friendly. When their assumptions are proven wrong, they and the other ThunderCats are forced to do battle to avoid the Kymera's destructive purposes and to help the Terator ... This episode represents a lesson we know from our own experiences to be true – that appearances may be deceiving and we must go beyond looks to determine the qualities of persons.'

Mad Bubbler

The Mad Bubbler appears only once, in an eponymous second season episode penned by Kimberly Morris. He resides in an abandoned Thundrillium mine near Hook Mountain and has the ability to extract underlying evil from even the most benevolent of victims (with the sole exception of Snarfs) as he encases them in his bubbles. The character was included in *ThunderCats* at the behest of toy manufacturer LJN Toys, who wished to market a bubble-making device (though the toy never reached any further than prototype stage). LJN designer Kevin Mowrer made the following notes on his designs for the character: '[It has a] chitinous arm socket. Large clear fluid bladder – ridged. Vestigial arms could be small PolyPro "snap-ins" for poseability and colour or could be moulded on ... [There is an] alternative design with eyes with integrated bellows: head cowl moves up and down to dip strip and pump bellows. Arms pump up and down with head.'

Mongor

Guest starring in Peter Lawrence's episode of the same name, Mongor is a physical manifestation of fear. With his fearsome scythe, he is unwittingly released upon the residents of Third Earth by the ThunderKittens. The script for 'Mongor' described the character thus: 'A monster, half human, half-goat, with heavy ram's horns and baleful yellow eyes, their pupils narrow vertical slits. NOTE: This first manifestation of MONGOR, though awe-inspiring, is no more than a fearsome, fiery preview of his final form, which will be fully revealed in later scenes. This fiery creature pounds the homestead, grinding the already ruined buildings into the ground.'

'Monsters' of Third Earth

The ThunderCats' adopted planet Third Earth is home to a vast array of native species. The many notable 'monsters' encountered include the Gaw Rak Rak (the twin-headed river monster that memorably pursues Lion-O during his Anointment Trials); the Tree Monster; the Tongue-A-Saurus; the Living Ooze; Crab Men; and Gargoyles, to name but a few.

Mossland Monster

The Mossland Monster is a resident of the Mosslands of New Thundera. The creature appears only once, in the second season adventure of the same name by writer Chris Trengove. Trengove's scripted description of the character read: 'In an underground cavern, a huge shape is spread over the rocky floor. This is the MONSTER OF THE MOSSLANDS. (A form of plant life, he is about 70 feet tall and vaguely humanoid in shape. Composed entirely of moss, he is more or less featureless. But he has eyes that blaze green, sending out a beam that covers his victims with moss, immobilising them.)'

Mumm-Ra's Disguises

In his quest to destroy the ThunderCats and reassert himself as supreme leader of Third Earth, Mumm-Ra adopts numerous disguises, often used to infiltrate Cats' Lair or obtain information from a reconnaissance mission. These impersonations, granted to him by the Ancient Spirits of Evil, usually fall into two categories; either emulating existing characters (for instance various ThunderCats and Third Earthers) or providing his own creations. Prominent examples of the latter include the false Thunderian Pumm-Ra and the Nether Witch. At other times, Mumm-Ra transforms into various creatures, including a Locust and a Diamond Fly. Additional personas he adopts include Silky, Gregory Gregian, Kudi and King Arthur.

Mutants of Plun-Darr

The Mutants of Plun-Darr are a race every bit as genealogically diverse as Thunderians. They are war-like creatures including species of Reptilians,

Monkians, Jackalmen and rodents. An army of Mutants forms an armoured convoy that attacks the royal ThunderCat flagship in the series' opening episode, Exodus, by Leonard Starr; and a variety of nameless Mutant workers are seen periodically in and around Castle Plundarr throughout the series.

Nemex

Nemex is responsible for imprisoning Jaga in Peter Lawrence's series one episode 'The Astral Prison'. He is determined to learn Jaga's secrets but is ultimately thwarted by Lion-O, who travels to the Astral World and frees his mentor.

Nemex's original character description, which differed from his final televised form, is revealed in the episode's script: 'The spectral form of JAGA is chained to the wall of the cell. Standing before him is the small, wizened form of NEMEX, the Warden of the Astral Prison. Like JAGA (and like everything else in the Astral World), NEMEX is ghost-like, his body faintly translucent. His eyes glow green. His hands and feet are clawed and he wears a cloak at the centre of which is a jewelled insignia [with] glowing colours [matching] his eyes.'

Plutar

The criminal Plutar makes a brief appearance on Third Earth in Bill Overgard's first season episode 'Mandora – The Evil Chaser'. After a brief escape from his incarceration, he is returned to captivity. Overgard's script described Plutar as: 'filthy, his face is a black mask, whites of his eyes and red gummed teeth in sharp contrast to a dark, sinister countenance. Spiky hair sticks straight up and his clothes are an abstract series of patches. A tattered cape trails him like a smoky cloud.'

Pyron

Pyron appears in the series' final episode, Bill Overgard's 'Book of Omens'. He is the champion of the Ancient Spirits of Evil, summoned into the Book to aid Mumm-Ra in preventing Lion-O from his ultimate victory in restoring Thundera to its former glory. He is defeated by fire after a brief battle with the Lord of the ThunderCats.

Queen Tartara

The eponymous star of the season one episode 'The Crystal Queen', Tartara is a ruthless collector who cages the gentle Arietta Bird and is eventually thwarted by Lion-O. Dr Robert Kuisis made the following observations about her in his moral analysis of the episode: 'One way persons of all ages contribute and feel necessary is through giving. Animals, like the Ariettabird, freely respond to their place in the balance of nature by playing their appropriate roles. The Ariettabird's role is helping to produce a fruitful harvest of Berbilfruit by singing. For persons, it is giving to others and making a contribution to society. This is in contrast to Tartara, who never learned the pleasures of sharing. Instead, she hoarded treasures and therefore never felt necessary or part of a group. We should accept the treasures of human companionship and seek to play a role in contributing to society. Then we will find in our giving to and receiving from others that we are useful and necessary.'

Ratar-O

The Mutant Ratar-O is a Plun-Darrian military commander who debuts in the first season two-part epic 'Feliner', written by Steve Perry. His weapons of choice are twin Rat's Eye daggers and he travels the galaxy in his armoured spacecraft, the RatStar. Though he at one time allies himself with Vultureman, Ratar-O typically views his fellow Mutants with contempt, and he usurps Slithe as their leader stranded on Third Earth. He proves to be a formidable opponent for the ThunderCats, but is subsequently defeated. An image of Ratar-O appears to Lion-O during the events of the first season finale 'Fond Memories', and he returns for a final appearance in the second season opener 'ThunderCats Ho!' He is a descendent of the Mutant warlord Ratilla.

Ratilla

Ratilla the Terrible was a Mutant warlord who threatened Thundera during the reign of Claudus. He is first seen in flashback in Peter Lawrence's 'ThunderCubs Part I', engaged in battle with Jaga. His weapon is the powerful Sword of Plun-Darr, which comes close to rivalling the Sword of Omens' mystical properties. Ratilla is defeated by Jaga and his Sword is cast into the core of Thundera, inadvertently resulting in the cataclysmic event that destroys the planet. The Sword is later retrieved by Mumm-Ra in his quest to destroy the ThunderCats.

Robots

Throughout both seasons of ThunderCats, a variety of robots plague Lion-O and his team. Memorable examples include: the Wolfrat, one of Vultureman's sinister inventions; and the Warbot, a Plun-Darrian robot the construction of which on Third Earth wreaks havoc for the ThunderCats. Peter Lawrence's first season episode 'Mechanical Plague' sees the ThunderCats faced with a combined force of robotic creations, including a return appearance by the Technopede, which previously attacked the Tuska Warriors in Chris Trengove's 'Turmagar the Tuska'.

Rock Giant

Appearing in an eponymous first season episode by Peter Lawrence, the Rock Giant is released after a volcanic eruption on Third Earth. The script for the episode gave the following description of the creature: 'The mountain range and the VOLCANO itself are moving, the contours flowing, great folds of earth and rock being forced into strangely distorted shapes. From these shifts in the mountains' contours, the eventual shape of THE ROCK GIANT begins to emerge in front of MUMM-RA ... eyes open ... mouth, nose and ears become defined [...] THE ROCK GIANT inexorably breaks away from the VOLCANO, creating rockslides and volcanic explosions as it does so. (NOTE: THE ROCK GIANT is huge. Upright, he will stand half the height of THE CATS' LAIR.)'

After pursuing the ThunderCats, the Giant is destroyed by Lion-O's application of intense heat, followed by cold, which shatters it.

Safari Joe and Mule

The intergalactic hunter Safari Joe debuts in an eponymous first season episode. With his trademark catchphrase 'Safari Joe does it again,' he is a dedicated 'sportsman' and has travelled to Third Earth to capture the ThunderCats and add them to his list of victories. With his robotic assistant Mule, he calculates the weaknesses of each of his victims and lays traps accordingly. He is defeated when he underestimates his latest opponents. Steve Perry's original script for 'Safari Joe' summarised the character's appearance, complete with a variant spelling of his name: 'Jo's a regulation BIG GAME HUNTER – khaki, bush hat, etc – and holds a gleaming MULT-BARRELED "GATLING" rifle. MULE, his robot "bearer," is a semi-humanised version of a CANAL MULE locomotive.'

Safari Joe returns, briefly, in the final first season episode 'Fond Memories', courtesy of Mumm-Ra's magic.

Scrape

Scrape represents an environmental hazard to the inhabitants of Third Earth in his appearance in Bill Overgard's first season episode 'Doctor Dometone'. With his mechanical submersible Eel, he wishes to drain Third Earth's Great Oceanic Plug in order to retrieve a viable fuel source for his own planet, Blue Plunder. An extract from the script for 'Doctor Dometone' introduces the character: 'SCRAPE gets out. He wears a transparent underwater suit. Under it the hardhat and cigar are visible. SCRAPE picks up the intercom from the underwater console. Clicking it on, he talks, his voice sounding gargled.'

Shadowmaster

The Shadowmaster is introduced during the final run of *ThunderCats* episodes, in an adventure entitled 'Shadowmaster'. Upon the destruction of Thundera, he captured the former ruler of the planet (and father to Lion-O) Claudus. Having been a powerful force for evil on the 'old' Thundera, he had been banished to the Shadow Realm by Claudus and had waited patiently to exact his revenge. He is eventually encased in rock when the combined forces of Lion-O and Claudus prove too powerful for him.

Dennis Woodyard's script for 'Shadowmaster' described the Shadow Realm as having a 'dark and moody look, think of dark blues and greys. The land is rocky and barren, as if in a perpetual winter. The sky is always grey and heavily overcast [...] WE SEE the SHADOWMASTER standing in the chamber looking at his shadow on the wall. (This WALL SHADOW serves as his version of MUMM-RA's CAULRON.)'

Spidera

Spidera features in the first season adventure 'Queen of 8 Legs' by Steve Perry.

Residing in the Kingdom of Webs on Third Earth, she is defeated by the combined force of the ThunderCats, despite having ensnared both Lion-O and Snarf in her giant webs. Perry's script for the episode reveals the following early character description: 'THE EGG in the KINGDOM OF WEBS. Sudden LOUD SCREECHING. THE EGG explodes. Shell fragments and dust settle. SPIDERA is revealed. SPIDERA SCREECHES in horrible frenzy and rage. (NOTE: SPIDERA is hairy and big as a bus. A HUMAN TORSO joins a SPIDER's BODY such as a centaur so that her arms and legs are semi-human.)'

Ta-She

Ta-She is an Egyptian princess who is summoned by Mumm-Ra in an attempt to learn the powers of the Doomgaze. She possesses the power to entrance the minds of men with her beauty. A perpetual inmate of the Time Warp prison, she seeks her freedom in Steve Perry's first season episode 'The Doomgaze'. During the events of this episode, her powers almost overwhelm the ThunderCats, but she is defeated as a result of Cheetara's immunity to her charms. Child psychologist Dr Robert Kuisis made the following comments on this scenario: 'Lion-O becomes infatuated by Ta-She's beauty and falls under her hypnotic spell. Even in the face of imminent danger to himself, Ro-Bear Belle and the other ThunderCats, he is unable to see through her appearance and grasp the essential evil beneath her charm. Only when rescued by Cheetara does he regain his judgment, discern the superficiality of her looks, and reflect on the dissimilarities between them.'

Trollogs

Introduced as servants of the Giantors in the series' third episode, 'Berbils', the cave-dwelling Trollogs are primitive Third Earthers with an aggressive nature. In the first season episode 'Eye of the Beholder' it is revealed that they are Mutant informants. Leonard Starr's writers' bible referred to the creatures as 'Trollers': 'The fray is not going well for the Berbils as LION-EL and COO-BER [later called Ro-Bear Bill] join in. The BERBILS fight bravely, their principal weapon being a blowgun that shoots little luminous stun darts, but the TROLLERS, while not much larger than the BERBILS, are much more muscular, very ugly, and armed with battle-axes, spiked clubs etc. LION-EL plunges into their midst, scattering them like tenpins. As the TROLLERS regroup to charge again, LION-EL draws his sword, and whirling it above his head, creates a forcefield that flings the TROLLERS back, and they retreat in disorder. The TROLLERS periodically raid the BERBIL village for their stores of Berbilfruit and Tingo juice. COO-BER explains that the TROLLERS can only eat the leaves of the Beevilberry bush, and while these bushes grow in abundance on the mountain tops above their caves, the GIGANTORS who inhabit that region won't let the TROLLERS pick them unless they supply the GIGANTORS with Berbilfruit and especially Tingo juice, which while simply nourishing to the Berbils, is intoxicating to the giants.'

Two-Time

First encountered in the third instalment of Peter Lawrence's 'Return to Thundera' serial, the robot Two-Time possesses two heads and commands his huge vessel, Dome-Down. After imprisoning Thunderian refugees, Two-Time comes face to face with Lion-O who, after almost succumbing to the robot, defeats him. Two-Time returns for a final appearance in Bill Overgard's second season episode 'Swan Song'. In this instance, he finds himself being pursued by an intergalactic ecology inspector. Using Dome-Down, he has been surreptitiously stealing precious landscapes across the galaxy and selling them to eager purchasers whose worlds have been polluted. He is eventually jettisoned from Dome-Down and the craft is recommissioned to benefit environmental efforts.

Peter Lawrence's script for 'Return to Thundera Part III' described Two-Time as: 'A bizarre and malicious robot-like creature who has a head and feet at both ends of his body so that he can walk with one head up – no matter what Dome-Down's gravity field is doing. On each of his foreheads he has a large button and a projector lens. He can control Dome-Down's gravity field by pressing a button on whichever of his two foreheads is upright.'

Zaxx

Zaxx formerly reigned over Third Earth's southern territories. Mumm-Ra, ruler of the northern territories, desired total domination of the planet, and so fought him for this. After his powerful medallion was stolen by Mumm-Ra, Zaxx was defeated. In Matthew Malach's second season adventure 'The Zaxx Factor', Vultureman brings about Zaxx's temporary return, and he resumes his age-old battle with Mumm-Ra before being consumed in the Black Pyramid's cauldron. Malach's script described him as: 'A four-armed super being ... Zaxx's head is that of an Ibis, with a long, curving beak and tiny black eyes. Zaxx is able to attach himself to any kind of body (as we shall soon see). The arms are covered in feathers, wings droop from behind. Zaxx wears a large silver medallion/chest plate around his neck.'

Principal Locations

Black Pyramid

The Black Onyx Pyramid is the ancient home of Third Earth's devil priest Mumm-Ra. Inside is a network of passageways and vaults that all lead to Mumm-Ra's Tomb Chamber. The Pyramid first appears in the series' second episode, 'The Unholy Alliance', and was referenced in the writers' bible: 'As the MUTANTS explore the land, they see a black onyx pyramid in the distance, an OBELISK standing at each corner. As S-S-S-Slithe approaches, daggers spring out of the ground. Passage seems hopeless when suddenly the daggers withdraw. Beyond the FIELD OF DAGGERS lies a desert, and they have not traversed it by much when they find themselves being rapidly sucked under. Here too, just as they appear doomed, they are suddenly able to extricate themselves. Something or someone is permitting them to approach the BLACK PYRAMID, which now looms ominously before them. There is an inscription on one of its smooth, black, polished sides. "THOSE WHO WOULD PLUNDER THE TOMB OF THE GREAT MUMM-RA BEWARE! ... LEST YOU UNLEASH HIS EVIL MAGIC!" Magic is exactly what the MUTANTS need, and the more evil the better.'

When the ThunderCats return to their home world in the second season, the Ancient Spirits of Evil grant Mumm-Ra's appeal to erect a similar building on New Thundera.

Castle Plun-Darr

Stranded on Third Earth, the Mutants of Plun-Darr began construction of a fortress to serve as a base for their onslaught of attacks against the ThunderCats. Representing the very finest in Plun-Darrian technology, Castle Plun-Darr is surrounded by a moat to aid in defending the building. The Castle is designed in the image of a Mutant, complete with retractable wings that make the entrance impregnable. Inside there sit a myriad of dungeons and quarters and a control room. The Castle first appears in Leonard Starr's season one episode 'The Slaves of Castle Plun-Darr', in which it is constructed by an enslaved army of Brutemen. Though its architect is unknown, many of its systems and technological installations are later designed and maintained by Vultureman.

Cats' Lair

After the destruction of Thundera, the architect Tygra drafts plans to recreate the ThunderCats' home, Cats' Lair, utilising natural materials found on their adopted planet Third Earth and technological embellishments gleaned from their crashed starship. The Berbils aid the ThunderCats in the construction of the building.

Cats' Lair first appears in Leonard Starr's episode 'The Slaves of Castle Plun-Darr'. Animation production artwork bore the following annotations: 'The Cats' Lair is built with equipments salvaged from the mothership and is against the BG cliff (marble rock). It is 165 feet tall. The Paw is made of metal goods. When the ThunderTank goes out from the Paw, it lifts up 45 degrees. The bridge in the centre extends forward over the valley, sliding open, and reaches the opposite ground.'

Upon the ThunderCats' return to New Thundera, a workforce of Snarfs begins construction on a new Lair. After a short delay, this is completed by the time of the second season adventure 'Leah'. While the design and appearance of Cats' Lair on Third Earth stayed close to the ThunderCats' ancestral home on Thundera, the new Lair features a radical redesign and appears significantly larger.

Sky Tomb

Sky Tomb is the home of the Lunataks of Plun-Darr. However, unlike the ThunderCats' and Mutants' respective fortresses, this one is mobile. First appearing in Leonard Starr's five-part serial 'Mumm-Ra Lives!', the giant device is fuelled by large quantities of Thundrillium. Extracts from the script for 'Mumm-Ra Lives! Part II' reveal the device was excavated from the lava that encased the Lunataks on Third Earth and was restored with the aid of Third Earth slaves: 'SKYTOMB will be THE LUNA-TICS' [the original working name for the Lunataks] sinister, mobile headquarters. A team of BRUTEMEN, WOLLOS and BOLKINS, shackled together and driven on by MONKIAN and JACKALMAN (both carrying whips), is freeing SKYTOMB from the remains of its lava prison (it was encased along with THE LUNA-TICS) and refurbishing it. The work is nearing completion [...] THE COMMAND CENTRE serves the same function as THE CATS' LAIR HEAD COUNTROL ROOM and is similarly equipped – although the technology is very different, very spacey and alien.'

Third Earth

Third Earth becomes the ThunderCats' adopted homeworld after the destruction of Thundera. It is also home to countless other species, and has wildly unpredictable terrain. *ThunderCats* head writer Leonard Starr envisaged the world as planet Earth in its third stage of evolution, following an atomic disaster that had, presumably, removed all but a remnant of human civilisation. The writers' bible made extensive notes about the various environments on the planet, correlated to a map drawn by Starr:

> The ship crashes in the African jungle, scattering the suspension capsules containing the THUNDERCATS. THE CATS' LAIR will be built facing THE PLAIN OF FERTILITY, the BERBILS' farmland, as a visible warning to any invaders or plunderers. A river separates the area they have staked out from the strongholds of the MUTANTS and MUMM-RA, but on their own side of the river there are dangers aplenty.
>
> The FOREST OF SILENCE, where nothing is heard, not one's own footsteps, not the roars and cries of the beasts and birds that inhabit it, not one's loudest shout. It is a silence so oppressive as to be vice-like, and to enter the Forest is to risk madness.
>
> The GARDEN OF DELIGHTS, seemingly a paradise, the scent of flowers so powerful as to be intoxicating, music so exquisite that one is lulled into a false sense of security, hot springs to further sooth and enervate one, beautiful maidens to serve one's every wish .... To enter is to wish never to leave, leaving one unconcerned and therefore vulnerable to the ever-present dangers lurking beyond.
>
> In the swamps bordering the river, the LIVING OOZE lies in wait. Actually a live creature, it can reach out to snare and engulf unwary passers-by. Beyond is the MIGGIT SWARM MONSTER, also a creature, but composed of millions of biting, stinging gnat-like insects. The GREAT VOID is seen as a humanoid white silhouette against whatever background he appears. To wrestle with him is to risk slowly losing one's own form and disappear into nothingness.
>
> Both the THUNDERCATS and the MUTANTS must try to effect an alliance with the SNOWMEN OF HOOK MOUNTAIN. They are large, obviously covered with fur beneath their clothes, in appearance somewhere between the Yeti and Bigfoot. Their kingdom and lifestyle are medieval. Their stronghold can only be reached by climbing the inside face of the hook-shaped mountain that their castle is perched upon. The SNOWMEN's friendship is necessary because of their ruby mines, the rubies being needed to power the laser weapons the THUNDERCATS and the MUTANTS brought with them and that are

now growing weak. The THUNDERCATS will achieve a grudging friendship with the SNOWMEN by helping them fight off the SNOWMEN's traditional enemies, the VULTUREMEN.

A slip while climbing HOOK MOUNTAIN means falling directly before the cave home of THE VORTEX. It is not necessary to enter the cave to be exposed to its danger. The VORTEX's tornado-like, funnel-shaped whirlwind comes sweeping out of the cave to swallow up the unwary into its greedy, swirling mouth.

In their continuing war with MUMM-RA, S-S-S-SLITHE and the MUTANTS, the THUNDERCATS must confront them on their own territory. To do this they must cross the RIVER OF DESPAIR, so called because its waters are too swift and treacherous for any sort of boat. To attempt swimming across is suicidal. There are two bridges. At the upper reaches of the river is the BRIDGE OF LIGHT, but this only appears when the furnace at the foot of the bridge is stoked in the nearby forest. [THE UNICONS who inhabit the forest] are friendly with the THUNDERCATS, especially so because the THUNDERCATS have protected the lovely, gentle, enchanted creatures from the GORGONS, BASILISKS and MANTICORES in the forest beyond theirs. Despite the UNICORNS' willingness to help, however, there is not always a sufficient supply to bring the BRIDGE OF LIGHT into being, and so the bridge at the nether end of the river must be attempted.

This is the BRIDGE OF SLIME. As its name suggests, it is difficult enough to get to the top of its high arch, but then extreme care must be taken not to slip off, for if one falls into the river one is swept inexorably into the WHIRLPOOL OF INFINITY, and if that is survived somehow, one must then face the horrible GAW RAK-RAK OF THE TWO HEADS atop its craggy rock. If one slides down the BRIDGE OF SLIME, it is almost impossible to avoid falling onto the PIT OF THE NETHERWITCH. She is a creature who can take many forms, at times beautiful and beguiling, at times horrid and deadly.

Even when able to cross the BRIDGE OF LIGHT, dangers abound. To get to MUMM-RA's or the MUTANTS' strongholds, the THUNDERCATS must go through the PASS OF THE ROCKMEN. These creatures are able to merge with the rocky faces of the mountains on either side of the pass, their presence unsuspected until their arms shoot out form the walls to snatch at their victims. In battle, however, they tend to shatter when struck.

Beyond lies the SPONGE FOG, an ever-present murky mass of air that is so heavy and oppressive that it drains one's last bit of strength, so that one must rest before attempting to get through the CAVE OF TIME. This is actually a tunnel, and one must try to run through it as quickly as possible, for one ages visibly while in the Cave. This is extremely difficult for one must inevitably age to some degree, and the older he gets the slower he goes, and of course, the slower he goes, the more he ages.

The only way to regain one's youth is to bathe in the GEYSER OF

LIFE. This secret is known by WILLA, QUEEN OF THE WARRIOR MAIDENS.

The FIRETREE FOREST seems ordinary at first, but the beasts who live within are so cowardly that the intensity of their panic sets the trees aflame. It is WILLA who knows where the shallow streams run through the forest so that it can be safely traversed.

It is also WILLA who supplies the special boots needed to cross the DESERT OF PHOSPHOROUS SANDS that fuel the FIRETREE FOREST. In certain cases, the services of the FIRETHROWER will be required, but he is mercenary and will work only for gold, just as readily for the MUTANTS as for THUNDERCATS. He is a creature of living flame who lives in a volcano and is able to hurl deadly fireballs. He must periodically bathe in molten gold in order to refurbish his powers. The THUNDERCATS must also cross the BOTTOMLESS CHASM, where the people of SECOND EARTH dumped their nuclear waste. Laser-like blasts shoot up at intervals in no particular spot and are extremely deadly. The THUNDERCATS will also face the perils of the FOREST OF GIANT INSECTS [and] THE SWAMP OF SERPENTS, confront MOLEMEN, CRABMEN, RATMEN, etc. The mystic secrets of all time and space will be called upon to aid the THUNDERCATS in their continuing struggle for a peaceful world on THIRD EARTH.

Thundera

Thundera is the home world of a huge variety of species; dominated by the feline Thunderians and governed by the ancestral order of the ThunderCats. Renowned for its pacifism and civilised world order, it was defended from attack throughout the ages by the powers of the mystic Eye of Thundera, which sits in the hilt of the Sword of Omens. The planet was destroyed during the reign of the ThunderCat Claudus after a geological catastrophe. Having escaped the devastation of the planet, the ThunderCats travel to Third Earth, where they live by the spirit of the Code of Thundera: justice, truth, honour and loyalty. In Bob Haney's 'Return to Thundera', Lion-O is granted a glimpse of his home world when he travels back in time to an image of the planet. The following extract is transcribed from that episode's script: 'The image of ThunDERa projected from the CAPSULE shimmers like a mirage; GAUDI-ESQUE futuristic buildings and ramps. LION-O trotting toward the city's main gate, which is in the form of a big THUNDERCAT head, with open mouth through which one enters-exits. TWO GUARDS, armed with ray pistols, at the gate. LION-O moving stealthily down street … [The streets] are really ramps curving and twisting and rising and descending. CAT motifs here and there. But some buildings are cracked, some ramps tilted, rubble has fallen here and there, effects of earth tremors.'

In Peter Lawrence's second season, five-part epic 'ThunderCubs', the ThunderCats learn that Thundera is reforming and, after a period of exploration, they returned to New Thundera to retrieve their countrymen and rebuild their civilisation.

Tower of Omens

With the addition of Bengali, Lynx-O and Pumyra to their ranks, the ThunderCats realise a second base on Third Earth is necessary to combat the increased threat posed by the Lunataks. Like Cats' Lair before it, the Tower of Omens is designed by Tygra and constructed by the Berbils. This occurs in Leonard Starr's five-part serial 'Mumm-Ra Lives!' The building serves as an observation tower and features an integrated Braille Board, which assists Lynx-O in monitoring activity on Third Earth.

PART FOUR
MERCHANDISE

8. ALL THAT GLITTERS
The Toy Story

Throughout the 1980s, television-led merchandising was abundant. With the He-Man cartoon series, *Masters of the Universe*, having enjoyed healthy sales, producers were becoming ever-more aware of licensing potential. The He-Man series had actually been engineered around an existing toy line from Mattel and, as increasing numbers of television tie-in toys appeared on the shop shelves, the manufacturers began to assert control over programme content. Cartoon characters began to be carefully embellished to maximise toy sales, with a constant stream of weaponry and accessories introduced to meet commercial needs, and the *ThunderCats* toy line would become one of the most memorable and successful of the decade.

Rankin/Bass was happy to maximise the licensing potential of their property, and the *ThunderCats* licensee, LJN Toys, became a hugely influential player in its development – although the show would never be compromised by it being dictated solely by market forces. Programme content would remain the domain of Rankin/Bass, thus avoiding the conflict between integrity and profit that affected so many series during this era in their quest for absolute domination of the toy market.

When *ThunderCats* was deep in pre-production, Stan Weston, President of Leisure Concepts Inc, was charged with selecting a toy maker to take it to market. The winning company was LJN Toys, a medium-sized manufacturer based in New York. The company had been founded by Jack Friedman, who understood the value of manufacturing toys linked to action/adventure serials. Paul Samulski, who was in charge of product development at LJN, explains how the company obtained the license for *ThunderCats*:

'We knew from first glance that it was going to be a "special" product line for us, and it was exactly what we were looking for at that time ... Something to go head-to-head with Mattel's He-Man and *Masters of the Universe*. I assigned José Longoria to it and we jumped in head first. Obviously the show was the vehicle that was going to initially drive the success of the property, but you have to remember that this was the time when licensing was truly coming into its own. The success of the toy line would guarantee continued interest in the show and everyone knew that. Sure, the success of the show also guaranteed interest in the toy line, but that's why we worked together as one unit ... to make sure that all the requirements were covered, for the animation as well as for the toy line.

'We had a very good relationship with Stan Weston. In addition to my relationship with him (from a product design and development point of view), he was also very friendly with both Jack Friedman (our President and CEO) and Karen Weiss (our Director of Licensing). We did not have to make a pitch presentation, [but] I don't remember a lengthy bidding process (as there were for other licenses at that time). One of the reasons we went after *ThunderCats* was because we were hoping to take away some of the market share from Mattel and their *Masters of the Universe* line of products. I remember a couple of early meetings with Rankin/Bass (with Ted Wolf and Arthur Rankin) and the *ThunderCats* production team (prior to us actually signing the licence) during which we seemed to "hit it off" as creative groups who both "got it". I had chosen José to be the head of our internal *ThunderCats* development (for a variety of reasons) and he and I never had any problems fitting in with the show's development team.'

As detailed in the first section of this book, Stan Weston's company, Leisure Concepts Inc, had been the catalyst for the production of *ThunderCats* after the show's initial creator, Ted Wolf, had visited Weston, who in turn had shared the concept with Rankin/Bass producers Jules Bass and Lee Dannacher. Furthermore, LCI employee Mike Germakian was responsible for a large amount of initial design work on the series, having been 'loaned' to Rankin/Bass to work on its development.

'For years, LCI repped Rankin/Bass for worldwide licensing,' explains Stan Weston. 'LJN was just one of the many toy companies we worked with – for whatever reasons, we just made a deal with them at the time. It was good for all concerned. A very good and profitable time was enjoyed by all.'

The issue of the profitability of the *ThunderCats* merchandising effort is briefly addressed in a book published in 1998 by writer Norma Odom Pecora. *The Business of Children's Entertainment* (pages 74-78) discusses the effect of merchandising children's programming and, based on information provided by Leisure Concepts in 1986, states that there were 'in excess of 65 domestic and 80 international licenses' granted for *ThunderCats* including, 'party favours, beach towels, toys, games, linen, crayons, juvenile clothing and shows, lunch pails and thermoses, Halloween masks, dinnerware, sleeping bags, sunglasses, balloons, stickers and books.' The book also asserts: 'The licensing activity for *ThunderCats* generated close to $10 million in gross royalties (1985-1987)'; and 'Agreements included 8% of toy revenues to Telepictures and a percentage of Telepictures' net profits on syndication revenue, videocassette sales, and program licensing fees to LCI.'

At LJN, the *ThunderCats* brand was overseen by line manager José Longoria. 'I must have been about three years out of college when I went to work for LJN toys,' says Longoria. 'It was a very promotional company. Jack Friedman, the principal, had figured out that toys sold better when they were associated with licensed properties that had a presence on TV and the movies. When I was hired, the company was already handling quite a few entertainment properties like *ET*, a Brooke Shields fashion doll, Spielberg's *Gremlins* and quite a few others. I think the Michael Jackson dolls and the Boy George doll came after *ThunderCats* were in place. The property, as I'm sure you know, was originated by Ted Wolf, and by the time we started working on it the characters were outlined and Rankin/Bass was starting to plan the scripts. For the toys, we had a business model in place: [to replicate the success of] Mattel's He-Man line, which was hugely popular already. We would eventually replace it as the number one boys' property. Our advantage was that we were promised that we would have input into the design of the cartoons before they were produced. We got rough sketches from Rankin/Bass (or maybe they came from Wolf) and we still had time to "toy them up" before they went to the Japanese animators.

'My boss Paul Samulski and I started to meet with Rankin/Bass weekly to make sure we had toy presence in the animation. The person that seemed to manage things there was a woman named Lee Dannacher. They had their office above the broadcasting museum in Manhattan. I remember they had an internal artist in place and we liked what they had done with the Cats' Lair. It was already a very cool variation of the Sphinx, but with a cat's head. I still have that head sculpture in my studio. I think an outside inventor brought us the idea of using the concept from Tin Can Alley, which was an old Ideal Toys target shoot game using light sensors. We hired Kevin Mowrer to design the toy version, and an outfit in Canada, Deadline Engineering, to make the tools. The sculpt was done by Bert Brooks.

'Most of the other vehicles and weapons [Rankin/Bass] had in mind were boring to us, so we insisted on redesigning them to be sure we had interesting merchandise. Eventually, with some help from freelance artists, sculptors and designers, my team orchestrated the series of vehicles and gadgets that we knew we could merchandise as toys. Among the contributions I was in charge of were the ThunderTank, the Feliner, Hammerhand and the Berserkers and a few others. Most made it into the animation and the toys.'

While it is true that LJN toys were in regular contact with Rankin/Bass, supervising producer Lee Dannacher explains that there were challenges to the relationship: 'It was very difficult adding a whole dimension that we were only just touching upon in regards to input. With *SilverHawks*, we were at the table from the beginning with the toy company, which was a different way of producing. With *ThunderCats*, Rankin/Bass created the whole world of the show, and we knew that the toy line was going to be there, so we needed to be mindful in the scripts and the character development that these were going to be toys. We had discussions [along the lines] that, "Okay, every good guy, every ThunderCat, needs to have a weapon" – because they sold the weapons in the blister packs, and Lion-O needed his sword and Cheetara had her damn stick, and what did Tygra have, his balls? And Panthro had his nun-chucks. So we were mindful of that – that there would be a whole subsidiary line of weapons and vehicles in the show – but it was all our ball game.

'If they wanted to send over design ideas, we could take a look at them, and we had the choice of using them or not using them. Over the course of the episodes, we gave our designs to LJN, whether they were characters or vehicles, but there was absolutely no pressure. We were producing the shows; the toys could take what they wanted to use from us. But I think that relationship changed a little in the second 65 episodes, and it was hugely different on *SilverHawks*, because then it was like, "The toy company (Kenner) will give their needs to you and you'll have to fit them in." With *ThunderCats*, as far as those things went – those character models, weapons and vehicles – when they got their act into gear, Leisure Concepts were producing the toothbrushes or the sheets, the secondary licence for the comic world [and so on]. That was their ball game; they could make whatever deals they wanted, with the caveat that everything came past our desk for approval. They'd send us some prototypes and the arms would be articulated or the toothbrush would have lights on it and they'd want us to take a look at it, but our responsibility was to make sure the moulding they had done in China as closely resembled Lion-O [and the other characters] as possible, and the colours were correct, and there was nothing offensive about it that would get us into trouble with the children's advisory groups out there. So they all came past us for approval, those subsidiary licences. But as far as developing the show went, and deciding on original designs for characters and vehicles, it was all Rankin/Bass.'

Paul Samulski adds his recollections about LJN's input: 'We had a great deal of influence on what made it into the show. Of course, we were still just the toy licensee and they weren't going to bow down to us and blindly accept every suggestion we made, however the dialogue was always open, and we definitely left our mark on the show. José and I got involved right from the get-go and were contributors to the actual character design of the lead and secondary characters. From costumes to weapons to names, we were always included in the decision-making sessions. Obviously, one of the reasons we were attracted to *ThunderCats* as a property was that, from our first look, we always thought it was wonderfully conceived and fantastically designed. There really wasn't a need to "throw out" many designs, but we did definitely request lots of changes (large and small), and the production group almost always accommodated us. Some were based on manufacturing limitations, some were based on our knowledge of what kids like and don't like, and some were simply based on suggestions we made that we thought improved the "look and feel" of the product. We were like an extension of the staff at Rankin/Bass and they treated us as such. We would get together to review both product and series designs, discuss storylines and identify what products might be hiding between the lines ... and also just to "blue-sky" as a group.'

Exactly how much the televised episodes of *ThunderCats* were influenced by LJN Toys is difficult to discern. Undoubtedly, however, LJN had minimal input into the scripts. Any changes the company would suggest would most likely have been cosmetic adaptations that would support the toy line. A good example of this is the 1987 figure the Tongue-A-Saurus. Though the character most certainly originated at LJN toys, it appears on screen for only a few seconds, in the episode 'Time Switch', therefore its presence is incidental to the story as a whole. 'I remember that the Tongue-A-Saurus was an independent inventor submission,' recalls José Longoria. 'We stylised it and submitted it to the animators.'

Another illustration of the relationship between character and toy is provided by Hammerhand and the Berserkers. Originally appearing in the 1985 episode 'The Terror of Hammerhand', the characters were conceived by writer Ron Goulart and designed by Rankin/Bass. However, in the second season opener, 'ThunderCats Ho!', they returned sporting a revised design. While they still resembled the originals, designer and sculptor Kevin Mowrer had adapted them for LJN's upcoming Berserkers series of toys. Hammerhand's associates had previously been a rather unremarkable group of (unnamed) humanoids, but Mowrer's work transformed them into the memorable characters of Ram-Bam, Top-Spinner and Cruncher. Again, though, this must count as a revision of the original Berserker characters rather than an outright creation.

While LJN's contribution to the series was certainly notable, it was seldom intrusive, and *ThunderCats* was never dominated by the quest to sell merchandise. Perhaps the most significant role the toymakers played in the show's evolution was a series of suggestions made in response to early drawings by character designer Mike Germakian. (See Chapter 7 for Leonard Starr's response to this commentary.) Having reviewed these drawings, LJN collaborated with Rankin/Bass to tweak the designs (and most notably those of the characters' accessories) to make them more suitable to take to market.

In most instances throughout the duration of their licence, LJN's role would be advisory, and they made only the occasional suggestion that a character or device be included in a script. While these additions would usually be relatively minor (and as such would not affect the show's continuity – e.g. the Astral Moat Monster), a few more prominent figures did originate from LJN. A good example can be seen in Kimberly Morris's second season adventure 'The Mad Bubbler'. In this instance, LJN requested that Rankin/Bass include a plot to introduce their prototype bubbling machine. The designs for the character were created by LJN associate Kevin Mowrer. This was thus a rare case of an episode crafted almost entirely to facilitate the toy manufacturer. 'I came up with the idea of doing a bubbler because, at the time, bubble-blowing toys became popular,' reveals José Longoria. 'I'm not sure, but it might have been CAP Toys, a Cleveland company, that were blowing out sales with bubble items. I knew management would like the idea of marketing a bubble toy. I then submitted the idea along with a bunch of others to the production people at Rankin/Bass. After it was okayed as something they were willing to write into the story, I asked Kevin Mowrer at Mowrer Design to flesh it out. Russ Whitman, a model maker at Product Dynamics (who is an amazing talent), worked on it for weeks, but couldn't come up with anything that didn't make a mess. We showed it at toy fair but never took it into production. Russ did the patterns for the ThunderTank, the Stilts, the Wings, the Driller, the Feliner, all the Berserkers and almost every character requiring moving parts. A typical way to come up with toy concepts was to use outside inventors. An outside guy would come in unsolicited with a cool mechanism. If we liked it, we would license the idea for royalty and adapt it for the *ThunderCats* stories and submit the design to be written into the series. Tongue-A-Saurus and Fist Pounder were in that group.'

Designer Kevin Mowrer describes the relationship with Rankin/Bass as 'give and take': 'The folks developing the show were really running those decisions,' but if they saw something creatively that worked well and also drove toys, it was good for the property and they'd put it in the show. Definitely not a case of the toy company creating the show.'

LJN Toys, the initials standing for Lewis J Norman, had been formed in 1970. The company's founder Jack Friedman had received initial backing from his previous employer, fellow toymaker Norman J Lewis, hence the use of a reversal of the latter's initials. Pursuing both toy manufacture and video game publishing, the company had enjoyed modest success with toy lines including *Dungeons & Dragons* and WWF action figures. Asked about the success of the *ThunderCats* acquisition, Paul Samulski reveals LJN knew they had the potential to make huge inroads into the action figure market: '*ThunderCats* was very successful for LJN. It was actually our most successful articulated figure and accessory line.'

Sculptor Steve Kiwus agrees that LJN were determined to maximise the possibilities of their license: 'I assume it was very successful, because they rode it to the end. Back then, a really good license lasted three years; that was the life cycle. If you sold toys on a property, you expected to get three years out of it. That changed with *Ninja Turtles* because all of a sudden it was in year four, year five, and people were saying, "When's this going to die? It keeps going and going." These are just my impressions, but it seemed to me [*ThunderCats*] was their golden child, their main thing that they were doing – the big money maker. I know it wasn't *Dune* [an

LJN toy line based on the 1984 film that performed disastrously], because *Dune* was at the same time. I have a complete set of *Dune* figures, which are probably quite valuable!'

Managing The Line

'LJN had a huge international distribution network,' says product development manager Paul Samulski. 'All of our key international people were like family, and we worked very closely together. With regard to manufacturing, almost all of the worldwide production was done in the same factories in the Orient.'

Asked about small variations in the materials used to manufacture the toys between series, Samulski replies, 'I don't remember us switching manufacturers (because of our ongoing relationship), but we might have done so in order to keep the hard costs within budget. I honestly don't think we did. Even so, there could have been changes in the basic materials used during manufacturing. Many times during production, we had to make material and/or chemical adjustments in order to guarantee the safety standards of the basic products and the paint/decoration.

'I had a design team at LJN that was second to none. I often told people (at that time) that I would put the LJN product design team up against any other in the industry ... domestic or foreign. We were good ... and we were quite varied in our strengths and focus. That's what made it the perfect team. I was also a bastard when it came to detail and design. I wouldn't accept something if I knew it could be done better. We pushed the manufacturing envelope so often that we definitely had our photos hanging in Hong Kong factories being used as dartboards or throwing-star targets. José was right at the top. He and I worked quite well together because we both had an appreciation for doing things the right way. We both knew that our work reflected ourselves ... and we wanted to be proud of what we did. We were very proud of *ThunderCats*.'

As regard the decisions on which characters and accessories should be selected for manufacture, Samulski reveals he was the driving force behind the release schedule: 'Obviously I would work closely with our marketing department, but no-one knew the property better than José and me, so it was difficult [for them] to challenge my direction as to which figures should be manufactured in which order and how the roll-out should occur. All product ideas came from José and me. It was my responsibility to "see the big picture" and create enough SKUs (stock-keeping units) to make sure the line could be profitable. But almost more important was the fact that it was my responsibility to make sure that we produced enough product to allow the kids to properly play with the *ThunderCats* toys. They needed it to feel "real". They needed to have enough elements to allow them to play out the episodes they saw on TV, and to expand on those using their own creativity. You can't do that with a limited line. The Cats' Lair and Mumm-Ra's Tomb were no-brainers. The action figures needed a home, both good and evil. They needed a base to operate from. The kids needed to be able to play "capture the fort", and these were the forts. Vehicles were also necessary for a toy line. We actually influenced the addition of vehicles to the show. The ThunderTank was a great vehicle ... and it didn't exist until we got involved. The Thunder-Claw, Feliner, Hover-Cat and Thunder-Strike were also important to the line, but obviously none of the vehicles sold as well as the figures. It was all about price points and what people could afford and/or would agree to spend.'

Samulski is delighted at the longevity of the *ThunderCats* line: 'I am indeed surprised, but very pleased. It is perhaps the most satisfying design accomplishment I have had in my career in toys and then video games. It's great to see people still wearing *ThunderCats* T-shirts and to hear it described by some (many) as the best cartoon/toy line combination ever. *Masters of the Universe* didn't give birth to a cult that is still alive so many years later. Only *ThunderCats* did that. I am constantly surprised when I hear younger people talk about *ThunderCats*, as if it was still "active" today. The design of the characters and the environments was great. The storylines were somewhat edgy, as was the idea of involving all members of the [cat] families. Kind of an "ethnically and racially balance approach" to cartoon casting.'

While Samulski oversaw the broad formation of the *ThunderCats* toy range, it was José Longoria who was given day-to-day responsibility for it. 'I was in charge of all R&D for the *ThunderCats* line from design to manufacturing,' he confirms. 'Staying involved with Rankin/Bass as they managed the production of the cartoon was part of what I did for LJN. The other was to make sure the toys were designed, engineered and manufactured in China. We managed the design and looked for cool gadget inventions and features for the action figures and vehicles. The main feature was "battlematic action". Each figure had a lever in the back and when you pushed it, it would move its arms, waving the weapon around. We had perfected this in the *Dungeons & Dragons* line that Dan Muldoon directed. The idea came to us from UK inventors Dixon-Manning (John Dixon and Peter Manning, who I think were based outside of London).

'There was some very innovative design work that distinguished us in the trade. At the time, Mattel's *Masters of the Universe* and Hasbro's *GI Joe* were the industry standards. The main thrust in those action figures was to make them poseable and articulated. The torsos, arms and legs in those figures were practically interchangeable. A limb from any one figure would fit the next, so they all looked the same. The freelance sculptors I would hire, who were usually freelancing for Mattel and Hasbro at the same time, would confirm that they would get a [figure] from Hasbro and modify it into the next *GI Joe* character to save time and ensure uniformity. I wanted to make each *ThunderCats* figure unique and have its own attitude. I knew I could rely on the story to create demand for the individual characters. I pushed to get each figure as different from the others as possible. Lion-O had his chest out in a proud attitude – standing tall with knees locked. Panthro was totally different, hunched over, ready to pounce. He was the enforcer. Cheetara was tiny by comparison, very graceful and feminine. So, unlike the competitors' ranges, each of our characters was different from the rest of the line! The best figure was Slithe. I wanted yucky leathery skin and we couldn't injection-mould that, so we used rotational moulding to mould his head out of soft vinyl.

'Some of the designs stayed true to the original concepts. The Cats' Lair, the Sword of Omens and the cast of characters stayed pretty much [as they had first been thought up]. We redesigned the characters [from the original drawings] with the help of freelancers. Rankin/Bass refined them again and organised the final designs incorporating what we wanted; to make good toys and what made sense for animation. The ThunderTank's styling, the weapons and all the vehicles were our exclusive contributions. For year two, we took a lot of the characters that were done by the producers pretty much as they were and made them into toys. Among them were WilyKit and Kat, Vultureman, Berbils, Hachiman, Cracker etc. We also originated some of the designs that had toy features, and they were worked into the show.

'I generated the concepts for characters and vehicles like the ThunderClaw, Cruncher, ThunderWings, HoverCat, TopSpinner, RamBam and the Feliner. At the time, LJN was ahead of the cartoon producers in the need for merchandise. This need drove the creation of new toys that would then be written into the story later (most of the time). After a toy was conceived, I would send a sketch or chat with a freelance designer on the phone and hire them to complete the work. Among those guys were Kevin Mowrer, Finn Tornquist, Joe Moll, Ann Jasperson, Ira Guilford, Russ Whitman … I recall other characters as having a combination of authors. Rankin/Bass designers would draw up the characters as they needed them for the stories. As an example, the Driller was illustrated by Rankin/Bass. I translated the motion into a mechanism that could be manufactured. Instead of a tornado, I changed the lower body into a three-legged rotator that the kid could operate with his fingers and knock other figures down during play. Kevin Mowrer did the control drawings.'

Longoria had joined LJN in 1982, having come from a background in industrial design. 'When I joined they had already manufactured *Dungeons & Dragons* action figures, which were not a great success,' he says. 'Their big hits were the Brooke Shields fashion dolls and a ton of *ET, The Extra Terrestrial* novelties. There was no plan with *ThunderCats*. Once the series aired, we were totally overwhelmed by demand, and basically we were making the toys as fast as we could while the product flew off the shelf. Management was based in NYC, manufacturing in Hong Kong. I would go back and forth. I remember when I started, even before *ThunderCats'* success, my boss explained they were making a couple of million US dollars per employee. There were fewer than 100 of us, in New York and Hong Kong included. It was kind of fun to know that we were competing successfully with teams of thousands at Mattel and Hasbro.

'For *ThunderCats*, the licensor approval process was painless, really casual by today's standards. All the parties seemed interested in doing their job well and not getting in each other's way. I'm not sure that Rankin/Bass ever really took us seriously enough to scrutinise what we were doing on the toy side. They never gave us on-screen credit for our contribution and we didn't really get that upset, although now I think it would have been cool. I don't ever remember discussing product details with the *ThunderCats* people. Take a look at the difference between the animated Slithe character and the action figure. It's a huge difference, because we had to release tooling without final review.'

One of the Rankin/Bass staff-members in charge of toy approvals was Peter Bakalian. 'LJN would bring in things and we would approve certain designs,' he recalls. 'They'd bring in prototypes of stuff and they'd try to find ways to extend the toy line by suggesting new vehicles and stuff. The show, while it had a strong relationship with the toy arm, wasn't driven by the toys themselves. It wasn't the case that the toy company would dictate things to us, how to write a show or what vehicles were in there. They'd be thrilled when we came up with stuff or they would suggest new stuff because it extended what they could offer the consumer.

It could be, "Could they change Lion-O's outfit to green?" And we'd say "No". But they might suggest something else and we'd think it was a good idea. They were very creative and enthusiastic their end, and they knew the shows as we went along, I had to deal with all of that. In many cases, I'd take a toy proposal to Arthur Rankin or Jules Bass (usually Jules) and I would say, "This is what they're thinking of doing, is it okay with you, do you have any suggestions?"'

Sculpting

With the *ThunderCats* licensing deal signed and José Longoria in post as line manager, LJN turned their attentions to finding the right sculptors to bring the cartoon characters to the toy shelves.

For the initial figures, LJN turned to established sculptors Rick Hughes, Bert Brookes and Ira Guilford. 'I've lost touch with Ira Gilford since he went to Hollywood,' says Longoria. 'I think he worked on the movie *Titanic* as a production designer. He was an old toy designer from Mattel who had already helped Ted Wolf develop some of the original *ThunderCats* material before JLN got involved. Ira had a lot to do with the final ThunderTank design. He must be in his late sixties by now, maybe retired. The same with Bert Brooks. Bert helped design and sculpt some of the main characters like Mumm-Ra and Slithe. We traded Christmas cards for years while he lived in Yonkers NY.'

As the line progressed, designers and sculptors such as Kevin Mowrer, Steve Kiwus and Ron Shrubbe were brought onto the project. 'Kevin Mowrer was a schoolmate,' says Longoria. 'At that time, he was working for Wang computers. I knew he was a toy guy at heart and I lured him away from his employer to freelance for us. Kev was hugely influential in designing a lot of the characters and vehicles before they went into the series. For instance, we designed the Feliner together. (There was a version Rankin/Bass did, but when they saw ours it was no contest.) We also did Hammerhand and the Berserkers, as a way of adding toys to the series. After the *ThunderCats* work dried up, Kevin went on to head Kenner boys toys, and eventually all of the Hasbro boys division. Another incredible talent was Steve Kiwus. Steve and I competed for the product manager job at LJN. We both worked together at CBS toys and we knew we were interviewing for the same job. I got the job, but he did even better. I immediately started to hire him to sculpt action figures for me at twice my income! He had no experience, but the talent was obvious to me. To keep him humble, I initially let him sculpt only Lion-O's glove, nothing else. After he didn't screw that up, he demanded to sculpt a ThunderCat. His long-legged girlfriend would model.'

Steve Kiwus is modest about his contribution to the *ThunderCats* toy line: 'I was not the most important sculptor on this line. It was the first real action figure line I ever worked on, right at the beginning of my career. I went to college to be a jeweller. I graduated with a Bachelor of Fine Arts in Metalsmithing, and I spent a year being a jeweller and hated it. This was in New York City. I moved back to Minnesota, where I was from, and I stumbled into an internship at a toy company. I was helping in the graphics department. I also worked in a full-time job as a product designer. The company I worked for were in a bad financial situation and they moved away and didn't make me an offer. I moved back to New York to take a job there, and I just hated it. It was in a huge company. My first company had been a tiny place; I'd do a drawing, go to the model shop and make it after I'd done some rendering. I'd do everything involved in getting it done. Then I went to this large company, where I was supposed to sketch all day long – which frankly, I'm not that good at. After exactly one year I left, because I'd been placed there by a headhunting firm, and if I had left earlier than that, I would have had to repay the headhunting fee. But the company did sculpting, so I saw sculpting, which the little company hadn't done. I looked at it and thought that I could do that, and I started trying to put together a portfolio and beating down doors to toy companies saying, "I think I can sculpt", which isn't the best way to do it!

'I was lucky enough that I knew José Longoria and I went to see him at LJN and he gave me a shot doing tiny things – my very first job was Lion-O's Power Glove, just the little piece of plastic that goes on the Lion-O action figure's hand, not the sculpt, not the figure. He just kept giving me tiny little projects, then he worked me up to trying me on some figures. My first figures were actually WWF wrestling figures that they were doing at the time. They were ten inches tall and solid vinyl. Once I was doing okay on that, José let me do some *ThunderCats* figures, because I had proved myself. That was their prestige line at the time; *ThunderCats* was the big one for LJN, and they weren't going to let just anybody work on it. I think the guy that did most of the stuff was called Bert Brookes – he was an older guy.

'I recall that LJN was kind of a medium-sized company. The owner was a guy called Jack Friedman who is now Jack's Pacific. The head of the department was a guy called Paul Samulski. When I started working there, there were two or three designers, but at the time LJN went out of business, there were about five or six. But it was a relatively small company, and for a starting-out freelancer it was an amazing place. It was almost like I was employed there. I had an apartment in New York at the time, and I would bring my work over and show José, he would give comments, and I'd go back to my apartment, which was only two or three blocks away, make the changes, and bring it back that afternoon. José was a great art director. That's how I learnt to sculpt, from his techniques. I still, to this day, hear his voice in my head saying, "The eye is a ball" or "Convex curves are more attractive than concave curves", that sort of thing. It was a wonderful place. This was long before you had computers and security cards to get in every doorway in a building. You only had to stop by the reception and be buzzed in. I didn't have to be stopped, I just walked into the office and I went to lunch with the designers. It was a wonderful time, and I have wonderful memories of it.'

'My first ever toy sculpture was that Power Glove. Mumm-Ra's staff was next, then Ma-Mutt, Pumyra, Captain Shiner and Hammerhand. I think that is in the order I did them in. The Ma-Mutt character was so textural that once you got the form right, I suppose José didn't think I could screw it up too badly! You could hide a lot of sins in the texture. It's still one of my favourite sculptures to this day – it's a fun figure. I don't draw well, only good enough to communicate an idea. Nobody would look at my drawing and say, "That's it!" So I'd go straight to sculpting. I remember a conversation with José saying, "This is what they've given us, straight shots," and I told him that I'd always been a huge proponent of, "You can tell a lot about a character by the pose". Even though we were doing very limited articulation – which from a sculptor's point of view is great – I'd rather have no joints, then the figure would have total character. I do lots of *GI Joe* figures now and those are just parts; they have no character. I'm not denigrating them, but that's what they want. The theory is that kids add the poses. But as a sculptor, that's not what I would prefer to do. We gave Pumyra a shy, coy little attitude, which was the first time that I got to do that and play with the pose. I think it was kind of my idea to do it that way, then I really went nuts when I took over Marvel figures eight years later; we really started giving them attitude. Pumyra was kind of the start of that. If you look at the earlier *ThunderCats*, they're all kind of straight, almost the da Vinci pose.'

Kiwus adds that LJN placed immense importance on producing cartoon-accurate figures: 'Rankin/Bass would give you a line-up and it would show you all the characters standing next to each other in scale, and that's basically the reason for differences in height between the toys. Some of the characters are just smaller. What's interesting is that there is such love in the world for the *ThunderCats* toys, yet José and I look back at them and think, "Man, they are so crude by today's standards." They're not embarrassing, they were state of the art at the time, but seeing what McFarlane have done now, you think, "Wow, they were simple." It never even crossed our minds to depart from the model sheet for a character. We could have fun with the pose, but the model sheet was like the Bible, and the toy had to look just like that. Later on, when I was doing Marvel stuff, the relationship was such that they'd say, "We want Wolverine this tall, he's wearing a blue costume, but other than that, we don't care, do whatever you come up with." But back at LJN, it had to be as close to the model sheet as we could make it.

'My process then was that I would start with a rough clay sculpture. You have to make all the joints that go into the figure, then I'd do a clay armature around those parts, and it would give me the forms that I needed later. Then I would make a mould of that and pour sculpting wax into the mould, then do all the final finishing and detailing and making the face in the wax. As far as approvals go, I very rarely, even to this day, get involved in that part of it. Now I send pictures, but back then I had to send the actual sculptures. Then [Rankin/Bass would] send the sculptures all over the place, and it could take a couple of weeks to get comments back, and then you'd make the changes that were needed. Nobody wanted to do this two week process. Now it's like, "I'm done; I'll e-mail some pictures," and one second later, they're in New York and California and they sit on someone's desk. It's no effort for them; they don't even have to pack the sculpture up and return it.

'Once that was done, we'd make more moulds and cast resin parts, which were the hard patterns, and I'd send those to the client, which was LJN. After that, it just disappeared and magically, nine months later, toys showed up. After that point, I was no longer involved; it went over to China or Hong Kong or wherever they were doing it. That's where the tools are made for toys, and someone has to do the paint masters.'

'José was the designer and he reported to Paul,' confirms Kiwus. 'I don't know what happened there, in relation to other freelancers working on it. I know Bert Brookes was the lead sculptor who did most of the toys. Maybe a guy called Rick Hughes was involved. José was the line manager for the whole line. He brought all the figures round to my apartment and photographed them; I let him use my apartment as long as he left one of each figure. I had completely forgotten about using my girlfriend Liza – now my wife – to model for Pumyra. It's funny that José remembers that, since they were not the type of photos I would have ever shown him. I had an idea for a pose for the toy and thought that using a model would make the sculpt better. I asked her to pose and she did. The extra effort is not readily apparent when looking at the toy – but, hey, an excuse to take pictures of one's girlfriend is always a good thing.'

Asked how his career has progressed since he worked for LJN, Kiwus replies: 'You can visit my website, toysculpting.com. My big claim to fame and my big break in my career was taking over the Marvel line in '91, and that's what I did for pretty much all the '90s. They were great times for me. I could pretty much charge what I liked for a sculpt. That's all changed over the last ten years. Now there's digital sculpting in China, and McFarlane has changed a lot; it's now a lot about comic book geeks and people living in Mom's basement wanting to do sculpting. Some are really good and willing to do it for a tenth of what I was charging. There are very few people who can tell excellent sculpture from decent sculpture.'

Another influential figure in the development of the *ThunderCats* action figures was designer and artist Kevin Mowrer. In addition to designing products and vehicles, he was responsible for many of the illustrations that adorned the larger *ThunderCats* packaging. 'I have a varied professional background,' says Mowrer. 'I'm a trained industrial designer as well as a trained illustrator, sculptor, storyteller, producer (TV) and author. Presently, I am one of only a couple of people who practice "meta-story" development (the development of stories to be told across many different forms of media and product). I've run Hasbro's R&D, founded their entertainment division and lots more. At LJN, I was a consultant hired by José Longoria to develop some of the toys for the toy line for several years. They liked the toy designs well enough that some of them ended up in the show (such as the Berserker designs). I remember there were two or three sculptors on the line. I did some of the box illustrations for LJN as well as the designs, but I don' know who else was doing them. (I did the Fist Pounder, the Thunder Wing, the Stilt Walker/Thunder Strider, the ride on bike and several others.) José did some of the additional designs himself as well for the toys.'

Mowrer confirms that it was Longoria who decided which specific figures to take to market: 'This was always a process of what was going to be shown in the show, mixed with which figures, vehicles and playsets might have the best features that could be developed for them. José was the mastermind on that mix. The line was always prototyped for toy fair and shown to the buyers. Depending on what orders they could write, they'd decide which toys to proceed with. In this way, there were occasionally toys that got designed and prototyped, but didn't get sufficient orders at the toy fair and didn't get produced. José would define what figure, and often what kind of feature, he wanted, based on what was going to happen in the TV show and his own toy-gut. He would call me or another toy design contractor and I'd develop concept sketches, showing him what the toy might look like and often working out a new mechanism for how it would work. After a few comments and refinement rounds, a layout drawing would be created and would go to a sculptor or prototype shop to be modelled in wax and plastic. The sculptor could be at Product Dynamics or might be Steve Kiwis or someone else, depending on what José was looking for and who was available.

'There's always some interpretation involved in sculpting from a flat drawing, no matter how good the drawing is. Some sculptors (like Steve Kiwus; I'm a big fan of his work) just put that extra something into the sculpt. From there, a non-working casting of the figure was made, and José would have it painted up to colour specifications (also on the drawings) to be used as paint masters that would be sent to the Orient for a clear guide. These paint masters were critical because, sometimes, the smallest addition or subtraction of a colour spot or shape really changed what the figure looked like. The paint masters were very few and therefore very rare. José often did final touch-ups on the paint masters and occasionally even painted them himself. Many were done by the very talented folks over at Product Dynamics.

'With the paint masters, a working prototype and a full set of design and layout drawings, the factories over in China could create the moulds and shape the assembly and paint line to produce the toy or figure. The paint master would be shown to buyers (often at toy fairs) and orders written. The package was designed as soon as the definition of the toy was clear, and often while it was being shipped to China to have moulds made. This usually meant that I'd move from toy design to package illustration seamlessly.'

Asked which figures he designed, Mowrer lists the Beserkers (Ram-Bam, Cruncher and Top Spinner), many versions of the main characters (Mumm-Ra, Lion-O, Cheetara, Panthro, Snarf, WilyKit and Kat etc), the Mad Bubbler (unproduced), vehicles, accessories and several of the playsets. He expands on some of the prerequisites for taking an action figure to market: 'It's the nature of toy design that you have to be able to be creative and make cool toys, but they have to be able to be manufactured, articulated and cost engineered (keeping things like too many paint operations to a minimum). They also have to be safety engineered, represent good value for money, be full of unique play-patterns and be highly demonstrable on a toy commercial.'

Asked to identify the sculptors responsible for specific figures, José Longoria notes: 'I art-directed all of the sculptures. I often would make changes to the sculpts and eventually became pretty decent at it, but admittedly I had *never* done this before, so we were flying without a parachute! The other individual that had a lot to do with the design of the figures was Finn Tornquist. Finn was/is a great artist and I hired him to provide "control art" for all of the sculpts.

'Lion-O was sculpted by Rick Hughes. Originally we wanted Rick to sculpt everything to keep the look uniform, but scheduling didn't permit it. Rick could never get the hair right on Lion-O ... I re-sculpted the hair, so what you see in production was my hair sculpt, which was only a minor improvement. Steve Kiwus sculpted the glove. That was the first action figure he ever was involved with. I wanted to bring Steve in because I could see his talent in spite of his inexperience, so I gave him all the shitty jobs. In my view, Steve became the best sculptor in the business later. He sculpted the majority of the Marvel figures for Toy Biz. I recommended him for that job and he just blossomed!

'Rick Hughes rushed through the first sculpt of Tygra, and we had to release it. Rick was *great*, but he would need two weeks per action figure, so we really rushed him. Bert Brooks did the second one, which was much better. We had to get the first year figures out fast. Whenever we had to [do a retooling], it was a chance to make improvements. Tygra's less "wimpy" re-birth was a result of that.

'The vehicles and playsets were more important for us in the toy company than they were in the inception of the *ThunderCats* concept. You can tell a good story without the wide variety of these accessories, but you really couldn't generate sales of toys unless you had many options, and new ones every year. If I remember correctly, before LJN got involved, they had the Cats' Lair, which was the stylised version of the Sphinx; we liked and kept that. The characters travelled around in a Jeep Wrangler type of vehicle, with machine guns mounted on it. We changed that to the ThunderTank. All the other playsets and vehicles were added to fill the variety of price points needed to generate our sales. Going into a bit of manufacturing detail, playsets and vehicles normally don't get "sculpted". They were sketched up by me or industrial designers, or artists I would hire. Then they would go to industrial designers and engineers to draw up in scale and come up with the mechanisms and features. Eventually, they were turned over to pattern-makers and model-makers to make the samples you see in the showrooms at a toy fair. Once we got orders from stores, I would work with Chinese engineers who would tool up and begin production.

'Jaga was Bert Brooks' work, and the first time we added fabric to any action figure. I don't remember a lot about that, only discussing that the ghost form is hard to represent in an action figure. We always needed to plan new characters and often requested to be involved in the hatching process. We would make suggestions, and Rankin/Bass would usually weigh in and then pass our sketches to the animators, who would do the final design.'

Design and Marketing

With a toy range designed, sculpted and ready for manufacture, the responsibility for packaging the *ThunderCats* line fell to graphic designer Laura Morehouse. 'I've been in the toy business for 30 years,' she explains. 'I started at Matchbox in 1982 or so, doing packaging, product graphics and decorating, comps, sales materials etc. I was hired by Paul Samulski, whom I had met previously at a little graphic design agency called Graphics Workshop in New Jersey. After Matchbox was sold, I went to a graphics agency in New York, worked for about a year and then was hired again by Paul when he went to LJN as Product Design Director. He made me Director of Packaging. (I think I was 23 or so.) My Packaging Group (three of us at the time) did everything – packaging, instructions, sales stuff, catalogue design etc. There was no line look, nothing but a logo, I believe.'

Under Morehouse's direction, the *ThunderCats* packaging encased the toys beautifully. Resisting the temptation to overcomplicate the graphic design elements, she gave the main line figures only a black backing card (later featuring a distinctive white splash) and the iconic *ThunderCats* logo. Not only did this maximise brand recognition, but it drew attention to the toys themselves, whose colourful features were enhanced by the stark contrast of the simple packaging. For larger toys such as playsets, hand-painted illustrations were commissioned in a similar vein to those used on Mattel's *Masters of the Universe* line. For character names, stickers and headings, the typeface Revue, designed by Colin Brignall in 1969, was used.

Morehouse explains how all of the graphic design requirements for *ThunderCats* were handled internally: 'I worked with the product managers to highlight the features of the product in illustration and photography. The product managers were José Longoria on the figures and some of the playsets and Mark

Morehouse (my future husband!) on a vehicle or two and the one and only "ride-on". I was also the art director, for the most part.'

Speaking of the box illustrations, Morehouse recalls the primary painters that worked on the artwork: 'Sally Bhandhugravi (Sally B for short) did all of the blister card art and Kevin Mowher did the playsets.'

Kevin Mowrer recalls there was one further illustrator who contributed to the packaging: 'Larry Elmore (he's the fella who did a lot of the *Dragonlance* books back then) was a talented guy. I never met him, but I remember his work.'

Discussing the practical processes involved in manufacturing, Morehouse recalls that the packaging masters were created from wax, using breadboard models of the figures to select an appropriate size. 'We also worked with marketing as far as price point/perceived value/package type were concerned,' she adds. 'We generally worked from non-working paint masters for photography, and hoped for the best! Most of the packaging was separated and printed in Hong Kong, handled by my Chinese counterpart, Danny So. We wrote all of the copy and off it went to market!'

In addition to packaging design, Morehouse's team oversaw the production of catalogues to promote the LJN line to industry and consumers. Those for latter appeared in the form of mini-booklets placed behind each figure. 'For photography, we primarily used Judd Pilosoff in New York,' recalls Morehouse. 'We drove him crazy trying to get him to show action and to differentiate the good guys (blue background I think) from the evil (purple). We had a Director of Licensing (Karyn Weiss), and she dealt directly with the licensor. We just gave her everything to be approved, and made the changes [Rankin/Bass] requested.'

José Longoria also recalls attending the photographic sessions: 'I'm sure I was at the shoots, making sure the models worked, and would always take a model-maker with me, because we always had to shoot them at the last minute and never had production samples for the shoot.'

'I was with LJN for five years,' concludes Morehouse. 'After we went to MCA, we were all laid off, so I freelanced with Matchbox, and eventually went to work for Viewmaster/Ideal, which was then sold to Tyco Toys. Having had just about enough of that, my husband and I started our own business, servicing many of the same companies, and two years later, merged with our current partners, forming One Flight Up Design. We've been in business for 19 years, *still* working a great deal in the crazy toy industry!'

While design and packaging of the *ThunderCats* toys was handled internally, LJN decided (as is the industry norm) to outsource the production of television and print advertisements. For television, they employed the services of an established toy commercials agency, DuRona Studios, formed by filmmaker André DuRona. 'They had a studio in New Rochelle, New York,' confirms José Longoria. 'That was a production company we used all the time. We always used outside agencies. One of the agencies we would hire most often was headed by Ira Kaltenik'.

Another agency utilised by the toymakers was Ross Enterprises, a small company operated by Jan and Cheryl Ross. They were hired to create and assemble sets for the promotion of the *ThunderCats* action figure line at leading toy fairs. A freelancer working for Ross Enterprises in the 1980s, Peter Pryor, picks up the story: 'My background is in fine arts. After receiving my second degree – a BFA from Pratt Institute – I started working in graphic design, doing freelance work. I was hired by a small firm specialising in licensing, Ross Enterprises. They produced voiceovers for commercials and corporate side shows. I left them around 1983, because I received a grant for some experimental film work and to produce some recordings, however I returned to do work for them over the coming years. Ross Enterprises grew rapidly and gained lucrative contracts – one of which was LJN. They moved from 86th Street to West 26th Street into larger office and studio premises, just three blocks from the national toy fair building on 23rd Street – big money.

'I signed on to design sets for the toy fair and do design work for the licensing of their toy line. Everything was new back then and I was trusted to come up with whatever I wanted, for presentation – slideshows – and licensing of projects. I did also review scripts from the cartoon series, and being a somewhat jaded young artist was astonished to see that they had morals put into the storylines by corporate psychologists and ethics professionals. The cartoon series was released in conjunction with the toys, which also was an eye-opener for me, that they were each there to promote the other.

'I reviewed the cartoons in order to get graphic references for presenting the product line in sets, and also to create art for the slideshows that we presented to people interested in licensing the *ThunderCats* images. Sets would be used at the toy fairs to place the toys in and photograph them. That required all kinds of skills, especially in a pre-digital environment. I worked with *ThunderCats* and LJN on the '85 toy fair show particularly.'

International Distribution

LJN toys engaged an international distribution network to ensure the toys succeeded abroad as well as domestically in the USA. 'Our primary international distribution territories included Canada, Italy, Germany, Japan, and the UK,' explains Paul Samulski. 'Each of the heads of those companies (sub-divisions) had been friends/business acquaintances with Jack [Friedman – founder of LJN] for many years. We also created most of the international packaging in the NY office as well. Almost all of the time, we would oversee the creation of the artwork and the basic package templates and then either drop in the international type and images or at least advise them (the international 2D art groups) as to what they should be doing. Laura Morehouse was my Head of Package Design and 2D Art in NYC and Theresa Bracchi was her number one … and also the person who, I believe, handled most of the *ThunderCats* stuff.'

As the *ThunderCats* brand swept across the world, the LJN action figure line appeared under the following imprints:

Rainbow Toys & Toy Options – Britain
Grand Toys – Canada
Childbro – Hong Kong and Asia
Playful – South America
Glasslite – Brazil
Mac Play – Mexico
LJN Europe – Continental Europe (including 'CosmoCats' line)
Otto Simon – Eastern Europe

In the vast majority of cases, the figures released internationally were identical to their US counterparts (aside from occasional small paint and accessory variations), with only Playful and Glasslite making significant changes to moulds and packaging. Owing to the large amount of territories the *ThunderCats* figures appeared in, there are also a few sub-branded and relabelled packages in existence. For instance, it was common to see LJN US-packaged figures in other countries, as the overflow of stock was consumed. In addition to the licensed lines manufactured by LJN, *ThunderCats* suffered the usual barrage of counterfeit toys sweeping the market, with varying resemblance to the official releases.

While the LJN line in America ran from 1985 to 1987, many other countries extended their distribution run into the early 1990s owing to the continued transmission of *ThunderCats* episodes around the world. More or less the complete range of figures was available in certain countries, including Britain, but not in others; the later figures in particular were not in mass circulation.

End of the Line

Having enjoyed three years of healthy sales, the six-inch *ThunderCats* action figure line ceased manufacture in 1987. 'We never really had a chance to take it as far as we envisioned,' says Paul Samulski, 'which was too bad. At the time, nobody really understood how special the *ThunderCats* license was. As a product line, it still came in #2 to *Masters of the Universe*, so even though we knew it was a success, it was still just #2 in the industry … maybe even #3, depending on how you want to slot in *GI Joe*. The decision to end the line was based on sales numbers, future projections and of course [how well] the show [was doing]. It was not an easy decision, and I remember the discussions being very heated during management meetings … pitting sides for and against.'

'This is pretty normal in the toy industry,' confirms José Longoria. 'Especially in those days when companies shot from the hip in making decisions about what new products to develop. To stay in business, you had to develop twice the products you really intended to manufacture and go into toy fairs "loaded for bear". LJN was a very high-energy risk-taker. They placed their bets with *ThunderCats* every year, but eventually decided it was "over" and turned their attention to video games. After the early, overwhelming success of the first year, I do remember that if you went to Toys 'R Us in the US, the whole *ThunderCats* shelf would be full of Slithe figures instead of a full range. Obviously, the inventory was not being managed well. I'm not sure what caused the decline in sales, but clearly the series was still extremely popular while sales tanked and LJN turned their attention to other properties.'

Kevin Mowrer adds his thoughts on the demise of the line: 'This would have been because the toy buyers thought that the line and TV show were declining and weren't willing to place sufficient orders for the toys at that point. Keep in mind that they are the first customer for toys, and what they buy or don't, is what gets made.'

When the line was ended, a further range of toys was already in pre-production. These sculpts and designs were destined to remain unrealised prototypes, and the much-anticipated figures that had featured in sales catalogues of forthcoming products would frustrate may parents as they tried in vain to 'complete' their children's collections. Amongst the unproduced prototypes were *ThunderCats* vehicles based on the popular Feliner and ThunderStrike. New figures for the standard line of action figures included Red-Eye (although there were no immediate plans for the release of the other Lunataks) and a range of new LJN-created Berserkers (which did not appear on screen).

'I initiated the design of all of these items with the intention of manufacturing,' reveals Longoria. 'But as the series got older and less popular, it didn't sustain the ability to tool up new items. I still have the model of Quick Jaws and Cannon Blaster in my studio. The working name for Quick Jaws was "the flasher" for obvious reasons. Very often, my process was to look for a fun gadget or a classic toy that I knew kids would like, and turn it into a character. I would sketch it out or hire someone to do it, then submit it to Rankin/Bass for a commitment that they would incorporate it into the show. LJN would submit what we thought it should look like and then design the product. Often, the Japanese animators would simplify it or change it for their reasons. That accounts for the differences between cartoons and toys. Some examples include: bubble blower gun (Mad Bubbler); pull-string helicopter (Red Eye shot props out of his chest); disc shooting gun (LunaTaker); and spinning top (Driller).

'Other times, we would get ideas from outside inventors, like Tongue-A-Saurus and the Fist Pounder. One time, my boss Paul and I were taking the subway to the broadcasting museum in NYC, where Rankin/Bass had their offices. We noticed an ad for the Museum of Modern Art, which had a picture of a dirty old man wearing a raincoat and presumably nothing underneath. The caption read "Expose Yourself to Art." That was the idea for "the flasher" or Quick Jaws. The mechanism came from a classic novelty. The idea for the Tongue-A-Saurus (which was released) came from whistles that they sell for New Year parties. They unfurl when you blow, like a frog's tongue, so we built a product around that.

'Cannon Blaster was a take-off on the *Mad Max* movie. Remember that – before Mel Gibson was popular? There was a little guy and a big guy that travelled together, brain and brawn. For fun, we put a bullet head hat on the little guy and made the big guy into a spring loaded cannon that would blast the dwarf 20 inches! An unfortunate cross between Master Blaster from *Mad Max* and the politically incorrect sport of midget tossing. None of these products existed in the show. We invented them, not so much because we were more creative, but because we needed the exposure to sell toys. The writers could have kept writing new stories around the same characters for years to come, but kids already owned those toys and Toys 'R Us wanted new merchandise from us.'

While these last-conceived figures would never be released, a great deal of work had already been invested in their preparation. Not only had they been designed and sculpted, but illustrator Kevin Mowrer had even completed the box art. 'A fair amount of the prototype work (including some of the figures) was done by Product Dynamics out of New Jersey,' recalls Mowrer. 'The company, which was established in 1976, specialised in the production of workable prototypes that could be painted and photographed. In the case of *ThunderCats*, the working prototypes were then included in sales catalogues, complete with assortment numbers and detailed photographs. Some of the original prototype sculptures have survived (occasionally traded on the internet for vast sums), however some may have been lost forever – the only footnote to their existence being captured on film.'

During its three-year run, the LJN *ThunderCats* toy line produced over 30 action figures of unrivalled quality (by the standards of the time), as well as a range of accessories, vehicles and playsets. Additionally, the company had released a 'plush' version of Snarf, and full-size action toys for children including the Sword of Omens and a 'Pedal Power' trike. Where other toy companies had based an entire line around a set of interchangeable limbs and body parts, with only individually sculpted heads to distinguish characters, every one of the *ThunderCats* figures had been individually designed and sculpted. While the standard did vary across the range, it was, overall, a superb toy line, with character sculpts that boasted likenesses of a degree of fidelity to their on-screen counterparts that is remarkable even by today's standards.

From Toys to Collectables

While the *ThunderCats* toys had disappeared from mainstream toy sellers by the early 1990s, remaining warehouse stock appeared sporadically in a variety of discount retailers throughout the decade. There then followed a slow drying up of the flow of available toys, and the *ThunderCats* brand seemed consigned to history, with only the odd loose figure appearing at second-hand fairs and junk sales.

With the emergence of the online auction site eBay, however, the *ThunderCats* figures were set to make a comeback. By now, the children who had once persuaded their parents to buy the *ThunderCats* toys, had grown up and become adult collectors. Soon, they were engaged in enthusiastic trading, trying to complete their collections of figures – in many cases, trying to obtain copies still sealed in original, undamaged packaging.

While the original toys had cost only a few dollars each, pristine and rare figures (such as third wave, or Series 3, releases, including Bengali and Lynx-O) were suddenly trading in hundreds of dollars each. Given that very few original shop-bought examples survived unopened, the pristine ones comprised mostly of unsold stock that had been acquired over the years from various distribution chains.

Commenting on why the *ThunderCats* line continues to be highly collectable, Steve Kiwus says: '[I think people got into the toys] before [they] were really collectible, so people weren't speculating like they do now. I have a friend I met when I was [doing the figures for] Marvel … When the whole Marvel [collecting] thing started, he'd buy 12 of every figure and store them. This was at the beginning of the '90s, and all of the speculation and collecting started. With *ThunderCats*, people weren't doing that, they were just buying them and playing with them, so pristine items are rare. It wasn't [designed to be] a collector's line, it was a toy line.'

While the *ThunderCats* series earned its place in children's programming history, the toy line supported it every step of the way. The toy-playing public filled the gaps between episodes with their range of action figures and, to a generation that yearned to complete their collections, the line will never be forgotten.

Toy Guide

The list below aims to provide a guide to the principal *ThunderCats* toy line released by LJN. While it gives details of every figure produced, it should be noted that minor variations have not been listed separately. These include variations in packaging and differences in paintwork. Details of the individual sculptors and designers that worked on each toy are listed where they have been identified.

The reference given in brackets after each character name indicates the number of figures available as stated on the back of the packaging: 8 Back (Series One figures); 14 Back (Series Two figures); 22 Back (Series Three figures); 7 Back (Companions); 4 Back (Berserkers); and 25 Back (Ram-Pagers).

NOTE: 'Sculptor' denotes the artist who modelled a specific figure. 'Product Design' refers to figures whose parts were tooled directly from design blueprints and drawings. More often than not, both stages were involved in the creation of a figure, with the 'Product Designer' typically dictating working parts and articulation, and a 'sculptor' realising likenesses.

1985 Series I

Lion-O (8 Back)
Assortment Number: 3500
Accessories: Sword of Omens, Claw Shield and Power Ring
Sculptor: Rick Hughes (Hair by José Longoria, Glove by Steve Kiwus)

Lion-O (8 Back) (With Free Battery)
Assortment Number: 3527
Accessories: Sword of Omens, Claw Shield and Power Ring
Sculptor: Rick Hughes (Hair by José Longoria, Glove by Steve Kiwus)

Tygra (8 Back)
Assortment Number: 3500
Accessories: Bolo Whip
Sculptor: Rick Hughes

Tygra and WilyKat (8 Back)
Assortment Number: 3500
Accessories: Bolo Whip

Cheetara (8 Back)
Assortment Number: 3500
Accessories: Staff
Sculptor: Rick Hughes

Cheetara and WilyKit (8 Back)
Assortment Number: 3500
Accessories: Staff

Panthro (8 Back)
Assortment Number: 3500
Accessories: Nunchaku
Sculptor: Rick Hughes

Mumm-Ra (8 Back)
Assortment Number: 3515
Accessories: Sword, Dagger and Power Ring (Removable Headdress)
Sculptor: Bert Brooks

Mumm-Ra (8 Back) (With Free Battery)
Assortment Number: 3515
Accessories: Sword, Dagger and Power
Ring (Removable Headdress)
Sculptor: Bert Brooks

S-S-Slithe (8 Back)
Assortment Number: 3545
Accessories: Axe
Sculptor: Bert Brooks

Jackalman (8 Back)
Assortment Number: 3515
Accessories: Club (Removable Shoulder
Strap)
Sculptor: Ron Shrubbe

Monkian (8 Back)
Assortment Number: 3545
Accessories: Mace on a Chain
(Removable Helmet)
Sculptor: Ron Shrubbe

Astral Moat Monster (8 Back)
Assortment Number: 3535
Accessories: (Removable Wings)

ThunderTank
Assortment Number: 3540
Accessories: (Removable Wheel Treads)
Product Designers: José Longoria and Ira
Gilford

Skycutter
Assortment Number: 3530
Accessories: N/A
Product Designer: José Longoria

Nosediver
Assortment Number: 3530
Accessories: Sticker Sheet
Product Designer: José Longoria

Sword of Omens
Assortment Number: 3570
Accessories: N/A

1986 Series II

Lion-O & Snarf (14 Back)
Assortment Number: 3522
Accessories: Sword of Omens, Claw
Shield and Power Ring

Tygra (Resculpt) (14 Back)
Assortment Number: 3500
Accessories: Bolo Whip
Sculptor: Bert Brooks

Tygra (Resculpt) and WilyKat (14 Back)
Assortment Number: 3545
Accessories: Bolo Whip

Panthro (14 Back)
Assortment Number: 3500
Accessories: Nunchaku
Sculptor: Rick Hughes

Cheetara and WilyKit (14 Back)
Assortment Number: 3545
Accessories: Staff

Cheetara (14 Back)
Assortment Number: 3545
Accessories: Staff
Sculptor: Rick Hughes

Tuska Warrior (14 Back)
Assortment Number: 3545
Accessories: Rifle

Snowman of Hook Mountain (14 Back)
Assortment Number: 3500
Accessories: Spear, Shield (Removable
Helmet)

Hachiman (14 Back)
Assortment Number: 3500
Accessories: Thunder-Cutter Sword
(Removable Helmet)
Sculptor: Rick Hughes

Grune the Destroyer (14 Back)
Assortment Number: 3545
Accessories: Mace and Knuckleduster

Mumm-Ra (14 Back)
Assortment Number: 3510
Accessories: Sword, Dagger and Power
Ring (Removable Headdress)
Sculptor: Bert Brooks

Mumm-Ra and Ravage (14 Back)
Assortment Number: 3522
Accessories: Sword, Dagger and Power
Ring (Removable Headdress)
Sculptor: Bert Brooks (Mumm-Ra)
Product Designer: Kevin Mowrer

S-S-Slithe (14 Back)
Assortment Number: 3515
Accessories: Axe
Sculptor: Bert Brooks

Jackalman (14 Back)
Assortment Number: 3515
Accessories: Club (Removable Shoulder
Strap)
Sculptor: Ron Shrubbe

Monkian (14 Back)
Assortment Number: 3515
Accessories: Mace on a Chain
(Removable Helmet)
Sculptor: Ron Shrubbe

Ratar-O (14 Back)
Assortment Number: 3515
Accessories: 2 x Daggers

Vultureman (14 Back)
Assortment Number: 3545
Accessories: Forked Staff

WilyKit (Companions Series)
Assortment Number: 3544
Accessories: Space Board

WilyKat (Companions Series)
Assortment Number: 3544
Accessories: Space Board

Snarf (Companions Series)
Assortment Number: 3544
Accessories: Space Board
Product Designer: Kevin Mowrer

Ma-Mutt (Companions Series)
Assortment Number: 3544
Accessories: Chain
Sculptor: Steve Kiwus

Berbil Bill (Companions Series)
Assortment Number: 3544
Accessories: N/A

Berbil Belle (Companions Series)
Assortment Number: 3544
Accessories: N/A

Berbil Bert (Companions Series)
Assortment Number: 3544
Accessories: N/A

Hammerhand (Berserkers Series)
Assortment Number: 3526
Accessories: N/A
Sculptor: Steve Kiwus
Product Designer: Kevin Mowrer

Ram Bam (Berserkers Series)
Assortment Number: 3526
Accessories: N/A
Product Designer: Kevin Mowrer

Top Spinner (Berserkers Series)
Assortment Number: 3526
Accessories: Shield
Product Designer: Kevin Mowrer

Cruncher (Berserkers Series)
Assortment Number: 3526
Accessories: N/A

Thunderclaw
Assortment Number: 3534
Accessories: N/A

Hovercat
Assortment Number: 3534
Accessories: N/A
Product Designer: Kevin Mowrer

Fist Pounder
Assortment Number: 3563
Accessories: N/A
Product Designer: Kevin Mowrer

Cats' Lair
Assortment Number: 3550
Accessories: Attack Sled, Ion Cannon, Ladder
Sculptor: Bert Brooks

Mumm-Ra's Tomb Fortress
Assortment Number: 3565
Accessories: Mummy Mumm-Ra

Plush Snarf
Assortment Number: 3575
Accessories: N/A

Mummy Mumm-Ra (Mailaway Exclusive)
Assortment Number: N/A
Accessories: Staff
Sculptor: Ron Shrubbe (Staff by Steve Kiwus)

1987 Series III

Lion-O (22 Back)
Assortment Number: 3501
Accessories: Sword of Omens, Claw Shield and Power Ring
Sculptor: Rick Hughes (Hair by José Longoria, Glove by Steve Kiwus)

Jaga (14 Back)
Assortment Number: 3500
Accessories: Sword of Omens (Removable Helmet)
Sculptor: Bert Brooks

Bengali (14 Back)
Assortment Number: 3500
Accessories: Hammer
Sculptor: Bert Brooks

Lynx-O (14 Back)
Assortment Number: 3500
Accessories: Shield
Sculptor: Bert Brooks

Pumyra (14 Back)
Assortment Number: 3500
Accessories: Sling
Sculptor: Steve Kiwus

Mumm-Ra (22 Back)
Assortment Number: 3501
Accessories: Sword, Dagger and Power Ring (Removable Headdress)
Sculptor: Bert Brooks

Mongor
Assortment Number: 3515
Accessories: Scythe

Safari Joe (14 Back)
Assortment Number: 3515
Accessories: Rifle
Sculptor: Bert Brooks

Captain Cracker
Assortment Number: 3515
Accessories: Pirate Cutlass

Captain Shiner
Assortment Number: 3545
Accessories: Gun
Sculptor: Steve Kiwus

Tongue-A-Saurus
Assortment Number: 3561
Accessories: N/A
Product Designer: Mark Morehouse

The Driller (Ram-Pagers Series)
Assortment Number: 3580
Accessories: N/A
Product Designer: Kevin Mowrer

The Stinger (Ram-Pagers Series)
Assortment Number: 3580
Accessories: N/A
Product Designer: Kevin Mowrer

Laser Sabers (Blue, Orange, Black, Red)
Assortment Number: 3566/3567
Accessories: N/A

Thunderwings Lion-O
Assortment Number: 3620
Accessories: N/A
Product Designer: Kevin Mowrer

Luna Lasher Mumm-Ra
Assortment Number: 3620
Accessories: N/A

Luna Lasher
Assortment Number: 3590
Accessories: N/A
Product Designer: Kevin Mowrer

Thunderwings
Assortment Number: 3590
Accessories: N/A
Product Designer: Kevin Mowrer

Stilt Runner
Assortment Number: 3590
Accessories: N/A
Product Designer: Kevin Mowrer

PART FIVE
SILVERHAWKS

9. *SilverHawks*
Partly Metal, Partly Real

'They fly on silver wings ... They fight with nerves of steel; partly metal, partly real. They are the SilverHawks! Born of a time beyond time, they sacrificed their human bodies – modified to withstand the stress of their long journey through space to the Galaxy of Limbo, sent there to defend the Universe against the terrible Mon*Star [...] The SilverHawks, their leader Quick Silver and his companion Tally Hawk – the invincible Spy Satellite and Interceptor. The tough-as-nails super twins, Steelheart and Steelwill – true to their names in heart, soul and spirit. Bluegrass – guitar-picking ace pilot of their incredible ship, The Mirage. And, from the Planet of the Mines, the Copper Kid. Their commander, Stargazer, directs the team from his orbiting headquarters, Hawkhaven. The SilverHawks, the first super androids with the minds of men and the muscles of machines.'
Opening Monologue – 'The Origin Story'

Three months prior to the broadcast of the pilot episode of *ThunderCats*, Rankin/Bass took the brave step of developing a second series for the action/adventure market – a genre as yet untested by the company. Where *ThunderCats* had been a fantasy-based series, revolving around mythical archetypes of good and evil, *SilverHawks* would be more science fiction-orientated, riding on the back of the success of blockbuster movies such as the *Star Wars* and *Star Trek* franchises of the 1970s and 80s. While *ThunderCats* and *SilverHawks* made no on screen connection, they were developed by an almost identical production team of writers, artists and voice actors. They were produced in tandem, with crew members crossing seamlessly from one to the other. Brimming with originality and eccentricity, *SilverHawks* was a distinctive member of the 1980s cartoon family, and anyone exploring the history of *ThunderCats* will find the two inextricably linked.

Developing *SilverHawks*

Toward the end of 1984, Jules Bass approached his team with a concept for a second series to be developed by Rankin/Bass. Though *ThunderCats* had been a gamble by the company to break into the action/adventure market, it was decided that, to capitalise fully upon the boom in the industry, an even more ambitious undertaking was required. Duly commissioned by Telepictures in January 1985, *SilverHawks* was slated to run for 65 episodes, placing immense pressure on the creative team already entrenched in work on *ThunderCats*.

Though *ThunderCats* had yet to air, production had progressed well, and Rankin/Bass was convinced that a separate series was achievable utilising the same creative teams. Production on *SilverHawks* would mirror that of *ThunderCats* in nearly every way. However, one key difference was the early involvement of Peter Lawrence. On *ThunderCats*, Leonard Starr had been commissioned to create the series bible and early story ideas, and Lawrence had joined only after a dozen scripts had already been completed. He had quickly found himself responsible for the show's entire script department, and soon became integral to various production decisions. On *SilverHawks*, Lawrence's services were secured from the very beginning.

'I wrote the bible, and *SilverHawks* is, to a very large extent, "my" show,' asserts Lawrence, 'building on Jules's base concept and accepting a lot of input from him. Jules presented the name and the concept: [creatures that were] partly metal, partly real. Also some, if not all, of the characters. I loved the show, edited and rewrote and edited and rewrote ... which is why I had only time to write a handful of original scripts.

'I did not care about credits and still don't, which is rather self-sabotaging. I was the showrunner and, effectively, an executive producer. I went to Japan to get the Pacific Animation Corporation guys on board and understanding the concepts ... I oversaw all the designs ... went through every storyboard ... and so on and so forth. Lee Dannacher, as ever, worked herself to death to keep it all together. Whatever the show's failings or successes, I think I was largely the "brain" (such as it was) behind the development (that is, taking it from concept to show, with big time input from Jules) and behind the creative execution; along with Lee who, of course, directed the voice tracks. I will therefore take the brickbats and the credits.

'Unlike *ThunderCats*, *SilverHawks* was home-grown. Jules Bass came up with the theme – "partly metal/partly real" – and the thought that each of the hero group would be missing an organic part ... hence Steelheart etc ... all commanded by an earlier generation of the partly metal/partly real concept: Commander Stargazer, who was basically a riff on the tough, grizzled, incorruptible cop. As I remember it – and these are my personal memories and therefore fallible – the concept was presented to Lorimar/Telepictures in a simple slideshow, along with the theme song written by Jules with Bernie Hoffer. I was part of that pitch, for some reason wearing a very flash white suit, a leftover from my days as an alleged advertising star. At that point, nothing else about the show was in place. No villains. No world. No real clue as to what the underlying theme might be. Not that that mattered, because Lorimar bought it right then and there – and Jules handed the package to me to develop.

'Lee Dannacher and the minimalist *ThunderCats* production crew were overwhelmed with that show. All the more so when the second season order came in. Therefore, they could not spend much time on the development of *SilverHawks*. That's one reason why the initial work was so heavily word-orientated: the first drafts of the show bible were effectively a workshop manual of the *SilverHawks* universe, without designs, and the immediate criticism from Jules was that we needed to be more story-driven. I believe that's what motivated him to become more involved for a period, and to invent the Mon*Star double persona, some of the bad guys and, in particular, Zeek and Seymour.

'Show development is a strange process that illuminates the paradox between the single vision/voice of a show "creator" and the infamous "collaborative process", which is alleged to define the entertainment business. There's a constant tension. The single voice welcomes real creative input and collaboration, but abhors the committee mentality that often entails. The collaborators chafe under the single voice's dictation and all want to see their particular contribution both appear on screen and be recognised by the audience. It makes me smile to see the various claims for credit that have been made about both *ThunderCats* and *SilverHawks*. Frankly, I was too naive to understand that by claiming my own roles, I would further my career and reputation. I was just having fun – and earning too well to be concerned about credits and kudos, which is odd because I certainly have my own ego! In this disregard for the claiming of "who done what", I was joined by Lee Dannacher, perhaps the hardest-working and most single-minded person I have ever known. Without her, none of these shows would have seen the light of day – or, if they had, they would not have achieved the high standards she demanded. I say this because she has never claimed her roles in either show and needs to be seen as central to the development, just as she was central to the production.'

A transcription of the on-screen credits for *SilverHawks* (taken from the first episode, 'The Origin Story') illustrates the similarity between the production teams working on *ThunderCats* and *SilverHawks*:

Executive Producers
ARTHUR RANKIN JR
&
JULES BASS

Supervising Producer
LEE DANNACHER

Animation By
PACIFIC ANIMATION
CORPORATION

In Charge Of Production
MASAKI IIZUKA

Animation Staff
TSUGU KUBO
MINORU NISHIDA
SHIGEO KOSHI
AKIHIKO TAKAHASHI
YUJI YATABE

Script Supervision
PETER LAWRENCE

Project Development
LEISURE CONCEPTS INC

Music
BERNARD HOFFER

Voice Characterizations
ROBERT McFADDEN
EARL HAMMOND
LARRY KENNEY
PETER NEWMAN
MAGGIE JAKOBSON
DOUG PREIS
ADOLPH CAESAR

Script Editor
LEE SCHNEIDER

Recording Staff
JOHN CURCIO – Dialogue
TOM PERKINS – Editorial
TOM GRETO – Music
LARRY FRANKE – Editorial
MICHAEL UNGAR – Editorial
PETE CANNAROZZI – Effects

Character Designs
MICHAEL GERMAKIAN

Soundtrack Supervisors
MATTHEW MALACH
STEVE GRUSKIN
TONY GIOVANNIELLO

enspenspenspenspenspenspenspenspenspensp SILVERHAWKS

Production Staff
SUSAN GILMAN-HARTS
KAREN SEIGEL
HEATHER WINTERS
CONSTANCE LONG

Secondary Character Designs
BOB CAMP

Scientific Consultant
For Epilogue Test Segments
DR. WILLIAM A.GUTSCH JR
American Museum-Hayden Planetarium

Psychological Consultant
ROBERT KUISIS PhD

While *ThunderCats* had featured its fair share of weird and wonderful creatures, locations and characters, its core premise had been grounded in classical mythology and storytelling techniques. Though it had, at times, ventured into outer space, it did not rely on science fiction concepts to propel it, and in this regard the two series parted company. Envisaged as an almost entirely space-bound adventure, *SilverHawks* broke with convention and became one of the most distinctive series to emerge from the genre. While admittedly idiosyncratic, the adventures of Commander Stargazer's metallic heroes captivated viewers and helped Rankin/Bass achieve number one ratings for the second time.

'The development process continued,' adds Lawrence, 'with Jules Bass and me knocking material back and forth – the rules of the universe, the stories, the characters – and Lee riding shotgun, until we had enough to bring some of the writers and designers into the loop. I do not remember who exactly worked on the show in these early days. I believe Mike Germakian did a lot of the character design work, his drawings being sent on to Pacific Animation Corporation to be transformed into animation designs. I'm sure I took a lot of input from Bill Overgard, because the bizarreness of *SilverHawks* appealed to us both. Steve Perry has said he was heavily involved in the development. I don't remember that, but perhaps he was – particularly in the first few scripts? Frankly, I much preferred *SilverHawks* to *ThunderCats*, not just because I was so intimately involved in the development (whereas I was only brought onto *ThunderCats* a little later, by which time we were working so hard and fast that we had no time to go back and straighten out some of the backstory, the world and the "rules"), but because it is profoundly eccentric. That's both its strength (and the reason that *SilverHawks* fans are quite fanatical and often a bit "out there" themselves) and its weakness: I do recognise, and accept responsibility for, the fact that the show's eccentricity is the reason that it was not as successful as *ThunderCats* – that, and the fact that the market was changing quite radically when *SilverHawks* debuted. I think it would, now, make a great camp CGI movie …'

As with *ThunderCats*, the lynch-pin of *SilverHawks*' production team was undoubtedly Lee Dannacher, who worked tirelessly to bring the show to air. 'All in all, *SilverHawks* was great fun to produce,' says Dannacher. 'When we got the green light for 65 episodes of *SilverHawks*, we were only at the actor recording stage for episode 40 of *ThunderCats*, but we had a pretty well-oiled production "structure" in place. We expanded the New York art department and production crew by a few artists and staff, and had to take over more studio space for soundtrack production, essentially contracting +audio rooms for our exclusive use. (I even negotiated that one of our rooms must have a ballet bar! My reasoning escapes me, since it soon

enspenspenspenspenspenspenspenspenspensp 420

became a coat rack.) For 'Hawks, it was great fun working with an expert at the Natural Museum of Science to produce the end tags (where our Copper Kid character is quizzed on science/astrological facts). I think, because the two series were so different, producing both shows simultaneously kept everyone's adrenaline pumping nicely. I can truthfully say that there wasn't a day when someone or something didn't present a huge laugh or a challenge that we could all get behind. There continued to be this mutual admiration society between our New York crew and Masaki's Pacific Animation Corporation, which Masaki and I encouraged and abetted, working out problems before they could jeopardise Arthur's golden rule: "On quality – on time – on budget."

'We moved through 130 episodes of *ThunderCats*, 65 episodes of *SilverHawks*, 13 half-hours each of *Karate Kat*, *Mini Monsters* and *Street Frogs*, and 26 half-hours of *TigerSharks*. Not to mention the continuous development of new concepts for other [clients], all produced in roughly five to six years. So much was wondrously blurred in the details. But it's amazing to look back and realise how tight we all stayed. For me personally, I've never had another production experience where everyone had each other's backs on a daily basis; and that overriding desire to entertain each other all the way through. There was just so much creativity and good humour in every department, igniting each other's contributions … It was magic, really. We worked a hard and gruelling schedule – but the laughter is what I remember most.'

SilverHawks benefited from the vast creative talents available to *ThunderCats*, yet its legacy would not be as pervasive as its predecessor's. With *ThunderCats*, Rankin/Bass's gambit had paid off, and though the production schedule had been frantic, their foray into the action/adventure cartoon serial market had been perfectly timed. Released the following year, *SilverHawks* had to compete in a far more tougher environment. '*ThunderCats* was lucky enough to be released in the heyday of action/adventure/fantasy,' admits Peter Lawrence. 'That's not to detract from its qualities, but it was one important component of its success. Then again, it operated in quite familiar territory, not quite sword-and-sandals but something like it. By the time *SilverHawks* was released, the genre – stripped action/adventure/fantasy – was dying. That does not explain or excuse the show's relative failure (though it was the top-rated new show of the season), but it did compound some of the innate faults. So what were those faults? In no particular order … It was probably a mistake to produce it in the same general style as *ThunderCats* – the voice cast, the rhythm and flow of the piece. You could argue this both ways, but perhaps *SilverHawks* really needed a more radical style and "delivery". The Mumm-Ra/Mon*Star transformations were perhaps too similar, particularly considering the voice casting. [There was] … an imperative … to have a transformation. Everyone demanded it, and it never occurred to me to argue against it. But perhaps Earl's wonderful delivery did make Mon*Star too similar to Mumm-Ra, and perhaps an entirely different execution of the transformation would have given this aspect of the show an intrigue that it missed. I'm not certain one way or another.

'The show has receded so far into the distance that I don't remember the finer details of the characters, but [another fault was that] *SilverHawks*' gallery of villains was substantially more interesting than its hero group. That does apply to a lot of shows and, for me, Mumm-Ra is the most interesting of all the *ThunderCats* characters – but the balance was way off in *SilverHawks*. The best of the heroes was Stargazer, an older man, far removed from the mass of the audience and based on an earlier tradition (from pulp magazines through to old cop movies) that did not resonate with the kids. Wonderful to write for – and there's a story editor's mistake of self-indulgence, right there. I loved the episode 'Stargazer's Refit' and its revelation of his old flame, Maeve, but I should have seen that it had no relevance to, and no resonance with, the kids who watched the show. One might make the same criticism about a lot of the interactions, PokerFace's particularly. So … too many adult themes and subtexts.

'Speaking of the hero group, if people were irritated by Snarf in *ThunderCats* – and many were – and exasperated by WilyKat and WilyKit – and some were – imagine the reaction to the Copper Kid, who annoyed the hell out of me! But he was *SilverHawks'* concession to the younger audience and to the need to have some kind of educational content to mollify the pressure groups of the time. I could write whole chapters about the horrible and ultimately self-sabotaging effects of some of the more fatuous parental groups and broadcast standards bureaucrats. Obviously, we should ensure that shows are appropriate for their audiences, but if the stretch to devise something "positive" leads to an idiocy like the Copper Kid, then something's wrong somewhere. (And do *not* ask me about Operation Push and *Street Frogs*.) Again, I should have opposed that addition – the Copper Kid and his ridiculous whistle voice and astronomy lessons – much more fiercely. At the time, it didn't seem one of those "to-die-for" causes but, looking back, the one character who should have endeared *SilverHawks* to the younger members of the audience was just plain annoying!

'Did the musical element work: bluegrass and melodia? Probably not. A good idea – and not badly executed considering the production process – but again maybe we didn't get the characterisation and the voices right. Easy to make these comments in retrospect.

'A summary, perhaps: in my vehement and still-held belief that kids are way smarter than most shows, producers and, especially, programme buyers give them credit for, I probably thought that "eccentric" and "out there" was closer to the mainstream than it actually was. *SilverHawks* could have had a more interesting hero group and a somewhat more mainstream overall approach to story – notwithstanding eccentric moments. I got the balance wrong. But let me not mount that hobby horse.'

For the series' musical score, Rankin/Bass turned once more to *ThunderCats* composer Bernard Hoffer. He was sent the series' opening scripts in April 1985, and began orchestral recording sessions on 20 May. He again contributed over a hundred unique cues for the series; a superb library of work that was perfectly selected and integrated into the episodes by the same team of recording engineers as on *ThunderCats*.

'It's telling that my most salient memory from *SilverHawks* is the music,' comments Lee Dannacher. 'I adored Bernie Hoffer's work on *ThunderCats*, and it was so amazing to me that he could take on a completely different series so soon after that. There were such distinctive differences in design and characterisation between the two shows ('*Cats* was "organic" in that the characters were half cat/half human and lived on an "Earth", but the '*Hawks* main cast was "partly metal/party real", with space as the environment). Bernie created such a new sound, completely and beautifully different, by varying instrument choices, rhythms and atmosphere. I can't stress strongly enough how Bernie's music permeated all aspects of the shows and gave all of us the energy and drive necessary to push animation production through our dizzying schedule from recording to airdates! I remember being over with the animation team in Tokyo and seeing a lot of the storyboard artists listening to music through their earphones. I figured they were listening to the latest pop music of the day – only to find out they were listening to Bernie's scores!'

'I have to admit, I have never watched *SilverHawks*,' says Hoffer. 'I will say this, however. I felt at the time that my score for *SilverHawks* was better than that for *ThunderCats*, mainly for two reasons. First, I already had one series under my belt and had a good idea what I should be doing. Secondly, the idea of these characters flying around through space allowed me to write more fluent and flamboyant music. I was sorry that the show wasn't as big a hit as *ThunderCats*, but I believe it was hampered by interference from the toy company, which insisted on too many characters (so that they could make more dolls), consequently making the stories less immediate to understand. The edge between a hit and an "also-ran" is very narrow indeed. If everybody knew the correct formula then, of course, there would never be any flops.'

The following promotional bulletin, entitled 'SilverGram', was issued to participating television stations by Lorimar-Telepictures. It reveals that comparisons with *ThunderCats* were actively encouraged when marketing *SilverHawks*:

Summer is upon us, and the fall TV season is not far behind. As you begin to make your programming plans for September, we feel compelled to remind you of an extraordinary opportunity that your station has at hand.

Your station is in the enviable position of owning the highest-rated animated strip with children 2-11 years old in America, *ThunderCats*. Waiting in the wings, prepared to soar to equally exhilarating ratings this fall, is *SilverHawks*. *SilverHawks*, like *ThunderCats*, is produced by Arthur Rankin and Jules Bass and has been specially crafted to run as a companion half-hour with *ThunderCats*. With these two shows, stations have the chance to programme the most formidable one-hour block of animation this business has ever seen. While on the surface the two programmes appear different, key similarities and strengths have been reinforced and expanded to help make a *ThunderCats* loyalist equally dedicated to *SilverHawks*. The key to this lies below the surface of our programmes' state-of-the-art animation and involves what we consider to be the most important ingredient for the long-term potential of these programmes; it's called *story*.

To truly understand our dedication to this concept and its benefits to you, it is necessary to briefly look back on how *ThunderCats* evolved into an overnight hit. When *ThunderCats* previewed last Fall, the programme was thrown into an animated, first-run competitive fray, the likes of which had never before existed in this business.

Initially, it appeared that the decks might be stacked against

ThunderCats rising above many of its first-run competition. Why? Consider this, *ThunderCats* debuted on television as a virginal property. It had no pre-existing history as a toy, greeting card, comic or children's property of any kind. The programme had to make its mark with children as a television programme only. Not so with many of its competitors. *G I Joe* from Hasbro had existed for over 20 years as a toy before its animated introduction. Hasbro also expanded *Transformers*, which had run as a weekly programme for one year, to a strip, and its two year history as a toy was gigantic. *He-Man* [sic] had two years as a television property behind it and generated toy sales in excess of $300 million dollars. *She-Ra*, a *He-Man* spin-off, was a first-run clone of *He-Man* and obvious beneficiary of all pre-existing toy and merchandising awareness. How then do we explain *ThunderCats'* success in lieu of a smaller station line-up than these other shows, no super-station carriage and virtually no pre-existing toy or merchandising influence? It all boils down to story and character development. The same essential factors that have contributed to the long-term success of many network programmes.

There was no 'gimmick' to the success of *M.A.S.H.*, *Barney Miller* or *Three's Company* on the network and ultimately in syndication. They worked because they were written better than many other programmes and were able to develop strong emotional ties between their characters and viewers.

ThunderCats is succeeding for the same reasons, and *SilverHawks* should do likewise. The programmes are conceived, crafted and produced to work over and over again because their stories are so strong. Terrific stories become a kind of protective armour against fads, trends and elements that can corrode a programme's strength over time.

This is why we so emphatically recommend programming these two shows as companions. Children are keenly perceptive and have an incredible ability to absorb and respond to the most minute details and programme nuances. In other words, the shared chemistry between these two shows is planned and devised as an explosive asset we hope you will take advantage of. Put Thunder and lightning to work for you, programme the 'Power Hour!'

Best Regards, Scott Carlin

Writing *SilverHawks*

The approach to commissioning and editing of writers was the same on *SilverHawks* as on *ThunderCats*, with Peter Lawrence again in charge. Says Lawrence: 'Story editing *ThunderCats* taught me a lot about the need to have a coherent and logical framework within which to set the "suspension of disbelief" on which all these shows depend. There have to be rules and physics if drama and tension are going to affect the audience. Writer's convenience has to be eliminated – and that, of course, is always a problem in children's programming. Many writers think that "because it's just for kids" they can make any jump of logic. If they want a chocolate blancmange to save the hero, so be it. The reality is that unless the heroic chocolate blancmange is part of the fabric of the show – or, at least, a believable development of that fabric – then the writer has cheated the audience; the show's dramatic structure can't be trusted; and no-one cares about the alleged jeopardy.

'I make these rather self-evident comments because *SilverHawks* was such a strange concept, a bizarre world, that it was really important to me to define it clearly in the materials that went out to the writers and animators. Effectively, and even physically, I drew a circle in space, and within that circle were certain rules that could not be broken – a world that existed on its own. For example, there was night and day – which does not exist in space; there was a particular gravity; sound travelled (witness Melodia); characters could breath and survive; pressure was sustainable; and so on. I felt that this world had to exist, clearly, before the stories could be developed, the characters designed, and so on. Others felt the world was irrelevant and that the stories and characters had to bring the world into being. I don't think there's a right or a wrong about all this – and perhaps the conflict helped the show. Certainly, without the base rules, it would have been impossible to story edit and maybe impossible to write.

'I'm certain that some of the stories, or elements within them, were simply too weird for a mass audience. I edited every episode myself, so I bear a lot of the blame – I wrote eight episodes (including the first, 'The Origin Story'), which were more appropriate to college cult kids than to the show's designated audience. I didn't realise it at the time, and was quite proud of some of the writing, but I do see the problems, looking back.'

In all, 23 writers contributed scripts to *SilverHawks*, with 16 of them having also written for *ThunderCats*. Often they were commissioned to write for both series simultaneously. Notable by his near-absence was *ThunderCats* veteran Leonard Starr, who wrote only one script for *SilverHawks*. 'Jules wanted to start another show and I came up with a name for it: *SilverHawks*,' recalls Starr, who has a poor opinion of the series. 'I think I wrote one or two of those, but Jules wanted to run everything himself. He didn't ask me to be the story editor or anything on it. He had Peter Lawrence there by that time. He had a space-taxi cab driver and a guitar-strumming rock star in it and a lot of other elements that confused the main thrust of the thing. My feeling was to forget it. It might have worked if they had done it like *ThunderCats* and kept it within the bounds of its main premise, but he had it going all over the place. He knew nothing about cliffhangers or pace or that type of thing.'

Unaware that Starr had first coined the title '*SilverHawks*', Lawrence maintains that the writer had little or no involvement in the series. However, he acknowledges that Starr and Arthur Rankin had been friends for many years. 'There may have been private meetings between Len and R/B about which I know nothing,' he admits.

Returning from his tenure on *ThunderCats* and assisting in editorial duties on *SilverHawks* was writer Lee Schneider, who provided five scripts for the series. While Schneider was credited as a script editor, Peter Lawrence assumed the mantle of 'Script Supervision'. Lawrence explains the breakdown of work between him and Schneider: 'I think we discussed the storylines – some of them submitted from outside and some generated by us. We would then go over the outlines and commission the scripts. As often as not, we simply took the writers' first drafts, read them, made our notes, took Lee Dannacher's notes, and then rewrote the stuff ourselves. We probably divided the actual rewriting between us. I think I probably kept an eye on the overall balance of the show – such as it was – while Lee [Schneider] was more involved in the day to day. After a while, we began to develop *The Comic Strip*, and I think Lee worked on *Mini Monsters*, which was based on a summer camp for the children of Dracula, Frankenstein, etc. I knew fuck all about American summer camps (even though I wrote *The Burning*), whereas Lee had actually been to them, like so many Americans. As to actual credits, none us gave much of a toss about it, but by that time I was referred to as the Creative Director (among other soubriquets, no doubt).'

Lawrence's long-time friend and fellow Englishman Chris Trengove was also invited to make the transition from *ThunderCats* to *SilverHawks*. 'If I remember rightly, the selling pitch for *SilverHawks* was "*The Untouchables* in space",' recalls Trengove. 'That pretty much sums the show up: master criminal Mon*Star and his henchmen are pursued around the Galaxy of Limbo by supercop Commander Stargazer and his team. It was second up in a batch of four animation shows produced by Rankin/Bass at this time. A number of *ThunderCats* writers went straight on to write for *SilverHawks*, and I ended up writing six episodes. I've always enjoyed writing comedy, so *SilverHawks* was fun to write, as there were a handful of comic characters such as Seymour the cab driver, his sidekick Zeek the Beak, Harry the barman and the oleaginous Yes-Man. (In *ThunderCats*, pretty much the only character with comic possibilities was Snarf, and late in the series, Snarfer.) *SilverHawks* was a little surreal, insofar as it took place in space, but a space that had gravity – characters fell downwards – and breathable air. I don't think it was ever anything like as big as *ThunderCats*, but it certainly had a following, and was sold to a number of worldwide territories. I recently worked on a European animation project where one of the young creators was a *SilverHawks* fan as a child – major kudos when he found out I was one of the writers!'

Also returning to add a much-needed female perspective was Kimberly Morris. 'They asked me to write a script introducing a new SilverHawk,' she recalls. 'The character's superpower was the ability to time travel. They asked for a story that would introduce the character, but said I didn't need to use the time travel ability because that would probably be too hard. I took that as a challenge and wrote a script in which the time travel ability was absolutely central to the plot. The story begins in the future, and the SilverHawks are almost wiped out and defeated. Stargazer is old and failing and the bad guys are in charge. A last-ditch invention of the time travel SilverHawk is their last chance. He goes back in time, changes the outcome of one event, and thus, changes the chain of events that led to their defeat. It was great fun. I also recall a conversation that illustrates the cultural disconnect between New York and Los Angeles. Each SilverHawk character had a bird/weapon. I got a call asking me to write a script introducing the bird/weapon for each character. These directives originated in Los Angeles, and they gave me the list of bird/weapons. One of them was called "Gyro". This totally confused me, because in New York a gyro is a *sandwich*! I couldn't figure out how or why the character was supposed to be armed with a *sandwich*. But I guess if you live in Los Angeles, you don't pass a thousand food stands and coffee shops advertising

"Gyro! $2.99".'

'I was pulled off *ThunderCats* toward the end of the first season to work on *SilverHawks* right from its inception,' says Steve Perry, who crafted four episodes of the new show. 'While I was writing the *ThunderCats* episode "Trapped", I was also writing page after page of *SilverHawks*. I worked closely with Peter on all of this, and with the input of several other writers as well, the Galaxy of Limbo came about, the weirdness of *SilverHawks* came into being, and the show was hammered into a package, riding on the successful coat-tails of *ThunderCats*, that was presented to Kenner toys. They saw more dollar signs – cats and birds remember – and I honestly do not think any of the toy people ever bothered to read any of the stuff. It was all smoke and mirrors, it was all the "look" of the art, the character design. A lot of the strangeness that would become *SilverHawks* – and subsequently a lot of its failure – came out of my head. It was just too weird, and the Hawks failed miserably. A one season wonder – the wonder being it was remarkable than Kenner put up money to do it! It was now a game of momentum. *ThunderCats* had entered its second season, lots of new stuff was happening there, *SilverHawks* hit the airwaves and no-one knew what a disaster it would become. Rankin/Bass was on a roll, though – the 'Cats filled the bank accounts to overflowing, the 'Hawks got funded, and now a new show was in the works, namely *The Comic Strip*. *The Comic Strip* was Peter Lawrence through and through – three ten-minute segments, one action, one funny animal, one girl-orientated. I was slated to work on *TigerSharks*. Cats, birds and now fish.'

Once again assisting on the production of *SilverHawks*, in addition to writing scripts, was Matthew Malach. '*SilverHawks* differed from *ThunderCats* in that it had a "futurist" theme,' says Malach. 'It was almost like Rankin/Bass's answer to *Star Wars*. I wrote only one episode, "Zeek's Power", a comedy of sorts. Also, I seem to recall that writer Lee Schneider named a martial arts move (done by one of the characters) after me – "the Malach Manoeuvre".'

The following episodes comprised the 65 adventures of the SilverHawks in their battle with Mon*Star and his evil accomplices:

01. The Origin Story (Original US Broadcast Monday 8 September 1986)
Written by Peter Lawrence

02. Journey To Limbo (Original US Broadcast Tuesday 9 September 1986)
Written by Peter Lawrence

03. The Planet Eater (Original US Broadcast Wednesday 10 September 1986)
Written by William Overgard

04. Save The Sun (Original US Broadcast Thursday 11 September 1986)
Written by Peter Lawrence

05. Stop Timestopper (Original US Broadcast Friday 12 September 1986)
Written by Lee Schneider

06. Darkbird (Original US Broadcast Monday 15 September 1986)
Written by Steve Perry

07. The Backroom (Original US Broadcast Tuesday 16 September 1986)
Written by William Overgard

08. The Threat of Dritt (Original US Broadcast Wednesday 17 September 1986)
Written by Bruce Smith

09. Sky-Shadow (Original US Broadcast Thursday 18 September 1986)
Written by Kimberly Morris

10. Magnetic Attraction (Original US Broadcast Friday 19 September 1986)
Written by Chris Trengove

11. Gold Shield (Original US Broadcast Monday 22 September 1986)
Written by Bruce Smith

12. Zero The Memory Thief (Original US Broadcast Tuesday 23 September 1986)
Written by Jeri Craden

13. The Milk Run (Original US Broadcast Wednesday 24 September 1986)
Written by Lee Schneider

14. The Hardware Trap Part I (Original US Broadcast Thursday 25 September 1986)
Written by Peter Lawrence

15. The Hardware Trap Part II (Original US Broadcast Friday 26 September 1986)
Written by Lee Schneider

16. Race Against Time (Original US Broadcast Monday 29 September 1986)
Written by Chris Trengove

17. Operation Big Freeze (Original US Broadcast Tuesday 30 September 1986)
Written by Jeri Craden

18. The Ghost Ship (Original US Broadcast Wednesday 1 October 1986)
Written by Chris Trengove

19. The Great Galaxy Race (Original US Broadcast Thursday 2 October 1986)
Written by William Overgard

20. Fantascreen (Original US Broadcast Friday 3 October 1986)
Written by Steve Perry

21. Hotwing Hits Limbo (Original US Broadcast Monday 6 October 1986)
Written by Peter Lawrence

22. The Bounty Hunter (Original US Broadcast Tuesday 7 October 1986)

Written by J V P Mundy

23. Zeek's Fumble (Original US Broadcast Wednesday 8 October 1986)
Written by Peter Lawrence

24. The Fighting Hawks (Original US Broadcast Thursday 9 October 1986)
Written by Kimberly Morris

25. The Renegade Hero (Original US Broadcast Friday 10 October 1986)
Written by Leonard Starr

26. One on One (Original US Broadcast Monday 13 October 1986)
Written by William Overgard

27. No More Mr Nice Guy (Original US Broadcast Tuesday 14 October 1986)
Written by Chris Trengove

28. Music of the Spheres (Original US Broadcast Wednesday 15 October 1986)
Written by Lee Schneider

29. Limbo Gold Rush (Original US Broadcast Thursday 16 October 1986)
Written by Steve Perry

30. Countdown to Zero (Original US Broadcast Friday 17 October 1986)
Written by Chris Trengove

31. The Amber Amplifier (Original US Broadcast Monday 20 October 1986)
Written by Bill Ratter

32. The Saviour Stone (Original US Broadcast Tuesday 21 October 1986)
Written by Bob Haney

33. Smiley (Original US Broadcast Wednesday 22 October 1986)
Written by Bruce Shlain

34. Gotbucks (Original US Broadcast Thursday 23 October 1986)
Written by Bob Haney

35. Melodia's Siren Song (Original US Broadcast Friday 24 October 1986)
Written by Lawrence Dukore

36. Tally-Hawk Returns (Original US Broadcast Monday 27 October 1986)
Written by Stephanie Swafford

37. Undercover (Original US Broadcast Tuesday 28 October 1986)
Written by Danny Peary

38. Eye of Infinity (Original US Broadcast Wednesday 29 October 1986)

Written by Kenneth Vose

39. A Piece of the Action (Original US Broadcast Thursday 30 October 1986)
Written by Bruce Smith

40. Flashback (Original US Broadcast Friday 31 October 1986)
Written by Kimberly Morris

41. Super Birds (Original US Broadcast Monday 3 November 1986)
Written by Bruce Shlain

42. The Blue Door (Original US Broadcast Tuesday 4 November 1986)
Written by Cy Young

43. The Star of Bedlama (Original US Broadcast Wednesday 5 November 1986)
Written by Kimberly Morris

44. The Illusionist (Original US Broadcast Thursday 6 November 1986)
Written by Jeri Craden

45. The Bounty Hunter Returns (Original US Broadcast Friday 7 November 1986)
Written by Steve Perry

46. The Chase (Original US Broadcast Monday 10 November 1986)
Written by Bruce Smith

47. Switch (Original US Broadcast Tuesday 11 November 1986)
Written by Beth Bornstein & J.V.P. Mundy

48. Junkyard Dog (Original US Broadcast Wednesday 12 November 1986)
Written by Bob Haney

49. Window in Time (Original US Broadcast Thursday 13 November 1986)
Written by J V P Mundy

50.Gangwar Part I (Original US Broadcast Friday 14 November 1986)
Written by William Overgard

51. Gangwar Part II (Original US Broadcast Monday 17 November 1986)
Written by William Overgard

52. Sneak Attack Part I (Original US Broadcast Tuesday 18 November 1986)
Written by William Overgard

53. Sneak Attack Part II (Original US Broadcast Wednesday 19 November 1986)
Written by Cy Young

54. Moon*Star (Original US Broadcast Thursday 20 November 1986)

Written by Peter Larson and Alice Knox

55. The Diamond Stick-Pin (Original US Broadcast Friday 21 November 1986)
Written by Peter Lawrence

56. Burnout (Original US Broadcast Monday 24 November 1986)
Written by Bill Ratter

57. Battle Cruiser (Original US Broadcast Tuesday 25 November 1986)
Written by Lee Schneider

58. Small World (Original US Broadcast Wednesday 26 November 1986)
Written by Kimberly Morris

59. Match-Up (Original US Broadcast Thursday 27 November 1986)
Written by Bruce Smith

60. Stargazer's Refit (Original US Broadcast Friday 28 November 1986)
Written by William Overgard

61. The Invisible Destroyer (Original US Broadcast Monday 1 December 1986)
Written by Dow Flint Kowalczyk

62. The Harder They Fall (Original US Broadcast Tuesday 2 December 1986)
Written by Chris Trengove

63. Uncle Rattler (Original US Broadcast Wednesday 3 December 1986)
Written by Beth Bornstein

64. Zeek's Power (Original US Broadcast Thursday 4 December 1986)
Written by Matthew Malach

65. Airshow (Original US Broadcast Friday 5 December 1986)
Written by Peter Lawrence

Voicing the Galaxy of Limbo

In April 1985, the cast of *SilverHawks* recorded the series' one hour pilot episode in New York. Assembled in the studios were Rankin/Bass stalwarts Bob McFadden and Earl Hammond, and existing *ThunderCats* actors Larry Kenney, Peter Newman and Doug Preis (who joined the *ThunderCats* cast for the second season). For the female lead characters, a new actress was required to match the vocal versatility of Lynne Lipton, after the actress found herself unable to commit to the series. Supervising producer Lee Dannacher gave this role to Maggie Wheeler (nee Jakobson), who successfully auditioned on 21 March 1985. Later to achieve fame with her powerful performance as Janice in the NBC sitcom *Friends*, Wheeler had an impressive vocal range.

'I started out in my teens, and I was bouncing around, trying to get work,' recalls Wheeler. 'It wasn't simple. I was doing a group read at a voiceover studio in New York and I was thrown in with a bunch of teenagers for a CBS record spot. It was for a band called the Rubinoos, and we all had to say, "Ooh, the Rubinoos". My voice was significantly lower than my compatriots'. From the other side of the booth they said, "Who is the one with the low voice?" I thought, oh my god, am I going to get fired? They pulled me aside and gave me the lead part. After that, they hired me many, many times, and it was the beginning of a long relationship.

'Along with everything else I was doing at that time, like extra work and whatever I could to string it all together, I had the opportunity to audition for a sketch comedy show that was being directed by Lorne Michaels of *Saturday Night Live*. It was his effort at doing a prime-time show, and it was called *The News Show*. In order to audition for that, I had to do five minutes of original stand-up (which I had never done before), so I tore my hair out and came up with five minutes of material. I did it the way that was most germane to the work I like to do, which is real character work rather than just jokes. I did a string of crazy characters, some from my life and some from my imagination, and once I had performed that for Lorne and the other people in the room, I had to do some improv with some of the Murray Brothers. It was extraordinary ,and an amazing opportunity; nerve racking and fantastic.

'All of this has a connection to *SilverHawks* because, when *The News Show* got cancelled, I left New York and went out to Los Angeles. I thought it was a good time to be out here on the heels of that NBC show. I was living in somebody else's place and working a little bit, and I'd just finished doing an episode of *The Paper Chase*, a show about law school. I got a call from Lee Dannacher, who was looking for somebody to take over the female roles on *SilverHawks* cartoon. Lee [knew] Lorne and had asked him if he had anything she could look at. He had sent her my audition tape, so she called me and said, "I've seen this wild thing, and I want to know if you would be interested in flying yourself back to New York to record the pilot of the show. I can't guarantee you the series, but we'd like to come and record the pilot if you're interested." I did have to fly myself back, but by that time, I'd been out here long enough and was excited about getting back to New York – which is where I'm from. I was very interested in a 65 episode order of a superhero cartoon series! I got on the plane to New York, and the rest is history!'

Wheeler recalls that she was made to feel extremely welcome by the established cast and crew: 'I think I was a bit blissfully innocent about what preceded my arrival. I wasn't watching *ThunderCats* and I missed all the hoopla. I had a great time with them and I loved being in their company. It was endlessly entertaining and they were very sweet to me. I'd frequently worked in this way with other people on other projects, so it didn't feel that different to me, and I'd come up from the theatre so it felt a very comfortable environment for me being in a room and throwing things back and forth. When they were writing a new script or bringing in a new character, we would have a little round-table meeting and throw out voice ideas for each new character. So I actually had as much of an opportunity to read for male characters as I did for female characters, and frequently the guys threw in and tried to get the girl roles from me, but that didn't happen very often. I loved the challenge. I've never been in another situation exactly like that; sitting around in front of each other and all having a go at it. It was very spirited and it was fun. We all had enough to do, so anything extra that came down the pipe was just gravy!'

Speaking of the Rankin/Bass method of assembling the entire cast to perform together in one studio, Wheeler reveals her enthusiasm for any method that offers an engaging role: 'A few years ago, I worked on *Justice League*, and the director had the whole cast assembled and we had a great time doing that – it felt like the old days. The exchange and the playfulness were really there. I've been working recently on *Archer* for FX, which is an adult cartoon, and that's at the opposite end of the spectrum. Not only am I alone in the booth, but my director, Adam Read, is in Atlanta. But we also had a lot of fun, so I feel like the medium itself is always fun, very creative and playful – but it's wonderful to be with everybody.'

Wheeler adds that it is impossible to choose a preference between voice and screen acting: 'I started in voice work early and I happen to love it. I love on-camera work also, it's fun and wonderful, but the beauty of doing animation is that not only can I play anything from an infant to a crone, but I can show up in my sweat pants, which is of course an added plus. I can't say what I love more. I love performing and I love to play characters that inspire me, but I love the process of animation work and having the freedom to do absolutely anything and not being bound by physical stereotypes and limitations that maybe Hollywood places on an actress. The availability of work is more limited for on-camera work for me.

'I certainly remember the way it was in the booth on *SilverHawks*. Bob McFadden was hysterical. They were still recording *ThunderCats* simultaneously and these guys had a long history with Rankin/Bass, so there were lots of references to past creative endeavours – all the Animagic Christmas shows the company did. Bob was in every single one of them, and he would digress given the slightest inspiration into 20 or 30 different voices and impressions – characters he played in those specials. We'd all fall down with laughter until Earl Hammond would boom in his voice on high and say, "Let us be about the Lord's work", and we'd go back to work. I remember things like that, and I certainly remember we had a great time and we laughed a lot.

'I went on to do several other things with Rankin/Bass when all that was done – they were lively times, I loved it. At the time, people were starting to buy little televisions that they could take with them, the beginning of that technology. Quite clumsy, but it was quite the thing to get to the Sony Store and get your little TV. I remember watching *SilverHawks* on that little thing. I thought the show was quirky and insane, and wild and funny. The kids were enjoying it – who knew that later it was college students who'd be watching it? Around that time, they also did a show at Madison Square Gardens that included *SilverHawks* and that we all went to see.

'Steelheart was my main character and Melodia was the villainess I played, and I loved doing that. I sent the recording engineers crazy shrieking that horrible song of hers, and any song she played. I also did all the incidental Lab-tech women and various male roles, although it's been too long and I don't remember who they were. But from time to time, monsters and creatures would come up and I'd do those. If it was female, it was always me, but if it was male, there were other little space invaders that I portrayed. They were very good at throwing up a sound clip if you needed to refer to something, so that was very useful in helping us to be consistent over time.'

Maggie Wheeler is incredibly proud of her work on *SilverHawks* and, though her career would boast much greater achievements, she is delighted to have played a part in so many people's childhoods: 'Without a doubt, there are moments in time of importance, and *SilverHawks* was a divine time for me. It was a steady job, which was fabulous and hard to come by. I was working with fabulous people. I loved Rankin/Bass; I loved the organisation and the people I worked with. I'd do it all again tomorrow! I've been very fortunate. I've performed on some wonderful, wonderful shows. *Friends* is my claim to fame, proudly; it was a great opportunity. Again, wonderful people, wonderful writers and a fabulous character that I got to pay. I had a wonderful time on *Everybody Loves Raymond*, again as a recurring character. My time on *The News Show* with Lorne Michaels was a really, really key experience, because I had a chance to work with amazing people: Steve Martin, Penny Marshall, Raul Julia, John Candy, Catherine O'Hara – just amazing people that I had a chance to perform with when I was doing that show. Then I did a movie when I was much younger, called *New Year's Day*. It was a great experience too, and it sort of put me on the map in a different way. I got on *The Johnny Carson Show*, and the film represented the US in the Venice Film Festival that year. I've been so lucky to work with some great people. I've worked on *Dream On* with Brian Benben and *Seinfeld*. I was on the first season of Ellen DeGeneres's show – she's a brilliant comedian, actress and person – and I did *The Parent Trap* for Disney when Lindsay Lohan was born onto the scene.

'I've had great opportunities to do sound work too. I played the villainess in the animated *Barbie* movie and various chickens in *Doctor Doolittle 3*, and things like that are fun and memorable. I also sing, so I had an opportunity to record some music for an episode of *The X-Files*, where I sing an accappella version of "Michael Row Your Boat Ashore" in five parts – my own arrangement – and I get a lot of requests for that!

'I've had a very varied journey, not over yet I surely hope. Most recently, I've just played an aging Irish rock and roller called Flame Bang Bang on *Glenn Martin, DDS*, and Chrissie Hynde of the Pretenders voiced one of the other band members. I'm currently working on *Archer* playing a hooker with a heart of gold from Brooklyn. I've done some wild things recently, including a craft show for children on which I got to work with some very creative people. That's called *Magpie*, and we're trying to sell that. Oddly enough, I also direct a choir in Hollywood, and I love that work. I've travelled the US and Canada bringing people together to sing. Amazingly, I was on my way to Portland a few weeks ago and I ran into Matthew Malach and his wife Karen, who I haven't seen forever, and we were on the same plane reminiscing about the old days!'

A second addition to the *SilverHawks* cast list was accomplished actor Adolph Caesar, fresh from Academy Award and Golden Globe nominations for his role in Norman Jewison's film *A Soldier's Story*. Cast by Lee Dannacher to play one character (rather than a myriad of voices – much like Earle Hyman on *ThunderCats*), Caesar performed the voice of Hotwing. 'Caesar had a remarkable voice,' recalls Matthew Malach. 'I had grown up hearing his voiceovers in countless commercials, so I was thrilled with the opportunity to work with him. However, he frequently showed up to our sessions in a daze. He had trouble reading his lines – and in some cases, staying awake. He blamed it on "jet lag", but we never quite found out what the issue was, because he died of a heart attack while working on a film in LA. After his death, Doug Preis (also newly cast in

SilverHawks) took over the Hotwing role, matching Adolph's voice very closely.'

Adding her memories of Caesar, Maggie Wheeler comments, 'I remember him swooping in with a white suit and a hat. He looked like some kind of angel in his white suit. He was a true character – very funny. I think he slept a lot in the corner when he wasn't recording. But he had an incredible presence in that little tiny studio where we were all together.'

Speaking about the casting of both Maggie Wheeler and Adolph Caesar, supervising producer Lee Dannacher recalls her desire to distinguish *SilverHawks* from *ThunderCats*: 'The casting of Maggie and Adolph – mixing them in with some of our known actors who were still working on *ThunderCats* shows – was simply a result of our desire to expand *SilverHawks* with the infusion of new talents and sounds. We did the same thing in other departments (new artists, Masaki assigned new storyboarding and animation directors under Kubo, etc). The new show had a sensibility and style much different from those of *ThunderCats*, so adding new talent served to shake it up for the rest of the cast as well as presenting new challenges for those of us directing the voice tracks. Maggie was phenomenal. Like Lynne Lipton on *ThunderCats*, she brought energy and a real "animatable" flavour to the characters she voiced. Adolph Caesar had this incredible voice of "gold", that was so distinctive and rich. He was not a voice-over actor in the traditional sense, so we knew we weren't going to use him for multiple roles, but we cast him for a specific character that, again, we felt would add depth to the whole of the soundtrack.'

Addressing the issue of Caesar's studio conduct, Dannacher insists he was both professional and hugely talented: 'Adolph was not temperamental in the studio. It's just that he showed up one day, well, let's say, not on top form, and we had to re-record. No biggie. *Not* newsworthy. He was a lovely man, as I remember, and apologised for the misstep. It would not be correct to reference Mr Caesar in any other way.'

One final, uncredited, member of the voice cast was Pete Cannarozzi, who had performed synthesizer sequences on both the *ThunderCats* and *SilverHawks* music scores. Having previously brought life to the electronic voices of the Ro-bear Berbils on *ThunderCats*, he was invited to perform the role of the Copper Kid on the new show. 'It was my voice on the Roland SVC 350 Vocoder,' he reveals. 'Basically, I was given a script or character voice. Then I would read the part into the mic connected to the SVC 350. The next process was the carrier, probably my Roland Jupiter 8 synth, and we would adjust tone and pitch by programming the oscillators and filters on that. However, the SVC 350 also had a decent filtering system, so we could tweak it even further. The tricky part was speaking and playing the keyboard simultaneously to actually produce the sound, but after a while we got the hang of it.'

Matthew Malach explains that there was an 'electronic/hard rock' feel to *SilverHawks*: 'That included the score. The Mon*Star voice was electronically affected in the studio. The Copper Kid was also a synthesized voice, but more elaborately done and hence, in my opinion, the most annoying voice on the show. The voice was actually synthesised and performed by Pete, a whiz with synthesisers and electronic music. Pete not only read the lines into his machines, but operated the vocoder we used to synthesise the voice. The Copper Kid sessions were all done separately from the rest of the cast recordings. Pete had the equivalent of a roadie who, for every session, lugged in what appeared to be countless cases of keyboards and filters and equalisers. It seemed a pity that we were only recording one voice with all that crap. We probably could have communicated with extraterrestrials or opened a Radio Shack!'

The Toy Line

Like *ThunderCats* before it, *SilverHawks* was supported by an extensive line of merchandise that brought the many heroes, villains and accessories from the series to the toy shelves. Whereas the licence for *ThunderCats* had been granted to New York-based LJN Toys, the *SilverHawks* toy line was developed by Ohio's Kenner Toys. Founded in 1947, the company was best known for having produced figures for the *Star Wars* franchise, and had a wealth of experience in the TV/toy tie-in arena.

By the time *SilverHawks* was in active production, the *ThunderCats* toy line had shattered all expectations and was fast becoming a merchandising phenomenon. This called for a rethink by Rankin/Bass of the importance they attached to merchandising in supporting the growth of a show. Kenner would consequently assert a much more powerful force on the creative team at Rankin/Bass than LJN had previously, and *SilverHawks* was developed to maximise its commercial potential. 'Personally,' says Peter Lawrence, 'I liked the Kenner guys, and they were always quite respectful of the show – but they did have more influence than Leisure Concepts and LJN had on *ThunderCats*. Consequently, we had god knows how many supernumerary accessories to incorporate – all those bloody weapons and personal "birds". I remember Masaki Iizuka sitting back in one meeting with the toy guys, in New York, saying, in his wonderful but heavily accented English: "Soon we have so many fucking birds flying around, we have no room for story." And he was right. As Jules Bass hammered – and I concur – story is everything. And if there's no room for story, no time for its development, then ... I guess you have a perfect show for an ADD-addled audience. Which is, perhaps, where we're headed – in TV, movies and the printed word'.

Tom McGrath, a Director of Marketing at Kenner during the 1980s, worked on the *SilverHawks* toy line. He explains why Rankin/Bass made the decision to turn away from LJN: 'Kenner was a much bigger player in the boys' action category at the time, so I think the licensors were excited to have us on board. We were interested, in part, because of their success with *ThunderCats*, but more because we thought the space sci-fi fantasy, metallic uniforms and flight fantasy would translate into pretty unique toys.'

Despite the reputation the line subsequently acquired as a 'market failure', McGrath reveals it was not as catastrophic as is often suggested: 'The line did fairly well, but was not a hit. It lasted two years, with the first year matching expectations, but rather than building in year two it declined a lot, so we dropped it for year three. It's hard to know for sure why it didn't perform as well as *ThunderCats*, but I believe the competition had a lot to do with it. *SilverHawks'* big year was '87, but that was also when our own *MASK* series really kicked in, and *Ghostbusters* was huge the next year. Also, *Star Wars* was still strong, Hasbro's *Transformers* and *GI Joe* were hot, and I believe *Masters of the Universe* was at its peak – a very competitive time.'

Commenting on Kenner's involvement in the development of the television series, McGrath maintains that they enjoyed a symbiotic relationship with Rankin/Bass: 'Kenner certainly consulted with the Rankin/Bass folks and lobbied for elements that we thought would be good for both the show and the toy line. However, Rankin/Bass had the final call on all show elements, and they certainly said no to some of our requests. I think it was a good working relationship – we both wanted the show to be entertaining and successful first and foremost. If kids weren't watching the show, they certainly wouldn't buy the toys.'

Though *SilverHawks* serves as only a footnote in McGrath's career, he remembers the distinctive visual appeal of the series: 'The most dramatic element of the toy line was the metallic (vacuum-metalised) suits – they really popped at retail shelves. Kids loved that look, and were immediately drawn to it because it was so different from most other action figures. However, the line really had only a couple of truly aspirational, cool heroes, and once kids bought those, there weren't a lot of great additional purchase options to keep them coming back. During that time, I was a Director of Marketing, working on *SilverHawks*, *MASK* and a number of other properties. I stayed with Kenner/Hasbro (Hasbro bought us in '91) for 16 years, running boys' toys for much of the '90s and ultimately as General Manager for the Hasbro Toy Group. I left Hasbro in 2000, and a year later started my own consulting business, which thankfully continues strong to this day.'

Throughout its two year run, Kenner Toys released the following *SilverHawks* figures to market:

1987 – Series One

Bluegrass with Sideman, Buzz-Saw with Shredator, Copper Kid with May Day, Flashback with Backlash, Hotwing with Gyro, Mo-Lec-U-Lar with Volt-Ure, MonStar with Sky-Shadow, Mumbo-Jumbo with Airshock, Quicksilver with Tally-Hawk, Stargazer with Sly-Bird, Steelheart with Rayzor, Steelwill with Stronghold

1988 – Series Two

Bluegrass Ultrasonic Suit, Condor with Jet Stream, Hardware with Prowler, Moon Stryker with Tail-Spin, Quicksilver Ultrasonic Suit, Steelwill Ultrasonic Suit, Windhammer with Tuning Fork

Playsets

Maraj, Tally-Hawk, Sky-Runner, Sky-Shadow, Sprint Hawk, Stronghold

Remembering *SilverHawks*

Undoubtedly *SilverHawks* has not enjoyed the legacy of *ThunderCats*, but it remains a much-beloved series for a generation of children. When the final episode aired on 5 December 1986, the show was not renewed for a second series. Rankin/Bass were, at this stage, continuing to produce a second order of 65 shows for *ThunderCats* as well as a new series, *The Comic Strip*, containing four separate adventure serials: *The Mini-Monsters, Street Frogs, Karate Kat* and *TigerSharks. The Comic Strip* first aired in 1987. By the conclusion of the second series of *ThunderCats*, Rankin/Bass had produced 260 half-hour action/adventure cartoon episodes, and the market was beginning to dry-up. Regrettably for *SilverHawks*, no subsequent episodes were commissioned and the genre began to recede. At the height of its popularity, *SilverHawks* had achieved number one status in its time slot and demographic, as well as spawning numerous publications and items of merchandise. Along with the usual swathe of board games, stationery and branded merchandise, selected episodes were released on VHS during the 1980s. The adventures of the SilverHawks were also continued in a comic range from Star Comics (an imprint of Marvel), and other supplementary publications included a colouring book and a storybook released in the early 1990s.

The adventures of the SilverHawks in the 29th Century introduced some incredibly creative and imaginative concepts to the world of television animation. Like *ThunderCats, SilverHawks* benefited from superb standards of writing, design animation and music, yet it was more idiosyncratic than its predecessor. While the *ThunderCats* toy line from LJN helped maintain that series' appeal (and original mint items still trade for hundreds of dollars), *SilverHawks* was not so fortunate. The Kenner toys enjoyed only modest sales and, two decades later, are all but forgotten to anyone but the most ardent collector. Furthermore, *SilverHawks* was not exported to the variety of overseas territories that broadcast *ThunderCats*. Indeed, it was never shown in the UK where, arguably, *ThunderCats* enjoyed some of its greatest success. Though it would be easy to conclude that *SilverHawks* slipped into obscurity due to issues of its own making (particularly its eccentric style), its fate may, perhaps, say more about the wild success of *ThunderCats* by comparison.

PART SIX
THE *THUNDERCATS* LEGACY

10. RETURN TO THUNDERA
The Ongoing Saga

The final episode of *ThunderCats* debuted in 1989. Over the course of 130 episodes, the series had entranced a generation of children; but a change in the television industry meant that no further episodes were commissioned. With action/adventure cartoon serials on the wane, *ThunderCats* and its compatriots were banished from the schedules to make way for a new generation of programming for the 1990s.

During both its first and second seasons, *ThunderCats* had achieved an 85% coverage of the US television audience and been broadcast on over 100 local stations. According to Nielsen Broadcast Data Systems (BDS) information, by the November 1989 sweeps period, repeats of both seasons were achieving a reduced coverage of 50% of the US audience; and by the final local broadcasts in July 1991, the figure had fallen to only 32%. Throughout the early part of the 1990s, episodes of the series could still be seen in syndication on a few stations around the world (many of which had purchased the series after its initial US run). However, by the middle of the decade, the show had all but disappeared from the schedules, and the adventures of the ThunderCats seemed destined to be forgotten. Although remembered fondly by its original audience, the series had fallen out of mainstream interest. Until, that is it returned in the form of reruns on a Cartoon Network cable channel in 1997.

Launched as part of the network's new Toonami programming block, all 130 episodes of *ThunderCats* were replayed. The network's license to broadcast the show ran from 25 December 1996 to 28 February 2003, and there were a myriad of repeats throughout this period across various time slots and dates. These revived broadcasts marked the beginning of a resurgence for the series, attracting a new legion of fans in addition to reawakening the interest of its original audience. Having emerged from a short period of dormancy, the legacy of *ThunderCats* was suddenly assured ...

The *ThunderCats* Legacy

The overwhelming success enjoyed by *ThunderCats* is indubitable, although the question of why it has bucked the trend for ephemera and continues to thrive is less easy to answer. Certainly it was meticulously constructed, and the artistic and creative efforts involved in producing it were of the highest order. However, comparable programmes (not least *SilverHawks*) had benefited from a similar fastidiousness, but have fallen short of achieving the longevity of *ThunderCats*. While the many writers, musicians, designers and producers credit the show's achievements to the collective group, they openly acknowledge the serendipitous way in which the show has stuck in the affections of its audience.

'I remember saying once that it was the humanity of it,' notes supervising producer Lee Dannacher. 'It just had something that no other animated series had in the action/adventure genre. It had this warmth, and the type of humanity that touched on everybody's development – childhood development or young adult development … Lion-O never grew up, so our episodes had to deal with the issue, "What would those lessons have been between 12 and 20 that Lion-O didn't get?" Issues of trust and friendship and being honest, along with, "We've got to deal with the jeopardy of the day". So I guess, at its core, it was the humanity and a sense of what a younger population goes through during those adolescent years that the other action/adventure fantasy shows didn't incorporate. We were constantly entertaining ourselves and we were just like kids in a candy store, saying, "Look what I've done with this, look how I added a layer to that". Whether it was the actors improvising well or adding to lines given, or what the recording engineers did, it was just extraordinary. I don't think anyone would have hung around and made the magic we created if we weren't all working on top of what was given to us along the line. I've been really, really fortunate … that *ThunderCats* attracted such outrageously great talents who have all, retrospectively, expressed such fond memories of the whole experience. I guess that's why, when someone asks why I think *ThunderCats* found such a loyal and lasting fan base, I think its knowing what a fantastic world of work and professional camaraderie was taking place behind the scenes. How could the series not reflect some of that magic?'

'It would be interesting to ask Warner Brothers what made *ThunderCats* a success,' adds script editor Peter Lawrence. 'I don't think they have a clue. My guess is this: that the characters by and large are all multi-dimensional. Lion-O was never a completely mature superhero – never enough that the kids couldn't relate to him. Everyone would like an uncle like Panthro – the strong protector. To my amazement, people I've met were really affected by Cheetara, not necessarily sexually, but boys really fell in love with her. She was an acceptable female hero for the boys. And the girls fell in love with the ThunderCats because they were accessible, they weren't all slam-bam, transforming, they had human characteristics and personalities.

'Even the most basic stories – and there were some basic ones – were real stories; they had a beginning, a middle and an end, they had tension and a lot of humour. Even the most ADD kids, if you sit them down and tell them a story, will listen to you. I think our stories were compelling, at least enough of them. Mumm-Ra is magnificent; he's both frightening and funny, and in a way reassuring because he's predictable – kids like that. Every now and then, you'd have something completely out of left field. That's what I think works for the target audience.

'They put on a live action *ThunderCats* show in Madison Square Gardens and there were 25,000 kids all waving their sword and chanting "ThunderCats Ho!", and you realise things like that connect with people. For some reason, *ThunderCats* picked up a cult college audience. I don't understand that, but maybe it was camp – not so camp that it lost its drama, but it didn't take itself that seriously. Slithe, Vultureman, Monkian, even the ThunderCats, didn't take themselves too seriously. I think that the main characters of *SilverHawks* don't have the same charm. Stargazer does. The best episode (which Bill Overgard wrote) is where he goes back to Earth for a refit and finds an old girlfriend. It's so adult. Stargazer had that warmth and humanity, but others didn't. I have to admit that WilyKit and Kat and

Snarf added humour to *ThunderCats*. Copper Kid a bit to *SilverHawks*, but not in the same way. I think *SilverHawks'* villains are better than *ThunderCats'* Mutants, but the main characters didn't have the same charm.'

Writer Lee Schneider believes *ThunderCats* had a cinematic sensibility that was unheard of for a cartoon: 'There was a sense of adventure and wonder that *ThunderCats* had throughout every story. The animators took on the series as though it were a feature film, with POV shots, vibrant camera angles, and a sense of energy and mission that didn't exist in American television animation at the time, to my knowledge. It was quality stuff, and the viewers, though they were just kids, sensed the quality and seemed to remain attached to it. I think that's why the show is fondly remembered. That, and the phallic nature of Lion-O's Sword!'

'Who can tell about popularity?' ponders writer Leonard Starr. 'I was there when *Superman* began, and I was a fan of Joe Shuster's and Jerry Siegel's private eye character *Slam Bradley*, which ran in Detective Comics. Then all of a sudden, here comes *Superman*, and I looked at it and thought, "What the hell is this? He's wearing a blue leotard and red bathing trunks and red booties and a cape." And to my great surprise, it became popular immediately, so I figured that it was a fad, and like all fads it would last two to three years until something else came along to replace it, and then that would be replaced and so on. It's now been 80 years and they still haven't replaced it. So that gives you an idea of how good I am at detecting these trends. Why one show works and another show doesn't? Who knows. You never know why. I think when *ThunderCats* came out, there were a couple of other new shows at the same time. *Rambo* was one of them, and I don't remember the other one, but the animation on the other one was first rate, exceptional in fact. All I remember is noticing it and then not noticing it. One minute it was there and then it was gone. Even *Masters of the Universe* didn't stand the test of time like *ThunderCats* did. It was very popular when it was running, but I never hear any references to it on the internet and I don't know how often it ran after its initial syndication run was done.'

Peter Bakalian, who worked for Rankin/Bass, believes the success of *ThunderCats* could be contextual: 'If *SilverHawks* had come first and *ThunderCats* second, it's conceivable we'd be talking about what a great show *SilverHawks* was. When *SilverHawks* came out, a lot of people didn't get to see it, because competition had become so intense for syndication. Things like *Masters of the Universe* were making a lot of money for the people who got in early, and it's conceivable some shows just got pushed under the bus and you couldn't see them. The level of artistry on *ThunderCats* was pretty high, the quality of the animation and writing. It could well be that the team working on it were fresher to it. When *SilverHawks* came around, I'm not saying people were tired, but it might not have had the same energy or stakes. Frankly, I like *SilverHawks* more. I think it was a funnier show. I like the genre. *ThunderCats* was a different show. You were almost in the land of *The Hobbit*; it had a high level of fantasy and medieval elements. It had the whole royal family thing with the *ThunderCats*. *SilverHawks* was kind of a space police show and, in that sense, it was more conventional. *ThunderCats* was out there; you didn't see characters like Tygra, Cheetara and Lion-O every day. The work that went into them, with Peter Lawrence's writing and Lee Dannacher making sure it was executed properly, really shows. Sometimes the difference between [success and failure] is very small, maybe just five percent, but it makes a difference.'

Scriptwriter James Rose believes *ThunderCats'* morality endeared parents to it: 'I believe it has a lot to do with the fact that parents could watch *ThunderCats* with their kids and enjoy the show. The stories had an ethical outlook that eschewed violence between individuals. That and the dynamic characters, the overall design and the show's huge mythic component really delivered to the viewers.'

Writer Heather Winters suggests another reason for the show's lasting impact: 'I think *ThunderCats* was one of the first shows of its kind that created other worlds where superheroes came from. It looked different and was so strong – from the show title, to the character names and designs, through to the writing. There was an inherent "power" to the show, and I think that made it very appealing and different from other show on air at the time. The characters were so well drawn, well designed and so compelling and likeable – people were naturally drawn to them. The writing, music, animation and voice talents were all excellent and drew viewers in. And of course, "Thunder, Thunder, Thunder, ThunderCats Ho!" gets ingrained in the brain! It's very addictive.'

Though the series was widely praised by its contributors, not everyone expected its success. Writer Beth Bornstein admits to being surprised at its longevity: 'I thought that *SilverHawks* would be equally successful. Does anyone even remember *SilverHawks* now?' Scriptwriter Doug Bernstein also feels that *ThunderCats* was an acquired taste: 'It seemed to have a high camp quotient to me, but the fan base belies that. They really bought into the show's mythology, and I think perhaps what it had was a truly scary and weird (if overacted) villain in Mumm-Ra.'

'The show was, in its day, somewhat edgy,' submits writer Larry Carroll. 'Lion-O always came off a lot less preppy than, say, He-Man. He could also screw up, and it wasn't unusual for the other ThunderCats to have to bail him out. And they're cats, which is kind of cool.'

Writer Jeri Craden lists her reasons for the show's staying-power: 'It was the music, the type of animation, the heroic plotlines and the humanity and friendships of the characters!' Another writer, Herb Englehardt, opines: 'It must be the mix of art and character and the timelessness of fantasy.'

'They are good stories with solid writing (under Peter Lawrence's reign),' says writer and episodic director Matthew Malach. 'It was a crack production team (under Lee Dannacher), and an astonishing cast of only about six people who did *all* the voices – including new characters – for the first 65 episodes!'

Recording engineer Tom Perkins concludes that *ThunderCats* transcends cultural barriers, maximising its appeal across ages and locales: 'I'm not sure I understand why it's had such an impact other than, as with *Star Wars* and such, the themes are universal and the morality clear and defined. It also happened to go on air at a time when the television industry itself was in flux; a new broadcast network (Fox) was shaking up the established order, cable was beginning to take hold, and the children of the first TV generation (the baby boomers) were now the viewers. TV was on the verge of becoming more than a mere source of entertainment; it was becoming central to the lives of people, and it captured the boomers' kids. Cable enabled *ThunderCats* to live on in syndication, where those themes of morality were ingested by yet another generation. The simple need of broadcasters for programming helped to extend the life of a lot of shows, and *ThunderCats* was there at the right time.'

A Global Phenomenon

At the peak of its original transmission run, *ThunderCats* was broadcast by 132 local stations across America. Rather than getting transmission tapes from Lorimar-Telepictures, participating stations would receive satellite transmissions direct from the distributors in California. They would be asked to retain their copies only long enough for transmission, and not to library their collections. For overseas transmissions, standards conversions would be required (for instance from the NTSC format native to America to the PAL format used in Europe, Asia and South America). Broadcast tapes would then be sent abroad via the distributor.

Though there is no complete record of all international sales of *ThunderCats*, it has been broadcast in the following countries: United Kingdom, Canada, Greece, Turkey, Brazil, India, Indonesia, Israel, France, Pakistan, Guatemala, Mexico, Thailand, Sweden, Iceland, Italy, Venezuela, Gibraltar, Kuwait, Uruguay, Portugal and South Africa.

Though these countries have all seen the series at one time or another, not all of them participated in its original run during the mid 1980s. Some saw episodes aired well into the early 1990s, while others had to wait for satellite channels to debut the episodes later in the same decade.

One of the most successful *ThunderCats* exports was to the United Kingdom, where the show was broadcast on BBC1. Arriving two years behind its American debut, the pilot episode, 'Exodus', went out on 2 January 1987. The series was subsequently shown as part of the Saturday morning children's magazine series *Going Live!*, *UP2U* and *On the Waterfront*. Additionally, it was shown as a stand-alone programme. While the episodes had been designed to be run consecutively across Mondays to Fridays, the BBC would typically air only one per week, vastly lengthening the show's transmission run and building added anticipation for each new adventure. *ThunderCats* catapulted into the consciousness of the British public with an explosion of popularity and merchandise sales that rivalled even the American response to the series.

In 1986, the BBC had appointed Theresa Plummer-Andrews as its Head of Children's Acquisitions and Co-Productions, and it was she who was responsible for bringing *ThunderCats* to UK screens. 'It was amongst a batch of programming shown to us by the distributor,' explains Plummer-Andrews. 'It was exciting, fun, not too violent, and outside what the BBC had normally purchased before. We felt it was time to spice up our schedules. The BBC did not have a "strip schedule" at that time. To transmit once or twice per week was perfectly normal, and it was thus until we launched our own digital channels, when stripping across the week became usual. The BBC produced a huge amount of programming in-house, and the animation I bought was only meant to complement and supplement what the BBC produced itself.'

Asked whether the series' pro-social credentials affected her decision to purchase it, Plummer-Andrews maintains that her decision was based purely on its appeal and suitability: 'Having a child psychologist involved made absolutely no difference to our thoughts about this series. In those days it wasn't the norm to have psychologists, child "specialists" or "experts" involved with children's programming. The BBC had their own in-house guidelines on all programmes produced or purchased, and we stuck to those guidelines without any outside influences.

'We were told about the success of the series, but we didn't care what the ratings were in other countries. We had to ensure it was going to work with English children. It's the same now. Some programmes are huge hits in one country but die a death in another. It's up to the broadcaster to know their home audience. American animation is very, very popular in the UK – with the children. They like the stories and style of scripting and the pace. Parents aren't so overawed by it! You might know that anything purchased for the under fives all has to be re-voiced into English, as parents don't want their kids to grow up saying things like "garbage" and "check this out". After five, no-one seems to care, and the series are broadcast in whatever language they were produced in! At one point there was a huge resistance to American animation, and the European Broadcasting Union set up a children's committee to work towards bringing more European animation to our screens. The outcome was series such as *Animals of Farthing Wood, Noah's Island, Pitt and Kantrop* etc. However, the cost of animating in Europe gets higher by the year, and studios are falling by the wayside. The current animation is not made in the USA. The concept, writing, voicing, etc are controlled there, but the animation itself is done in India, China, the Philippines, Malaysia, Korea etc. The same applies for most countries. France produces a lot of animated series, but the actual animation is done in the countries previously mentioned.

'*ThunderCats* was the first of its genre to be aired on the BBC. Plus, it didn't have a lot of competition. Remember, there were no cable or satellite channels to compete for the audience then, so the audience didn't have too many places to go. Notwithstanding all that, it was a good series, and kids just loved it! I was the buyer at ITV when they bought *Masters of the Universe*, then was head-hunted by the BBC and bought *ThunderCats*! Both purchases were on the basis of good stories and great characters. And yes, of course we were competing with each other – whatever side I was on at the time!'

Though *ThunderCats'* popularity was undeniable, the BBC took the decision not to purchase the second season, and the original run of episodes concluded on British television on the 20 May 1991 with the first season finale 'Fond Memories'. 'We had the rights [to give the first season] I think something like three runs over five years,' says Plummer-Andrews, 'which meant that we didn't really need to buy any further episodes. The series was on air over a long period of time and kept picking up new viewers. After this we felt we needed something new to replenish the schedule and keep it fresh.'

Having omitted one episode ('Spitting Image') from the original run, the BBC also edited some to remove 'excessive violence'. In practice, this involved excising many sequences featuring Panthro's use of nunchaku, which were frowned upon by British censors. 'Every episode of everything the BBC buys is pre-edited to take out items that are considered unsuitable for transmission on the BBC,' explains Plummer-Andrews. 'This, as you can imagine, takes a great deal of time, when taking into account the amount of series the BBC buys. The reason the episodes were originally transmitted over a long period of time is that the contract would have specified delivery of a certain number by a certain date (not all at once), which meant the transmission (and the pre-editing) was spread out.'

Though no longer working for the BBC, Plummer-Andrews remains involved in the world of children's television. 'Programming has changed since those days,' she concludes. 'Sometimes not for the better, as the violence has gone up a ratchet or four! It seems to be more apparent on the cable/satellite networks and, quite frankly, I have seen programmes transmitted on these channels that I certainly wouldn't allow any child of mine to watch. The world has changed, but I think the main terrestrial broadcasters try to keep up good editorial standards, and their compliance teams do everything they can to ensure the viewer sees only pretty good programming.'

Over a five year run (broken by periods of hiatus), *ThunderCats* had captured the hearts and minds of children across Britain. Decades after its arrival, the series remains one of the most successful children's imports originating in the USA.

Comic Possibilities

For many children, the televised episodes of *ThunderCats* proved to be just one of many ways to enjoy the adventures of their favourite characters. In 1985, a range of *ThunderCats* comics began publication in the US by Star Comics (a subsidiary of Marvel). It eventually ran for four years across 24 issues. This comic line proved incredibly popular and helped bring an additional audience to the series, with readers quickly converting to viewers. The majority of the issues featured adaptations of televised *ThunderCats* episodes, restructured to work in a comic format by a talented group of writers and artists.

In the UK, a similar line emerged from Marvel Comics. This lasted from 1987 until 1990. Far surpassing its US counterpart, it ran to an incredible 135 issues, going far beyond TV adaptations to present specially-crafted new plots, characters and environments. Seasonal comic compilations and annuals were also released periodically, featured previously-published content from the Marvel UK comics.

One of the editors assigned to the original US line of *ThunderCats* comics was Don Daley, who recalls that Marvel may have became interested in the property on the advice of industry luminaries Sid Jacobson and Tom DeFalco: 'I was assigned the title after Mike (who'd been editing the book), left Marvel for DC. I was basically trying to get going what Mike had gotten up and running. If you look at the first few issues, they're pretty faithful to the parent property, and that's what we tried to do. If it ain't broke ... All of us wanted to do a faithful, loving comic book version of the already successful series. We all watched the original series on VHS (don't they seem bulky now?), to learn the characters and their "voices", to get a sense of the feel and pace of it. We liked it!'

Asked how successful the comic was, Daley replies: 'The fact that Marvel published *ThunderCats* as long as it did (24 issues), suggests to me that it made money for them – although the fact that it was then cancelled suggests that either the profit dropped to a point below Marvel's target range, or the licence renewal was seen as too expensive, or both. My sense at the time, with Marvel, was that the people working in editorial and creative tried to give every title a chance at success. You have to, not only from a business point of view, but also from the creative side. The people who create comics generally love the medium and love working on a title, and our crew loved *ThunderCats*. I suspect that sales dipped to a point at which Marvel was better off financially allocating those resources to other titles. It's par for the course. Remember that licensed titles cost a publisher more, generally, because it has to pay licensing fees, so they have to sell more copies just to cover the initial investment. Of course, at the same time, you have the TV show out there as a "free ad" helping (one hopes) to drive sales. Ultimately, publisher and property owner have to craft a deal that each believes to be beneficial.

'Mike Carlin picked the initial team to work on the comic, and anyone who's worked with Mike knows that he's very, very, very knowledgeable in terms of personnel, styles, individuals' work habits, preferences and productivity. So I inherited a book that was already in pretty good shape, and I made changes only when I thought I had to. Particularly with an existing property (as opposed to a cold start-up of a new one), the editor's job is to "zoom in" on the core of the property, because it's that core that formed the basis for its initial appeal. I was fortunate to work on *GI Joe* with Denny O'Neil and Larry Hama, and at lunch one day, Larry said, "You know what *GI Joe* is about? Camaraderie!" And if you look at the issues, he's right. *X-Men* seemed to say that if you're a teen who feels alienated, you're special, and Chris Claremont and John Byrne drove that home in every issue, in a nuanced way. You can look at most comics and boil them down into a core, and with *ThunderCats*, I inherited a turnkey operation. The core was there, the crew was there, my job was to keep it running on time and within budget.'

Daley believes that *ThunderCats* was extremely compatible with the comic book medium, thanks in part to the fact that many of its writers – Leonard Starr, Howard Post, Bob Haney et al – had originally hailed from the comics industry: 'I thought that the TV show's approach made our work very easy to transition the material to comics. Many of the people who'd worked on the show knew comics already, and like most people working in animation, they thought in pictures. Maybe Temple Grandin (who wrote *Animals in Translation, Unwritten Rules of Social Relationships* and many other great books) could be a great animator, because her autism has her thinking in pictures, not words as most people think.'

As regards his team's collaboration with the Rankin/Bass production office, Daley comments: 'Anytime anyone does something based upon an original property as part of a licensing deal, it's standard operating procedure to get approval in writing prior to release. That protects the owner from damage to the brand, or duplication of, say, a film that's in the works, by a comic that has a shorter lead time, and it also insulates the licensee from being sued by the property owner. So with *GI Joe, Transformers, ThunderCats*, any of the licensed properties Marvel published, we always secured approval for story and art. What was tricky was when you were running late, submitted what you hoped would be the finished product to the licensor, sent the book out to the printer so they could start work on it, and then heard back from the licensor that there was a problem. One time with *GI Joe* we had an issue that featured a nuke as the MacGuffin. Book's all set, colour's in, time's tight, we submit it to Hasbro. They say, "No nukes". Larry Hama and Denny and I order sandwiches and call in three pencillers. Larry's doing thumbnails and blowing them up, and he scripts from them. We letter it on vellum as the pencillers tighten the thumbnails and ink it. We colour from the blow-ups of the thumbnails. We put out a 21-page comic, finished, in less than 24 hours. So, short story long, you need licensor approval when you're a licensee.'

Asked about the added longevity of the range internationally, Daley says: 'The US and UK markets, obviously, differ. *Doctor Who* has succeeded over here in the States, but it's been a major property in the UK to a much greater extent, and I think part of it has to do with what I see as a longer attention span in the UK. The fans there are even more devoted, even more attentive and appreciative of detail, than the US fans. That's been my experience, at least. Look at *Transformers*, which ran forever in the UK. When they love a property, they love it longer. Just my take on it, and I hope I don't offend all the great fans in the US who read this, but I've been long struck by the devotion to titles by the UK fan base.'

Daley is extremely positive about his time on *ThunderCats* and acknowledges the show's continuing appeal: 'My memory of working on *ThunderCats* consists mostly of working with Jose Delbo, who's a sweet guy, and with a bunch of writers, including the late George Caragonne and the late Steve Perry. If you look at the original television series, there's a lot of love there. The visuals are fairly fresh, and the whole "furry" thing helps drive it. How many of us dressed up, at some point or other, as an animal? And the variety of cats in *ThunderCats* enabled everyone to find a cat they related to.'

Another integral member of the *ThunderCats* comic team was the aforementioned writer and editor Tom DeFalco, who achieved fame with his work on the *Spiderman* comic series. 'Don Daley was the editor and I told him that the book absolutely, positively, had to ship on time,' says DeFalco. 'It was a comic that sold primarily on the newsstand, and there was no margin for error. He responded by handing me a script for one of the shows and telling me to help him make his deadlines by adapting it. I took the animation script, broke it down into a 22-page comic story and turned in a script that described each panel. After my script was approved, it was sent to an artist. Since I rarely look at my published work, I'm afraid I don't even remember who drew it. I guess Don liked what I did, because he asked me to do a few more.

'Marvel/Star was actively courting younger readers and the animation market. Unlike today, when a score of publishers are licensing children's properties, we were pretty much the only game in town. I don't remember if the *ThunderCats* people approached us or we approached them. Whatever! It was good match. I wanted to translate each animated adventure into the most exciting comic book story that I could. I watched a few episodes to get the feel of the show and the way the characters talked and reacted to each other. I liked what I saw. Animation and comics may seem similar, but they employ two very different types of visual storytelling. One uses continual motion. The other employs snapshots. While the content of *ThunderCats* was very compatible for comic books, the actual scripts needed to be adjusted to fit the medium. *ThunderCats* is/was an exciting and well-done show and quality always lasts!'

The Star/Marvel lines of the 1980s would not prove to be *ThunderCats* final foray into the world of comics. In 2002, the property was revived in the form of several comic book mini-series publications from WildStorm Comics (an imprint of DC Comics). Whereas the original Marvel line had effectively been promoted by the television series, the WildStorm one faced the unenviable task of reviving a brand from nearly two decades previously. Fortunately, nostalgic buyers still held a deep affection for *ThunderCats*, which led to sales far in excess of the publisher's predictions, and issues continued to be published until 2004.

The WildStorm line began with *Reclaiming Thundera*, a five-part serial that continued where the TV series had ended and successfully replicated its tone. After this came the five-issue serial *The Return*. This offered a darker and more adult interpretation of *ThunderCats* in an epic story that initially witnessed the devastating victory of Mumm-Ra and his subjugation of the ThunderCats in the absence of Lion-O. After the latter's return to Thundera, the story then focused on the restoration of peace and ThunderCat rule. WildStorm produced further mini-serials entitled *Dogs of War*, *Hammerhand's Revenge* and *Enemy's Pride*, as well as a number of special editions, including a brief guide to the world and characters contained within WildStorm's volumes.

One of the most influential figures in the development of the revived comic line was writer Ford Lytle Gilmore, who worked on the first few issues. 'If memory serves correctly, the idea to do it was really Jim Lee's and John Nee's doing,' he says. 'Before the whole nostalgia wave hit comics, I know Jim was interested in *GI Joe*, *Transformers* and *ThunderCats* and understood that there was an audience there for a number of the big '80s cartoons. When other companies licensed the rights to the first two and found great success with them, I'm sure that was more than enough ammo for Jim to re-approach DC and convince them to do *ThunderCats* – especially since DC is part of the Time-Warner family and its sister company Warner Brothers controls the rights to *ThunderCats*.

'I had worked with a number of the folks at WildStorm back when I was trying to license from them the film/TV rights to a comic (Jeff Mariotte's *Desparados*) shortly before they were acquired by DC. That experience led me to writing a creator-owned series at WildStorm called *Nightfall: The Black Chronicles*, and I continued to work with the folks over there off and on. John Nee knew I grew up in the '80s and thought I might be a fan of *ThunderCats*, and approached me about pitching for it when they were looking at publishing. I had fond memories of the show, but confessed I hadn't seen it since I was a kid, and was intrigued. Long story short, my pitch was accepted and we started down the road of creating the series.'

Gilmore believes that the line between honouring the original series and reinvigorating the brand was difficult to tread: 'First and foremost, it was decided to do a slightly more contemporary updating of the ThunderCats, building upon their mythology and telling stories that would be most appreciated by fans who already had at least a passing familiarity with the show but weren't necessarily die-hards. Accessible, entertaining, and telling more PG kinds of deeper stories. I really wanted to avoid matching the tone of some of the goofier, funnier episodes from later in the run, and focus on the action/adventure elements that were so cool to me as a kid. Knowing that most of the audience for the comic would be in their mid-twenties and older, the idea was to do a darker, self-contained mini-series, and I had described it to WildStorm initially as kind of a *The Dark Knight Returns* with the *ThunderCats*. That was *ThunderCats: The Return*. Somewhere along the way, someone higher up the foodchain at DC decided that we needed to do something much more in tone with episodes of the series – lighter, and all self-contained stories, ideally showcasing different "favourite" characters each issue. So we ended up doing the *Reclaiming Thundera* mini-series first, with the knowledge that I'd get to do *The Return* afterwards.

'You have to be aware of the existing fans, but if you always second-guess yourself and try to cater to them, you risk losing sight of the forest for the trees – especially since not all fans are 100% in agreement about everything, so you're never going to be able to placate them all. I think it's important to treat the material – and the audience – with respect, while concentrating on telling the best stories possible. Ironically, that was part of the impetus behind *The Return* for me. I figured that most of the fans, those who were still collecting comics at least, would be more interested in seeing new stories that built upon what went before and felt a little more adult, as opposed to re-tellings of episodes or stories crafted to feel like "lost episodes".

'I'd seen a number of *ThunderCats* episodes as a kid, and probably most of the first season. I loved it then – what could be cooler than ninja cats fighting monsters and aliens? I thought there was a lot of fertile ground to mine. I confess I was less of a fan of the later episodes, as they seemed to have more licensing-driven stories/characters, and more gags that were just beyond the pale in my opinion. Not that there weren't awesome episodes or characters in there; I just thought it worked better straighter, without things like Luna going on about Amok again and again or throwaway bits about Snarf loving burritos from the planet with Mexican food.'

Commenting on the artists that contributed to the WildStar comic, Gilmore believes that fans often underestimate the calibre of talent involved: 'The artists were selected by WildStorm editorial. They got J Scott Campbell to do the "0" issue, then Ed McGuinness for the first mini and eventually Ed Benes for the second. It was crazy, really, as they were three of the biggest artists in the industry at the time (and still are), so it was just a great show of WildStar's commitment to the material to go get such heavy hitters to draw the books. I know that some of the *ThunderCats* fans who weren't comics readers didn't know it at the time – and I know some of them weren't happy with the fact that the art didn't look just like the cartoons – but it can't be stressed enough how big those artists were and how cool it was to be working with them on the project. I think the Wildstorm comics were very compatible with the television medium, because both really allowed you to play with visual storytelling. Bridging the gap from animation to comics was relatively easy when there were guys like Jeff and Ed and Ed drawing the stories.

'I don't remember exact sales figures, but I know the first mini-series was a much bigger success than a lot of folks anticipated, and was WildStorm's best-selling title by a wide margin. I couldn't tell you why the line eventually ended, as I was just a freelancer writing some of it. I assume it was the age-old issue of shrinking sales. I remember very clearly flying out to the Wizard World East convention in Philadelphia when they were getting ready to announce the comic. There had been rumours for a while, and everyone assumed something would be happening just in light of the success of *GI Joe* and *Transformers*, and that DC would be doing it since Warner controlled the rights, but nothing was ever said until that convention. I remember the slide coming up – with J Scott Campbell's cover to the '0' issue – as DC's Patty Jeres was announcing to an unsuspecting crowd that they were doing the book, and this one woman a few rows back exclaimed loudly "Oh my god! You're bringing back *ThunderCats*! Too cool!" There were other folks reacting and plenty of excitement, so it let me know immediately that the book would be a hit.

'I think there are a number of reasons, honestly, why *ThunderCats* is still remembered. First and foremost, the original show was just plain cool, and featured some of the best-looking animation of the era. There was also a lot more depth to the characters than most cartoons have, and a real sense of family and community within the core group; they were relatable, and felt deeper. The fact that there were multiple strong, well-crafted female characters, kid characters who weren't just goofy comic relief, and males who did more than just kick butt, is a huge part of it, too. Finally, it's the fandom. *ThunderCats* fans are awesome, vocal, and passionate, with a lot of them feeling like it's their mission to keep the flame burning. Fans like that are never going to let their show die, and never let it fade into oblivion.'

The Stage Show

In 1987, during the height of popularity of Rankin/Bass's animated cartoon series, the company's distributor, Lorimar/Telepictures, took the unusual move of producing a tie-in stage show. This extravaganza, entitled ThunderCats Live!, was billed as featuring 'ThunderCats, SilverHawks & their special friends, Gumby & Pokey, TigerSharks, Street Frogs [and] Karate Kat'. Though the stage production's main selling point was the *ThunderCats* connection, Lorimar were keen to exploit the popularity of both *SilverHawks* and *The Comic Strip* as well. The popular Gumby character, first seen on American screens in 1957, was also included to tie in with a revival by Lorimar, who had recently acquired the property.

Produced by Steven Goldberg, the show premiered at the famous Madison Square Garden arena in Manhattan, New York in September 1987. The writer, director and choreographer, Nancy Gregory, recalls the many team members who brought the show to life: 'Steve was the producer and initiated the entire production. He hired me. It was our third show together, and there would be another after this in the early '90s for Warner Bros. Jeremy Railton was the scenic designer, Randy Gale was associate producer and Phillip Dennis was costume designer. Lee Dannacher was the soundtrack supervisor. The famous Foys designed my flying rigs.

'The show opened in 1987 and I think it toured the country for about two years. Jeremy Railton is now a very successful designer and we have collaborated on several shows since then. Phillip Dennis went on to work with Barry Manilow for years, and passed away unfortunately a few years back. Steve did one more show and then quasi-retired in Carmel. He started a company that sold cosmetics on TV that made him very wealthy.'

Asked about the storylines used in the stage show, Nancy Gregory recalls the problems inherent in incorporating so many elements in to one project: 'There were six different programmes that had to be connected in one show, so it was an interesting challenge. The basic storyline was that Gumby and Pokey decided to go into the TV set (like they used to do with books) and have a "live" cartoon adventure. This took them into the various worlds of the characters. Of course, *ThunderCats* had the most action, with Mumm-Ra and the Mutants in pursuit of Lion-O. Gumby and Pokey got in the middle of this and had to be saved.'

Gregory remains in the industry today and remembers her involvement in ThunderCats Live! with a great sense of pride: 'I have many memories of the production, including meeting with the Flying Foys in Las Vegas so I could fly the *SilverHawks* across an arena. The show was done "in-the-round"[8], with big ramps

---

[8] A theatre set up with the audience surrounding the stage.

around the main stage, and some of the characters roller-skated, so it was a fabulous creative staging challenge. I also remember the thousands of kids screaming with the characters. The production was a success and broke all attendance records at Madison Square Garden at that time.'

The complete credits for ThunderCats Live!, as printed in the show's souvenir booklet, are reproduced below:

STAFF

Executive Producer: Steven Goldberg
Director/Choreographer: Nancy Gregory
Writer: Nancy Gregory
Associate Producer: Randolph Gale
Set Design: Jeremy Railton
Costume Design: Phillip Dennis
Soundtrack Supervisor: Lee Dannacher
Lighting Supervisor: Kirk Bookman
Music Supervisor: Earl Manky
Assistant to Mr. Goldberg: Bianka Lunecke-Branstner
Office Assistant: Kathleen Becket

MARKETING STAFF

Director of Booking and Marketing: Ivy Bauer
Marketing Assistant: Marte Christman
Promoters: Herbert Frank, Larry Frank, Fred Frank, Suzan Harrison, Robert Vrooman

ROAD PRODUCTION STAFF

Production Manager and Coordinator: Jimmy Lewis
Rigger: Russell Draeger
Carpenter: Kevin Spinks
Lighting Board Operator: Jim Bauman
Audio Engineer/Stage Manager: Jim Slater
Wardrobe Assistant: Frieda M Paras
2nd Carpenter: Dana Vanella
Electrical Technician: Jim Cozad
2nd Wardrobe Assistant: Kari Ann Messina
Dance Captain: Evel
Rollerskating Captain: Billy Richardson
Assistant to Ms Gregory: Randy Doney

THE CAST

Marty Almaraz, Chris Bethards, Jeff Biggs, Greg Carrillo, Christy Curtis, Derek J K Delanoza, Marcie Dinardo, Evel, Vernon David Gallegos, Gregory Gonzales, Tracy Ann Guaderrama, Enrique Hernandez, Michael Jefferson, Judy Kathleen, Peter

Lajos, Chuck Merrell, Michelle Miracle, Jane Phillips, Billy Richardson, Allison Spinella, Micheal Spinella, Kimberly Talbert, Gavin Van, Deanna Wilshire

Soundtrack Production: Rankin/Bass, New York, NY
Business Management: Duitch & Franklin – Richard Parness
Accounting: Lorimar – Rick Endelson
Legal Counsel: Don Biederman
Lighting: Showlites, Compton, CA
Flying: Flying by Foy, Las Vegas, NV
Sound: Sound on Stage, San Francisco, CA
Set Construction: Sunrise Sets, Burbank, CA
Trucking: Entertainment Transportation
Bussing: Jarrel Summar Tours
Commercial: Bozell, Jacobs, Kenyon & Eckhardt – Jim Bardwil, Foster Hurley
Security Systems: Recreation Technologies

THE TOUR BOOK
Tour Book Design: John Coulter, John Coulter Design
Front Cover Art Direction/Graphics: Ron Ascher
Front Cover Illustration: Greg Martin
Color Separations: Steve Uslan, Prestone Graphics
Printing: Stanley Marks, Spencer Graphics Service, Jersey City, NJ
Merchandising: Tom Collins, Tom Collins Enterprises, Inc.
Riedell Shoes Inc is the official skate boot used by *ThunderCats Live!*

SPECIAL THANKS
Dick Robertson, Michael Garin, Stephen Ross, Jim Moloshak, Lee Dannacher, Jim McGillen, Scott Carlin, Keith Samples, Mary Van Houten, Allen Bohbot, Stan Westen, Steve Westen, Sid Kaufman, Jules Bass, Arthur Rankin, Cy Schneider

The Merchandising Machine

In addition to the extensive *ThunderCats* toy line and series of comics, Rankin/Bass's licensing agent Stan Weston was keen to exploit the series across as many merchandise items (and companies) as possible. Supervising producer Lee Dannacher comments: 'Leisure Concepts were handling the licensing, but I don't know what their deal was with Telepictures. I don't know if they had to go back to them for toothbrush or bed sheet deals. (Incidentally, *ThunderCats* bed sheets ended up in the Tom Hanks movie *Big*. His character goes into his new Manhattan apartment and they have them on the bed.) I assume, though, that LCI had to at least pass all of their deals past Telepictures for approval.'

Below is a brief and non-exhaustive list of some of the more memorable items to emerge sporting the *ThunderCats* brand:

Mini Figures: A range of two-inch PVC miniatures released by Kidsworks, including playsets and a belt for carrying the figures.

Annuals: Released between 1985 and 1992 in the UK, the *ThunderCats* annuals

454

included character drawings, information, puzzles, and comic strips taken from the comic line.

Books and Magazines: A wide variety of books emerged exploring the world of the ThunderCats. These included adventure novels, booklets accompanying an audio cassette narrated episode, and a range of sticker books, colouring books and activity packs. A *ThunderCats* magazine was also released in the late 1980s featuring comic strips and a host of puzzles, information and activities.

Branded Items: At the height of the show's popularity, thousands of items emerged from a variety of companies across the globe featuring the *ThunderCats* logo. These included items as varied as erasers, Gro-ThunderCats, Mighty Fighting Tops, alarm clocks, plastic pencils, wind socks, kites, pencil sharpeners, a bow and arrow set, Eye of Thundera necklace, paint by numbers pictures, reproduction cel art, a sticker book, book light with bookmark, Burger King kids meal toys and cups, drinking glasses, toothbrushes, clothing, bed covers and curtains, posters, jigsaws, greetings cards, games, puzzles, costumes and others too numerous to mention.

Video Cassettes: In several territories including the US and the UK, a selection of *ThunderCats* episodes emerged on videocassette, usually with two episodes on one release. Notable examples include the 'Exodus' release (featuring a compiled version of the opening episodes, complete with additional scenes from the episodic versions) and the 'ThunderCats Ho!' movie, a compilation of the five-part introduction to the second season.

DVDs: During the mid 2000s, all 130 episodes of ThunderCats were released across four DVD box sets by Warner Home Video. Special features included featurettes on the making of the series and a DVD adventure game.

Statues: Beginning in 2010, collectable statues of a variety of *ThunderCats* characters were released. The initial prestige figures, in 1:7 scale, were courtesy of US company Hard Hero, who had obtained the licence from Warner Brothers. Further companies later acquiring licences included Pop Culture Shock, who engineered 1:4 scale statues, and Icon Heroes, who manufactured six-inch 'stactions' (static action figures).

A Fan Community

By the mid 1990s, the internet was really starting to take off with the general public – including *ThunderCats* fans. One of the earliest websites dedicated to the show was launched in 1995, a mere six years after the final episode had aired. This was the Ultimate *ThunderCats* Webpage (now located at www.ThunderCatsho.com), which slowly evolved into the first useful resource for the series. In addition to showcasing digital illustrations by the author, the site also featured a wealth of information, including both an episode guide and a character summary. Other early adopters of the technology included Cheezey's *ThunderCats* Zone (www.cheezey.org) and Queen Cheetah's Domain (www.queencheetah.com), which both emerged in early forms during 1997.

As the internet swept the globe, more and more fan websites began to appear. Most were relatively modest web pages, presenting viewers' personal memories of *ThunderCats*, along with images and small snippets of information. However, the beginning of the new millennium brought with it a range of ever-more-ambitious endeavours. Notable examples from this period include Angie Hill's Return to Thundera webpage (www.thunderCatsfans.org), which from humble beginnings in 2001 grew to offer the first tantalising glimpse of the behind-the-scenes production processes of the show. Futhermore, it boasted a popular message board that, alongside others, offered fans the opportunity to share memories of the series. In 2005, *ThunderCats* Lair (www.ThunderCatslair.org) was launched, and fast became one of the most comprehensive internet guides to both the series and the LJN toy line.

As well as sharing recollections and information about the series, the countless fans and enthusiasts who interacted online put their creative talents to work in creating original artwork and fan fiction, which continued the adventures of the *ThunderCats* in a variety of formats.

As the internet has grown to be an all-encompassing resource, *ThunderCats* has had its fair share of representation, having now spawned hundreds of individual websites and established a strong presence on websites such as YouTube (www.youtube.com) and Facebook (www.facebook.com).

As the original child audience that followed the series grew into adults, and parents, a generation of *ThunderCats* fans began to share it with their own children, citing a dearth of contemporary programming to match the 'magic' of the show. With future official projects continuing to unfold for the property, programme-makers undoubtedly owe a huge debt of gratitude to the countless fans who kept the spirit of *ThunderCats* alive for over two decades of inactivity, and it is a fitting testament to the series that its original audience feels such continued affection towards it.

Michigan-based Angie Hill shares her memories of how the series shaped her childhood: 'I was nearly 11 years old when *ThunderCats* made its US debut in the fall of 1985. Though the toons of *Voltron* (both lion and vehicle versions) and He-Man were other favourites of mine at the time, I was most taken with *ThunderCats*. Perhaps this was due to the fact that, a few years earlier, I had created a tribe of feral-looking cat people from a distant planet via drawings, so I enjoyed the humanoid feline bent on the heroes. That may have drawn me in, but what kept me watching were many things – the animation, the characters (I found WilyKit most relatable back then, being as she was a pre-teen character), and the fantastic adventures.

'Many people may have moved on, grown up and forgotten about a cartoon show they liked as a kid. But for me, the moment came in '97 when I caught both *Voltron* and *ThunderCats* on reruns on Cartoon Network. I was swept up in the nostalgia. But yet again, I was most taken with *ThunderCats*. The stories and the characters stuck in my head. And even though parts of it seemed corny to me now, there was enough there to keep me interested all over again as an adult. Good, imaginative storytelling is always a classic.

'Then came the internet. I got online in February of '01, and one of the first things I did was to search for sites and info about *ThunderCats*. I saw that I wasn't the only adult who still fondly remembered the show, and allowed myself to feel less ridiculous about it. I even got my son into the show for a time, and dug my old action figures out of my parents' attic for him to use. Soon it became more than a cartoon show I still liked. It was the subject of my first foray into a web presence, where I eventually learned HTML (that, being a skill that actually landed me my current job!) and inspired me to explore my creative side more. I did decide to take a more humorous approach to the subject online, inspired by Cheezey's *ThunderCats* Zone. The site grew as I also became a collector of facts and memorabilia on the old show. The involvement with the site and its growing popularity allowed me other opportunities such as being able to contact writers, voice actors and people involved with the WildStorm Comics to submit their thoughts either via e-mail interviews or live chats with other fans. A common question was if they were surprised at the interest in the show after all these years. Maybe nobody can really point to one reason why the show endures, but it clearly does. Sites that have come along since have taken up the gauntlet and vastly improved the variety and presentation of the interview concept, but it still amazes me how accessible those involved with the series have made themselves to fans. I have been involved with other toon fandoms online and have to say *ThunderCats* is special in that regard. As an adult fan, it's fantastic to learn about behind-the-scenes things, as well as meet the personalities behind the stories and the characters. I thank everyone that has indulged the fans, and I look forward to the next chapter in the *ThunderCats* story.'

Celesta Johnston-Krantz is an illustrator and *ThunderCats* fan from Arizona. Having been inspired to paint and draw characters from the series, she a created a website (www.ThunderCatsillustrated.com) to showcase her work and explore the series. '*ThunderCats* is "just a cartoon," yes and no,' insists Johnston-Krantz. 'I disagree with those who dismiss this art form as anything but good or life–lasting, because of the impact the show has in my life. I was a child of the '80s, so I watched cartoons like *Transformers*, *GI Joe* and *Masters of the Universe*. The shows were entertaining, I just didn't identify with the characters as much as I did with those in *ThunderCats*. The show had people who were a combination of humans and cats, two subjects in life that I love. *ThunderCats* was set in the far-off future, revealing to me a hope that life goes on, possibly life that started on Earth and returned here again. There were three children at the beginning of the show; I identified with all of them throughout, as was intended. However, I connected with the younger Lion-O due to his reaction to losing his world. Why? When I was kid, I lost my world every time I moved around with my family due to my father's work. I finally realised animation as an art form due to the excellent work created for the series. The music by Bernard Hoffer revealed to me how much music can go hand in hand with art and resulted in my love of scores; listening to them to set a mood as I create art. Granted, the stories of *ThunderCats* were camp at times, but the morals are still needed as reminders to be and do "good" deeds, whatever our age.'

'What made *ThunderCats* so popular was the fact that it appealed to many different kinds of people,' asserts Jesse Goliath from West Virginia. 'It had science, technology, magic and fantasy all in one. It dealt with the trials of growing up and learning right from wrong. It helped children understand how we should treat each other and have respect for ourselves and for other people, as well as for the environment. Some quotes that come to mind include, "We can always replace the

ThunderTank, we can never replace a life" from Panthro in reference to a baby seahorse trapped behind the tank. Or, the immortal words of Jaga in response to Lion-O's misuse of the Sword to go hunting, "Fun? Your food supplies are plentiful at present and those gentle creatures have as much right to the life force as you do. The Sword will only come to life to combat evil." It helped to develop the moral fibre of a generation, unlike many other shows at the time that were glorified, extended commercials. Even now, I talk to people about *ThunderCats* and always hear great things about what the show meant to them. Despite it being a cartoon, it served as a guide, a moral compass for many children of the '80s.'

Fans of *ThunderCats* are abundant not only in the US but also in Europe and across the world. 'When you are a young kid, the capability to evaluate extensively and delve into the source of your enthusiasm (while maintaining a critical eye) is reasonably limited,' notes Orestis Makrydimitris from Athens, Greece. 'You simply like what you see without giving too much thought about it. I experienced an intense feeling during the summer of 1989 when I watched *ThunderCats* on TV for the first time. The show was broadcast in the absence of Greek dubbing, late in the afternoon, and despite it being difficult for a five-year-old boy to understand the foreign language, the unique magic of this new series had me totally captivated. Growing up, I realised there were more fundamental reasons than merely the nostalgia for a beloved childhood memory that urged me to watch the cartoon once again, but from a mature and analytical standpoint this time. The significant and distinctive elements constituting the *ThunderCats* world can be individually assessed, and even to this day, given the abundance of animation developments and diverse styles, can be reckoned as top-quality works of art, standing proudly next to the modern cartoon productions.

'Much like the Golden Age of comic books when the archetypal heroes were created and comics arrived as a mainstream art form enjoying an unexpected surge of popularity, *ThunderCats* signified the beginning of an era, ushering in an alternative format of storytelling known as cartoon animation, presenting the rare fusion of an American concept with Japanese anime. Moreover, even though *ThunderCats* was initially considered as a kid-orientated series, its overall standards were actually so good that it transcended that idea and became a critically-acclaimed pop culture phenomenon, where fans of a wide age range praised its sophisticated tone and masterfully-developed characteristics. Unlike other '80s cartoons, which admittedly have gone through a revival process every now and then, *ThunderCats* has managed to stay alive during a period of 25 years, relying entirely on its original 130 episodes and, to some degree, the classic (and much sought-after) LJN toy line. Perhaps it was the unparalleled visual designs, the clever, absorbing storylines, maybe the intriguing characters, or just the dynamic introduction sequence accompanied by an epic theme song that made the show a success? I really can't explain the grounds of success ... But I do know for sure that *ThunderCats* was ahead of its time, introducing groundbreaking features and, furthermore, inspiring (positively) a whole generation. Like any great artistic achievement, it proved that quality alone *is* enough to ensure longevity, even when devoid of a plenitude of merchandise-related products to keep the franchise in existence.'

'This is how important and real *ThunderCats* was for me as a kid,' exclaims Cliff Laureys from Hoeilaart, Belgium. 'I remember vividly that, before there was any *ThunderCats* merchandise available out here, I ran around the neighbourhood wearing one of my mom's yellow mittens with a blunt potato knife stuffed inside, imitating Lion-O. Until she caught me, that is. Years later, when I finally got my Sword of Omens toy, I remember running in an open cornfield at night in the pouring rain, desperately hoping that its "sight beyond sight" would show me where my missing Husky had gone. Also, when I was a little boy, I didn't pray just to God. Every night, I prayed to God and Jaga. That's how much impact the show had on me. You can't forget stuff like that, not even more than 20 years later. They sure don't make shows like that anymore.'

Jonathan Prideaux from Toronto, Canada agrees that the series stands out amongst its contemporaries: 'I can't point my finger at any one thing I enjoyed. I liked the wide range of characters, and found that I liked watching the supporting cast just as much as the main cast, both hero and villain. The stories were often beautifully crafted, and filled with top-notch animation and music. It wasn't always positives. I'm sure everyone has their character or story that they dislike, but I often found that for every "Snarfer" or "Cracker's Revenge" there was a "Chilla" or "Psych Out" waiting around the corner. And that's the beauty of a series like this: it's got something for almost everyone, so if you don't like what you're seeing, you just have to wait for the next episode. Through my life, I've explored other fandoms, but in the end I keep being drawn back to *ThunderCats*.'

Though they may adore the series, the legion of *ThunderCats* followers are not blind to its occasional faults. 'The critics are right: the very concept of *ThunderCats* was ridiculous,' declares Nick Mills from Glasgow, Scotland. 'But who cares?' Half the things we like in society are a bit far-fetched – *RoboCop*, *Star Wars*, even the idea of a cartoon mouse downright torturing a grown cat in *Tom & Jerry*. But it was ours – every child that grew up watching it remembers it fondly. I remember every morning putting in a VHS tape of *ThunderCats*, Lion-O statue in hand, and watching nearly every episode that was available at the time. I actually didn't speak properly until six years old, when I decided to scream Mumm-Ra's transformation out, to the fright of my parents. *ThunderCats* stayed with me even until my adult life when I decided to go to college and study media. Now, I'm a member of the ThunderCatslair.org website and have interviewed many cast members, writers and even the man that created the music. I was always curious about how the show was created and what kind of legacy it had – and it definitely shows. Even today, the show commands a large amount of respect from all young adults, and you'll definitely see someone wearing a *ThunderCats* T-shirt from time to time! It's amazing how a show with so much corny dialogue and so many ridiculous plotlines is so loved – but then look at *Masters of the Universe* and you'll see what I mean.'

Another member of the popular ThunderCatslair.org web team is Neil Sheldon from Nottinghamshire, England. He still recalls the occasion he first saw *ThunderCats*: 'It was a weekday, but it must have been a Bank Holiday or close to one as my dad was on holiday from work, and it was he who noticed it in the TV guide. This would be my earliest memory of being exposed to *ThunderCats*. It wasn't until years later, when researching on the internet, that I confirmed that it was indeed just after Christmas 1986, as the show debuted on Friday 2 January 1987 in the UK. At the time, my brother and I were mad on the worlds of He-Man and She-Ra, and I remember feeling worried that this was put on TV to replace

Masters Of The Universe (even though they aired on different channels)! However, the more I watched *ThunderCats*, the more I got into the show. Episodes that sealed my love were 'Snarf Takes Up The Challenge', which showed the audience not to give up before you try, and my favourite, 'The Shifter' (for the sheer hilarity of it!).

'My first exposure to the LJN toys (distributed in the UK by Rainbow Toys) was on holiday in Blackpool during the summer of 1988. My brother and I got a Lion-O each, which we played with so much that I had to buy a second Lion-O a few years later after the first broke! We loved the "battle-matic" action and light-up features of the toy, which offered something that the *Masters of the Universe* toys lacked. I have fond memories of visits into town and going into the Woolworths shop and looking at the figures. If I was lucky enough to have saved enough pocket money, I could buy one. I had most of the main characters, but never owned them all. Years later, in early 2001, I rediscovered my love for *ThunderCats*, looking it up online. Since then I've amassed a near complete loose action figure collection, as well as an extensive carded/mint-in-package collection!'

'For some fans, *ThunderCats* is about fun, escapism and entertainment,' suggests Sussex, England resident Chris Davis from ThunderCatslair.org. He believes the series played a crucial role in his personal development. 'It's all of those things to me, too. But, for me, it means more than just those things. When I was a kid growing up, it actually helped to shape the person I became. Watching Lion-O grow from a boy in a man's body into an adult, I learned the same lessons he learned – idolising those characters. I wanted to be just like them, and that included their sense of morality, decency, fairness and compassion. My aspiration to live up to the same ideals that the ThunderCats lived up to is something that shaped me into the person I am today. Over the last few years, I've been glad to share my passion for *ThunderCats* with the online community, and proud of what, as a fantastic team, we've all been able to achieve. But more than that, I'm proud of the values and beliefs that *ThunderCats* instilled into me – proof that the Code of Thundera lives on within a whole generation of 1980s kids!'

Another member of the ThunderCatslair.org team is Kyle Lambert from Manchester, England. '*ThunderCats* was the first cartoon that completely captured my imagination as a child,' he says. 'It was both conceptually and visually exciting, with imaginative and engaging storylines, characters and environments. The series was accompanied by a brilliant range of merchandise, including the multitude of accurate action figures produced by LJN, many of which I still own to this day. Looking back at the series now, it can be difficult to look past the "cheese factor". But for me, the concept is still as strong as it was in the '80s, and the animation, which was cutting-edge back then, is still beautiful to watch. With Warner Brothers taking ownership of the franchise, I can see a big future for Lion-O and *ThunderCats*.'

'ThunderCats seem like they've been part of my life from the beginning,' says Tim Shrimpton from South Dakota, USA, who believes that the series is intrinsically connected with his memories of childhood. 'One of my earliest memories is being about three years old and watching TV with my Dad downstairs. I remember first seeing the flashy introduction to the show and wondering what ThunderCats were. I was hooked from then on. *ThunderCats* has tied in a lot with my family life beyond that as well. From my Dad calling warehouses before Christmas to see if anyone had a Panthro figure anywhere, to my grandparents buying me the amazingly awesome light-up Sword of Omens. I even remember imagining that the tree stump in their front yard was a high mountain top from which to shine the iconic cat symbol! There are just a lot of good memories tied in with the show in my mind, beyond just sitting down in front of the TV on a given afternoon. As a parent myself now, re-watching the episodes on their DVD releases, I find some of the material is cringe-inducingly corny (yet perhaps that's one of the reasons we love it so much!), but the moral fibre runs deep in the show's messages as well. The Code of Thundera is something we don't often see in today's selfish, "me-first", rude TV climate, especially in a show geared for children. Having these classic cartoons archived for my son to share when he's older is an exciting prospect. I hope he can end up with the fond, family-based memories I've cherished for many years of being gathered around Lion-O and the gang.'

Though fans' interest in *ThunderCats* is often restricted to the stories themselves, others admire the series for its technical prowess. ThunderCatslair.org member Mark Sheard from Ontario, Canada marvels at the standard of animation on display, and has a large collection of production cels. 'What is the allure of animation art?' he ponders. 'Why does the very sight of it seem to spark an uncontrollable urge for some people to own and caress cels, to stare at pencil sketches and admire the minor details that went into the creation of a single frame of cartoon history? Why is it that I, and people like me, are so fascinated with the production process that created our favourite cartoons? And what possesses us to fork over large sums of money to buy cels from TV shows from the '80s? It's partly a hobby, but more of an obsession, really. Something about seeing, first hand, the original pieces of art that were made over 20 years ago that led to me lying in the classic kid-watching-TV pose – on my living room carpet, belly down, head first, facing the TV. I was about four feet away from the screen, head resting between my hands and supported by my elbows, which were placed directly in front of me with a pillow between them. My legs were bent and my feet swayed slowly from side to side as Lion-O leapt away from Mumm-Ra's energy beam, and Cheetara raced across the screen, legs blurring faster than the Road Runner. I loved *ThunderCats* then, and I love *ThunderCats* now. I loved watching the show then, but I *love* owning pieces of the show now. I love holding a frame of *ThunderCats* history in my hands and knowing that I have a one-of-a-kind, rare, hand-drawn, hand-painted piece of the show. This, to me, is better than owning a rare toy or a hard-to-find comic. As a fan of cartoons and of comic books, I love owning original artworks, and it's even more special that I can own art from my favourite childhood shows.

'Not many people know very much about how cartoons are put together. The more you learn, the more you can appreciate the hard work and creativity that goes into it. This amazing art has been available since the first cartoon movies and shows were made – Disney and other studios have been selling artwork since the 1930s – but it hasn't really become a mainstream collecting habit for the public until recently. What is ironic about that is now that it's a popular hobby, the new shows that are mostly digital won't be creating any "real" animation art for fans to collect. The hand-drawn process has been replaced with digital software that creates cartoon shows, meaning that cels are no longer used as part of the process. This makes owning cels an expensive proposition, and means that only older shows will have produced any art worthy of collecting. What's great about *ThunderCats* cels is that they are always far more impressive to see in person than on the TV screen. In comparing screencaps with cel scans, you'll soon see that much of the detail is lost in the translation from cel to cartoon frame. The colours in the cels are more vibrant, the detail is greater and there is more to see on the cel than finally made it to the screen. Often a background was created before the cel, and you don't even get to see whole sections of the background in the show because the cel covers the details. When you own the set-up yourself, and you can peel back the cel, amazing things often become visible to you. To truly appreciate the cartoon magic of *ThunderCats* is to truly love the beautiful frames of art that made the animation jump into life. That's what the cels are to me.'

Whether they have crafted websites or simply acknowledge the series as having instilled action, adventure and morality into their childhoods, the fans of *ThunderCats* will always cherish the series. While some may have huge collections of pristine and boxed toys from the 1980s, others may have only their original Lion-O figures, perhaps chewed, broken or incomplete. The *ThunderCats* fanbase speaks volumes about the success of the programme-makers' efforts to develop a truly refreshing series, and everyone at Rankin/Bass can be assured of the heritage of their work. To the children who watched the series, *ThunderCats* will never be forgotten. Through fans sharing the adventures of Third Earth with their own children, the original series continues to live on and be enjoyed by the next generation, for whom it remains as relevant and imaginative as, and ultimately more satisfying than, its contemporary rivals.

The Return Of The ThunderCats

On 2 June 2010, Warner Brothers issued a press release announcing the return of *ThunderCats* after an absence of more than 20 years. The 2011 series will mark a collaboration between the property owners Warner Brothers and the Japanese animation group Studio4°C, who have worked on such projects as *The Animatrix*, *Transformers Animated* and *Batman: Gotham Knight*. Production will thus mirror that on the original series, with writing and design taking place in America and animation being carried out in Japan.

An extract from Warners' press release reveals the intention to placate the series' original fans as well as return the property to a mainstream audience:

The new *ThunderCats* will appeal to viewers who have loved the characters all their lives as well as young newcomers to the franchise. A sweeping tale combining swords and science and boasting ferocious battles with the highest of stakes, the grand origin story of Prince Lion-O's ascension to the throne – and of those who would thwart his destiny at any cost – takes on epic dimensions in this sharp new telling. As the forces of good and evil battle each other in the quest for the fabled Stones of Power, Lion-O and his champions learn valuable lessons of loyalty, honour and morality in every episode. *ThunderCats* is executive produced by Sam Register (*Teen Titans, Ben 10, Batman: The Brave and the Bold*). Michael Jelenic (*Batman: The Brave and the Bold, Wonder Woman*) and Ethan Spaulding (*Avatar: The Last Airbender*) are the producers.

The announcement of the new series marked the end of an intense period of speculation that had surrounded the property throughout the 2000s. Following the successful movie revival of the *Transformers* franchise in 2007, many assumed *ThunderCats* would be in line to follow suit. Indeed, rumblings of future productions had included several mooted movie adaptations (including both live action and animated projects), perhaps the most substantial of these being one that was planned to be produced by Warner Brothers. Both a script and test sequences were reportedly commissioned, yet the project fell into development limbo prior to being, seemingly, replaced by the new series.

With a new team at the helm, a new chapter in the *ThunderCats* story is set to begin. With new writers, artists and musicians bringing their ideas to the table, the revived series will be in many ways a new entity, separate from the original, but nevertheless representing the next progression of the property. While, to many, it will never be able to replicate the sheer imagination and timelessness of the classic series, *ThunderCats* once again has the opportunity to affect a generation of children. Regardless of its success or failure, the legacy of *ThunderCats* is secured, and the timeless nature of the series continues to resonate within its audience with its spirit of adventure, morality and the Code of Thundera: *Justice, truth, honour and loyalty.*

APPENDIX A
THUNDERCATS 2011

Background

Since the original publication of this book, a reboot of *ThunderCats* was developed by Warner Bros which began with an hour-long premiere on Cartoon Network on July 29, 2011. Seeking to replicate the formula of the original, the series was animated in America by Warner Bros. Animation, and Japan by Studio 4°C and combined elements of western animation with Japanese anime.

Initially planned for 52 episodes, it was confirmed by *ThunderCats* art-director Dan Norton in early 2013 that the show had been canceled after only one season of 26x 20 minute episodes.

While well intentioned, and lovingly put-together, the series failed to replicate the success of its predecessor, despite establishing a fan base, gaining positive reviews, and the widespread consensus that it probably deserved a second season, if only to allow it to conclude the series properly.

The series is notable for facilitating the return of Larry Kenney (the voice of Lion-O in the classic series), as Lion-o's father, Claudus. This lends a much-needed note of familiarity and nostalgia to the opening episodes. The series sticks fairly close to the characters and overall story themes from the original throughout while still trying to establish itself in its own right. Another link with the original series is through writer and Script Editor Peter Lawrence, who wrote the episode, Forest of Magi Oar, though was reportedly unhappy with the subsequent changes made to his original script.

Despite the production team's best efforts to establish itself as something new, and 'darker' than the original, comparisons are inevitable. And where the 2011 series fares particularly unfavourably is perhaps in character design and music. Design, because each of the characters are altogether less distinctive and captivating than their originals. Where the 1980's character designs were colourful and vibrant – unlike anything seen before or since, and (much like The Simpsons) were instantly recognisable, the new characters are fairly generic, less feline and too similar to countless other cartoons. Finally, the music isn't a patch on Bernard Hoffer's iconic original score which is a missed opportunity, and one that the series' successor would seek to correct…

Episodes

1 Omens: Episode 1
Written by Michael Jelenic & Ethan Spaulding
Directed by Yoshiharu Ashino & Sean Song
Airdate: 29 July 2011
US Viewers: 2.414

Official Synopsis
An epic, all-new reimagining of the classic and beloved 1980s animated series,
ThunderCats tells the story of a hero's journey to fulfill his ultimate destiny. On Third
Earth, the kingdom of Thundera is being threatened by the evil sorcerer Mumm-Ra,
and Lion-O, the young heir to the throne, embarks on a great quest to take his
rightful place as king. The unlikely champion must work with his faithful comrades
Tygra, Cheetara, Panthro, WilyKit, WilyKat and his loyal pet, Snarf, who join him on
his journey to save their world from darkness.

2 Omens: Episode 2
Written by Tab Murphy
Directed by Yasuhiro Geshi & Rokou Ogiharu
Airdate: 29 July 2011
US Viewers: 2.414

Official Synopsis
An epic, all-new reimagining of the classic and beloved 1980s animated series,
ThunderCats tells the story of a hero's journey to fulfill his ultimate destiny. On Third
Earth, the kingdom of Thundera is being threatened by the evil sorcerer Mumm-Ra,
and Lion-O, the young heir to the throne, embarks on a great quest to take his
rightful place as king. The unlikely champion must work with his faithful comrades
Tygra, Cheetara, Panthro, WilyKit, WilyKat and his loyal pet, Snarf, who join him on
his journey to save their world from darkness.

3 Ramlak Rising
Written by Todd Casey
Directed by Yoshiharu Ashino & Sean Song
Airdate: 5 August 2011
US Viewers: 1.483

Official Synopsis
After escaping their destroyed city with the Sword of Omens, the team encounters
the Fishmen, who sail the quicksand sea in search of a massive sea creature. The
ThunderCats' quest is to find the Book of Omens but Lion-O is more interested in
revenge on Mumm-Ra.

4 Song of the Petalars
Written by J. M. DeMatteis
Directed by Yasuhiro Geshi & Sean Song
Airdate: 12 August 2011
US Viewers: 1.845

Official Synopsis
On the run from the unstoppable lizard army, Lion-O fears for his life. While hiding,
he encounters a race of creatures who live out their entire lifetime in 24 hours, and
learns a valuable lesson about hope. Plus, Panthro and Thundertank are introduced.

5 Old Friends
Written by Tab Murphy
Directed by Yoshiharu Ashino & Sean Song
Airdate: 19 August 2011
US Viewers: 1.753

Official Synopsis
Panthro finally joins the team, but his gruff demeanor intimidates Lion-O. Despite his best efforts, Panthro can't dissuade the Cats from following him on a mission to get Thundrillium to fuel the Thundertank. Plus, a mission leads Panthro to his old nemesis: Grune!

6 Journey to the Tower of Omens
Written by Tab Murphy
Directed by Kazuo Nogami & Sean Song
Airdate: 26 August 2011
US Viewers: 1.617

Official Synopsis
The Cats must pass a series of obstacles in order to finally get the Book of Omens, but Mumm-Ra is hot on their trail. Lion-O must stop him from getting the book first, for the book will lead whoever finds it to the Stones of Power.

7 Legacy
Written by Todd Casey
Directed by Kazuyoshi Takeuchi & Sean Song
Airdate: 2 September 2011
US Viewers: 1.650

Official Synopsis
Lion-O ventures into the Book of Omens where he becomes the incarnation of his renowned ancestor, the valiant Leo, who led the rebellion against Mumm-Ra in a previous millennium. In this landmark episode, we learn the origin of the Stones of Power and the Cats' relationship to Mumm-Ra and the other animals.

8 The Duelist and the Drifter
Written by Tab Murphy
Directed by Shingo Uchida & Sean Song
Airdate: 9 September 2011
US Viewers: 1.615

Official Synopsis
While traveling through a village built on swordsmanship, Lion-O's cockiness loses him the Sword of Omens to the Duelist, a villainous sword-collector. With the help of the listless Drifter, Lion-O must get it back.

9 Berbils
Written by Tab Murphy
Directed by Yasuhiro Geshi & Takahiro Tanaka
Airdate: 28 October 2011
US Viewers: 1.576

Official Synopsis
Tiny robot bears solicit the help of the ThunderCats to save them from a slave trader who values their technical and construction skills. The Cats help to rescue enslaved Berbils and defend their village. Panthro learns that's he's not the only "wrench monkey" and bonds with Robear Bill.

10 Sight Beyond Sight
Written by Todd Casey
Directed by Yoshiharu Ashino
Airdate 4 November 2011
US Viewers: 1.675

Official Synopsis
The Cats track the location of the first stone to the mystical Elephant Village, but Lion-O can't find the specific location and the forgetful Elephants no longer remember where it is. Lion-O must learn to use Sight Beyond Sight and interpret the consequences of his actions when he inadvertently invites an attack on the village.

11 The Forest of Magi Oar
Written by Peter Lawrence
Directed by Tomoya Takahashi
Airdate: 11 November 2011
US Viewers: 1.432

Official Synopsis
Sent by the Elephants to the Forest of Magi Oar, Lion-O must learn to master Sight Beyond Sight before returning to the Elephant Village. The Cats encounter a group of paper warriors with a dark secret.

12 Into the Astral Plane
Written by Paul Giacoppo
Directed by Yoshiharu Ashino
Airdate: 18 November 2011
US Viewers: 1.334

Official Synopsis
The Cats are ready to retrieve the stone from the "Astral Plane" in the Elephant Village, but find it overtaken by Grunea and Mumm-Ra's forces. Plus, Tygra and Cheetara's early relationship to one another is revealed.

13 Between Brothers
Written by Paul Giacoppo
Directed by Shingo Uchida
Airdate: 25 November 2011
US Viewers: 1.433

Official Synopsis
Tygra and Lion-O enter the Astral Plane to retrieve the stone, but encounter Mumm-Ra in the process. Grune and Panthro have their final duel. Cheetara finally chooses her beau.

14 New Alliances
Written by J. M. DeMatteis
Directed by Yoshiharu Ashino
Airdate: 24 March 2012
US Viewers: N/A

Official Synopsis
The ThunderCats go on the offensive taking down Mumm-Ra's lizard army piece by piece. Lion-O appeals to the soldiers to turn against their overlord, but Mumm-Ra won't see his army crushed so easily. He tasks Slithe with recruiting two new and vicious Generals — Addicus and Kaynar — to retaliate against the Cats. Meanwhile, the Robear Berbils make Panthro a new set of robotic arms and trick out the Thundertank.

15 Trials of Lion-O: Episode 1
Written by Todd Casey
Directed by Yoshiharu Ashino
Airdate: 31 March 2012
US Viewers: N/A

Official Synopsis
Mumm-Ra's generals stage an ambush and, while the other Cats are captured, Lion-O falls to his death. Thanks to the Spirit Stone, he encounters Jaga in the Astral Plane and is given a second chance at life. If he is able to pass a series of trials that pit him against each of his teammates, he can win back his life and save the other Cats. First up are Kit and Kat, followed by Cheetara. But the clock is ticking because Mumm-Ra has the Sword of Omens!

16 Trials of Lion-O: Episode 2
Written by Will Friedle
Directed by Yutaka Kagawa
Airdate: 7 April 2012
US Viewers: N/A

Official Synopsis
The other cats remain trapped in Mumm-Ra's Pyramid and, believing Lion-O is dead, attempt to escape to prevent Mumm-Ra from getting the Eye of Thundera out

of the sword. Lion-O has two trials left: Panthro and Tygra, but he fails to defeat the latter. Pleading for a chance to save his friends, Jaga grants him life until sunrise to try and save his friends ... and stop Mumm-Ra.

17 Native Son
Written by Tab Murphy
Directed by Mitsuo Kusakabe
Airdate: 14 April 2012
US Viewers: N/A

Official Synopsis
While traveling through snowy mountains in search of safe passage, Tygra and Lion-O come upon a lost tiger village and in it they find Tygra's real father. Tygra learns why his father sent him away as a baby — to save his life. But all is not as it seems in this village as the brothers learn these tigers are cursed and Tygra may be the answer to saving them — but at the cost of his own life.

18 Survival of the Fittest
Written by J. M. DeMatteis
Directed by Riki Matsuura
Airdate: 21 April 2012
US Viewers: N/A

Official Synopsis
While Tygra and Lion-O search for a mountain pass, Panthro, Cheetara, WilyKit and WilyKat stay in the woods. Panthro and Cheetara decide it's time for the kids to learn some hunting skills. In the process, Kit and Kat flash back to reveal how they began to live on their own and separate from their family, and it turns out these two cubs have sacrificed more than the ThunderCats could imagine.

19 The Pit
Written by Todd Garfield
Directed by Mitsuo Kusakabe
Airdate: 28 April 2012
US Viewers: N/A

Official Synopsis
Lion-O and company come upon a Dog City where they unexpectedly find a cat: Pumyra. This comes as a surprise since they believed all the cats were enslaved by Mumm-Ra, but an even greater surprise is that this cat has no love for Lion-O and, in the end, he's forced to face the cat down in a death match — and she's not pulling any punches. Meanwhile, Panthro runs into an old friend turned enemy, Dobo.

20 Curse of Ratilla
Written by Todd Casey
Directed by Tomoya Takahashi
Airdate: 5 May 2012
US Viewers: 1.551

Official Synopsis
The ThunderCats must infiltrate the mines of Mount Plundarr where Ratar-O is holding Cats as slaves. There they learn the legend of the Sword of Plundarr, which they must now retrieve while also freeing their people.

21 Birth of the Blades
Written by Will Friedle
Directed by Masayuki Kato
Airdate: 12 May 2012
US Viewers: N/A

Official Synopsis
As Lion-O and Pumyra try to evade Mumm-Ra and his forces in the mines of Mount Plundarr in an effort to keep the Sword of Plundarr out his hands, we flash back in time and discover its origin ... and its relationship with the Sword of Omens.

22 The Forever Bag
Written by Tab Murphy
Directed by Yoshiharu Ashino
Airdate: 19 May 2012
US Viewers: 1.755

Official Synopsis
Kit and Kat follow Tookit into his magical Forever Bag - a seemingly normal bag that is infinitely big on the inside - where they meet a group of orphans. Seduced by the their fun loving lifestyle of Tookit and the orphans, Kit and Kat are tricked by Tookit into becoming thieves again. Now they must turn the tables on the charming rogue Tookit or end up in jail.

23 Recipe for Disaster
Written by Tab Murphy
Directed by Riki Matsuura
Airdate: 26 May 2012
US Viewers: N/A

Official Synopsis
When Mumm-Ra unleashes the deadly Sycorax upon them, the ThunderCats must turn to an unlikely savior — a snake oil salesman named Ponzi whose potion is the only thing that repels the beast. Ponzi also provides Lion-O some helpful romantic advice as he begins to pursue Pumyra.

24 The Soul Sever
Written by Brandon Easton
Directed by Kenichi Maejima
Airdate: 2 June 2012
US Viewers: 1.428

Official Synopsis
While trying to uncover the location of the next stone, the ThunderCats cross paths
with a mad man, Soul Sever, who is trying to insert the souls of his long-lost family
into machines. When Soul Sever steals the Book of Omens in pursuit of this goal,
Lion-O risks being turned into one of his mechanical monstrosities.

25 What Lies Above: Episode 1
Written by Paul Giacoppo
Directed by Shin'ichi Matsumi
Airdate: 9 June 2012
US Viewers: 1.596

Official Synopsis
The ThunderCats' search for the next stone leads them high above Thundera to the
floating bird city of Avista. The Birds possess the Tech Stone but have no intention of
handing it over to the Cats as it's the power source for their city. The stakes are high
when Tygra challenges the birds' leader, Vultar, to an aerial battle where the winner
gets the stone.

26 What Lies Above: Episode 2
Written by Paul Giacoppo
Directed by Shin'ichi Matsumi
Airdate: 16 June 2012
US Viewers: 1.523

Official Synopsis
In the season finale, Mumm-Ra's forces find the ThunderCats and the Tech Stone in
Avista City. There's an incredible battle for the stone as Lion-O is betrayed by a
trusted ally.

APPENDIX B
THUNDERCATS ROAR

Background

On May 18, 2018, it was announced that a third *ThunderCats* cartoon, *ThunderCats Roar*, was in development and was picked up by Cartoon Network. It was originally scheduled to premiere in 2019 but was delayed to 2020. The first two episodes were released on the Cartoon Network app on January 10, 2020. *ThunderCats Roar* premiered on Cartoon Network UK on April 6, 2020. *ThunderCats Roar* later premiered on Cartoon Network Africa on May 25, 2020.

    ThunderCats Roar is undoubtedly the most divisive project to emerge from the *ThunderCats* brand. It's a series that was deliberately designed to be childlike and 'goofy', and is happy to parody the original and gently poke fun at its fans. Some enjoy it for what it is and encourage people not to take it too seriously, others thoroughly despise it, and find it an insult to the original. Whatever your thoughts, it's notable for once again welcoming Larry Kenney back to the series, this time to provide the voice of Jaga. The show also features the welcome return of Bernard Hoffer's original *ThunderCats* score, and reuses a number of original music cues throughout the series. This tricks the ear, if not the eye into occasionally thinking you may be watching a programme that's at least distantly related to the original.

    An honoruble (or dishonourable) mention goes to another Cartoon Network series, *Teen Titans Go!*, from which *ThunderCats Roar* clearly draws its inspiration. In the season 5 episode, Teen Titans Roar!, the *ThunderCats Roar!* characters also feature, and – somewhat inexplicably – meet the 1980's version of Lion-O, voiced by Larry Kenney. There's even a cameo from the original Snarf!

    Love it or loathe it, *ThunderCats Roar* continues to show the brand is here to stay. There is, as you might say, life in the old Cat yet.

Episodes

1 Exodus Part 1
2 Exodus Part 2
Story by Joan Ford
Teleplay by Victor Courtright
Directed by George Kaprielian
Airdate: February 22, 2020
US Viewers: 0.37

Official Synopsis
Fleeing the destruction of their home planet Thundera, Lion-O and the ThunderCats land on the mysterious, dangerous, all-around awesome world of

APPENDIX B: THUNDERCATS ROAR

Third Earth! But their enemies, the Mutants of Plun-Darr have followed them and it turns out Third Earth already has a Mumm-Ra problem – can Lion-O learn the ropes of being a leader in time?

3 The Legend of Boggy Ben
Written by Victor Courtright
Directed by Victor Courtright
Airdate: February 29, 2020
US Viewers: 0.42

Official Synopsis
Lion-O has gotten ahold of the last jar of Thundersnaps – the best cookies Thundera had to offer! But a difficult to open cookie jar sends Lion-O and Cheetara chasing down the legend of Boggy Ben.

4 Prank Call
Story by Victor Courtright
Teleplay by: Marly Halpern-Graser
Directed by Jeremy Polgar
Airdate: February 29, 2020
US Viewers: 0.36

Official Synopsis
Trying to prove to the Thunderkittens that he's not just some boring old adult (like Tygra), Lion-O ignores his instincts and messes with an obviously evil crystal.

5 Driller
Story by Joan Ford
Teleplay by Bryan Condon
Directed by George Kaprielian
Airdate: March 7, 2020
US Viewers: 0.33

Official Synopsis
Panthro is getting a little fed up with having to fix things around the Cats' Lair constantly, which is unfortunate because the ThunderCats are about to be attacked by an unstoppable drilling robot – and he's going to break everything!

6 Secret of the Unicorn
Story by Joan Ford
Teleplay by Ben Crouse
Directed by Angelo Hatgistavrou
Airdate: March 7, 2020
US Viewers: 0.32

Official Synopsis
A crying unicorn appears at the Cats' Lair and weepily tells the ThunderCats that all of her unicorn friends have been captured! Tygra thinks he's just the unicorn

expert to help the last of the unicorns – He just needs her to stop sobbing long enough to tell him who took her friends. Easier said than done, pal.

7 Panthro Plagiarized!
Story by Joan Ford
Teleplay by Lesley Tsina
Directed by Jeremy Polgar
Airdate: March 14, 2020
US Viewers: 0.42

Official Synopsis
Vultureman has got a brand-new invention, but there's one big problem: he stole the idea from Panthro! Oh, also Vultureman is using his invention to take over Third Earth. So, there are actually two big problems.

8 Warrior Maiden Invasion
Story by Joan Ford
Teleplay by Molly Knox Ostertag
Directed by Angelo Hatgistavrou
Airdate: March 14, 2020
US Viewers: 0.41

Official Synopsis
Third Earth is being overrun by super-tough, super-buff Warrior Maidens, and it looks like the ThunderCats are next on their hit list! Now, it's going to be up to the ThunderKittens to save the day even though the kittens are so small and the Warrior Maidens are so big.

9 Lost Sword
Written by Victor Courtright
Directed by George Kaprielian
Airdate: March 21, 2020
US Viewers: 0.27

Official Synopsis
Lion-O is reminded that he needs to plug the Sword of Omens into the Cats' Lair each night or else the base will run out of power. That's fine; it's not as if Lion-O's going to accidentally lose the sword or anything. Right?

10 The Horror of Hook Mountain
Story by Joan Ford
Teleplay by Eric Knobel
Directed by Jeremy Polgar
Airdate: March 21, 2020
US Viewers: 0.28

Official Synopsis
Tygra takes Lion-O climbing up the peak of Hook Mountain to teach him a lesson

about trust. But when they get trapped by a snowstorm and take refuge in a creepy cabin, owned by the creepy Snowman, it's Tygra's ability to the trust that's going to be tested.

11 ThunderSlobs
Story by Joan Ford
Teleplay by Ben Joseph
Directed by Jessica Borutski & Angelo Hatgistavrou
Airdate: March 28, 2020
US Viewers: 0.26

Official Synopsis
Feeling underappreciated by the other ThunderCats, Tygra starts hanging out with Mumm-Ra and cleaning his black pyramid. Whaaaat?

12 Working Grrrl
Written by Joan Ford
Directed by George Kaprielian
Airdate: March 28, 2020
US Viewers: 0.26

Official Synopsis
Cheetara is the fastest living being in the universe, until Monkian beats her in a race! Now Cheetara has to find something else to be the best at, while the rest of the ThunderCats find out how Monkian got so darn fast!

13 Mandora - The Evil Chaser
Story by Joan Ford
Teleplay by Cait Raft
Directed by Jeremy Polgar
Airdate: April 4, 2020
US Viewers: 0.38

Official Synopsis
Lion-O accidentally releases a whole space prison-full of space criminals and winds up on the wrong side of the law. On the right side of the law is Mandora the Evil Chaser, a no-nonsense space cop! Lion-O's going to have to work very hard to prove he's not a criminal, just a little bit of an oaf!

14 Dr. Dometome
Story by Joan Ford
Teleplay by Justin Becker
Directed by Jessica Borutski
Airdate: April 4, 2020
US Viewers: 0.37

Official Synopsis
Lion-O is tasked with mapping the beaches of Third Earth, which leads to him

somehow draining the oceans of all water entirely. But a mysterious scientist with a robotic frog says they can fix everything by traveling under the earth – which is just the type of crazy adventure Lion-O is all about!

15 Study Time
Story by Joan Ford
Teleplay by Bryan Condon
Directed by George Kaprielian
Airdate: April 11, 2020
US Viewers: 0.44

Official Synopsis
Lion-O never pays attention during Tygra's training sessions so when he's asked to do a pop quiz on 'sword magic' he accidentally opens a portal to the Astral Plane and releases the Nether Witch! When the Witch imprisons Lion-O and Tygra in her nightmare realm, it's going to take a lot of studying to figure out a way home. Wonder if the Astral Plane has any great teachers lying around?

16 Mumm-Ra, the Ever-Living
Story by Joan Ford
Teleplay by Lesley Tsina
Directed by Jeremy Polgar
Airdate: April 11, 2020
US Viewers: 0.41

Official Synopsis
Every time Mumm-Ra gets hold of a magic artifact to restore his powers, the ThunderCats just smash it, turning him into a dinky skeleton again. Until today that is, because Mumm-Ra just remembered he's got the Ancient Spirits of Evil – and now he can get whole whenever he wants.

17 Berserkers
Story by Joan Ford
Teleplay by Molly Knox Ostertag
Directed by N/A
Airdate: April 18, 2020
US Viewers: 0.32

Official Synopsis
The Cats' Lair is attacked by gold-loving robot pirates – the Berserkers! This is a good thing, really, since it means Lion-O and the ThunderKittens can ditch their chores and fight robo-pirates instead! Just don't tell Tygra!

18 Jaga History
Story by Joan Ford
Teleplay by Ben Crouse
Directed by George Kaprielian
Airdate: April 18, 2020

US Viewers: 0.38

Official Synopsis
Freed from the Astral Plane, Jaga – ghost of the ThunderCats mentor – is now free to visit the Cats' Lair. Which means he can finally tell them why Thundera, their home world, exploded. It's story time!

19 Barbastella
Written by Joan Ford
Directed by Jeremy Polgar
Airdate: April 25, 2020
US Viewers: 0.30

Official Synopsis
While flying with his new invention, Panthro hits it off with a new friend – Barbastella, the Queen of the Bats! Now Panthro needs help getting ready for his big date with her – because it turns out Panthro is terrified of bats! Lion-O and Cheetara are happy to help but… wow, that is a lot to unpack!

20 Adopt a Jackal
Story by Joan Ford
Teleplay by Bryan Condon
Directed by Keith Pakiz
Airdate: April 25, 2020
US Viewers: 0.28

Official Synopsis
After a battle with the Mutants, Jackalman gets confused and accidentally returns to the Cats' Lair with the Thundercats (he is the dumbest mutant). Jackalman pretends to be a Thundercat so his enemies won't catch him and the Thundercats pretend to play along because they feel bad for him!

21 Summer Fun Day!
Story by Joan Ford
Teleplay by Justin Becker
Directed by George Kaprielian
Airdate: May 2, 2020
US Viewers: 0.29

Official Synopsis
Exhausted from fighting bad guys all the time, Lion-O suggests the ThunderCats spend a relaxing summer fun day at the beach – with no fighting! Unfortunately, the beach is home to the Crabmen – giant, clawed humanoids that fight anyone who steps on their sand! Looks like summer fun day might involve some fighting!

22 Safari Joe
Written by Joan Ford
Directed by Jeremy Polgar

Airdate: May 2, 2020
US Viewers: 0.32

Official Synopsis
While minding her own business, Cheetara is caught in a trap set by Safari Joe, the
famously annoying hunter! After escaping, she rallies the other ThunderCats to
help her stop Joe once and for all – by turning the tables and capturing him!

23 Ratar-O
Story by Joan Ford
Teleplay by Bryan Condon
Directed by Keith Pakiz
Airdate: May 9, 2020
US Viewers: 0.26

Official Synopsis
The ThunderCats have gotten so good at defeating the Mutants of Plun-Darr that
it's basically become routine. That all changes with the arrival of the Mutants' old
leader: Ratar-O, wielder of the Sword of Plun-Darr! Uh-oh!\

24 Prince Starling's Quest
Story by Marly Halpern-Graser
Teleplay by Molly Knox Ostertag
Directed by George Kaprielian
Airdate: May 9, 2020
US Viewers: 0.22

Official Synopsis
Lion-O is happily playing with Snarf in their "Frolicking Field" and doesn't have a
care in the world – unfortunately he's accidentally stomping all over the miniature
village of the Micrits! The tiny people want to defeat the "giant orange monster"
but such a quest would require a brave hero. Luckily, the Micrits have such a hero:
Prince Starling! Now, let us the tell you the epic tale of Prince Starling as he
journeys to find the fountain of growth and defeat the wicked Lion-O (who has no
idea any of this is going on)!

25 Lion-S
Story by Joan Ford
Teleplay by Cait Raft
Directed by Jeremy Polgar
Airdate: May 16, 2020
US Viewers: 0.23

Official Synopsis
Lion-O and the other ThunderCats are thrilled to meet a brand new Thunderian:
Lion-S! She's cool, good at fighting robots and, most importantly, thinks Lion-O
and his Sword of Omens are really interesting! Looks like the ThunderCats have a
new best friend! Maybe even... a new ThunderCat?

26 Snarf's Day Off
Story by Joan Ford
Teleplay by Justin Becker
Directed by Keith Pakiz
Airdate: May 16, 2020
US Viewers: 0.21

Official Synopsis
On Snarf's monthly day off, he leaves Cats' Lair to get a needed vacation – by transforming into a normal cat and hanging out with a nice old lady on a farm! But his relaxing day is threatened when Snarf and the nice old lady cross paths with Mumm-Ra!

27 Mumm-Ra of Plun-Darr Part 1
28 Mumm-Ra of Plun-Darr Part 2
Story by Joan Ford
Teleplay by Bryan Condon
Directed by George Kaprielian
Airdate: May 23, 2020
US Viewers: 0.22

Official Synopsis
In the first of a two-part episode, the Thundercats' worst nightmare comes true when their worst enemies, Mumm-Ra and The Mutants, team up after Mumm-Ra acquires The Sword of Plun-Darr!

In the second of a two-part episode, chaos reigns over Third Earth now that the Mutants and Mumm-Ra control the Cats' Lair! The Thundercats' only hope is to sneak back in and get a super-secret weapon Panthro has hidden at the heart of the Lair.

From left: Robert Kuisis, Jules Bass & Peter Lawrence review scripts in a production meeting

Masaki Iizuka (foreground) holds up a cartoon of Peter Lawrence drawn by Tsugo Kubo (background)

From left: Arthur Rankin, Masaki Iizuka and Jules Bass enjoy an evening out

Peter Lawrence at work in his offices at Rankin/Bass

William Overgard pictured with his wife Gloria

Leonard Starr pictured just prior to his work on ThunderCats in 1982

Mike Germakian pictured at the offices of Leisure Concepts Inc in 1987

Peter Bakalian and Lee Dannacher attend a party in New York City

The former Rankin/Bass office building at One East 53rd Street, New York as it appears today

ONE EAST 53

The following page comprises of stills taken from VHS footage recorded during voice recording sessions on *ThunderCats*. © LYNNE LIPTON

From left: Peter Newman, Earle Hyman and Larry Kenney perform a *ThunderCats* script in Studio B at RCA Studios on Sixth Avenue, New York City

Bob McFadden performs Snarf

Bob McFadden and Earl Hammond perform together

Earl Hammond mid-rant as Mumm-Ra

Earle Hyman vocalising the Ancient Spirits of Evil

Larry Kenney takes a break from recording

Larry Kenney performs Lion-O's 'ThunderCats Ho!'

Lee Dannacher and Peter Newman pose for the camera

Lee Dannacher reviews takes

Lynne Lipton in full swing as Cheetara

Larry Kenney and Lynne Lipton share a scene

Peter Newman as Monkian

Earle Hyman mid performance

Back row from left: Matthew Malach,
Michael Ungar, Rob Schaeffer, Tony Giovanniello
Front from left: Larry Franke & John Crenshaw

© LARRY FRANKE

© LARRY FRANKE

Earl Hammond attends a New York
party complete with neck brace!

Bob McFadden and John Crenshaw
smile for the camera

© LARRY FRANKE

Lee Dannacher
pictured at
Howard Schwartz
Recording Studios,
Lexington Ave,
New York City.

© LARRY FRANKE

Larry Kenney and Maggie Jakobson

© LARRY FRANKE

The following pages represent the majority of action figures released by LJN Toys for *ThunderCats* (excluding some variants and rereleases).

Toys are pictured on a variety of American and European cards from the collection of Andrew Marczenko

ALL IMAGES © ANDREW MARCZENKO

LJN
COME SHARE THE MAGIC

LION-O 1985   TYGRA 1985   TYGRA AND WILYKAT 1985

CHEETARA 1985   CHEETARA AND WILYKIT 1985   PANTHRO 1985   MUMM-RA 1985   S-S-SLITHE 1985

JACKALMAN 1985   MONKIAN 1985   LIONO AND SNARF 1986   TYGRA 1986   TYGRA AND WILYKAT 1986

PANTHRO 1986   CHEETARA 1986   CHEETARA 1986   TUSKA WARRIOR 1986   SNOWMAN 1986

HACHIMAN 1986   GRUNE THE DESTROYER 1986   MUMM-RA 1986   MUMM-RA AND RAVAGE 1986   S-S-SLITHE 1986

JACKALMAN 1986   MONKIAN 1986   RATAR-O 1986   VULTUREMAN 1986   WILYKIT 1986

WILYKAT 1986   SNARF 1986   MA-MUTT 1986   BERBIL BILL 1986   BERBIL BELLE 1986

BERBIL BERT 1986   HAMMERHAND 1986   RAM-BAM 1986   TOP-SPINNER 1986   CRUNCHER 1986

JAGA 1987   BEN GALI 1987   LYNX-O 1987   PUMYRA 1987   MONGOR 1987

SAFARI JOE 1987   CAPT CRACKER 1987   CAPT SHINER 1987   THE DRILLER 1987   THE STINGER 1987

The 'Red-Eye' unpainted prototype sculpt by Bert Brooks

A working model of the abandoned 'Luna Tacker' [sic] vehicle designed by Jose Longoria

Two prototype figures for the 'Mad Bubbler'. The left model was eventually developed into a character for the TV series, before both toys were abandoned

The painted prototype of 'Cannon Blaster' by Russ Witman awaits photography

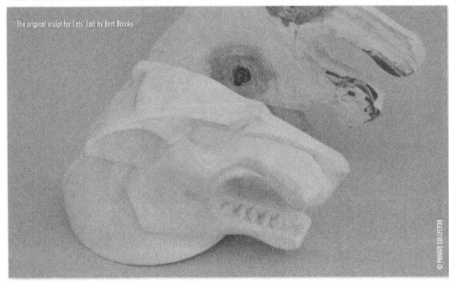

The original sculpt for Cats' Lair by Bert Brooks

© PRIVATE COLLECTOR

Other Cult TV Titles
From Telos Publishing

Back to the Vortex: *Doctor Who* 2005
J Shaun Lyon

Second Flight: *Doctor Who* 2006
J Shaun Lyon

Third Dimension: *Doctor Who* 2007
Stephen James Walker

Monsters Within: *Doctor Who* 2008
Stephen James Walker

End of Ten: *Doctor Who* 2009
Stephen James Walker

Cracks in Time: *Doctor Who* 2010
Stephen James Walker

River's Run: *Doctor Who* 2011
Stephen James Walker

Time of the Doctor: *Doctor Who* 2012 and 2013
Stephen James Walker

The Television Companion (*Doctor Who*) Vols 1 and 2
David J Howe, Stephen James Walker

The Handbook (*Doctor Who*) Vols 1 and 2
David J Howe, Stephen James Walker, Mark Stammers

Talkback (*Doctor Who* Interview Books) Vols 1, 2 and 3
Ed. Stephen James Walker

The Target Book (*Doctor Who* Novelisations)
David J Howe

Doctor Who Exhibitions
Bedwyr Gullidge

Inside the Hub (Guide to *Torchwood* Season 1)
Something in the Darkness (Guide to *Torchwood* Season 2)
Stephen James Walker

A Day in the Life (Guide to Season 1 of 24)
Keith Topping

Liberation (Guide to *Blake's 7*)
Alan Stevens and Fiona Moore

Fall Out (Guide to *The Prisoner*)
Alan Stevens and Fiona Moore

A Family at War (Guide to *Till Death Us Do Part*)
Mark Ward

Destination Moonbase Alpha (Guide to *Space 1999*)
Robert E Wood

Assigned (Guide to *Sapphire and Steel*)
Richard Callaghan

Hear the Roar (Guide to *Thundercats*)
David Crichton

Hunted (Guide to *Supernatural* Seasons 1-3)
Sam Ford and Antony Fogg

Triquetra (Guide to *Charmed*)
Keith Topping

Bowler Hats and Kinky Boots (Guide to *The Avengers*)
Michael Richardson

By Your Command (Guide to *Battlestar Galactica*, 2 Vols)
Alan Stevens and Fiona Moore

Transform and Roll Out (Guide to The Transformers Franchise)
Ryan Frost

The Complete Slayer (Guide to *Buffy the Vampire Slayer*)
Keith Topping

Songs for Europe (Guide to the UK in the Eurovision Song Contest: 4 Volumes)
Gordon Roxburgh

Prophets of Doom (Guide to *Doomwatch*)
Michael Seely and Phil Ware

**All available online from
www.telos.co.uk**

Printed in Great Britain
by Amazon

84386768R00281